DATE DUE

			PRINTED IN U.S.A.

SOMETHING ABOUT THE AUTHOR

ISSN 0276-816X

SOMETHING ABOUT THE AUTHOR

**Facts and Pictures about Authors
and Illustrators of Books for Young People**

EDITED BY
ANNE COMMIRE

VOLUME 45

GALE RESEARCH COMPANY
BOOK TOWER
DETROIT, MICHIGAN
48226

Editor: Anne Commire

Associate Editors: Agnes Garrett, Helga P. McCue

Assistant Editors: Dianne H. Anderson, Elisa Ann Ferraro, Eunice L. Petrini, Linda Shedd

Sketchwriter: Rachel Koenig

Researchers: Kathleen Betsko, Catherine Ruello

Editorial Assistant: Lisa Bryon

Permissions Assistant: Susan Pfanner

In cooperation with the Young People's Literature staff

Editor: Joyce Nakamura

Assistant Editor: Heidi Ellerman

Research Coordinator: Cynthia J. Walker

External Production Supervisor: Mary Beth Trimper

External Senior Production Associate: Dorothy Kalleberg

External Production Assistant: Michael B. Vargas

Internal Senior Production Assistant: Sandy Rock

Internal Production Assistant: Lisa Woods

Layout Artist: Elizabeth Lewis Patryjak

Art Director: Arthur Chartow

Special acknowledgment is due to the members of the *Contemporary Authors* staff
who assisted in the preparation of this volume.

Publisher: Frederick G. Ruffner

Editorial Director: Dedria Bryfonski

Associate Editorial Director: Ellen Crowley

Director, Literature Division: Christine Nasso

Senior Editor, Something about the Author: Adele Sarkissian

Library of Congress Catalog Card Number 72-27107
ISBN 0-8103-2255-2
ISSN 0276-816X
Computerized photocomposition by
Typographics, Incorporated
Kansas City, Missouri
Printed in the United States

Contents

Introduction   9   Acknowledgments   15
Illustrations Index   225   Author Index   243

A

Acuff, Selma Boyd   1924- 21

Alcock, Vivien   1924- 22

Alex, Ben [a pseudonym]   1946- 24

Alex, Marlee [a pseudonym]   1948- 27

Allen, Thomas B(enton)   1929- 27

Allen, Tom
   see Allen, Thomas B(enton) 27

Altschuler, Franz   1923- 29

Andrist, Ralph K.   1914- 30

Antolini, Margaret Fishback   1904-1985
   Obituary Notice 31

Antonacci, Robert J(oseph)   1916- 31

Aoki, Hisako   1942- 32

Appel, Martin E(liot)   1948- 33

Appel, Marty
   see Appel, Martin E(liot)...................33

Applebaum, Stan   1929- 33

Atticus
   see Davies, (Edward) Hunter 67

B

Baird, Thomas P.   1923- 35

Barbe, Walter Burke   1926- 35

Batherman, Muriel
   see Sheldon, Muriel 184

Beckman, Kaj
   see Beckman, Karin 37

Beckman, Karin   1913- 37

Beckman, Per (Frithiof)   1913- 41

Belair, Richard L.   1934- 43

Berenstain, Michael   1951-
   Brief Entry................................44

Bergey, Alyce (Mae)   1934- 44

Bernard, Jacqueline (de Sieyes)   1921-1983
   Obituary Notice 45

Blair, Jay   1953- 45

Boyd, Pauline
   see Schock, Pauline 183

Boyd, Selma
   see Acuff, Selma Boyd....................21

Britton, Louisa
   see McGuire, Leslie (Sarah) 150

Brooks, Maurice (Graham)   1900- 48

Brown, Buck   1936- 48

Browne, Anthony (Edward Tudor)   1946- 48

Bull, Angela (Mary)   1936- 53

Burton, Leslie
   see McGuire, Leslie (Sarah) 150

C

Calvert, Patricia   1931- 54

Campbell, Patricia J(ean)   1930- 56

Campbell, Patty
   see Campbell, Patricia J(ean) 56

Carlson, Nancy L(ee)   1953-
   Brief Entry................................57

Carroll, Elizabeth [Joint pseudonym]
   see James, Elizabeth.....................116

Cooke, Donald Ewin   1916-1985
   Obituary Notice 57

Copley, (Diana) Heather Pickering   1918- 57

Cormier, Robert (Edmund)   1925- 58

Costabel, Eva Deutsch   1924- 65

D

Davidson, Alice Joyce   1932-
   Brief Entry................................67

Davies, (Edward) Hunter   1936-
   Brief Entry................................67

5

Demarest, Chris(topher) L(ynn) 1951- 68

DeWeese, Gene
see DeWeese, Thomas Eugene 70

DeWeese, Jean
see DeWeese, Thomas Eugene 70

DeWeese, Thomas Eugene 1934-
Brief Entry....................................70

Dixon, Dougal 1947- 70

Dolan, Edward F(rancis), Jr. 1924- 71

Dudley, Martha Ward 1909(?)-1985
Obituary Notice 72

Duval, Katherine
see James, Elizabeth......................116

E

Evslin, Bernard 1922- 73

Eyre, Dorothy
see McGuire, Leslie (Sarah) 150

F

Farthing, Alison 1936- 74

Ferguson, Cecil 1931- 74

Fidler, Kathleen (Annie) 1899-1980
Obituary Notice 74

Fishback, Margaret
see Antolini, Margaret Fishback 31

Fitch, John IV
see Cormier, Robert (Edmund) 58

Fitzhugh, Louise (Perkins) 1928-1974 74

Fox, Eleanor
see St. John, Wylly Folk 181

Freeman, Peter J.
see Calvert, Patricia 54

G

Gans, Roma 1894- 79

Gérard, Jean Ignace Isidore 1803-1847........80

Gerrard, Roy 1935-
Brief Entry.................................89

Glenn, Mel 1943-
Brief Entry.................................90

Gough, Philip 1908- 90

Grace, F(rances Jane) 91

Graham-Cameron, M(alcolm) G(ordon) 1931-
Brief Entry.................................92

Graham-Cameron, Mike
see Graham-Cameron, M(alcolm) G(ordon) ...92

Grandville, J. J.
see Gérard, Jean Ignace Isidore 80

Grandville, Jean Ignace Isidore Gérard
see Gérard, Jean Ignace Isidore 80

Graves, Robert (von Ranke) 1895-1985 92

Gray, Marian
see Pierce, Edith Gray 167

Greenhaus, Thelma Nurenberg 1903-1984.....106

Gustafson, Anita 1942-
Brief Entry.............................106

H

Hague, Kathleen
Brief Entry.............................107

Handville, Robert (Tompkins) 1924- 107

Harmer, Mabel 1894- 110

Hastings, Beverly [Joint pseudonym]
see James, Elizabeth....................116

Hines, Anna G(rossnickle) 1946-
Brief Entry.............................111

Holmgren, George Ellen
see Holmgren, Helen Jean.................111

Holmgren, Helen Jean 1930- 111

Holton, Leonard
see Wibberley, Leonard
(Patrick O'Connor) 211

Horwitz, Elinor Lander......................112

Howard, Alan 1922- 115

Hunter, Bernice Thurman 1922-
Brief Entry.............................115

Hurd, Thacher 1949-
Brief Entry.............................115

J

James, Elizabeth 1942- 116

K

Keith, Robert
see Applebaum, Stan 33

Kent, Jack
see Kent, John Wellington 119

Kent, John Wellington 1920-1985
Obituary Notice 119

Keyser, Sarah
　see McGuire, Leslie (Sarah) 150

Klass, Sheila Solomon 1927- 119

Klein, Aaron E. 1930- 120

Klein, Robin 1936-
　Brief Entry.............................122

L

Lancaster, Matthew 1973(?)-1983
　Obituary Notice 122

Lantz, Paul 1908- 122

Larson, Eve
　see St. John, Wylly Folk 181

Lathrop, Francis
　see Leiber, Fritz 124

Leiber, Fritz 1910- 124

Leokum, Arkady 1916(?)- 126

Leslie, Sarah
　see McGuire, Leslie (Sarah) 150

Little, A. Edward
　see Klein, Aaron E. 120

Lloyd, E. James
　see James, Elizabeth..................116

Lloyd, James
　see James, Elizabeth..................116

Lubin, Leonard B. 1943- 127

M

Maris, Ron
　Brief Entry..........................142

Matthews, William Henry III 1919- 142

Max, Peter 1939- 143

McGuire, Leslie (Sarah) 1945-
　Brief Entry..........................150

McKay, Donald 1895- 151

McMahan, Ian
　Brief Entry..........................152

Mendonca, Susan 1950-
　Brief Entry..........................152

Mitsuhashi, Yoko.......................153

N

Nebel, Gustave E.......................153

Nebel, Mimouca
　see Nebel, Gustave E..................153

Newcombe, Jack........................155

North, Sterling 1906-1974 155

Nurenberg, Thelma
　see Greenhaus, Thelma Nurenberg 106

O

Obligado, Lilian (Isabel) 1931-
　Brief Entry..........................162

O'Connor Patrick
　see Wibberley, Leonard
　(Patrick O'Connor) 211

P

Partch, Virgil Franklin II 1916-1984.........163

Pennington, Lillian Boyer 1904- 166

Pierce, Edith Gray 1893-1977 167

Pierce, Katherine
　see St. John, Wylly Folk 181

Porte, Barbara Ann
　Brief Entry..........................168

R

Rhue, Morton
　see Strasser, Todd 196

Robinson, Shari
　see McGuire, Leslie (Sarah) 150

Roddenberry, Eugene Wesley 1921- 168

Roddenberry, Gene
　see Roddenberry, Eugene Wesley...........168

Rosenblatt, Arthur S. 1938-
　Brief Entry..........................180

Ross, John 1921- 180

S

Sadler, Catherine Edwards
　Brief Entry..........................180

St. John, Wylly Folk 1908-1985
　Obituary Notice 181

Sand, George X.........................181

Schock, Pauline 1928- 183

Schwartz, Julius 1907- 184

Sheldon, Muriel 1926- 184

Shenton, Edward 1895-1977 185

Shirer, William L(awrence) 1904- 190

Slepian, Jan(ice B.) 1921-
   Brief Entry.............................193

Smith, Samantha 1972-1985
   Obituary Notice 193

Smith, Winsome 1935- 193

Smits, Teo
   see Smits, Theodore R(ichard) 195

Smits, Theodore R(ichard) 1905- 195

Steinberg, Rafael (Mark) 1927- 195

Steiner, Charlotte 1900-1981 195

Strasser, Todd 1950- 196

Stratton, Thomas [Joint pseudonym]
   see DeWeese, Thomas Eugene 70

Strong, David
   see McGuire, Leslie (Sarah) 150

T

Teleki, Geza 1943- 200

Temple, Herbert 1919- 202

Terban, Marvin
   Brief Entry.............................202

Thiry, Joan (Marie) 1926- 202

Thomas, Victoria [Joint pseudonym]
   see DeWeese, Thomas Eugene 70

Truesdell, Sue
   see Truesdell, Susan G. 203

Truesdell, Susan G.
   Brief Entry.............................203

Tusiani, Joseph 1924- 203

V

Vevers, (Henry) Gwynne 1916- 204

Vincent, Mary Keith
   see St. John, Wylly Folk 181

Vip
   see Partch, Virgil Franklin II 163

Vogt, Gregory
   Brief Entry.............................206

Vogt, Marie Bollinger 1921- 206

W

Walker, (James) Braz(elton) 1934-1983 207

Walter, Mildred Pitts
   Brief Entry.............................207

Wangerin, Walter, Jr. 1944- 208

Webb, Christopher
   see Wibberley, Leonard
   (Patrick O'Connor) 211

Welch, Martha McKeen 1914-
   Brief Entry.............................211

Wibberley, Leonard (Patrick O'Connor)
   1915-1983 211

Williams, Michael
   see St. John, Wylly Folk 181

Winchester, James H(ugh) 1917-1985
   Obituary Notice.........................220

Work, Virginia 1946-
   Brief Entry.............................220

Introduction

As the only ongoing reference series that deals with the lives and works of authors and illustrators of children's books, *Something about the Author (SATA)* is a unique source of information. The *SATA* series includes not only well-known authors and illustrators whose books are most widely read, but also those less prominent people whose works are just coming to be recognized. *SATA* is often the only readily available information source for less well-known writers or artists. You'll find *SATA* informative and entertaining whether you are:

—a student in junior high school (or perhaps one to two grades higher or lower) who needs information for a book report or some other assignment for an English class;

—a children's librarian who is searching for the answer to yet another question from a young reader or collecting background material to use for a story hour;

—an English teacher who is drawing up an assignment for your students or gathering information for a book talk;

—a student in a college of education or library science who is studying children's literature and reference sources in the field;

—a parent who is looking for a new way to interest your child in reading something more than the school curriculum prescribes;

—an adult who enjoys children's literature for its own sake, knowing that a good children's book has no age limits.

Scope

In *SATA* you will find detailed information about authors and illustrators who span the full time range of children's literature, from early figures like John Newbery and L. Frank Baum to contemporary figures like Judy Blume and Richard Peck. Authors in the series represent primarily English-speaking countries, particularly the United States, Canada, and the United Kingdom. Also included, however, are authors from around the world whose works are available in English translation, for example: from France, Jean and Laurent De Brunhoff; from Italy, Emanuele Luzzati; from the Netherlands, Jaap ter Haar; from Germany, James Krüss; from Norway, Babbis Friis-Baastad; from Japan, Toshiko Kanzawa; from the Soviet Union, Kornei Chukovsky; from Switzerland, Alois Carigiet, to name only a few. Also appearing in *SATA* are Newbery medalists from Hendrik Van Loon (1922) to Patricia MacLachlan (1986). The writings represented in *SATA* include those created intentionally for children and young adults as well as those written for a general audience and known to interest younger readers. These writings cover the spectrum from picture books, humor, folk and fairy tales, animal stories, mystery and adventure, science fiction and fantasy, historical fiction, poetry and nonsense verse, to drama, biography, and nonfiction.

Information Features

In *SATA* you will find full-length entries that are being presented in the series for the first time. This volume, for example, marks the first full-length appearance of Karin and Per Beckman, Anthony Browne, Robert Handville, Elinor Lander Horwitz, Elizabeth James, Gene Roddenberry, Edward Shenton, Todd Strasser, and Walter Wangerin, Jr., among others. Since Volume 25, each *SATA* volume also includes newly revised and updated biographies for a selection of early *SATA* listees who remain of interest to today's readers and who have been active enough to require extensive revision of their earlier entries. The entry for a given biographee may be revised as often as there is substantial new information to provide. In Volume 45 you'll find revised entries for Robert Cormier, Louise Fitzhugh, Sterling North, and Leonard Wibberley.

Brief Entries, first introduced in Volume 27, are another regular feature of *SATA*. Brief Entries present essentially the same types of information found in a full entry but do so in a capsule form and without illustration. These entries are intended to give you useful and timely information while the more time-consuming process of compiling a full-length biography is in progress. In this volume you'll find Brief Entries for Michael Berenstain, Roy Gerrard, Mel Glenn, Kathleen Hague, Thacher Hurd, Ron Maris, Barbara Ann Porte, and Jan Slepian, among others.

Obituaries have been included in *SATA* since Volume 20. An Obituary is intended not only as a death notice but also as a concise view of a person's life and work. Obituaries may appear for persons who have entries in earlier *SATA* volumes, as well as for people who have not yet appeared in the series. In this volume Obituaries mark the recent deaths of Jacqueline Bernard, Donald Ewin Cooke, Kathleen Fidler, John Wellington Kent, Wylly Folk St. John, and others.

Each *SATA* volume provides a cumulative index in two parts: first, the Illustrations Index, arranged by the name of the illustrator, gives the number of the volume and page where the illustrator's work appears in the current volume as well as all preceding volumes in the series; second, the Author Index gives the number of the volume in which a person's biographical sketch, Brief Entry, or Obituary appears in the current volume as well as all preceding volumes in the series. These indexes also include references to authors and illustrators who appear in *Yesterday's Authors of Books for Children*. Beginning with Volume 36, the *SATA* Author Index provides cross-references to authors who are included in *Children's Literature Review*.

You will also find cross-references to authors who are included in the *Something about the Author Autobiography Series,* starting with Volume 42. This companion series to *SATA* is described in detail below.

Illustrations

While the textual information in *SATA* is its primary reason for existing, photographs and illustrations not only enliven the text but are an integral part of the information that *SATA* provides. Illustrations and text are wedded in such a special way in children's literature that artists and their works naturally occupy a prominent place among *SATA*'s listees. The illustrators that you'll find in the series include such past masters of children's book illustration as Randolph Caldecott, Kate Greenaway, Walter Crane, Arthur Rackham, and Ernest L. Shepard, as well as such noted contemporary artists as Maurice Sendak, Edward Gorey, Tomie de Paola, and Margot Zemach. There are Caldecott medalists from Dorothy Lathrop (the first recipient in 1938) to Chris Van Allsburg (the latest winner in 1986); cartoonists like Charles Schulz, ("Peanuts"), Walt Kelly ("Pogo"), Hank Ketcham ("Dennis the Menace"), and Georges Rémi ("Tintin"); photographers like Jill Krementz, Tana Hoban, Bruce McMillan, and Bruce Curtis; and filmmakers like Walt Disney, Alfred Hitchcock, and Steven Spielberg.

In more than a dozen years of recording the metamorphosis of children's literature from the printed page to other media, *SATA* has become something of a repository of photographs that are unique in themselves and exist nowhere else as a group, particularly many of the classics of motion picture and stage history and photographs that have been specially loaned to us from private collections.

What a *SATA* Entry Provides

Whether you're already familiar with the *SATA* series or just getting acquainted, you will want to be aware of the kind of information that an entry provides. In every *SATA* entry the editors attempt to give as complete a picture of the person's life and work as possible. In some cases that full range of information may simply be unavailable, or a biographee may choose not to reveal complete personal details. The information that the editors attempt to provide in every entry is arranged in the following categories:

1. The "head" of the entry gives

    —the most complete form of the name,
    —any part of the name not commonly used, included in parentheses,
    —birth and death dates, if known; a (?) indicates a discrepancy in published sources,

—pseudonyms or name variants under which the person has had books published or is publicly known, in parentheses in the second line.

2. "Personal" section gives

—date and place of birth and death,
—parents' names and occupations,
—name of spouse, date of marriage, and names of children,
—educational institutions attended, degrees received, and dates,
—religious and political affiliations,
—agent's name and address,
—home and / or office address.

3. "Career" section gives

—name of employer, position, and dates for each career post,
—military service,
—memberships,
—awards and honors.

4. "Writings" section gives

—title, first publisher and date of publication, and illustration information for each book written; revised editions and other significant editions for books with particularly long publishing histories; genre, when known.

5. "Adaptations" section gives

—title, major performers, producer, and date of all known reworkings of an author's material in another medium, like movies, filmstrips, television, recordings, plays, etc.

6. "Sidelights" section gives

—commentary on the life or work of the biographee either directly from the person (and often written specifically for the *SATA* entry), or gathered from biographies, diaries, letters, interviews, or other published sources.

7. "For More Information See" section gives

—books, feature articles, films, plays, and reviews in which the biographee's life or xwork has been treated.

How a *SATA* Entry Is Compiled

A *SATA* entry progresses through a series of steps. If the biographee is living, the *SATA* editors try to secure information directly from him or her through a questionnaire. From the information that the biographee supplies, the editors prepare an entry, filling in any essential missing details with research. The author or illustrator is then sent a copy of the entry to check for accuracy and completeness.

If the biographee is deceased or cannot be reached by questionnaire, the *SATA* editors examine a wide variety of published sources to gather information for an entry. Biographical sources are searched with the aid of Gale's *Biography and Genealogy Master Index*. Bibliographic sources like the *National Union Catalog*, the *Cumulative Book Index*, *American Book Publishing Record*, and the *British Museum Catalogue* are consulted, as are book reviews, feature articles, published interviews, and material sometimes obtained from the biographee's family, publishers, agent, or other associates.

For each entry presented in *SATA*, the editors also attempt to locate a photograph of the biographee as well as representative illustrations from his or her books. After surveying the available books which the biographee has written and / or illustrated, and then making a selection of appropriate photographs and illustrations, the editors request permission of the current copyright holders to reprint the material. In the case of older books for which the copyright may have passed through several hands, even locating the current copyright holder is often a long and involved process.

We invite you to examine the entire *SATA* series, starting with this volume. Described below are some of the people in Volume 45 that you may find particularly interesting.

Highlights of This Volume

ROBERT CORMIER......the author of psychological suspense novels for young adults, like *The Chocolate War, Beyond the Chocolate War, I Am the Cheese, After the First Death,* and *The Bumblebee Flies Anyway.* Cormier recalls past years when, as an insomniac writer, he would fill the empty hallways of his home with the tappings of his typewriter long after his teenaged children had returned home for the evening. Those times they stopped to talk remained as kernels of inspiration in Cormier's mind. "Your son will tell you things at one o'clock in the morning," he says, "that he won't tell you at one o'clock in the afternoon." Cormier knows that "teenagers do not live in a peppermint world of fun and frolic." Although extremely popular with young adult readers, his books have been viewed as pessimistic and depressive by some critics and parents. The reason for this, he believes, is because "everybody wants to have a happy ending. My books go against that. . . .People don't ride off into the sunset in my books, they walk off hobbled and crippled maybe, into the dark night."

JEAN IGNACE ISIDORE GÉRARD......a nineteenth-century French caricaturist and illustrator, best known under the name Grandville. While in his teens, Grandville's original approach to art caught the eye of the French painter Mansion, who urged the youth to travel to Paris to study. Heeding this advice, in 1829 Grandville found himself savoring success with the publication of *Les Métamorphoses du jour,* a collection of drawings that featured unusual combinations of human and animal anatomy. So fantastical and absurd are Grandville's detailed line drawings that he has been regarded as a precursor of surrealism, a label he would no doubt enjoy. "The eyes of the cartoonist," he once reflected, "are trained to perceive, in essence, the ridiculous. . . .The absurd contrasts which arouse our mirth are the result of an inconspicuous method." This master of the satirical cartoon also provided illustrations for children's classics, such as *Travels into Several Remote Nations of the World by Lemuel Gulliver, La Fontaine: Selected Fables,* and *The Life and Adventures of Robinson Crusoe.*

ROBERT GRAVES......who grew up in Victorian England, the product of an ancestral tree that boasted scholars, writers, and theologians. Graves' most direct link to the world of letters was his own father, the Irish poet and ballad writer Alfred Perceval Graves, a man he both respected and admired. It was their relationship that prevented Graves from developing "any false reverence of poets." A noted novelist, critic, mythographer, translator, and editor, Graves remained first and foremost a poet. For him, poetry was spontaneous expression—a force "like the tense headache before a thunderstorm, which is followed by an uncontrollable violence of feeling. . . ." Although best remembered for his numerous poetical works and novels like *I, Claudius,* Graves also wrote several children's books, including *The Big Green Book, Two Wise Children,* and *An Ancient Castle.*

LEONARD B. LUBIN......who, as a child, "did lots of drawing and went through sheets and sheets of paper." By the time he reached high school, however, his parents made it quite clear that drawing was *not* an acceptable profession. They considered electronics a much more lucrative field. "My grandfather worked downtown," he recalls, "and would often see the open-air artists drawing the bums lying in the street. He asked, 'Is this what *you* want to be?'" Despite his family's objections, that's exactly what Lubin wanted to be. During the past ten years, he has more than justified his career-making decision with the publication of award-winning illustrations in children's books like *The Pig-Tale, The Little Swineherd, and Other Tales,* and *The Birthday of the Infanta.* Lubin describes his lavish, rococo-like art work as "eccentric, with just a dash of nastiness. . . .I do love detail, but I still feel there is enough left to the imagination so that kids can dream about what's in the picture."

PETER MAX......known as the "prince of psychedelic art." This talented and prolific artist rose to fame during the 1960s and was largely responsible for inspiring the brightly-colored, "pop art" movement of the times. Born in Berlin, Max spent most of his childhood in Shanghai and Tibet where, he remembers, "the word 'America' had a magical ring to it, much like Baghdad or 'never-never land.'" In 1962 Max hit the advertising world of Madison Avenue in New York City, where he began to work his own magic. Eventually, he amassed a multi-million dollar fortune with innovative designs that appeared on everything from posters to shower curtains. A strong advocate of yoga, Max always tries to reflect the positive aspects of life in his work, to convey "a message of love, harmony, unity, and symmetry." His timely illustrations can be found in several books for children, including *The Peter Max Land of Blue (and How the Cousins Got There)* and *The Peter Max Land of Yellow (and How the Purple King Nearly Lost Himself There)*.

LEONARD WIBBERLEY......the author of more than fifty children's books, most notably historical works like his "Treegate" and "Thomas Jefferson Biography" series. The Revolutionary War was a favorite topic for Wibberley, who viewed it as "a war for the rights of *all* men." As a novelist, he learned to "listen to the insistent whisper of forgotten voices penetrating the centuries" and blended together real and imagined characters from the pages of American history. All the drama and excitement of times long past are brought vividly to life for young readers in Wibberley's books, among them *The King's Beard, The Life of Winston Churchill, John Treegate's Musket, Sea Captain from Salem,* and *Young Man from Piedmont*.

These are only a few of the authors and illustrators that you'll find in this volume. We hope you find all the entries in *SATA* both interesting and useful.

Something about the Author Autobiography Series

You can complement the information in *SATA* with the *Something about the Author Autobiography Series (SAAS),* which provides autobiographical essays written by important current authors and illustrators of books for children and young adults. In every volume of *SAAS* you will find about twenty specially commissioned autobiographies, each accompanied by a selection of personal photographs supplied by the authors. The wide range of contemporary writers and artists who describe their lives and interests in the *Autobiography Series* includes Joan Aiken, Betsy Byars, Leonard Everett Fisher, Milton Meltzer, Maia Wojciechowska, and Jane Yolen, among others. Though the information presented in the autobiographies is as varied and unique as the authors, you can learn about the people and events that influenced these writers' early lives, how they began their careers, what problems they faced in becoming established in their professions, what prompted them to write or illustrate particular books, what they now find most challenging or rewarding in their lives, and what advice they may have for young people interested in following in their footsteps, among many other subjects.

Autobiographies included in the *SATA Autobiography Series* can be located through both the *SATA* cumulative index and the *SAAS* cumulative index, which lists not only the authors' names but also the subjects mentioned in their essays, such as titles of works and geographical and personal names.

The *SATA Autobiography Series* gives you the opportunity to view "close up" some of the fascinating people who are included in the *SATA* parent series. The combined *SATA* series makes available to you an unequaled range of comprehensive and in-depth information about the authors and illustrators of young people's literature.

Please write and tell us if we can make *SATA* even more helpful to you.

Acknowledgments

Grateful acknowledgment is made to the following publishers, authors, and artists
for their kind permission to reproduce copyrighted material.

ACROPOLIS BOOKS LTD. Illustration and Sidelight excerpts from *Peter Max Paints America,* edited by Victor Zurbel. Reprinted by permission of Acropolis Books Ltd.

AMERICAN HERITAGE PUBLISHING CO., INC. Photograph from *Steamboats on the Mississippi* by the editors of American Heritage. Copyright © 1962 by American Heritage Publishing Co., Inc. Reprinted by permission of American Heritage Publishing Co., Inc.

ATHENEUM PUBLISHERS. Illustration by Eva Deutsch Costabel from *A New England Village.* Copyright © 1982, 1983 by Eva Deutsch Costabel. Reprinted by permission of Atheneum Publishers.

AUGSBURG PUBLISHING HOUSE. Illustration by George Ellen Holmgren from *Small Prayers for Small Children about Big and Little Things* by Paul A. Schreivogel. Copyright © 1971 by Augsburg Publishing House. Reprinted by permission of Augsburg Publishing House.

BANTAM BOOKS, INC. Jacket illustration by Quentin Blake from *The Mouse That Roared* by Leonard Wibberley. Copyright 1954, 1955 by the Curtis Publishing Co. Copyright 1955 by Leonard Wibberley. Reprinted by permission of Bantam Books, Inc.

BERKLEY PUBLISHING GROUP. Illustration by Paul Rivoch from "Black Glass" in *The Ghost Light Masterworks of Science Fiction and Fantasy* by Fritz Leiber. *The Ghost Light Masterworks of Science Fiction and Fantasy* copyright © 1984 by Byron Preiss Visual Publications, Inc. Stories copyright © 1984 by Fritz Leiber. Reprinted by permission of Berkley Publishing Group.

BETHANY HOUSE PUBLISHERS. Photographs by Ben Alex and Otto Wikkelsoe from *Grandpa and Me: We Learn about Death* by Marlee and Ben Alex. Text copyright © 1982 by Bethany House Publishers. Photograph copyright © 1981 by Forlaget Scandinavia. Both reprinted by permission of Bethany House Publishers.

THE BODLEY HEAD LTD. Illustration by Heather Copley and Christopher Chamberlain from *London's River: The Story of a City* by Eric de Maré. Text copyright © 1964 by Eric de Maré. Illustrations copyright © 1964 by The Bodley Head Ltd. / Illustration by Matthew Hillier from *Animal Cleaners* by Gwynne Vevers. Text copyright © 1982 by Gwynne Vevers. Illustrations copyright © 1982 by Matthew Hillier. Both reprinted by permission of The Bodley Head Ltd.

BRADBURY PRESS. Jacket illustration by Phil Franke from *Branigan's Dog* by Fran Grace. Copyright © 1981 by Fran Grace. Reprinted by permission of Bradbury Press.

CHILDRENS PRESS. Photograph from *The Circus* by Mabel Harmer. Copyright © 1981 by Regensteiner Publishing Enterprises, Inc. Reprinted by permission of Childrens Press.

THE CHILD'S WORLD, INC. Illustration by Franz Altschuler from *Bobbin's Land* by Carol Cornelius. Copyright © 1978 by The Child's World, Inc. Reprinted by permission of The Child's World, Inc.

COWARD, McCANN & GEOGHEGAN, INC. Jacket illustration by Judy Clifford from *Angel Dust Blues* by Todd Strasser. Copyright © 1979 by Todd Strasser. Reprinted by permission of Coward, McCann & Geoghegan, Inc.

THOMAS Y. CROWELL, INC. Illustration by Holly Keller from *Rock Collecting* by Roma Gans. Text copyright © 1984 by Roma Gans. Illustrations copyright © 1984 by Holly Keller./ Illustration by Yoko Mitsuhashi from *I Have a Horse of My Own* by Charlotte Zolotow. Text copyright © 1964 by Charlotte Zolotow. Illustrations copyright © 1980 by Yoko Mitsuhashi. Both reprinted by permission of Thomas Y. Crowell, Inc.

THE CROWELL—COLLIER PRESS. Illustrations by Maurice Sendak from *The Big Green Book* by Robert Graves. Text copyright © 1962 by International Authors, N.V. Illustrations copyright © 1962 by Maurice Sendak. Both reprinted by permission of The Crowell-Collier Press.

DELACORTE PRESS. Jacket illustration by Paul Tibbles from *The Sylvia Game* by Vivien Alcock. Text copyright © 1982 by Vivien Alcock. Jacket illustration copyright © 1984 by Paul Tibbles./ Jacket illustration by John Heinly from *The Strange Story of the Frog Who Became a Prince* by Elinor Lander Horwitz. Text copyright © 1971 by Elinor Horwitz. Illustrations copyright © 1971 by John Heinly./ Illustration by Leonard B. Lubin from *Aladdin and His Wonderful Lamp,* adapted by Leonard B. Lubin. Copyright © 1982 by Leonard B. Lubin. All reprinted by permission of Delacorte Press.

DODD, MEAD & CO. Jacket illustration by Robert Handville from *The Mysteries in the Commune* by Norah Smaridge. Copyright © 1982 by Norah Smaridge. Reprinted by permission of Dodd, Mead & Co.

DOUBLEDAY & CO., INC. Illustration by Dimitris Davis from *Greek Gods and Heroes* by Robert Graves. Copyright © 1960 by Robert Graves./ Illustration by C. Walter Hodges from *The Siege and Fall of Troy* by Robert Graves. Text copyright © 1962 by International Authors, N.V. Illustrations copyright © 1962 by Cassell & Co. Ltd./ Sidelight excerpts from an article "The Petals of Happiness" in *My Most Inspiring Moment: Encounters with Destiny Relived by Thirty-eight Best-Selling Authors,* edited by Robert Fitzgibbon and Ernest V. Heyn./ Illustration by Brad Holland from *So Dear to My Heart* by Sterling North. Text copyright 1947 by Sterling North. Illustrations copyright © 1968 by Doubleday & Co., Inc./ Illustration by Virgil Partch from *Joe, the Wounded Tennis Player* by Morton Thompson. Copyright 1929, 1944, 1945 by Morton Thompson./ Illustration by Richard Cuffari from *Little League Family* by Leonard Wibberley. Text copyright © 1978 by Leonard Wibberley./ Illustrations from *The Making of the Trek Conventions; or, How to Throw a Party for 12,000 of Your Most Intimate Friends* by Joan Winston. Copyright © 1977 by Joan Winston. All reprinted by permission of Doubleday & Co., Inc.

E. P. DUTTON, INC. Illustration by Leonard B. Lubin from "The Little Swineherd" in *The Little Swineherd and Other Tales* by Paula Fox. Text copyright © 1978 by Paula Fox. Illustrations copyright © 1978 by Leonard B. Lubin./ Frontispiece illustration by John Schoenherr and Sidelight excerpts from *Rascal: A Memoir of a Better Era* by Sterling North. Text copyright © 1963 by Sterling North. Illustrations copyright © 1963 by E. P. Dutton, Inc./ Illustration by John Schoenherr from *The Wolfling: A Documentary Novel of the Eighteen-Seventies* by Sterling North. Text copyright © 1969 by Sterling North. Illustrations copyright © 1969 by E. P. Dutton, Inc./ Illustration by Carl Burger from *Hurry, Spring!* by Sterling North. Text copyright © 1966 by Sterling North. Illustrations copyright © 1966 by Carl Burger./ Illustration by Carl Burger from *Little Rascal* by Sterling North. Text copyright © 1965 by Sterling North. Illustrations copyright © 1965 by Carl Burger. All reprinted by permission of E. P. Dutton, Inc.

FABER & FABER LTD. Illustration by Alan Howard from "Annie Norn and the Fin Folk" in *The Faber Book of Northern Folk-Tales,* edited by Kevin Crossley-Holland. Text copyright © 1980 by Kevin Crossley-Holland. Illustrations copyright © 1980 by Faber & Faber Ltd./ Illustration by Jill Bennett from *The Accidental Twins* by Angela Bull. Text copyright © 1982 by Angela Bull. Illustrations copyright © 1982 by Faber & Faber Ltd. Both reprinted by permission of Faber & Faber Ltd.

FARRAR, STRAUS & GIROUX, INC. Illustration by Louise Fitzhugh from *Nobody's Family Is Going to Change* by Louise Fitzhugh. Copyright © 1974 by Louise Fitzhugh./ Cover illustration by Eric Velasquez from *John Treegate's Musket* by Leonard Wibberley. Text copyright © 1959 by Leonard Wibberley. Illustrations copyright © 1986 by Eric Velasquez./ Jacket illustration by Enrico Arno from *Flint's Island* by Leonard Wibberley. Copyright © 1972 by Leonard Wibberley./ Jacket illustration by Enrico Arno from *The Gales of Spring: Thomas Jefferson, the Years 1789-1801* by Leonard Wibberley. Copyright © 1965 by Leonard Wibberley./ Jacket illustration by Richard Cuffari from *Guarneri: Story of a Genius* by Leonard Wibberley. Copyright © 1974 by Leonard Wibberley./ Jacket illustration by Enrico Arno from *Leopard's Prey* by Leonard Wibberley. Copyright © 1971 by Leonard Wibberley. All reprinted by permission of Farrar, Straus & Giroux, Inc.

FOUR WINDS PRESS. Illustration by Barbara Bascove from *The Green Hero: Early Adventures of Finn McCool* by Bernard Evslin. Copyright © 1975 by Bernard Evslin./ Photograph by George X. Sand from *The Everglades Today: Endangered Wilderness* by George X. Sand. Copyright © 1971 by George X. Sand. Both reprinted by permission of Four Winds Press.

GARRARD PUBLISHING CO. Illustration by Buck Brown from *Fritz, the Too-Long Dog* by Bee Lewi. Copyright © 1980 by Bee Lewi. Reprinted by permission of Garrard Publishing Co.

HARCOURT BRACE JOVANOVICH, INC. Illustration by Edward Shenton from *Blueberry Mountain* by Stephen W. Meader. Copyright 1941 by Harcourt, Brace & Co., Inc./ Illustration by Edward Shenton from *Shadow in the Pines* by Stephen W. Meader. Copyright 1942 by Harcourt, Brace & Co., Inc./ Illustration by Edward Shenton from *Boy with a Pack* by Stephen W. Meader. Copyright 1939 by Harcourt, Brace & Co., Inc. All reprinted by permission of Harcourt Brace Jovanovich, Inc.

HARLIN QUIST, INC. Illustration by Ralph Pinto from *Two Wise Children* by Robert Graves. Copyright © 1966 by International Authors, N.V. Copyright © 1966 by Harlin Quist, Inc. Reprinted by permission of Harlin Quist, Inc.

HARPER & ROW, PUBLISHERS INC. Jacket illustration by Robert Sabin from *Finding Fever* by Thomas Baird. Text copyright © 1982 by Thomas Baird. Jacket copyright © 1982 by Harper & Row, Publishers Inc./ Illustration by Louise Fitzhugh from *Harriet, the Spy* by Louise Fitzhugh. Copyright © 1964 by Louise Fitzhugh./ Jacket illustration by Ronald Keller from *The Book of the Dun Cow* by Walter Wangerin, Jr. Copyright © 1978 by Walter M. Wangerin, Jr./ Illustration by Marcia Sewall from *Thistle* by Walter Wangerin, Jr. Text copyright © 1983 by Walter M. Wangerin, Jr. Illustrations copyright © 1983 by Marcia Sewall./ Jacket illustration by Alan Mazzetti from *Ragman and Other Cries of Faith* by Walter Wangerin, Jr. Copyright © 1984 by Walter Wangerin, Jr./ Illustration by Per Beckman from "The Rooster That Fell in the Brew Vat" in *The Hen That Saved the World and Other Norwegian Folktales,* retold by Margaret Sperry. Copyright 1952 by Margaret Sperry. All reprinted by permission of Harper & Row, Publishers Inc.

HARVEY HOUSE, INC. Photograph from *The Story of Glaciers and the Ice Age* by William H. Matthews III. Copyright © 1974 by William H. Matthews III. Reprinted by permission of Harvey House, Inc.

HASTINGS HOUSE, PUBLISHERS INC. Illustration by Anne Mieke from *The Mystical Beast* by Alison Farthing. Text copyright © 1976 by Alison Farthing. Illustrations copyright © 1976 by Anne Mieke. Reprinted by permission of Hastings House, Publishers Inc.

HIGH COUNTRY PRESS. Illustration by Earle Gardner from *Snafu, the Littlest Clown* by Lillian Boyer Pennington. Reprinted by permission of High Country Press.

HODDER & STOUGHTON LTD. Illustration by John Schoenherr from *Rascal: A Memoir of a Better Era* by Sterling North. Text copyright © 1963 by Sterling North. Illustrations copyright © 1963 by E. P. Dutton, Inc. Reprinted by permission of Hodder & Stoughton Ltd.

HOLT, RINEHART & WINSTON. Photographs and Sidelight excerpts from *Robert Graves: His Life and Work* by Martin Seymour-Smith. Copyright © 1982 by Martin Seymour-Smith. All reprinted by permission of Holt, Rinehart & Winston.

THE HORN BOOK, INC. Sidelight excerpts from an article "An Interview with Robert Cormier" by Anita Silvey, May/June, 1985 in *Horn Book.* Copyright © 1985 by The Horn Book, Inc./ Sidelight excerpts from *Illustrators of Children's Books: 1946-1956,* edited by Bertha Mahony Miller & others. Copyright © 1958 by The Horn Book, Inc./ Sidelight excerpts from an article "I Go There Quite Often" by Leonard Wibberley, June, 1978 in *Horn Book.* Copyright © 1978 by The Horn Book, Inc./ Sidelight excerpts from an article "The Treegate Series" by Leonard Wibberley in *Horn Book Reflections on Children's Books and Reading,* edited by Elinor Whitney Field. All reprinted by permission of The Horn Book, Inc.

HOUGHTON MIFFLIN CO. Illustration by Victor Mays from *Captured by the Mohawks and Other Adventures of Radisson* by Sterling North. Copyright © 1960 by Sterling North. Reprinted by permission of Houghton Mifflin Co.

JOHNSON PUBLISHING CO., INC. Illustration by Herbert Temple from *The Legend of Africania* by Dorothy W. Robinson. Copyright © 1974 by Johnson Publishing Co., Inc. Reprinted by permission of Johnson Publishing Co., Inc.

KAYE & WARD LTD. Illustration by Kaj Beckman from *The Nightingale* by Hans Christian Andersen. Translated by M. R. James. Text copyright taken from *Hans Christian Andersen Forty-two Stories,* translated by M. R. James and published by Faber & Faber Ltd. Illustrations copyright © 1969 by Kaj Beckman./ Illustration by Kaj Beckman from *Thumbelina* by Hans Christian Andersen. Illustrations copyright © 1967 by Kaj Beckman. Both reprinted by permission of Kaye & Ward Ltd.

MICHAEL KESEND PUBLISHING LTD. Back cover photograph by Beryl Graves from *An Ancient Castle* by Robert Graves. Text copyright © 1980 by Robert Graves. Illustrations copyright © 1980 by Elizabeth Graves./ Illustration by Elizabeth Graves from *An Ancient*

Castle by Robert Graves. Text copyright © 1980 by Robert Graves. Illustrations copyright © 1980 by Elizabeth Graves. Both reprinted by permission of Michael Kesend Publishing Ltd.

ALFRED A. KNOPF, INC. Jacket illustration by Brad Holland from *Beyond the Chocolate War* by Robert Cormier. Text copyright © 1985 by Robert Cormier. Jacket illustration copyright © 1985 by Brad Holland./ Illustration by M. Nebel from *The Good Tiger* by Elizabeth Bowen. Copyright © 1965 by Elizabeth Bowen./ Illustration by Muriel Batherman from *The Little Chalk Man* by Václav Čtvrtek. Copyright © 1970 by Alfred A. Knopf, Inc./ Illustration by Charlotte Steiner from *The Hungry Book* by Charlotte Steiner. Copyright © 1967 by Charlotte Steiner./ Illustration by Anthony Browne from *Gorilla* by Anthony Browne. Copyright © 1983 by Anthony Browne./ Illustrations by Anthony Browne from *Willy the Champ* by Anthony Browne. Copyright © 1985 by Anthony Browne. All reprinted by permission of Alfred A. Knopf, Inc.

LAUREL-LEAF BOOKS. Jacket illustration from *Friends Till the End* by Todd Strasser. Copyright © 1981 by Todd Strasser. Reprinted by permission of Laurel-Leaf Books.

LITTLE, BROWN & CO., INC. Illustrations by Leonard B. Lubin from *The Pig-Tale* by Lewis Carroll. Illustrations copyright © 1975 by Leonard B. Lubin./ Illustration by Leonard B. Lubin from *Henny Penny,* retold by Veronica S. Hutchinson. Illustrations copyright © 1976 by Leonard B. Lubin./ Illustration by Leonard B. Lubin from *The White Cat* by Madame d'Aulnoy. Illustrations copyright © 1978 by Leonard B. Lubin. All reprinted by permission of Little, Brown & Co., Inc.

LOTHROP, LEE & SHEPARD BOOKS. Illustrations by Patience Brewster from *I Met a Polar Bear* by Selma and Pauline Boyd. Text copyright © 1983 by Selma and Pauline Boyd. Illustrations copyright © 1983 by Patience Brewster./ Illustration by Chris L. Demarest from *Clemen's Kingdom* by Chris L. Demarest. Copyright © 1983 by Chris L. Demarest./ Illustration by Joel Schick from *How to Grow a Hundred Dollars* by Elizabeth James and Carol Barkin. Copyright © 1979 by Elizabeth James and Carol Barkin./ Illustration by Joel Schick from *How to Keep a Secret: Writing and Talking in Code* by Elizabeth James and Carol Barkin. Copyright © 1978 by Elizabeth James and Carol Barkin./ Illustration by Leonard B. Lubin from *Kevin's Hat* by Isabelle Holland. Text copyright © 1984 by Isabelle Holland. Illustrations copyright © 1984 by Leonard B. Lubin. All reprinted by permission of Lothrop, Lee & Shepard Books.

McGRAW-HILL, INC. Illustration by Patti Boyd from *Soccer for Young Champions* by Robert J. Antonacci and Anthony J. Puglisi. Copyright © 1978 by Robert J. Antonacci and Anthony J. Puglisi./ Photograph by Norman R. Lightfoot from *The Life of the Mountains* by Maurice Brooks. Copyright © 1967 by McGraw-Hill, Inc./ Illustration by Peter Max from *Meditations,* selected by Peter Max. Copyright © 1972 by Peter Max Enterprises, Inc. All reprinted by permission of McGraw-Hill, Inc.

JULIAN MESSNER. Photograph by Jay Irving from *Bicycle Touring and Camping* by Edward F. Dolan, Jr. Copyright © 1982 by Edward F. Dolan, Jr. Reprinted by permission of Julian Messner.

METHUEN & CO. LTD. Illustration by Kaj Beckman from *The Happy Prince* by Oscar Wilde. Illustrations copyright © 1977 by Kaj Beckman. Reprinted by permission of Methuen & Co. Ltd.

WILLIAM MORROW & CO., INC. Sidelight excerpts from *The Shannon Sailors: A Voyage to the Heart of Ireland* by Leonard Wibberley./ Frontispiece illustration by Lydia Rosier from *The Hands of Cormac Joyce* by Leonard Wibberley. Copyright © 1960 by Leonard Wibberley. Copyright © 1960 by Curtis Publishing Co. Illustrations copyright © 1967 by Lydia Rosier./ Illustration by Peter Max from *Thought* by Peter Max Swami Satchidananda. Copyright © 1970 by Peter Max. All reprinted by permission of William Morrow & Co., Inc.

NEUGEBAUER PRESS, INC. Illustration by Ivan Gantschev from *Santa's Favorite Story* by Hisako Aoki. Copyright © 1982 by Kado-Sobo. Text copyright © 1982 by Neugebauer Press, Inc. Reprinted by permission of Neugebauer Press, Inc.

PANTHEON BOOKS, INC. Jacket illustration "Corner Seat" by Robert Vickrey from *I Am the Cheese* by Robert Cormier. Copyright © 1977 by Robert Cormier./ Jacket illustration by Norman Walker from *The Bumblebee Flies Anyway* by Robert Cormier. Copyright © 1983 by Robert Cormier./ Jacket illustration "Running Boy" by Robert Vickrey from *The Chocolate War* by Robert Cormier. Copyright © 1974 by Robert Cormier. All reprinted by permission of Pantheon Books, Inc.

PUFFIN BOOKS. Illustration by Philip Gough from "The Princess and the Pea" in *Hans Andersen's Fairy Tales,* compiled by Naomi Lewis. Text copyright © 1981 by Naomi Lewis. Illustrations copyright © 1981 by Philip Gough. Reprinted by permission of Puffin Books.

RAINTREE PUBLISHERS, INC. Illustration by Jay Blair from *Diana: Alone against the Sea* by Valjean McLenighan. Copyright © 1980 by Raintree Publishers, Inc. Reprinted by permission of Raintree Publishers, Inc.

RANDOM HOUSE, INC. Illustration by Donald McKay from *Gettysburg* by MacKinlay Kantor. Copyright 1952 by MacKinlay Kantor./ Photograph from *The Rise and Fall of Adolf Hitler* by William L. Shirer. Copyright © 1961 by William L. Shirer. Both reprinted by permission of Random House, Inc.

ST. JAMES PRESS. Sidelight excerpts from *The Annual Obituary,* edited by Janet Podell. Copyright © 1985 by St. James Press. Reprinted by permission of St. James Press.

SCHOLASTIC BOOK SERVICES. Illustration by Carol Nicklaus from *Elephant in the Kitchen* by Winsome Smith. Text copyright © 1980 by Winsome Smith. Illustrations copyright © 1980 by Scholastic, Inc. Reprinted by permission of Scholastic Book Services.

CHARLES SCRIBNER'S SONS. Jacket illustration by Debbi Chabrian from *The Stone Pony* by Patricia Calvert. Copyright © 1982 by Patricia Calvert./ Jacket illustration by Ted Lewin from *The Hour of the Wolf* by Patricia Calvert. Copyright © 1983 by Patricia Calvert./ Jacket illustration by Ronald Himler from *The Bennington Stitch* by Sheila Solomon Klass. Copyright © 1985 by Sheila Solomon Klass. All reprinted by permission of Charles Scribner's Sons.

SIMON & SCHUSTER, INC. Illustration by Vip from *Ludwig, the Dog Who Snored Symphonies* by Robert Kraus. Text copyright © 1971 by Robert Kraus. Illustrations copyright © 1971 by Virgil Partch./ Jacket illustration from *Star Trek—The Motion Picture* by Gene Roddenberry. Copyright © 1979 by Paramount Pictures Corporation and Gene Roddenberry. Both reprinted by permission of Simon & Schuster, Inc.

TIDEN FORLAG. Illustration by Per Beckman from *Vi busungar* ("We Bothering Children") by Lillie Björnstrand./ Illustration by Kaj Beckman from *Den staandaktige tennsoldaten (The Steadfast Tin Soldier)* by Hans Christian Andersen. Both reprinted by permission of Tiden Forlag.

VAN NOSTRAND REINHOLD CO., INC. Illustration by Kaj Beckman from *The Nightingale* by Hans Christian Andersen. Translated by M. R. James. Text copyright taken from *Hans Christian Andersen: Forty-two Stories* translated by M. R. James and published by Faber & Faber Ltd. Illustrations copyright © 1969 by Kaj Beckman. Reprinted by permission of Van Nostrand Reinhold Co., Inc.

VIKING KESTREL. Illustration by Anthony Browne from *The Visitors Who Came to Stay* by Annalena McAfee. Text copyright © 1984 by Annalena McAfee. Illustrations copyright © 1984 by Anthony Browne. Reprinted by permission of Viking Kestrel.

THE VIKING PRESS. Illustration by Robert Handville from *Lord of the Sky: Zeus* by Doris Gates. Copyright © 1972 by Doris Gates./ Illustration by Paul Lantz from *Blue Willow* by Doris Gates. Copyright 1940, © 1968 by Doris Gates./ Illustration by Leonard B. Lubin from *The Birthday of the Infanta* by Oscar Wilde. Illustrations copyright © 1979 by Leonard B. Lubin./ Illustrations by Leonard B. Lubin from *The Elegant Beast* by Leonard B. Lubin. Copyright © 1981 by Leonard B. Lubin./ Illustration by Leonard B. Lubin from "The Mikado" in *Gilbert without Sullivan.* Libretti by W. S. Gilbert. Illustrations copyright © 1981 by Leonard B. Lubin./ Illustration by Leonard B. Lubin from "H.M.S. Pinafore" in *Gilbert without Sullivan.* Libretti by W.S. Gilbert. Illustrations copyright © 1981 by Leonard B. Lubin. All reprinted by permission of The Viking Press.

FRANKLIN WATTS, INC. Frontispiece illustration by Michael Horen from *Auto Mechanics: An Introduction and Guide* by A. Edward Little. Copyright © 1974 by Franklin Watts, Inc./ Illustration by Peter Max from *The Peter Max Land of Blue* by Peter Max. Copyright © 1970 by Peter Max. Both reprinted by permission of Franklin Watts, Inc.

JOHN C. WINSTON CO. Illustration by Kurt Wiese from *Midnight and Jeremiah* by Sterling North. Copyright 1943 by John C. Winston Co. Reprinted by permission of John C. Winston Co.

Sidelight excerpts from an article "J. J. Grandville," in *Cahier de l'Art Mineur,* no. 14-15. Reprinted by permission of *Cahier de l'Art Mineur./* Sidelight excerpts from an article "Star Trek: The Motion Picture" by Don Shay, Spring, 1974 in *Cinefantastique.* Reprinted by permission of *Cinefantastique./* Sidelight excerpts from an interview "Robert Cormier: An Interview." Reprinted by permission of Robert Cormier./ Sidelight excerpts from an article "Star Trek" by Michael Delon, September, 1984 in *Film* (London), number 128. Reprinted by permission of *Film* (London)./ Sidelight excerpts from a translation of *J. J. Grandville* by

Laure Garcin. Reprinted by permission of Eric Losfeld./ Sidelight excerpts from an article "Peter Max," August, 1968 in *Mademoiselle.* Reprinted by permission of *Mademoiselle.*/ Sidelight excerpts from an article "I Was a Teenage Boy: An Interview with Todd Strasser," February, 1983 in *Media & Methods* magazine. Amended by Todd Strasser. Reprinted by permission of *Media & Methods* magazine./ Photograph by David R. Bridge from *Vanishing Wildlife of North America* by Thomas B. Allen. Copyright © 1974 by National Geographic Society. Reprinted by permission of National Geographic Society./ Sidelight excerpts from an article "Star Trek's Gene Roddenberry," March, 1976 in *Penthouse.* Copyright © 1976 by Penthouse International Ltd./ Sidelight excerpts from an article "Twenty Years of Wonderful Uncertainty" by George X. Sand, July, 1961 in *Writer's Digest.* Reprinted by permission of George X. Sand./ Ink drawing by Edward Shenton entitled "Burning Ship." Reprinted by permission of Edward Shenton./ Sidelight excerpts from an article "Gene Roddenberry: The Years Between, the Years Ahead" by Jeff Szalay, October, 1981 in *Starlog.* Reprinted by permission of *Starlog.*/ Cartoon by Partch in *True* magazine. Reprinted by permission of *True* magazine.

Appreciation also to the Performing Arts Research Center of the New York Public Library at Lincoln Center for permission to reprint the documentary film still "The Epic That Never Was."

PHOTOGRAPH CREDITS

Martin Appel: Beverly Scheiner; Patricia Campbell: David Shore Photo; Robert Cormier: Findle Photography; Edward F. Dolan, Jr.: Luther Greer; Louise Fitzhugh: Suzanne Singer; Louise Fitzhugh ("Tap Dance Kid"): Martha Swope; F. Grace: Florence Harrison; Robert Graves (with Elizabeth Graves and son, Robin): Beryl Graves; Sheila Solomon Klass: Morton Klass; Edward Shenton: Courtesy of The Pennsylvania Academy of Fine Arts; William L. Shirer: Clemens Kalischer, copyright © 1980; Walter Wangerin, Jr.: Najlah Feanny/*Sunday Courier & Press.*

SOMETHING ABOUT THE AUThOR

ACUFF, Selma Boyd   1924-
(Selma Boyd)

PERSONAL: Born April 10, 1924, in Chicago, Ill.; daughter of Lucius Virgil (a carpenter) and Eloise (Stroupe) Boyd; married Gale Acuff (a school principal), July 13, 1946; children: David, Kathy, Sally, Gale, Jr. *Education:* Western Carolina University, B.S. 1944; attended Emory University, 1952. *Politics:* Democrat. *Religion:* Episcopalian. *Home:* 1415 Glenwood Dr. SE, Huntsville, Ala. 35801.

CAREER: Teacher in Hampton, Va., 1944-45, and Marietta, Ga., 1951-53, 1958-61, and 1962-64; psychologist's assistant in Atlanta, Ga., 1945-46; writer, 1979—. *Member:* Society of Children's Book Writers, Academy of American Poets, Huntsville Literary Association.

WRITINGS—Under name Selma Boyd; children's books; with sister, Pauline Boyd: *The How: Making the Best of a Mistake* (illustrated by Peggy Luks), Human Sciences, 1981; *Footprints in the Refrigerator* (illustrated by Carol Nicklaus), F. Watts, 1982; *I Met a Polar Bear* (illustrated by Patience Brewster), Lothrop, 1983.

WORK IN PROGRESS: A children's novel, a picture book and an easy-to-read children's book, all with sister, Pauline Boyd.

SIDELIGHTS: "At the age of four, when I was living in Chicago, I developed rheumatic fever. As a consequence, I spent many hours in bed or resting. To help pass the time, my mother read to me and recited poetry. Poetry was and is my first love.

"We moved to North Carolina when I was eight. That year I wrote my first children's story, 'The Red Shoes,' for my sister and co-author, Pauline. I can remember the euphoria I felt when the story found a responsive audience in her.

"In school I spent my spare hours involved in dramatics and with the school newspaper. I continued in college, now spending more time on the newspaper and magazines and enjoying seeing my poems, essays, and short stories in print.

"After I married, I concentrated on rearing four children. We lived on or near school campuses while the children were growing up. I taught first and second grades off and on during these years, substituted in the first seven grades, and continued my writing. I piled papers into dresser drawers, an old trunk, and a suitcase.

"When my last child was in college, I took a creative writing course at the local university, along with my sister. We were encouraged to submit to publishers. The first book, *The How,*

SELMA BOYD ACUFF

I stopped at the corner for just a minute to look in the bakery window. ■ (From *I Met a Polar Bear* by Selma and Pauline Boyd. Illustrated by Patience Brewster.)

was an outcome of that class and of an experience with my first graders.

"I keep a schedule, flexible, of course. When an idea strikes, I grab paper and pencil. There are many rewritings involved and a great distance, usually, from the first pencilled scribblings to the final product. My co-author and I miss very few days working together.

"We choose to write for children because our lives have always been involved with them. We enjoy reading our books to them and observing their reactions. They are a wonderful, honest audience.

"I am amazed, though our books seem to be so different, to find a common thread in them: problem-solving. I suppose the subtle message running through our stories is that problems can be solved.

"I am a private person who spends most of her time reading and writing. Most of all, I suppose, I am an observer.

"I enjoy traveling especially visiting London. My sister, Pauline and I were brought up with the works of the English authors and feel at home in London. We especially enjoy the people, the plays, and the bookstores. We are fascinated by the manuscripts in the British Museum and overwhelmed by the grandeur of Westminster Abbey. Our third trip in 1984 was as exciting as the first one."

HOBBIES AND OTHER INTERESTS: Foreign travel. ("I hope to get to Italy this summer—for the museums.")

ALCOCK, Vivien 1924-

PERSONAL: Born September 23, 1924, in Worthing, England; daughter of John Forster (a scientist) and Molly (Pulman) Alcock; married Leon Garfield (a writer), October 23, 1947; children: Jane Angela. *Education:* Attended Ruskin School of Drawing and of Fine Arts, Oxford, 1940-42. *Politics:* Liberal. *Religion:* Church of England. *Home:* 59 Wood Lane, London N.6 5VD, England. *Agent:* John Johnson Ltd., Clerkenwell House, 45-47 Clerkenwell Green, London EC1R 0HT, England.

CAREER: Gestetner Ltd. (duplicating firm), London, England, artist, 1947-53; Whiltington Hospital, London, secretary, 1953-58. Writer. *Military service:* British Army, ambulance driver, 1942-46.

WRITINGS—For young people: *The Haunting of Cassie Palmer*, Methuen (London), 1980, Delacorte, 1982; *The Stonewalkers*, Methuen, 1981, Delacorte, 1983; *The Sylvia Game* (Junior Literary Guild selection), Methuen, 1982, Delacorte, 1984; *Travellers by Night,* Methuen, 1983, published as *Travelers by Night* (Junior Literary Guild selection; *Horn Book* Honor List) Delacorte, 1985; *Ghostly Companions* (collection of ten ghost stories), Methuen, 1984; *The Cuckoo Sister* (Junior Literary Guild selection) Methuen, 1985.

ADAPTATIONS: "The Haunting of Cassie Palmer" (television series), TVS (Television South), 1984; "Travellers by Night" (television series), TVS, 1985; "The Sylvia Game" (reading on "Jackanory"), BBC-TV, 1983; "Travellers by Night" (reading on "Jackanory"), BBC-TV, 1984.

WORK IN PROGRESS: A children's novel; an early reader for younger children.

SIDELIGHTS: "I should like to be able to say that I started writing stories from some noble motive, but it would not be true. It was because I had two pretty sisters. They were both bigger than me, with fair curly hair, pink cheeks and blue

"That's my dad's painting! The old liar!" She frowned. "He said it had gone wrong and he'd painted it out!" ∎ (Jacket illustration by Paul Tibbles from *The Sylvia Game* by Vivien Alcock.)

eyes. They learned to read before I did. They learned to swim before I did. They were chosen to be angels in the school nativity play, while I was disguised as a sheep somewhere at the back of the stage. It was difficult not to feel like an insignificant shadow trailing behind two bright stars.

"It is easy, however, to be the hero of a story if you write it yourself. I started telling myself stories in which the heroines were always small and skinny and dark, like me. It was comforting to find out how well they got on, facing up to incredible adventures and dangers—as long as I was writing the script. At first they were impossibly brave and resourceful, but this did not content me for long. I wanted them to be human, to have the same fears and uncertainties that I had, or their triumphs seemed phoney—unsatisfying.

"It was a form of escapism, I suppose, just as daydreams are. But I think it was a valuable one. In trying to invent characters, you have to look at people more closely, try to guess what they are thinking and what they are likely to say, and how the world looks through their eyes. Even in producing a disguised version of yourself as a heroine, you learn at least what strengths and virtues you would most like to have, and sometimes they are unexpected ones.

"When I became an ambulance driver, I gave up writing stories for a time. It was not that we were always so busy. We would often sit doing nothing for hours, just waiting in case

VIVIEN ALCOCK

we were called. But somehow it was difficult to settle down to work when one might have to leave in a hurry. In Belgium, the trains from the front always came in at night. We would be told to rest on our beds fully dressed, even down to our army boots, so that we should be ready when the signal came. Then we would drive in convoy to Ostend Station, park on the platform and wait. When the train came, the wounded soldiers were loaded onto the ambulances so quickly that we hardly saw them. They were just voices in the night.

"My husband was in the army medical corps and we met in an army canteen. Like me, he could not decide whether he wanted to be an artist or a writer. In the end, he became the writer and I became a commercial artist. I gave this up when our daughter was born, and it was through telling her bedtime stories that my desire to be a writer returned.

"I suppose like all writers, I am influenced to some extent by my own experience, though I do not draw on it consciously. My mother died when I was ten, and we were sent to live with some old friends of my father's in the country, far away from our old home and anyone we knew. I find I tend to write about children who are facing some great change or difficulty in their lives, and who learn to grow through it to a greater understanding of themselves and other people. I do not apologise for having happy endings. I firmly believe children are resilient and resourceful, and will make their own happiness somehow if given a chance. The end of childhood is not necessarily when the law decides it shall be.

"Although I have a liking for dramatic and sometimes fantastic plots, I try to make my characters as real as possible, and their relationships true. My heroines are no longer always small and skinny and dark. (But then nor am I now.) I suspect there is a little of me stilll lurking at the bottom of all the characters I create, though blown up out of all recognition. In *Travellers by Night,* two circus children kidnap an elderly elephant in an attempt to save it from the slaughterhouse, and hide it in a forest. I have never tried to hide an elephant. I can remember, however, hiding my favourite cat under my blankets at bedtime, and with a bit of imagination. . . ."

HOBBIES AND OTHER INTERESTS: Painting, patchwork, reading.

FOR MORE INFORMATION SEE: Times Literary Supplement, November 20, 1981, July 23, 1982.

ALEX, Ben [a pseudonym]   1946-

PERSONAL: Born February 17, 1946, in Copenhagen, Denmark; son of Alex (a dairy farmer) and Ruth (a housewife; maiden name, Larsen) Jensen; married Marlee Smith (an author and editor; known under pseudonym Marlee Alex), September 10, 1974; children: Tirza, Mathilde, Joy Melissa. *Education:* Attended University of Aarhus, 1966-72. *Religion:* Christian. *Home:* 122 Kildedalen, Hilleroed, 3400 Denmark. *Office:* Scandinavia Publishing House, 32 Noerregade, 1165 K. Copenhagen, Denmark.

CAREER: Udfordringen (magazine), Copenhagen, Denmark, editor, 1978-82; Scandinavia Publishing House, Copenhagen, managing editor, 1976—; writer, 1978—. *Awards, honors:* C. S. Lewis Gold Medal Award for best children's book with a Christian message, 1983, for *Grandpa and Me: We Learn about Death.*

BEN ALEX

WRITINGS—With wife, Marlee Alex; children's books in "Family Reality" series: *Dig og mig og vores ny baby,* Scandinavia Publishing House, 1981, translation published as *You and Me and Our New Little Baby* (illustrated with photographs by B. Alex and Joergen Vium Olesen), Zondervan, 1982, published as *Our New Baby,* Lion, 1982; *Bestefar og mig laer om doeden,* [Denmark], 1983, translation published as *Grandpa and Me: We Learn about Death* (illustrated with photographs by B. Alex and Otto Wikkesloe), Bethany House, 1983, published as *Grandpa and Me,* Lion, 1983.

For adults; with M. Alex: *Jeg elsker dig,* Scandinavia Publishing House, 1983, translation published as *I Love You: Notes from Our Marriage,* Bethany House, 1983; *Magic Moments in the Kingdom of Kids,* Thomas Nelson, 1986.

Also author of monthly column in *Udfordringen* magazine.

WORK IN PROGRESS: A Boy from Sao Paulo Brazil and *A Boy from Kenya,* both part of "Children Around the World" series; *Chebet and the Lost Goat; You and Me and Our Best Christmas; Essays.*

SIDELIGHTS: Alex's books have been translated into more than nine languages.

But still I dream that somewhere there must be
The spirit of a child that waits for me.

—Bayard Taylor

(From *Grandpa and Me: We Learn about Death* by Marlee and Ben Alex. Photographs by Ben Alex and Otto Wikkelsoe.)

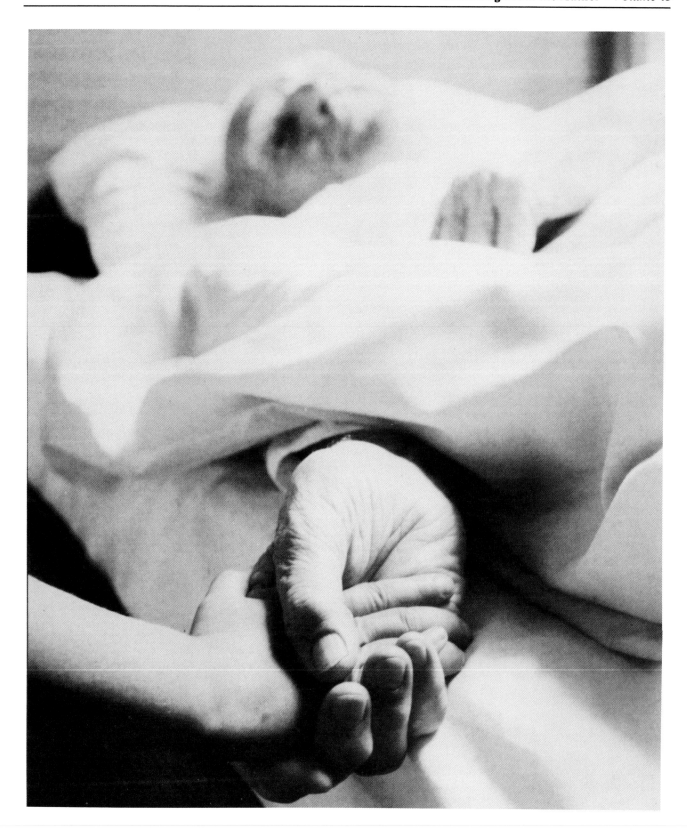

Grandpa lay completely still in his bed. ■ (From *Grandpa and Me: We Learn about Death* by Marlee and Ben Alex. Photographs by Ben Alex and Otto Wikkelsoe.)

MARLEE ALEX

ALEX, Marlee [a pseudonym] 1948-

PERSONAL: Born December 29, 1948, in Pratt, Kan.; daughter of Marvin Smith (an executive chartered life underwriter) and Virginia Cook (a secretary); married a managing editor and author, known under pseudonym Ben Alex, September 10, 1974; children: Tirza, Mathilde, Joy Melissa. *Education:* Attended Westmont College, 1967-69; San Diego State College (now University), B.A., 1971. *Religion:* Christian. *Home:* 122 Kildedalen, Hilleroed, 3400 Denmark. *Office:* Scandinavia Publishing House, 32 Noerregade, 1165 K. Copenhagen, Denmark.

CAREER: Writer, 1979; Scandinavia Publishing House, Copenhagen, Denmark, editor, 1983—. *Awards, honors:* C. S. Lewis Gold Medal Award for best children's book with a Christian message, 1983, for *Grandpa and Me: We Learn about Death.*

WRITINGS: Songs of Heaven and Earth, Scandinavia Publishing House, 1984; *Songs of Light,* Scandinavia Publishing House, 1984; *Songs from the Desert,* Scandinavia Publishing House, 1984.

Children's books in "Women of the Bible" series; all published by Scandinavia Publishing House: *The Story of Esther,* 1986; . . . *Ruth,* 1986; . . . *Sarah,* 1986; . . . *Mary,* 1986; . . . *Hannah,* 1987; . . . *Deborah,* 1987; . . . *Mary Magdalene,* 1987; . . . *Mary of Bethany,* 1987.

With husband, Ben Alex; children's books in "Family Reality" series: *Dig og mix og vores ny baby,* Scandinavia Publishing House, 1981, translation published as *You and Me and Our New Little Baby* (illustrated with photographs by B. Alex and Joergen Vium Olesen), Zondervan, 1982, published as *Our New Baby,* Lion, 1982; *Bestefar og mig laer om doeden,* [Denmark], 1983, translation published as *Grandpa and Me: We Learn about Death* (photographs by B. Alex and Otto Wikkesloe), Bethany House, 1983, published as *Grandpa and Me,* Lion, 1983.

For adults; with B. Alex: *Jeg elsker dig,* Scandinavia Publishing House, 1983, translation published as *I Love You: Notes from Our Marriage,* Bethany House, 1983; *Magic Moments in the Kingdom of Kids,* Thomas Nelson, 1986.

WORK IN PROGRESS: "A saga of three generations of women who struggle to find their way in the universal and timeless dilemmas of womanhood based on the life of my grandmother at the turn of the century in Missouri and the World War II romance and battlefield experience of my mother and father in California and in France."

SIDELIGHTS: "Although I grew up in California, I am proud of my roots in the heart of America, in a wheat-farming family. After college and two years of work and travel in Europe and Israel, I returned to the Midwest, where I met my Danish husband. It was he who later prompted me to write professionally. He would set up the typewriter after supper, insert a piece of paper, and type the first few words; then he removed the dishcloth from my hands and sat me down at the typewriter while he cleaned up the dishes.

"The wonder of pregnancy and the marvelous experience of giving birth, along with the challenge of raising three daughters, is a natural motivation for writing about and for children, along with my intense interest in the psychological and spiritual development of children. Our Christian beliefs and our commitment to family life are reflected in our writings."

Alex's books have been translated into more than nine languages.

ALLEN, Thomas B(enton) 1929-
(Tom Allen)

PERSONAL: Born March 20, 1929, in Bridgeport, Conn.; son of Walter Leo (a salesman) and Elizabeth (Reilly) Allen; married Florence MacBride (a potter), June 5, 1950; children: Christopher, Constance, Roger. *Education:* Attended Fairfield University, 1947-49; University of Bridgeport, B.A., 1955. *Politics:* Democrat. *Religion:* Unitarian Universalist. *Home and office:* 7820 Custer Rd., Bethesda, Md. 20014. *Agent:* Philip G. Spitzer Literary Agency, 111-25 76th Ave., Forest Hills, N.Y. 11375.

CAREER: Bridgeport Herald, Bridgeport, Conn., reporter, 1946-52, 1953-63; *New York Daily News,* New York, N.Y., feature writer, 1956-63; Chilton Book Co., Philadelphia, Pa., managing editor for trade books, 1963-65; National Geographic Society, Washington, D.C., book editor, 1965-81. Instructor in freshman English, Montgomery College, 1969-70; lecturer in creative writing, U.S. Naval Academy; instructor, Writers Center (Washington, D.C.) *Military service:* U.S. Navy, journalist, 1952-53. *Member:* Writer's Center (member of board of directors), Washington Independent Writers.

WRITINGS: (Under name Tom Allen; with Harold W. McCormick and William Young) *Shadows in the Sea: The Sharks, Skates, and Rays,* Chilton, 1963; *The Quest: A Report on Extraterrestrial Life,* Chilton, 1965; (editor and contributor) *Vacationland U.S.A.,* National Geographic Society, 1972; (with others) *Living in Washington: A Moving Experience,* Westover, 1972; (editor) *The Marvels of Animal Behavior,* National Geographic Society, 1972; *The Last Inmate* (novel), Charterhouse, 1973; *Vanishing Wildlife of North America,* National Geographic Society, 1974; (editor and contributor) *We Americans,* National Geographic Society, 1975; *A Short Life* (novel), Berkley Publishing, 1978; (editor and contributor) *Wild Animals of North America,* National Geographic Society, 1979; (with Norman Polmar) *Rickover* (biography), Simon & Schuster, 1981; (editor and contributor) *Images of the World,* National Geographic Society, 1981; (with N. Polmar) *Not Quite Treason* (novel), Macmillan, 1986. Contributing editor to *Seapower* and *National Geographic.* Also author of feature articles for Chicago Tribune-New York Daily News Syndicate and Field Enterprises Syndicate.

Contributor; all published by National Geographic Society: *Greece and Rome: Builders of Our World,* 1968; *The Age of Chivalry,* 1969; *Wilderness U.S.A.,* 1972; *The World of the American Indian,* 1974; *Our Continent,* 1976; *Visiting Our Past,* 1977; *Ancient Egypt,* 1978; *Romance of the Sea,* 1980; *Journey to China,* 1982; *England and Ireland,* 1985.

WORK IN PROGRESS: A novel; a nonfiction account of the experience of an adoptee searching for his natural parents.

SIDELIGHTS: Allen has been writing professionally since he was fifteen years old. He claims that he has always, even in his fiction, relied upon fact. "I write both fiction and nonfiction because, to me, there is no difference in style and little difference in approach. Words are words; English is English. I believe that I am still learning about this craft after more than thirty years. And I hope to keep on learning. I enjoy teaching or, rather, talking about writing. I believe I have to pay my dues by helping young writers. I do this teaching at the Washington Writer's Center. When I am not there, I am working, which is what I call writing."

Allen's novel *A Short Life,* based on a real incident involving the illegal dispersal of radioactive substances, has been sold to Time-Life Films as the television movie, "The Plutonium Incident." About the book, Allen wrote: "This, for me, is the best kind of writing—'factual fiction' which can shed light on a vital current issue."

Unloved and often unnoticed, many reptiles and amphibians face the same relentless pressure on their living space. ■ (From *Vanishing Wildlife of North America* by Thomas B. Allen. Photograph by David R. Bridge.)

THOMAS B. ALLEN

ALTSCHULER, Franz 1923-

PERSONAL: Born October 2, 1923, in Mannheim, Germany; became naturalized citizen. *Education:* Institute of Design, Chicago, Ill., B.F.A. *Agent:* (Paintings) Tria Gallery, Ellison Bay, Wis.

CAREER: Institute of Design, Chicago, Ill., instructor in drawing, 1954-65; commissioned designer and illustrator of books and periodicals, 1954-78; Art Institute of Chicago, Chicago, assistant professor of graphic design and illustration, 1973-77; Morehead State University, Morehead, Ky., assistant professor of graphic design and illustration, 1978—. Chairman of planning committee, Urban Renewal, Old Town Triangle Association, 1960-67. Work has been exhibited at various locations, including Art Institute of Chicago, Chicago, 1951-53, 1962; Society of Typographic Arts, Chicago, 1952-77; Art Directors Club, New York, N.Y., 1954-60, 1973, 1978; Denver Museum Annual, Denver, Colo., 1955; Society of Illustrators, 1967-78; Illinois State Museum, Lewiston, Ill., 1969; and is represented in several public collections. *Member:* American Institute of Graphic Arts, Society of Typographic Arts (director and vice-president), Friends of the Institute of Design (secretary), 27 Chicago Designers and Arts Club. *Awards, honors:* Pauline Palmer Prize, Art Institute of Chicago, 1953; Notable Book award, Southern California Council on Literature for Children and Young People, 1967, for *The Royal Dirk; Tales from Atop a Russian Stove* was selected one of Child Study Association's "Children's Books of the Year," 1973; first prize, Artists Guild of Chicago Watercolor Show, 1976.

ILLUSTRATOR—Of interest to young readers: Claudia L. Lewis, *The Strange Room*, Albert Whitman, 1964; Patricia

She acted as if she were a baby robin, begging for a worm. ■ (From *Bobbin's Land* by Carol Cornelius. Illustrated by Franz Altschuler.)

Beatty, *Squaw Dog,* Morrow, 1965; Mary L. Hansen, *Black Bear Adventures,* Allyn & Bacon, 1965; John Beatty and P. Beatty, *The Royal Dirk,* Morrow, 1966; (with James MacDonald) Ralph E. Bailey, *Guns over the Carolinas: The Story of Nathaniel Green,* Morrow, 1967; R. E. Bailey, *Fight for Royal Gorge,* Morrow, 1968; Allan W. Eckert, *The King Snake,* Little, Brown, 1968; P. Beatty, *The Sea Pair,* Morrow, 1970; Edythe W. Newell, *The Rescue of the Sun, and Other Tales from the Far North,* Albert Whitman, 1970; P. Beatty, *A Long Way to Whiskey Creek,* Morrow, 1971; Phyllis Savory, compiler, *Lion Outwitted by Hare, and Other African Tales,* Albert Whitman, 1971; Roger Elwood, compiler, *Monster Tales: Vampires, Werewolves, and Things,* Rand McNally, 1973; *Tales from Atop a Russian Stove,* Albert Whitman, 1973.

Ida Chittum, *Tales of Terror,* Rand McNally, 1975; Ruth Odor, *Cissy, the Pup,* Child's World, 1976, revised edition published as *The Pup Who Did as She Pleased,* 1979; Jane B. Moncure, *Barbara's Pony, Buttercup,* Child's World, 1977; Sylvia Root Tester, *Melinda,* Child's World, 1977; Carol Cornelius, *Bobbin's Land,* Child's World, 1978; C. Cornelius, *Hyla (Peep) Crucifer: The Story of the Spring Peeper Frog,* Child's World, 1978; C. Cornelius, *Isabella Wooly Bear Tiger Moth,* Child's World, 1978; Bill Maddox and Harold Beeson, *Rag and Patches,* Follett, 1978.

Other: *Human Evolution,* Rand McNally, 1974; *Advise and Consent,* Franklin Library, 1976. Also contributor of illustrations to *Sphere.*

ANDRIST, Ralph K.   1914-

PERSONAL: Born January 11, 1914, in Crookston, Minn.; son of John J. (a railroadman) and Mary (Knutson) Andrist; married Vivian Margaret Witt (an oral historian), February 22, 1941; children: Jill Andrist Miller, Mary Andrist Leech, Melissa Andrist Hardtke. *Education:* University of Minnesota, B.A. (magna cum laude), 1937; Columbia University, additional study, 1946-47. *Politics:* Democrat. *Home:* Meadow Dr., North Eastham, Mass. 02651.

CAREER: Held various jobs, including grave digging, carpentry, and free-lance publicity, 1937-45; Radio Station WCCO, Minneapolis, Minn., news editor, 1945-48; *Better Homes and Gardens,* Des Moines, Iowa, garden editor, 1948-50; Crusade for Freedom, New York City, press publicity director, 1951-52; Episcopal Church Foundation (fund-raising), New York City, associate director, 1952-60; free-lance writer, 1961-64, 1970-74; American Heritage Publishing Co., New York City, book editor, 1964-70; senior editor, Franklin Library, 1973-79. Member, New Canaan (Conn.) Democratic Town Committee, 1955-59. *Military service:* U.S. Naval Reserve, 1942-45; became lieutenant; awarded Bronze Star. *Member:* Authors Guild, Phi Beta Kappa. *Awards, honors:* Award of National Conference of Christians and Jews; *Variety* plaque award; Heywood Broun Award, 1947, for radio documentary series on juvenile delinquency; Golden Spur Award, Western Writers of America, 1967, for *To the Pacific with Lewis and Clark.*

WRITINGS—All published by American Heritage Press, except as noted: *The California Gold Rush,* 1961; *Steamboats on the Mississippi,* 1962; *Heroes of Polar Exploration,* 1962; *Andrew Jackson, Soldier and Statesman,* 1963; *The Erie Canal,* 1964; *The Long Death: The Last Days of the Plains Indians,* Macmillan, 1964; (editor) *The Great West,* 1965; (editor) *World War II,* 1966; (editor) *The Thirteen Colonies,* 1967; *To the Pacific with Lewis and Clark,* 1967; (editor) *The Making of the Nation,* 1969; (author of text) Ray Brosseau, compiler, *Looking Forward: Life in the Twentieth Century as Predicted in the Pages of American Magazines from 1895-1905,* 1970; (editor and contributor) *The '20s and '30s,* 1970; (editor) *George Washington: A Biography in His Own Words,* Newsweek, 1972;

Little more than the pilothouse of the Ouachita shows above her prodigious load of cotton. ▪
(From *Steamboats on the Mississippi* by the editors of American Heritage. Narrative by Ralph K. Andrist.)

RALPH K. ANDRIST

American Century, 1972; (contributor) *The Law in America*, 1974; (contributor) *The Very Rich*, 1974; (contributor) *Two Hundred Years*, U.S. News and World Report, 1976; (with Herbert Johnson) *Historic Courthouses of New York State*, Columbia University Press, 1977. Ghostwriter of two books for government officials. Also author of many radio documentary shows, 1945-48; contributor of numerous articles to periodicals including *Christian Science Monitor*, *American Heritage*, *Reader's Digest*, and *Smithsonian*.

WORK IN PROGRESS: The Lost Passage, a book "about the search for a northwest passage and especially the tragic Franklin expedition of 1845."

SIDELIGHTS: "I have been torn between wanting to be a writer or an editor. Happily, most of my editing jobs have also required a good deal of creative writing, so I have been able to indulge both bents. As for when I decided to be a writer, I suppose it was from the very beginning, and as a journalist I have always been putting words together in one way or another—publicity, ghostwriting, news, what have you—but I turned to the typewriter in earnest when I became intrigued by the possibilities that lay in history—and particularly American history. Here were characters and plots better than anything I could make up: good men and bad, heroism and cowardice, events on a grand scale and the human interest of obscure citizens. To bring history out of the schoolbook stuffiness of a mere catalogue of dates and events and to bring it to life has been a satisfying challenge. And always in the back of my mind has been the hope that, by making the past real and provocative, I can help at least some readers to better understand the present."

FOR MORE INFORMATION SEE: Christian Science Monitor, November 2, 1967; *Book World*, November 5, 1967; *New York Times Book Review*, February 4, 1968.

ANTOLINI, Margaret Fishback   1904-1985 (Margaret Fishback)

OBITUARY NOTICE: Professionally known under her maiden name, Margaret Fishback; born March 10, 1904, in Washington, D.C.; died September 25, 1985, in Camden, Me. Copywriter, poet, and author. Fishback, who wrote advertising copy for Macy's department store in New York City, became known for her light verse. Described as "the highest-paid advertising woman in the world" during the 1930s, she reportedly combined her successful copywriting career with an equally prof-

itable one as a free-lance writer. Fishback's verse appeared in numerous publications, including her collections *I Feel Better Now: Verses, I Take It Back: Verses*, and *One to a Customer: Collected Poems*. She also wrote several children's books, including *My Little Library* and *A Child's Book of Natural History*. Among the author's other writings are *Safe Conduct, Time for a Quick One*, and *Look Who's a Mother! A Book about Babies for Parents, Expectant and Otherwise*.

FOR MORE INFORMATION SEE: Everett S. Allen, *Famous American Humorous Poets* (juvenile), Dodd, 1968; *Current Biography*, H. W. Wilson, 1941. Obituaries: *New York Times*, September 28, 1985; *Washington Post*, September 29, 1985; *AB Bookman's Weekly*, November 11, 1985; *Current Biography*, November, 1985.

ANTONACCI, Robert J(oseph)   1916-

PERSONAL: Born January 21, 1916, in Toluca, Ill.; son of Nick and Angeline (Matterelli) Antonacci; married second wife, Amaryllis Boyd (a bacteriologist), September 16, 1953; children: (first marriage) Robert J., Jr.; (second marriage) Clarissa. *Education:* Indiana University, B.S., 1941; University of Michigan, M.S., 1946, Ed.D., 1956.

CAREER: Oregon State University, Corvallis, assistant professor of health and physical education and wrestling coach, 1946-50; University of Chicago, Chicago, Ill., member of staff of department of physical education and guidance, 1950-53; Wayne State University, Detroit, Mich., associate professor of health and physical education, 1953-57; director of health, physical education, and safety for public schools, Gary, Ind., beginning 1957; member of staff of department of physical education, Temple University, Philadelphia, Pa. Member of Indiana board of directors, Health Funds for Medical Research, 1962-64; member of board of directors, United Fund of Gary, 1961-63, and Gary Youth Commission, 1960-64. *Military service:* U.S. Navy, 1941-45; became chief specialist.

First match of British Ladies Football Club, 1895. ▪ (From *Soccer for Young Champions* by Robert J. Antonacci and Anthony J. Puglisi. Illustrated by Patti Boyd.)

MEMBER: American Association for Health, Physical Education and Recreation (chairman of Midwest association; vice-president of Indiana association), American Public Health Association, National Society for Study of Education, Phi Delta Kappa, Sigma Delta Psi, Phi Epsilon Kappa.

WRITINGS—Published by McGraw, except as indicated: (With others) *Sports Officiating,* Ronald, 1949; (with Jene Barr) *Baseball for Young Champions,* 1956, 2nd edition, 1977; (with J. Barr) *Football for Young Champions,* 1958, 2nd edition, 1976; (with J. Barr) *Basketball for Young Champions,* 1960, 2nd edition, 1979; (with J. Barr) *Physical Fitness for Young Champions,* 1962, 2nd edition, 1975; (with Gene Schoor) *Track and Field for Young Champions,* 1974; (with Anthony J. Puglisi) *Soccer for Young Champions* (illustrated by Patti Boyd), 1978; (with Barbara D. Lockhart) *Tennis for Young Champions,* 1982. Also editor of health and physical education teaching guides. Contributor to several books and to professional journals and newspapers.

WORK IN PROGRESS: Research on health habits and practices of elementary school children and on fitness status of boys and girls in secondary schools.

SIDELIGHTS: Robert J. Antonacci is a member of Indiana University's Hall of Fame as national collegiate wrestling champion.

FOR MORE INFORMATION SEE: Michigan Authors, 2nd edition, Michigan Association for Media in Education, 1980.

HISAKO AOKI

AOKI, Hisako   1942-

PERSONAL: Born July 27, 1942, in Nishinomiya City, Japan; daughter of Shoichi (an importer) and Fumiko (Yamazaki) Aoki. *Education:* International Christian University, B.A., 1965. *Home and office:* 9-1-515 Sanban-Cho, Chiyoda-Ku, Tokyo 102, Japan.

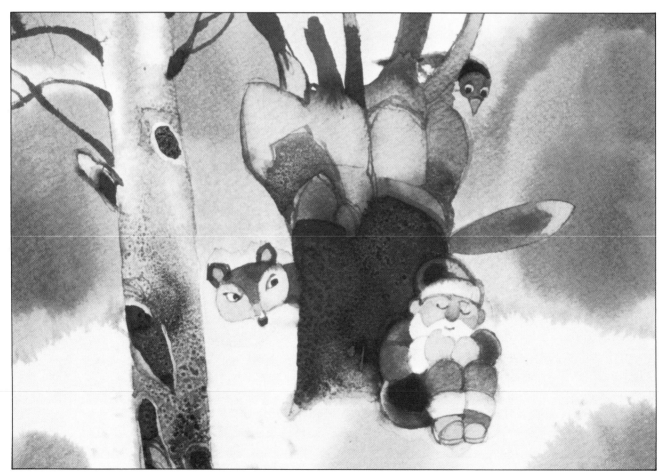

There, fast asleep against a tree, was Santa Claus! ■ (From *Santa's Favorite Story* by Hisako Aoki. Illustrated by Ivan Gantschev.)

CAREER: Shiko-Sha Co., Ltd., Tokyo, Japan, editor, 1972-79; Neugebauer Press, Salzburg, Austria, editor, 1979-80; Kado-Sobo, Tokyo, Japan, editor of picture books, 1980—. Freelance editor, translator, and coordinator.

WRITINGS: (With Yutaka Sugita) *Fly Hoops Fly,* Barron, 1978; (editor) *Henzeru to Greteru* (title means "Hansel and Gretel"), Kado-Sobo (Tokyo), 1981; (editor) Kenzo Kobayashi, *Noharo no chiisana ie* (title means "Two Little Ducks"), Kado-Sobo, 1981; *Oyayubi-hime* (title means "Thumbelina"), Kado-Sobo, 1982; *Santa's Favorite Story* (illustrated by Ivan Gantschev), Neugebauer Press, 1982.

Also translator of books from the English to the Japanese, including *How Santa Had a Long and Difficult Journey Delivering His Presents* by Fernando Krahn, *Children's Letters to Santa Claus,* compiled by Bill Adler, and *The Trial of Animal,* a Phillippine folktale. Contributor to *Horn Book.*

APPEL, Martin E(liot) 1948-
(Marty Appel)

PERSONAL: Surname is pronounced A-*pell;* born August 7, 1948, in Brooklyn, N.Y.; son of Irving (an insurance broker) and Celia (a secretary; maiden name, Mann) Appel; married Patricia Alkins (a social worker), October 26, 1975; children: Brian, Deborah. *Education:* State University of New York College at Oneoneta, B.A., 1970. *Home:* 4 Sherwood Dr., Larchmont, N.Y., 10538. *Office:* 11 WPIX Plaza, New York, N.Y. 10017.

MARTIN E. APPEL

CAREER: New York Yankees, Bronx, N.Y., director of public relations, 1968-77; Garagiola/Appel Enterprises, Tarrytown, N.Y., president, 1977-78; New York Apples (tennis team), New York City, director of public relations, 1979; Office of the Baseball Commissioner, New York City, 1978-80; WPIX, Inc., vice-president, 1980—. *Member:* Society of American Baseball Research. *Awards, honors: Baseball's Best* was named outstanding sports reference book by American Library Association, 1977.

WRITINGS: (With Matt Winick) *Illustrated Digest of Baseball,* five volumes, Stadia Sports Publishing, 1971-75; (with Burt Goldblatt) *Baseball's Best: The Hall of Fame Gallery,* McGraw, 1977; (with Thurman Munson) *Thurman Munson: An Autobiography* (Sports Illustrated Book Club selection), Coward, 1978; (editor, under name Marty Appel) *Batting Secrets of the Major Leaguers,* Wanderer Books, 1981; (contributor) *The Masked Marvels,* Random House, 1982; (with Tom Seaver) *Tom Seaver's All-Time Baseball Greats,* Wanderer Books, 1984. Contributor to *Baseball Digest* and *Encyclopedia Americana.*

WORK IN PROGRESS: A book with Bowie Kuhn for Times Books.

SIDELIGHTS: Appel, who was raised in New York as a Yankee fan, went from college to work in the team's front office and, later, the commissioner's office. He feels "few have managed to be this fortunate—crossing over from fan to the 'inside' and gaining the opportunity to write about it.

"How do I accomplish writing books? Two skills—I read a lot as a youngster, and thus book styles made an impression. And I learned to type with great speed, so all first drafts go straight from my mind to my fingertips rapidly. I couldn't have been an author before the electric typewriter era."

APPLEBAUM, Stan 1929-
(Robert Keith)

PERSONAL: Born March 1, 1929, in Newark, N.J.; son of William and Julia (Knoll) Applebaum; married second wife, Cecelia Notov (an educator and television personality), March 3, 1971; children: (first marriage) Jody Karin, Jonathan Todd; (second marriage) Edward Norman, Allison Joyce. *Home and office:* 330 West 58th St., New York, N.Y. 10019.

CAREER: Musical arranger, composer, conductor, and writer. Arranger for big band directors, including Harry James and Benny Goodman; musical arranger and orchestrator for "The Goldbergs," 1950-51, "Jimmy Durante," 1951-52, "Eddie Cantor" and "Martin and Lewis," 1953, "The Hit Parade," 1956-57, and "Studio One," 1960; eastern artists and repertory directory for Warner Brothers Records, 1961-63.

MEMBER: National Academy of Recording Arts and Sciences (member of board of governors), American Society of Composers, Authors, and Publishers, Society of Advertising Music Producers, Arrangers, Composers (head of technical and information committee). *Awards, honors:* Awards of merit from Communication Arts Society, 1967, for music campaigns for Bristol Myers Co. and Eastern Airlines; international broadcasting awards from Hollywood Radio and Television Society, 1967, for music in Pan American World Airlines advertisement, and 1969, for music in Sears, Roebuck & Co. advertisement; award from American Television and Radio Com-

STAN APPLEBAUM

mercials Festival, 1968, for music in Pan American World Airlines advertisement; award from Cannes International Festival of Film Publicity, 1969, for music in WTS Pharmacraft Products advertisement.

WRITINGS—Children's nature books; all published by Golden Press, except where indicated: (With Victoria Cox) *A Not So Ugly Friend*, Holt, 1973; *The Flying Janitor*, 1973; (with V. Cox) *Nature's Carpet Sweeper* (illustrated by George Sandstrom), 1973, *The Night in Crusty Armor*, 1973; *Nature's Smallest Grave-digger*, 1973; *The Laughing Garbage Disposal*, 1973; *Nature's Assistant*, 1973; *Going My Way?*, Harcourt, 1975; *Nature's Doubles*, 1975.

Music books: *How to Improvise*, C. Colin, 1954; *Advanced Trumpet Duets*, two volumes, C. Colin, 1955; *Folk Music: Bach Style*, Schroeder & Gunther, 1972; *Creative Rhythmic Reading at the Piano*, Schroeder & Gunther, 1972; *Sound/World*, Schroeder & Gunther, 1974; *Bach Music: Simple Style*, Schroeder & Gunther, 1975; *Double Play*, Schroeder & Gunther, 1975.

Also author of plays with Gerald Dietz, including "Heavenly Chase," "Hogan's Utopia," "Pithead," "Bride of the Bayou," "Mr. Nathan and the Nafke," and "Catherine's Daughter." Co-author with Mel Mandel and composer of musical comedy "Bright Lights," and arranger/orchestrator of musical "Raggedy Ann and Andy."

Composer of music for television and radio commercials, records for leading performers, motion pictures, pieces for band and orchestra, jazz instrumentals, chamber and choral music, choral arrangements, dance band music, piano music, and children's songs, some under pseudonym Robert Keith, many published by Chappell, Inc., E. Shuberth & Co., E. H. Morris, and other leading music publishers.

WORK IN PROGRESS—All children's books: *The Words We Live By; I See With My Ears; Three Different Places; I Can Be Positive; I've a Friendship With the Lord; The Apple, the Bee, the Bird, and Me; The Five of Us; Music Primer; Search and Discover*, science oriented series co-authored with Victoria Cox; *Buggy Books*, a series on small creatures; *A Very Special Vehicle*, the travels of a seed.

SIDELIGHTS: Applebaum's prolific career in music has spanned several generations and covered nearly all aspects of composition and arrangement. Beginning with the big-band era, he later moved into television and radio work. Subsequently, he arranged the music for hit records by such popular recording artists as Joanie Sommers, Bobby Vinton, Brook Benton, and Connie Francis. He has also composed dozens of pieces for beginning and advanced music students.

"I started writing children's books when an editor at Holt indicated that he was shy one title for a basic elementary reading series, and that the deadline for submissions was two weeks away. With my co-writer, Victoria Cox, we created a simple book about a worm, *A Not So Ugly Friend*. It was accepted and my career as an author emerged. This book, by the way, is very much a part of required reading in the schools today. With an avid interest in scientific subjects, it was a foregone conclusion that I'd write in this area. All my efforts in this area are first cleared with authorities at the Museum of Natural History prior to submission. Cleared for accuracy, that is.

"Writing books for children is a joy. The challenge of saying something simply and effectively is one that gives me immense pleasure."

HOBBIES AND OTHER INTERESTS: Archaeology, travel in Mexico, ham radio, carpentry, botany, painting, jogging, swimming, baseball.

THOMAS P. BAIRD

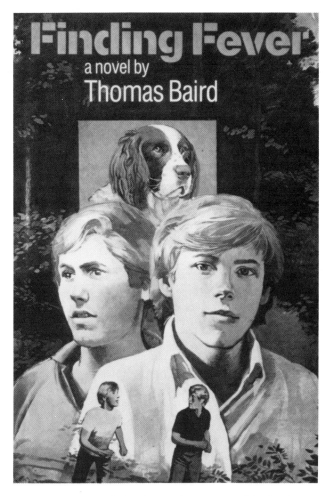

We live in a neighborhood where much of the land, once farmed, has run to trees and scrub, and there are always woods close by the houses. . . . ■ (Jacket illustration by Robert Sabin from *Finding Fever* by Thomas Baird.)

BAIRD, Thomas P.   1923-

PERSONAL: Born April 22, 1923, in Omaha, Neb.; son of Edgar A. and Alice (Kennard) Baird. *Education:* Princeton University, B.A., 1945, M.F.A., 1950. *Politics:* None. *Religion:* None. *Home:* 293 Oxford St., Hartford, Conn. 06105. *Agent:* Harold Ober Associates, Inc., 40 East 49th St., New York, N.Y. 10017. *Office:* Trinity College, Hartford, Conn. 06105.

CAREER: Writer. Princeton University, Princeton, N. J., instructor in art history, 1949-51, 1952-53; Frick Collection, New York, N.Y., lecturer in art history, 1954-57; National Gallery of Art, Washington, D.C., member of curatorial staff, 1957-60; Dumbarton Oaks, Washington, D.C., associate director, 1967-70; Trinity College, Hartford, Conn., associate professor of art history, 1970-79, professor of art history, 1979—. *Military service:* U.S. Naval Reserve, 1943-46.

WRITINGS—Novels; published by Harcourt, except as indicated: *Triumphal Entry,* 1962; *The Old Masters,* 1963; *Sheba's Landing,* 1964; *Nice Try,* 1965; *Finding Out,* 1967; *People Who Pull You Down,* 1970; *Losing People,* 1974; *The Way to the Old Sailors Home,* Harper, 1977; *Poor Millie,* Harper, 1978; *Finding Fever* (young adult), Harper, 1982; *Walk Out*

a Brother (young adult), Harper, 1983; *Villa Aphrodite,* St. Martin's Press, 1984.

BARBE, Walter Burke   1926-

PERSONAL: Born October 30, 1926, in Miami, Fla.; son of Victor Elza and Edith (Burris) Barbe; married Marilyn Wood (a high school guidance counselor), February 7, 1967; children: Frederick W. *Education:* Northwestern University, B.S., 1949, M.A., 1950, Ph.D., 1953. *Politics:* Democrat. *Religion:* Presbyterian. *Home:* R.D. 1, Narrowsburg, N.Y. 12764. *Office: Highlights for Children,* 803 Church St., Honesdale, Pa.

CAREER: Baylor University, Waco, Tex., instructor in psychology, 1950; Kent State University, Kent, Ohio, assistant professor of elementary education and director of reading clinic, 1950-52, professor of education and head of special education department, 1960-64; University of Chattanooga, Chattanooga, Tenn., professor of education and director of Junior League Reading Center, 1953-60; *Highlights for Children,* Honesdale, Pa., editor, 1964—. Adjunct professor, University of Pittsburg, 1964, Ohio State University, 1973—. Editor, Zaner-Bloser, Inc. *Military service:* U.S. Army, 1944-46. *Member:* Council for Exceptional Children, American Psychological Association (fellow), National Association for Gifted Children (president, 1958-60), National Education Association, The Association for the Gifted (president, 1967), International Reading Association, Council of State Directors of

WALTER BURKE BARBE

Programs for Gifted, Phi Delta, Kappa Delta Pi, Psi Chi, National Press Club. *Awards, honors:* Psi Chi research award, 1953; Meritorius Service Award from International Reading Association, 1982; Citation of Merit, Council for Exceptional Children, 1984.

WRITINGS: Directory of Reading Clinics, University of Chattanooga Press, 1955; (with Dorothy Hinman) *We Build Our Words,* Bookman Associates, 1957; (editor with others) *Teen-Age Tales,* Heath, 1957; (editor with Thomas M. Stephens) *Educating Tomorrow's Leaders,* Ohio State Department of Education, 1961; *Educator's Guide to Personalized Reading Instruction,* Prentice-Hall, 1961; *The Exceptional Child,* Center for Applied Research in Education, 1963; (editor) *Teaching Reading: Selected Materials,* Oxford University Press, 1965; (editor) *Psychology and Education of the Gifted: Selected Readings,* Appleton, 1965; (compiler) *Creative Writing Activities,* Highlights for Children, 1965; (editor with Edward C. Frierson) *Educating Children with Learning Disabilities: Selected Readings,* Appleton, 1967; (editor) Annette Wynne and others, *Children around the World,* Highlights for Children, 1968; (editor) *Searchlights on Literature* (basic reading program series), Harper, 1969.

(Editor) *Sports Handbook,* Highlights for Children, 1970; *Fables and Folktales from Many Lands,* Highlights for Children, 1972; *Classroom Activities for Children with Special Needs,* Center for Applied Research in Education, 1974; (editor with Joseph S. Renzulli) *Psychology and Education of the Gifted,* Irvington, 1975; (with Jerry L. Abbott) *Personalized Reading Instruction: New Techniques That Increase Reading Skill and Comprehension,* Parker, 1975; *Creative Growth with Handwriting,* Zaner-Bloser, 1975, 2nd edition, 1979; (editor with Virginia H. Lucas) *Approaches to the Problem of Reversals in Reading and Writing,* Zaner-Bloser, 1975; *Reading Skills Check Lists and Activities,* Center for Applied Research in Education, 1975; (editor) *What Supervisors Say about Handwriting Instruction,* Zaner-Bloser, 1975.

(Editor) *The Left-Handed Child in a Right-Handed World,* Zaner-Bloser, 1976; (editor) *Evaluating Handwriting Manuscript,* Zaner-Bloser, 1977; (editor) *Zaner-Bloser Handwriting Workbook: Cursive,* Zaner-Bloser, 1977; (editor) *Zaner-Bloser Handwriting Workbook: Manuscript,* Zaner-Bloser, 1977; (editor with Caroline Clark Myers) *Challenge of a Handicap: Understanding Differences, Accepting Limitations,* Highlights for Children, 1977; (editor) *Reading Adventures in Spanish and English,* Highlights for Children, 1977; (with Ida L. Shaw) *Handwriting Instruction: The Supervisor's Role,* Zaner-Bloser, 1978; *The Relationship of Reading and Handwriting Instruction,* Zaner-Bloser, 1978; (editor) *Teaching Handwriting: A Transparency Program for Teachers,* Zaner-Bloser, 1978; (editor) *Competency Tests for Basic Reading Skills,* Center for Applied Research in Education, 1978; (with Raymond H. Swassing) *Teaching through Modality Strengths: Concepts and Practices,* Zaner-Bloser, 1979; (with R. H. Swassing) *The Swassing-Barbe Modality Index,* Zaner-Bloser, 1979.

(With Michael N. Milone) *Why Manuscript Writing Should Come Before Cursive Writing,* Zaner-Bloser, 1980; (editor with others) *Basic Skills in Kindergarten: Foundations for Formal Learning,* Zaner-Bloser, 1980; (with V. H. Lucas) *Resource Book for the Kindergarten Teacher,* Zaner-Bloser, 1980; (with M. N. Milone) *Teaching Handwriting through Modality Strengths,* Zaner-Bloser, 1980; (with others) *The Zaner-Bloser Check Lists of Basic Kindergarten Skills,* Zaner-Bloser, 1980; (with R. H. Swassing and M. N. Milone) *The Swassing-Barbe Checklist of Observable Modality Strength Characteristics,* Zaner-Bloser, 1980; (with Azalia S. Francis and Lois A. Braun) *Spelling: Basic Skills for Effective Communication,* Zaner-Bloser, 1983; *Spelling: Basic Skills and Application,* Zaner-Bloser, 1983; *Handwriting: Basic Skills and Application,* Zaner-Bloser, 1984; (with V. H. Lucas and Thomas M. Wasylyk) *Handwriting: Basic Skills for Effective Communication,* Zaner-Bloser, 1984; (with R. H. Swassing and M. N. Milone) *Successful Language Arts Instruction Using Modality Strengths,* Zaner-Bloser, 1984; *Analyzing Spelling Errors to Determine Learning Styles,* Zaner-Bloser, 1984; *Growing Up Learning,* Acropolis, 1985.

Contributor of more than one hundred articles to educational and psychological journals.

SIDELIGHTS: "I try to write every day—something, anything, everything. The mere act of writing is a stabilizing influence. It brings order to the random thinking that I am plagued with, it allows me to visualize my thoughts in a more concrete fashion, it forces me to stop and say, 'There, that is exactly what I was thinking' or to say, 'No, that isn't what I meant.'

"I find that I can write more fluently when I am actively involved in reading something I like. The subject or type of material does not necessarily have to be of the same type. There appears to be some kind of language flow that reading causes to occur, and writing is easier when that flow is occurring.

"The process of reading is more enjoyable to me than to almost anyone I know. A close friend of many years, who is rather hard on me most of the time, criticized my reading habits by saying that I had no reading taste for I read everything. I have come to believe that he was right, for I discover myself reading whatever is in front of me and often thoroughly enjoy the process, even though I may not particularly care for the subject, the author, or the particular piece. I know that I like certain authors and certain of their works better than others, but I certainly would not want to limit myself to just those pieces.

"At one point I was asked to suggest materials to be included in an anthology for junior high school students. While I now philosophically am opposed to the anthology approach to teaching literature, I was in the enviable position of having to seek out all of the things I had previously read and loved, reread them and accept or reject them as suitable for this publication. I discovered that many of the things I thought I had read I apparently only remembered hearing about, other things that I had read did not seem so memorable, some things I remembered reading were not as I remembered—some were better, some not so good, and some apparently built on by me to be what I thought the author should have made them. The material was published, but the astounding thing to me even to this day is that I was paid to do a task which I would never have done otherwise but which I treasure as one of the most exciting experiences I have ever had.

"Being a very proficient hunt-and-peck typist, beginning long before adolescence to type everything I wrote, I have been unable as an adult to slow down to use the touch system. I regret this inability, and resent that I was not taught typing at the age of eight or nine when I bought my first typewriter for ten dollars (earned selling *Liberty* magazines). I sold the typewriter during World War II for fifteen dollars. And now I have discovered the word processor and have fallen in love with writing without a pair of scissors."

Tiden/FIB, 1970, 2nd edition, 1976; *Maans och Mari om sommaren* (title means "Maans and Mari in the Summer"), Tiden/FIB, 1971, 2nd edition, 1976; *Maans och Mari om hösten* (title means "Maans and Mari in the Fall"), Tiden/FIB, 1973, 2nd edition, 1976; *Maans och Mari om vintern* (title means "Maans and Marie in the Winter"), Tiden/FIB, 1974, 3rd edition, 1975; *Farfar och Trollet* (self-illustrated; title means "Grandfather and Troll"), Carlsen, 1975.

Jag ser paa mig själv och andra (illustrated with photographs by son, Mikael Beckman; title means "I Look at Myself and Others"), Rabén & Sjögren, 1976, new edition, 1981; *Bild och ord fraan A till Ö* (illustrated with photographs by M. Beckman; title means "Pictures and Words from A to Z"), Liber, 1977; *Maans och Mari fraan vaar till vinter* (self-illustrated; title means "Maans and Mari from Spring to Winter"), Tiden, 1979; *Matti, Maans och Mari* (self-illustrated; title means "Matti, Maans and Mari"), Tiden, 1980; *Sitta stilla och tänka efter* (poetry; illustrated with photographs by M. Beckman; title means "Sitting Quietly in Deep Thought"), Tiden, 1980.

Compiler: *Ord i bok* (poetry; self-illustrated; title means "Words in a Book"), Allhem, 1958; *Vaar* (poetry; self-illustrated; title means "Spring"), Fabel, 1965; *Host* (poetry; self-illustrated; title means "Autumn"), Fabel, 1965; *Sommar* (poetry; self-illustrated; title means "Summer"), Fabel, 1966; *Vinter* (poetry; self-illustrated; title means "Winter"), Fabel, 1966; *I världen* (poetry; self-illustrated; title means "In the World"), FIB, 1966; *Som en resa blott* (self-illustrated; title means "As a Journey"), Rabén & Sjögren, 1966; *Om fjärilars liv* (poetry; title means "About the Lives of Butterflies"), Piccolo, 1968; *Liten lyrikstund* (poetry; title means "A Little While with Poetry"), Sveriges radio, 1969; *Rödan guld* (poetry; illustrated by P. Beckman; title means "Red Gold"), Sveriges radio, 1969; *Under tiden* (poetry; self-illustrated; title means "In the Meantime"), Rabén & Sjögren, 1974; *Cirkusvärld* (prose and poetry; illustrated by P. Beckman; title means "World of the Circus"), Rabén & Sjögren, 1976.

Illustrator: May Höst, *Pricken* (title means "The Dot"), Bonniers, 1937; Daisy Reuterskiöld, *Lill-Pyrets äventyr* (title means "The Adventures of a Little One"), Bonniers, 1938.

Brita af Geijerstam, *Trasdockan och andra visor* (title means "The Ragdoll and Other Stories"), Gebers, 1944; Cecily Finn, *Om igen* (title means "Once Again"), Ljus, 1944; Gustaf Lindwall, compiler, *Barnvisor fraan när och fjärran* (title means "Nursery Songs from Different Countries"), Bonniers, 1948; Hans Christian Andersen, *Sagor I-IV* (title means "Tales I-IV"), Natur och kultur, 1949.

Britt G. Hallqvist, *Barn* (title means "Children"), Bonniers, 1953; Jan de Hartog, *Den lilla arken* (title means "The Little Ark"), Forum, 1954; Wolf Mankowitz, *En killing för en styver* (title means "A Kid for Two Farthings"), Forum, 1956; K. O. Hammarlund, *Album* (title means "Album"), Allhem, 1957; Oscar Wilde, *Den själviske jätten* (title means "The Selfish Giant"), Saga, 1958; Erik Blomberg, *100 Svenska dikter* (title means "One Hundred Swedish Poems"), Tiden, 1958; Harriet Hjorth, *Blomstervandringar* (title means "Flower Promenades"), Rabén & Sjögren, 1958-62; E. Blomberg, *100 Dikter ur världslyriken* (title means "One Hundred Poems from around the World"), Tiden, 1959.

H. Hjorth, compiler, *Flora poetica* (title means "Poetic Flora"), Tiden, 1960; Bo Setterlind, *Herrens moder* (title means "Our Lord's Mother"), Diakonistyrelsens bokförlag, 1962; Jeanna Oterdahl, *Franciskus, Guds lille spelman* (title means "Francis, God's Little Player"), Diakonistyrelsens bokförlag, 1963;

KARIN BECKMAN

BECKMAN, Karin 1913-
(Kaj Beckman)

PERSONAL: Born February 2, 1913, in Enköping, Sweden; daughter of Sven Henrik (a bank director) and Ingeborg (an artist; maiden name, Esbjörnson) Thelander; married Per Beckman (an illustrator), January 5, 1939; children: one son, Mikael. *Education:* Attended Konstfackskolan, Stockholm, Sweden, 1931-35. *Home:* Minerva, 170 11 Drottningholm, Sweden.

CAREER: Artist, illustrator, author, and compiler of books for children. *Exhibitions:* "Young Artists," National Museum, Stockholm, 1938-42; Swedish Women Artists Association, Gävle, 1938; Swedish Public Art Association, 1939-1941; "From the World of Fantasy and Fairytales," Stockholm, 1944; Stockholm (one-woman show), 1946. Her work is included in permanent collections at the National Museum; Museum of Art, Göteborg; and Sandviken's Museum. *Member:* Konstnärernas Riksorganization (state organization of artists), Associations for designers, artists and authors. *Awards, honors:* Unga Tecknare ("Young Designers"), 1942; Elsa Beskow plaque, 1973. Has won several bursaries and prizes from literary and artistic societies in Sweden.

WRITINGS: Ti och Bi (self-illustrated; title means "Ti and Bi"), Bonniers, 1941; *Lisen kan inte sova* (illustrated by husband, Per Beckman), Rabén & Sjögren, 1969, published in America as *Lisa Cannot Sleep*, F. Watts, 1970; *Maans och Mari om vaaren* (title means "Maans and Marie in the Spring"),

(From *Den staandaktige tennsoldaten* [*The Steadfast Tin Soldier*] by Hans Christian Andersen. Illustrated by Kaj Beckman.)

August Strindberg, *Blomstermaalningar* (title means "Flower Paintings"), Fabel, 1964; J. Oterdahl, *Albert Schweitzer: Pojken som inte kunde döda,* Diakonistyrelsens bokförlag, 1965, translation by Gene Lund and Louise Lund published as *Albert Schweitzer: The Boy Who Could Not Kill,* Augsburg, 1967; H. Hjorth, compiler, *Flora poetica exotica* (title means "Poetic and Exotic Flora"), Tiden, 1965.

Siv Widerberg, *Gertrud paa daghem,* Rabén & Sjögren, 1966, translation by Patricia Crampton published as *Judy at School,* Burke, 1968; Gunnar Turesson, compiler, *Visor fraan Kraakelund* (title means "Songs from Kraakelund"), Tiden, 1966; H. C. Andersen, *Tummelisa,* Tiden, 1967, translation from the Danish by M. R. James published as *Thumbelina,* Van Nostrand, 1972; H. C. Andersen, *John Blund,* Tiden, 1968, translation fron the Danish by L. W. Kingsland published as *Willie Winkie,* Kaye & Ward, 1974; S. Widerberg, *Alldeles vanliga Hjalmar och Hedvig,* Rabén & Sjögren, 1968, translation by Patricia Crampton published as *This Is Peter, This Is Jane,* Burke, 1969; P. Beckman, *Mias docka,* Rabén & Sjögren, 1969, translation published as *Mia's Doll,* Dent, 1975; H. C. Andersen, *Näktergalen,* Tiden, 1969, translation from the

Danish by M. R. James published as *The Nightingale,* Van Nostrand, 1972.

H. C. Andersen, *Den staandaktige tennsoldaten,* Tiden, 1976, translation from the Danish by L. W. Kingsland published as *The Steadfast Tin Soldier,* Kaye & Ward, 1976; Lennart Hellsing, compiler, *Spinn spinn dotter min* (title means "Spin Spin, My Daughter"), Carlsen, 1976; O. Wilde, *Den lycklige prinsen,* Tiden, 1977, translation published as *The Happy Prince,* Methuen, 1977; H. C. Andersen, *Aarets historia,* Tiden, 1979, translation from the Danish by Erik Christian Hangaard published as *The Story of the Year,* Kaye & Ward, 1979.

H. C. Andersen, *Den lilla flickan med svavelstickorna,* Tiden, 1981, translation from the Danish by L. W. Kingsland published as *The Little Match Girl,* Kaye & Ward, Kingswood, 1981; H. C. Andersen, *Soppa paa en korvsticka* (title means "Soup on a Sausage Stick"), Tiden, 1983; Monica Stein, compiler, *Herr gurka* (title means "Mr. Cucumber"), Carlson, 1984.

Also illustrator of other books published in Sweden, including Nanny Hammarström's *En sommar i tossarnas och paltarnas skog* (title means "A Summer in the Woods with Ragged Children"), 1938; Ellen Schlyter's *Vipp,* 1943; and Elsa Holm's *Gert Remsnidare* (title means "Gert, the Beltmaker"), 1960.

All illustrated with P. Beckman: Hjalmar Bergman, *Lasse i Rosengaard och andra sagor* (title means "Lasse at Rosehill and Other Fairytales"), Bonniers, 1942; Ester Salminen, *Den underbara trädgaarden och andra berättelser,* Gebers, 1944, translation by Eugene Gay-Tifft published as *God's First Children,* Roy, 1946; E. Salminen, *Den nye konungen och andra berättelser ur Nya Testamentet* (title means "The New King and Other Stories from the New Testament"), Gebers, 1946; Vassilissa Semenoff, *Ryska folksagor* (title means "Russian Folktales"), Gebers, 1947; Meta Öhman, compiler, *Första sagoboken* (title means "The First Book of Tales"), Carlson, 1948.

L. Hellsing, compiler, *Äppel Päppel* (title means "Apple Dumpling"), Carlsen, 1983. Also illustrators of books published in Sweden, including Harriet H. Wetterström's *Första blomboken* (title means "The First Book of Flowers"), 1950; Margot Lang's *Första färgboken* (title means "The First Book of Colors"), 1951; Bengt Cortin's *Första svampboken* (title means "The First Book of Mushrooms"), 1952; Harriet Hjort's *Första tradgaardsboken,* (title means "The First Book of Gardens"), 1952; Sven Rosendahl's *Första fjärilboken* (title means "The First Book of Butterflies"), 1952; Olga Wikström's *Första faagelboken* (title means "The First Book of Birds"), 1954; and S. Rosendahl's *Första naturboken* (title means "The First Book of Nature"), 1955.

WORK IN PROGRESS: A series of six programs about "The Stocking People," little hand dolls, for Swedish television; exhibition of collages and paintings in Stockholm.

SIDELIGHTS: "Fairytales were read to me from the age of two. . . . I loved the writings of Elsa Beskow, Jeanna Oterdahl, the Grimm Brothers, and, naturally, H. C. Andersen's adventures also." [Translation of *De tecknar för barn,* edited by Carl-Agnär Lövgren, 2nd revised edition, Lund, 1981.¹]

"I have wanted to illustrate children's books since the age of three or four. With understanding and supportive parents I was given the opportunity of studying art at Konstfackskolan in Stockholm. There I met my husband, Per Beckman, and since that time we have had a rich, intense life together.

"I see my work as an illustrator of children's books as a great responsibility in shaping the imaginary world of children. The experience of an image can follow a child for the rest of his life."

"Children think much more than we adults can imagine; this applies to small children also. They wonder about the dark, the night and death. To be able to convey a sense of safety and security in spite of all uncertainty, while being able to answer all their questions, is presently one of the most important obligations of youth literature and illustration. In *Maans och Mari om hösten* ('Maans and Mari in the Fall'), I presented death as a reality in a context which children understand. But 'All Saints Day' at the cemetery is, after all, only one episode in the book."

Thumbelina could sit and sail from one side of the plate to the other. ■ (From *Thumbelina* by Hans Christian Andersen. Illustrated by Kaj Beckman.)

"It's hard to know exactly how to convey security to children in illustrations and text. If one could go directly to the child without the 'in between' hands—suggestive adults, parents and others who 'know it all'—we would get a better result. Children are nonprejudicial; they readily accept the most fantastic, they can be stimulated to tell stories, and they can draw original pictures. To tell stories directly to a child can also turn out badly. When I was drawing the pictures for Oscar Wilde's *The Selfish Giant,* my son, Mikael, sat next to me and helped me 'draw the winds.' We thought we had been successful, but we apparently were wrong. It's true that the book was chosen among the twenty-five best books for that year but sales were so poor that most of the editions were burned!

"In my earlier storybooks and also in some vignettes from a few of the poetic anthologies which I have compiled, my creatures are presented like the elements from nature—slim, and a little stiff and ceramic. To me they seem much like impulsive expressions of Italian/Hungarian rashes, like we observed during our long research trips after the war. This concept is particularly obvious in the book *Franciskus, Guds lille spelman* (Francis, God's Little Player') by Jeanna Oterdahl. . . . Later, my characters became more soft and round, the children more plump and perhaps cuter, and colors were added. Earlier, many of my pictures were black and white, often for economic reasons, and I worked with lines to emphasize the silhouette effect. I like working with gray silhouettes. I have included some . . . in the collection of poems 'I Look at Myself and Others' published in the series *Easy Reading for Adults.* This happened in collaboration with my son's board of education.

"The books about Maans and Mari are now being used in the elementary schools, and I am very happy about that. There is a lot of nature and tradition included, two very important ideas in illustrating for children. Old traditions are mentioned and relived. The books have glimpses from before. We adults can mediate them.

"Reality and fantasy must be woven together. Our granddaughter Anna, then one and a half years, was looking in the book *Maans och Mari om sommaren* ('Maans and Mari in the Summer'). There were blueberries and raspberries growing on one page, appearing as in a botanical garden book. Very seriously, Anna took her little fingers and carefully began picking one raspberry after another and began putting them into her mouth. The raspberries 'tasted' good. After a while she

Her father will beat her if she does not bring home some money, and she is crying. ■ (From *The Happy Prince* by Oscar Wilde. Illustrated by Kaj Beckman.)

The Nightingale sang yet more delightfully, so that it went straight to his heart.... ■ (From *The Nightingale* by Hans Christian Andersen. Illustrated by Kaj Beckman.)

took the berries 'out of her mouth' and placed them back on the plant. She knew it was a picture, what she had done is possible in fantasy.'"[1]

Kaj Beckman's illustrations have served as the foundation for her son's television productions and as audio visual training materials for schools.

FOR MORE INFORMATION SEE: Bertha M. Miller and others, compilers, *Illustrators of Children's Books: 1946-1956,* Horn Book, 1958; Eva von Zweigbergk, *Barnboken i Sverige: 1750-1950* (title means "The Children's Book in Sweden: 1750-1950"), Rabén & Sjögren, 1965; *Svenska illustratörer* (title means "Swedish Illustrators"), National Museum/Swedish Illustrators Organization, 1972; Gunilla Noreen, *Barnboksbilder: Porträtt av 54 Svenska barnboksillustratörer* (title means "Portraits of Fifty-four Swedish Youth Illustrators"), Rabén & Sjögren, 1979; Carl-Agnar Lövgren, editor, *De tecknar för barn* (title means "They Draw for Children"), 2nd revised edition, Lund, 1981.

If we work upon marble, it will perish; if we work upon brass, time will efface it; if we rear temples, they will crumble into dust; but if we work upon immortal minds, if we imbue them with principles, with the just fear of God and love of our fellowmen, we engrave on those tablets something which will brighten to all eternity.

—Daniel Webster

BECKMAN, Per (Frithiof) 1913-

PERSONAL: Born July 11, 1913, in Vissefjärda, Sweden; son of Frithiof (a bank official) and Magdalene (Faie-Hansen) Beckman; married Karin Thelander (an author and illustrator), January 5, 1939; children: one son, Mikael. *Education:* Attended Konstfackskolan, Stockholm, Sweden, 1931-1935; Konstakademiens etsarskola (art academy etching school), 1938. *Home:* Minerva, 170 11 Drottningholm, Sweden.

CAREER: Artist, illustrator, teacher, author. Began career illustrating for magazines and books. A. B. Anders Beckman's School for Commercial Design and Illustration, Stockholm, Sweden, head teacher, 1943-1980, head master, 1967-1980. Has also designed book covers, posters, and other commercial art projects. *Exhibitions:* "Young Artists," Stockholm National Museum, 1938; Swedish Public Art Association, 1940; "From the World of Fantasy and Fairytales," Stockholm, 1944; Sandviken Museum. Work has also been represented in exhibitions in Paris, Zurich, London, Oslo, and Stockholm, and in collections of the National Museum, Stockholm, and the Museum of Modern Art, New York. *Member:* Art Graphic International, Föreningen Svenska Tecknare (Swedish Designers), Konstnärernas Riksorganisation (state organization of artists), Sveriges Författarförbund (Swedish League of Authors). *Awards, honors:* Bursaries and prizes from literary and artistic societies in Sweden.

WRITINGS: Lukas kommer till stan (self-illustrated), Rabén & Sjögren, 1967, translation published as *Looking for Lucas,*

David White, 1968; *Mias docka* (illustrated by wife, Kaj Beckman), Rabén & Sjögren, 1969, translation published as *Mia's Doll*, Dent, 1975; *Klunsen* (self-illustrated; title means "The Lump"), Rabén & Sjögren, 1971; *Röd och blaa* (self-illustrated; title means "Red and Blue"), Carlsen, 1972.

Illustrator: (With K. Beckman) Hjalmar Bergman, *Lasse i Rosengaard och andra sagor* (title means "Lasse at Rosehill and Other Fairytales"), Bonniers, 1942; (with K. Beckman) Ester Salminen, *Den underbara trädgaarden och andra berättelser*, Gebers, 1944, translation by Eugene Gay-Tifft published as *God's First Children*, Roy, 1946; (with K. Beckman) E. Salminen, *Den nye konungen och andra berättelser ur Nya Testamentet* (title means "The New King and Other Stories from the New Testament"), Gebers, 1946; (with K. Beckman) Vassilissa Semenoff, *Ryska folksagor* (title means "Russian Folktales"), Gebers, 1947; Cora Sandels, *Djur jag har känt* (title means "Animals I Knew"), Forum, 1947; (with K. Beckman) Meta Öhman, *Första sagoboken* (title means "The First Book of Tales"), A. V. Carlson, 1948.

Emil Zilliachus, *Romerska vandringar* (title means "Roman Walks"), Gebers, 1950; Margaret Sperry, reteller, *The Hen That Saved the World and Other Norwegian Folktales*, John Day, 1952; Johannes Edfelt, compiler, *Rysk lyrik* (title means "Russian Poetry"), Natur och kultur, 1953; H. Hjort, *Mykonos, duvornas ö* (title means "Mykonos, Island of Pigeons"), Rabén & Sjögren, 1956; Sixteen Belfrage, compiler, *Saanger ur psaltaren* (title means "Canticle Songs"), Allhem, 1956.

PER BECKMAN

In no time at all, kitchen and house walls and even the roof were smeared so thick with porridge no one could see how the house was made. ■ (From "The Rooster That Fell in the Brew Vat" in *The Hen That Saved the World and Other Norwegian Folktales*, retold by Margaret Sperry. Illustrated by Per Beckman.)

H. Hjort, *Champagne och annat festligt* (title means "Champagne and Other Festivities"), Rabén & Sjögren, 1964; Bo Setterlind, compiler, *Kyrkoaarets poesi* (title means "Poetry of the Church-year"), Diakonistyrelsens bokförlag, 1965; Sten Hagliden and Helmer Nyberg, *Bortom och här* (title means "Far Away and Here"), Läromedelsförlagen, 1968; K. Beckman, *Lisen kan inte sova*, Rabén & Sjögren, 1969, translation published in America as *Lisa Cannot Sleep*, F. Watts, 1970; Olle Hammarlund, *Stjärnornas barn* (title means "Children of the Stars"), Rabén & Sjögren, 1969; K. Beckman, compiler, *Rödan guld* (title means "Red Gold"), Sveriges Radio, 1969.

Lillie Björnstrand, *Vi barnungar* (title means "We Children"), Tiden, 1974; L. Björnstrand, *Vi busungar* (title means "We Bothering Children"), Tiden, 1975; Lennart Hellsing, compiler, *Vart ska du gaa lilla fänta* (title means "Where Are You Going, Little Girl"), Carlsen, 1976; K. Beckman, compiler, *Cirkusvärld* (title means "World of the Circus"), Rabén & Sjögren, 1976; L. Björnstrand, *Mellan faagel och äng* (title means "Between Bird and Meadow"), Tiden, 1978; L. Björn-

(From *Vi busungar* ["We Bothering Children"] by Lillie Björnstrand. Illustrated by Per Beckman.)

strand, *Malin och Birger* (title means "Malin and Birger"), Tiden, 1979.

(With K. Beckman) L. Hellsing, compiler, *Äppel Päppel* (title means "Apple Dumpling"), Carlsen, 1983; Monica Stein, compiler, *Ekorrn satt I granen* (title means "The Squirrel in the Spruce Pine"), Carlsen, 1984.

Illustrator of Erik Asklund's *Silverligan* (title means "The Silver Theft Ring"), 1950; Aake Holmberg's *Sweden*, 1962; L. Björnstrand's, *Vi tjejer* (title means "We Girls"), 1977. Also illustrator with K. Beckman of Harriet H. Wetterström's *Första blomboken* (title means "The First Book of Flowers"), 1950; Margot Lang's *Första färgboken* (title means "The First Book of Colors"), 1951; Bengt Cortin's *Första svampboken* (title means "The First Book of Mushrooms"), 1952; Harriet Hjort's *Första trädgaardsboken* (title means "The First Book of Gardens"), 1952; Sven Rosendahl's *Första fjärilboken* (title means "The First Book of Butterflies"), 1952; Olga Wikström's *Första faagelboken* (title means "The First Book of Birds"), 1954; S. Rosendahl's *Första naturboken* (title means "The First Book of Nature"), 1955.

SIDELIGHTS: "The illustration is lost if it does not strengthen the vision of the reader. Therefore, the image must be natural and important to both the author and the illustrator."

In one of Per Beckman's first illustrations, Hjalmar Bergman's *Lasse i Rosengaard och andra sagor* ("Lasse at Rosehill and Other Fairytales"), he worked in a graphical stroke manner with ink and attempted to produce a dramatic interplay between light and dark that well suited the Bergman stories, usually tied by traditions and folktales. The interplay with

black and white ink appears even more refined in the dramatic illustrations of Lillie Bjornstrand's *Vi barnungar* ("We Children"), and *Vi busungar* ("We Bothering Children").

Beckman collaborates with his wife—both write and illustrate.

FOR MORE INFORMATION SEE: Bertha E. Miller and others, compilers, *Illustrators of Children's Books: 1946-1956*, Horn Book, 1958; Gunilla Noreen, *Barnboksbilder: Porträtt av 54 Svenska barnboksillustratörer* (title means "Portrait of Fifty-four Swedish Youth Illustrators"), Rabén & Sjögren, 1979.

BELAIR, Richard L. 1934-

PERSONAL: Born June 11, 1934, in Central Falls, R.I.; son of Leo A. (a machinist) and Eva (Berard) Belair; married Pauline Lariviere, November 28, 1959; children: Alex, Aimee. *Education:* Assumption College, Worcester, Mass., A.B., 1960; Worcester State College, M.Ed., 1968; University of Connecticut, Certificate of Advanced Graduate Studies in media production, 1974. *Religion:* Catholic. *Home:* 7 Meadowbrook Rd., Auburn, Mass. 01501.

CAREER: Auburn High School, Auburn, Mass., English teacher, 1961—; Assumption College, Worcester, Mass., part-time writing instructor, 1984—. *Military service:* U.S. Army, 1953-56.

WRITINGS: Praying Mantis (play), produced at Assumption College, December 1958, National Catholic Theater Confer-

RICHARD L. BELAIR

ence, 1959; *Road Less Traveled* (novel), Doubleday, 1965; *Double Take* (novel), Morrow, 1979. Contributor of short stories and articles to *Ligourian* and other periodicals.

WORK IN PROGRESS: A historical novel, a biblical novel, various young adult novels.

SIDELIGHTS: "When I read *Rime of the Ancient Mariner* in my high school sophomore year, I could feel what the mariner went through, and I decided I wanted to write so that I could make people *feel* what my fictional characters experienced. I became a writer immediately when I sat down and completed something not required by any teacher but simply by my desire to try. At the time, I also set out to seek fame and fortune.

"Now I write during every spare hour because characters with problems keep coming to mind, and I can't ignore their call to see what they will do next and how they will make out. I think I have shared experiences with enough fictional characters to populate a small town. Few of them have gripped the attention of editors. Writing often means going all the way to rejection with characters you have loved. It also means regretting you don't yet have the skill, but resolving that you will work at it every day so that more of your characters will reach readers.

"I haven't found fame and fortune. But, readers have spent some time with a few of the characters who came out of my head. I hope they have experienced their pain and joy and loved them as much as I do."

BERENSTAIN, Michael 1951-

BRIEF ENTRY: Born December 21, 1951, in Philadelphia, Pa. This is the third Berenstain to appear on the children's literature scene. His parents, Stan and Jan, creators of the popular "Berenstain Bears," are prolific authors-illustrators. A former student of the Philadelphia College of Art and Pennsylvania Academy of Fine Arts, Berenstain worked briefly as a designer for Random House before becoming an author-illustrator in 1975. Two years later *The Castle Book* appeared, the first in a series published by McCay. *The Ship Book* (1978), *The Lighthouse Book* (1979), and *The Armor Book* (1979), like *The Castle Book,* are designed to provide a historical overview of their topics for elementary-grade readers. A reviewer for *Publishers Weekly* observed that the books "encompassed

full and absorbing information, excitingly illustrated" with black-and-white cutaway drawings.

Berenstain's sense of humor emerged in works like *The Troll Book* (Random House, 1980), and *The Creature Catalog* (Random House, 1982) as he increasingly began to concentrate on aspects of fantasy and the supernatural. *Publishers Weekly* called *The Troll Book* a "thorough, quietly comic report on the trolls of Scandinavia," complete with "full-color pictures of awesome forests and trees." According to *Booklist, The Creature Catalog* is "pretty creepy stuff," with everything "from cyclops to unicorns to Dr. Jekyll." Wizards, dragons, unicorns, and griffins all play a part in Berenstain's adventure entitled *The Sorcerer's Scrapbook; or, "Why I Am a Wizard": Being the Life and Times of Nicodemus Magnus, Doctor of Magick and Sorcerer to the Duke, Told in His Own Words* (Random House, 1981). "This spoof of things mystical is very funny," noted a *School Library Journal* reviewer, who further added that "the graphic layout is sensational. . . . and the realistic recreations of the dynamics of light . . . are superb."

Reviewers also reacted favorably to Berenstain's creation of odd little characters in *The Dwarks* (Bantam, 1981). The possum-like creatures appeared in a second adventure called *The Dwark Meets the Trash Monster* (Bantam, 1984). Berenstain is the illustrator of *K'tonton on an Island in the Sea* by Sadie Rose Weilerstein and *King Kong,* adapted by Judith Conaway. *Residence:* New Hope, Pa.

FOR MORE INFORMATION SEE: Contemporary Authors, New Revision Series, Volume 14, Gale, 1985.

BERGEY, Alyce (Mae) 1934-

PERSONAL: Born March 25, 1934, in Lanesboro, Minn.; daughter of Forrest Frank and Mabel Luella (Peterson) Bergey. *Education:* Attended Lanesboro (Minn.) schools. *Religion:* Protestant. *Residence:* 235 Nathan La., Plymouth, Minn. 55441.

WRITINGS: Rocky, the Rocket Mouse, Denison, 1961; (with Obata) *The World God Made,* Concordia, 1965; *The First Rainbow,* Denison, 1965; (with Betty Wind) *The Boy Who Saved His Family,* Concordia, 1966; *Fishermen's Surprise,* Concordia, 1967; *The Great Promise,* Concordia, 1968; *Beggar's Greatest Wish,* Concordia, 1969; *The Boy Who Was Lost,* Concordia, 1972; *The Secret of the Arrows,* Concordia, 1972.

ADAPTATIONS—Book with record and book with cassette; all produced by Concordia: "The World God Made," 1965, published as a coloring book, 1978; "The Boy Who Saved His Family," 1966; "Fishermen's Surprise," 1967; "The Great Promise," 1968; "Beggar's Greatest Wish," 1969; "The Boy Who Was Lost," 1972; "The Secret of the Arrows," 1972.

SIDELIGHTS: "I was born in Lanesboro, Minnesota, a small village almost hidden among the hills and bluffs of southeastern Minnesota. Among the memories of childhood I treasure most are those of afternoons spent with my family picking wild flowers and berries in those hills. We often took Sunday afternoon rides during the warm weather months. When my sisters and I spotted flowers along the roadside, we'd yell, 'Daddy, stop! Flowers!' And he always stopped the car by the side of the road to let his three little girls clamber up the hillside to gather their treasure.

ALYCE BERGEY

"In May of 1949, when I was fifteen, polio struck. I was rushed to Rochester, Minnesota, where I was hospitalized for fourteen months. After that time, I went home to Lanesboro to live with my parents. Unable to move either my legs or my arms, I was interested when, about ten years later, I saw someone demonstrating on TV how to type with a mouthstick. I began saving money to buy an electric typewriter. A good reconditioned one was $300, a huge amount of money to me at that time. When I'd purchased it and practiced a bit with a mouthstick, a friend who was a first-grade teacher, and who knew I'd always been interested in writing, urged me to begin work on a book for children. The idea appealed to me. Miraculously, my first book, *Rocky, the Rocket Mouse* was published. I wasn't surprised at the time, but looking back later, I marveled because I had known nothing at all about writing books for children—or for anyone! My five nephews and one niece, who were all at the age my books were aimed toward, were my best critics. I always read my stories to at least one of them, and could tell by watching them which parts weren't clear and which parts delighted them.

"In 1981 I moved to Courage Center, a transitional living center for the disabled. I spent a year at Courage Center and then moved to an apartment in Plymouth, a suburb of Minneapolis, where I still live with around-the-clock attendants.

"While I was at Courage Center I wrote articles for two of their newsletters. About a year ago I was asked to write an article 'from the patient's point of view' for the *Christian Medical Society Journal*. I'm still very much interested in writing and hope it will be possible for me to do more of it at

sometime in the future, but I have been finding talking to groups of school children great fun, and certainly stimulating. They ask marvelous questions about both writing and disabilities. I've also begun to talk to small groups of adults, something I vowed I would never do. I have come to enjoy it, but children will always be my favorite audience. Their openness and enthusiasm is delightful.''

FOR MORE INFORMATION SEE: St. Paul Pioneer Press, October 22, 1961; *Rochester Post-Bulletin,* October 25, 1961; *Minneapolis Morning Tribune,* November 4, 1961; *Minneapolis Star,* December 15, 1961.

BERNARD, Jacqueline (de Sieyes) 1921-1983

OBITUARY NOTICE—See sketch in *SATA* Volume 8: Born May 5, 1921, in Le Bourget du Lac, Savoie, France; died from strangulation, about August 1, 1983, in New York, N.Y. Journalist, social activist, and author. Bernard was co-founder and one time vice-president of Parents Without Partners, a highly successful national organization for unmarried parents and their children. Bernard participated in the group, established in 1956, for only eighteen months, leaving to pursue more political activities. Among the causes she espoused were prisoners' rights, women's rights, and minority rights. She also protested the Vietnam War and worked for nuclear disarmament. In addition, Bernard held a variety of posts throughout her career, including reporter for ABC News Service in the 1940s and advertising copywriter for B. L. Mazel in the late 1950s. The author-activist was found dead in her apartment on August 2, 1983. Investigation into her death revealed that she died of ''injuries indicative of homicide.'' Among her writings are *Journey Toward Freedom: The Story of Sojourner Truth, Voices from the Southwest,* and *The Children You Gave Us.*

FOR MORE INFORMATION SEE: Contemporary Authors, Volumes 21-24, revised, Gale, 1977. Obituaries: *New York Times,* August 21, 1983; *New York,* October 17, 1983.

BLAIR, Jay 1953-

PERSONAL: Born January 21, 1953, in Omaha, Neb.; son of William Jay (an artist) and Josephine (Dilorenzo) Blair; married Linda Cleary (a medical technician), February 8, 1975; children: Meagan Anna. *Education:* University of Wisconsin, Milwaukee, B.F.A., 1974. *Religion:* Lutheran. *Home:* 2247 W. Arbor Ave., Glendale, Wis. 53209. *Office:* Spectrum Creative, Inc., 7709 W. Lisbon Ave., Milwaukee, Wis. 53222.

CAREER: Free-lance illustrator, 1973-75; J. K. Art Directions, Milwaukee, Wis., illustrator/designer, 1975-78, art director, 1978-84; R. L. Meyer Advertising, Inc., Milwaukee, Wis., art director, 1984-85; Spectrum Creative, Inc., Milwaukee, illustrator/designer, 1985—. *Exhibitions:* University of Wisconsin, Milwaukee, 1974, 1980; University of Wisconsin, Stevens Point, 1975; Ozankee Art Center, 1978; Milwaukee Institute of Art and Design, 1981. *Member:* Illustrators and Designers of Milwaukee; American Institute of Graphic Arts. *Awards, honors:* Wisconsin University Prize for drawing, 1975; Milwaukee Society of Communicating Arts, first place, 1978; Business Persons Advertising Association, numerous awards, 1978-82; National Addy (merit), 1981; Madison Addy, first place, 1982.

As the night wore on, Diana's trainers became seriously worried about her swollen mouth. ∎
(From *Diana: Alone against the Sea* by Valjean McLenighan. Illustrated by Jay Blair.)

JAY BLAIR

ILLUSTRATOR: (With Marke Mille) Jim Johnson, *A Look Inside Lasers,* Raintree, 1981; Sharon Addy, *We Didn't Mean To,* Raintree, 1981; Valjean McLenighan, *Alone against the Sea: Diana Nyad,* Raintree, 1980, published as *Diana: Alone against the Sea,* 1982.

WORK IN PROGRESS: Posters for the city of Milwaukee, drawings of circus horses, assorted agency art.

SIDELIGHTS: ''I think as a working illustrator I value most the visual descriptions of events that are written. First comes the long period of learning techniques and perfecting your craft, then the immersion in the manuscript. You determine the look of the book on a whole and decide on techniques to be used, determine the design of each illustration and draw with any reference you need. You present these drawings and ideas, and reach accord with the art director, and proceed.

''I have often thought of publication art as a joy as opposed to a job. Certainly, it's much work, but very satisfying.

''I believe no experience, no classes are a waste because there is always something to learn and to help you later. Travel is important, and I have felt seeing things that change your view and sense of scale are good for your creativity. That's why I enjoy the American West, particularly Arizona.

''My goal is to work as a part of a creative team and 'put my mark' on things that reach many, as a designer, illustrator, and art director.''

The golden-mantled ground squirrel . . . is often mistaken for a chipmunk. . . . ■ (From *The Life of the Mountains* by Maurice Brooks. Photograph by Norman Lightfoot.)

BROOKS, Maurice (Graham)   1900-

PERSONAL: Born June 16, 1900, in French Creek, W.Va.; son of Fred Ernest and Hettie Grace (Coburn) Brooks; married Ruth Anna Brown, December 23, 1931; children: Fred Carson. *Education:* Attended Wesleyan College, 1918-21; West Virginia University, A.B., 1923, M.S., 1935; further study at University of Michigan, 1939-41.

CAREER: West Virginia State 4-H Club, agent, 1923-26; Upshur County High School, Buckhannon, W.Va., principal, 1926-34; West Virginia University, Morgantown, instructor in biology, 1935-38, professor of wildlife management, beginning 1938. Worked as a forester at the West Virginia Agricultural Explorational Station. Visiting professor at University of Virginia, summer, 1938, University of Minnesota, summer, 1941; chairman, West Virginia Biological Survey, 1936-46; chairman of recreation committee, West Virginia Planning Board, 1938-45; director, West Virginia Conservation School, beginning 1945; member, West Virginia Conservation Commission, 1945-54. *Member:* American Academy of Arts and Sciences (fellow), American Ornithologists Union, Wilson Ornithological Club (president, 1950-52), Society of American Foresters, Wildlife Society, Phi Beta Kappa, Sigma Xi, Alpha Zeta.

WRITINGS: The Pteridophytes of West Virginia (illustrated by A. S. Margolin), West Virginia University, 1938; *The Appalachians* (illustrated by Lois Darling and Louis Darling), Houghton, 1965; *The Life of the Mountains* (young adult), McGraw, 1967.

Contributor of articles to periodicals, including *National Wildlife*.

FOR MORE INFORMATION SEE: New York Times Book Review, November 14, 1965; *Book Week,* December 5, 1965.

BROWN, Buck   1936-

PERSONAL: Born February 3, 1936, in Morrison, Tenn.; son of Michael Fate and Doris (Lemings) Brown; married Mary Ellen Steverson, December 24, 1965; children: Robert, Tracy Elizabeth. *Education:* Wilson Junior College, Chicago, Ill.,

His long body tore the sports page. ■ (From *Fritz, the Too-Long Dog* by Bee Lewi. Illustrated by Buck Brown.)

A.A., 1962; University of Illinois, B.F.A., 1966. *Address:* c/o Playboy Enterprises, Inc., 747 Third Ave., New York, N.Y.

CAREER: Cartoonist and illustrator of books for children. Chicago Transit Authority, Chicago, Ill., bus driver, 1958-63; adult cartoonist, 1961—. Member, Vice-President's Task Force on Youth Motivation, 1968-70. *Military service:* U.S. Air Force, 1955-58. *Member:* Magazine Cartoonists Guild. *Awards, honors:* Named one of ten Outstanding Young Men by the Chicago chapter of the United States JayCees, 1970; New Jersey Authors Award, New Jersey Institute of Technology, 1978, for *ABC Pirate Adventure.*

ILLUSTRATOR—All fiction for children: Kathy Darling, *The Jelly Bean Contest,* Garrard, 1972; K. Darling, *Bug Circus,* Garrard, 1976; Ida DeLage, *ABC Pirate Adventure,* Garrard, 1977; Bee Lewi, *Fritz, the Too-Long Dog,* Garrard, 1980. Also contributor of adult cartoons to various publications.

BROWNE, Anthony (Edward Tudor)   1946-

PERSONAL: Born September 11, 1946, in Sheffield, England; son of Jack Holgate (a teacher) and Doris May (Sugden) Browne; married Jane Franklin (a violin teacher), July 26, 1980; children: Joseph, Ellen. *Education:* Leeds College of Art, degree in graphic design (with honors), 1967. *Home and office:* The Chalk Garden, The Length, St. Nicholas-at-Wade, Kent, England.

CAREER: Victoria University of Manchester, Manchester, England, medical artist at Royal Infirmary, 1968-70; Gordon Fraser Greeting Cards, London, England, designer, 1971—; author and illustrator of children's books, 1975—. *Awards, honors:* Kate Greenaway Medal commendation from the British Library Association, 1982, for *Hansel and Gretel;* Kurt Maschler/'Emil' Award, 1983, and Kate Greenaway Medal, 1984, both for *Gorilla;* Deutscher Jugendliteratur Preis (German Youth Literature Prize), 1985, for *The Visitors Who Came to Stay.*

WRITINGS—Self-illustrated children's books: *Through the Magic Mirror,* Hamish Hamilton, 1976, Greenwillow, 1977; *A Walk in the Park,* Hamish Hamilton, 1977; *Bear Hunt,* Atheneum, 1979; *Look What I've Got,* F. Watts, 1980; (reteller) Jacob Grimm and Wilhelm Grimm, *Hansel and Gretel,* Macrae, 1981, F. Watts, 1982; *Bear Goes to Town,* Hamish Hamilton, 1982; *Gorilla* (*Horn Book* honor list), Macrae, 1983, F. Watts, 1985; *Willy the Wimp,* Knopf, 1985; *Willy the Champ,* Macrae, 1985, Knopf, 1986.

Illustrator: Annalena McAfee, *The Visitors Who Came to Stay,* Viking, 1985; Sally Grindley, *Knock, Knock! Who's There?,* Knopf, 1986.

ADAPTATIONS: "Bear Hunt" (filmstrip), Weston Woods, 1982.

WORK IN PROGRESS: Piggybook, to be published by Knopf.

SIDELIGHTS: Browne was born in Sheffield, England. He was educated at Leeds College of Art, where he received a degree in graphic design. "At Leeds Polytechnic Institute I did graphic design and hated it. I wanted to be a painter. I found that illustration was treated as a kind of second-class art. At the college I attended, we were meant to be advertising executives—people who could organize, illustrate, present their

ANTHONY BROWNE

work, tell other people what to do, and not do the physical work—while I actually enjoyed drawing.

"I turned against graphic design in general; I just wanted to be a painter. . . . My father died when I had just started art school at Leeds, and I got this morbid interest in death and insides of people's bodies. I used to spend a lot of time in Life Class, and quite often instead of drawing the outsides of bodies, I did what little I knew of the insides—gruesome imagery. So that's what attracted me to medical art. I totally avoided what I thought was commercial.

"In Manchester I got a job, which was pretty well paid, as an assistant lecturer in medical art. I enjoyed it, and it exorcised that gruesome fascination with the insides. Eventually, lecturing became repetitive. Nobody, understandably, was interested in my work as paintings or drawings. But medical art was great training; it was much better than actually being in art school, because I wasn't being judged on the quality of the paint or design or balanced composition—just on whether the artwork did the job. I had to explain something visually that was very difficult to explain any other way.

"I nearly went to teacher training college. When I first left Leeds, I applied to Goldsmiths. I only spent a morning there studying teaching theory. I went back and taught a day a week at the Art College in Leeds. After I left medical art, I taught realistic drawing, which was the most difficult job I ever held. I spent a lot of time in the library feeling guilty about how much money I was being paid and designing greeting cards for Gordon Fraser. The cards continue to be a major source

(From the filmstrip "Bear Hunt." Produced by Weston Woods, 1982.)

of my income.'' [Sylvia Marantz and Kenneth Marantz, ''An Interview with Anthony Browne,'' *Horn Book,* November/December, 1985. Amended by Anthony Browne.[1]]

Browne began working as a designer of the world-famous Gordon Fraser greeting cards in 1971. Although he still designs greeting cards for them, his work as an illustrator and writer of children's books is paramount to his career. To date, Browne has written and illustrated eight books for children and retold and illustrated the classic Grimm Brothers' tale *Hansel and Gretel.* He has also illustrated *The Visitors Who Came to Stay* by Annalena McAfee and *Knock, Knock* by Sally Grindley. ''I use watercolor, semi-moist and concentrated liquid—no tubes. The artwork is usually the same size as it will appear in the book. When I was a kid, I drew what would now be called surrealist jokes—but I thought of them as funny things going on and labeled them with arrows. My artwork hasn't changed that much. It has so often been said that Magritte is an influence on my work that I decided to come out of the closet with blatant references to him. Surrealism is, or at least was, such a common influence on art students in England that his images have become almost ordinary because they've been exposed so much. There have been so many imitators.

''When I first designed books, I adopted a page design in which I used a small picture on one page and a large one on the facing page. Well, that was a period I was going through. I have not used that design recently. *Willy* has opened things up. I think I got a bit conscious that I was tending to put a formula around things. *Gorilla* certainly used that design. I became aware that I was tending to use it automatically. I got away from the design a little with *The Visitors Who Came to Stay.* Where I had a big picture and a little picture, I still used the form, but the little picture was an object.''[1]

With encouragement from his publisher Browne decided to retell and illustrate *Hansel and Gretel.* ''I read as many versions of *Hansel and Gretel* as I could find. I amalgamated them. I suspected the book was going to be controversial because I was bringing the pictures up to date. Therefore, I thought I'd not meddle too much with the story. I was very conscious, I think, of not wanting to do a pretty book in contrast to other versions. I've occasionally used a pretty style for greeting cards, but it's not really me. *Hansel and Gretel* was my most difficult book because I knew I was going to be judged purely on the illustrative qualities of the book, whereas before I was doing both story and illustration. Because I was

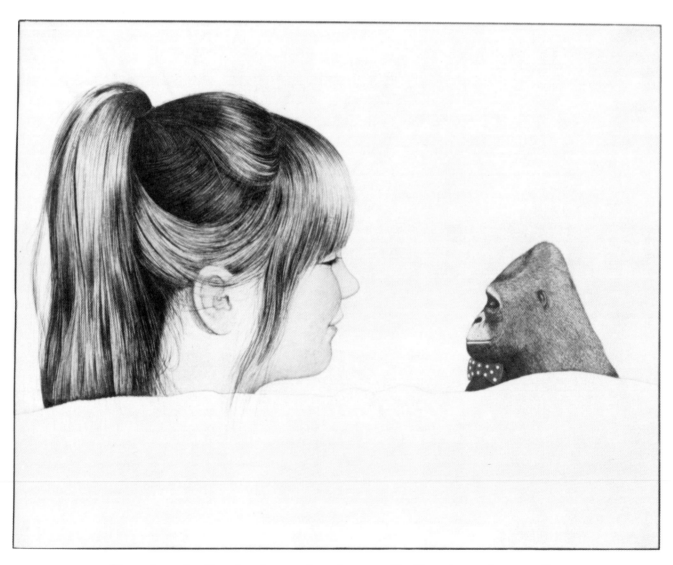

The next morning Hannah woke up and saw the toy gorilla. She smiled. ■ (From *Gorilla* by Anthony Browne. Illustrated by the author.)

(From *The Visitors Who Came to Stay* by Annalena McAfee. Illustrated by Anthony Browne.)

illustrating a traditional story, I knew I was making myself vulnerable on a technical level. So I spent more time on these illustrations than I had in any previous books.''[1]

In 1984, Browne's book *Gorilla* was awarded the Kate Greenaway Medal from the British Library Association for the "most distinguished work in the illustration of a children's book."
"*Gorilla* is about the relationship between a child and her father. My father was the kind of man who never actually found a career. He did lots of things. He was a boxer; he taught art for a while; he was in the army; he tried rugby. He died when I was seventeen. I really didn't know where the

Willy didn't seem to be any good at anything.

(From *Willy the Champ* by Anthony Browne. Illustrated by the author.)

story came from, but I think it has something to do with my father. He was a big man, and I was always a small boy. He was very keen on sports and encouraged my brother and me to be good at them. And yet he also drew and made delicate little models. I think that in some way the contrast of his strength and masculinity with his delicateness and his encouragement of our efforts to draw and write poetry has something to do with *Gorilla.*

''I wasn't thunderstruck; there was no searing light when I saw my first gorilla. Particularly, I remember seeing Guy, who was a very large gorilla in the London Zoo. I used to go and spend a lot of time looking at him.

''I was doing a school program for Thames Television. I'd finished the artwork for *Gorilla,* but it hadn't been published. They wanted me to write and present a program about children's books. They saw the *Gorilla* pictures and said, 'Wouldn't it be great to have some shots of you in a cage with a gorilla?' I thought it would be very exciting and a little bit frightening.

They said, 'Oh, you'll be fully insured. Don't worry about it. We'll make sure it's O.K.'

''The keepers suggested that I go into the cage with a couple of females a few times before the filming so they could get used to me. It was wonderful—one of the most wonderful experiences I've ever had! I went in twice for about a half-hour at a time. I was wrestling with them and carrying them on my back, sort of play-fighting. It was scary, but incredibly exhilarating.

''Then we went one day for the filming, with the camera people there. It seemed different. As soon as I went in, one of the gorillas came up and seemed to be sniffing my calf. I patted her on the back as I would a dog, because she was an old friend. Although I'd only been with them twice, those were such memorable experiences that I felt I really knew this gorilla. Then suddenly she sank her teeth into my leg, and I've never known pain like it. It was the shock as well. It seemed as though a friend had turned on me. It was like a dream when a friend's face suddenly turns into something horrible. Here I was with the microphone, and the expensive film running, supposed to be describing what it was like to meet my first gorilla.

"It turned out that the owner of the zoo had some sort of argument with the television people about how much he was going to be paid. He decided to feed the gorillas just as I was going into the cage. I was in there for twenty minutes before they could see how badly hurt I was. I kept looking down at the leg, but I was so embarrassed, I didn't want to say, 'Please can I get out?' They rushed me to the hospital eventually. It wasn't quite what we had had in mind.

"*The Visitors Who Came to Stay* is the first book I've illustrated that's been written by somebody else—Annalena McAfee, a friend of mine who lives in the village. Some people consider the book a follow-up to *Gorilla.* I certainly don't. It was quite difficult to convince Annalena that a story could be told in the pictures as well as in the words, but we worked closely together and the book developed quite smoothly.

"*Knock Knock* is the second book I've illustrated written by someone else. It's aimed at younger children. It's not written by somebody with any great pretentions to be a writer, but she's run a children's book club for some time and knows a great deal about what works with children. There is a lot of chanting: 'Knock, knock. Who's there?'—using the idea without the jokes. I wanted to put in some jokes, but she, I think quite rightly, said that the book was aimed at an age group that wouldn't appreciate them.

"For the book I worked on some drawings of children, and drawing them doesn't come very easily to me. The text has a simplicity and a repetitive chant, which I find quite appealing. I don't think I would have come up with the chant by myself. The little girl always has control of some potentially frightening images. She can always say, 'But I won't let you in.' It is also quite difficult to do some of these creatures which are potentially frightening.

"I like to have something in illustrations that might not be spotted the first time, so the child can go back and discover things in the pictures. That technique makes the books something one would want to go back to."[1]

HOBBIES AND OTHER INTERESTS: Reading, swimming, music, theatre, films, tennis, squash. "I play cricket for the local village team."

BULL, Angela (Mary) 1936-

PERSONAL: Born September 28, 1936, in Halifax, Yorkshire, England; daughter of Eric Alexander (a company director) and Joyce (Benson) Leach; married Martin Wells Bull (a Church of England clergyman), September 15, 1962; children: Timothy Martin, Priscilla Emily. *Education:* University of Edinburgh, M.A. (with honors), 1959; St. Hugh's College, Oxford, graduate study, 1959-61. *Religion:* Church of England. *Home:* The Vicarage, Hall Bank Dr., Bingley, West Yorkshire BD16 4BZ, England.

CAREER: Writer. Casterton School, Kirkby Lonsdale, Westmorland, England, teacher of English, 1961-62; Bodleian Library, Oxford University, Oxford, England, assistant to keeper of western manuscripts, 1963. *Awards, honors:* Other Award, 1980, for *The Machine Breakers: The Story of the Luddites.*

ANGELA BULL

WRITINGS—Published by Collins, except as indicated: *The Friend with a Secret,* 1965, Holt, 1966; (with Gillian Avery) *Nineteenth Century Children,* Hodder & Stoughton, 1965; *Wayland's Keep,* 1966, Holt, 1967; *Child of Ebenezer,* 1974; *Treasure in the Fog,* 1976; *Griselda,* 1977; *The Doll in the Wall* (illustrated by Gareth Floyd), 1978; *The Machine Breakers: The Story of the Luddites,* 1980; *The Bicycle Parcel* (illustrated by Jane Paton), Hamish Hamilton, 1981; *The Accidental Twins* (illustrated by Jill Bennett), Faber, 1982; *Noel Streatfeild,* 1984; *Anne Frank,* David & Charles, 1984; *Florence Nightingale,* David & Charles, 1985; *A Hat for Emily,* 1985.

WORK IN PROGRESS: A biography of Marie Curie, for Hamish Hamilton.

SIDELIGHTS: "Being brought up, as I was, in an English middle class home, just before and during the Second World War, was not unlike being brought up in Victorian England. Old ways lingered. I was one of five children, brought up in a big old house, with a Nannie, and afternoon walks whatever the weather, and nursery tea followed by stories round the fire. The house was full of books, including many Victorian children's books handed down through the family, and as I enjoyed them so much, I chose them for the subject of my research at Oxford. So when, after that, I began to write my own stories, to use a Victorian setting seemed the easiest, most natural thing in the world.

"A strong religious background helped equally towards my stories. Most of them have the theme of reconciliation between

Sally was skipping an endless series of "double-throughs,"... and no one had any attention to spare for Susan's careful skipping and expensive rope. ■
(From *The Accidental Twins* by Angela Bull. Illustrated by Jill Bennett.)

characters of opposing temperaments or upbringings. I did not choose this consciously, but later, looking back, I realized that I really always wanted to write about reconciliation.

"Diverted mainly now into non-fiction, since historical novels are out of fashion with English publishers, I have enjoyed working on biographies, especially when I can make an emotional identification with my subject. The biography of Noel Streatfeild was useful in introducing me to many half-forgotten writers of the 1930s and 1940s—a new field to me, as I had only worked on the Victorians before. Some of these books of fifty years ago deserve to be revived, and I hope to do further work in this field."

CALVERT, Patricia 1931-
(Peter J. Freeman)

PERSONAL: Born July 22, 1931, in Great Falls, Mont.; daughter of Edgar C. (a railroad worker) and Helen P. (a children's wear buyer; maiden name, Freeman) Dunlap; married George J. Calvert (in insurance business), January 27, 1951; children: Brianne L. Calvert Elias, Dana J. Calvert Halbert. *Education:* Winona State University, B.A., 1976, graduate study, 1976—. *Politics:* Liberal Democrat. *Religion:* Unitarian-Universalist.

Home: Foxwood Farm, R.R.2, Box 91, Chatfield, Minn. 55923. *Office:* Mayo Clinic, 200 Southwest First St., Rochester, Minn. 55901.

CAREER: St. Mary's Hospital, Great Falls, Mont., laboratory clerk, 1948-49; clerk typist at General Motors Acceptance Corp., 1950-51; Mayo Clinic, Rochester, Minn., cardiac laboratory technician, 1961-64, enzyme laboratory technician, 1964-70, senior editorial assistant in section of publications, 1970—. *Member:* American Medical Writers Association, Children's Reading Round Table, Society of Children's Book Writers, Society of Midland Authors. *Awards, honors:* "Best Book" Award from American Library Association, 1980, Society of Midland Authors Juvenile Fiction Award, Friends of American Writers Juvenile Award, and Young Women's Christian Association Award for outstanding achievement in the arts, all 1981, all for *The Snowbird;* nominated for Mark Twain Award from Missouri Association of School Libraries, 1984, for *The Money Creek Mare;* nominated for Maude Hart Lovelace Award for *The Stone Pony,* 1985.

WRITINGS: (Contributor) Lyle L. Miller, editor, *Developing Reading Efficiency,* 4th edition, Burgess, 1980; *The Snowbird* (young adult), Scribner, 1980; *The Money Creek Mare* (young adult), Scribner, 1981; *The Stone Pony* (young adult), Scribner, 1982; *The Hour of the Wolf* (young adult), Scribner, 1983; *Hadder MacColl* (young adult), Scribner, 1985. Contributor of more than one hundred articles and stories to children's magazines (sometimes under pseudonym Peter J. Freeman), including *Highlights for Children, Friend, Junior Life,* and *Jack and Jill.*

PATRICIA CALVERT

WORK IN PROGRESS: The Rainbow Comes and Goes, a book dealing with illegitimacy; *Catching Tigers in Red Weather;* a sequel to *Hadder MacColl; This Other Eden,* an adult historical novel set in America between 1885 and 1930.

SIDELIGHTS: 'My parents were eighteen years old when they married at the height of the Great Depression. Jobs were non-existent; for a penniless couple who were soon to be responsible for two small children it was next to impossible to find a home to rent, much less to own.

''But on an idle summer outing into a range of mountains eighty miles east of Great Falls, Montana, my father chanced to discover an abandoned miner's shack. The cabin, constructed nearly forty years before, was windowless; its puncheon floor had rotted away; rats and mice were its only inhabitants.

''The surrounding countryside, however, once the scene of gold-and-silver mining activity during the 1890s, was lively with wild game, and the nearby creeks were full of slim, silver trout. In such a place, my father reasoned, a man and his family might live off the land—and so, in October 1933, he moved a wife, a two-year-old daughter, and an infant son into that inhospitable cabin and set about to make it livable.

Jake hunched his shoulders against the morning chill and squinted across the snow-covered valley. . . . ■ (Jacket illustration by Ted Lewin from *The Hour of the Wolf* by Patricia Calvert.)

The only horse JoBeth had ever liked at all was the stone pony. ■ (Jacket illustration by Debbi Chabrian from *The Stone Pony* by Patricia Calvert.)

''The mountains that ringed the home where I grew up were known by such sonorous names as Thunder Mountain, Monument Peak, and Old Baldy; the brooks where I learned to fish were called Pilgrim Creek, Tenderfoot, Big Timber; the gold and silver mines that dotted the hillsides were labeled the Silver Bell, the Admiral Dewey, and the Gold Bug. It was a magic world for any child, one in which lodgepole pines grew like arrows toward a sky that seemed always blue. When I was older I had a sassy little horse named Redbird to ride, a collie named Bruno to keep me company, and a calico cat named Agamemnon to sleep at the foot of my bed.

''But it was also an isolated life, and two of the few recreations available to me and to my brother (who was my only playmate) were story-telling and reading. It was our good fortune to have a mother who was a lively story-teller; she was black-haired and green-eyed and had been raised in an Irish family of ten children—and she never tired of telling us sad and funny (and often outrageous!) tales about her own childhood.

''In addition, my mother read to us almost every evening by the light of a smoky kerosene lamp—not the traditional classics that most children hear, but a crazy assortment of detective, adventure, and love stories from such popular magazines as *Liberty* and *Saturday Evening Post*—stories I am sure no schoolteacher would have thought appropriate fare but which acquainted me early with the art and craft of a good yarn. It was in such magazines I later learned, that authors such as F.

Scott Fitzgerald, Ernest Hemingway, and William Faulkner gained their wide audiences.

"By the time I was ten years old, I knew that what I wanted to be most in life was a writer. At that time I also read two books that crystallized my desire to write for a young-adult audience. The first was Armstrong Sperry's gripping tale, _Call It Courage,_ and the second was Kate Seredy's wonderful saga, _The White Stag._ Those books embraced things that were important to me: each dealt with themes of honor and courage; each took place in the out-of-doors; each was written in an artful, elegant manner.

"But years were to pass before I was able to write the kind of books that I wanted to write. I grew up and left the mountains; I married and had two children of my own; eventually, I went to work as an editorial assistant in the Section of Publications at the Mayo Clinic in Rochester, Minnesota. When my daughters, Brianne and Dana, were married and had families of their own, I moved back into the country where I belonged. My husband and I bought a small farm and named it Foxwood; we turned our acres into a wildlife preserve where deer, fox, and raccoon could wander where they wished.

"I converted an old chicken coop into a place to write, and when I did I returned to scenes from my childhood and to those half-forgotten tales told to me by my mother about her own childhood. I hoped that my first book, _The Snowbird,_ would bring to young-adult readers some of the pleasure that came to me when I read _Call It Courage_ and _The White Stag._ More than that, I hoped I could pass on to my readers my pet philosophy: that no matter how young one is, it is sometimes necessary to declare to the world _I am accountable._

"In a modest way, perhaps I succeeded. _The Snowbird_ was named a 'Best Book' by the American Library Association; later it received awards from the Friends of American Writers and a second one from the Society of Midland Authors. Then I wrote _The Money Creek Mare, The Stone Pony,_ and _The Hour of the Wolf._ When William Faulkner accepted the Nobel Prize for Literature in 1950, he said that it had been his privilege to 'create out of the materials of the human spirit something which did not exist before.' In my own way, I have tried to do the same for young-adult readers.

"I am everlastingly fascinated by that country from which we are all emigrants: the land of childhood—and that is the reason why my fiction is for (and about) children. When an acquaintance recently expressed to me the hope that, since I'd now had a couple of children's books published, I could write 'a real one' (that is, a novel for adults), I had to discourage him quickly. To write for and about children—and to write for and about the child in myself—is really all I intend to do."

HOBBIES AND OTHER INTERESTS: Reading, hiking around the farm.

CAMPBELL, Patricia J(ean) 1930-
(Patty Campbell)

PERSONAL: Born November 20, 1930, in Hollywood, Calif.; daughter of Fred Duane and Frances (Griffith) Cowan; married Billy Wilmon Campbell, April 20, 1951 (divorced, September, 1970); married David Pildas Shore (a writer), February 9, 1984; children: (first marriage) Fred Campbell-Craven, Broos, Aisha, Cameron. _Education:_ University of California, Los Angeles, B.A., 1952; University of California, Berkeley, M.L.S.,

PATRICIA J. CAMPBELL

1953. _Politics:_ Democrat. _Religion:_ "Liberal Christian." _Home:_ 1437 Lucile Ave., Los Angeles, Calif. 90026.

CAREER: Library of Hawaii, Honolulu, librarian, 1954-55; Office of Economic Opportunity, Los Angeles, Calif., housing organizer, 1967-69; Los Angeles Public Library, Los Angeles, young adult librarian, 1969-72, assistant coordinator of young adult services, 1972-78; writer, consultant, and columnist, 1978—; instructor, UCLA Extension, 1980-84. _Member:_ American Library Association (member of board of directors of Young Adult Services Division, 1979-81), Southern California Council on Literature for Children and Young People, Young Adult Reviewers of Southern California (president, 1975), Phi Beta Kappa.

WRITINGS: Sex Education Books for Young Adults, 1892-1979, Bowker, 1979; _Passing the Hat: Street Performers in America_ (illustrated with photographs by Alice Belkin), Delacorte, 1985; _Presenting Robert Cormier_ (young adult), Twayne, 1985; _Sex Guides: Books and Film on Sexuality for Young Adults,_ Garland, 1986.

Author of a column on young adult library services in _Booklegger,_ 1975-77, and a column of young adult book reviews, "The YA Perplex," in _Wilson Library Bulletin,_ 1978—. Contributor to library magazines and the _New York Times Book Review._

WORK IN PROGRESS: Europe Free!, a book on van travel in Europe with David Shore; _The Sidewalks of Y'urp,_ a factual novel about street performers in Europe.

CARLSON, Nancy L(ee) 1953-

BRIEF ENTRY: Born October 10, 1953, in Minneapolis, Minn. Artist, author and illustrator of picture books for children. After attending the University of Minnesota at Duluth for one year, Carlson enrolled at the Minneapolis College of Art and Design where she received her B.F.A. in 1976. Her work has been exhibited in both solo and group showings; in 1975 she won printmaking awards from the Northshore Arts Festival. Along with her role as an artist, she is a card buyer for the Center Book Shop and Walter Art Center as well as an arts and crafts specialist for the city of South St. Paul, Minn. Carlson described herself as "an artist who enjoys making up stories for children." To this end, she has produced over a dozen picture books. "All the stories are based on things that happened to me as a kid," she related, "and each has a simple moral."

In several series of books, Carlson anthropomorphizes characters like Harriet the dog, Loudmouth George the rabbit, and Louanne Pig. *Booklist* called her stories "smooth little vignettes that have both strong child appeal and something to say," while *School Library Journal* took note of the "fine black lines, bold colors and attention to detail" in her illustrations. Among Carlson's titles, all published by Carolrhoda, are *Harriet and Walt, Harriet and the Garden, Harriet's Halloween Candy* (all 1982), *Loudmouth George and the New Neighbors, Loudmouth George and the Sixth-Grade Bully* (both 1983), *Bunnies and Their Hobbies* (1984), *Louanne Pig in Making the Team,* and *Louanne Pig in the Mysterious Valentine* (both 1985). She also illustrated Joyce Kessel's *Halloween* and Geoffrey Scott's *Egyptian Boats. Home and office:* 4825 Upton Ave. S., Minneapolis, Minn. 55410.

FOR MORE INFORMATION SEE: Contemporary Authors, Volume 110, Gale, 1984.

COOKE, Donald Ewin 1916-1985

OBITUARY NOTICE—See sketch in *SATA* Volume 2: Born August 5, 1916, in Philadelphia, Pa.; died after a long illness, in Pennsylvania. Artist, educator, publisher, journalist, illus-trator, and author. Cooke was founder of Edraydo publishers, now known as Haverford House. He was also a distinguished water-colorist and illustrator whose work appeared in exhibits, as limited edition art prints, in books, and even on note cards. Among his many writings are *The Firebird, Little Wolf Slayer, Johnny on-the-Spot, The Silver Horn of Robin Hood, Fathers of American Freedom,* and *Our Nation's Great Heritage.*

FOR MORE INFORMATION SEE: Contemporary Authors, New Revision Series, Volume 4, Gale, 1981; *Philadelphia Enquirer,* August 19, 1985.

COPLEY, (Diana) Heather Pickering 1918-

PERSONAL: Born December 13, 1918, in Brewood Hall, Brewood Staffs, England; daughter of Eric Oswald Pickering (a land agent) and Doris Kathleen (Metcalfe) Copley; married Christopher Chamberlain (an artist), November 5, 1940 (deceased); children: Diana Saskia. *Education:* Attended Clapham School of Art, 1936-39; Royal College of Art, diploma, 1946, post graduate work, 1948. *Home:* 43 Edith Grove, Chelsea, London SW10 0LB, England.

CAREER: Painter, and children's book illustrator. Part-time lecturer in art, St. Martin's School of Art, 1948-83. Commissions include a printer's calendar, 1962, and a series of drawings for Tinlings of Liverpool, London, England, 1964. Paintings have been exhibited regularly at the Royal Academy of Arts, London. *Wartime service:* World War II, served in Civil Defense in England. *Awards, honors: London's River: The Story of a City* was commended as a Carnegie Medal book by the British Library Association, 1965.

ILLUSTRATOR: Drawings of the Katydid, Katydid Press, 1958; Arthur H. Naylor, *The Study Book of Time and Clocks* (juvenile), Dufour, 1959; (with husband, Christopher Chamberlain) Roger L. Green, reteller, *Heroes of Greece and Troy* (young adult), Bodley Head, 1960, Walck, 1961, revised edition, Bodley Head, 1973; Geoffrey Middleton, *The Study Book of Canals,* Bodley Head, 1961; Leonard Clark, editor, *Drums and Trumpets* (juvenile), Bodley Head, 1962, Dufour, 1963, published as *Drums and Trumpets: Poetry for the Youngest,*

The skyline is dominated by the dome of St. Paul's Cathedral and the spires of many of Wren's new parish churches. ■ (From *London's River: The Story of a City* by Eric de Maré. Illustrated by Heather Copley and Christopher Chamberlain.)

Merrimack Book Service, 1979; (with C. Chamberlain) Eric Baxter, *The Study Book of Ships* (juvenile), Dufour, 1963; (with C. Chamberlain) E. Baxter, *The Study Book of Railways* (juvenile), Dufour, 1964; (with C. Chamberlain) Eric de Maré, *London's River: The Story of a City* (juvenile), Bodley Head, 1964, McGraw, 1965, revised edition, Bodley Head, 1972, Merrimack Book Service, 1978; R. L. Green, compiler and reteller, *Tales of Ancient Egypt,* Bodley Head, 1967; Dorothy Canfield, *Betsy,* Bodley Head, 1973.

Also contributor of illustrations and an article on Benjamin Franklin to *Book Design and Production,* 1961.

SIDELIGHTS: ''[I] always wanted to be an artist. . . . I like drawing but I prefer to be thought of as a painter who draws rather than an illustrator.'' [Lee Kingman and others, compilers, *Illustrators of Children's Books: 1957-1966,* Horn Book, 1968.[1]]

''I would rather draw directly from life because working in any other way does not seem convincing to me.'' [John Ryder, *Artists of a Certain Line,* Bodley Head, 1960.[2]]

''I have paintings in New York and Hollywood. I come from the same family that produced John Singleton Copley of Boston (1737-1815).''

FOR MORE INFORMATION SEE: John Ryder, *Artists of a Certain Line,* Bodley Head, 1960; Lee Kingman and others, compilers, *Illustrators of Children's Books: 1957-1966,* Horn Book, 1968.

CORMIER, Robert (Edmund) 1925-
(John Fitch IV)

PERSONAL: Born January 17, 1925, in Leominster, Mass.; son of Lucien Joseph (a factory worker) and Irma (Collins) Cormier; married Constance B. Senay, 1948; children: Rob-

ROBERT CORMIER

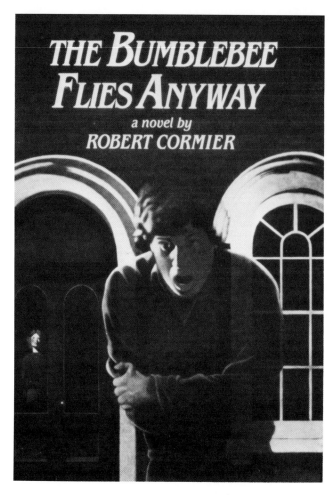

His breath came in terrifying gasps and his heart threatened to explode from his body. ■ (Jacket illustration by Norman Walker from *The Bumblebee Flies Anyway* by Robert Cormier.)

erta S., Peter J., Christine J., Renee E. *Education:* Attended Fitchburg State College, one year. *Home:* 1177 Main St., Leominster, Mass. 01453.

CAREER: Radio station WTAG, Worcester, Mass., writer, 1946-48; *Telegram & Gazette,* Worcester, reporter, 1948-55, writing consultant, 1980-83; *Fitchburg Sentinel,* Fitchburg, Mass., reporter, 1955-59, wire editor, 1959-66, associate editor, 1969-78; free-lance writer, 1978—. *Member:* L'Union St. Jean Baptiste d'Amerique.

AWARDS, HONORS: Prize for best news writing, Associated Press in New England, 1959, 1973; best newspaper column, K. R. Thomson Newspapers, Inc., 1974; *New York Times* Outstanding Book of the Year Award, 1974, for *The Chocolate War,* 1977, for *I Am the Cheese,* and 1979, for *After the First Death; The Chocolate War, I Am the Cheese, After the First Death,* and *The Bumblebee Flies Anyway* were chosen as a ''Best Book for Young Adults'' by the American Library Association, 1974, 1977, 1979, and 1983 respectively; Media & Methods Maxi Award from *Media & Methods,* 1976, Lewis Carroll Shelf award, 1979, and included on *School Library Journal*'s ''Best of the Best 1966-1978'' list, 1979, all for *The Chocolate War;* Doctor of Letters, Fitchburg State College, 1977; Woodward Park School Annual Book Award, 1978, for *I Am the Cheese; Eight Plus One* was selected as a Notable Children's Trade Book in the Field of Social Studies by the

The three sophomores awaited in tense and silent anticipation, a little nervous about what was going to happen. ■ (Jacket illustration by Brad Holland from *Beyond the Chocolate War* by Robert Cormier.)

joint committee of the National Council for Social Studies and Children's Book Council, 1980; Assembly on Literature for Adolescents (ALAN) Award of the National Council of Teachers of English, 1982, for significant contributions to the field of adolescent literature; *The Chocolate War, I Am the Cheese,* and *After the First Death* were chosen for American Library Association's "Best of the Best Books 1970-1983"; *The Bumblebee Flies Anyway* was included on *School Library Journal*'s "Best Books 1983" list.

WRITINGS—Novels, except as indicated: *Now and at the Hour,* Coward, 1960; *A Little Raw on Monday Mornings,* Sheed, 1963; *Take Me Where the Good Times Are,* Macmillan, 1965; *The Chocolate War* (ALA Notable Book; with teacher's guide), Pantheon, 1974; *I Am the Cheese* (ALA Notable Book; *Horn Book* Honor List; with teacher's guide), Pantheon, 1977; *After the First Death* (with teacher's guide), Pantheon, 1979; *Eight Plus One* (short stories; with teacher's guide), Pantheon, 1980; *The Bumblebee Flies Anyway* (ALA Notable Book), Pantheon, 1983; (contributor) *Sixteen: Short Stories by Outstanding Writers for Young Adults,* Delacorte, 1984; *Beyond the Chocolate War* (*Horn Book* Honor List), Knopf, 1985.

Fitchburg Sentinel, author of human interest column, 1964-78, and under pseudonym, John Fitch IV, of a book review column, "The Sentinel Bookman," 1966-78; also author of monthly human interest column, "1177 Main Street," *St. An-*

thony Messenger, 1972-80. Contributor of articles and short stories to periodicals, including *McCalls, Redbook, Saturday Evening Post, Sign,* and *Woman's Day.*

ADAPTATIONS: "The Chocolate War" (recording and cassette), Miller Brody, 1982; "I Am the Cheese" (recording and cassette), Miller Brody, 1982; "After the First Death" (recording and cassette), Miller Brody, 1982; "I Am the Cheese" (motion picture), starring Robert Wagner, Hope Lange, Don Murray, Robert MacNaughton, and Robert Cormier, Almi Group, 1983.

WORK IN PROGRESS: "I am working on a new novel. I never discuss plot, title, etc., before a novel is completed."

SIDELIGHTS: **January 17, 1925.** Born in Leominster, Massachusetts. In a 1982 taped interview for Random House/Miller Brody, Cormier commented on his youth, his early career, and his major works. "I wasn't the physical type, the ball-playing type, and I never got chosen for the team. I was out under a tree reading a book, probably. The streets were terrible. It was depression and it was bleak, but home was warm. We had a large family, a warm family. But really, I was a skinny kid living in a ghetto type of neighborhood wanting the world to know I existed. I'd listen to the radio programs at night, Jack Benny, or famous singers and other people. I felt

I am afraid of a thousand things, a million. Like, is it possible to be claustrophobic and yet fear open spaces, too? ■ (Jacket illustration "Corner Seat" by Robert Vickrey from *I Am the Cheese* by Robert Cormier.)

so unknown and so lost that I said, 'Someday I want them to know that I'm here. I exist.'

"'. . . If a kid wanted to be a baseball player he would go to Fenway Park, that was where his heroes were. My heroes were in the library, in those books. One of the greatest thrills in my life was when I graduated from the childhood section to the adult section. Then you could go into the stacks—that was a big moment. The stacks were behind the circulation desk and not just anybody could go in there. They gave it to me at a very early age because I just zipped through all those children's books. So I went from *Penrod and Sam* (Booth Tarkington) right into Thomas Wolfe. In fact, the discovery of Thomas Wolfe occurred in a library, and had probably the greatest single effect on me as a writer.

"I discovered that Thomas Wolfe book when I was thirteen years old. The book was *The Web and the Rock*. It was under new fiction; it had just been published. The book jacket said, 'This is a novel of man's longing in his youth.' It's about a boy from a small town who wanted to be a writer, and wanted to go to the big city (which was the rock), and become famous and have people know who he was. ''And I said 'That's me! I want to be a writer.' Then I realized there was someone else like me, who felt the same way.

"That book meant so much to me. Emotionally it was a great thing to me; in a literary way it wasn't. Thomas Wolfe was the kind of a writer who wrote mountain torrents of prose— all those adjectives. I tried to write the way he did and it was frustrating. I figured if he's my model then I must write like that. I spent months just pouring out this awful, terrible prose that I knew wasn't right, but I didn't know what to do about it. Thank God, that particular thing ended; it ended when I discovered some other writers.

"If Wolfe opened the door emotionally to me as a writer, Hemingway opened it stylistically. He made me realize you didn't have to have the mountain torrent of prose. You could have a clear, thin stream. He used the simple word. I realized the *one* great adjective or the *one* great verb can do it. You don't need all these other words. His stuff was like music. The opening passage of *A Farewell to Arms* is like a simple melody, part of a great symphony. William Saroyan *also* wrote simply. Hemingway wrote these great romantic things, the war hero, the wounded war hero in *The Sun Also Rises*. But Saroyan wrote about people like me, his neighborhood in Fresno, California—the Armenian neighborhood. There I was in a French Canadian one. I thought God, this stuff can be the stuff of drama. I don't have to imitate Wolfe and I don't have to be a war hero. I can write about what's happening here on French Hill.'' [Taken from a taped interview of Robert Cormier. Produced by Random House/Miller Brody, 1982.[1]]

1943. Enrolled in Fitchburg State College, Fitchburg, Massachusetts. ''I was very fortunate with my teachers. When I was a college freshman I had an art teacher . . . [who] read one of my theme papers, and she brought me up after class and said, 'This shows a lot of talent, Bob. Evidently you like to write, or you'd like to be a writer.' Of course in my heart I knew that I *was* a writer. I said 'Yes.' She said, 'The next time you write something I'd love to see it.' I was looking for an audience in those days. I had all these plots and emotions hanging around so I just went home that day and on the kitchen table, with pencil and paper wrote a story called 'The Little Things That Count,' and brought it in to her. She read it, said she liked it, and then she said a puzzling thing to me. She said, 'Do you mind if I hold onto it for awhile?' I said fine. Without telling me, she had it typed and sent it to a magazine.

Later that year, during the summer, her car pulled up in front of our house and out she got waving this check. She had sold the story for me, for seventy-five dollars, to a national Catholic magazine. It wasn't a particularly Catholic story but it was a story about a family living in a place like French Hill. So, there I had a teacher acting as an agent. I didn't give her ten percent but I did send her a bouquet of flowers—roses, red roses. That was a great moment. Suddenly I was a professional writer. Until then, I was that strange kid who was always in his room scribbling. But with our American system of the dollar economy, the dollar society, as soon as you sell, you are a writer. My cousins and uncles and aunts who had thought that I was just a strange, eccentric little kid said, 'My God!, he made seventy-five dollars by putting words on paper.' This was miraculous to them.'''[1]

1946. Began working for radio station WTAG in Worcester, Massachusetts. ''I wanted to earn my living with words, and I became a reporter, but first I worked for a radio station and wrote commercials for two years, which was the worst experience of my work life. If you think commercials are terrible to listen to, they're awful to write. Yet I learned so much. Minute commercials were one hundred words and station break commercials were thirty words. You have to be clever. You have to get in all the specials the store owners want to sell, and you have to write them for the *ear* not the eye, so an announcer can pronounce them correctly. You're doing a lot of things: you're being clever, you're doing it in a hundred words, you're covering all the material they want to get in there, and you're writing for the ear. I hated it, but I realized looking back that this was one of the greatest disciplines that I ever went through and it really affected me. I graduated from there to newspaper work. I say graduated because my original intention was to work for newspapers. I got sidetracked when I got into radio.'''[1]

1948. Began working as a reporter for the Leominster bureau of the Worcester *Telegram & Gazette*. ''I became a reporter and was a reporter for most of my life and loved it. Luckily, I covered many beats: I started on the police beat, went into politics, and did human interest columns.'''[1]

1955. Became a reporter for the *Fitchburg Sentinel*. ''Writing for a newspaper after awhile is very constricting. It's very formularized. There are just so many ways you can write a three-alarm fire or a two-car accident or cover court. I was lucky, I moved sideways into an editing position where I wrote headlines, which was a different kind of writing, but it was working with words. Everything was contributing to what I wanted to do—learn to use words. Then I became an associate editor. I started writing editorials, and then I wrote a human interest column which allowed me to create rather than write the standard, routine, ordinary story. So my experience in newspaper work was very rewarding because I kept changing. . . . I was very fortunate.'''[1]

1959. Promoted to wire editor of the *Sentinel*. One of his feature stories was selected as the best human-interest story of the year by the Associated Press in New England. While a reporter, Cormier wrote in his free time, developing his techniques as a novelist. ''. . . Reporting was the means to the end. I regarded myself as a novelist who was being a reporter to support my family. There has to be a certain amount of obsession in being a writer, a certain amount of madness; I always knew I had choices. I'd get up from the supper table in the evening, there'd be a good television show on, and I'd say to myself, 'What are you, a television watcher or are you a writer?' Some men played golf, I wrote. I had a growing family, yet I never had a door to my writing room. My writing, my typewriter was never off limits to the kids. I remember writing when they were very small crawling up my leg. In fact, recently my daughter . . . said, 'Dad, I remember falling asleep to the sound of that typewriter, that faint click, clicking coming from downstairs. What a marvelous feeling that was. You were awake and writing and I'd go off to sleep. . . .'

''I think the guy who went out and played golf probably saw less of his family. Even though I was enshrouded in this little world of mine at the typewriter, at least I was available to the kids. Having insomnia when they were teenagers, I was always up half the night and I'd be there when they came home from dances or dates or movies. A lot of nights they'd just go to bed, 'Goodnight Dad,' then up the stairs. Sometimes they didn't. My son and I would sit and talk. . . . Your son will tell you things at one o'clock in the morning that he won't tell you at one o'clock in the afternoon and you'll tell your son things at that hour that you wouldn't earlier. I think those insights helped when I began writing novels that started to appeal to young adults.''[1]

1960. First novel, *Now and at the Hour* was published. It was followed three years later with *A Little Raw on Monday Mornings.* ''I'm always conscious of the reader and wanting to affect that reader. You either make that reader laugh or you make him angry or frightened. I use everything I can. I go for

clarity and I keep to those simple words and simple sentences. But simplicity doesn't mean that a thing has to be without meaning or depth. I try to write to let the reader supply the emotion, . . . and I do that by setting up scenes and describing the situation. In other words *I* would never say 'this man is sad.' I would write in such a way that the reader feels the emotions of that person and comes to the conclusion that this man is sad.

''Actually I think of myself as a rewriter rather than a writer. I rewrite and rewrite and rewrite. With each novel, I fill a shopping bag of material that has been rewritten. I think for every page that appears finally in the finished product there are probably three to four pages that don't. What makes my wife start climbing walls is [the fact that] I don't throw anything away, so I have boxes and boxes of manuscripts. These have now been collected at a college near my home.''[1]

1965. Third novel, *Take Me Where the Good Times Are* was published. ''. . . I love to tinker with the words. I hate to let novels go when they are done. One of my novels, *Take Me Where the Good Times Are,* I actually wrote over completely after it was all done and ready to go to the publisher. . . . I get pretty involved with the characters.'' [Patricia J. Campbell, *Presenting Robert Cormier,* Twayne, 1985.[2]]

(From the movie "I Am the Cheese," starring Robert Macnaughton and Cynthia Nixon. Released by Almi Films. Copyright © 1983 by I Am The Cheese Co.)

1974. Inspired by a true life experience, Cormier wrote his controversial book for young adults, *The Chocolate War*. The book was based on his teenage son's experience. "My son was going to a high school much like the school in the book. They were having a chocolate sale, and Peter refused to sell the chocolates. It was a family decision, a matter of principle. . . . He was the only kid in the place who didn't sell the chocolates. Nothing happened to him but something happened to me. I used the thing all writers use: 'What if? What if there had been peer pressure; what if there had been faculty pressure?' The emotional content was there.

"When Peter brought those chocolates back the next day, I was apprehensive for him, I was fearful. I felt guilty that we allowed him to do this. He was fourteen years old, a freshman in a new school, in a different city—these emotions got me to the typewriter. Then I saw a chance to explore themes, the individual against society, manipulation. That's how *The Chocolate War* began."[1]

The Chocolate War became a turning point in Cormier's writing life. It won numerous awards and was extremely popular with young adults. Although the book won rave reviews by numerous critics, it also received a great many negative comments from other reviewers. Many teachers, parents, and librarians were uncomfortable with the effect the book would have on young people. "My books have never been banned outright; they have been criticized, and they have been up for banning. . . . I called Proctor, Vermont to find out whether my book *The Chocolate War,* had been banned. There had been

a vote by the trustees [of the library]. The librarian said, 'Bob, they voted three to two to keep your book in the school.' That sounded like a victory but she added, 'However, the book has to be labeled. It has to be on a special shelf in some cases. . . . It can be taken out, but with special permission.'

"This [situation] is being repeated all over the country with a great many books. . . . People get upset by language in books but they don't look at the meanings. This worries me because I think there are more subversive books being published, but because the language is okay people are reading them and probably being more influenced by them."[1]

When asked why he thought his books were so controversial, Cormier offered the following observation: "I think it makes some people uncomfortable because I recognize that life isn't always a series of happy endings; everybody likes to aspire to that. You know they talk about the violence on television but it's a phoney violence because we know at the end of the show, with the last commercial to protect your underarms, that 'Starsky and Hutch' or 'Magnum P.I.'or whoever, is going to get his man. We have a whole generation that has been brought up with this idea that at ten o'clock all's well. We're brought up to expect happy endings. Everybody wants to have a happy ending. My books go against that: the hero doesn't always win, and sometimes you're not sure who the bad guy is as in *I Am the Cheese*. This upsets people; they like labels; they like clear identification. They like riding off into the sunset. People don't ride off into the sunset in my books, they walk off hobbled and crippled maybe, into the dark night.

Robert Cormier (center) played Mr. Hertz in the film version of his novel. ■ (From the movie "I Am the Cheese." Released by Almi Films. Copyright © 1983 by I Am The Cheese Co.)

''I remember Robert Frost said a marvelous thing. He said 'Poetry is saying one thing and meaning another.' I try to apply that in my books. People think they're reading one thing and suddenly it dawns on them, about three quarters of the way through, 'Hey this isn't what I thought it was going to be.' This upsets people. When I say upsets people I'm talking about adults; it doesn't upset the children.

''Sometimes I'm irritated by even having to come to the defense of a book. . . . The book itself is a defense, the seeds of all my defenses are in the books themselves. I don't feel that I ought to be an attorney on behalf of my own books. I said it in the book. Other people defend them, thank goodness.''[1]

The Chocolate War was followed by another psychological suspense novel entitled *I Am the Cheese* in 1977, which was in turn followed by *After the First Death* in 1979. All three books deal with violence and have downbeat endings, and, because of those books, Cormier was labeled a pessimistic writer, a label he staunchly opposed. ''I'm an optimist and yet entirely a realist, if that can be. A man can be like myself: love old Beatle songs, and be a romantic. Yet a part of me is very realistic. I know there seems to be a dichotomy there, but I think we're none of us all of one thing. We love labels—people apply labels all the time, but I think that within the labels there are variations. We're mixtures of heaven and hell—I think I am too. I have my demons and I have my angels. It works in all of us—this heaven-hell idea. It happens that more of a hell comes out in my writing than the heaven part of it.

''Jerry Renault got terribly beaten up at the end of *The Chocolate War*. He was the protagonist, the kid readers identified with. But Jerry gave it the good fight. He went against society, *his* society, that school. He was alone and he tried to beat the odds. What a lot of kids respond to is that he *tried*. He *did* it. The fact that he failed was almost beside the point. Some critics who feel my books are too downbeat only look at the ending and say, 'Gee, that poor kid got beaten up and was kind of dispirited about it.' They forget what came before: that he made the great effort. And to me that's always been the big thing.

''In *I Am the Cheese* this poor traumatized, drugged kid has an awful future. But he's on that bicycle pumping away, peddling away, doing something. Kate, in *After the First Death*, had a terrible fate. Yet to the final moment she tried. Tried to rescue those kids, tried to start the bus. She even resorted to feminine wiles, which she hated doing because she was a feminist. My protagonists put up the good fight.

''I really think kids recognize this; that's why, although parents and adults are disturbed about these things, they're not. I've never had a letter from a young person saying, 'This was too downbeat, this was awful.' They do say, 'I wish Kate hadn't died.' But add, 'We knew it was inevitable.' ''[1]

Cormier is fond of the variety of letters he receives from his teenage readers and the long-distance phone calls. ''I get a lot of mail because there are things about the characters in my work that are ambiguous and this intrigues the kids. . . . I try for the shock of recognition. Kate is a lovely American cheerleader, always-has-a-date-for-the-prom type. She's been brought up protected all her life and suddenly she is in this terrible position of stress. I get mail from girls about *After the First Death* because I think they identify with Kate. In . . . *The Chocolate War, I Am the Cheese* and *After the First Death*, she is my first full-scale female character. So I get mail from girls, twelve to sixteen, about it. They ask a lot of questions.

''I have answers but I like to stretch their minds a little, challenge them a bit. So I don't give them the answers they think they'd like. I write letters like the kind of novels I write. . . . I give them alternatives, options. . . .

''I [also] get long distance calls. . . . The young adult audience is a marvelous audience because it is so responsive. A thirty-eight year old adult would *never* call an author. Fifteen-year-old readers will because they identify with you, because you're their friend. They feel you know the shocks of recognition, 'I'll call him because I know he wouldn't mind.' This is a marvelous relationship to have with your readership.''[1]

1977. Received an honorary Doctor of Letters from Fitchburg State College, the college that he had attended as an undergraduate student.

Cormier commented on his writing and the influences on his style: ''There are so many rewards [to writing]. When you get the ideas, that's a thrill; when you're writing the book and it's coming out well, that's a thrill; when you finish it and other people read it, that's a thrill. There are going to be reviews, of course; not everyone's going to love it. You feel . . . naked and vulnerable in a way. That's just a minor part of the process, really. If you can't take that part, you shouldn't be in the business. There is the sense of so many people having been involved. There are a lot of people who have contributed, people whose lives you have affected. An artist had to design the book; another person worked on the promotion. It has set a whole world going.

''I think there are two great influences on my writing. One is current. I read a lot of detective stories because they always deliver. They give you a beginning, a middle, and an end—a resolution. The modern novels I read don't always deliver because I'm looking essentially for a story. As in Shakespeare, 'The play's the thing.' In particular, I read detective stories for pacing, plot and suspense. Ed McBain's Seventy-sixth Precinct mysteries are probably the most underrated detective stories in the world today.

''I also like police procedural novels. I was brought up on Ellery Queen, and, of course, those books were puzzles rather than mysteries. But I learned plotting technique and gradual disclosure from Queen.

''The earliest influence on me was the movies of the thirties when I was growing up. Those were stories. . . . My mother didn't go to the movies because of a religious promise she made early in her life, and I used to go to movies and come home and tell her the plots of those old Warner Brothers/James Cagney/Bette Davis movies, the old romantic love stories. Through these movies . . . I absorbed drama, sense of pacing, and plot.

''When I write, I never think of segments as chapters; I think of them as scenes. I always visualize them in my mind. Then I try to get the scene down on paper as closely as I can. That's the one thing that readers don't see—what you have in your mind. The reader can only see what you get on the page.

''Even with these influences I don't think I [became] a professional writer until I learned my weaknesses and what I couldn't do. This forced me to compensate. I use a lot of similes and metaphors when I work, simply because it's my best way of describing a building or a scene. I'm terrible at describing landscapes—trees, buildings. The inanimate things don't interest me: I always think, 'Oh, no, here comes another building I have to describe.' So I usually use a simile or metaphor.

His mouth encountered gravel, and he spat frantically, afraid that some of his teeth had been knocked out. ■ (Jacket illustration "Running Boy" by Robert Vickrey from *The Chocolate War* by Robert Cormier.)

When I first started out writing and heard about figures of speech, I thought they were 'fancy writing,' but I realize they're not. Graham Greene showed me the use of metaphor to evoke emotion, scene, and place.

"There is very little that is accidental in my work. I believe in serendipity for developments of plot, but the actual writing is arrived at by very hard work. I mentioned the joy of writing, but that doesn't mean that you don't get the backaches and headaches and the days when it's not coming." [Anita Silvey, "An Interview with Robert Cormier," *Horn Book,* May/June, 1985.[3] Amended by R. Cormier.]

1978. Began writing full time as a free-lancer. ". . . I act as though I'm going into the office each day, and I try to be very businesslike. I get up and dress and shave, read the paper, and go to the typewriter. I plan a good full morning that might be two-and-a-half or four hours. I find that intense writing at the typewriter is very exhausting. I rest in the afternoon and see friends or watch something I've taped on my VCR. Again, in the evening I bring out my writing and look at it. If it reads well, it makes me feel like writing again the next morning; and if it doesn't, it still makes me feel like correcting the material. I try to set up a continuity, a momentum. Even though I set up these artificial times, the book is always with me. I probably get the greatest idea of the week standing in line at the bank or driving the car. I'm always telling myself as I write that I'm not really writing a novel; I'm just going to fool around with a character or an idea. I have a whole pile of manuscripts that are different books in different stages. Until the sequel, I drove my editors crazy because I never told them what I was working on. Until Fabio Coen saw *I Am the Cheese,* he had no idea that I was working on it—nor did my wife.

"I don't even number my pages. There again, I don't think that I'm writing a novel. I also don't like to think in terms of writing ten or twelve pages a day. Usually I'm writing a scene, and it's always with the idea, 'I wonder what is going to happen.' Or sometimes I write about something that affected me emotionally the day before and that I don't want to lose. I'm very unorganized at first; but finally it comes into a structure where consciously I'm working on a novel per se.

". . . I'm always afraid I'll wake up some morning and it will all be gone. And you never reach the stage when you say, 'I've done it.' The blank page is there every day; that's what keeps you humble. That's what keeps your feet on the ground. No one can do it for you; and the page can be terrifyingly blank. As much as there is joy in writing, there's always the little bit of terror to keep you on edge, on your toes. It is a strange way to occupy yourself—to enjoy your life on a daily basis. There is no guarantee that something great is going to come next. That's why I don't sign three book contracts ahead of time; I don't like to write against deadlines, demands.

"I've always wanted to write a love story. *After the First Death* I thought would be my adolescent love story. But what I would like to write and what I am going to write are usually two different things."[3]

1981. The Robert E. Cormier Collection was established at Fitchburg (Mass.) State College. "All of my manuscripts, correspondence, articles, interviews, reviews, etc. have been gathered at the college and housed in a special area. It is planned for these materials to be available to young people interested in a writer's development as well as any other interested persons."

1983. Another book about teenagers faced with intense and painful situations, *The Bumblebee Flies Anyway,* was published. The setting for the novel is a hospital for terminally ill young people. "A bleak setting. People die in this book. They also fall in love; know bliss as well as pain.

"I have no hesitation or twinges of conscience as I anticipate young people reading this novel. Because I know that in their teenage world people also die. And fall in love. And stumble into bliss as well as pain.

"The fact is that teenagers do not live in a peppermint world of fun and frolic. Their world is vividly real, perhaps harsher and more tragedy prone than the everyday world their mothers and fathers inhabit.

"Teachers know this. Everyone who works with young people on a day-to-day basis knows this. They have witnessed the strength of 'young adults'—their resilience, their ability to absorb the blows that teenage life delivers.

"Parents have a tendency to tell young people, 'These are the happiest days of your life.' But young people know this isn't true. They are lacerated by the lashes of adolescence. Oh, there are good times, of course. Peaks of pleasure to balance the unavoidable pits.

"They also aspire to happy endings. In their lives and in the books they read and the movies they see.

"But they don't flee friends who are unhappy or ignore books and movies that present them with tragedy. They already know that tragedy is part of existence." [Robert Cormier, "Do We Underestimate Teenagers?" *Dell Catalog,* winter, 1984-1985.[4]]

1985. Eleven years after *The Chocolate War,* its sequel, *Beyond the Chocolate War,* was published. The power of Cormier's writing has been compared to J. D. Salinger, an author whom Cormier greatly admires. ". . . Salinger is such a terrific writer; he did so many great things. He is one of those writers that I still reread simply because he makes me see the possibilities and makes me feel like writing. There are certain writers who put you in the mood to write. In the way a whiff of a cigar will bring back memories of a ballgame on a Saturday afternoon, reading Salinger makes me want to get to the typewriter. *The Catcher in the Rye* is on my list of best books."[4]

Other books on Cormier's list of best books and authors are: ". . . Graham Greene's *The End of the Affair, The Heart of the Matter,* and *The Power and the Glory.* It's amazing that one man wrote three masterpieces. *The Daring Young Man on the Flying Trapeze* by William Saroyan. Hemingway is looked down on now, but he was such a door-opener for us in his time. *The Sun Also Rises* is really my favorite of his books, for that time in his life; *The Old Man and the Sea,* later. I'd also include *Appointment in Samarra* by John O'Hara. He writes very differently from the way I write; he never used a metaphor in his life. Brian Moore's *The Lonely Passion of Judith Hearne.* They are the people who write the kind of books I love so much."[4]

When asked what he would write for his own epitaph, Cormier replied: "I think it would say 'It has all been very interesting.' Now to explain a little bit. Interesting is a very intriguing word. The Chinese say 'May you live in interesting times,' and that's a curse. But I don't use it in the complete sense of a curse. The fact that life has been interesting has a lot of levels and depths. It means I've never been bored and never hope to be. But it means that everything hasn't always been sunset and roses and music. So I think that would sum it up for me. It has all been very interesting."[1]

FOR MORE INFORMATION SEE: Library Journal, June 1, 1960; *Kirkus Review,* June 1, 1960; *Leominster Daily Enterprise,* July 28, 1960; *New York Herald Tribune Book Review,* July 31, 1960; *Time,* August 1, 1960; *Fitchburg Sentinel,* August 2, 1960; *Atlantic,* September, 1960; *Catholic World,* December, 1960; *Best Sellers,* October 1, 1963, April 15, 1974; *New York Times Book Review,* April 25, 1965, May 5, 1974, May 1, 1977, May 22, 1977, April 29, 1979, November 9, 1980; *America,* May 15, 1965; *Commonweal,* July 2, 1965; *American Libraries,* October, 1974; *Times Literary Supplement,* April 4, 1975, December 2, 1977; *Junior Bookshelf,* June, 1975; *Growing Point,* July, 1975, April, 1978; *English Journal,* September, 1975, September, 1977, November, 1984; *Signal,* September, 1975; *School Library Journal,* May, 1977, March, 1979; *Horn Book,* August, 1977, April, 1979, April, 1985, June, 1985; *Washington Post Book World,* May 13, 1979, January 11, 1981; *Christian Science Monitor,* June 1, 1979; *Manchester Guardian,* June 22, 1979; *Newsweek,* July 16, 1979.

Contemporary Literary Criticism, Volume XII, Gale, 1980; Robert Cormier, *Eight Plus One,* Pantheon, 1980; *Boston Globe Magazine,* November 16, 1980; *Boston Magazine,* December, 1980; *Voice of Youth Advocates,* December, 1980; Betsy Hearne and Marilyn Kaye, editors, *Celebrating Children's Books: Essays on Children's Literature in Honor of Zena Sutherland,* Lothrop, 1981; *Contemporary Authors, New Revision Series,* Volume 5, Gale, 1982; "Robert Cormier: An Interview" (cassette), Random House/Miller Brody, 1982; *Media & Methods,* February, 1983; Laurel Graeber, "PW Interviews: Robert Cormier," *Publishers Weekly,* October 7, 1983; Sally Holmes Holtz, editor, *Fifth Book of Junior Authors and Illustrators,* H. W. Wilson, 1983; *Wilson Library Bulletin,* December, 1984; Patricia J. Campbell, *Presenting Robert Cormier,* Twayne, 1985.

COSTABEL, Eva Deutsch   1924-

PERSONAL: Born November 20, 1924, in Zagreb, Yugoslavia; daughter of Arnold (a chemical merchant) and Ann (an owner of a children's clothing boutique; maiden name, Weinberger) Deutsch. *Education:* Attended the Academy of Fine Arts, Rome, Italy and Pratt Institute, Brooklyn, N.Y. *Politics:* Democrat. *Religion:* Jewish. *Home:* 33-43 Crescent St., Long Island City, N.Y. 11106.

CAREER: Package designer, graphic designer, design teacher, writer. Barton's Bonbonniere, Inc., assistant to the art director, 1953-55; Mitchell Studios, package designer, 1955-65; J. C. Penney Co., senior graphic and package designer, 1965-68; Clairol, Inc., senior package designer, 1968-71; Parsons School of Design, New York, N.Y., instructor, 1982-85. *Member:* Greater Astoria Historical Society, Graphic Artists Guild, Appalachian Mountain Club, American Museum of Natural History.

WRITINGS—All self-illustrated: *Full Color Floral Needlepoint Designs,* Dover, 1976; *Design and Make Your Own Floral Applique,* Dover, 1976; *A New England Village,* Atheneum, 1983.

WORK IN PROGRESS: Book on Pennsylvania art and lifestyles entitled *The Pennsylvania Dutch: Craftsmen and Farmers,* for Atheneum.

SIDELIGHTS: "I was born in Yugoslavia to a middle class Viennese family. I fled Zagreb, my native town, in 1941 during the Nazi occupation, then began the odyssey and flight from Nazi murderers to the end of the war. I spent about eighteen months as a prisoner in an Italian concentration camp. The humanity of the Italian soldiers of the camp left a deep impression on me, and I feel they contributed to my survival.

"After the Italian capitulation in 1943, I joined the Yugoslavian resistance, first as an army nurse, later as staff artist for the resistance publications.

"I arrived at New York Harbour on June 10, 1949 where I still reside.

"I credit Yugoslavian peasant art as well as contemporary New York painting as an important influence on my work. In 1953, I was further influenced by my teacher Franz Kline, famous painter of the New York School of Abstract Art with whom I studied at Pratt Institute in Brooklyn.

"My art training began at the Academy of Fine Arts in Rome, Italy, where I studied painting, anatomy, and the history of art. I was accepted at the Academy in spite of the fact that my entrance requirements were insufficient. Years of schooling had been lost with the holocaust. The Academy's vice-president, a sculptor, helped to register me. Once again the Italians proved their humanity towards me.

"The classic and thorough training in one of the most beautiful art centers in Europe proved to be the most joyful experience. It represented the crossroad in my life—the beginning of the long, painful healing process after witnessing the horrors of the holocaust and after having lost my father, as well as virtually everyone I grew up with.

"The holocaust thrust me into a dark pit of vipers, snakes, creatures of the underworld, creatures of total evil, creatures

In the dipping method, the string wicks were dipped over and over again into the hot tallow until the layers of tallow formed a candle. . . . ■ (From *A New England Village* by Eva Deutsch Costabel. Illustrated by the author.)

Self-portrait of Eva Deutsch Costabel.

without a grain of human compassion. To be captive of those monsters and their cruel accomplices, apathetic people whom I was faced with at the age of fifteen, left an impression so powerful that the happy grin of childhood was forever wiped from my lips.

"As an artist it is my aim to express life's vibrancy, optimism and joy. Since the holocaust I have with great effort climbed from that dark pit towards the light and towards enlightenment. My aim is to overcome, to surround myself with goodness, kindness, compassion and humanity—to celebrate light, color; to rejoice in the greatness of life.

"Above all, I am a painter and a poet wounded by the events of my time. I lived in the eye of the hurricane and made myself into a person, truly human.

"My first historical book for children, *A New England Village,* was published in 1983 by Atheneum. This historically accurate book has been well received by schools and libraries all over the country as a tool for teaching social studies to children.

"I've been a package designer since 1953 and have expanded my skills, designing textiles, embroidery, china, silverware, and housewares."

DAVIDSON, Alice Joyce   1932-

BRIEF ENTRY: Born September 2, 1932, in Cincinnati, Ohio. Editor, poet, author, and artist. Davidson began her career at Gibson Greeting Cards in Cincinnati where she held the position of editor from 1963 to 1965. During the next seven years she worked as a free-lance writer for advertising agencies and greeting card companies, as continuity director at WXIX-TV, and as promotion manager at WCPO-TV. In 1972 Davidson

returned to Gibson Greeting Cards as editorial director and, later, inspirational manager. Her first book of poems, *A Cat Called Cindy,* written for children, appeared in 1981. It was followed by *Because I Love You* (Fleming Revell, 1982), a collection of inspirational poems accompanied by Davidson's own illustrations. She dedicated this book to her longtime friend, the late Helen Steiner Rice, who wrote the introduction. In addition to two other books of poems, *Reflections of Love* (Fleming Revell, 1983) and *Loving One Another* (Fleming Revell, 1984), Davidson is the author of over a dozen children's books in her "Alice in Bibleland" series. Published by C. R. Gibson, the titles include *The Story of Creation, The Story of Jonah, Psalms and Proverbs for You* (all 1984), *The Story of David and Goliath,* and *The Story of the Loaves and Fishes* (both 1985). She has also written television stories for children and is the creator of greeting cards, calendars, and gift books. *Home:* 6315 Elbrook Ave., Cincinnati, Ohio 45237.

FOR MORE INFORMATION SEE: Contemporary Authors, Volume 115, Gale, 1985.

DAVIES, (Edward) Hunter   1936- (Atticus)

BRIEF ENTRY: Born January 7, 1936, in Renfrew, Scotland. Although primarily an adult novelist (*Here We Go, Round the Mulberry Bush* and *The Rise and Fall of Jake Sullivan*), Davies has produced a biography for young adults as well as three stories for children. In *William Wordsworth: A Biography* (Atheneum, 1981), he explores Wordsworth's poetical development within the framework of the other Lake District poets. *School Library Journal* observed that Davies succeeds in creating "a lively biography of a man often previously depicted as pompous and dull." *New York Times Book Review* agreed, describing the book as "easy-going . . . written in a familiar, cheeky style. . . . Slangy and conversational, the book is fun to read." For a younger audience, Davies mixes fantasy with good humor in three related titles, beginning with *Flossie Teacake's Fur Coat* (Bodley Head, 1982). When nine-year-old Flossie dons her older sister's fur coat, she suddenly finds herself transformed into a very grown up eighteen-year-old, with some unexpected results. Davies continues the adventures in *Flossie Teacake—Again!* (Bodley Head, 1983) and *Flossie Teacake Strikes Back!* (Bodley Head, 1984). His other works include *The Beatles: The Authorized Biography.* First published by McGraw-Hill in 1968, the second revised edition appeared in 1985. According to *Wilson Library Bulletin,* the book has endured as a "pioneering biography" amidst masses of material produced on the Fabulous Four.

During the 1960s, Davies was employed as a reporter for the *Evening Chronicle* in Manchester and the *Sunday Times* in London, for which he also wrote a column under the pseudonym Atticus. He has worked as editor of *Colour* magazine and, since 1979, as a columnist for *Punch. Home:* 11 Boscastle Rd., London NW5, England.

FOR MORE INFORMATION SEE: The Writers Directory: 1984-1986, St. James Press, 1983; *Contemporary Authors, New Revision Series,* Volume 12, Gale, 1984; *Who's Who: 1985-1986,* St. Martin's, 1985.

What blockheads are those wise persons, who think it necessary that a child should comprehend everything it reads.

—Robert Southey

DEMAREST, Chris(topher) L(ynn) 1951-

PERSONAL: Born April 18, 1951, in Hartford, Conn.; son of Robert (a salesperson) and Shirley Mavis (a librarian; maiden name, Johnston) Demarest; married Larkin Dorsey Upson (a finish carpenter), February 2, 1982. *Education:* University of Massachusetts, B.F.A., 1976. *Home and office:* 47 Portsmith Ave., Exeter, N.H. 03833. *Agent:* Whit Stillman, Edward T. Riley, Inc., 81 Greene St., New York, N.Y. 10012.

CAREER: Cartoonist, author, and illustrator of books for children. *Member:* Society of Childrens Book Writers.

WRITINGS—Self-illustrated children's books: *Benedict Finds a Home,* Lothrop, 1982; *Clemens' Kingdom,* Lothrop, 1983; *Orville's Odyssey,* Simon & Schuster, 1986.

Illustrator: Rose Greydanus, *Tree House Fun,* Troll Associates, 1980; Elizabeth Isele, *Pooks,* Lippincott, 1983; Betty Jo

and into a big, sunny room.

(From *Clemen's Kingdom* by Chris L. Demarest. Illustrated by author.)

Stanovich, *Hedgehog and Friends,* Lothrop, 1983; B. J. Stanovich, *Hedgehog Adventures,* Lothrop, 1983; B. J. Stanovich, *Hedgehog Surprises,* Lothrop, 1984; Sue Alexander, *World Famous Muriel,* Little, Brown, 1984; S. Alexander, *World Famous Muriel and the Dragon,* Little, Brown, 1985.

Illustrator of greeting cards and newspaper columns.

WORK IN PROGRESS: The Adventures of Kitman and Willy, No Peas for Nelson, and *Morton and Sidney* (tentative title).

SIDELIGHTS: "Whether doing my own books or illustrating others, the temptation to throw in whimsey is always there. That way even if the storyline contains a moral, it is hopefully handled in a humorous way.

"I've always loved cartoons and animation in general and when I started drawing, the first images were of many of my cartoon heroes. It wasn't until finishing college, after years of realism in my art, that cartooning returned. Even then humor

Chris Demarest's notion of himself.

was always just below the surface and when I could finally accept life outside of fine arts it emerged.

"After a few years of straight cartooning for magazines and newspapers, I was introduced to the world of children's books by the late Emilie McLeod of Unicorn Books. It was she who enabled me to expand beyond the single panel format to the thirty-two plus pages.

"When developing a story the visuals are worked out first—usually in storyboard fashion to allow an overall view. Seldom is the ending known. What happens is a character is born and sent upon an adventure which keeps developing from page to page. In other words the story line is very much a puzzle which has to be assembled before the story works.

"Except for one year in Seattle immediately after college, I've lived in the Northeast all my life (so far). I grew up always active, playing whatever sports were available from season to season, both team and individual. Having a physical release has been essential for my sanity. The longer I'm stationary, the shorter my attention-span and thus my work truly becomes demented.

"Sports and cartooning go hand-in-hand for another reason. Since much of my work involves moving figures, having an understanding of body motion helps to translate that to paper. Most of my cartoons are captionless so this too is where motion comes in handy. The next logical step would be to get into animation. Then I would feel I'd come full circle.

"As for long range plans, my wife and I would love to live in France for a year or so. It's a fantasy at this point but for me to be in the same country as some of my favorite cartoonists and the Tour de France bicycle race, well . . . that's heaven."

HOBBIES AND OTHER INTERESTS: Sailing, cycling, music, rock 'n' roll, and tennis.

There is more treasure in books than in all the pirates' loot on Treasure Island. . .and best of all, you can enjoy these riches every day of your life.
—Walt Disney

DeWEESE, Thomas Eugene 1934-
(Gene DeWeese; Jean DeWeese, a pseudonym; Thomas Stratton, Victoria Thomas, joint pseudonyms)

BRIEF ENTRY: Born January 31, 1934, in Rochester, Ind. A free-lance writer since 1974, DeWeese formerly worked as a radio technician and technical writer. He writes in a variety of genres—including nonfiction, science fiction, and gothic romance—and for different reading audiences. His first book, *Making American Folk Art Dolls* (Chilton, 1975), written with Gini Rogowski, was followed by a number of science fiction/horror works. Some of these, like *Gates of the Universe* (Laser Books, 1975), were written in collaboration with Robert Coulson for young adults and adults. Others, like *Nightmares from Space* (F. Watts, 1981) and *The Adventures of a Two-Minute Werewolf* (Doubleday, 1983), appeal to younger readers. In 1980 DeWeese received the best juvenile book award from the Council for Wisconsin Writers for *Major Corby and the Unidentified Flapping Object* (Doubleday, 1979). Other science fiction works include several "Man from U.N.C.L.E." adventures written with Coulson, under the joint pseudonym Thoams Stratton. Another pseudonym, Jean DeWeese, appears on the covers of nearly a dozen gothic romances like *The Reimann Curse* (Ballantine, 1975), *Cave of the Moaning Wind* (Ballantine, 1976), *Nightmare in Pewter* (Doubleday, 1978), and *The Backhoe Gothic* (Doubleday, 1981). *Home and office:* 2718 North Prospect, Milwaukee, Wis. 53211.

FOR MORE INFORMATION SEE: Peter Nicholas, *The Encyclopedia of Science Fiction: An Illustrated A to Z*, Grenada, 1979; *Contemporary Authors, New Revision Series*, Volume 9, Gale, 1983; *The Writers Directory: 1984-1986*, St. James Press, 1983.

DIXON, Dougal 1947-

PERSONAL: Born March 1, 1947, in Dumfries, Scotland; son of Thomas Bell (an engineer) and Margaret (Hurst) Dixon; married Jean Mary Young, April 3, 1971; children: Gavin Thomas, Lindsay Kathleen. *Education:* University of St. Andrews, B.Sc. (with honors), 1970, M.Sc., 1972. *Home:* 55 Mill La., Wareham, Dorsetshire BH20 4QY, England.

CAREER: Mitchell-Beazley Ltd. (publisher), London, England, book editor, 1973-78; Blandford Press, Poole, England, book editor, 1978-80; free-lance writer and editor, 1980—. Civilian instructor for Air Training Corps. *Member:* Bournemouth Science Fiction and Fantasy Group (vice-chairman, 1980-81; chairman, 1981-82), British Sub-Aqua Club. *Awards, honors:* Hugo Award nomination for special achievement in science fiction, 1982.

WRITINGS: (Contributor) James Mitchell, editor, *The Joy of Knowledge*, Mitchell-Beazley, 1976; (contributor) Michael Chinery, editor, *Enjoying Nature With Your Family*, Crown, 1977; *After Man: A Zoology of the Future*, St. Martin's, 1981; (contributor) M. A. Janulewicz, editor, *The Forest*, Mitchell-Beazley, 1981; *Science World: Geology* (illustrated by Chris Forsey and others), Aladdin Books, 1982, F. Watts, 1983; *Science World: Geography* (illustrated by C. Forsey and others), Aladdin Books, 1983, F. Watts, 1984; *Find Out about Jungles*, Hamish Hamilton, 1984; *Find Out about Prehistoric Reptiles*, Hamish Hamilton, 1984; *Minerals, Rocks and Fossils*, Macdonald, 1984; (with Jane Burton) *Time Exposure: A Photographic Record of the Dinosaur Age*, Beaufort, 1984; *Mountains*, F. Watts, 1984; *Deserts and Wastelands*, F. Watts,

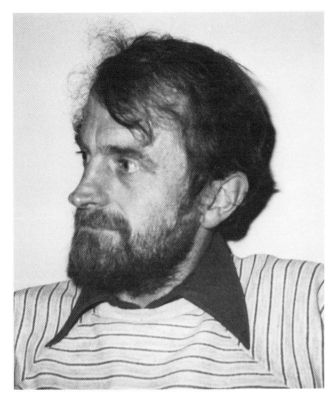

DOUGAL DIXON

1984; *Forests,* F. Watts, 1984; *Time Machine: Ice Age Adventurer,* Byron Preiss, 1985; *Find Out about Dinosaurs,* Hamlyn, in press; *Secrets of the Earth,* Hamlyn, in press.

Consultant and animator for video program "Dinosaurs: Fun, Fact and Fantasy," Longman Video, 1982. Contributor to *World Reference Encyclopaedia, Encyclopaedia of Knowledge, Everyman Encyclopedia,* and *Factopaedia.* Contributor to magazines, including *Omni, Cineagic,* and *Film Making.* Geology editor of *The Joy of Knowledge, Atlas of the Oceans,* and *Life and Science Encyclopedia.*

WORK IN PROGRESS: An Ice Age follow-up to *Time Exposure* with Jane Burton.

SIDELIGHTS: "My education was almost purely scientific but my interests are primarily artistic. I entered publishing as a career to combine both inclinations. The speculation about the future processes of evolution, the subject of *After Man,* began in the 1960's from a chance remark my father made about extinction. My interest was rekindled in 1979 when I saw a 'save the whale' badge; I started the book after that.

"I suppose I can trace my writing career back to my early school days when I devoted a lot of spare time to drawing and writing comic strips for my own amusement. The strips were generally on science fiction or futuristic themes and usually contained some strange-looking animals—obviously a foretaste of *After Man.* I also contributed regularly to the school magazine. It was not until after my university education and until I had taken up a career in publishing that I appreciated the mechanics of having work published and began writing seriously.

"With *After Man* I intended to put forward and describe salient points of evolution and ecology—but in a totally novel and, I hoped, attractive way. I also used the book to indulge my

fantasies of weird animals and was most gratified to have it nominated for a special achievement in science fiction award in 1982. The philosophy behind the book is optimistic—it is all about survival—despite my device of dismissing man in the introductory section. Happily most reviewers realized this, but a number still think that the book is 'really' about the extinction of man. The science fiction film industry is showing a great deal of interest in *After Man* as the background for a film, and I do not think that this will detract from its instructional theme in any way. The book is currently published in sixteen foreign editions."

HOBBIES AND OTHER INTERESTS: Film and video.

FOR MORE INFORMATION SEE: New York Times Book Review, April 4, 1982.

DOLAN, Edward F(rancis), Jr.   1924-

WRITINGS: Pasteur and the Invisible Giants, Dodd, 1958; *Green Universe: The Story of Alexander von Humboldt,* Dodd, 1959; *Jenner and the Miracle of Vaccine,* Dodd, 1960; *White Battleground: The Conquest of the Arctic,* Dodd, 1961; *Vanquishing Yellow Fever: Dr. Walter Reed,* Britannica Press, 1962; *Adventure with a Microscope: A Story of Robert Koch,* Dodd, 1964; *The Camera,* Messner, 1965; *Disaster 1906: The San Francisco Earthquake and Fire* (Junior Literary Guild selection), Messner, 1967; *Explorers of the Arctic and Antarctic,* Crowell Collier, 1968; (with H.T. Silver) *William Crawford Gorgas: Warrior in White,* Dodd, 1968.

The Explorers: Adventures in Courage, Reilly & Lee, 1970; *Inventors for Medicine,* Crown, 1971; *Engines Work Like This,* McGraw, 1971; *Legal Action: A Layman's Guide,* Regnery, 1972; (with Frederick J. Hass) *The Foot Book,* Regnery, 1973; (with F. J. Hass) *What You Can Do about Your Headache,*

EDWARD F. DOLAN, JR.

Gus and Gertie give up. ∎ (From *Bicycle Touring and Camping* by Edward F. Dolan, Jr. Photograph by Jay Irving.)

Regnery, 1973; *A Lion in the Sun: A Background Book for Young Pepole on the Rise and Fall of the British Empire*, Parents Magazine Press, 1973; *The Complete Beginner's Guide to Bowling*, Doubleday, 1974; *The Complete Beginner's Guide to Ice Skating*, Doubleday, 1974.

Starting Soccer: A Handbook for Boys and Girls (illustrated with photographs by Jameson C. Goldner), Harper, 1976; *Basic Football Strategy: An Introduction for Young Players*, foreword by Duffy Daugherty, Doubleday, 1976; *Amnesty: The American Puzzle*, F. Watts, 1976; *The Complete Beginner's Guide to Making and Flying Kites*, Doubleday, 1977; *How to Leave Home—And Make Everybody Like It*, Dodd, 1977; (with Richard B. Lyttle) *Archie Griffin*, Doubleday, 1977; (with R. B. Lyttle) *Bobby Clarke*, Doubleday, 1977; *The Complete Beginner's Guide to Magic*, Doubleday, 1977; (with R. B. Lyttle) *Martina Navratilova*, Doubleday, 1977; (with R. B. Lyttle) *Scott May: Basketball Champion*, Doubleday, 1978; (with R. B. Lyttle) *Fred Lynn: The Hero from Boston*, Doubleday, 1978; (with R. B. Lyttle) *Janet Guthrie: First Woman Driver at Indianapolis*, Doubleday, 1978; *Gun Control: A Decision for Americans*, F. Watts, 1978, revised edition, 1982; (with R. B. Lyttle) *Dorothy Hamill: Olympic Skating Champion*, Doubleday, 1979; *Matthew Hewnson: Black Explorer*, Dodd, 1979; (with R. B. Lyttle) *Kyle Rote, Jr.: American-Born Soccer Star*, Doubleday, 1979; (with R. B. Lyttle) *Jimmy Young: Heavyweight Challenger*, Doubleday, 1979.

The Complete Beginner's Guide to Gymnastics (illustrated with photographs by James Stewart), Doubleday, 1980; *Child Abuse*, F. Watts, 1980; *The Bermuda Triangle and Other Mysteries of Nature*, F. Watts, 1980; *Let's Make Magic*, Doubleday, 1980; *It Sounds Like Fun: How to Use and Enjoy Your Tape Recorder and Stereo*, Simon & Schuster, 1981; *Adolf Hitler: A Portrait in Tyranny*, Dodd, 1981; *Calling the Play: A Beginner's Guide to Amateur Sports Officiating*, Atheneum, 1981;

Great Moments in the World Series, F. Watts, 1982; *Great Moments in the Indianapolis 500*, F. Watts, 1982; *Great Moments in the Super Bowl*, F. Watts, 1982; *Great Moments in the NBA Championships*, F. Watts, 1982; *Bicycle Touring and Camping*, Simon & Schuster, 1982; *Matters of Life and Death*, F. Watts, 1982.

Protect Your Legal Rights: A Handbook for Teenagers, Simon & Schuster, 1983; (with Shan Finney) *The New Japan*, F. Watts, 1983; *Great Mysteries of the Air*, Dodd, 1983; *History of the Movies*, Bison, 1983; *Great Mysteries of the Sea*, Dodd, 1984; *The Insanity Plea*, F. Watts, 1984; (with S. Finney) *Youth Gangs*, Simon & Schuster, 1984; *The Simon & Schuster Sports Question and Answer Book*, Simon & Schuster, 1984; *Be Your Own Man*, Prentice-Hall, 1984; *International Drug Traffic*, F. Watts, 1985; *Anti-Semitism*, F. Watts, 1985; *Great Mysteries of the Ice and Snow*, Dodd, 1985; *Hollywood Goes to War*, Bison, 1985.

FOR MORE INFORMATION SEE: Young Readers' Review, November, 1967; *New York Times Book Review*, May 19, 1968; *Best Sellers*, June 1, 1968, December 15, 1971; Martha E. Ward and Dorothy A. Marquardt, *Authors of Books for Young People*, supplement to the second edition, Scarecrow, 1979.

DUDLEY, Martha Ward   1909(?)-1985

OBITUARY NOTICE: Born about 1909 in Rochester, N.Y.; died of cancer, November 22, 1985, in Washington, D.C. Educator, social worker, political activist, and author. Dudley began her career as a teacher in public schools in Washington, D.C. She was an activist and ardent Democrat who supported numerous programs to benefit the underprivileged. Dudley taught Sunday school, participated in volunteer classes to educate the elderly, lobbied on Capitol Hill for the peace and civil-rights movements, and published a political newsletter. During the 1940s she also ran a church settlement house in Washington, D.C. She wrote several books for children, including the book *Bad Mousie*.

FOR MORE INFORMATION SEE—Obituaries: *Washington Post,* November 25, 1985.

EVSLIN, Bernard 1922-

PERSONAL: Born April 9, 1922, in Philadelphia, Pa.; son of Leo (an inventor) and Tillie (Stalberg) Evslin; married Dorothy Shapiro (a writer and teacher), April 18, 1942; children: Thomas, Lee, Pamela, Janet. *Education:* Attended Rutgers University. *Home:* 158 Sutton Manor, New Rochelle, N.Y. 10805.

CAREER: Full-time professional writer and producer of documentaries filmed in United States and various parts of Europe and Asia. *Military service:* U.S. Army, 1942-45. *Awards, honors:* "Face of the Land" was named best television film of 1959 in *Variety* poll; National Education Association Award, 1961, for best television documentary on an educational theme; *The Green Hero* was nominated for a National Book Award, 1975.

WRITINGS: Merchants of Venus, Fawcett, 1964; *The Greek Gods* (also see below), Scholastic Book Services, 1966; *Heroes and Monsters of Greek Myth* (also see below), Scholastic Book Services, 1967; *Heroes, Gods and Monsters of the Greek Myths* (includes *The Greek Gods* and *Heroes and Monsters of Greek Myth*), Four Winds, 1967; *Adventures of Ulysses* (also see below), Scholastic Book Services, 1969; *The Trojan War* (also see below), Scholastic Book Services, 1971; *Gods, De-*

When he had stripped all the meat away, he cracked the head of the huge bone between his teeth and sucked the marrow. ■ (From *The Green Hero: Early Adventures of Finn McCool* by Bernard Evslin. Illustrated by Barbara Bascove.)

migods and Heroes, Scholastic Book Services, 1975; *The Green Hero: Early Adventures of Finn McCool* (illustrated by Barbara Bascove; *Horn Book* honor list), Four Winds, 1975; *The Dolphin Rider,* Scholastic Book Services, 1976; *Greeks Bearing Gifts: The Epics of Achilles and Ulysses* (illustrated by Lucy Martin Bitzer; includes *Adventures of Ulysses* and *The Trojan War*), Four Winds, 1976; *Heraclea: A Legend of Warrior Women* (illustrated by L. M. Bitzer), Four Winds, 1978; *Signs and Wonders: Tales from the Old Testament,* Bantam, 1979; *Hercules* (illustrated by Jos. A. Smith), Morrow, 1984; *Jason and the Argonauts,* Morrow, 1986.

Also author of two plays, "Step on a Crack," first produced on Broadway at Ethel Barrymore Theatre, October, 1962, and "Geranium Hat," first produced off Broadway at Orpheum Theatre, March 17, 1969. Author of scripts for many documentaries and shorts.

WORK IN PROGRESS: Serving the Goddess, a novel.

SIDELIGHTS: Several of Evslin's books have been translated into Japanese.

FOR MORE INFORMATION SEE: Martha E. Ward and Dorothy A. Marquardt, *Authors of Books for Young People,* supplement to the second edition, Scarecrow, 1979.

BERNARD EVSLIN

The rabbit landed with a thump on the ground. . . . ■
(From *The Mystical Beast* by Alison Farthing. Illustrated by Anne Mieke.)

FARTHING, Alison 1936-

PERSONAL: Born May 11, 1936, in Gloucester, England. *Education:* Attended Froebel Educational Institute. *Home:* 23 Bolton Gardens, Teddington, Middlesex, England.

CAREER: Author of books for children. Has worked as a teacher in England. *Member:* Society of Authors.

WRITINGS—All fiction for children: *The Queen's Flowerpot* (illustrated by George Adamson), Oliver & Boyd, 1968; *The Hollycock Race* (illustrated by Lynette Hemmant), Chatto, Boyd, & Oliver, 1969; *Skip Saturday* (illustrated by Prudence Seward), Chatto, Boyd, & Oliver, 1972; *The Gauntlet Fair* (illustrated by Shirley Hughes), Chatto & Windus, 1974; *The Mystical Beast* (illustrated by Anne Mieke), Chatto & Windus, 1976, Hastings House, 1978.

CECIL FERGUSON

FERGUSON, Cecil 1931-

PERSONAL: Born March 13, 1931, in Chicago, Ill.; married Irene Fox, about 1957; children: Mark. *Education:* Attended Art Institute of Chicago and Illinois Institute of Technology Institute of Design; graduated from American Academy of Art. *Home:* 501 East 32nd St., Chicago, Ill. 60616. *Office:* 820 South Michigan Ave., Chicago, Ill. 60605.

CAREER: Illustrator and graphic artist. Johnson Publishing Co., Chicago, Ill., assistant art director of *Ebony,* designer of "Ebony Success Library" and other books, and promotional illustrations and layout artist for various Johnson publications.

ILLUSTRATOR: Margaret Peters, *The Ebony Book of Black Achievement* (juvenile), Johnson Publishing, 1970, revised edition, 1974.

FIDLER, Kathleen (Annie) 1899-1980

OBITUARY NOTICE—See sketch in *SATA* Volume 3: Born August 10, 1899, in Coalville, Leicestershire, England; died in 1980. Educator, playwright and author of children's fiction. Fidler taught in girls' schools in England during the 1920s and was a scriptwriter for the Authors' Panel for Schools Broadcasting in Scotland from 1938 to 1962. In 1944 she began writing fiction for children and was the author of more than eighty books, including *The Borrowed Garden, Fingal's Ghost, The Brydons at Smugglers' Creek, The Lost Cave,* and *The Ghosts of Sandeel Bay.* Fidler also wrote for British Broadcasting Corp. programs, including "Children's Hour." In 1967 "Flash the Sheep Dog," a motion picture based on her book of the same name, received the first award for a children's film at the Moscow Film Festival.

FOR MORE INFORMATION SEE: Contemporary Authors, Volumes 25-28, revised, Gale, 1977; *Twentieth-Century Children's Writers,* 2nd edition, St. Martin's, 1983.

FITZHUGH, Louise (Perkins) 1928-1974

PERSONAL: Born October 5, 1928, in Memphis, Tenn.; died of an aneurism, November 19, 1974, in New Milford, Conn.; daughter of Millsaps (an attorney) and Louise (Perkins) Fitzhugh. *Education:* Attended Southwestern College, Florida Southern College, Bard College, and New York University; studied painting at Art Students League, in Bologna, Italy, and at Cooper Union. *Residence:* Bridgewater, Conn. *Agent:* McIntosh & Otis, 475 Fifth Ave., New York, N.Y. 10017.

CAREER: Author, illustrator, and artist. Her oil paintings were exhibited at several galleries, including Banfer Gallery, New York City, 1963. *Awards, honors:* New York Times Outstanding Books of the Year, 1964, and Sequoyah Children's Book Award, 1967, both for *Harriet the Spy; New York Times* Choice of Best Illustrated Books of the Year, 1969, and Brooklyn Art Books for Children citation, 1974, both for *Bang, Bang, You're Dead;* Other Award from *Children's Book Bulletin,* 1976, for *Nobody's Family Is Going to Change;* Emmy Award for children's entertainment special, 1979, for "The Tap Dance Kid."

WRITINGS—All for children; all self-illustrated, except as noted: (With Sandra Scoppettone) *Suzuki Beane,* Doubleday, 1961; *Harriet the Spy* (ALA Notable Book), Harper, 1964; *The Long Secret,* Harper, 1965; (with S. Scoppettone) *Bang, Bang, You're*

LOUISE FITZHUGH

Dead, Harper, 1969; *Nobody's Family Is Going to Change,* Farrar, Straus, 1974; *I Am Five,* Delacourt, 1978; *Sport,* Delacourt, 1979; *I Am Three* (illustrated by Susanna Natti), Delacorte, 1982; *I Am Four* (illustrated by Susan Bonners), Delacorte, 1982.

ADAPTATIONS: "The Tap Dance Kid" (television; based on *Nobody's Family Is Going to Change*), NBC "Special Treat," 1978; "The Tap Dance Kid" (film; teacher's guide available), Learning Corporation of America, 1978; "The Tap Dance Kid" (play), first produced at Broadhurst Theater, New York, N.Y., December 21, 1983 (the play won two Tony Awards).

SIDELIGHTS: Fitzhugh was born in Memphis, Tennessee, the daughter of an attorney. She began writing stories at eleven, and attended the Hutchinson School and later Southwestern College in Memphis. During her college years, she also attended Florida Southern College in Lakeland, Florida, Bard College at Annandale-on-Hudson in New York, and the School of Education at New York University. Six months before completing her degree in literature, Fitzhugh left school to pursue an interest in art.

She enrolled at the Art Students League and later at Cooper Union, in New York. In 1954 Fitzhugh's painting sent her to Europe for six months, and to Italy for a year in 1957. Her oil paintings were termed realistic, and were exhibited at several galleries over the years.

Fitzhugh's humorous illustrations attracted attention in her first published book, *Suzuki Beane.* It was written in collaboration with Sandra Scoppettone and published in 1961.

Now widely regarded as a milestone in children's literature, Fitzhugh's second book, *Harriet the Spy,* was met by mixed reviews when it first appeared in 1964. The novel, set in New York and illustrated by Fitzhugh, told the story of young Harriet M. Welsch, whose eavesdropping and occasional lying exposed the hypocrisies of the adult world. Harriet, who aspires to be a famous writer, has been keeping a notebook since she was eight. Now that she is eleven, she spies for practice, and records her often acute observations of those around her. Though the book is written in the third person, the notebook entries, written in first person, record Harriet's actual language and reveal the content and thinking process of her mind. About her classmates, who apparently have not discovered their own special interests or abilities, Harriet notes in her typically blunt fashion, "THEY ARE JUST BATS. HALF OF THEM DON'T

EVEN HAVE A PROFESSION." About mothers, she observes, "I WOULDN'T LIKE TO HAVE A DUMB MOTHER. IT MUST MAKE YOU FEEL VERY UNPOPULAR."

Upon publication of *Harriet the Spy,* Fitzhugh was called "one of the brightest talents of 1964," by the *New York Times Book Review,* which praised the book for its vigor and originality of style and content. Ellen Rudden in *Library Journal* wrote, "Harriet is one of the meatiest heroines in modern juvenile fiction . . . [the novel is] a *tour de force* . . . [and]. . . bursts with life." A reviewer for *The Junior Bookshelf* noted: "Despite . . . a heroine who seems at first merely an uninhibited all-American child—and despite the illustrations which suggest one much younger than Harriet's eleven years—[*Harriet the Spy*] is a remarkable book. Quite *why* one finds it becoming an addiction is hard to pinpoint: amid the welter of apparent realism, it takes a long time to realise the strong underlying fantasy . . . From this reprehensible pastime [spying], Harriet gains real understanding of the nature of tragedy and happiness. It is extraordinary how deeply involved one becomes, almost against one's will, with these characters."

In the most extensive review of *Harriet the Spy,* however, critic Ruth Hill Viguers of the highly respected publication,

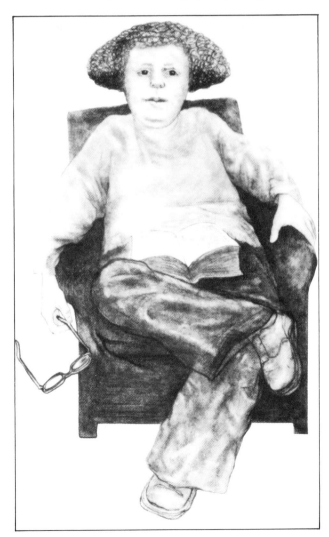

Emma Sheridan. ▪ (From *Nobody's Family Is Going to Change* by Louise Fitzhugh. Illustrated by the author.)

(From the movie "The Tap Dance Kid," based on the novel *Nobody's Family Is Going to Change* by Louise Fitzhugh. Produced by Learning Corporation of America, 1978.)

Horn Book, objected strongly to its "disagreeable people and situations" and questioned its "realism" and suitability for children. She wrote: "The arrival of *Harriet the Spy* with fanfare and announcements of approval for its 'realism' makes me wonder again why that word is invariably applied to stories about disagreeable people and situations. Are there really no amiable children? No loyal friends? No parents who are fundamentally loving and understanding? I challenge the implication that New York City harbors only people who are abnormal, ill-adjusted, and egocentric . . . the objects of Harriet's spying are merely depressing types. Her schoolmates . . . represent not reality but the distortion of caricature . . . the heroines . . . stoical containment of her personal tragedy arouses strong but reluctant sympathy. . . . Many adult readers appreciating the sophistication of the book will find it funny and penetrating. Children, however, do not enjoy cynicism. I doubt its appeal to many to them."

Upon discovering that *Horn Book* had reviewed the book so harshly, critic Maggie Stern found occasion to write an article entitled, "A Second Look: *Harriet the Spy*" [*Horn Book,* August, 1980]. She wrote: "None of the reviewers . . . truly looked at what Louise Fitzhugh had so brilliantly done. Louise Fitzhugh was talking about the balance of life. And this balance, and loss of balance, is all seen through Harriet. In a sense Harriet is within us all: that feistiness, fire, honesty, quickness to be hurt, softness, loudness, and loneliness. Ruth Hill Viguers missed the essence of the book. She missed its humor, richness and texture. Time has shown that *Harriet the Spy* is still read, still loved by children. It appears that children have not found Harriet disagreeable, abnormal, ill-adjusted, or egocentric as Mrs. Viguers suggested. Harriet is a real child, living in a real world. And that is not easy. . . . Through Harriet one sees the process of life, the human struggle. From unawareness to awareness—from order to chaos to new order. Louise Fitzhugh wrote a remarkable book."

Twenty years after the book's initial publication, critic Virginia L. Wolf reflected: "Today, now that many books are even more overt and harsh in their criticism of contemporary society, such objections [as Ruth Hill Viguers raised] are less common. Nevertheless, in my part of the country, the midwest, such objections have been, and continue to be the basis for censorship of the novel. It has been periodically removed

(From the Broadway musical "The Tap Dance Kid," based on the novel *Nobody's Family Is Going to Change* by Louise Fitzhugh, which opened at the Broadhurst Theater, December, 1983. It starred Hinton Battle who won a Tony Award for Best Featured Actor in a Musical, 1984.)

from the shelves of school libraries, as recently as the spring of 1974, because adults have complained that children are imitating or might imitate Harriet's window peeping.''

In response to these objections, Wolf argued: ''. . . The novel can be read as social criticism. It is, on one level, an illuminating portrait of contemporary, urban, American Life. . . . To read the novel as social criticism, however, is to see it in only one dimension . . . [and] to ignore its structure . . . the novel is more than the overt, simplistic social criticism of so many of the recent realistic novels for children. *Harriet the Spy* is not a message book. It is first and foremost an experience. On the primary level, we are immersed in Harriet and, by means of her, her world. . . . Obviously, I believe that *Harriet the Spy* will survive. Harriet and her adventures are memorable. Like all good literature, the novel transcends the particular, evoking the inner spirit of a character and her world to explore eternal questions about love and happiness and truth. Significantly, the novel is not a fantasy like so many children's masterpieces. Perhaps this is revelatory of the mid-twentieth century. In any case, it is fortuitous for children's literature. Louise Fitzhugh has proven that contemporary, realistic fiction of psychological and philosophical depth is a viable possibility for children. *Harriet the Spy* is a milestone and a masterpiece of children's literature—perhaps *the* masterpiece of the mid-twentieth century.''

The Long Secret, the sequel to *Harriet the Spy,* was published a year later and received favorable reviews as well. The two books introduced a new realism into children's literature. *School Library Journal* commented: ''With subtlety, compassion, and her remarkable ability to see inside the minds and hearts of pre-adolescent children while portraying them from the world of the adult, Fitzhugh has written a second story about Harriet and her friends. . . . The breezy, irreverent style and story line are deceptive; [*The Long Secret*] offers a sensitive and realistic description of young girls' reactions to the onset of puberty. This second book may be less of a bombshell to timid librarians and reviewers, but its impact may be more durable than that of *Harriet the Spy*.''

Fitzhugh collaborated again with Sandra Scoppettone for the 1969 publication of *Bang, Bang, You're Dead.* The anti-war book was selected by the Brooklyn Museum and the Brooklyn Public Library for the Brooklyn Art Books for Children citation.

Nobody's Family Is Going to Change was filled with comedy and topical issues. The book centered around a black, middle-class, New York family complete with maid and two private-school children, Emma and Willie. The children did not, however, live up to parental expectations. Emma aspired to become a lawyer, and Willie a professional dancer. Their parents disapproved of both female lawyers and male dancers. Reviewers of the book commended Fitzhugh for revealing sympathy and understanding of children.

In 1974, the author and illustrator died suddenly at the age of forty-six of an aneurism. At the time of her death, Fitzhugh was working on the text and illustrations of *I Am Five,* part of an uncompleted series. Delacorte Press published the book and its sequels posthumously in 1978, 1979, and 1982.

HOBBIES AND OTHER INTERESTS: Tennis and playing the flute.

FOR MORE INFORMATION SEE: New York Times Book Review, November 5, 1967, February 25, 1968; Martha E. Ward and Dorothy A. Marquardt, *Authors of Books for Young People,*

Just as she reached the parlor floor there was a terrible loud creak. She sat there horrified. . . . ■ (From *Harriet, the Spy* by Louise Fitzhugh. Illustrated by the author.)

Scarecrow, 1967; Doris de Montreville and Donna Hill, editors, *Third Book of Junior Authors,* H. W. Wilson, 1972; D. L. Kirkpatrick editor, *Twentieth-Century Children's Writers,* St. Martin's, 1978; *Horn Book,* August, 1980.

Obituaries: *New York Times,* November 21, 1974; *Publishers Weekly,* December 2, 1974; *AB Bookman's Weekly,* December 16, 1974.

GANS, Roma   1894-

PERSONAL: Born February 23, 1894, in St. Cloud, Minn.; daughter of Hubert W. (a musician and businessman) and Mary Anne (Ley) Gans. *Education:* Columbia University, B.S., 1926, Ph.D., 1940. *Politics:* Democrat. *Religion:* Roman Catholic. *Home and office address:* Wayside Lane, West Redding, Conn. 06896.

CAREER: Junior high school mathematics teacher in Clearwater, Minn., 1917; high school mathematics teacher in St. Cloud, Minn., 1918-23; director of primary grades at Community School in St. Louis, Mo., 1924-25; assistant superintendent of schools and research director in Superior, Wis., 1925-29; Columbia University, Teachers College, New York,

N.Y., 1929-59, began as assistant professor, then associate professor, professor of education, 1940-59; writer, 1959—. Co-founder and chairman of New York City's Citizens Committee for Children. Vice-president of New York State Liberal Party. Member of editorial boards, Thomas Y. Crowell Co. and Harper & Row. Lecturer at colleges and universities in Canada, Italy, England, and the United States, including University of Pennsylvania and University of Illinois. *Awards, honors:* Awards from Child Study Association International and Delta Kappa Gamma, 1963, for *Common Sense in Reading; Birds at Night* was selected one of Child Study Association's "Children's Books of the Year," 1968, *Hummingbirds in the Garden,* 1969, *Bird Talk,* 1971, and *Oil: The Buried Treasure,* 1975.

WRITINGS—Juvenile; all published by Crowell: *Birds Eat and Eat and Eat* (illustrated by Ed Emberley), 1963; *The Wonder of Stones* (illustrated by Joan Berg), 1963; *It's Nesting Time* (illustrated by Kazue Mizumura), 1964; *Icebergs* (illustrated by Bobri), 1964; *Birds at Night* (illustrated by Aliki) 1968; *Hummingbirds in the Garden* (illustrated by Grambs Miller), 1969; *Bird Talk* (illustrated by Jo Polseno), 1971; *Water for Dinosaurs and You* (illustrated by Richard Cuffari), 1972; *Millions and Millions of Crystals* (illustrated by Giulio Maestro), 1973; *Oil: The Buried Treasure* (illustrated by G. Maestro), 1975; *Caves* (illustrated by G. Maestro), 1976; *When Birds*

The oldest things you can collect are rocks. ■ (From *Rock Collecting* by Roma Gans. Illustrated by Holly Keller.)

ROMA GANS

Change Their Feathers (illustrated by Felicia Bond), 1980; *Rock Collecting* (illustrated by Holly Keller), 1984; *Danger: Icebergs,* 1986.

Other: *A Study of Critical Reading Comprehension in the Intermediate Grades,* Teachers College, Columbia University, 1940, reprinted, AMS Press, 1972; *Guiding Children's Reading Through Experiences: Practical Suggestions for Teaching,* Teachers College, Columbia University, 1941; *Reading Is Fun,* Teachers College, Columbia University, 1949; (with Celia Burns Stendler and Millie Almy) *Teaching Young Children in Nursery School, Kindergarten, and the Primary Grades,* World Book Co., 1952; *Common Sense in Teaching Reading: A Practical Guide,* Bobbs-Merrill, 1963; *Common Sense in Teaching Reading,* Bobbs-Merrill, 1963; *Fact and Fiction About Phonics,* Bobbs-Merrill, 1964. Also author of *Reading Is Fun,* published by Teachers College, Columbia University. Contributor of several hundred articles to educational journals.

SIDELIGHTS: "I've always enjoyed talking with children and watching the beauty of their faces as they latch on to a word or an idea. Their eyes send out a quick glow, the mouth registers a silent 'oh.' I write and visualize faces before me who are reading as I write. I love children."

How beautiful is youth! how bright it gleams
With its illusions, aspirations, dreams!
Book of Beginnings, Story without End,
Each maid a heroine, and each man a friend!
—Henry Wadsworth Longfellow

GÉRARD, Jean Ignace Isidore 1803-1847
(Jean Ignace Isidore Gérard Grandville; J. J. Grandville, pseudonym)

PERSONAL: Born September 3, 1803, in Nancy, France; died March 17, 1847; son of Jean Baptiste (a miniaturist portrait painter) and Catherine Emilie (Viot) Gérard; married Marguerite Henriette Fisher, 1833 (deceased, 1842); married Madeleine Lhuillier, 1843; children: (first marriage) three children; (second marriage) Armand.

CAREER: Caricaturist and illustrator. Gained fame with his illustrated contributions to the satirical journals *La Silhouette, La Caricature, Le Magazin Pittoresque,* and *Charivari.* In much of his satire, he portrayed people as animals, such as in the series *Les Metamorphoses du jour,* 1828.

ILLUSTRATOR—All under pseudonym J. J. Grandville; of special interest to young readers: Jonathan Swift, *Voyages de Gulliver,* with a biography by Walter Scott, [Paris], 1838, another edition published as *Travels into Several Remote Nations of the World by Lemuel Gulliver,* with notes and biography by W. C. Taylor, Hayward & Moore (London), 1840; George M. Bussey, *Fables: Original and Selected,* Charles Tilt (London), 1839; Jean de La Fontaine, *Fables,* [Paris], 1839, reissued as *La Fontaine: Selected Fables,* translated by James Michie and with an introduction by Geoffrey Grigson, Viking, 1979; Jean P. C. de Florian, *Fables,* Willoughby, 1839; Daniel Defoe, *Aventures de Robinson Crusoe,* [Paris], 1840, reissued as *The Life and Adventures of Robinson Crusoe: Part I,* G. Routledge (London), 1853, reprinted, with an

Jean Ignace Gérard, self-portrait.

introduction by Edward Lucie-Smith, Paddington 1978; (with G. Seguin) Sourdille La Valette, *Fables* [Paris], 1841; P. J. Stahl (pseudonym of Pierre J. Hetzel) and others, *Scènes de la vie privée et publique des animaux* (fables), J. Hetzel et Paulin (Paris), 1842, translation and adaptation by J. Thomason published as *Public and Private Life of Animals,* Sampson Low & Co. (London), 1877, reprinted, Paddington, 1977; Paul Alverdes, adapter and editor, *Rabe, Fuchs und Loewe: Fabeln der Welt* (fables), Ehrenwirth (Munich), 1962; Abraham Aesop (pseudonym of John Newbery), *Fables from Aesop,* adapted by Ennis Rees, Oxford University Press (New York), 1966; Klara Maria Veider, compiler, *Die schoensten Tierfabeln* (fables), Umschau-Verlag (Frankfurt/Main), 1967.

Other: *Les Métamorphoses du jour,* circa 1828, with text by Alberic Second and others, [Paris], 1854; (with Raffet) Pierre J. Beranger, *OEuvres completes* (title means "Complete Works"), [Paris], 1837; (with Tony Johannot and Deveria) Nicolas Boileau-Despreaux, *OEuvres* (title means "Works"), [Paris], 1840; Johann W. Von Goethe, *History of Renard, the Fox* (poem; adapted from the German), Joseph Thomas (London), 1840; (contributor) Louis Huart, *Museum Parisien,* [Paris], 1841; *Un Autre Monde: Transformations, visions, incarnations . . . et autres choses* (humor), H. Fournier (Paris), 1844; *Cent proverbes,* (title means "One Hundred Proverbs"), H. Fournier, 1845; Marie R. L. Reybaud, *Jérôme Paturot à la recherche d'une position sociale,* [Paris], 1846; *Les Fleurs animées* with text by Delord, [Paris], 1847, translation by N. Cleaveland published as *The Flowers Personified,* R. Martin (New York), 1847-49, also published as *The Court of Flora: The Engraved Illustrations of J. J. Grandville,* Braziller, 1981; Miguel de Cervantes Saavedra, *L'Ingenieux Chevalier Don Quichotte de la Manche,* [Tours, France], 1848; Joseph Mery, *Les Etoiles: Derniere feerie,* G. de Gonet (Paris), 1849; with Penguilly and J. David) Theophrastus (pseudonym of Jean de La Bruyere), *Les caractères, ou les moeurs de ce siecle,* [Paris], 1864; *Familiar Tables,* 1866; (with Gavarni and others) *Le*

Night and day he dreamed. ■ (From *Scènes de la vie privée et publique des animaux* by P. J. Stahl and others. Illustrated by J. J. Grandville.)

Diable à Paris: Paris et les Parisiens, J. Hetzel, 1868; Louis C. A. de Musset, *The White Blackbird,* translated from the French by Julian Jacobs (originally published as "Histoire d'un merle blanc" in *Scènes de la vie privée et publique des animaux*), Rodale Press, 1955.

Collections: *Album Beranger par Grandville,* [Paris], circa 1848; *Comical People,* D. Bogue (London), 1852; *Quadru-Biped Characters after Grandville,* [Edinburgh, Scotland], 1865; *Das gesamte Werk,* (title means "The Complete Works") Rogner und Bernhard (Munich), 1969; *Bizarreries and Fantasies of Grandville: 266 Illustrations from Un autre monde [and] Les animaux,* introduction and commentary by Stanley Appelbaum, Dover, 1974; *Grandville: Caricatures et illustrations,* Musee des Beaux-Arts (Nancy, France), 1975; Hans-Burkhard Schlichting, compiler, *Die Phantasien des Grandville: Druckgraphik 1829-1847,* Melzer (Darmstadt, West Germany), 1976; A. Avila, *Grandville en ses secrets,* Limage, (Paris), 1978; *Grandville's Animals: The World's Vaudeville,* with an introduction by Bryan Holme, Thames & Hudson, 1981.

SIDELIGHTS: **September 3, 1803.** Born in Nancy, France to a family involved with the arts and the theater. His father was a miniaturist portrait painter. His grandparents, whose professional name of Grandville he later adopted, were famed actors.

Illness played a central part in Grandville's childhood. In his memoirs, Alexandre Dumas devoted a chapter to his recollections of his friend Grandville. "When he was born he was so weak that for a moment his parents believed he only came into this world to die." [Translation of *Mes Mémoires* by Alexandre Dumas, Cadot, 1852-54.[1]]

The cat and the mirror. ■ (From *Fables* by Jean P. C. de Florian. Illustrated by J. J. Grandville.)

(From *Les Métamorphoses du jour* by Alberic Second and others. Illustrated by J. J. Grandville.)

1815. Entered the local high school in Nancy. "What did it matter whether Grandville learned Latin, Greek or even French! He had a language of his own which he spoke under his breath. . . .'' noted Dumas. "Young, he was taciturn but observant, looking at everything with big melancholic eyes. He seemed to look for and to discover in everything some unknown aspect which remained invisible to others.''[1]

1817. Left school to apprentice in his father's workshop, learning the technical foundations of drawing, painting and lithography. Although he was taught the well-established conventions of portraiture, Grandville's paintings of his father's models were so original and startling they attracted the attention of the French painter Mansion during his visit to Nancy. Impressed by his talent, Mansion urged Grandville to come to cosmopolitan Paris where he would be able to develop his talent to its full measure.

Grandville's father, who was interested in all forms of art, also taught his son music which was to have a lasting influence on Grandville's art.

1820-1825. Some time between the age of seventeen and twenty-two, Grandville, with a small sum of money from his father, moved to Paris where he took lodging with his cousin Lemétayer, a stage manager at the Opera Comique. Grandville was introduced to the world of theater and became friendly with many artists, including the famous French actor Talma. Theater, ballet movements and dance were to remain constant themes in Grandville's art.

Became a student of Mansion who exploited Grandville's talent. Mansion often signed his own name to the drawings of his pupil. "Mansion's student kept an old grudge against his teacher,'' Dumas recalled. "Grandville, with his inventive spirit, had during his association with Mansion designed a deck of fifty cards. Mansion thought the game so remarkable, he pub-

lished it under his own name. . . . I saw that deck of cards one day, when Grandville was in a good mood and was going through some old boxes. It was a fantastic work of art.''[1]

Dumas met Grandville around **1826.** "[Grandville's] mocking smile, eyes sparkling with wit, small height, big hearted with a delightful melancholy over it all—that is you dear Grandville! Do you remember the time when I visited you in your studio? What long and lovely discussions we had! . . . You smiled sadly at life and at the future, because you always had some sadness pouring out from the depth of your heart.''[1]

Grandville left Mansion and gained admittance to Hippolyte Lecomte's studio. Dumas related: "At Hippolyte Lecomte it was no longer a question of learning how to draw but how to paint. Painting was not Grandville's forte; but the pencil, pen and ink! Yes indeed!''[1]

Disappointed with Lecomte's academic method of teaching, Grandville left to start working as an independent artist. "Grandville was a searcher,'' according to Dumas, "always unhappy about what others had discovered for him, sometimes unhappy about what he himself hit upon.''[1]

From this period on, Grandville surrendered to the fantasy of his own imagination and worked in complete isolation. In a letter to his friend Charon, he wrote: "I have never followed anyone and very few painters, very few artists, have answered my expectations regarding the question of the essential which lies at the very foundation of every true work of art.'' [Translation of *J. J. Grandville* by Laure Garcin, Eric Losfeld, 1970.[2]]

Throughout the remainder of the decade of the twenties and into the thirties, Grandville developed his art through many small series of lithographs. Dumas commented: "Grandville executed his lithographs like an engraver. He sliced the stone with a hard pencil, hatched the shadows, precised the forms

J. J. G.

The portrait was finished in spite of their remonstrances. ■ (From _Scènes de la vie privée et publique des animaux_ by P. J. Stahl and others. Illustrated by J. J. Grandville.)

and no longer drew, but engraved. During those years he created [two series of lithographs] 'The Sundays of a Parisian Bourgeois' and 'Every Age Has Its Pleasures.'"[1]

1829. Dumas recalled how Grandville loved animals and studied them with great care. "When I entered Grandville's studio, I usually found him with a lizard in his hand, or whistling to a canary in its cage, or crumbling some bread for his red fish. What was he drawing?"[1] asked Dumas. "He himself was not sure. A sudden outburst of feeling was driving his paint brush. The result was birds with monkey's head, monkeys with fishes' heads, faces of bipedals with four-/footed bodies. It was a world more fantastic than the temptations of Callot, or the devilries of Breughel."[1] Grandville's first satirical drawings with combinations of people and animals first appeared in *Les Métamorphoses du jour*.

The success of *Les Métamorphoses*, which secured for Grandville some immediate work, was largely due to the regulars of the Duchess de Berry's salon, who publicized one of the satirical drawings referring to the amorous misadventures of the Duke de Chartres, the son of Louis-Philippe who was soon to become King of France.

1830. Fought on the barricades during the struggle of the Revolution of July 30, which succeeded in dethroning Charles X in favor of Louis-Philippe. As a result, restrictions of the press were considerably eased and Grandville was able to work as a cartoonist for the new political humor sheet, *La Silhouette*. He was well acquainted with the works of Lavater on physiognomy and Gall on phrenology, but Grandville's use of distortions and animal characters to caricature human behavior and personality traits always obeyed his own law of fantasy and observation. "The eyes of the cartoonist are trained to perceive, in essence, the ridiculous characteristics of each face. He can render more expressions, outlines or shapes than the language can. The absurd contrasts which arouse our mirth are the result of an inconspicuous method."[2]

1831. *La Silhouette* stopped publication. Grandville began working for *La Caricature*, which was the beginning of a

Amiable author who rocks with one hand and writes with the other. ■ (From *Scènes de la vie privée et publique des animaux* by P. J. Stahl and others. Illustrated by J. J. Grandville.)

social and active period in his life. His studio was a place of meetings and discussions.... Present were (Charles) Phillipon, founder of *La Caricature*, the architect Horeau, the painter Huet ... and Dumas, who recalled, "When we were rich we drank beer, otherwise we were just as happy to smoke, talk, and laugh. Grandville didn't talk, smoke, laugh or drink much. He sat at a table, a piece of paper always in front of him, and pen or ink in hand. Sometimes he smiled but he always drew ... and when two hours had passed, full of laughter and noises from the others, Grandville had extracted from his brain an Ark of fantastic new creatures who belonged to him as surely as the one destroyed in the deluge had belonged to God. And it was all so witty, so delightful, saying so well what it was meant to say ... that we always spent at least thirty minutes or an hour trying to find the meaning of those illustrations improvised from some untold tales of Hoffman."[1]

Unlike his fellow-workers, Grandville always insisted on writing the political captions for his cartoons. Feeling Louis-Philippe had betrayed the ideas of the revolution of July, 1830, Grandville's caricatures took on a mocking tone toward the regime, the censors and the ultra-conservatives. One of his contemporaries called his cartoons ". . . [A] philosophy, social science done by a thinker for other thinkers, improved by the use of Pictures."[2]

1833. Married a cousin from Nancy, Marguerite Henriette Fisher, and moved to Quai des Grands Augustins. Fisher was a domineering woman with conventional views. Edward Charon, a friend of the family described the way she kept Grandville under her control. "He undertook nothing, he didn't make a

The animal in the moon. ■ (From *Fables* by Jean de La Fontaine. Illustrated by J. J. Grandville.)

and he turned to book illustration for a more stable source of income. Over the next twelve years he produced nearly 3000 drawings.

1838. The Industrial Revolution, the emergence of a middle class asking for illustrated books, and the improvement in printing practices, all contributed to the demand for men with Grandville's talent.

Lithography was no longer used for book illustration, steel engraving was too expensive, so wood engraving—over which the artist had very little control—was adopted. Grandville was fortunate to work with publishers who hired the best engravers. In a letter to engraver Godard, Grandville thanked him ''. . . for lending me a hand with La Fontaine and especially with the second series. I eagerly take this opportunity to pay tribute (like the animals in Alexander) to the rare and extraordinary talent you displayed engraving my drawings. . . . But let's see, nobody is listening to us, so let's put aside any silly modesty, and let's in turn pat each other on the back for there are not so many loving friends who would be willing to praise our most sensitive spots. Indeed, show me a fellow capable of understanding entirely the quality of the Rooster, and the fox engraving . . . please agree with me on one point: most of my drawings pleased you and even amused you. I cannot otherwise explain the loving care with which you have shaped the Traveller's face, reproduced so accurately the likeness of the cat . . . but excuse me, I am forgetting myself and flattery is making a full circle to fall back on me. I beg you not to think for a moment that I've been praising this work so that the compliment will rub off on me. We are fair, and we agree that if the sort of painter who looks for the perfect expression is a rare bird, the engraver qualified to reproduce it is also rarely encountered.''[4]

A ballet in full wind. . . . ■ (From *Un Autre Monde: Transformations, visions, incarnations . . . et autres choses.* Illustrated by J. J. Grandville.)

pencil stroke without consulting her, and all her suggestions were full of taste and good sense. He admired her, he rubbed his hands together comfortably while listening to her, he was delighted to seem dominated, indeed to *be* dominated so properly and so usefully. The way in which he said, 'Madame Grandville thinks this sketch offensive,' was truly curious and touching. Sometimes he pretended to rebel; but his pencil obeyed and behaved itself. As long as she lived, he didn't deviate from the respectable path along which public approval had followed him.'' [Translation of *Grandville* by Charles Blanc, E. Audois (Paris), 1855.[3]]

Although he respected his wife and adored his three children, Grandville's marriage was not a happy one. Marguerite Fisher, who was distrustful of the fantastic aspect of her husband's imagination, made curling-paper for her hair out of the drawings which failed to meet her approval. With bitter irony, Grandville used to say to his rare friends, ''Madame Grandville uses more valuable curling-paper than the Queen . . . herself.''[2] A later drawing portrayed his wife, candlestick in hand, demanding a harvest of sketches for her curling-paper; the caption read: ''Drawings forbidden by. . . .''

1834. Contributed to *Le Magazin Pittoresque*, his favorite publication, edited by Edward Charon. Grandville's association with *Le Magazin Pittoresque* and his friendship with Charon endured the rest of his life. Three weeks before his death, Grandville wrote to Charon: ''I am still entirely devoted and possessed by the dear 'Magazine': such a glutton for ideas.'' [''J. J. Grandville,'' special issue of *Cahier de l'Art Mineur*, number 14-15, n.d.[4]]

The Repressive Law of September, 1835, which censored the press, closed down *La Caricature,* in reaction to an attempt made on King Louis-Philippe's life. The censorship of political cartoons left Grandville in a precarious financial situation,

So much animal passion bursts out in mankind that we cannot doubt our affinities. ■ (From *Scènes de la vie privée et publique des animaux* by P. J. Stahl and others. Illustrated by J. J. Grandville.)

Three little ones caught in the act of poaching. ■ (From *Un Autre Monde: Transformations, visions, incarnations . . . et autres choses.* Illustrated by J. J. Grandville.)

When one has observed mankind a little too closely, one is quite proud to be a giraffe. ■ (From *Scènes de la vie privée et publique des animaux* by P. J. Stahl and others. Illustrated by J. J. Grandville.)

Like most of the artists of the time, Grandville drew on paper and an artisan copied the drawings onto the blocks which were then sent to the engraver. As a result there were misunderstandings at times about the meaning of the original drawings. Grandville wrote to engraver Godard: ''Generally speaking, I would reproach you for too many details concerning the shadows. I like them heavy, dense and soothing. Some outlines or some touches are too black in the midst of white areas which are light and soft, like feathers, flesh. . . . You will of course forgive me these small complaints, they are not true criticisms but rather my particular and individual way of seeing. . . . I, for my part, am absolutely convinced that whenever the surface is covered by white and delicate areas, their shadows can never come close to the vigor and the blackness of the harsh, hard and dark areas. Once again a thousand apologies for these remarks, but it is because I know that the engraver is often inconvenienced by the grey of the pencil, which he sometimes interprets as a solid black when a grey shade was in fact expressed.''[4]

1841. To Godard, he wrote: ''I don't think Mr. Fournier [publisher of Grandville's editions of La Fontaine's *Fables*] will edit another book for a long time, and I was running the risk of remaining idle if I hadn't turned toward [publishers] MM Paulin and Hezel. They will ask for your help on my account. . . . They will be publishing *Scenes of the Public and Private Life of Animals*. They will send you a woodblock with their letter . . . and I will make a few recommendations:

1) To persist in shaping and polishing the details and to keep on looking for the exact expressions since they are of the greatest importance.

2) To entrust only the most insignificant tasks to your helpers. First of all the master's eyes and hands! Always!''[4]

Scenes of the Public and Private Life of Animals was a big success, and Honoré de Balzac, who wrote some of the text, related in a letter to Hetzel that statuettes of the 'Animals' were being manufactured and sold illegally. *Scenes of the Public and Private Life of Animals* was crowded with details from Grandville's knowledge of natural history combined with a dream-like atmosphere. ''In my opinion we never dream of any objects that we haven't seen or imagined in a state of sleeplessness. And it is this amalgam of diverse objects perceived by the mind which shapes the atmosphere of the dream, so strange, so disparate, and also, at the mercy of the level of the blood activity.''[2]

1842. ''Then, in the middle of all this lively creation escaped from his pencil, the deepest sorrow, the saddest bitterness befell him: His wife and (two) children died, was no more studio life for him, no more juvenile pleasantry; he talks of the future life towards which he moves, of the immortality of the soul whose secret he will soon possess.''[1]

On her death bed, Grandville's wife made him promise to marry the woman she had chosen for him, Madeleine Lhuil-

(From *Un Autre Monde: Transformations, visions, incarnations . . . et autres choses.* Illustrated by J. J. Grandville.)

lier. Grandville had kept a close correspondence with her for the past several years.

1843. Married Madeleine Lhuillier, who was also from Nancy. Left his home of Saint-Mande with its bad memories to move into a small studio at 26 rue des Saint Péres. "For the first time in my life I feel carefree and allow myself to live happily. I am hoping for everything I have the right to expect in return for so much suffering."[2]

Well before the invention of animation, or the experiments of the cubists, Grandville became preoccupied with the representation of the concept of time in plastic arts and searched for a new way of expressing dynamism, and of extending a movement which would vibrate like a sound. In a letter to a friend, he attempted to describe, through music, his conception of the object in time. "I wanted to create an effect similar to those produced by a musician when he ... modulates through a succession of chords and harmonic progressions, and then brings his audience back to the original tonality, thus giving them a most enjoyable pleasure."[2]

1845. Began illustrating Marie R. L. Reybaud's *Jérôme Paturot*. "I'm not satisfied with that book, the work is out of date ... the satire is now weak for having been retold too many times, as the book has been published in serial form for the past two or three years. To come back to it again will be very boring and the public will remain indifferent: it is a vampire in constant need of new blood. Man is never satisfied and maybe I'm harder to please than anyone else, but frankly, I'm worried and I fear those illustrations ... I dread to be ill at ease."[2]

Eight months later he added, "I had the greatest difficulties from the beginning to classify, to choose, to decide the style, the effects, the relevance of the subject. I could see how I could take advantage of the cutting remarks on our bad habits, our quackeries, but ... to renew oneself, to follow the text step by step, to comment on it, to study it, to tighten it, all that was not an easy task...."[2]

1846. Created *The Personified Flowers*. "What did I imagine? Gracious monstrosities for a public who always wants something new at all cost. But with that work I've not invented anything. I merely associated dissimilar components, and grafted antipathetic and incongruous forms one onto the others."[2]

1847. Began sketching his dreams and nightmares, and was fascinated by the transmutations of forms in dreams. "What will our title be? Metamorphosis During Sleep? ... Transformation, Distortions, Restorations of Dreams? ... Chains of Ideas During Dreams, Nightmares? Ecstasies etc.... Or else Harmonic Transfigurations During Sleep? ... But here I think is the real title ... Nocturnal Visions and Transformations...."[2]

"The art of distorting and restoring images, with their metamorphoses always following one another in a parallel direction with a moral sense: this is not without difficulties or surprising oddities, but nevertheless, it seems to me a matter of interest to people with a dreamy imagination who enjoy the tricks that the mind can play. Until now, in no other work of art ... dream was expressed or understood in this way."[4]

The last son of his first marriage died in his arms. "Unhappiness," one of his friend's wrote, "strikes with such a fatal perserverance ... that even the tenderness and the devotion of his second wife could not save him from his silent despair. This was when he had the presentiment of his own death....

He saw it come, he announced it in a resolute voice.... He didn't show any anxiety as the last hour drew near ... maybe ... he was wishing it!"[2]

Twelve days before his death, he displayed the same feeling in a letter to Charon concerning *The Personified Stars*. "Besides, cut out, convert, change, do the best you can, I still have a few days to devote to you ... Good bye!"[2]

March 17, 1847. Died of a septic throat ailment late in the afternoon at the sanitorium of Vanves, near Paris. Grandville was buried at the cemetery of Saint-Mande. The epitaph he had composed for himself reads, "Here lies Grandville; he endowed everything with life, and after God made everything speak and walk. Alone, he did not know how to make his way into the world."[2]

FOR MORE INFORMATION SEE: Alexandre Dumas, *Mes Mémoires,* Cadot, 1852-1854; Charles Blanc, *Grandville: Les Métamorphoses du Jour,* F. Havard (Paris), 1854; C. Blanc, *Grandville,* E. Audois (Paris), 1855; Pierre Fusman, *Le Livre et L'Estampe,* Albert Morance (Paris), 1923; Marguerite Mespoulet, *Creators of Wonderland,* Arrow Editions, 1934; *Gazette des Beaux-Arts,* December, 1948; *Time,* August 30, 1968; Laure Garcin, *J. J. Grandville,* Eric Losfeld, 1970; M. Praz, "Two Masters of the Absurd: Grandville and Carroll," *The Artist and the Writer in France: Essays in Honour of Jean Seznec,* edited by Francis Haskell, Anthony Levi and Robert Schackleton, Oxford University Press, 1974; William E. Maloney, *The Illustrated Cat,* Harmony Books, 1976; *Cahier de l'Art Mineur,* number 1, 1976, special edition, number 14-15, n.d.; *Smithsonian,* September, 1978.

GERRARD, Roy   1935-

BRIEF ENTRY: Born January 25, 1935, in Atherton, England. A former student of the Salford School of Art, Gerrard worked as an art teacher and department head at grammar schools in England for more than twenty years, beginning in the late 1950s. An artist and author-illustrator of children's books since 1980, he described his art work as having "a sense of whimsy which owes much to Lewis Carroll and Edward Lear." Married to children's author Jean Gerrard, he provided the illustrations for her picture book *Matilda Jane* (Gollancz, 1981), a runner-up for the Mother Goose Award in 1982. Gerrard's own children's works, *The Favershams* (Farrar, 1983) and *Sir Cedric* (Farrar, 1984), are both written in rhyming text.

Critics took note of the unusual and detailed illustrations in *The Favershams,* described by *Horn Book* as "a quirky picture book ... a spoof on the life and times of Victorian England." *Washington Post Book World* put it in "the classic class of [Sendak] ... with watercolor illustrations of hypnotic fascination." The people in these illustrations, according to *New York Times Book Review,* are "all roly-poly and squashed flat on top, as if crushed beneath the weight of their own importance." In 1983 *The Favershams* was one of *New York Time*'s Choice of Best Illustrated Children's Books of the Year. It also received the Children's Graphic Art Prize at the Bologna Children's Book Fair and the Parents' Choice Award fot Illustration in Children's Books. Gerrard used the same illustrative style in *Sir Cedric,* the amusing tale of an adventurous little knight. *School Library Journal* observed that the epic poem was accompanied by "colorful, detailed paintings of short, round people with large heads (many bald)," while *Booklist* praised the "fluid rhyming and stunning embellishments [that] exert vivacious appeal.'' *Home:* 117 Moor End Rd., Mellor, via Stockport, Cheshire, England.

FOR MORE INFORMATION SEE: Contemporary Authors, Volume 110, Gale, 1984.

GLENN, Mel 1943-

BRIEF ENTRY: Born May 10, 1943, in Zurich, Switzerland. Educator and author. After graduating from New York University in 1964, Glenn began a two-year stint with the Peace Corps, serving as an English teacher in Sierra Leone, West Africa. Upon his return to the United States, he started teaching at the junior high school level and three years later, in 1970, found himself employed as an instructor at Abraham Lincoln High School in Brooklyn, the same school from which he had graduated in 1960. Glenn is the author of *Class Dismissed! High School Poems* (Clarion Books, 1982), a collection of seventy poems which are based on his observations of the students who surround him daily. Each piece of free verse, told in the first person, represents a fictional student. *Booklist* described the individualized poems as ''revealing expressions about adolescence, laced with touches of humor and poignancy,'' while *School Library Journal* commented on the ''authenticity of the feelings and experiences.'' In 1982 *Class Dismissed!* was chosen one of the best young adult books of the year by the American Library Association and received an Honor Book plaque in the Golden Kite Awards presentation sponsored by the Society of Children's Book Writers. Glenn is also the author of *One Order to Go* (Clarion Books, 1984), a novel for young adults that follows the conflict between a father and his high school son. Recently, Glenn completed his second novel entitled *Play-by-Play* (Houghton, 1986). *Home:* 4288 Bedford Ave., Brooklyn, N.Y. 11229.

GOUGH, Philip 1908-

PERSONAL: Born June 11, 1908, in Warrington, Lancashire, England. *Education:* Attended Liverpool School of Art, England, also art schools in Chelsea and Penzance, England. *Home:* Chelsea, England.

CAREER: Artist, book illustrator. Stage designer, London, for about twenty-five productions, including ''The Two Bouquets,'' ''Land of the Christmas Stocking,'' and ''Where the Rainbow Ends.''

ILLUSTRATOR: Hans Christian Andersen, *Hans Andersen's Fairy Tales,* Peter Lunn, 1946, Penguin, 1981; Jane Austen, *Emma,* Macdonald & Co., 1948; Barbara L. Picard, *The Mermaid and the Simpleton,* Oxford University Press (New York), 1949, reprinted, Criterion, 1970; Eleanor Farjeon, *The Old Nurse's Stocking Basket,* University of London Press, 1949; J. Austen, *Pride and Prejudice,* Macdonald & Co., 1951, Coward, 1953; Mary Clive, *Christmas with the Savages,* St. Martin's, 1955; Doris Leslie, *Peridot Flight,* Hutchinson, 1956, reprinted, Heinemann, 1971; (with M. W. Hawes) E. Farjeon, *The New Book of Days,* Walck, 1961; Philip Turner, *Colonel Sheperton's Clock,* Oxford University Press (London), 1964, World Publishing, 1966.

Philip Rush, *Frost Fair,* Collins, 1965, Roy, 1967; Jean Blathwayt, *On the Run for Home,* Macdonald & Co., 1965; Rosalie K. Fry, *Gypsy Princess,* Dutton, 1969; Ann Stone, *The Balloon People,* Lutterworth, 1971, McGraw, 1974; Henry S. Merriman, *Barlasch of the Guard,* Dent, 1971; Gordon Cooper,

The water ran down her hair and her clothes, through the tips of her shoes and out at the heels. Still, she said she was a real princess. ■ (From "The Princess and the Pea" in *Hans Andersen's Fairy Tales,* compiled by Naomi Lewis. Illustrated by Philip Gough.)

An Hour in the Morning, Oxford University Press, 1971, Dutton, 1974; Geoffrey Chaucer, *The Franklin's Tale,* adapted by Ian Serraillier, Warne, 1972; Roger L. Green, editor, *Ten Tales of Adventure,* Dent, 1972, Dutton, 1973; B. L. Picard, adapter, *Three Ancient Kings: Gilgamesh, Hrolf Kraki, Conary,* Warne, 1972; John R. Townsend, *A Wish for Wings,* Heinemann, 1972.

SIDELIGHTS: ''I trained as a stage designer at the Liverpool School of Art and in 1928 did my first full-scale production, *A Midsummer Night's Dream,* at the Liverpool Repertory Theatre. In 1929 I designed the original production of *Toad of Toad Hall* by A. A. Milne. Following the failure of the family fortunes, I worked for two years in a commercial studio in London. I then began to design for London theatres. The twenty-five-odd productions include the original 'The Two Bouquets' by Eleanor and Herbert Farjeon, and children's plays designed by me include 'Land of the Christmas Stocking' and 'Where the Rainbow Ends,' which I re-designed.

''Since the second world war, I have devoted more time to books than to the theatre, and have illustrated, decorated, and designed covers for innumerable books.

''I have always been an ardent disciple of Claude Lorraine, Poussin, Tiepolo and Wilson. They are some of the principal painters who have been constant sources of inspiration to me. My great interest, however, is in architecture, furniture and decoration of the late eighteenth and early nineteenth centuries.'' [Bertha E. Miller and others, compilers, *Illustrators of Children's Books: 1946-1956,* Horn Book, 1958.]

GRACE, F(rances Jane)

PERSONAL: Born in Santa Monica, Calif.; daughter of Emile Albert (in business) and Hazel (Webster) Simons; married Jack Kenneth Grace (a consulting engineer); children: Jack Kenneth, Jr., Edward Webster. *Education:* Santa Monica College, A.A.; Woodbury College (now University), B.B.A.; University of California, Los Angeles, B.A., 1977. *Residence:* Manhattan Beach, Calif. *Agent:* Marilyn Marlow, Curtis Brown Ltd., 10 Astor Place, New York, N.Y. 10003.

CAREER: Writer. Worked as staff writer for *Santa Monica Evening Outlook, Long Beach Independent* (now *Independent-Press Telegram*), and KSKY-Radio in Dallas, Tex.; associated with Civil Service in Washington, D.C. *Member:* Society of Children's Book Writers, Surfwriters, American Association of University Women, Southwest Manuscripters, Southern California Council on Literature for Children and Young People. *Awards, honors: Branigan's Dog* listed among best books in Young Adult Service Division by American Library Association, 1981.

WRITINGS: Branigan's Dog (young adult), Bradbury, 1981; *A Very Private Performance* (young adult), Bradbury, 1983. Author of scripts for CBS-Radio. Contributor to periodicals, including *Westways, Transitions,* and *Christian Science Monitor.*

WORK IN PROGRESS: Q, a novel for young adults; a book for younger readers.

SIDELIGHTS: "I've been a reader and a writer since grade school. My failed first novel, written at age twelve in my Venice, California, 'studio' (the upstairs bedroom), was a purple-sage saga directly attributable to a summer of reading Zane

(Jacket illustration by Phil Franké from *Branigan's Dog* by Fran Grace.)

Grey. Although I wrote several other books at a young age, it wasn't until after many years and a university education in literature that I actually sold a book. Consequently, I can't say enough for a wide academic education (everything is grist for the writer's mill), and especially for education in literature. English and American literature, and Greek and Latin literature in translation, were my stepping stones not only to winnowing the best from the rest, but to the process of writing and creative thought.

"*Branigan's Dog,* first written in white-hot haste, then tediously rewritten under the cool, discerning eye of my Bradbury Press editor, Richard Jackson, grew out of the painful experience of losing a pet. Its predecessor, which I finally cut into quarters to serve as scratch pads, was an attempt to magnify the same incident in a book for younger readers. That story ended up didactic and dull, anathema to readers of any age. *Branigan's Dog* was named one of the 'Fifty Best Books for Young Adults' for 1981 by the American Library Association, proving that in my case it isn't writing, but rewriting, that's the name of the game.

"Sonia Levitin, award-winning writer of novels for young people, gave my second book its title, *A Very Private Performance,* when my editor and I reached a stalemate. Sonia's choice also triggered a new plan for the denouement.

"Proving again that everything experienced personally or vicariously can feed into the writer's IBM Selectric (I have re-

F. GRACE

cently taken on the IBM PC), the young protagonist of *A Very Private Performance* sprang to life after I had seen a street mime perform in Berkeley. The enigmatic and tortured girl violinist of the story is a composite of many gifted performers I have known or known of. This book involved considerable research, which I enjoy. A trip to the Cajun country of Louisiana established the character of the mime's girlfriend, and hours of listening to classical records helped define the violinist's passion.

"While I hadn't set out to write for the youth market—my background is in journalism and radio—I was plunged into it by the fine writing in the field being done in the weekly workshop I attend, especially by such authors as Mildred Ames. Among my impersonal mentors are the books of M. E. Kerr, Richard Peck and Paul Zindel."

HOBBIES AND OTHER INTERESTS: Travel, music, art, jogging, theater.

GRAHAM-CAMERON, M(alcolm) G(ordon) 1931-
(Mike Graham-Cameron)

BRIEF ENTRY: Born January 18, 1931, in London, England. Publisher, editor, and author of children's books. After serving in the Royal Air Force for twelve years, from 1948 to 1960, Graham-Cameron joined a printing and design company in Cambridge, England as sales director. After several years of hard work, he turned a declining business into a successful enterprise with the added services of advertising and marketing activities. In 1969 he and his first wife co-founded Dinosaur Publications, a small publisher of children's books. About 1984 the company was taken over by a much larger publisher, and Graham-Cameron, with his second wife, artist and illustrator Helen Herbert, founded Graham-Cameron Publishing. Graham-Cameron has written nearly a dozen works for children, including *The Farmer, Home Sweet Home, Life in an Edwardian Country Household, Rural Life in Roman Suffolk,* and *Shopping at the Co-op.* He also serves as external assessor at the Cambridge School of Art. *Home and office:* 10 Church St., Willingham, Cambridge CB4 5NE, England.

GRAVES, Robert (von Ranke)   1895-1985

PERSONAL: Born July 24, 1895, in London, England; died at his home in Deyá, Majorca, Spain, December 7, 1985; son of Alfred Perceval (an Irish poet and ballad writer) and Amalia (von Ranke) Graves; married Nancy Nicholson, 1918 (marriage ended, 1929); married Beryl Pritchard; children: (first marriage) Jenny, David, Catherine, Samuel; (second marriage) William, Lucia, Juan, Tomas. *Education:* Attended Charterhouse School; Oxford University, B. Litt., 1926. *Religion:* Anglican. *Residence:* Majorca, Spain. *Agent:* A. P. Watt Ltd., 26/28 Bedford Row, London WC1, England.

CAREER: Egyptian University, Cairo, Egypt, professor of English literature, 1926; Oxford University, Oxford, England, professor of poetry, 1961-65. Clarke Lecturer, Trinity College, Cambridge University, 1954. Lectured in the United States, 1958, 1966-67. *Military service:* Royal Welch Fusiliers, 1914-18; served in France; became captain. *Awards, honors:* James Tait Black Memorial Prize, 1935, for *I, Claudius* and *Claudius, the God and his Wife Messalina;* Hawthornden Prize, 1935, for *I, Claudius;* Femina-Vie Heureuse Prize and the

Stock Prize, 1939, for *Count Belisarius;* Russell Loines Memorial Fund Award, 1958; Gold Medal of the Poetry Society of America, 1959; M.A., Oxford University, 1961; Queen's Gold Medal for Poetry, 1969.

WRITINGS—Juvenile: The Big Green Book (illustrated by Maurice Sendak), Crowell, 1962; *Two Wise Children,* Harlin Quist, 1966; *The Poor Boy Who Followed His Star,* Cassell, 1968, Doubleday, 1969; *An Ancient Castle* (illustrated by Elizabeth Graves), P. Owen, 1980, Michael Kesend, 1982.

Poetry: *Over the Brazier,* Poetry Bookshop, 1916; *Fairies and Fusiliers,* Heinemann, 1917, Knopf, 1918; *Country Sentiment,* Knopf, 1920: *The Pier-Glass,* Knopf, 1921; *The Feather Red,* L. and V. Woolf, 1923; *Whipperginny,* Knopf, 1923; *Mock Beggar Hall,* Hogarth Press, 1924; *Welchman's Hose,* The Fleuron, 1925; *John Kemp's Wager: A Ballad Opera,* S. French, 1925; *Robert Graves,* Benn, 1925; *Poems, 1914-26,* Heinemann, 1927, Doubleday, Doran & Co., 1929; *Poems, 1929,* Seizin Press, 1929.

Ten Poems More, Hours Press (Paris), 1930; *Poems, 1926-30,* Heinemann, 1931; *Poems, 1930-33,* Barker, 1933; *Collected Poems,* Random House, 1938; *No More Ghosts,* Faber, 1940; (with Alan Hodge and Norman Cameron) *Work in Hand,* Hogarth, 1942; *Poems, 1938-45,* Creative Age Press, 1946; *Collected Poems, 1914-47,* Cassell, 1948; *Poems and Satires,* Cassell, 1951; *Poems, 1953,* Cassell, 1953; *Collected Poems, 1955,* Doubleday, 1955; *Robert Graves: Poems Selected by Himself,* Penguin Books, 1957; *The Poems of Robert Graves Chosen by Himself,* Doubleday, 1958; *Collected Poems, 1959,* Cassell, 1959, Doubleday, 1961, 3rd edition, Cassell, 1962.

Portrait of Robert Graves. (Copyright © 1966 by Aemilia Laracuen.)

In spite of the state police who tried to stop her at the crossroads, she drove ten miles at full speed to the nearest hospital. . . . ■ (From *Two Wise Children* by Robert Graves. Illustrated by Ralph Pinto.)

The Penny Fiddle: Poems for Children, Cassell, 1960, Doubleday, 1961; *More Poems, 1961*, Cassell, 1961; *Selected Poetry and Prose* (chosen, introduced, and annotated by James Reeves), Hutchinson, 1961; *Poems, Collected by Himself*, Doubleday, 1961; *The More Deserving Cases: Eighteen Old Poems for Reconsideration*, Marlborough College Press, 1962; *New Poems*, Cassell, 1962, Doubleday, 1963; *Ann at Highwood Hall: Poems for Children*, Cassell, 1964; *Man Does, Woman Is*, Doubleday, 1964; *Love Respelt*, Cassell, 1965, Doubleday, 1966; *Collected Poems, 1965*, Cassell, 1965; *Collected Poems, 1966*, Doubleday, 1966; *Seventeen Poems Missing from Love Respelt*, Stellar Press, 1966; *Colophon to Love Respelt*, Bertram Rota, 1967; *Poems 1965-1968*, Cassell, 1968; *Beyond Giving*, Bertram Rota, 1969; *Love Respelt Again*, Doubleday, 1969; *Poems about Love*, Cassell, 1969.

Poems 1968-70, Cassell, 1970, Doubleday, 1971; *Green-Sailed Vessel*, Bertram Rota, 1971; *Poems 1970-72*, Cassell, 1972; *Timeless Meeting*, Bertram Rota, 1973; *At the Gate*, Bertram Rota, 1974; *Collected Poems*, Cassell, 1975.

Fiction: *My Head! My Head! Being the History of Elisha and the Shunamite Woman; with the History of Moses as Elisha Related It, and Her Questions Put to Him*, Secker, 1925; *The Shout*, Mathews and Marrot, 1929; *But It Still Goes On: An Accumulation*, J. Cape, 1930, J. Cape and H. Smith, 1931; *I, Claudius*, Smith & Haas, 1934; *Claudius, the God and His Wife Messalina*, Barker, 1934, Smith & Haas, 1935; "*Antigua, Penny, Puce*," Seizen Press and Constable, 1936, published as *The Antigua Stamp*, Random House, 1937; *Count Belisarius*, Random House, 1938.

Sergeant Lamb of the Ninth, Methuen, 1940, published as *Sergeant Lamb's America*, Random House, 1940; *Proceed, Sergeant Lamb*, Random House, 1941; *The Story of Marie Powell, Wife to Mr. Milton*, Cassell, 1943, published as *Wife to Mr. Milton: The Story of Marie Powell*, Creative Age Press, 1944; *The Golden Fleece*, Cassell, 1944, published as *Hercules, My Shipmate*, Creative Age Press, 1945; *King Jesus*, Creative Age Press, 1946, 6th edition, Cassell, 1962; *The Islands of Unwisdom*, Doubleday, 1949; *Seven Days in New*

Crete, Cassell, 1949, published as *Watch the North Wind Rise*, Creative Age Press, 1949.

Occupation: Writer, Creative Age Press, 1950; *Homer's Daughter*, Doubleday, 1955; *Catacrok! Mostly Stories, Mostly Funny*, Cassell, 1956; *They Hanged My Saintly Billy: The Life and Death of Dr. William Palmer*, Doubleday, 1957; *Collected Short Stories*, Doubleday, 1964.

Nonfiction: *On English Poetry; Being an Irregular Approach to the Psychology of This Art, from Evidence Mainly Subjective*, Knopf, 1922; *The Meaning of Dreams*, Palmer, 1924; *Poetic Unreason and Other Studies*, Palmer, 1925; *Contemporary Techniques of Poetry: A Political Analogy*, Hogarth Press, 1925; *Another Future of Poetry*, Hogarth Press, 1926; *Impenetrability; or, The Proper Habit of English*, L. and V. Woolf, 1926; *Lawrence and the Arabs*, J. Cape, 1927, published as *Lawrence and the Arabian Adventure*, Doubleday, Doran & Co., 1928; *Lars Porsena; or, The Future of Swearing and Improper Language*, Dutton, 1927, revised edition published as *The Future of Swearing and Improper Language*, K. Paul, Trench, Trubner & Co., 1936; *Mrs. Fisher; or, The Future of Humour*, K. Paul, Trench, Trubner & Co., 1928; (with Laura Riding) *A Pamphlet Against Anthologies*, J. Cape, 1928; *Good-Bye to All That: An Autobiography*, J. Cape, 1929, J. Cape & H. Smith, 1930, revised edition, Doubleday, 1957.

The Real David Copperfield, Barker, 1933; (with Laura Riding) *No Decency Left*, J. Cape, 1935; *T. E. Lawrence to His Biographer*, Doubleday, 1938, published with Liddell Hart's work as *T. E. Lawrence to His Biographers*, Doubleday, 1963, 2nd edition, Cassell, 1963; (with Alan Hodge) *The Long Week-End: A Social History of Great Britain, 1918-1939*, Faber, 1940, Macmillan, 1941; (with Alan Hodge) *The Reader over Your Shoulder: A Handbook for Writers of English Prose*, Macmillan, 1943; *The White Goddess: A Historical Grammar of Poetic Myth*, Creative Age Press, 1948, amended and enlarged edition, Vintage Books, 1958; *The Common Asphodel: Collected Essays on Poetry, 1922-1949*, H. Hamilton, 1949.

(With Joshua Podro) *The Nazarene Gospel Restored*, Cassell, 1953, Doubleday, 1954; (with Joshua Podro) *Nazarene Gos-*

pel, Cassell, 1955; *Adam's Rib, and Other Anomalous Elements in the Hebrew Creation Myth: A New View*, Trianon Press, 1955, Yoseloff, 1958; *The Greek Myths*, two volumes, Penguin Books, 1955; *The Crowning Privilege: The Clark Lectures, 1954-1955* (includes sixteen new poems), Cassell, 1955, Doubleday, 1956; (with Joshua Podro) *Jesus in Rome: A Historical Conjecture*, Cassell, 1957; *5 Pens in Hand*, Doubleday, 1958; *Steps: Stories, Talks, Essays, Poems, Studies in History*, Cassell, 1958.

Food for Centaurs: Stories, Talks, Critical Studies, Poems, Doubleday, 1960; *Greek Gods and Heroes*, Doubleday, 1960 (published in England as *Myths of Ancient Greece*, Cassell, 1961); *Oxford Addresses on Poetry*, Doubleday, 1962; *The Siege and Fall of Troy*, Cassell, 1962, Doubleday, 1963; *Nine Hundred Iron Chariots*, Massachusetts Institute of Technology, 1963; (with Raphael Patal) *Hebrew Myths: The Book of Genesis*, Doubleday, 1964; *Mammon* (lecture; also see below), London School of Economics, 1964; *Mammon and the Black Goddess* (one section previously published as *Mammon*), Doubleday, 1965; *Majorca Observed*, Doubleday, 1965; *Spiritual Quixote*, Oxford University Press, 1967; *Poetic Craft and Principle* (collection of Oxford lectures), Cassell, 1967; (author of introduction) *Greece, Gods, and Art*, Viking, 1968; *The Crane Bag*, Cassell, 1969; *Difficult Questions, Easy Answers*, Cassell, 1972, Doubleday, 1973; *In Broken Images: Selected Letters of Robert Graves 1914-1946*, edited by Paul O'Prey, Hutchinson, 1982; *Between Moon and Moon: Selected Letters of Robert Graves 1946-1972*, edited by P. O'Prey, Hutchinson, 1984.

Graves during his school days at Charterhouse.

Editor: *The English Ballad: A Short Critical Survey*, Benn, 1927; (compiler) *The Less Familiar Nursery Rhymes*, Benn, 1927; (and author of foreword) Swinburne, *An Old Saying*, J. S. Mayfield, 1947; *English and Scottish Ballads*, Macmillan, 1957; (and author of foreword) *The Comedies of Terence*, Doubleday, 1962, published as *Comedies*, Aldine, 1962. Condensed Merrill P. Paine's edition of *David Copperfield*, by Charles Dickens, Harcourt, 1934. Edited, with Laura Riding, a semi-annual called *Epilogue: A Critical Summary*, 1935-37.

Translator: (With Laura Riding) Georg Schwarz, *Almost Forgotten Germany*, Random House, 1937; Lucius Apuleius, *The Transformations of Lucius, Otherwise Known as "The Golden Ass,"* Farrar, Straus, 1951; Manuel de Jesus Galvan, *Cross and the Sword*, Indiana University Press, 1954; Pedro Antonio de Alarcon, *Infant with the Globe*, Faber, 1955; Marcus Annaeus Lucanus, *Pharsalia: Dramatic Episodes of the Civil Wars*, Penguin Books, 1956; George Sand, *Winter in Majorca*, Cassell, 1956; Seutonius, *The Twelve Caesars*, Cassell, 1957; *The Anger of Achilles: Homer's "Illiad"* (produced at Lincoln Center, New York, 1967), Doubleday, 1959; Hesiodu Stamperia del Santuccio, *Fable of the Hawk and the Nightingale*, 1959: (with Omar Ali-Shah) *The Rubaiyyat of Omar Khayaam* (based on the 12th-century manuscript), Cassell, 1967, published as *The Original Rubaiyyat of Omar Khayaam*, Doubleday, 1968; *Solomon's "Song of Songs,"* Cassell, 1968, Doubleday, 1969.

ADAPTATIONS: "I, Claudius" (television series; based on *I, Claudius* and *Claudius, the God and His Wife Messalina*), BBC-TV 1976; broadcast in America on PBS-TV, 1978; "The Shout," Rank/Recorded Picture, 1978.

SIDELIGHTS: **July 24, 1895.** Born in London, England, to the Irish poet and ballad writer Alfred Perceval Graves. "I am glad in a way that my father was a poet. This at least saved me from any false reverence of poets, and his work was never an oppression to me. I am even very pleased when I meet people who know his work and not mine. Some of his songs I sing without prejudice; when washing up after meals or shelling peas or on similar occasions. He never once tried to teach me how to write, or showed any understanding of my serious work; he was always more ready to ask advice about his own work than to offer it for mine. He never tried to stop me writing and was glad of my first successes. His light-hearted early work is the best. . . .

"My mother married my father largely, it seems, to help him out with his five motherless children. Having any herself was a secondary consideration. But first she had a girl, then she had another girl, and it was very nice of course to have them, but slightly disappointing, because she belonged to the generation and the tradition that made a son the really important event; then I came and I was a fine healthy child. She was forty when I was born and my father was forty-nine. Four years later she had another son and four years later she had still another son. The desired preponderance of male over female was established and twice five made ten. The gap of two generations between my parents and me was easier in a way to bridge than a single generation gap. Children seldom quarrel with their grandparents, and I have been able to think of my mother and father as grandparents. Also, a family of ten means a dilution of parental affection; the members tend to become indistinct. I have often been called: 'Philip, Richard, Charles, I mean Robert.'

"My father was a very busy man, an inspector of schools for the Southwark district of London, and we children saw practically nothing of him except during the holidays. Then he was

When Trojan scouts went out at dawn they found the horse towering over the burned camp. ■ (From *The Siege and Fall of Troy* by Robert Graves. Illustrated by C. Walter Hodges.)

very sweet and playful and told us stories with the formal beginning, not 'once upon a time,' but always 'and so the old gardener blew his nose on a red pocket handkerchief.' He occasionally played games with us, but for the most part when he was not doing educational work he was doing literary work. . . .'' [Robert Graves, *Good-Bye to All That: An Autobiography*, Blue Ribbon Books, 1930.¹]

Graves' family were members of the well-to-do class in Victorian England and their ancestors included scholars, writers and theologians. ''My mother and father were never of the aggressive, shoot-'em-down type. They were Liberals or, more strictly, Liberal-Unionists. In religious theory, at least, they treated their employees as fellow-creatures. But social distinctions remained clearly defined. . . .

''I can well recall the tone of my mother's voice when she informed the maids that they could have what was left of the pudding, or scolded the cook for some carelessness. It was a forced hardness, made almost harsh by embarrassment. My mother was *gemütlich* by nature. She would, I believe, have given a lot to be able to dispense with servants altogether. They were a foreign body in the house. . . .

'The bridge between the servants and ourselves was our nurse. She gave us her own passport on the first day she came: 'Emily

Dykes is my name; England is my nation; Netheravon is my dwelling-place, and Christ is my salvation.' Though she called us Miss and Master she spoke it in no servant tone. In a practical way she came to be more to us than our mother. I began to despise her at about the age of twelve—she was then nurse to my younger brothers—when I found that my education was now in advance of hers, and that if I struggled with her I was able to trip her up and bruise her quite easily. . . .''¹

1901. Sent to first of many preparatory schools. ''I went to six preparatory schools. The first was a dame's school at Wimbledon. I went there at the age of six. My father, as an educational expert, did not let me stay here long. He found me crying one day at the difficulty of the twenty-three-times table. . . .

''So I went to the lowest class of King's College School, Wimbledon. I was just seven years old, the youngest boy there, and they went up to nineteen. I was taken away after a couple of terms because I was found to be using naughty words. I was glad to leave that school because I did not understand a word of the lessons. I had started Latin and I did not know what Latin was or meant; its declensions and conjugations were pure incantations to me. For that matter so were the strings of naughty words. And I was oppressed by the huge hall, the enormous boys, the frightening rowdiness of the corridors, and compulsory Rugby football of which nobody told me the rules. I went from there to another preparatory school of the ordinary type, also at Wimbledon, where I stayed for about three years. Here I began playing games seriously, was quarrelsome, boastful, and talkative, won prizes, and collected things. The only difference between me and the other boys was that I collected coins instead of stamps. . . .

But whenever he tried to pick any of the fruit that dangled against his shoulders, a wind always swept the branch away. ■ (From *Greek Gods and Heroes* by Robert Graves. Illustrated by Dimitris Davis.)

Graves, Beryl, and a guest, 1943.

"I left that day-school at Wimbledon because my father decided that the standard of work was not good enough to enable me to win a scholarship at a public school. He sent me to another preparatory school in the Midlands; because the headmaster's wife was a sister of an old literary friend of his. It proved later that these were inadequate grounds. It was a queer place and I did not like it. There was a secret about the headmaster which a few of the elder boys shared. It was somehow sinister, but I never exactly knew what it was. . . . He was succeeded by the second master, a good man, who had taught me how to write English by eliminating all phrases that could be done without, and using verbs and nouns instead of adjectives and adverbs wherever possible. And where to start new paragraphs, and the difference between O and Oh. . . .

". . . What surprised me most at this school was when a boy of about twelve, whose father and mother were in India, was told by cable that they had both suddenly died of cholera. We all watched him sympathetically for weeks after, expecting him to die of grief or turn black in the face, or do something to match the occasion. Yet he seemed entirely unmoved, and since nobody dared discuss the tragedy with him he seemed to forget what had happened; he played about and ragged as he had done before. We found that rather monstrous. But he could not have been expected to behave otherwise. He had not seen his parents for two years. And preparatory schoolboys live in a world completely dissociated from home life. They have a different vocabulary, different moral system, different voice, and on their return to school from the holidays the change over from home-self to school-self is almost instantaneous, the reverse process takes a fortnight at least. A pre-

paratory-school boy, when off his guard, will often call his mother, 'Please, matron,' and will always address any man relation or friend of the family as 'Sir,' as though he were a master. I used to do it. School life becomes the reality and home life the illusion. In England parents of the governing classes virtually finish all intimate life with their children from about the age of eight, and any attempt on their part to insinuate home feeling into school life is resented.

"Next I went to a typically good school in Sussex. The headmaster was chary of admitting me at my age, particularly from a school with such a bad recent history. Family literary connections did the trick, however, and the headmaster saw that I was advanced enough to win a scholarship and do the school credit. The depressed state I had been in since the last school ended the moment I arrived."[1]

The preparatory school in Sussex, called Copthorne, prepared Graves for admission to Charterhouse, one of the leading English public schools. He hated Charterhouse, however, with a vengeance that lasted throughout his lifetime. "From the moment I arrived at the school I suffered an oppression of spirit that I hesitate now to recall in its full intensity. . . . The school consisted of about six hundred boys. The chief interests were games and romantic friendships. School-work was despised by everyone; the scholars, of whom there were about fifty in the school at any given time, were not concentrated in a single dormitory-house as at Winchester, but divided among ten. They were known as 'pro's,' and unless they were good at games and willing to pretend that they hated work as much as or more than the non-scholars, and ready whenever called on to

He went inside, changed back into a little boy, clothes and all, put the big green book under the sack in the attic, and came down again. ■ (From *The Big Green Book* by Robert Graves. Illustrated by Maurice Sendak.)

help these with their work, they usually had a bad time. I was a scholar and really liked work, and I was surprised and disappointed at the apathy of the classrooms. My first term I was left alone more or less, it being a school convention that new boys should be neither encouraged nor baited.... But my second term the trouble began. There were a number of things that naturally made for my unpopularity. Besides being a scholar and not outstandingly good at games, I was always short of pocket-money. I could not conform to the social custom of treating my contemporaries to food at the school shop, and because I could not treat them I could not accept their treating. My clothes were all wrong; they conformed outwardly to the school pattern, but they were ready-made and not of the best-quality cloth that the other boys all wore. Even so, I had not been taught how to make the best of them.... The other boys in my house, except for five scholars, were nearly all the sons of business men; it was a class of whose interests and prejudices I knew nothing, having hitherto only met boys of the professional class. And I talked too much for their liking...."[1]

1909. Attempted to translate poems by Catullus and to adapt Welsh technical procedures, amongst the most complicated in world poetry, to English. By the age of fifteen Graves had decided to become a poet. "Being thrown entirely on myself I began to write poetry. This was considered stronger proof of insanity than the formal straws I wore in my hair. The poetry I wrote was not the easy showing-off witty stuff that all the Graves write and have written for the last couple of centuries. It was poetry that was dissatisfied with itself. When, later, things went better with me at Charterhouse, I became literary once more."[1]

1913-1914. During his last year at Charterhouse, Graves was co-editor of the school magazine. "My last year at Charterhouse I devoted myself to doing everything I could to show how little respect I had for the school tradition. In the winter of 1913 I won a classical exhibition at St. John's College, Oxford, so that I could go slow on school work. Nevill Barbour and I were editing *The Carthusian,* and a good deal of my time went in that. Nevill, who as a scholar had met the same sort of difficulties as myself, also had a dislike of most Charterhouse traditions...."[1]

August 12, 1914. Enlisted in the Royal Welch Fusiliers, and spent the next few months in training. "I was at Harlech when war was declared; I decided to enlist a day or two later. In the first place, though only a very short war was expected—two or three months at the very outside—I thought that it might last just long enough to delay my going to Oxford in October, which I dreaded. I did not work out the possibilities of being actively engaged in the war. I thought that it would mean garrison service at home while the regular forces were away. In the second place, I entirely believed that France and England had been drawn into a war which they had never contemplated and for which they were entirely unprepared. It never occurred to me that newspapers and statesmen could lie. I forgot my pacifism—I was ready to believe the worst of the Germans. I was outraged to read of the cynical violation of Belgian neutrality. I wrote a poem promising vengeance for Louvain. I discounted perhaps twenty per cent. of the atrocity details as war-time exaggeration. That was not, of course, enough."[1]

December, 1914. Sent to fight in the trenches of France. "These were early days of trench-warfare, the days of the jam-tin bomb and the gas-pipe trench-mortar. It was before Lewis or Stokes guns, steel helmets, telescopic rifle-sights, gas-shells, pill-boxes, tanks, trench-raids, or any of the later improvements of trench-warfare.

"The trench was wet and slippery. The guide was giving hoarse directions all the time. 'Hole right.' 'Wire high.' 'Wire low.' 'Deep place here, sir.' 'Wire low.' I had never been told about the field telephone wires. They were fastened by staples to the side of the trench, and when it rained the staples were always falling out and the wire falling down and tripping people up. If it sagged too much one stretched it across the top of the trench to the other side to correct the sag, and then it would catch one's head. The holes were the sump-pits used for draining the trenches. We were now under rifle-fire. I always found rifle-fire more trying than shell-fire. The gunner was usually, I knew, firing not at people but at map-references—crossroads, likely artillery positions, houses that suggested billets for troops, and so on. Even when an observation officer in an aeroplane or captive balloon or on a church spire was directing the gun-fire it seemed unaimed, somehow. But a rifle bullet even when fired blindly always had the effect of seeming aimed. And we could hear a shell coming and take some sort of cover, but the rifle bullet gave no warning. So though we learned not to duck to a rifle bullet, because once it was heard it must have missed, it gave us a worse feeling of danger. Rifle bullets in the open went hissing into the grass without much noise, but when we were in a trench the bullets, going over the hollow, made a tremendous crack.

"Aside from wounds, gas, and the accidents of war, the life of the trench soldier was, for the most part, not unhealthy. Food was plentiful and hard work in the open air made up for the discomfort of wet feet and clothes and draughty billets. A continual need for alertness discouraged minor illnesses; a cold was thrown off in a few hours, an attack of indigestion was hardly noticed. This was true, at least, in a good battalion, where the men were bent on going home either with an honourable wound or not at all.... In a really good battalion, as the Second Battalion was when I went to it first, the question of getting wounded and going home was not permitted to be raised."[1]

Graves began writing poetry in earnest. Before the war ended, he had two volumes of verse published.

September 9, 1915. Went home to London on leave. Upon his return to the trenches, he was engaged in the Battle of Loos, during which Graves lost most of his fellow officers. In eight days he snatched a mere eight hours of sleep. Soon after the Battle of Loos he was raised to rank of Special Reserve Captain. "Like everyone else I had a carefully worked out formula for taking risks. We would all take any risk, even the certainty of death, to save life or to maintain an important position. To take life we would run, say, a one-in-five risk, particularly if there was some wider object than merely reducing the enemy's man-power; for instance, picking off a well-known sniper, or getting fire ascendancy in trenches where the lines were dangerously close."[1]

1916. Wounded during a German shelling of his battalion. "My memory of what happened then is vague. Apparently Doctor Dunn came up through the barrage with a stretcher-party, dressed my wound, and got me down to the old German dressing-station at the north end of Mametz Wood. I just remember being put on the stretcher.... The dressing-station was overworked that day; I was laid in a corner on a stretcher and remained unconscious for more than twenty-four hours.

"It was about ten o'clock on the 20th that I was hit. Late that night the colonel came to the dressing-station; he saw me lying in the corner and was told that I was done for. The next morning, the 21st, when they were clearing away the dead, I was found to be still breathing; so they put me on an ambulance for Heilly, the nearest field-hospital. The pain of being jolted down the Happy Valley, with a shell-hole at every three or four yards of the roads, woke me for awhile. I remember screaming. But once back on the better roads I became unconscious again. . . .''[1]

Graves was at first listed as killed in action, and his family received notification of his apparent death on his twenty-first birthday. He was actually taken to a hospital at Rouen where he recuperated from his wounds. The war, he later remarked, changed his entire outlook of the world, and scarred him for life.

January, 1918. Married Nancy Nicholson.

November, 1918. "In November came the Armistice. . . . Armistice-night hysteria did not touch the camp much, though some of the Canadians stationed there went down to Rhyl to celebrate in true overseas style. The news sent me out walking alone along the dyke above the marshes of Rhuddlan (an ancient battle-field, the Flodden of Wales) cursing and sobbing and thinking of the dead.''[1]

January, 1919. First daughter, Jenny Nicholson, born. She became the best-known of Graves' eight children, eventually becoming a journalist.

When Graves was demobilized he was officially suffering from neurasthenia or shell shock. "I was very thin, very nervous,

"Why do you laugh, old man?" asked the uncle. ■ (From *The Big Green Book* by Robert Graves. Illustrated by Maurice Sendak.)

Robert Graves in his farmhouse kitchen, 1944.

and had about four years' loss of sleep to make up. I found that I was suffering from a large sort of intestinal worm which came from drinking bad water in France. I was now waiting until I should be well enough to go to Oxford with the Government educational grant; it seemed the easiest thing to do. I knew that it would be years before I was fit for anything besides a quiet country life. There was no profession that I wished to take up, though for awhile I considered schoolmastering. My disabilities were many; I could not use a telephone, I was sick every time I travelled in a train, and if I saw more than two new people in a single day it prevented me from sleeping. I was ashamed of myself as a drag on Nancy.

"In **October 1919** I went up to Oxford at last. . . . The city was overcrowded; the lodging-house keepers, some of whom had nearly starved during the war, now had their rooms booked up terms ahead and charged accordingly. Keble College had put up many huts for its surplus students. There was not an unfurnished house to be had anywhere within the three-mile radius. I solved the difficulty by getting permission from my college authorities to live five miles out, on Boar's Hill; I pleaded my lungs. John Masefield, who liked my poetry, offered to rent us a cottage at the bottom of his garden."[1]

1920. Met and befriended T. E. Lawrence. "I met T. E. Lawrence first at a guest-night at All Souls'. Lawrence had just been given a college fellowship, and it was the first time for many years that he had worn evening dress. The restlessness of his eyes was the first thing about him I noticed. He told me that he had read my poems in Egypt during one of his flying visits from Arabia; he and my brother Philip had been together in the Intelligence Department at Cairo, before his part in the Arab revolt had begun, working out the Turkish order of battle. I knew nothing about his organization of the Arab revolt, his exploits and sufferings in the desert, and his final entry into Damascus. He was merely, to me, a fellow-soldier who had come back to Oxford for a rest after the war."[1]

June, 1921. Became ill. Left Oxford and moved with his family to a house in Islip, which they rented from Graves' mother. "Islip was a name of good omen to me: it was associated with Abbot Islip, a poor boy of the village who had become Abbot of Westminster and befriended John Skelton when he took sanctuary in the Abbey from the anger of Wolsey. I had come more and more to associate myself with Skelton, discovering a curious affinity. Whenever I wanted a motto for a new book I always found exactly the right one somewhere or other in Skelton's poems. We moved into the Islip cottage and a new chapter started. I did not sit for my finals.

"These four years I spent chiefly on housework and being nurse to the children. Catherine was born in 1922 and Sam in 1924. By the end of 1925 we had lived for eight successive years in an atmosphere of teething, minor accidents, epidemics, and perpetual washing of children's napkins. I did not dislike this sort of life except for the money difficulties. I liked my life with the children. But the strain told on Nancy. She was constantly ill, and often I had to take charge of everything. She tried occasionally to draw; but by the time she had got her materials together some alarm from the nursery would always disturb her. She said at last that she would not start again until all the children were house-trained and old enough for school. I kept on writing because the responsibility for making money rested chiefly on me, and because nothing has ever stopped me writing when I have had something to write. We kept the cottage cleaned and polished in a routine that left us little time for anything else. We had accumulated a number of brass ornaments and utensils and allowed them to become

a tyranny, and our children wore five times as many clean dresses as our neighbours' children did.

"I found that I had the faculty of working through constant interruptions. I could recognize the principal varieties of babies' screams—hunger, indigestion, wetness, pins, boredom, wanting to be played with—and learned to disregard all but the more important ones. But most of the books that I wrote in these years betray the conditions under which I worked; they are scrappy, not properly considered and obviously written out of reach of a proper reference-library. Only poetry did not suffer. When I was working at a poem nothing else mattered; I went on doing my mechanical tasks in a trance until I had time to sit down to write it out. At one period I only allowed myself half an hour's writing a day, but once I did write I always had too much to put down; I never sat chewing my pen. My poetry-writing has always been a painful process of continual corrections and corrections on top of corrections and persistent dissatisfaction. I have never written a poem in less than three drafts; the greatest number I recall is thirty-five ('The Troll's Nosegay')."[1]

Between the years 1920 and 1925, Graves published a volume of poems every year.

So they all went up the ladder. . . .Only the secretary with the glasses stayed behind. He said that he was afraid of climbing up ladders. ■ (From *An Ancient Castle* by Robert Graves. Illustrated by Elizabeth Graves.)

Robert Graves. Photograph by Freya Edwards.

1926. Granted a B.Litt. degree from Oxford. Taught English in Egypt for one year. ''The only possible job that I could undertake was teaching. But I needed a degree, so I completed my thesis, which I published under the title of *Poetic Unreason* and handed in, when in print, to the examining board. I was most surprised when they accepted it and I had my bachelor's degree. But the problem of an appointment remained. I did not want a preparatory or secondary-school job which would keep me away from home all day. Nancy did not want anyone else but myself and her looking after the children, so there seemed no solution. And then the doctor told Nancy that if she wished to regain her health she must spend the winter in

Egypt. In fact, the only appointment that would be at all suitable would be a teaching job in Egypt, at a very high salary, where there was little work to do. And a week or two later (for this is the way things have always happened to me in emergencies) I was asked to offer myself as a candidate for the post of professor of English Literature at the newly-founded Egyptian University at Cairo. . . .

''I did two useful pieces of educational work in Egypt. I ordered a library of standard textbooks of English literature for the Faculty Library at the University (from which I hope Mr. Bonamy Dobree, my successor, profited). And I acted as examiner to the diploma class of the Higher Training College which provided English teachers for the primary and secondary schools.''[1] Upon his return to London, Graves vowed he would never take another job.

1927. ''Jonathan Cape [publishers] wrote to me suggesting that I should write a book for boys about Lawrence. There was not much time to do it to have it ready for autumn publication (about two months)—and Lawrence was in India and I had to get his permission and send parts of the manuscript there for him to read and pass. Lowell Thomas anticipated me with a *Boy's Book of Colonel Lawrence;* so I decided to make mine a general book, three times the length of his, working eighteen hours a day at it. Most of those to whom I wrote for information about Lawrence, including His Majesty the King, gave me their help. The only rebuff I got was from George Bernard Shaw. . . .''[1]

1929. Marriage to Nancy Nicholson ended. Left England for Majorca with fellow poet Laura Riding. Wrote autobiography, *Good-Bye to All That: An Autobiography,* which became a best-seller. At the time, critics said that Graves' move to the tiny Spanish island of Majorca was a phase, but the poet remained an inhabitant for the remainder of his lifetime.

1934. The novel, *I, Claudius,* was published, and became a financial success. The book won the Hawthornden and James Tait Black Prizes. Graves' historical novels, magazine essays and translations enabled him to work on his poetry without financial pressure.

1937. Movie based on *I, Claudius,* starring Charles Laughton and Merle Oberon. Project was abandoned. Twenty-eight years later, in 1965, British Broadcasting Corporation made a documentary of the abandoned movie entitled ''The Epic That Never Was.''

1939. Broke off personal and professional relations with Laura Riding. Graves subsequently married Beryl Pritchard. Three sons and a daughter were born to this marriage.

1945. After an exile in England during World War II, Graves returned to Majorca with his wife to raise his second family and to write poetry.

1946. ''I have at last got off that complicated book, now called *The White Goddess,* to Faber's, & Macmillan in U.S.A. If I hadn't it would have stayed and stayed and swelled for another few years. I went on inserting things up to the last moment. . . .

(From the documentary film "The Epic That Never Was," produced by BBC in 1965. It was an assemblage of surviving footage from the abandoned 1937 movie "I, Claudius," starring Charles Laughton and directed by Joseph von Sternberg.)

"And *King Jesus* is page proofing and looks very nice.

"And now I'll have a big tidy-up, including tidying-up my *Collected Poems* definitely for the new edition. It will be fun watching the reviews of my *Poems* [1938-1945] to see which way the wind of fashion is blowing." [Martin Seymour-Smith, *Robert Graves: His Life and Work*, Holt, 1982.[2]]

1948. Published *The White Goddess: A Historical Grammar of Poetic Myth.* The origin of the work was pure inspiration, according to Graves, who believed most emphatically in a personal muse. "As I was working on *King Jesus* these ideas began to pop in on me one by one. Then a friend sent me [a ring] from Africa; while at the same time another friend gave me . . . what seemed to be a very ancient coin—and shortly afterward I found this print. All those things taken together started me on the track. . . . How much do you believe in intuition? If a writer doesn't work by intuition, what good is he?

"I've been criticized because of my allegiance to the White Goddess. After all, it's not *my* White Goddess. I'm merely her interpreter. She was here long before me. In fact, being the spirit of poetry, I should say she was rather eternal. . . . "

[John Haller, "Conversations with Robert Graves," *Southwest Review,* Volume 42, 1957.[3]]

1951. Mother died; Graves remembered her mainly for the following piece of advice: "Robert, this is a great secret, never forget it! *Work is far more interesting than play.*"[2] It became his motto throughout his lifetime, to the extent that he came to regard work as his "habit."

1959. Awarded the Gold Medal of the Poetry Society of America. "I felt my mother's ghost present with me at the Waldorf-Astoria, New York, where the National Poetry Society of America were celebrating their Golden Jubilee. Though an Englishman, I had been judged worthy of the Prince Alexander Droutzkoy Memorial Award: a gold medal for Services to Poetry. An alarming experience, since I have always considered poetry as a private and, indeed, almost anti-social obsession, and been at pains to discount its more public manifestations. There I was, in evening dress, among six hundred fellow-obsessionists as well-groomed as myself, sitting down to dinner in the great Sbert Banqueting Hall. The Committee had placed me with a row of award-winners on a lofty dais.

"Robert Frost, the Society's Honorary President, sat near me, making mischievous *sotto voce* comments. I have known and

(From the television series "I, Claudius," starring Derek Jacobi. Produced by BBC-TV in 1976. Broadcast on PBS-TV, 1978.)

Robert Graves with niece Elizabeth and her son, Robin, in Majorca.

loved him since 1914, when we first met accidentally in a London bookshop; and his carefree mood gave me courage. Marianne Moore, whom I had not known before, but always respected for her unchanging dry wit, was there too. . . .'' [Robert Graves, *Oxford Addresses on Poetry,* Doubleday, 1962.⁴]

1961-1965. Lectured at Oxford University. Wrote to a friend: ''The village is very much the same. So, oddly enough, is

Oxford: surprising. . . . I met two or three undergraduates who had something *to* them.''²

1969. Awarded the Queen's Gold Medal for Poetry. ''Poetry does not count as work somehow. It can't be planned or discovered. It forces itself upon you without your knowing what it's all about. It comes like the tense headache before a thunderstorm, which is followed by an uncontrollable violence of feeling, and the whole air is ionized. You feel absolutely wonderful when you get the first line or two down on paper. Naturally, it takes three or four days before you bring the poem to its final state, and even then, years later, you may spot a word that's wrong. You know that it's been worrying you in the back of your mind all along." ["Playboy Interview: Robert Graves," *Playboy,* December, 1970.[5]]

1970-1975. Concentrated his efforts almost exclusively on poetry, publishing six volumes of his poems. ". . .Now well into my seventy-sixth year, I had been increasingly concerned with hidden powers of poetic thought, which raise and solve problems of advanced mathematics and physics. The word 'poetry' meant in Greek the 'act of making'—a sense that has survived in the old Scottish word for a poet, namely 'Maker.' . . . The poetic power to make things happen, as understood for instance by the early medieval Irish master-poets, and by their Middle Eastern Sufic contemporaries, raises simply love-alliances to a point where physical absence supplies living presence. These experiences occur not only in the fourth dimension, where prison walls are easily cheated . . . but in the fifth, where time proves as manipulable as is vertical or lateral space in the usual third dimension, and where seemingly impossible coincidences and so-called 'Acts of God' occur almost as a matter of course. In poetry, the fifth-dimensional coidentification of lovers is truth rather than idealistic fancy. . . ."[2]

1978. The highly successful series, "I, Claudius," based on his book and first produced in England by the BBC, was shown in America.

December 7, 1985. Died at the age of ninety at his home in Deyá on the island of Majorca. Graves' health had been failing for ten years, during which time he lived in seclusion and was unable to write. Before his death he had been bedridden for several months.

FOR MORE INFORMATION SEE— Books: Robert Graves. *Good-Bye to All That: An Autobiography,* J. Cape, 1929, Blue Ribbon Books, 1930, revised edition, Doubleday, 1957; Frank Swinnerton, *The Georgian Literary Scene,* Dent, 1951; J. M. Cohen, *Robert Graves,* Oliver & Boyd, 1960; R. Graves, *Oxford Addresses on Poetry,* Doubleday, 1962; Douglas Day, *Swifter Than Reason: The Poetry and Criticism of Robert Graves,* University of North Carolina Press, 1963; Howard Nemerov, *Poetry and Fiction,* Rutgers University Press, 1963; Martin Seymour-Smith, *Robert Graves,* revised edition, Longman Group, 1965; F. H. Higginson, *A Bibliography of the Works of Robert Graves,* Shoe String, 1966; D. J. Enright, *Conspirators and Poets,* Dufour, 1966; D. G. Hoffman, *Barbarous Knowledge,* Oxford University Press, 1967; Randall Jarrell, *The Third Book of Criticism,* Farrar, Straus, 1969; Peter Quennell, *Casanova in London,* Stein & Day, 1971; *Contemporary Literary Criticism,* Gale, Volume I, 1973, Volume II, 1974, Volume VI, 1976, Volume XI, 1979; Martin Seymour-Smith, *Robert Graves: His Life and Work,* Holt, 1982.

Periodicals: John Haller, "Conversations with Robert Graves," *Southwest Review,* Volume 42, 1957; *Arizona Quarterly,* Volume 15, 1959; *Horizon,* January, 1962; *Show,* December, 1962; *Life,* June 24, 1963, October 15, 1965; *New York Times,* November 20, 1964, December 1, 1966, October 26, 1967, September 20, 1979; *Literary Times,* April, 1965; *Sewanee Review,* fall, 1965; *Times Literary Supplement,* October 7, 1965, December 7, 1967, June 26, 1969, November 21, 1980; *New Statesman,* December 3, 1965; *Atlantic,* January, 1966; *Shenandoah,* spring, 1966; *New York Times Magazine,* October 30, 1966; *Commentary,* February, 1967; *Hudson Review,* spring, 1967; *Listener,* May 4, 1967, November 9, 1967, December 24, 1970; *Harper's,* August, 1967; *Time,* November 3, 1967,

May 31, 1968; *Newsweek,* May 20, 1968, July 28, 1969; *Observations,* July, 1968; *Yale Review,* autumn, 1968; *Poetry,* January, 1969; *London Magazine,* February, 1969; *National Observer,* March 17, 1969; *New York Times Book Review,* July 20, 1969, October 12, 1969, March 11, 1973, April 29, 1979; *New Leader,* October 27, 1969; *Prairie Schooner,* summer, 1970; "Playboy Interview: Robert Graves," *Playboy,* December, 1970; *Variety,* July 26, 1972; *Publishers Weekly,* August 11, 1975; *Nation,* March 18, 1978.

Obituaries: *New York Times,* December 8, 1985; *Variety,* December 11, 1985; *School Library Journal,* February, 1986.

GREENHAUS, Thelma Nurenberg 1903-1984 (Thelma Nurenberg)

PERSONAL: Born December 25, 1903, in Warsaw, Poland; died of an apparent heart attack, August 8, 1984, in New York, N.Y.; married Charles Greenhaus; children: Carla Lord. *Education:* Attended Columbia University, 1923-26, and Jewish Theological Seminary, 1925-27. *Religion:* Jewish. *Home:* New York, N.Y.

CAREER: Journalist and author. Worked as reporter for *Brooklyn Daily Eagle,* Brooklyn, N.Y., and *New York Evening Graphic,* New York City. *Member:* Authors Guild, Authors League of America. *Awards, honors: The Time of Anger* was chosen as a Notable Children's Trade Book in the Field of Social Studies by the National Council for Social Studies and the Children's Book Council.

WRITINGS—Under name Thelma Nurenberg: *The New Red Freedom,* Wadsworth, 1932; *My Cousin, the Arab,* Abelard, 1965; *New York Colony* (history), Crowell, 1969; *The Time of Anger* (novel) Abelard, 1975. Author of "The Refugee Story" (television play), 1958. Editor of *Woman Today,* 1936-38.

SIDELIGHTS: Following a stay in the Soviet Union during the 1920s, Greenhaus contributed articles about the details of her experiences to the *Brooklyn Daily Eagle* and the *New York Times.* In 1932 these articles were collected and published in book form as *The New Red Freedom.* She wrote her two books *My Cousin, the Arab* and *The Time of Anger* to encourage peaceful relations between Israel and its Arab neighbors.

FOR MORE INFORMATION SEE: Martha E. Ward and Dorothy A. Marquardt, *Authors of Books for Young People,* Scarecrow, 1971. Obituaries: *New York Times,* August 24, 1984.

GUSTAFSON, Anita   1942-

BRIEF ENTRY: Born December 29, 1942, in Hastings, Neb. Author and playwright. Gustafson graduated with honors from Buena Vista College and received her M.A. from Drake University in 1973. A free-lance writer since 1975, she previously worked as a high school teacher and lecturer in theater arts at Drake University. Her first book for children was a retelling of American legends entitled *Monster Rolling Skull and Other Native American Tales* (Crowell, 1980). It was followed by two nonfiction works, *Burrowing Birds* (Lothrop, 1981) and *Some Feet Have Noses* (Lothrop, 1983), a look at the evolution of feet in both humans and non-humans. In addition to her juvenile works, Gustafson has written several plays, including

"Fox Boy's Night Vision" which was named a semifinalist at the Eugene O'Neill Playwright's Conference in 1978. Among her more recent writings are the young adult books *What Happened to Them?* (Scholastic Book Services, 1984) and *Guilty or Innocent?* (Holt, 1985). *Residence:* Des Moines, Iowa.

FOR MORE INFORMATION SEE: Contemporary Authors, Volume 112, Gale, 1985.

HAGUE, Kathleen

BRIEF ENTRY: Born in Ventura, Calif. Artist, photographer, and author of books for children. A former student of the Art Center College of Design in Los Angeles, Hague has collaborated with her husband, Michael, on four books for which he provided illustrations. The Hagues are retellers of *East of the Sun and West of the Moon* (Harcourt, 1980), an old Scandinavian tale about a farmer who gives away his youngest daughter to a mysterious white bear in exchange for promised riches. *Booklist* called the Hagues' interpretation "spirited and free-flowing," emphasized by watercolors in "dark, dramatic tones." Another retelling, appropriately titled *The Man Who Kept House* (Harcourt, 1981), tells the tale of a man who trades work with his wife for the day—with surprising results. In *The Legend of the Veery Bird* (Harcourt, 1985), Kathleen Hague unfolds her own fantasy about a shy boy, a lovely lady known as Keeper of the Forest, and a lost love that becomes the beautiful song of a forest bird. The husband-and-wife team also produced *Alphabears: An ABC Book* (Holt, 1984). *Residence:* Colorado Springs, Colo.

HANDVILLE, Robert (Tompkins)   1924-

PERSONAL: Born March 23, 1924, in Paterson, N.J.; son of Robert Ray (a railroad engineer) and Olive (Tompkins) Handville; married wife, Marylee (a painter), November 25, 1948; children: Robert, David. *Education:* Pratt Institute, certificate (with honors), 1948; studied painting with Ruben Tam at Brooklyn Museum Art School, 1960-64. *Home and office:* 99 Woodland Dr., Pleasantville, N.Y. 10570.

CAREER: Painter and illustrator. Charles E. Cooper Studios, illustrator, 1950-53; free-lance illustrator, 1950—; *Sports Illustrated*, New York, N.Y., illustrator and artist/reporter, 1962—; Fashion Institute of Technology, State University of New York, faculty member, 1978—. Past chairman, Artists in the Parks Program, National Park Service, Department of the Interior. Commissioned by the Presidential Citizens Advisory Stamp Council to design the Yellowstone National Park U.S. commemorative stamp, 1971-72, and the Alfred Verville U.S. commemorative air mail stamp, 1981.

EXHIBITIONS: Work has appeared in various exhibitions, including "200 Years of American Watercolor Painting," Metropolitan Museum of Art, New York City, 1966; Exhibition of the Olympic Games, Museo de la Acuarella, Instituto de Arte de Mexico, 1968; New England Silvermine Guild, New Canaan, Conn., 1970; Smithsonian Institution, Washington, D.C.; Audubon Artists; American Watercolor Society; City Center, New York; Butler Institute of American Art, Youngstown, Ohio; Woods Hole Gallery, Woods Hole, Mass.; American Institute of Graphic Arts; Royal Society of Watercolour Painters, London, England; Katonah Gallery, Katonah, N.Y.; 155th Annual Exhibition, National Academy of Design; "Champions of American Sport Show," National Portrait

Gallery, Washington, D.C., 1981 and Museum of Natural History, New York, N.Y., 1982.

Work is represented in permanent collections, including those of the John F. Kennedy White House, UNICEF, University of Denver, Syracuse University, and the University of Oklahoma. *Military service:* U.S. Air Force, 1941-45; flight radio operator, 1950-51. *Member:* American Watercolor Society (director, 1973-75), National Academy of Design, Society of Illustrators, Westchester Art Society.

AWARDS, HONORS: Has won numerous awards, including Anonymous Prize from Audubon Artists, Twenty-First New England Exhibition Award from Silvermine Guild Artists, Salamugundi Award from the American Watercolor Society, American Canadian County Award from the Twenty-Seventh New England Exhibition, Arthur Butler Award, First Honorable Mention from the American Watercolor Society, Mary Pleissner Memorial Award from the 114th Annual Exhibition of the American Watercolor Society, 1981, Ellin P. Speyer Prize from the 157th Annual Exhibition of the National Academy of Design, 1982, and Mario Cooper Award, 1983.

ILLUSTRATOR— All juvenile: William Heuman, *Missouri River Boy,* Dodd, 1959; Mary Malone, *This Was Bridget,* Dodd, 1960; Richard A. Boning, *The Long Search,* Dexter & Westbrook, 1972; Doris Gates, *Lord of the Sky: Zeus,* Viking, 1972; Bud Wilkinson (pseudonym of Charles B. Wilkinson), *Sports Illustrated Football: Offense,* Lippincott, 1972; B. Wilkinson, *Sports Illustrated Football: Defense,* Lippincott, 1973; B. Wilkinson, *Sports Illustrated Football: Quarterback,* Lippincott, 1976; Pat Jordan, *Sports Illustrated Pitching,* Lippincott, 1977; James F. Fixx, *The Complete Book of Running,* Random House, 1977; Norah Smaridge, *The Mystery of Greystone Hall,* Dodd, 1979; N. Smaridge, *The Mystery in the Old Mansions,* Dodd, 1981; N. Smaridge, *The Mysteries in the Commune,* Dodd, 1982; Robert J. Antonacci and Barbara D. Lockhart, *Tennis for Young Champions,* McGraw, 1982. Contributor of illustrations to periodicals, including *Elks* magazine and *Sports Illustrated.*

SIDELIGHTS: Born in Paterson, New Jersey in 1924, Handville's younger years were spent riding on the Lackawanna Railroad with his engineer father. His interest in art began early in grammar school on rolled paper with cheap paints. "I liked it because it was one of the things I could do successfully. One summer I worked for a farmer in Vermont and did a watercolor of us loading hay, entered it in a scholastic competition and won a prize for it."

Another of Handville's early influences was one of his high school art teachers "who took an interest in me and offered much encouragement. She took me to a one-man show in New York City. It was Andrew Wyeth's first show."

At the age of seventeen Handville enlisted in the Air Force. "'Let him try; he won't make it,' was my father's response, but I came home with papers for him to sign. I served in the Air Force for four years during World War II and was later recalled for the Korean War.

"After I came out of the service, I went back to Pratt. When I finished there I took a job with an ad agency. The job, however, was misrepresented to me, and I was out looking again. I found another job with an ad agency as a sketch artist, making good illustrations out of rough layouts. It was for embellishment to give the client an idea of what his ad was going to look like."

A cloud dark as smoke circled up from the opened box as millions of insect-like creatures flew forth. ■ (From *Lord of the Sky: Zeus* by Doris Gates. Illustrated by Robert Handville.)

(Jacket illustration by Robert Handville from *The Mysteries in the Commune* by Norah Smaridge. Illustrated by Robert Handville.)

Took a job with Charles E. Cooper Studios in 1950. "It was like a finishing school or prep school. We were about forty artists doing editorial and advertising art work.

"In 1962, I started working for *Sports Illustrated* on the editorial end. I would go out on assignment with a writer who would have a story line. He'd do the writing and I'd produce the art work. Illustrations brought variety to the work. Photographs are rigid giving [the character] a frozen form look. On the other hand, drawings are more flexible. You can make them do whatever you want them to do."

Illustrated a running book by Jim Fixx. "'What about royalties?' I asked art director Carol Owens who told me that historically this was not done with trade books. You get a flat fee. Owens expected that Fixx's book would break even. The result was, I believe, that Fixx made seven million dollars out of the book."

Commissioned by the Presidential Citizens Advisory Stamp Council to design two postage stamps. "One of the members of the Council knew that I had just returned from a trip to Yellowstone National Park and gave me the assignment. I made roughs which were presented to the committee for approval. At first they told me to do sketches of everything but the geyser. I did seven or eight such sketches of everything in the park except the geyser. Then they returned with 'I think we'll do the geyser.' Too much." Handville's second stamp has not been used as yet.

One of his paintings is in the John F. Kennedy Collection in the White House. "It was one of the first assignments I ever did for *Sports Illustrated*. I was given a script done by Kennedy on the subject of vigor and told on that Thursday that the sketch would have to be done by Sunday at the latest. The sketch was accepted and everybody was real happy. I received a letter from the White House." The sketch depicted the President walking, shown from the knees up. Handville used "a composite of photographs, a head I liked here, a stride of the body there. The kind of clothing I wanted. . . ." The dynamics of showing the President from the knees up was to give the portrait greater impact. "So I made a striding figure by showing one leg back and one forward" and the result was a figure with great vigor.

Handville is a past chairman of the "Artists in the Parks" program for the National Park Service, responsible for the selection and sending of artists to various National Parks to record their impressions with paintings, sketches, graphics, and sculpture. The works are donated to the National Park Service and form a touring exhibition to be seen in area museums throughout the United States.

FOR MORE INFORMATION SEE: M. Tinkleman, "Robert Handville," *American Artist,* July, 1977; Henry C. Pitz, *Two Hundred Years of American Illustration,* Random House, 1977; Walt Reed and Roger Reed, *The Illustrator in America 1880-1980,* Society of Illustrators, 1984.

The bookful blockhead, ignorantly read,
With loads of learned lumber in his head.
　　　　　　　　　　　—Alexander Pope

MABEL HARMER

HARMER, Mabel 1894-

PERSONAL: Born September 28, 1894, in Logan, Utah; daughter of John Jacob (a merchant) and Bertine (Berg) Spande; married Earl W. Harmer (a realtor), September 14, 1922; children: Marian Harmer Nelson, Earl W., Jr., Patricia Harmer Spencer, John Loren, Alan Spande. *Education:* Utah State University, B.S., 1923. *Politics:* Republican. *Religion:* Church of Jesus Christ of Latter-Day Saints. *Home:* 515 10 East 702, Salt Lake City, Utah 84102.

CAREER: Teacher in Logan, Utah, 1916-21; writer, 1932—; teacher of creative writing at Brigham Young University Adult Education Center, Salt Lake City, Utah, 1967-77. *Member:* National League of American Pen Women (state president, 1951-52; president, Salt Lake chapter, 1958-60), League of Utah Writers (president, Salt Lake chapter, 1945-46; state president, 1954-55), American Association of University Women, Daughters of the Utah Pioneers, Ladies Literary Club. *Awards, honors:* Named "Writer of the Year" at the annual convention of the League of Utah Writers, 1985. Has received over twenty awards for short stories, books, and articles from Utah Fine Arts Council, League of Utah Writers, and National League of American Pen Women.

WRITINGS: (With Clarissa Y. Spencer) *Brigham Young at Home,* Caxton, 1940; (with C. Y. Spencer) *One Who Was Valiant,* Caxton, 1940; *The Story of the Mormon Pioneers,* Deseret, 1943; *Famous Mascots and K-9s,* Deseret, 1945; *The Youngest Soldier,* Deseret, 1953; *Dennis of the Mormon Battalion,* Deseret, 1954; *The True Book of the Circus,* Childrens Press, 1955, published as *The Circus,* 1981; *The True Book of Pioneers* (Junior Literary Guild selection), Childrens Press, 1957, reissued as *My Easy-to-Read True Book of Pioneers,*

Grosset, 1957; *About Dams,* Melmont, 1963; *About Penguins, and Other Antarctic Animals,* Melmont, 1964; *Our Utah Pioneers,* Deseret, 1966; *The Boy Who Became a Prophet,* Bookcraft, 1969; *Lizzie: The Lost Toys Witch,* Macrae, 1970; *Upstairs to a Mine,* Utah State University Press, 1975. Contributor of daily juvenile story to *Deseret News,* 1947-57.

SIDELIGHTS: "My parents were both immigrants from Norway and my maternal grandmother lived with us during my childhood. She told me stories of Norwegian folklore and customs, which I used later in my writing. I was the eldest of seven girls—no boys. Our father died when I was fourteen and my mother had a struggle in rearing her young family.

"I taught school for seven years before my marriage to Earl W. Harmer and we became the parents of five children.

"I began writing in 1932 during the Depression when my small checks were an important part of our income. My first story to *The Friend* brought $1.25. A story in 1985 brought $125. I had the good fortune to write the home life of Brigham Young with his daughter Clarissa Young Spencer. It was in print for forty years and serves as the textbook for guides at the Beehive House, the home of Brigham Young. Another book, *The True Book of Pioneers* was the first book by a Utah author to make the Junior Literary Guild.

Emmett Kelly and Jack LeClair. ■ (From *The Circus* by Mabel Harmer. Photograph courtesy of Circus World Museum, Baraboo, Wisconsin.)

"Since my memories go back to the turn of the century, I have vivid recollections of our first telephone, electric light, and my first automobile ride (at age sixteen). In 1918 I watched a local flier land his plane out in a field. I little dreamed that in the years to come I would fly across the ocean more than a dozen times.

"I have traveled in almost every country in Europe (including Russia), the Orient, Alaska, Israel, the Caribbean and nearly all of the states.

"I am blessed with remarkably good health and at ninety enjoy a swim every morning in our indoor pool. I am also active in half a dozen clubs, including American Pen Women and the League of Utah Writers and still make at least one trip a year."

HOBBIES AND OTHER INTERESTS: Travel, classical music, book reviews.

HINES, Anna G(rossnickle) 1946-

BRIEF ENTRY: Born July 13, 1946, in Cincinnati, Ohio. A full-time author and illustrator of books for children since 1978, Hines was previously employed as a preschool and elementary-grade teacher in the California school system. Since 1983 she has produced seven picture books, all self-illustrated, and one juvenile novel. Hines related that her stories "are mostly about the discovery, imagination, playfulness, and wonder in young children's everyday lives, so often missed by busy adults." These simple joys include walking in the rain in *Taste the Raindrops* (Greenwillow, 1983), discovering spring wildflowers and birds in *Come to the Meadow* (Clarion Books, 1984), and fixing a damaged but beloved doll in *Maybe a Band-Aid Will Help* (Dutton, 1984). For middle-grade readers, *Cassie Bowen Takes Witch Lessons* (Dutton, 1985) is a novel that explores the beginning and ending of friendships and the effects of cruel teasing on someone who dares to be different. "I wrote it as a result of a dream I had," said Hines. "The basic plot and characters were all in that dream." She is currently working on another self-illustrated picture book entitled *Just Emily. Address:* P.O. Box 923, Twain Harte, Calif. 95383.

FOR MORE INFORMATION SEE: Contemporary Authors, Volume 114, Gale, 1985.

HOLMGREN, Helen Jean 1930- (George Ellen Holmgren)

PERSONAL: Born June 2, 1930, in Chicago, Ill.; daughter of George R. (a sheet metal worker) and Helen (Jesky) Holmgren. *Education:* Chicago Academy of Fine Arts, certificate, 1950; Rosary College, A.B., 1958; Pius XII Institute, M.A., 1961. *Politics:* Democrat. *Home and office:* 1515 West Ogden Ave., La Grange Park, Ill. 60525.

CAREER: Walgreen Agency, Chicago, Ill., layout artist and illustrator, 1950-51; entered Congregation of the Sisters of St. Joseph of La Grange (C.S.J.), 1952, began religious profession, 1958—. Art teacher and department chairman at private academy in La Grange Park, Ill., 1958-59; part-time instructor in art at College of DuPage, Glen Ellyn, Ill., 1968-73; founder and director of IKON School of Art, 1973—. Artist and lecturer, with art exhibits all over the United States and paintings in private collections; designer of stained glass works at Emil Frei Studio, summers, 1965-66. Member of summer faculty

HELEN JEAN HOLMGREN

at Rosary College, La Grange campus, 1961, and Edgewood College, 1966. *Member:* Chicago Art Institute, Chicago Calligraphy Collective. *Awards, honors:* First prize from Hinsdale Community Artists, 1964; honorable mention from Oakbrook Fine Arts Promenade, 1964.

ILLUSTRATOR—Under name George Ellen Holmgren: Florence Marie Gerdes, C.S.J., *The Aeneid: A Retelling for Young People,* St. Martin's Press, 1969; Paul A. Schreivogel, *Small Prayers to Small Children about Big and Little Things,* Augsburg, 1970; Francis B. Connors, *Voyages in English,* Loyola University Press, 1979. Cover art for *Saints and Feast Days: Lives of the Saints,* Loyola University Press, 1985. Contributor to education and art magazines.

WORK IN PROGRESS: Tell Me about Your Father, a self-illustrated children's religious book; an autobiography; *I Can See,* a self-illustrated children's book on perceptions.

SIDELIGHTS: "I was born and raised on the west side of Chicago, and I have always loved this city. Each time I go to the Loop, or the lakefront, a feeling of excitement comes over me. I find it vital and refreshing.

"As an only child in a middle-class family, I devoted much time to cut-outs, drawing, sewing for my doll, and even building a doghouse. At one time I thought I would like to be an architect. My first painting of 'Hunting Dogs' was a gift to my father.

"After my art studies and work as a commercial artist, I made the decision to join the religious profession. Looking back to my childhood days has provided me with happy memories and ideas for children's stories.

"*The Aeneid: A Retelling for Young People* came about after my return from Europe and studies in Florence. I was truly in love with that country and its people, and the opportunity to bring the riches of that land to our American children was a thrilling concept. I delighted in studying the Etruscan vases and sources that related to the time of the *Aeneid* in order that the young reader might absorb the spirit of the art work (in its stylized manner) in context.

"Return trips to Europe bring a different understanding, appreciation, and empathy with friends and other people there. Traveling as an artist in Israel, France, and Scandinavia brought

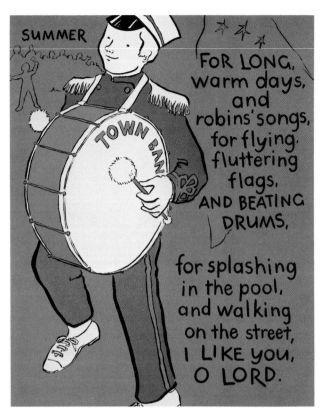

SUMMER

FoR LONG,
warm days,
and
robins' songs,
for flying
fluttering
flags,
AND BEATING
DRUMS,

for splashing
in the pool,
and walking
on the street,
I LIKE you,
O LORD.

TOWN BAN...

(From *Small Prayers for Small Children about Big and Little Things* by Paul A. Schreivogel. Illustrated by George Ellen Holmgren.)

a deep awareness of the people and their land, as they allowed me to make portraits, and hear stories.

"My love of color shows itself in my painting and stained glass work in an expressive way. Designing eleven hundred square feet of glass for the Motherhouse chapel in La Grange was a high point in my professional career. I enjoy designing beautiful works for the church, such as vestments, tabernacles, and candlesticks. Study in liturgical art and stained glass provided a fine background, and I have a special reverence for icons."

HORWITZ, Elinor Lander

PERSONAL: Born in New Haven, Conn.; daughter of Harry P. (a lawyer) and Gertrude (a reporter; maiden name, Pearson) Lander; married Norman H. Horwitz (a neurosurgeon); children: Erica, Joshua, Anthony. *Education:* Smith College, A.B. *Home:* 3807 Bradley Lane, Chevy Chase, Md. 20815. *Agent:* Marilyn Marlow, Curtis Brown Ltd., 575 Madison Ave., New York, N.Y. 10022.

CAREER: Writer. *Awards, honors:* Science Writer's Award, American Dental Association, 1973, for article on orthodontics in *Washingtonian* magazine; *Mountain People, Mountain Crafts* was included on *School Library Journal*'s Book List, 1974; *Contemporary American Folk Artists* was selected one of the "Children's Books of the Year," 1975, by the Child Study Association; *When the Sky Is Like Lace* was chosen one of *New York Times* Outstanding Book of the Year, 1975.

WRITINGS—Juvenile; nonfiction, except as indicated; published by Lippincott, except as indicated: *The Strange Story of the Frog Who Became a Prince* (fiction; illustrated by John Heinly), Delacorte, 1971; *The Soothsayer's Handbook: A Guide to Bad Signs and Good Vibrations,* 1972; *Communes in America: A Place Just Right,* 1972; *Capital Punishment U.S.A.,* 1973; *Mountain People, Mountain Crafts* (illustrated with photographs by sons, Joshua Horwitz and Anthony Horwitz), 1974; *When the Sky Is Like Lace* (fiction; illustrated by Barbara Cooney), 1975; *Contemporary American Folk Artists* (illustrated with photographs by J. Horwitz), 1975; *The Bird, the Banner and Uncle Sam: Images of America in Folk and Popular Art,* 1976; *A Child's Garden of Sculpture,* Washingtonian Books, 1976; *Madness, Magic, and Medicine: The Treatment and Mistreatment of the Mentally Ill,* 1977; *On the Land: American Agriculture from Past to Present,* Atheneum, 1980; *Sometimes It Happens* (fiction; illustrated by Susan Jeschke), Harper, 1981; *How to Wreck a Building* (ALA Notable Book; illustrated with photographs by J. Horwitz), Pantheon, 1982.

Other: *Our Nation's Wetlands,* U.S. Government Printing Office, 1978; *Our Nation's Lakes,* U.S. Government Printing Office, 1980.

Author of column "The Uncommon Shopper" in the *Washington Star* for four years. Contributor to *Washington Post* and other newspapers and national magazines.

ADAPTATIONS: "The Strange Story of the Frog Who Became a Prince" (animated cartoon), Xerox Corp., 1974. *The Strange Story of the Frog Who Became a Prince* was made into an opera by Edward Barnes in 1981.

HOBBIES AND OTHER INTERESTS: Art, environment, science and medicine, travel, birdwatching.

FOR MORE INFORMATION SEE: New York Times Book Review, June 2, 1974, September 14, 1975, April 25, 1982.

Elinor Lander Horwitz with son, Joshua.

She took a wet newspaper out of her wet pocket. ■ (From *The Strange Story of the Frog Who Became a Prince* by Elinor Lander Horwitz. Illustrated by John Heinly.)

(From "Annie Norn and the Fin Folk" in *The Faber Book of Northern Folk-Tales*, edited by Kevin Crossley-Holland. Illustrated by Alan Howard.)

HOWARD, Alan 1922-

PERSONAL: Born December 1, 1922, in Nottingham, England; son of Cecil (a teacher) and Mabel (a housewife; maiden name, Beeton) Howard; married Margaret Collins (an artist), October, 1953; children: three. *Education:* Caius College, Cambridge, B.A., 1942, M.A., 1952; studied at School of Oriental and African Studies, London, England, 1943-45, and Nottingham College of Arts and Crafts, 1949-51. *Home:* 53 Powis Rd., Ashton-on-Ribble, Preston PR2 1AD, England.

CAREER: Graphic designer and illustrator of books for children. *Military service:* British Intelligence Corps, 1941-45.

*ILLUSTRATOR—*All for children: Sergei Prokofiev, *Peter and the Wolf,* Faber, 1951, reissued, 1979; Erik Hutchinson, *Roof-Top World,* Faber, 1956; David E. Walker, *Fat Cat Pimpernel,* Faber, 1958, Barnes, 1960; Walter de la Mare, *Tales Told Again,* Knopf, 1959.

D. E. Walker, *Pimpernel and the Poodle,* Barnes, 1960; E. Hutchinson, *Night of the Michaelmas Moon,* Faber, 1961, Transatlantic, 1975; Kathleen Lines, editor, *The Faber Storybook,* Faber, 1961; E. Hutchinson, *Limping Ginger of London Town,* Faber, 1962; Kornei Chukovsky, *Crocodile,* adapted by Richard Coe, Faber, 1964; Jill Tomlinson, *The Bus That Went to Church,* Faber, 1965; K. Lines, editor, *Tales of Magic and Enchantment,* Faber, 1966; J. Tomlinson, *Patti Finds an Orchestra,* Faber, 1966; Robert Browning, *The Pied Piper of Hamelin,* Faber, 1967; *Dick Whittington and His Cat,* Faber, 1967; Donald Mitchell, compiler, *The Faber Book of Nursery Songs,* arranged by Carey Blyton, Faber, 1968, published as *Every Child's Book of Nursery Songs,* Crown, 1969; Eilís Dillon, *The Voyage of Mael Duin,* Faber, 1969.

David and Goliath, Faber, 1970; Rhiannon Davies Jones, *Hwiangerddi Gwreiddiol* (poetry; title means ''Original Nursery Rhymes''), Gwasg Gomer (Llandysul, Wales), 1973; Buddug Medi Williams, *Chwyrlibwm* (title means ''Whizz-bang''), Llyfrau'r Faner, 1974; T. Llew Jones, *Helicopter! Help! a Storïau Evaill* (title means ''Helicopter! Help! and Other Stories''), Christopher Davies, 1975; Elfyn Pritchard, *Y Gath a Gollodd ei Grwndi* (title means ''The Cat That Lost Her Purr''), Gwasg Gomer, 1975; Catherine Storr, *The Painter and the Fish,* Faber, 1975; Anwen P. Williams, *Antur Elin a Gwenno* (title means ''Elin and Gwenno's Adventure''), Gwasg Gomer, 1976; Kevin Crossley-Holland, editor, *The Faber Book of Northern Legends,* Faber, 1977; Megan Williams, *Pecyn Deg* (title means ''Pack of Ten''), Gwasg Gomer, 1977; K. Crossley-Holland, editor, *The Faber Book of Northern Folktales,* Faber, 1980; W. de la Mare, *Tales Told Again,* Faber, 1980; K. Lines, editor, *The Faber Book of Magical Tales,* Faber, 1985.

SIDELIGHTS: ''I work full-time as a graphic designer and regard children's book illustration as a pastime. In recent years I have become more concerned with trying to stop the damage that people are inflicting on the real world and have had less time for the imaginary world of children's books.

''As an illustrator I am not interested in medium or technique as such, but regard the finished result as what really matters. I use rapidograph and felt tip markers quite a lot. I used litho and crayon in my earlier work, but discarded them as too limiting.

''My favorite authors are E. Nesbit, C. S. Lewis, J.R.R. Tolkien, Lewis Carroll, Charles Williams, George MacDonald, Anthony Trollop; Botticelli and Henri Rousseau, my favorite artists.''

HOBBIES AND OTHER INTERESTS: Countryside, beautiful buildings (old and new), Beethoven, Beatles, walking, dancing, conducting tourists around historic towns.

FOR MORE INFORMATION SEE: Lee Kingman and others, compilers, *Illustrators of Children's Books: 1957-1966,* Horn Book, 1968; Bettina Hürlimann, *Picture-Book World,* World Publishing, 1969.

HUNTER, Bernice Thurman 1922-

BRIEF ENTRY: Born November 3, 1922, in Toronto, Ontario, Canada. Canadian author of short stories and books for children. At the age of fourteen, Hunter received some advice from well-known Canadian author L. M. Montgomery that, unfortunately, delayed her writing career for many years. Montgomery told Hunter that the one thing a writer must have above all else is a higher education. For Hunter, growing up during the Depression in a poverty stricken family, this proved to be an insurmountable obstacle. She became a bookkeeper instead, although she never ceased to write stories. Years later, following the birth of her first grandchild, Hunter submitted an article entitled ''A Grandchild Can Make Life Beautiful Again'' to the *Toronto Star.* Alexander Ross, then a columnist for the newspaper, ran the piece and encouraged Hunter to continue writing. Acting upon this advice, she subsequently became the author of *That Scatterbrain Booky* (Scholastic-Tab, 1981), a nostalgic look at life in Toronto during the Depression era. Autobiographical in nature, this children's novel received the 1981 IODE Book Award and was a finalist in the 1982 Toronto Book Awards. Hunter also produced two sequels, *With Love from Booky* (Scholastic-Tab, 1983), a Ruth Schwartz Book Award finalist, and *As Ever, Booky* (Scholastic-Tab, 1985). Hunter's other works include *A Place for Margaret* (Scholastic-Tab, 1984), for which she also drew from her childhood memories. Currently, she is working on a sequel tentatively titled *Margaret, On Her Way. Home:* 39 Leeswood Cres, Scarborough, Ontario, Canada M1S 2P4.

FOR MORE INFORMATION SEE: Toronto Star, October 15, 1981; *Scarborough Mirror,* October 21, 1981; *Children's Book News,* December, 1983.

HURD, Thacher 1949-

BRIEF ENTRY: Born March 6, 1949, in Burlington, Vt. Author and illustrator of picture books for children. Hurd's first book, *Little Dog Dreaming* (Harper, 1965), was written in collaboration with his mother, Edith Thacher Hurd, and illustrated by his father, Clement Hurd. As the son of respected contributors to children's literature, Hurd's chosen field seemed almost inevitable. He remembers ''an air of creativity around the house'' while growing up and a feeling that he ''would end up doing something in the creative arts.'' Hurd did not, however, plunge directly into children's books. After attending the University of California at Berkeley for one year and working as an apprentice printer, he received his B.F.A. from the California College of Arts and Crafts in 1972. He then became a self-employed builder, designer, and cabinetmaker until 1978, beginning his career as an author and illustrator in 1974. Since 1983 Hurd, his wife Olivia, and his father have been responsible for the operation of the Peaceable Kingdom Press, which reproduces illustrations from children's books in poster form.

Hurd described his first attempted children's works as ''stiff, pale fairy tales with watery morals and dangling plots.'' The turning point came when he ''became aware of my own childhood memories and childlike feelings within myself.'' His first self-illustrated picture book, *The Old Chair* (Greenwillow, 1978), resulted from past remembrances of a comfortable family chair. ''Spare sketches of homey scenes,'' observed *School Library Journal,* ''echo the soothing tone of the story.'' The same gentleness pervades Hurd's bedtime story, *The Quiet Evening* (Greenwillow, 1978), labeled ''a dreamlike mood piece'' by *Horn Book.* ''The serene, nighttime mood is textually established,'' added *Booklist.* ''. . . Lovely, soothing, and appropriately quiet.''

Hurd also strives to provide characters and scenes easily identified by city-dwelling children. Thus, in *Hobo Dog* (Scholastic Book Services, 1980) the main character lives in a junkyard by the railroad tracks, while the tom in *Axle the Freeway Cat* (Harper, 1981) makes his home in an abandoned car under a freeway overpass. In 1985 Hurd received first prize for illustration in the *Boston Globe-Horn Book* Awards competition for *Mama Don't Allow* (Harper, 1984), based on the old jazz song. According to *School Library Journal,* this story of a young possum and his raucous Swamp Band contains ''multicolored full-spread watercolor illustrations [that] are stunningly bright and full of movement.'' *Wilson Library Bulletin* agreed, noting that ''Hurd uses bright, bold color with no concern for tradition. . . . [He] knows the rules, but is simply being discriminating in their use.'' Hurd's other books are *Mystery on the Docks* (Harper, 1983) and *Hobo Dog in the Ghost Town* (Scholastic Book Services, 1985). *Home:* 2954 Hillegass, Berkeley, Calif. 94705.

FOR MORE INFORMATION SEE: Oakland Tribune, November 26, 1981; *Contemporary Authors,* Volume 106, Gale, 1982; *Horn Book,* January-February, 1986.

JAMES, Elizabeth   1942-
(Katherine Duval, James Lloyd, E. James Lloyd; Elizabeth Carroll, Beverly Hastings, joint pseudonyms)

PERSONAL: Born November 5, 1942, in Pittsburgh, Pa.; daughter of Curtis Blakeslee (a salesman) and Sally (a banker; maiden name, Lloyd) James; married J. David Marks (a motion picture executive), June 24, 1973. *Education:* Colorado College, B.A., 1963. *Residence:* Beverly Hills, Calif.

CAREER: United Air Lines, Los Angeles, Calif., stewardess, 1963-65, Otis Productions, Los Angeles, Calif., writer and female lead in the motion picture ''Born Losers,'' 1965-67; free-lance writer, 1965—. Assistant director, Sullivan Educational Systems (publisher), 1970-72; consultant to Stanford Research Institute in evaluating Project Follow Through, 1972; consultant to Education Commission of the States, Denver, Colo., developing television programs on early childhood development, 1972-73. Member of the board of directors, Neighbors of Watts, 1978—. *Member:* Screen Actors Guild, Society of Children's Book Writers, Authors Guild, Women's National Book Association, Writers Guild of America (West), Southern California Council on Literature for Children and Young People, Mystery Writers of America, P.E.N.

WRITINGS—Juvenile; all with Carol Barkin, except as noted; all published by Lothrop, except as noted: *The Simple Facts of Simple Machines* (illustrated with photographs by Daniel Dorn, Jr. and with diagrams by Susan Stan), 1975; *Slapdash Sewing* (illustrated by Rita Flodén Leydon), 1975; (with Lee Arthur and Judith B. Taylor) *Sportsmath: How It Works,* 1975; *Slapdash Cooking* (illustrated by R. F. Leydon), 1976; *Slapdash Alterations: How to Recycle Your Wardrobe* (illustrated by R. F. Leydon), 1977; *Slapdash Decorating* (illustrated by

For privacy, use a flashlight at midnight under the covers! ■ (From *How to Keep a Secret: Writing and Talking in Code* by Elizabeth James and Carol Barkin. Illustrated by Joel Schick.)

The time anyone spends working is worth whatever an employer is willing to pay for it. ■ (From *How to Grow a Hundred Dollars* by Elizabeth James and Carol Barkin. Illustrated by Joel Schick.)

R. F. Leydon), 1977; *How to Keep a Secret: Writing and Talking in Code* (illustrated by Joel Schick), 1978; *What Do You Mean by "Average"? Means, Medians, and Modes* (illustrated by J. Schick), 1978; *How to Grow a Hundred Dollars* (illustrated by J. Schick), 1979.

How to Write a Term Paper, introduction by Leland B. Jacobs, 1980; *The Complete Babysitter's Handbook* (illustrated by R. F. Leydon), Wanderer, 1980; *A Place of Your Own* (illustrated with photographs by Lou Jacobs, Jr.), Dutton, 1981; (with Malka Drucker) *Series TV: How a Show Is Made*, Clarion, 1983; *How to Write a Great School Report*, introduction by M. Jean Greenlaw, 1983; *The Scary Halloween Costume Book* (illustrated by Katherine Coville), 1983; (under joint pseudonym Elizabeth Carroll) *Summer Love*, Wanderer, 1983; (under joint pseudonym Beverly Hastings) *Watcher in the Dark*, Pacer, 1986; *How to Write Your Best Book Report*, 1986.

"Transition" series; all with C. Barkin; all illustrated with photographs by Heinz Kluetmeier; all published by Raintree, 1975: *Are We Still Best Friends?*; *Doing Things Together*; *I'd Rather Stay Home*; *Sometimes I Hate School*.

"Money" series; all with C. Barkin; all published by Raintree, 1977: *Managing Your Money* (illustrated by Santos Paniagua); *What Is Money?* (illustrated by Dennis Hockerman); *Understanding Money* (illustrated by D. Hockerman).

Adult: *Ziegfeld: The Man and His Women* (novelization; under pseudonym Katherine Duval), Paradise, 1978; (with Carol Barkin, under joint pseudonym Beverly Hastings) *Don't Talk to Strangers* (novel), Jove, 1980; *Secrets* (novel), Berkley, 1983; (with C. Barkin) *Helpful Hints for Your Pregnancy*, Fireside, 1984; (with C. Barkin, under joint pseudonym Beverly Hastings) *Don't Walk Home Alone* (novel), Jove, 1985.

Also author of several screenplays and television dramas, including (under pseudonym James Lloyd) "Born Losers," starring Tom Laughlin and Elizabeth James, American International Pictures, 1967, and (under pseudonym E. James Lloyd) "Loose Change," Willgeorge Productions, 1971.

WORK IN PROGRESS: Another adult novel; *Don't Cry Little Girl*, an adult novel with Carol Barkin under joint pseudonym Beverly Hastings; several juvenile and young adult projects, both fiction and nonfiction with Carol Barkin.

SIDELIGHTS: "As described to me by college recruiters, jobs in mathematics sounded incredibly boring. So upon graduation I took a job as an airline stewardess in order to see the world.

"I had moved to Los Angeles, and the magic of the movies beckoned. My first screenplay, 'Born Losers,' was produced independently and released by American International Pictures in 1967. It was the first of the 'Billy Jack' films and I played the female lead opposite Tom Laughlin who played Billy Jack.

"After that, I wrote a number of other screenplays for Fox, American International Pictures, and independent producers, as well as a television Movie-of-the-Week.

"I also did some consulting for educational films and then began writing books. The first one was published in 1975.

"For the past several years I have been engaged primarily in writing books and occasional screenplays. I enjoy the different and unique challenges in both collaborative writing and working alone, and I have produced scripts and books both ways.

"My formal education did not include courses in writing. Though writing classes may be helpful, I have found that extensive reading, life experience, a good grasp of the language, and logical thought processes are invaluable in writing both fiction and nonfiction.

"Every book requires research, but I find it impossible to write from library research alone. For both fiction and nonfiction I must have some sort of intuitive grasp of the subject matter before I can begin. I need to already know something about the topic, to be interested in that theme or problem, to care about it. If parts of the book are set in locations I'm unfamiliar with, I go there. I require the details of ambience from my own experience to provide an environment for my characters;

I can't pick up this feel for a setting by reading about it. Similarly, if a book has projects and instructions, I try everything out to make sure it works and that it works by following the directions I've written. I am forced to follow the old adage 'write what you know.'

"In doing travel research, the one item I find indispensable is a good camera. I take terrible notes; my handwriting is almost illegible, even to me. And I can't encompass in a few phrases the wealth of details I recapture in a bunch of snapshots. I don't waste time taking postcard-type pictures; I buy those. Instead, I look for everyday items—street signs, crowds on sidewalks, passing cars and buses and taxis and emergency vehicles, garden arrangements, odd bits of architecture. I find it jarring to read about a city I know and see mistakes in geography or the colors of the police cars or the look of the houses, no matter how interesting the story. I also get comprehensive local maps and mark them as I go. And I save matchbooks, leaflets, and brochures. They bring back all sorts of related memories when I sift through them as I write.

"As to writing itself, I agree with many of my writer friends who say it's always nicest to 'have written.' In retrospect, everything I've done was fairly easy. I tend to forget the time and the agonizing and the rewriting and am always surprised at how difficult it is to face that blank page at the beginning of a project. I have no solutions other than to start at the beginning and just keep plugging along until you reach the end. Whether fiction or nonfiction, working in collaboration

(From the movie "Born Losers," starring Tom Laughlin. Screenplay by E. James Lloyd. Produced by American International, 1967.)

ELIZABETH JAMES

or alone, I find it essential to have a mental map of where I'm going and how I plan to get there. However, there is no substitute for that putting of one word after another to create a gripping word-picture that captures the vision of the mind's eye.

"Every experience I have, every place I go, every person I meet, all provide grist for the mill. Everything just gets shoved into the pot we all have bubbling away on the back burner of the brain."

HOBBIES AND OTHER INTERESTS: Reading, traveling, tennis, gardening, and living life.

KENT, John Wellington   1920-1985
(Jack Kent)

OBITUARY NOTICE—See sketch in *SATA* Volume 24: Born March 10, 1920, in Burlington, Iowa; died of leukemia, October 18, 1985, in San Antonio, Tex. Cartoonist, illustrator, and author. Kent worked as a free-lance commercial artist and cartoonist between 1935 and 1950. During this time, he began drawing the syndicated comic strip "King Aroo" which ran for fifteen years. In 1965 Kent returned to free-lance work, and in 1968 he became a full-time author and illustrator of children's books. Kent subsequently produced over seventy juvenile works, including *Just Only John, Fly Away Home, The Blah, The Scribble Monster, Joey,* and *Joey Runs Away.*

FOR MORE INFORMATION SEE: Contemporary Authors, Volumes 85-88, Gale, 1980. Obituaries: *San Antonio Express-News,* October 21, 1985; *Publishers Weekly,* November 8, 1985; *School Library Journal,* December, 1985.

KLASS, Sheila Solomon   1927-

PERSONAL: Born November 6, 1927, in Brooklyn, N.Y.; daughter of Abraham Louis (a presser) and Virginia (Glatter) Solomon; married Morton Klass (a professor of anthropology), May 2, 1953; children: Perri Elizabeth, David Arnold, Judith Alexandra. *Education:* Brooklyn College (now Brooklyn College of the City University of New York), B.A., 1949; University of Iowa, M.A., 1951, M.F.A., 1953. *Religion:* Jewish. *Home:* 330 Sylvan Ave., Leonia, N.J. 07605. *Agent:* Molly Friedrich, Aaron M. Priest Literary Agency, 565 Fifth Ave., New York, N.Y. 10017. *Office:* Department of English, Manhattan Community College of the City University of New York, 199 Chambers Street, New York, N.Y. 10007.

CAREER: Worked as an aide in a psychopathic hospital in Iowa City, Iowa, 1949-51; English teacher in junior high school in New York City, 1951-57; Manhattan Community College of the City University of New York, New York City, assistant professor, 1968-73, associate professor, 1973-82, professor of English, 1982—. Guest at Yaddo colony, 1974. *Member:* International P.E.N. *Awards, honors:* Bicentennial Prize from Leonia Drama Guild, 1976, for one-act play, "Otherwise It Only Makes One Hundred Ninety-Nine."

WRITINGS—Young adult novels: *Nobody Knows Me in Miami,* Scribner, 1981; *To See My Mother Dance,* Scribner, 1981; *Alive and Starting Over,* Scribner, 1983; *The Bennington Stitch,* Scribner, 1985.

Other: *Come Back on Monday,* Abelard, 1960; *Everyone in This House Makes Babies,* Doubleday, 1964; *Bahadur Means Hero,* Gambit, 1969; *A Perpetual Surprise,* Apple-wood, 1981. Also author of one-act play, "Otherwise It Only Makes One Hundred Ninety-Nine." Contributor of short stories and humorous articles to *Hadassah, Bergen Record, New York Times,* and other publications.

SHEILA SOLOMON KLASS

WORK IN PROGRESS: A young adult novel.

SIDELIGHTS: "I've been a writer since adolescence. I write because writing is supreme pleasure. Creating a story on paper is a peculiar joy unlike any other. Just the writing itself is the first reward. Later, if a relative or a friend reads the work, and admires it, the delight is heightened. Then, if an editor likes it well enough to print it, the delight bursts all boundaries. And if the book is printed and makes money, that is sheer ecstasy. But it is irrelevant to the writing itself.

"My life and what happens around me, what I hear about and read about—these are the sources that initiate the act of writing. But, almost immediately, imagination takes over and the story acquires its own energy and direction. What *really* happened is not pertinent. It's forgotten. Fiction is not autobiography. It is experience transmuted by the imagination in inexplicable ways. It has its own truth and its own life.

"Sometimes a character I create is so interesting and real to me, I cannot desert him/her and so I do a second book. Thus, Bahadur, an illiterate humorous Nepali in *Bahadur Means Hero* reappears in *A Perpetual Surprise* twelve years after I thought I was through with him, and Jessica Van Norden in *To See My Mother Dance* continues as the main character in *Alive and Starting Over*.

"I hope my writing entertains, for while it may instruct the mind, or purge the emotions, or ennoble the spirit, if it doesn't offer diversion I feel it is unsuccessful.

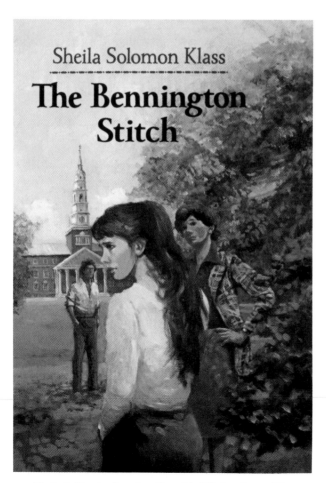

(Jacket illustration by Ronald Himler from *The Bennington Stitch* by Sheila Solomon Klass.)

"I write about people dealing with important issues in their lives; my book *The Bennington Stitch,* for example, follows several seniors through that last year in high school when test results and college applications can cause so much stress.

"The pleasure in the act of writing makes teaching writing a delightful job. What I am doing is introducing students to the highest high in the whole world—the high that is achieved by creating new and wonderful works out of their heads.

"All three of my children are writers. This I think, is my greatest delight: That my children love writing so much."

FOR MORE INFORMATION SEE: Los Angeles Times, March 19, 1982.

KLEIN, Aaron E. 1930-
(A. Edward Little)

PERSONAL: Born July 8, 1930, in Atlanta, Ga.; son of Samuel Joseph and Pearl (Natkoff) Klein; married Cynthia Lee (a choral director and teacher); children: Eric, Jason. *Education:* University of Pennsylvania, B.A., 1953; University of Bridgeport, M.S., 1958; additional graduate study at Yale University, 1960, 1964-65, and Wesleyan University, Middletown, Conn., 1961-64. *Politics:* "No party affiliation—liberal orientation." *Religion:* "No affiliation—Jewish background." *Home:* 2346 Redwood Rd., Scotch Plains, N.J. 07076.

CAREER: Worked as driving instructor, veterinary assistant, Good Humor man, salesman, and window shade-maker, among other jobs, to get through college and augment his teacher's pay; junior high school teacher in New Haven, Conn., 1957-58; high school science and mathematics teacher in Woodbridge, Conn., 1958-63; Western Connecticut State College, Danbury, instructor in biology, 1963-66; Silver Burdett Co., Morristown, N.J., science editor, 1966-68; John Wiley & Sons, Inc., New York, N.Y., science project editor, 1968-70; Xerox Publishing Division, Middletown, Conn., managing editor, 1970-78; writer and editor of articles, newsletters, books, and visual materials, New Haven, Conn., 1978-81; Patient Care Communications, Darien, Conn., senior editor, 1981-83; Medical Education Programs, Wilton, Conn., senior medical writer, 1984; MED Communications, Woodbridge, N.J., director of scientific services, 1984-86. University of Bridgeport, visiting lecturer, 1961-64; Museum of Art, Science, and Industry, Bridgeport, Conn., visiting scientist, 1964-66. *Military service:* U.S. Navy, 1955-57. *Member:* American Association for the Advancement of Science, National Science Teachers Association, National Association of Biology Teachers, American Institute of Biological Sciences.

WRITINGS: (Ghost writer) *Table Top Physics,* Doubleday, 1970; *Threads of Life: Genetics from Aristotle to DNA,* Natural History Press, 1970; *The Hidden Contributors: Black Scientists and Inventors in America,* Doubleday, 1971; (with W. E. Pearce) *Transistors and Circuits: Electronics for Young Experimenters,* Doubleday, 1971; *Trial by Fury: The Polio Vaccine Controversy,* Scribner, 1972; *Test Tubes and Beakers,* Doubleday, 1972; (with C. T. Prime) *Seedlings and Soil: Botany for Young Experimenters,* Doubleday, 1973; *Beyond Time and Matter: A Sensory Look at ESP,* Doubleday, 1973; *The Electron Microscope: A Tool of Discovery,* McGraw, 1974; (under pseudonym A. Edward Little) *Automobile Mechanics,* F. Watts, 1974.

(With John E. DeWaard) *Electric Cars,* Doubleday, 1977; *You and Your Body: A Book of Experiments to Perform on Your-*

self, Doubleday, 1977; *Medical Tests and You,* Grosset, 1978; *Science and the Supernatural: A Scientific Overview of the Occult,* Doubleday, 1979; (with wife, Cynthia L. Klein) *Mind Trips: The Story of Consciousness-Raising Movement,* Doubleday, 1979; *How to Watch and Control Your Blood Pressure,* Grosset, 1979.

The Complete Beginners Guide to Microscopes and Telescopes, Doubleday, 1981; *The Parasites We Humans Harbor,* Elsevier/Nelson, 1982; (with C. L. Klein) *The Better Mousetrap: A Miscellany of Gadgets, Labor-Saving Devices, and Inventions That Intrigue,* Beaufort Books, 1982; *Super Trains,* Bison, 1985; *The New York Central,* Bison, 1985; *Encyclopedia of North American Railways,* Bison, 1986.

"Doubleday Companion to . . ." series; all published by Doubleday, except as noted: *Doubleday Companion to Animals and Their Ways,* 1968; . . . *Crust of the Earth,* 1968, (workbook) Natural History Press, 1968; . . . *World Beneath the Oceans,* 1968, (workbook) Natural History Press, 1968; . . . *Men Without Machines,* 1969.

Writer of teaching materials in biology for Standard Publishing; ghost-writer of life science laboratory manual for Harcourt; editor of *Current Science* magazine, 1972-78.

Contributor to *Patient Care, A Nursing Dictionary, The New Book of Knowledge, Science Update, Dictionary of American History, Dictionary of Black History, The Science Teacher* and *Current Science.*

WORK IN PROGRESS: A book of fiction. *The Men Who Built the Railroads,* an account of the contributions of several key people in the building of railroads in the U.S. and in Canada.

Few people in the world today are not affected in some way by automobiles. ■ (From *Auto Mechanics: An Introduction and Guide* by A. Edward Little. Illustrated by Michael Horen.)

SIDELIGHTS: "I suppose I have always wanted to write. When I was eight or nine I produced a little neighborhood newspaper that had a circulation of about two—myself and my older sister. At seventeen I did a newspaper for a boys' club and when I was in the Navy I wrote a newspaper for my unit.

"After being discharged from the Navy I started to teach at a junior high school in New Haven, Connecticut. In subsequent years I taught life sciences at a high school and a couple of small colleges. It turned out that some of my students at the college were associated with publishing. They encouraged me to try writing and made some key introductions to people in the business. I started by writing some small activity booklets to accompany a juvenile science series published by Doubleday. My first hardcover book, *Threads of Life,* was published in 1970, and since that time I have made my living as an editor and writer."

Klein's goal is to become known as a science writer for the laity. He is fluent in Yiddish; reads, writes, and speaks German; reads, writes, and understands a little Russian.

FOR MORE INFORMATION SEE: Dorothy A. Marquardt and Martha E. Ward, *Authors of Books for Young People,* 2nd edition supplement, Scarecrow, 1979.

KLEIN, Robin 1936-

BRIEF ENTRY: Born February 28, 1936, in Kempsey, Australia. The author of nearly twenty books for children, Klein has been a full-time writer since 1981. Prior to that time, she held such positions as warehouse "tea lady," bookshop assistant, and copper enamelist. Klein revealed that she writes for children "because I adore their company, honesty, and sense of fun." She added: "Most of my books seem to have a strong female character, capable of dealing with any problem that arises, perhaps because I was a very cowardly child and admired people like that." She has received several awards for her works, including a special mention in the Critici in Erba Awards at the 1979 Bologna Children's Book Fair for her first book, *The Giraffe in Pepperell Street* (Hodder & Stoughton, 1978); the Australian Children's Book of the Year Award, 1983, for *Thing* (Oxford University Press, 1982); and a "highly commended" book of the year award from the Children's Book Council of Australia, 1984, for *Penny Pollard's Diary* (Oxford University Press, 1983). In addition, she was the recipient of a senior fellowship grant from the Arts Council of Australia literature board in 1985.

Among Klein's other books for children are *People Might Hear You* (Penguin, 1983), *Hating Alison Ashley* (Penguin, 1984), *Brock and the Dragon* (Hodder & Stoughton, 1984), a sequel to *Thing* entitled *Thingnapped!* (Oxford University Press, 1984), *Halfway across the World and Turn Left* (Penguin, 1985), *The Princess Who Hated It* (Omnibus Books, 1986), and *Boss of the Pool,* (Omnibus Books, 1986). She is also a contributor of stories, poems, and plays to *New South Wales School Magazine* and publications of the Victorian Department of Education. *Home:* 38 Monbulk Rd., Belgrave, Victoria 3160, Australia.

FOR MORE INFORMATION SEE: Contemporary Authors, Volume 116, Gale, 1986.

Some of my best friends are children. In fact, all of my best friends are children.

—J.D. Salinger

LANCASTER, Matthew 1973(?)-1983

OBITUARY NOTICE: Born about 1973; died March, 1983. Author and illustrator. Lancaster wrote his first and only book, *Hang Toughf,* after becoming stricken with Ewing's sarcoma—a form of cancer—around the age of ten. *Hang Toughf,* dedicated to "all people with cancer," describes the young writer's experience with radiation therapy and chemotherapy, offering advice and encouragement to other cancer victims with what *Los Angeles Times Book Review* critic Kristiana Gregory called "wisdom exceeding his few years." Lancaster's original drawings accompany a poignant but simple text, complete with misspelled words. Taking the stance that his disease "wasn't fair," he notes nevertheless that "it happened, and you and I have to except it." Gregory concluded in her review that "Matthew's spirit is so like every child's, and his wish to give comfort is an endearing gift. He left quite a legacy when he died."

FOR MORE INFORMATION SEE: Los Angeles Times Book Review, September 22, 1985.

LANTZ, Paul 1908-

PERSONAL: Born February 14, 1908, in Stromberg, Neb.; married; children: two daughters, one son. *Education:* Attended Kansas City Art Institute, National Academy of Design, and Art Students' League. *Home:* Woodstock, N.Y.

CAREER: Painter and illustrator. Work has appeared in one-man shows and group exhibitions, including those at the New York World's Fair, San Francisco World's Fair, Texas Centennial, 460 Park Avenue Galleries, New York, N.Y., Marshall Gallery, Roswell Museum and Art Center, New Mexico. Work is represented in the permanent collections of the Metropolitan Museum of Art and the New York Historical Society, and is in many private collections, including those of Mrs. Marshall Field and Theodore Roosevelt, Jr. *Military service:* U.S. Army, World War II. *Awards, honors:* Illustrator of 1941 Newbery honor book, *Blue Willow* by Doris Gates; illustrator of 1942 Newbery Medal book, *Matchlock Gun* by Walter Edmonds.

ILLUSTRATOR: Harlan Thompson, *Spook, the Mustang,* Dodd, 1936; Doris Gates, *Blue Willow* (ALA Notable Book), Viking, 1940; Walter D. Edmonds, *Matchlock Gun* (ALA Notable Book), Dodd, 1941; W. D. Edmonds, *Tom Whipple,* Dodd, 1942; Betty Holdridge, *Island Boy,* Holiday House, 1942; Ann N. Clark, *Little Navajo Bluebird,* Viking, 1943.

Robert E. Pinkerton, *The First Overland Mail,* Random House, 1953; Samuel Epstein and Beryl Williams Epstein, *First Book of Hawaii,* F. Watts, 1954; D. Gates, *Becky and the Bandit,* Ginn, 1955; Evelyn S. Lampman, *Navajo Sister,* Doubleday, 1956; Florence Means, *Knock at the Door, Emmy,* Houghton, 1956; Priscilla Hallowell, *Dinah and Virginia,* Viking, 1956; J. K. McClarren, *Mexican Assignment,* Funk, 1957; Dorothy Koch, *When the Cows Got Out,* Holiday House, 1958; Jack M. MacLeod, *Theirs Is the Kingdom,* Westminster Press, 1959.

Clyde R. Bulla, *Three-Dollar Mule,* Crowell, 1960; Maureen Daly, *Patrick Visits the Library,* Dodd, 1961; Mary Barker, *Milenka's Happy Summer,* Dodd, 1961; Lavinia R. Davis, *Clown Dog,* Doubleday, 1961; Edwin W. Teale, *Lost Dog,* Dodd, 1961; Adelaide W. Arnold, *Traveler's Moon,* Doubleday, 1962. Also illustrator of *Peary at the North Pole.*

(From *Blue Willow* by Doris Gates. Illustrated by Paul Lantz.)

SIDELIGHTS: Lantz, who grew up on a farm, has been interested in art since he was five years old when someone gave him a tablet and some crayons. ''I set to work and produced a picture of a man walking down the boardwalk to the hen-house. Now I concentrate on murals, portraits, illustrations for children's books, and depictions of the western scene. I have never consciously painted in the tradition of any school of aesthetic expression. My purpose has been to master the craft of drawing, design and painting in order to portray life and nature as I see and feel them, with as much understanding and power as possible. In illustrating, my only roots are in the story itself. I try to depict the character and locale as vividly as possible, and that alone, as far as I know, determines the character of the work. I really love children and like to illustrate the type of story that would inspire in them a love of nature and good music, a respect for the traditions of civilized behavior.'' [Bertha E. Mahony and others, compilers, *Illustrators of Children's Books: 1744-1945*, Horn Book, 1947.]

FOR MORE INFORMATION SEE: Art Digest, March 1, 1940; Bertha E. Mahony and others, compilers, *Illustrators of Children's Books: 1744-1945*, Horn Book, 1947; Bertha E. Miller and others, compilers, *Illustrators of Children's Books: 1946-1956*, Horn Book, 1958.

LEIBER, Fritz 1910-
(Francis Lathrop)

PERSONAL: Born December 25, 1910, in Chicago, Ill.; son of Fritz (a Shakespearean actor) and Virginia (a Shakespearean actress; maiden name, Bronson) Leiber; married Jonquil Stephens (a writer), January 16, 1936 (died September, 1969); children: Justin. *Education:* University of Chicago, Ph.B., 1932; attended Episcopal General Theological Seminary. *Home and office:* 565 Geary St., Apt. 604, San Francisco, Calif. 94102.

CAREER: Episcopal minister at two missionary churches in New Jersey, 1932-33; Shakespearean actor, 1934-36; Consolidated Book Publishers, Chicago, Ill., editor, 1937-41; Occidental College, Los Angeles, Calif., instructor in speech and drama, 1941-42; Douglas Aircraft Co., Santa Monica, Calif., precision inspector, 1942-44; *Science Digest,* Chicago, Ill., associate editor, 1944-56; free-lance writer, 1956—. Lecturer at science fiction and fantasy writing workshops, Clarion State College, summers, 1968, 1969, 1970.

AWARDS, HONORS: World Science Fiction Convention Guest of Honor, 1951; Eighth Annual Mrs. Ann Radcliffe Award

Fritz Leiber in front of "Books of Wonder," a childern's bookstore in New York City. For one morning it was renamed "The Ghost Light." (Photograph courtesy of Ben Asen.)

(From "Black Glass" in *The Ghost Light Masterworks of Science Fiction and Fantasy* by Fritz Leiber. Illustrated by Paul Rivoche.)

for *Conjure Wife,* 1953; Hugo Award, 1958, for *The Big Time,* 1965, for *The Wanderer,* 1968, for best novelette "Gonna Roll the Bones", 1970, for best novella "Ship of Shadows", 1971, for best novella "Ill Met in Lankhmar!," and 1976, for "Catch That Zeppelin!"; Science Fiction Writers of America Nebula award, 1967, for "Gonna Roll the Bones," 1970, for "Ill Met in Lankhmar!," and 1975, for "Catch That Zeppelin"; Gandalf Award for Achievement in Fantasy, 1975; August Derleth Fantasy Award, 1976, for "Belsen Express"; Lovecraft Award from the World Fantasy Convention for body of work and for short story, "Belsen Express," both 1976, and for novel, *Our Lady of Darkness,* 1978; named the American Guest of Honor at the World Science Fiction Convention held in Brighton, England, 1979.

WRITINGS—All science fiction novels, except as indicated: *Night's Black Agents,* Arkham House, 1947. abridged edition published as *Tales from Night's Black Agents,* Ballantine, 1961; *The Girl with the Hungry Eyes, and Other Stories,* Avon, 1949; *Gather Darkness!* (first published in *Astounding Stories,* 1943), Pellegrini & Cudahy, 1950, new edition, Grosset, 1951; *Conjure Wife* (first published in *Unknown Worlds,* 1943), Twayne, 1953, reissued, Universal Publishing and Distributing, 1970, another edition published as *Burn Witch Burn,* Berkley, 1962; (with David Williams) *Bulls, Blood, and Passion by David Williams* [and] *The Sinful Ones by Fritz Leiber,* Universal Publishing and Distributing, 1953; *The Green Millennium,* Abelard Press, 1953; *Two Sought Adventure: Exploits of Fafhrd and the Gray Mouser,* Gnome Press, 1957; *Destiny Times Three,* Galaxy, 1957.

The Silver Eggheads (first published in *Magazine of Fantasy and Science Fiction,* 1958), Ballantine, 1961; *The Big Time,* Ace Books, 1961, reprinted, 1972; *The Mind Spider,* Ace Books, 1961; *Shadows with Eyes,* Ballantine, 1962; (with others) *H. P. Lovecraft: A Symposium* (speeches), Science Fiction Society, 1963, reprinted, R. West, 1973; *Ships to the Stars,* Ace Books, 1964; *A Pail of Air,* Ballantine, 1964; *The Wanderer,* Ballantine, 1964; *The Night of the Wolf,* Ballantine, 1966; *Tarzan and the Valley of Gold,* Ballantine, 1966; *The Swords of Lankhmar,* Ace Books, 1968; *The Secret Songs,* Hart-Davis, 1968; *Swords against Wizardry,* Ace Books, 1968; *Swords in the Mist,* Ace Books, 1968; *A Spectre Is Haunting Texas,* Walker & Co., 1969; *The Demons of the Upper Air,* privately printed, 1969; *Night Monsters,* Ace Books, 1969.

Swords against Death, Ace Books, 1970; *Swords and Deviltry: Fafhrd and the Gray Mouser,* Ace Books, 1970; *You're All Alone,* Ace Books, 1972 (originally published as *The Sinful Ones,* 1953); *The Book of Fritz Leiber,* Daw Books, 1974; *The Best of Fritz Leiber,* Ballantine, 1974; *The Second Book of Fritz Leiber,* Daw Books, 1975; *The Worlds of Fritz Leiber,* Ace Books, 1976; *Swords and Ice Magic,* Ace Books, 1977; *Rime Isle,* Whispers Press, 1977; *Our Lady of Darkness* (occult fantasy), Putnam, 1977; *Bazaar of the Bizarre,* Grant, 1978; *Heroes and Horrors* (illustrated by Tim Kirk), Whispers Press, 1979; *The Ship of Shadows,* Gollancz, 1979; (author of introduction) John Stanley, *The Creature Feature Movie Guide, or an A to Z Encyclopedia of Fantastic Films, or Is There a Mad Doctor in the House?* (illustrated by Ken Davis), Creatures at Large, 1981; *In the Beginning* (illustrated by Alicia Austin), Cheap St., 1983; *The Ghost Light,* Berkley, 1984.

ADAPTATIONS: "Weird Woman" (motion picture; based on *Conjure Wife*), Universal, 1944; "Conjure Wife" (television show), NBC-TV, 1960; "Burn, Witch, Burn," (motion picture; based on *Conjure Wife*), American International, 1962; two short stories have been dramatized for Rod Sterling's "Night

Gallery" show entitled "The Girl with the Hungry Eyes," 1970, and "The Dead Man," 1971.

SIDELIGHTS: Leiber, who has occasionally used the pseudonym Francis Lathrop, and whose books have been translated into many languages, has a number of interests, including science, metaphysics, history, backgammon, chess (he was the champion of Santa Monica in 1958), poetry reading, cats, all games of skill and chance, and acting (he acted in his father's Shakespearean repertory company and received screen credits in Greta Garbo's "Camille" and in "Equinox").

He writes: "Except for a couple of friends living nearby and an occasional guest or visitor, I live alone in a top-floor apartment in downtown San Francisco. From its roof I study the moon and stars, the planets and the weather. For exercise, I walk, taking an especial interest in the city's hills and high-rise buildings. I am a frequent film-goer, taking a more sporadic interest in music and the theater."

FOR MORE INFORMATION SEE: Sam Moscowitz, *Seekers of Tomorrow,* World Publishing, 1966; Judith Merril, "Fritz Leiber," *Magazine of Fantasy and Science Fiction,* July, 1969; Jim Purviance, "*Algol* Interview: Fritz Leiber," *Algol,* summer-fall, 1978; Paul Walker, *Speaking of Science Fiction: The Paul Walker Interviews,* Luna, 1978.

LEOKUM, Arkady 1916(?)-

PERSONAL: Surname rhymes with "yokum"; born about 1916 in Russia; married; children: Leonard, Peter. *Education:* City College (now of the City University of New York), B.A. *Residence:* Stockbridge, Mass.; and New York City. *Agent:* Gilbert Parker, William Morris Agency, 1350 Avenue of the Americas, New York, N.Y. 10019.

CAREER: Free-lance writer. Grey Advertising Agency, creative director, 1953-58; has also worked as a reporter.

WRITINGS—Juvenile: *The Quiz Book* (illustrated by John Huehnergarth), Grosset, 1968; *The Curious Book: Fascinating Facts about People, Places, and Things,* Sterling, 1976; (with Paul Posnick and Stanley Corwin) *Where Words Were Born,* Corwin, 1977.

"Tell Me Why" series; all published by Grosset: *Tell Me Why* (illustrated by Herb Mott and others), 1965; *More Tell Me Why: Answers to Over 400 Questions Children Ask Most Often* (illustrated by Cynthia Koehler and Alvin Koehler), 1967; *Still More Tell Me Why: Answers to Hundreds of Questions Children Ask* (illustrated by C. Koehler and A. Koehler), 1968; *Puzzles, Stunts, Brain Teasers, and Tricks from Tell Me Why* (illustrated by J. Huehnergarth), 1969; *Lots More Tell Me Why: Answers to Hundreds of Questions Children Ask* (illustrated by C. Koehler and A. Koehler), 1972; *Quizzes, Tricks, Stunts, Puzzles and Brain Teasers from Tell Me Why* (illustrated by J. Huehnergarth), Grosset, 1973; *Tell Me Why: Answers to Questions Children Ask about Love, Sex, and Babies* (illustrated by Richard Powers), 1974; *Animals, Insects, Fishes, and Birds: How They Live and Do What They Do* (originally published in *Tell Me Why*), 1976; *How Things Are Made: How They Work . . . Where They Come From* (originally published in *Tell Me Why*), 1976; *How Things Began: Who Made Them First . . . How New Ideas Got Started* (originally published in *Tell Me Why*), 1976; *How Things Got Started: How We Use, Enjoy, and Believe in Them* (originally published in *More Tell Me Why*), 1976; *The Human Body: How It Works . . . How

ARKADY LEOKUM

Things Happen to It (originally published in *More Tell Me Why*), 1976; *The World We Live In: How and Why Things Happen on Earth* (originally published in *Tell Me Why*), 1976; *Another Tell Me Why: Enlightening Answers to Questions Children Ask* (illustrated by Frank Aloise), 1977.

Adult novels: *Please Send Me, Absolutely Free . . .* , Harper, 1946; *The Temple,* World Publishing, 1969.

Plays: *Friends [and] Enemies* (two one-act; first produced in New York City at Theatre East, September 16, 1965), Samuel French, 1966; *Neighbors: A Play,* Dramatists Play Service, 1972.

Author of syndicated column, "Tell Me Why."

ADAPTATIONS—Movies: "Enemies" (television special), starring Sam Jaffe and Ned Glass, Public Broadcasting Service, 1971; "Neighbors" (television special), starring Andrew Duggan, Jane Wyatt, and Cicely Tyson, Public Broadcasting Service, 1971.

WORK IN PROGRESS: Plays and novels.

SIDELIGHTS: In the advertising world, Leokum may be best known for his slogan for the Chock Full O' Nuts coffee ad campaign, a slogan that pushed Chock Full O' Nuts from a seventh-rank position to third, in what is considered America's toughest taste market—New York City. "Don't spend the extra money for this coffee . . . unless you're just plain crazy about good coffee!" became the operative phrase for the campaign. It appealed directly to the consumer's true "taste" in coffee, a concept with subtle implications about a person's social sophistication. Leokum wrote "negative copy" but used a positive advertising approach to suggest buyer refinement, if not snobbery, in choosing Chock Full O' Nuts.

Leokum is also known in the writer's world as an author of both adult and children's books, and as a playwright. His "Tell Me Why" juvenile series of over ten books not only answers hundreds of questions often asked by children but attempts to stimulate their further curiosity of, and inquiry into, new topics. The series has been praised by children's book critics for being more than just a continuing set of questions and answers.

Leokum's plays have faired equally well, with "Neighbors" and "Enemies" adapted into Public Broadcasting Service television specials. The social commentary in Leokum's plays, particularly in "Neighbors," stabs unmercifully at the prejudices of its viewers, and the success of this play seems to lay in the cunning with which Leokum writes the dialogue between the two main couples, creating the uneasiness that characteristically shrouds "nonprejudiced" society.

FOR MORE INFORMATION SEE: Printer's Ink, September 7, 1956.

LUBIN, Leonard B.   1943-

PERSONAL: Born November 27, 1943, in Detroit, Mich.; son of Arnold and Annette (Wexler) Lubin. *Education:* Attended John Herron School of Art, Indianapolis, Ind., diploma, 1965. *Home:* 367 6th St., Brooklyn, N.Y. 11215. *Agent:* Dilys Evans, 1123 Broadway, New York, N.Y. 10010.

CAREER: Artist, author and illustrator of books for children. *Awards, honors:* Lewis Carroll Shelf Award, and *New York Times* choice of Best Illustrated Children's Books of the Year, both 1975, and Children's Book Council's Children's Book Showcase title, 1976, all for *The Pig-Tale; The Little Swineherd, and Other Tales* was included in the American Institute of Graphic Arts Book Show, 1979; American Book Award for illustration, 1980, and chosen one of *School Library Journal's* Best Books, 1981, both for *The Birthday of the Infanta.*

WRITINGS—Juvenile; all self-illustrated: (Adapter) Madame d'Aulnoy, *The White Cat,* Little, Brown, 1978; *The Elegant Beast,* Viking, 1981; (adapter) Richard F. Burton, *Aladdin and His Wonderful Lamp,* Delacorte, 1982; *This Little Pig: A Mother Goose Favorite,* Lothrop, 1985.

Illustrator; all for children, except as noted: Lewis Carroll (pseudonym of Charles Lutwidge Dodgson), *The Pig-Tale,* Little, Brown, 1975; Veronica S. Hutchinson, reteller, *Henny Penny,* Little, Brown, 1976; Stephen Schwartz, *The Perfect Peach: A Story,* Little, Brown, 1977; Paula Fox, *The Little Swineherd, and Other Tales,* Dutton, 1978; Oscar Wilde, *The Birthday of the Infanta,* Viking, 1979; W. S. Gilbert, *Gilbert without Sullivan* (adult; libretti selection), Viking, 1981; Isabelle Holland, *Kevin's Hat,* Lothrop, 1984.

WORK IN PROGRESS: "Right now, I'm working on another nursery rhyme, *Sing a Song of Sixpence,* in the same kind of color and with the same format as *This Little Pig*"; *The Emperor's New Clothes.*

SIDELIGHTS: **November 27, 1943.** Born in Detroit, Michigan. "I was the eldest of three children and, as a child, did lots of drawing and went through sheets and sheets of paper. The art teachers, even in grade school, were wonderful and very supportive. The librarian was also very helpful; she took an interest in my work and encouraged me."

La Belle Epoque, 1910-1915. With the coming of the war, fashion took a back seat to far more pertinent issues. ■ (From *The Elegant Beast* by Leonard B. Lubin. Illustrated by the author.)

Directoire, 1795-1800. With the rise of Napoleon, this sartorial splendor was diluted and then jelled into what became the Empire Style. ■ (From *The Elegant Beast* by Leonard B. Lubin. Illustrated by the author.)

Attended Mumford High School. "At Mumford there were two art teachers, one of whom went on to teach at Cass Technical, which was highly regarded as far as the arts. This teacher fostered my interest a great deal. She was a disciplinarian as far as technique, which was good for me at the time; but was also very open and therefore learned from us, too. My parents weren't too happy that the school was located in downtown Detroit—the neighborhood was a little dangerous and quite a distance from home. Therefore I wasn't allowed to transfer to Cass Tech.

"I had a group of friends. We took art classes and hung around together but didn't go to the football games or student meetings. We weren't too interested in school activities.

"In my last three years of high school, Raymond De Vleeschouwer came to teach art. He was an artist, and it was fantastic to work with him. I don't remember the rest of high school, I spent most of my time in the art room and managed to accumulate so many art credits that I put myself ahead and was ready to graduate in my third year. Then I discovered I had too many of the wrong credits—all art credits—so I had to double up on my English and social science courses.

"I was also attending Saturday morning classes for special art students sponsored by the Detroit Institute of Art. We had full use of all the facilities and every week there was a different three-hour session. We used the museum to get historical as well as artistic background. It taught us that we had to constantly reinterpret what we were seeing from the past in order to apply it to the present. Later, when I was in art school, I taught similar classes in Indianapolis for special high school students during the summers. I used my earlier experience as a base.

"My parents were ambivalent about my pursuit of art and it was very uncomfortable. My father, a tool and die engineer, had artistic ability and talent. He could draw just about anything and showed an interest in my work. However, there were discouraging influences: My mother's family had a great deal of money and had always intended to provide for my education. Unfortunately, they felt I should do what they thought best, and art was definitely not what they had in mind. It wasn't their idea of a career. There was also, at the time, what was called a 'trash can' movement in art. People were drawing from nature and, in a city like Detroit, portraying the seamier side of life. My grandfather worked downtown and would often see the open-air artists drawing the bums lying in the street. He asked, 'Is this what *you* want to be?' Then insisted I go into electronics. We went round and round. Electronics was the up and coming field. For years they had humored my 'nice little hobby,' even giving me an easel and watercolor paints, in hopes that I would 'get over' my interest in art. In the end my father sided with me, and my mother, of course, with her parents.

"In spite of the family conflict over my future, I started applying for art scholarships and entered the Scholastic Art Award competition. When I won a full scholarship to John Herron School of Art in Indianapolis, I decided to go. I didn't say anything to my parents until the scholarship was a fact. Then I announced that I would study art, and that they had nothing whatsoever to say about it. They were not too happy, but decided to go along with it."

Attended Herron School of Art. Received a diploma in 1965. "I had a hard time in art school. I have fond memories of Indianapolis, despite the school, which was very conservative. Indianapolis was a good change from Detroit; it was the next

step up for me. What I objected to, and almost violently so, was the small town, bigoted attitudes of the school itself which did not, in any way, foster creativity. Herron was very inbred, partly because most of the faculty consisted of Herron alumnae. Even the young instructors were ingrained, which I felt was a terrible shame. The emphasis was on technique to the absurd extent that we would spend weeks learning the different grades of graphite—and even the methods of sharpening pencils. I felt this had nothing to do with art. I only learned one useful technique there, which I have since abandoned: a pencil-drawing method in which you stress where two lines meet to create dimension.

"I began to question authority which was not welcome and got me in trouble. Still, the other students were wonderful. We laughed at the prejudice and I secretly printed a small edition of lithographs satirizing the faculty. The challenge got my blood going and taught me a lot about myself and other people. I might have learned faster at another school, but I don't have any regrets. In any case, most of what I do know about art, I've come by naturally.

"After graduation, I worked for a friend in Indianapolis who was an antique dealer. I opened my own antique shop but after two years decided it was a dead end. I worked for various decorators and continued painting and drawing for private buyers; I set up an easel in the shop and worked while waiting for customers to come in. I was doing all right, and I'm sure I would have made a comfortable living, but there was no challenge. Yet, all I was qualified to do was paint and draw. I had what was called a 'fine-art' education, and hadn't learned the aspects of commercial art because I wanted no part of it. I knew I would never fit into that field.

"I met many people traveling through Indianapolis and some of them were in the Metropolitan Opera Company. I became friends with those working behind the scenes like Jane Greenwood, a costume designer, and Harry Lyons, a set designer. They repeatedly tried to convince me to come to New York. Jane felt she could find me work immediately. She looked at my work and said, 'I could make a costume from this drawing, the detailing is so correct. Did you study sewing or pattern making?' I hadn't, and told her so. 'How do you know this is where the seam belongs? It's amazing. . . .' I couldn't tell her how I knew, it just *looked* right. Other people had suggested I go into costuming. I would have enjoyed it, but there were already plenty of talented people out of work in that field. Eventually I did move to New York and realized that there was definitely a different way of dealing in New York than in Indianapolis. It was strange at first, but I learned fast not to depend on connections.

"I could paint, and I could draw, but that was it. What could I do with what I knew? I had considered book or magazine illustration, but it wasn't until I got to New York that I thought about doing children's books. I didn't know where to start, so I got a job in a display house, and worked there for a few years. It was fun and a good experience—a lot like what I imagined set designing to be. We worked on scaffolds, in large scale 14′ x 8′ screens, etc. After a year and a half at the studio, I was transferred to their design area where I worked at a drawing table for three years. I then took a job at a smaller studio where there was more room for creativity. The man who ran it was interested in anything that was elegant, so I did a lot of costume design for him. After a year and a half, they couldn't afford to keep me on.

"I had learned to do window displays while I was in art school and had some experience. I had no problem finding jobs and

Every day, Mrs. Gudge said to him, "If it hadn't been for us, who knows what would have become of you?" ■ (From "The Little Swineherd" in *The Little Swineherd and Other Tales* by Paula Fox. Illustrated by Leonard B. Lubin.)

When the Princess passed by, Aladdin was struck dumb by her loveliness and grace. ■ (From *Aladdin and His Wonderful Lamp,* adapted and illustrated by Leonard B. Lubin.)

made window displays for various stores in Manhattan, which I enjoyed. There are so many bookstores here in New York, that I started to spend a lot of my time browsing and buying books. At some point I thought, 'Well, I could do this,' [book illustration] but got sidetracked making a living. After awhile, I quit doing window displays and decided I was going to put all my energy into breaking into publishing. I got a list of all the art directors and took my portfolio around to anyone who would see me. Most of the time, I was not even seeing the person in charge, but a third assistant. Nothing came of it.

"In 1975, I took a sales job at the Doubleday bookstore with the idea that I would eventually get into the art and editorial office. My shift started at 4:30 in the afternoon, so during the day I went around with my portfolio. Nothing happened until I ran into an old friend from school who was living in Boston and working for Little, Brown and Houghton-Mifflin. He suggested I come to Boston so he could introduce me to some people in the art departments. I had nothing to lose, so I went. When I came back, two weeks later, there were calls from both houses. Little, Brown said they had work and assigned me Lewis Carroll's _The Pig-Tale,_ without even knowing I had an interest in pigs. It was a happy solution for all.

"I feel the reason I had trouble finding assignments in New York was because the publishers didn't know what to do with me. Although they were enthusiastic about my work, they didn't know how to apply my particular talents to book illus-

He rode on the carousel. The music was Spanish and made him sad. ■ (From _Kevin's Hat_ by Isabelle Holland. Illustrated by Leonard B. Lubin.)

And I copied all the letters in a big round hand—. ■ (From "H.M.S. Pinafore" in *Gilbert without Sullivan*. Libretti by W. S. Gilbert. Illustrated by Leonard B. Lubin.)

So Henny Penny, Cocky Locky, Ducky Daddles, Goosey Poosey, and Turkey Lurkey went on to tell the King the sky was falling. ■ (From *Henny Penny*, retold by Veronica S. Hutchinson. Illustrated by Leonard B. Lubin.)

tration. In fact many of the books I have illustrated are not specifically children's books, including *The Birthday of the Infanta, The Pig-Tale,* and my own, *The Elegant Beast.* One of my books, *Kevin's Hat,* was a real breakthrough for me. At least that's what my agent says. It was not all powdered wigs and hoop skirts and crystal chandeliers with very elegant Victorian or Edwardian or rococo settings and costumes. The story deals with a troubled little crocodile. It was charming and quite different to work on. A lot of the drawings were inspired by actual streets and places in my Brooklyn neighborhood.

"I didn't work directly with the author, Isabelle Holland, though she later wrote me a note saying how happy she was with the book. In fact, the first sketches I made portrayed the alligator as a grown-up loser with a pathetic look in double-pleated pants with cuffs, penny-loafers, and an 'Izod' shirt with a little man on it. When I showed it to the editor, she got hysterical with laughter and said, 'You know, Kevin is supposed to be about ten years old.' Here I thought he was just a yuppie loser! Instead he was a kid who couldn't make up his mind about a dumb hat.

"Most publishers like to keep the author and illustrator separate and leave it to the editors to run interference. But on *The Perfect Peach,* I worked with composer, Stephen Schwartz, quite closely. We talked at length, not necessarily about what it should or shouldn't look like, but about how we felt about the story. He'd go off to rehearse some musical he was involved with and I'd go home to draw. Then we'd meet in a studio someplace and he'd say, 'This is exactly what I had in mind.' And I'd say 'Fine.' It worked out very nicely.

"One thing I'm notoriously known for is refusing to do preliminary sketches. When I know exactly how I see something, I can explain it without going through the time and effort involved in making sketches. Some editors are very visual and understand this, others understand but can't really *see* what I have in mind.

"Books without a great deal of text, such as tales and nursery rhymes do spark my imagination. Minimum text allows me to be very creative; the text becomes a take off point for the illustrations.

"I use a kind of writer's sense in plotting illustrations. I begin before the actual verse or story begins. For example, in my book, *Sing a Song of Sixpence*, the first illustration shows a fowler trapping some blackbirds in a field to bring back to the king's kitchen. The book takes place during the reign of Henry VIII. I am using a lot of historical background and some symbolism in the illustrations, as they did that back then. I've put in badges and emblems. Henry the VIII's was the Tudor rose, Catherine's was a pomegranate and Anne's was a white falcon.

"*The Elegant Beast* was my idea. I had done some 'costume plates' of animals in eighteenth-century costumes. I went to Barbara Burn, the head of Viking Studio Books. Her husband is a veterinarian and she's very fond of all animals, particularly dogs and horses. She saw my drawings, went crazy, and asked, 'What kind of book could we do using all of these historical costumes and animals.' I suggested a history of costume and she said, 'Wonderful!' It was that simple."

In his introduction to *The Elegant Beast*, Lubin wrote: "If humans can be referred to as eagle-eyed, hawk-nosed, pigeon-toed, leonine, and goatish, or as lame ducks or real dogs, why not outfit our furry, feathered and scaly chums in clothing that might just show how human they can be?"

"I look at animals and I laugh and see people. Though many of the expressions on animal faces are not human at all—they do *look* human. Many of the characters I created in the book were suggested by the costumes of each period. I just couldn't picture any other animal than the one I chose to draw in that costume. The attitudes and ambiance of each period, what went on back then, who they were, what they were doing, what they looked like, suggested definite animal counterparts. One of the most perfect examples is the hippos in the Dutch baroque period; the people who would wear the costumes of this particular epoch were overfed and amply proportioned, very rich and their costumes showed this.

"I did all of the drawings for *The Elegant Beast* first and then worked on the text. I really overwrote. The editor worked very closely with me, and did a great job of cutting it down to a workable size. I would love to do another book in the same style, though I would skip the Greeks, because they walked around in nothing but sheets and towels anyway. The Egyptians I could do, and I'd like to do the Romans and portray them as goats. I'd love to bring the book all the way up from the twenties to the sixties. Perhaps, even into the eighties. I think the British punkers with their mohawk-spiked hair would have to be some kind of wild birds."

The throne itself. . . . ■ (From *The Birthday of the Infanta* by Oscar Wilde. Illustrated by Leonard B. Lubin.)

My object all sublime
I shall achieve in time
To let the punishment fit the crime—.

■ (From "The Mikado" in *Gilbert without Sullivan*. Libretti by W. S. Gilbert. Illustrated by Leonard B. Lubin.)

About his working method, Lubin commented, "First I do drawings, then I put on color, then I use pastel pencils to shade. Sometimes just small touches with a pastel pencil brings an illustration together. I draw in pen and ink and then mix up 'bathtubs' full of watercolor. Once I mix up a batch, I have to be careful because the colors can change in a subtle way with time and I've had problems matching shades. Now I wait until I have finished all the drawings for a book before I put on the color. Paper can change color, too. Once I had trouble because I ran out of paper and though I bought the same type, the new paper took color differently and I had to start playing little games. Then, of course, the printers can screw things up, too. Sometimes they do a damn good job; but many times, the reproductions are less than desirable."

When asked about the special problems involved in bringing animals to life, Lubin responded, " You can't find reference material on a pig singing, but you can find pictures of pigs with their mouths open. I combine a number of things and adapt my reference to the situation. I can get a sense of movement and how clothes might hang on an animal by looking at a person. I have a huge reference library of my own—books and books. Many of the figures in *The Perfect Peach* were inspired by photographs I'd collected of Chinese Opera. The drums were Japanese, but the gods we used were Chinese. For the character of Peachy, I looked at many different Chinese calendars I had, with delightful pictures of little children. I picked one and based Peachy on him. I enjoyed the whimsy and the fantasy of that book, particularly the double-page illustrations.

"I had read Oscar Wilde's short stories in art school and always loved *The Birthday of the Infanta*. I brought the idea of making it into a book to Viking and they picked up on it right away. I felt the illustrations should have been much more detailed in terms of finished rendering, which the publishers liked but couldn't afford to reproduce. I also wanted the book to be in color with larger drawings, but it wasn't possible.

"The character of the Infanta was based on my roommate's daughter, Elizabeth, who at the time was twelve years old. When I started to work on the story I thought of her immediately, because, although the Infanta was not an evil or nasty child, she was very icy. Elizabeth had a very aloof manner, so I used her as a base for the drawings. Sometimes the feeling for a character can come from a person I know.

"Reading the story, I thought of the dwarf as uglier than my final portrayal in the book. Somehow, I just couldn't make him as grotesque as I originally saw him. Enough was enough and besides, there was something about him I liked. I looked at some of the Velazquez drawings of court jesters and dwarfs for inspiration.

"I used actual tapestries as models for the tapestry in *The Birthday of the Infanta,* as I'm sure Wilde did in his story. I'm also using a tapestry in *Sing a Song of Sixpence,* and I'll probably use part of my work on . . . *Infanta* as reference. I find I'm using my own work as reference more and more now. I go back to what I've done to see how I approached the problem before.

"Perspective has never been a real trouble area for me. A friend of mine who is taking perspective classes asked me, 'How do you do it?' I told her I just put down what looks right to me. She couldn't understand, but it's true. In art school, I took perspective over and over and over. I could not grasp the technicalities; it was just too cut and dry for me. Then I began to put down whatever looked right, because sometimes, something can be technically correct and still look way off. I don't bother with that technical business. I build my own scale and what looks right to the eye *is* right, as far as I'm concerned.

"My interest in costume goes all the way back to high school. I always felt particularly interested in 17th- and 18th-century costume design. I learned about costume through my art teacher who had a number of books which I borrowed frequently. The museum in Detroit didn't have a costume collection per se, but they did have period rooms in which they'd often display a mannequin in period costume. I feel a definite connection to the 18th century, and always have. I was even told by an astrologer, years ago, that one of my past lives was in 18th-century France. Someday, I would love to go to Versailles. I have books and books and books on that period in French history, including biographies of the various kings and queens and mistresses. I keep thinking I have to go there. I'd like to walk through the palace rooms because I'm sure I'll feel something—like I've been there before. I went to the 18th-Century costume show at the Metropolitan Museum of Art umpteen times. It was fabulous. I spent hours and hours there and wanted to make sketches, but it was not permitted. I have managed to build up a very good reference library of my own. If I'm working on a project and need something I usually have it. If I don't, I find it and buy it, rather than go to the library.

"For *Gilbert without Sullivan* I looked at some of their old production stills, but I wasn't crazy about them, so reimagined the space. When I finished the illustrations for the libretti, I realized that a lot of my drawings could be used as production designs, though that wasn't my original intention.

"My humor is not a political humor, it's a humorous way of seeing things in general, though other people seeing my work often find political overtones.

"I like what I'm doing and I want to stick with book illustration, but it's got to start paying more. A lot of people can't understand that. Each book takes me hours and hours of work. I'm in the red, I've been in the red for years. It doesn't matter whether a publisher pays me $500 or $7,000. I can only do the best work I can. It's a vocation. Definitely. And if I didn't enjoy doing it, I certainly wouldn't be doing it. People tell me it takes a long time to earn a decent living in the field. I just don't feel I have that kind of time. I don't want to wait another twenty years before I have a comfortable income.

"I work every day. I'm usually up by 6:30, doing what has to be done around the house. By 9:30 I'm downstairs in my studio working till six in the evening. I used to go back down around 8:30 and work till late at night, but I can't do that anymore. Enough is enough. I keep music on in the studio all the time and it influences me. At certain times I'll think, why am I listening to this? It has nothing to do with what I'm working on. Then they'll play some Mozart or Handel or Bach, which is absolutely perfect. I'll listen hour after hour. I even listened to Gilbert and Sullivan constantly while I was working on that book.

"I usually see a book in a certain way, right away, and then I start thinking in terms of what I want to illustrate in the story. I think about character, I illustrate what's important, and then go back and fill in the spaces. I have to decide how each page should go and plot out the pictures. I generally want to do more illustrations than I am allotted, but lately I've been realizing how less can be more.

**Little Birds are teaching
Tigresses to smile,
Innocent of guile. . . .**

■ (From *The Pig-Tale* by Lewis Carroll. Illustrated by Leonard B. Lubin.)

That Camel scanned him, dreamy-eyed.
"Methinks you are too plump.
I never knew a Pig so wide—
That wobbled so from side to side—...."

■ (From *The Pig-Tale* by Lewis Carroll. Illustrated by Leonard B. Lubin.)

In gay amusements days went past,   The time to go did come at last.

(From *The White Cat* by Madame d'Aulnoy. Adapted and illustrated by Leonard B. Lubin.)

''I often get reactions to my books from kids who live right on my block. Daniel, a four year old, took *Kevin's Hat* to nursery school with him every day—the book is all banged up now, and he's been driving his parents crazy, asking them to read it again and again. *This Little Pig* got good response from the eight year old who said, 'It's very pretty.' Strange what appeals to who and at what age. I gave *This Little Pig* to Daniel's parents who are both teachers. They felt it was too sophisticated for a four year old. Then I sat down with Daniel and told him the story of the illustrations, involving the nursery rhyme and he loved it! Some people don't understand there is a story all its own in the pictures themselves.

''I illustrated *Aladdin and His Wonderful Lamp* in a French-rococo-Chinese style. For the tale, we went back as far as we could to the old versions. We had some trouble adapting it as there was quite a bit of anti-semitism in the original which we did away with. Some of it was quite funny, but it wasn't meant to be. Then we had to decide whether or not to use 'Thee' and 'Thou.' Finally I gave up—it just sounded so silly. Some of *The Emperor's New Clothes* had been difficult, too. It is a very short story, many of the scenes are not very pictorial, and I saw more in the tale than there was in the original.

''I write in longhand because I can't type. Then I either have the manuscript typed by someone or take it to the editor and

say, 'Here, you decipher it and have your secretary type it.' I write straight through from beginning to end and I usually have done the pictures before hand, or at least know what the pictures will involve. I include in the writing what I have already drawn or what I'm going to draw.

''I know a number of people in the business but for some reason, we don't socialize. Actually, I like being isolated, to a point, but there are times when I go absolutely crazy. Sometimes the phone doesn't ring for days on end. As far as other artists are concerned, I don't miss a community—we're all too much on our own ego trips, we don't have time for someone else's ego, especially when we're doing books. It's a selfish thing to say, I wish them all well, but I'm really not interested in what they are doing. I have enough to do with just keeping up with my own work, and I'm sure they feel the same way. I know the ups and downs, and other artists have the same problems. When I have time, I want to spend it with people who have different lives. I would never choose to call other illustrators I know and say, 'Let's go out for a drink.' I would rather go out with someone else.

''I read for relaxation, and when I go out it's usually to a bookstore. I love the Strand in New York, as well as the Pagaent, and, of course, all the fine art book stores. I rarely go see theatre or opera, I haven't even been to the movies in years. I'd rather go buy a book—something I can use for my work rather than sit in an opera house. I especially enjoy reading historical fiction and biographies.

"I would describe my illustration as very meticulous. Though people often describe my work as baroque, I would say it has more rococo feeling. No matter how detailed or heavy it may be, there is still a feeling of fun. My work is eccentric, with just a dash of nastiness.

"In *The Emperor's New Clothes* there is an illustration in which the characters are ironing. I had to call up a friend whom I've nicknamed, 'The Authority.' He's a teacher from Virginia who also helped me figure out what kind of oven they may have used in the days of *This Little Pig*. I want to make sure my details are right. I think kids have an instinct for what's right or wrong in a picture. They'll question things. If I were to put a microwave oven in that picture, they'd know something was wrong. In *The Emperor's New Clothes* I have one drawing where they are ironing nonexistent clothes. I have to find out what kind of irons were used back in the eighteenth century. I've seen pictures, but they are not very clear. I am using a hand-molded iron in a wedge shape, though sometimes they used heated bricks. I haven't caught myself doing something that wasn't accurate. When I run up against something that I'm not sure how to draw, it becomes a challenge.

"Sometimes too much imagination in illustration is just that: too much. Perhaps what I do is too literal sometimes. I do love detail, but I still feel there is enough left to the imagination so that kids can dream about what's in the picture. There's also enough going on in the illustrations for kids to be able to make up little stories of their own, as well as go back and find details they have missed.

"I deeply admire the work of Arthur Rackham, Leslie Brooks, Walter Crane, and Grandville. People have often come to me with ideas like 'You should do *Alice in Wonderland*', and I tell them 'No way!' because as far as I'm concerned, even Rackham had no business touching it after Tenniel. The Tenniel version is perfect. Trina Shart Hyman's *Snow White* is perfect and so is her *Sleeping Beauty* and *The Little Red Riding Hood*. She has done the epitome of illustration for those tales, they are beautiful and nobody should touch them. I'd still love to do *Cinderella* as well as an animal 'ABC' book and, perhaps, *The Nutcracker*.

"I would say a book generally takes about six months, but some have taken a little longer. Ideally, I'd like to do more than two books a year, but I can only do what I can. If I lived by myself I think I probably would sit down and work seven days a week both mornings and evenings, but I don't know how good that would be for me. I wouldn't do anything else.

"Sometimes, there are days when I realize it's getting dark already, and I think I have to stop; there are other days when I only want to go on. I often lose sense of time, depending on what the project is."

Twinkle, twinkle, little bat!
How I wonder what you're at!
Up above the world you fly!
Like a teatray in the sky.

—Lewis Carroll
(pseudonym of Charles Lutwidge Dodgson)

MARIS, Ron

BRIEF ENTRY: The author and illustrator of five picture books, Maris is also senior lecturer in art and design at Huddersfield Polytechnic in West Yorkshire, England. His first book, *Better Move On, Frog!* (F. Watts, 1982), was followed by *My Book* (F. Watts, 1984), a runner-up for the Kate Greenaway Medal. *My Book* introduces preschoolers to the various possessions of a family cat through the use of split pages alternating with full ones. "The illustrations," noted *School Library Journal*, "are charming, colorful and full of amusing details." Colorful pictures also abound in Maris's *The Punch and Judy Book* (Gollancz, 1984), a look at the classic puppet show which was described by *Times Literary Supplement* as "a beautifully designed book . . . in the tradition of Harold Jones and Peter Spier." In his fourth book, *Are You There, Bear?* (Greenwillow, 1985), Maris utilizes another unusual illustrative technique as the search for Bear is undertaken by a child holding a flashlight. "The story's gentle simplicity blooms under Maris' inventive graphic treatment," observed *Booklist*, as "circles and half circles of golden light . . . [are] pleasing contrast to the darkened reaches of the room." At the story's end, Bear is found reading a book, none other than Maris' own *My Book*. His most recent work is entitled *Is Anyone Home* (MacRae, 1985). Maris is married and the father of three sons. *Residence:* Yorkshire, England.

MATTHEWS, William Henry III   1919-

PERSONAL: Born March 1, 1919, in Henrietta, Okla.; son of William Henry (an engineer) and Douglass (Fain) Matthews; married Jennie Anzalone (a registered nurse), September 7, 1940; children: William Henry IV, James Douglas. *Education:* Texas Christian University, B.A., 1948, M.A., 1949; graduate study at University of Texas, 1950-51. *Religion:* Episcopal. *Home:* 5795 Sul Ross Lane, Beaumont, Tex. 77706. *Office:* Department of Geology, Lamar State College of Technology, Beaumont, Tex. 77704.

CAREER: Texas Christian University, Fort Worth, assistant professor, 1948-52; Texaco, Inc., subsurface geologist, 1952-55; Lamar State College of Technology, Beaumont, Tex., professor, 1955—. Visiting professor, Sul Ross State College, summers, 1961, 1962. Research scientist, Bureau of Economic Geology, University of Texas, summers, 1958, 1959, 1960. Consulting geologist to Texas Portland Cement Co. and Texas State Highway Department; consultant to various other agencies. *Member:* American Association for the Advancement of Science, National Association of Geology Teachers (president, Texas Section, 1960-61; national president, 1969-70), Geological Society of America, American Association of Petroleum Geologists, Society of Economic Paleontologists and Mineralogists, Paleontological Society, National Science Teachers Association, Texas Association of College Teachers, Texas Academy of Science, Beaumont Geological Society (former president). *Awards, honors:* Neil Miner Award, 1965, for his service to the National Association of Geology Teachers.

WRITINGS—Juvenile: *Wonders of the Dinosaur World*, Dodd, 1963; *Exploring the World of Fossils*, Childrens Press, 1964 (published in England as *The World of Fossils*, Odhams, 1966); *The Story of the Earth* (illustrated by John E. Alexander), Harvey House, 1968; *Wonders of Fossils*, Dodd, 1968; *The Story of Volcanoes and Earthquakes*, Harvey House, 1969; *Soils*, F. Watts, 1970; *The Earth's Crust*, F. Watts, 1971; *Introducing the Earth: Geology, Environment and Man*, Dodd,

This **Arctic iceberg in Baffin Bay dwarfs the Coast Guard cutter** *Eastwind.* ■ (From *The Story of Glaciers and the Ice Age* by William H. Matthews III. Photograph courtesy of the U.S. Coast Guard.)

1972; *The Story of Glaciers and the Ice Age,* Harvey House, 1974.

Other: *Marine Ecology as an Aid in Teaching Invertebrate Paleontology,* Lamar State College of Technology, c. 1957; *The Paleontology and Paleoecology of the Biostrome Fauna of the Edwards Formation of Texas,* Lamar State College of Technology, 1957; *Texas Fossils: An Amateur Collector's Handbook,* Bureau of Economic Geology, University of Texas, 1960; *Fossils: An Introduction to Prehistoric Life,* Barnes & Noble, 1962; *Bathymetry of Powell Lake, British Columbia,* Institute of Oceanography, University of British Columbia, 1962; *The Geologic Story of Longhorn Cavern,* Bureau of Economic Geology, University of Texas, 1963; *Quaternary Stratigraphy and Geomorphology of the Fort St. John Area, Northeastern British Columbia,* British Columbia Department of Mines and Petroleum Resources, 1963; *Thirteen Potassium-Argon Dates of Cenozoic Volcanic Rocks from British Columbia,* Department of Geology, University of British Columbia, 1963.

Geology Made Simple, Doubleday, 1967, revised edition, W. H. Allen, 1970; *A Guide to the National Parks: Their Landscape and Geology,* Natural History Press for American Museum of Natural History, Volume I: *The Western Parks,* 1968; Volume II: *The Eastern Parks,* 1968; *The Geologic Story of Palo Duro Canyon,* Bureau of Economic Geology, University of Texas, 1969; *Science Probes the Earth: New Frontiers of Geology,* Sterling, 1969; *Invitation to Geology: The Earth through Time and Space,* Natural History Press for American Museum of Natural History, 1971; (compiler) *Helping Children Learn Earth-Space Science,* National Science Teachers Association, 1971.

General editor, "Earth Science Curriculum Project" series, Prentice-Hall, 1964-65. Contributor to professional and popular publications.

FOR MORE INFORMATION SEE: Commonweal, May 24, 1968; *Best Sellers,* March 1, 1970; *Library Journal,* March 15, 1970, October 15, 1982; Martha E. Ward and Dorothy A. Marquardt, *Authors of Books for Young People,* 2nd edition supplement, Scarecrow, 1979.

MAX, Peter 1939-

PERSONAL: Born October 19, 1939, in Berlin, Germany; came to United States in 1953; son of Jacob (a pearl merchant) and Salla (Zeisel) Finkelstein; married Elizabeth Ann Nance, May 1, 1963 (divorced); children: Adam Cosmo, Libra Astro (a daughter). *Education:* Attended Art Students' League, Pratt Graphic Arts Center, and School of Visual Arts. *Office:* Peter Max Enterprises, 118 Riverside Dr., New York, N.Y. 10024.

CAREER: Artist, graphic designer, entrepreneur. Daly-Max Design Studio (graphic arts studio), New York City, co-owner, director, 1962-65; Peter Max Posters (printers), New York City, co-owner, designer, 1967; Peter Max Enterprises, New York City, president, beginning 1967. Recipient of numerous commissions, including Tin Lizzie Steak House interior, Manhattan, N.Y., 1967; Metro Transit Advertising Co., New York City, series of posters for buses and subways in ten U.S. cities, 1968; U.S. postage stamp, "Cosmic Jumper," 1974; series of seven murals for 135 U.S. border stations, 1976; six Statue of Liberty paintings, 1981. Work has appeared in numerous exhibits, including: "The World of Peter Max," M. H. De Young Memorial Museum, San Francisco, Calif., and other U.S. cities, 1970; five-year retrospective, London Arts Gallery, 1970; Smithsonian Institution, Washington, D.C., 1972-74; nationwide touring retrospective, 1974; Riverside Gallery, Shreveport, La.; Munic Art Gallery, Los Angeles, Calif.; Corcoran Gallery of Art, Washington, D.C., 1981; and over forty one-man shows. *Awards, honors:* Recipient of awards from

Peter Max in his studio.

American Institute of Graphic Arts, Society of Illustrators, and International Poster Competition of Poland, and of over sixty awards for graphic design.

WRITINGS—All self-illustrated: (With Swami Satchidananda) *God,* Morrow, 1970; (with Satchidananda) *Love,* Morrow, 1970; *The Peter Max Land of Blue (and How the Cousins Got There)* (juvenile), F. Watts, 1970; *The Peter Max Land of Red* (juvenile), F. Watts, 1970; *The Peter Max Land of Yellow (and How the Purple King Nearly Lost Himself There)* (juvenile), F. Watts, 1970; (with Satchidananda) *Peace,* Morrow, 1970; *Peter Max Poster Book,* Crown, 1970; (with Satchidananda) *Thought,* Morrow, 1970; (with Ronwen Vathsala Proust) *The Peter Max New Age Organic Vegetarian Cookbook,* Pyramid Communications, 1971; *Peter Max Superposter Book,* Crown, 1971; *Meditations,* McGraw, 1972; (with Betty Staal) *The Peter Max Book of Crochet,* Pyramid Communications, 1972; (with Susan Sommers Winer), *The Peter Max Book of Needlepoint,* Pyramid Communications, 1972; *Peter Max Paints America,* edited by Victor Zurbel, Acropolis Books, 1976.

Illustrator: Abby Gail Kirsch and Sandra Bangilsdorf Klein, *Teen Cuisine: A Beginner's Guide to French Cooking* (juvenile), Parents Magazine Press, 1969.

SIDELIGHTS: **October 19, 1939.** Born in Berlin, Germany. Max spent most of his childhood in the Orient, first in Shanghai, where his father had a successful business, and later in Tibet. "I had a magical and adventurous childhood. I was born in Berlin and at the age of one was transported to China.

It was there I spent the first decade of my life. Then my family and I embarked on another odyssey. We traveled by boat from China around southernmost Africa and arrived in Israel during the time of its rebirth as a nation. After a few years in the Biblical land we then journeyed through the European continent, finally ending up on the shores of America.

"I first learned about America when I was a small boy about six years of age. I was playing with a friend in a spacious garden in Shanghai, amidst exotic pagodas and Eastern temples. My friend told me about a wonderful gift he had received from his uncle in New York, which was a city in far-off America. The word 'America' had a magical ring to it, much like Baghdad or 'never-never land.'

"I would hear strange and delightful new sounds from America every Thursday at 4:30 p.m. on the radio. Hearing the beat of Benny Goodman after listening all week to the ancient sounds and songs of the Orient was an experience not to be forgotten by an impressionable child from the West, growing up in a land with a culture that was over five thousand years old. The thought that these new, interesting sounds came to us in ancient Shanghai from a place not yet even 200 years old challenged the imagination only slightly less than visualizing the far-off land of Tarzan, Flash Gordon, Buck Rogers, Captain Marvel, Wonder Woman and Submariner.

"These, to a little boy and his friends in China, were the fantasies of America come to us in comic books and on the screen. They introduced an appealing art style somewhat resembling sumi drawings, in miniature. This was a time when every day I looked out of my pagoda window into a temple to see sumi artists painting on the floor on huge sheets of rice paper, providing imagery to tremendous events with the graceful movements of their bodies.

"It was the movement of the comic books, however, which carried me away to different environs and fantasies of the future. They led me to pursue a great interest in astronomy, further developed while residing in Israel." [Victor Zurbel, editor, *Peter Max Paints America,* Acropolis Books, 1976.[1]]

At the age of thirteen Max enrolled at Haifa University in Israel to study astronomy. Travels to Italy and Paris followed.

1953. Moved to New York with his family. Enrolled at the Art Students' League, after completing a general education at Lafayette High School. As a student at the Art Students' League, Max drew all day long and often into the evening. "I slowly started drawing the things that grew out of my interests: astronomy, evolution, philosophical aspects. I also love people and their profiles, their hats, bodies, flowers. That's how I began. Art was my whole life. I played it, I lived it, I breathed it, I ate it. And slowly a style developed." ["Peter Max: The Wizard of Ahs Paints a Vivid Self-Portrait," *Seventeen,* April, 1970.[2]]

1962. Opened a graphic arts business with partner, Tom Daly, called Daly-Max Design Studio. Within two years the company's commercial success caused Max to be called the "wonder boy of Madison Avenue." In one year he won more than seventy awards for advertising art.

1963. Married Elizabeth Ann Nance. The couple had two children, a son and a daughter.

1965. After two years of commercial success, Max went into a self-imposed retreat. He moved into his studio with his wife and two young children. "Through this success, I discovered that I really had something. I hadn't thought that before. So I went into a creative retreat for two years to develop my art. The result was five thousand pieces of art and four and one-half thousand more written ideas. Then I went back into the field and did my thing."[2]

1967. Began designing and producing "Peter Max" posters. The new-age posters were youth-oriented in color and design. His posters led to commissions in other product fields, including clothes, towels, sheets, clocks, and so on. "People are finding a new importance in art as an enhancement to a product. Why should a shower curtain, for example, be only a repeated pattern of fish and seashells? Why shouldn't it be a complex, fantastic mural that lets you discover something new each time you look at it? Why can't one of my clock

Peter Max, age six, with his parents in Shanghai.

designs be blown up to become the colorful ceiling of a building?" ["Hot Mod Artist Gets in Commercial Groove," *Business Week,* March 16, 1968.[3]]

Known as the "prince of psychedelic art" in the 1960s, Max had amassed a four-million-dollar empire. By 1969 his posters could be seen on 20,000 buses in ten major cities. "I produce between thirty and forty-five pieces of art a day that are completely original. In the studio, with assistants' help, still sort of under my guidance and my own creativity, we put out anywhere between three and six or seven finished items a day, which would mean a line of watch faces, or a line of blankets, or pillows, or a line of wallpapers. Every day or two, a line of this gets out of here. But my own drawings, that are usually done in between—usually on the phone or during interviews . . . usually I have a pen in hand and I just draw, and within an hour or two of conversation or being on the phone, or being at a meeting, I will do at least twelve drawings. These drawings get filed and cleaned up, and there I have my reservoir. I have a reservoir of close to ten thousand things now. I sort of touch every subject, phase and mood, in art, you know. It's really a good way to work, so when an assignment comes up, I just pick something I've done.

"I find working in industry and working for businessmen to be supercreative. The average artist cannot stomach working with a businessman. I understand their problems, their facilities, their financial responsibilities, risks and so forth." [Donald Moffitt and B. Martin Pedersen, "A Conversation with Peter Max," in *Peter Max Poster Book,* Crown, 1970.[4]]

To withstand the pace, Max lived a lifestyle of relative simplicity, which included meditation and yoga practices. "What fascinates and drives me is that man and his acts are insignif-

icant, microscopic in terms of the continual evolution of the universe according to a master plan or an omnipresent law that governs the state of existence." ["Peter Max: The Ubiquitous Designer," *Publishers Weekly,* April 27, 1970.[5]]

1970. Wrote and illustrated his first book with guru, Swami Satchidananda. "I found the Swami Satchidananda in Paris and brought him here to be my guru. Before that I had an art studio, but I was like everybody else. Yoga isn't a religion; it's a way of life, a practice of moral and ethical codes and discovery of cosmological laws. There's an absence of a spiritual background in this country. Our parents and our culture have never showed us a direction. Eastern thinking has been constant, continuous development for 4,000 years. Now there's a great blend of East and West; we have the technological advances that we're giving to the East; in turn we're getting Eastern spiritual aspects. The role of artists and writers all over the world is to bring out this spiritual aspect and influence the masses toward beauty and subtlety.

"The things I've learned under yoga—a message of love, harmony, unity, and symmetry—I try to change into art for the masses through this mass commercial vehicle. The business people are a vehicle through which I distribute my very intimate ideas." ["Peter Max," *Mademoiselle,* August, 1968.[6]]

Max's way of life and his yoga practices had a direct influence on his art. "The lines, the colors, the shapes, the subjects, the compositions are very carefully planned to be in a positive nature. There's no negativity here. There's no 'anti' something there. It is all pro-life, it is all pro-beauty, it is all pro-good. Even the lines are very carefully selected. Very seldom do I ever use pointed lines. . . . I have something specific to show, because pointed things are like, pointy, and round things are

(From *Peter Max Paints America,* edited by Victor Zurbel. Illustrated by Peter Max.)

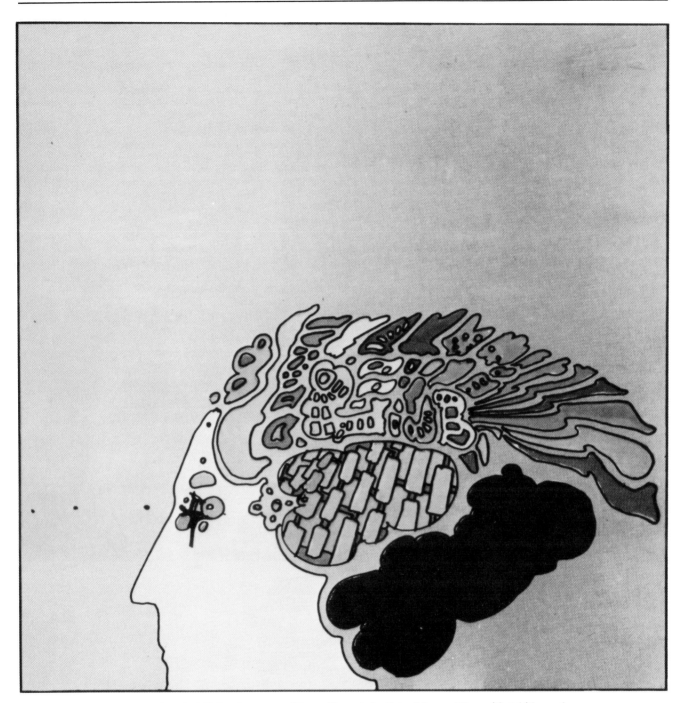

Thought is a vital, living force.... ■ (From *Thought* by Peter Max and Swami Satchidananda. Illustrated by Peter Max.)

smooth. You very seldom see pointed things in nature, only things that are sort of on the defense—you know, like a rose has these pointed things, these barbs—thorns—to hurt, to fight back.''[4]

A traveling art show, ''The World of Peter Max,'' opened at the M. H. De Young Memorial Museum in San Francisco.

1971. Made plans for a World Spiritual Festival in Oregon (the Pope had been invited), but the plans failed to materialize. ''The eastern peoples have their own symbols; the demon, the flower, and the symmetry of their designs. The symbols of the new culture in America in the 1960s are words like 'love' and 'peace.' The word for the 70s will be cosmology.''

1973. Went into a self-imposed ''creative retreat.'' Although still prolific, Max chose to allow companies to use his designs. ''I am an original. I am as original as an original can be. I am also a real American because Americans are immigrants. And, my friend, I am a real American immigrant.

''Artists are seers, visionaries. I was blessed with this without knowing it. One day I was living just like my friends and my art school buddies and the next I was a visionary. America, the whole world, grabbed me, so fast, so much. I expressed my art fast and big but it was received bigger. It just wiped me out. I had to pull back. I had to stop. They were just taking too much from me.

ORANGE BOY HAD BEEN FEELING VERY *RED*
AND WANTED SOMETHING TO COOL OUT HIS HEAD

(From *The Peter Max Land of Blue* by Peter Max. Illustrated by the author.)

"A canvas shouldn't be framed and called finished. It should be copied, reproduced, displayed, distributed as far and wide as possible; like the rays of the sun.

"My creativity is going mass again. I feel that people are waiting, that I'm being called back again. It's like the first two hundred years were an outline, a rough outline of what's to be. It's really going to take off now; via self-realization, via communication, via Max.'' ["Peter Max," *Crawdaddy*, September, 1976.[6]]

1978. Peter Max posters were placed at 135 ports of entry into the United States along the Canadian and Mexican borders to welcome visitors to America.

Speaking about his art, Max said: "The devotion and respect I have for my audience comes across. My work is an 'up' thing. It's happy.

"There's a tremendous hunger out there in America for some excitement. My art brings some satisfaction for their thirst.

"People think I'm in this for money. That's not my motivation. This art of mine is a cause, a mission." [Eleanor Kalter "Color Him Green . . . As in Money," *Sunday News,* April 20, 1969.[7]]

To young people Max gave the following advice: ". . . Accept society, but understand it, that it's only in the process of evolution—they're the new evolution, society is the old one. To work with the facilities the society has given us. Most people today, when they get the bug, rebel completely, rebel themselves out of a relationship with society. Then they can't get a job or an education or use the facilities.

"Don't make the rebellion obvious. Keep it hidden as a motive. Don't throw it up all at once. Take a lifetime and do it through your work. Be responsible.

"Today is the first day of the rest of your life."
                                                    Anonymous

(From *Meditations,* selected and illustrated by Peter Max.)

"Second, get involved in yoga. It's the first time a true, determined, powerful spiritual force has taken hold and is willing to work with your society.'"[5]

FOR MORE INFORMATION SEE: "The Kaleidoscopic World of Peter Max," *Interior Design,* June, 1967; *New York Times,* February 20, 1968, March 31, 1974, July 25, 1978, February 16, 1982; "Hot Mod Artist Gets in Commercial Groove," *Business Week,* March 16, 1968; "Commercial Graffiti," *Time,* June 7, 1968; "Peter Max," *Mademoiselle,* August, 1968; "Month's Cover Artist: Peter Max," *Wilson Library Bulletin,* April, 1969; *Newsweek,* April 14, 1969, June 23, 1980; Eleanor Kalter, "Color Him Green . . . As in Money," *Sunday News,* April 20, 1969; *Newsday,* May 15, 1969; *Washington Post,* June 28, 1969; "Mark of Max is Everywhere," *Life,* September 5, 1969; *Cue,* October 4, 1969; "Peter Max: The Wizard of Ahs Paints a Vivid Self-Portrait," *Seventeen,* April, 1970; *Peter Max Poster Book,* Crown, 1970; "Peter Max: The Ubiquitous Designer," *Publishers Weekly,* April 27, 1970; David L. Goodrich, *Horatio Alger Is Alive and Well and Living in America: Success Stories of the Under-30 Generation,* Cowles, 1971; *Current Biography Yearbook,* H. W. Wilson, 1972; *Dallas News,* September 13, 1974; J. Kutner, "Max Visits Dallas to Sell New Image," *Biography News,* November, 1974; Martha E. Ward and Dorothy A. Marquardt, *Illustrators of Books for Young People,* Scarecrow, 1975; "Peter Max," *Crawdaddy,* September, 1976; "America My Love," *American Home,* February, 1977; "Border Disputes," *Art News,* November, 1977; "A Burst of Color for Visitors to U.S.," *U.S. News,* May 28, 1979.

McGUIRE, Leslie (Sarah) 1945-
(Louisa Britton, Leslie Burton, Dorothy Eyre, Sarah Keyser, Sarah Leslie, Shari Robinson, David Strong)

BRIEF ENTRY: Born January 18, 1945, in New York, N.Y. Artist, author and illustrator of children's books. A graduate of Barnard College, McGuire has worked as a public relations assistant and teacher of special reading in New York City. From 1969 to 1977 she was employed as an editor at Platt & Munk. The author of more than thirty books for children, McGuire writes under a variety of pseudonyms. Although most of her books have been illustrated by others, she provided the pictures for *This Farm Is a Mess* (Parents Magazine Press, 1981). Her other books include *Farm Animals* (Platt, 1970), *Petrouchka: From an Old Russian Legend* (Platt, 1971), *You: How Your Body Works* (Platt, 1974), *Numbers, Signs, and Pictures: A First Number Book* (Platt, 1975), *Who Invented It and What Makes It Work?* (Platt, 1976), *Scooter Computer and Mr. Chips in the Computer in the Candy Store* (Golden Press, 1984), and *The Saggy Baggy Elephant and the New Dance* (Golden Press, 1985). *Home:* 420 Riverside Dr., New York, N.Y. 10025.

FOR MORE INFORMATION SEE: Contemporary Authors, Volume 107, Gale, 1983.

Little Boy kneels at the foot of the bed,
Droops on the little hands little gold head.
Hush! Hush! Whisper who dares!
Christopher Robin is saying his prayers.
                                                    —A.A. Milne
                                    (From *When We Were Very Young*)

Ewell rode proudly, one hand resting on his wooden leg. ■ (From *Gettysburg* by MacKinlay Kantor. Illustrated by Donald McKay.)

McKAY, Donald 1895-

PERSONAL: Born in 1895, in San Francisco, Calif.; *Education:* Attended Mark Hopkins Art School.

CAREER: Illustrator and artist. Has also designed and decorated Christmas cards, and has worked as a cartoonist for *Esquire. Military service:* U.S. Army, Artillery, World War I. *Awards, honors:* Lewis Carroll Shelf Award, 1962, for *The Adventures of Huckleberry Finn.*

ILLUSTRATOR: Mark Twain, (pseudonym of Samuel Langhorne Clemens), *The Adventures of Tom Sawyer,* Random House, 1930; Richard Aldrich Summers, *Conquerors of the River,* Oxford University Press, 1939.

Hartzell Spence, *One Foot in Heaven,* McGraw, 1940; R. A. Summers, *Cavalcade to California,* Oxford University Press, 1941; Irwin Shapiro, *How Old Stormalong Captured Mocha Dick,* Messner, 1942; I. Shapiro, *Steamboat Bill and the Captain's Top Hat,* Messner, 1943; I. Shapiro, *Gremlins of Lieu-*

tenant Oggins, Messner, 1943; Charles Dickens, *Posthumous Papers of the Pickwick Club,* Modern Library, 1943; C. Dickens, *Dickens Digest,* McGraw, 1943; Caroline Dyer, *Tale of Two Houses,* McGraw, 1944; Philip H. Reisman, Jr., *Please Don't Streamline Mother While I'm Gone,* McGraw, 1944; I. Shapiro, *Casey Jones and Locomotive Number 638,* Messner, 1944; Rosemary Taylor, *Ridin' the Rainbow: Father's Life in Tucson,* McGraw, 1944; Anthony Trollope, *Barchester Towers,* Doubleday, 1945; C. Dyer, *Three Famous Ugly Sisters,* McGraw, 1946; Moritz A. Jagendorf, *New England Bean-Pot: American Folk Stories to Read and to Tell,* Vanguard, 1948; M. Twain, *The Adventures of Huckleberry Finn,* Grosset, 1948.

MacKinlay Kantor, *Lee and Grant at Appomattox,* Random House, 1950; Robert Burns, *Some Poems, Songs, and Epistles,* Oliver, 1951; Walter M. Teller, *Island Summer,* Knopf, 1951; M. Kantor, *Gettysburg,* Random House, 1952; Joan Howard (pseudonym of Patricia Gordon), *The Story of Mark Twain,* Grosset, 1953; Doris Shannon Garst, *John Jewitt's Adventure,* Houghton, 1955; Jean Gould, *Young Mariner, Melville,* Dodd, 1956; (with James Daugherty), I. Shapiro, *Heroes in American Folklore,* Messner, 1962.

Tom listened a moment, but no sound disturbed the quiet. Then he gave a low, distinct whistle. ■
(From *The Adventures of Tom Sawyer* by Mark Twain. Illustrated by Donald McKay.)

FOR MORE INFORMATION SEE: Bertha Mahony Miller and others, compilers, *Illustrators of Children's Books: 1946-1956,* Horn Book, 1958.

McMAHAN, Ian

BRIEF ENTRY: Author of fiction and nonfiction for children and adults. Among McMahon's works for children are three mysteries aimed at middle-grade readers. According to *Booklist, ESP McGee and the Ghost Ship* (Avon/Camelot, 1984) features a "brainy Sleuth" and his best friend, Matt, who together manage to work themselves around a number of predicaments. Both *The Fox's Lair* (1983) and *Lake Fear* (1985) are part of Macmillan's "Microkid Mystery" series which combines mystery with microcomputer wizardry. McMahan's adult books include the novel *From the Shamrock Shore,* inspired by his interest in the folk music of the British Isles. *Residence:* New York, N.Y.

Some books are to be tasted, others to be swallowed, and some few to be chewed and digested: that is, some books are to be read only in parts, others to be read, but not curiously, and some few to be read wholly, and with diligence and attention.

—Francis Bacon

MENDONCA, Susan   1950-

BRIEF ENTRY: Born June 6, 1950, in Harrow, England; came to the United States in 1957. Author of novels for young adults. A writer since 1973, Mendonca previously worked as a secretary and a designer-producer of wetsuits in California. In her first novel, *Tough Choices* (Dial, 1980), Mendonca focuses on fourteen-year-old Crystal Borne who, when her parents divorce, must decide whether she would prefer to live with her reliable father or irresponsible mother. "The California-set story . . . has conviction and a certain poignancy . . . ," observed *Horn Book.* "The characters are well-defined," added *Bulletin of the Center for Children's Books,* "the writing style smooth, and the dialogue natural. . . ." Mendonca is also the author of three romance novels: *The Problem with Love* (Bantam, 1982), *Broken Dreams* (Scholastic Inc., 1984), and *Once Upon a Kiss* (Scholastic Inc., 1985). Her work is represented in anthologies, and she is a contributor of articles and stories to magazines. *Home and office:* 1101 North Branciforte Ave., Santa Cruz, Calif. 95062.

FOR MORE INFORMATION SEE: Contemporary Authors, Volume 102, Gale, 1981.

The school system has much to say these days of the virtue of reading widely, and not enough about the virtues of reading less but in depth.

—John Ciardi

(From *I Have a Horse of My Own* by Charlotte Zolotow. Illustrated by Yoko Mitsuhashi.)

MITSUHASHI, Yoko

PERSONAL: Born in Tokyo, Japan. *Education:* Graduated, Women's College of Fine Arts, Tokyo, Japan.

CAREER: Illustrator and designer. Has worked for the Nippon Design Center, Japan and, beginning 1962, in New York. *Member:* Japan Advertising Artists Club. *Awards, honors: Such Is the Way of the World* was selected one of Child Study Association's "Children's Books of the Year," 1968, and *The King's Choice: A Folktale from India*, 1971.

ILLUSTRATOR— All for children: Charlotte Zolotow, *I Have a Horse of My Own*, Abelard, 1964, new edition, Crowell, 1979; Eve Titus, adapter, *The Two Stonecutters*, Doubleday, 1967; Benjamin Elkin, *Such Is the Way of the World*, Parents Magazine Press, 1968; Kermit Krueger, *The Serpent Prince: Folk Tales from Northeastern Thailand*, World Publishing, 1969; Mary Leister, *The Silent Concert*, Bobbs-Merrill, 1970; K. Shivkumar (pseudonym of K. Shanker Pillai), reteller, *The King's Choice: A Folktale from India*, Parents Magazine Press, 1970; Naomi Sellers, *The Little Elephant Who Liked to Play*, Ginn (England), 1974.

FOR MORE INFORMATION SEE: Martha E. Ward and Dorothy A. Marquardt, *Illustrators of Books for Young People*, Scarecrow, 1975.

NEBEL, Gustave E.
(Mimouca Nebel)

PERSONAL: Born in Paris, France; became American citizen; married: Lydie Vallois (an actress and author of children's books). *Education:* Attended Académie Julian, École des Arts Décoratifs, and École National des Beaux Arts. *Residence:* New York, N.Y.

CAREER: Artist and illustrator of books for young readers. Work has been exhibited both in the United States and abroad, and is represented in private collections. *Military service:* French Army, World War II. *Awards, honors: Think about It: Experiments in Psychology* and *My Village, My World* were both chosen one of Child Study Association's Children's Books of the Year, 1968 and 1969, respectively; *Book World*'s Children's Spring Book Festival honor book, 1969, for *My Village, My World*.

ILLUSTRATOR—Of interest to young readers: (Under pseudonym Mimouca Nebel) Elizabeth Bowen, *The Good Tiger*, Knopf, 1965; Sylvia Sherry, *Secret of the Jade Pavilion*, Lippincott, 1967; Eve Hanley, *A New Song*, Weybright & Talley, 1967; Laurence J. Gould and William G. Martin, *Think about It: Experiments in Psychology*, Prentice-Hall, 1968; Edmund Lindop, *The First Book of Elections*, F. Watts, 1968, revised edition, 1972; Julia C. Mahon, *The First Book of Creative Writing*, F. Watts, 1968; Norah Smaridge, *Teacher's Pest*, Hawthorn, 1968; Lydie Nebel, *Happy Old Engine*, Funk, 1968; Ida DeLage, *The Old Witch Goes to the Ball*, Garrard, 1969; Marie Niemeyer, *The Moon Guitar*, F. Watts, 1969; David E. Sanford, *My Village, My World*, Crown, 1969; Ronald Seth, *Spies: Their Trade and Their Tricks*, Hawthorn, 1969.

Anne Alexander, *Little Foreign Devil*, Atheneum, 1970; Edmund Wallace Hildick, *The Secret Winners* (Junior Literary Guild selection), Crown, 1970; Elizabeth Comstock Mooney, *The Sandy Shoes Mystery*, Lippincott, 1970; E. W. Hildick, *The Secret Spenders*, Crown, 1971; Miriam Chaikin, *The Happpy Pairr and Other Love Stories*, Putnam, 1972; Carol York, *Mystery at Dark Wood*, F. Watts, 1972. Contributor of illustrations to magazines in the U.S., France, and Italy.

SIDELIGHTS: Nebel's works are included in the Kerlan Collection at the University of Minnesota.

FOR MORE INFORMATION SEE: Martha E. Ward and Dorothy A. Marquardt, *Illustrators of Books for Young People*, Scarecrow, 1975.

(From *The Good Tiger* by Elizabeth Bowen. Illustrated by M. Nebel.)

NEWCOMBE, Jack

PERSONAL: Born in Burlington, Vt. *Education:* Received B.A. from Brown University; attended University of Missouri, University of California, Pomona College, and American University at Biarritz. *Residence:* Los Angeles, Calif.

CAREER: Editor, journalist, and author. Has been employed as managing editor of *Sport,* and text editor of *Life. Military service:* U.S. Army.

WRITINGS—Of interest to young readers, except as indicated; all nonfiction, except as indicated: *Floyd Patterson: Heavyweight King,* Bartholomew House, 1961; *The Fireballers: Baseball's Fastest Pitchers,* Putnam, 1964; (editor) *The Fireside Book of Football,* Simon & Schuster, 1964; *The Game of Football* (illustrated by Paul Frame), Garrard, 1967; *Six Days to Saturday: Joe Paterno and Penn State* (illustrated with photographs by Dick Swanson), Farrar, Straus, 1974; *The Best of the Athletic Boys: The White Man's Impact on Jim Thorpe,* Doubleday, 1975; (editor) *A Christmas Treasury* (anthology; fiction), Viking, 1982; *In Search of Billy Cole* (adult novel), Arbor House, 1984; *Northern California: A History and Guide,* Random House, in press.

FOR MORE INFORMATION SEE: Martha E. Ward and Dorothy A. Marquardt, *Authors of Books for Young People,* Scarecrow Press, 1971; *Sport,* July, 1980.

NORTH, Sterling　1906-1974

PERSONAL: Born November 4, 1906, in Edgerton, Wis.; died of a stroke, December 22, 1974, in Morristown, N.J.; son of David Willard (a real estate salesman, farm owner, and expert on Indian artifacts) and Elizabeth (a linguist, biologist, and history teacher; maiden name, Nelson) North; married Gladys Dolores Buchanan, June 23, 1927; children: David Sterling, Arielle (Mrs. C. E. Olson). *Education:* University of Chicago, A.B., 1929. *Residence:* Morristown, N.J. *Agent:* (Films) H. N. Swanson, Inc., 8523 Sunset Blvd., Hollywood, Calif.

CAREER: Chicago *Daily News,* Chicago, Ill., reporter, 1929-31, literary editor, 1932-43; *Post,* New York, N.Y., literary editor, 1943-49; *World Telegram and Sun,* New York, N.Y., literary editor, 1949-1956; Houghton Mifflin Co., (publishers), founder and general editor of North Star Books (historical series for children), 1957-64; author. Syndicated columnist for several years before 1957. Master of ceremonies for radio program, ''Books on Trial,'' four years. *Member:* Authors League of America. *Awards, honors:* Witter Bynner Poetry Award; *Poetry* magazine's Young Poet's Prize; *New York Herald Tribune*'s Spring Book Festival honor book, 1956, for *Abe Lincoln: Log Cabin to White House;* Dutton Animal Book Award, New Jersey Institute of Technology Authors Award, both 1963, Newbery Honor Book, 1964, Lewis Carroll Shelf Award, 1964, Dorothy Canfield Fisher Children's Book Award, 1965, Aurianne Award, 1965, William Allen White Children's Book

STERLING NORTH

Award, 1966, Pacific Northwest Library Association Young Readers' Choice Award, 1966, and Sequoyah Children's Book Award, 1966, all for *Rascal: A Memoir of a Better Era;* New Jersey Institute of Technology Authors Award, 1965, for *Little Rascal;* New Jersey Institute of Technology Children's Book Writer of the Year Award, 1966; Dutton Animal Book Award, 1969, for *The Wolfling.*

WRITINGS—Juvenile: *The Five Little Bears* (illustrated by Clarence Biers and Hazel Frazee), Rand McNally, 1935; *The Zipper ABC Book* (illustrated by Keith Ward), Rand McNally, 1937; *Greased Lightning* (illustrated by Kurt Wiese), Winston, 1940; *Midnight and Jeremiah* (Junior Literary Guild selection; illustrated by K. Wiese), Winston, 1943; *The Birthday of Little Jesus* (illustrated by Valenti Angelo), Grosset, 1952; *Son of the Lamp Maker: The Story of a Boy Who Knew Jesus* (illustrated by Manning Lee), Rand McNally, 1956.

The First Steamboat on the Mississippi (illustrated by Victor Mays), Houghton, 1962; *Rascal: A Memoir of a Better Era* (ALA Notable Book; *Horn Book* honor list; illustrated by John Schoenherr), Dutton, 1963, reissued, 1984 (published in England as *Rascal: The True Story of a Pet Raccoon,* Hodder & Stoughton, 1963); *Little Rascal* (based on *Rascal: A Memoir of a Better Era;* illustrated by Carl Burger), Dutton, 1965; *Raccoons Are the Brightest People,* Dutton, 1966 (published in England as *The Raccoons of My Life,* Hodder & Stoughton, 1967); *The Wolfling: A Documentary Novel of the Eighteen-Seventies* (illustrated by J. Schoenherr), Dutton, 1969.

Biographies for young readers: *Abe Lincoln: Log Cabin to White House* (illustrated by Lee Ames), Random House, 1956; *George Washington, Frontier Colonel* (illustrated by L. Ames), Random House, 1957; *Young Thomas Edison* (illustrated by William Barss), Houghton, 1958; *Thoreau of Walden Pond* (illustrated by Harve Stein), Houghton, 1959; *Captured by the Mohawks, and Other Adventures of Radisson* (illustrated by V. Mays), Houghton, 1960; *Mark Twain and the River* (illustrated by V. Mays), Houghton, 1961.

Novels: *Plowing on Sunday,* Reilly & Lee, 1933; *Night Outlasts the Whippoorwill,* Macmillan, 1936; *Seven against the Years,* Macmillan, 1939; *So Dear to My Heart,* Doubleday, 1947; *Reunion on the Wabash,* Doubleday, 1952.

Other: (With Harry Dean) *The Pedro Gorino: The Adventures of a Negro Sea-Captain in Africa* (autobiography of H. Dean), Houghton, 1929 (published in England as *Umbala,* Harrap, 1929); *Midsummer Madness,* Grosset, 1933; *Tiger,* Reilly & Lee, 1933; *The Writings of Mazo De La Roche,* Little Brown, n.d.; (with wife, Gladys North) *Being a Literary Map of These United States Depicting a Renaissance No Less Astonishing Than That of Periclean Athens or Elizabethan London,* Putnam, 1942; *Hurry, Spring!,* Dutton, 1966. Also author of a book of lyric poems, published by University of Chicago Press, 1925.

Editor: (With Carl Kroch) *So Red the Nose, or Breath in the Afternoon: Literary Cocktails,* Farrar & Rinehart, 1935; (with

(From the movie "Rascal," starring Bill Mumy. Produced by Buena Vista Films, 1969.)

C. B. Boutell) *Speak of the Devil: An Anthology of the Appearances of the Devil in the Literature of the Western World*, Doubleday, 1945. Editor of about twenty-three other books. Contributor to anthologies and of poems, articles, and stories to *Dial, Atlantic Monthly, Esquire, Saturday Review, Har-* *per's, Yale Review, Poetry, Nation, Reader's Digest, Holiday*, and other periodicals.

ADAPTATIONS: "So Dear to My Heart" (motion picture), RKO, 1948; "Rascal: A Memoir of a Better Era" (motion

(From the movie "So Dear to My Heart," starring Burl Ives and Bobby Driscoll. Released by RKO Radio Pictures. Copyright 1948 by Walt Disney Productions.)

Using a small barrel of gunpowder, he lighted a fuse, and lifted this improvised bomb over the wall. . . . ■ (From *Captured by the Mohawks and Other Adventures of Radisson* by Sterling North. Illustrated by Victor Mays.)

picture), Disney Studios, 1969; ''Rascal'' (record or cassette), Miller-Brody, 1979.

SIDELIGHTS: **November 4, 1906.** Born in a farmhouse on Lake Koshkonong in southern Wisconsin. North's father was a real-estate speculator, who was also an expert on Indian artifacts and nature. ''In his real-estate business, my father speculated largely in farm properties,'' wrote North in his autobiographical novel *Rascal: A Memoir of a Better Era*. ''He mortgaged each farm he acquired, used the money to buy another farm, then repeated the process. This reckless pyramiding of paper profits brought him close to disaster in every farm recession. But it paid off well in 1918, which was a boom year for farms, and he often put a sign on the door announcing that he was 'Gone for the Day' or longer.

''At home my father was usually immersed in endless research for a novel about the Fox and Winnebago Indians. Somehow the book never got written, but his fund of tribal lore, as he pointed out this Indian trail or that, was always fascinating.'' [Sterling North, ''Rascal: A Memoir of a Better Era,'' *Reader's Digest,* September, 1963.[1]]

North's mother was a linguist, biologist, and history teacher who had graduated from college at the head of her class at the age of eighteen. She taught her children to read and write at an early age.

1913. Mother died. North was raised by his father and sister, Jessica Nelson North, who later became a well-known poet.

1914. First published poem appeared in *St. Nicholas* magazine. '''Eager faces looking up/filled with wonder, like a cup.' I wonder who wrote that inspired couplet. The world is created anew for each child. My desire to write (particularly for children) began with a poem I published in *St. Nicholas* magazine at the age of eight and has continued ever since.

''The impulse to write, I believe, is the desire to communicate a memory, a mood, a distillation of delight that might otherwise be lost forever. It is mortal man's feeble attempt to stay the hand of time. I know that many modern writers could not care less about such attempts to perfect and perpetuate a perception. Words today are often used merely as weapons, blunt and brutal weapons. They seek to kill or wound more frequently than to inspire.

''But in children we have an innocent audience not yet hardened and brutalized and made cynical. They look to us trustingly for information and enchantment. How very few of us are worthy of such trust.

''I feel that I was blessed by a richly rewarding childhood in a far off time before the genocide of the human race seemed probable. There were in those days certain 'enduring' values, only a few of which still survive. If I have captured the ear and the imagination of a few million children around the globe I feel I have not lived in vain.''

1918. ''I was 11 years old . . . and lived alone with my father in our big ten-room house. He was an absentminded, scholarly man whose real-estate business frequently took him away on trips, and since my brother, Herschel, was fighting in France and my two grown sisters lived elsewhere, I was often left to myself. But I did not lack for companionship.

''My numerous pets included several cats and four yearling skunks (until a slight accident occurred and a delegation of neighbors urged me to give them up); Wowser, my huge, affectionate, perpetually hungry Saint Bernard; and Edgar Allan Poe, the crow, who lived in the belfry of the Methodist Church next door, and shouted, 'What fun! What fun!,' the only phrase he knew, as dignified parishioners came to church services, weddings and funerals. But my newest friend and most constant companion was Rascal, my pet raccoon.

''I had raised him from a kit, and now he ate at the table with Dad and me, occupying my old high chair and drinking warm milk from a bowl. He reached the milk by standing in the chair and placing his hands on the edge of the tray. His table manners were excellent—much better than those of most children—and he chirred and trilled his satisfaction with the arrangement. Rascal slept with me, too, and at night his comforting furry presence made me feel less lonesome when my father was away.

''He went fishing with me and explored the Wisconsin woods around Brailsford Junction, where we lived. He fitted nicely into the basket on my bicycle and soon became a cycling maniac. He stood on the wire mesh with his feet apart, his hands gripping the front edge of the basket. As we tore down the hills his tail plumed out behind, and the natural black goggles around his bright eyes made him look like Barney Oldfield coming down the stretch. He was a demon for speed, and I took him everywhere.

"On the morning of November 11, the real Armistice was signed, and a sudden silence fell over the trenches of Europe. In Brailsford Junction, the celebration began early. The decorated fire engines, automobiles and horse-drawn conveyances crowded the streets in a noisy, happy parade. I interwove the spokes of my bicycle wheels with red, white and blue crepe-paper ribbons. With Rascal in the basket, I pedaled through the throng, ringing my bell as a small contribution to the joyous pandemonium of fire whistles and church bells.

"But by afternoon my elation had subsided and I returned home to begin oiling my muskrat traps for the season ahead. As usual Rascal was interested in what I was doing. But when he came to sniff and feel the traps, a terrible thought slowed my fingers. Putting my traps aside, I opened a catalogue from a St. Louis fur buyer. There on the first page was a handsome raccoon, his paw caught in a powerful trap.

"How could anyone mutilate the sensitive, questing hands of an animal like Rascal? I picked up my raccoon and hugged him in a passion of remorse.

"I burned my fur catalogues in the furnace and hung my traps in the loft of the barn, never to use them again. Men had stopped killing other men in France that day; and on that day I signed a permanent peace treaty with the animals and the birds."[1]

Eventually, North gave Rascal freedom, but their relationship was immortalized many years later in the award-winning book *Rascal: A Memoir of a Better Era.*

1924. Entered the University of Chicago, where he paid his tuition by such odd jobs as spray-painting cars, keeping books for a large sanitarium, selling cigars, and running a commercial truck garden. In his spare time he also managed to edit the campus literary magazine, to write lyrics for student musicals, and to publish his poetry and short stories in *Dial* and other national magazines.

1925. A slender volume of his poetry was published by the University of Chicago Press, when he was nineteen.

June 23, 1927. Married Gladys Dolores Buchanan, his childhood sweetheart. North was twenty, and a junior at the University of Chicago. "We had been in love since we first met at 15 and had married while I was still earning my way through the University of Chicago. We were as poor as all proverbial poets, but hard-working and hopeful. A full schedule at school and a full-time job took much of our time. Somehow we also

This young ram is a champion in every sense of the word.... ■ (From *So Dear to My Heart* by Sterling North. Illustrated by Brad Holland.)

found the energy to write verse for many national magazines, furnish the lyrics for the campus musical comedy (Beatrice Lillie sang my 'Helen of Troy' on three continents), and write a book.

"The first book and the first baby were more than casually related. We have found over the years that either a book or a baby takes some nine months of gestation, plus a certain amount of misery before the ultimate joy. But the immediate acceptance of my first book by Houghton Mifflin in Boston and publishers in Berlin and London made a baby economically possible. . . ." [Sterling North, ''The Petals of Happiness,'' *My Most Inspiring Moment: Encounters with Destiny Relived by Thirty-Eight Best-Selling Authors,* edited by Robert Fitzgibbon and Ernest V. Heyn, Doubleday, 1965.²]

February, 1929. North's first baby was born on the day his first book was published. "A Chinese sage once wrote that there are 'three petals to the Flower of Happiness': a man must write a book, become a father of a son, and build a house.

"It would be many years before Gladys and I could build our present house beside our waterfall. But late in February, . . . when we were young and almost penniless, the first two petals of this flower of happiness unfolded.

"The book was my romantic but factual biography of a fascinating old sea captain who had signed on as a cabin boy at the age of 12 and who owned his tramp schooner in his 20s. We called the book, *The Pedro Gorino,* after the strange name of his schooner.

Wolf licked her cheek. She didn't sound very dangerous to him. ■ (From *The Wolfling: A Documentary Novel of the Eighteen-Seventies* by Sterling North. Illustrated by John Schoenherr.)

They never take "no" for an answer, and will perch on the shoulders of a scarecrow. . . . ■ (From *Hurry, Spring!* by Sterling North. Illustrated by Carl Burger.)

"Now on the evening of Monday, Feb. 25th, . . . —20 months after Gladys and I had taken our vows in a Methodist parsonage in Waukegan, Ill.—it was apparent that book and baby would complicate my senior year but enrich it quite beyond measure.

"During the afternoon I had cut all my classes to help arrange a window at Marshall Field's—ivory tusks, native drums and spears, lion skins, and a great pyramid of my book. I came home elated through a freezing rain to find Gladys at work on a poster which was needed to go with this display.

"She continued to work industriously with her India ink and lettering pens, doing a beautiful job of calligraphy. At about 8 in the evening, she paused for a few minutes and closed her eyes. With characteristic courage, she refused to admit that she had felt her first birth pain. But there was no way to hide the next pain or the next."²

North and his wife named their first child David. Three years later, a daughter named Arielle was born.

1929-1943. Worked for the Chicago *Daily News,* first as a reporter and later becoming literary editor. North worked in the company of such notable American writers as Carl Sandburg and John Gunther. During those years he also wrote novels and juveniles. "Discovering that three cannot go through college as inexpensively as one, I found it expedient to take a full-time job with the Chicago *Daily News.* 'From cub reporter to literary editor in three years' time' might be the caption of the years of the depression. During those years I covered every sort of assignment from night police reporting in gang-infested Chicago to 'Toonerville Trolley'—it meets all the trains.''

1943. Left Chicago to become literary editor of the New York *Post*. He worked on the *Post* for six years until joining the staff of *World Telegram and Sun* as their literary editor. After moving east, the North family built their house on a twenty-seven-acre plot of land on a small lake in Morristown, New Jersey.

1957. Quit newspaper work to devote more time to his New Jersey farm and his books. Became general editor of Houghton Mifflin's North Star Books, an American history series for children. His own contributions to the series included six biographies of famous Americans, such as George Washington, Thomas Edison, and Henry David Thoreau. About the famous nature philosopher, North remarked: ''Henry Thoreau once voluntarily spent an entire day submerged in a marsh up to his neck, to get a frog's-eye view of nature. Most of his biographers have found themselves in a similar bog.

''Thoreau had a practical turn of mind when needful. Emerson's Harvard-trained handyman could graft an appletree, manure and plant a good garden, and build a house, a cabin, or a boat. He invented and refined processes for making the best pencils in America. And he could out-walk, out-skate, out-botanize, and out-teach anyone in Concord.'' [Sterling North, ''A Frog's-Eye View at Walden Pond,'' *Saturday Review,* January 15, 1966.[3]]

In his books for young people, North went beyond the intention to entertain and amuse. ''What America desperately needs is a better educational system. We must teach children not only how to read well at a very early age, but must inspire in them a love of books and of knowledge. It has been my life-long crusade to fight the comics and the terror TV shows, while editing and writing books which I hope will give bright young Americans a deeper and richer sense of our culture, past and present.''

North's books have been translated into more than fifty languages.

December 22, 1974. Died of a stroke in Morristown, New Jersey. He was sixty-eight years old. ''If a man cannot stand alone on his own two feet and be judged by his own work he is not a very strong man.''

HOBBIES AND OTHER INTERESTS: Reading, fishing, swimming, and good conversation.

FOR MORE INFORMATION SEE: Stanley J. Kunitz and Howard Haycraft, editors, *Twentieth Century Authors,* H. W. Wilson, 1942; *Current Biography,* H. W. Wilson, 1943; *Editor and Publisher,* September 24, 1949; Harry R. Warfel, *American Novelists of Today,* American Book, 1951; *Publishers Weekly,* December 31, 1956; *Saturday Review,* November 7, 1959, January, 15, 1966.

Kirkus Service, March 15, 1961; *Horn Book,* August, 1961; *New York Times Book Review,* August 25, 1963, August 22, 1965, April 24, 1966; Sterling North, ''Rascal: A Memoir of a Better Era,'' *Reader's Digest,* September, 1963; *Best Sellers,* September 1, 1963, August 15, 1966; *Library Journal,* March 15, 1964, July, 1966; Robert Fitzgibbon and Ernest V.

After a supper of cornmeal mush and cream, Granny had started to decorate the tree. . . . ■
(From *Midnight and Jeremiah* by Sterling North. Illustrated by Kurt Wiese.)

I would float on my back and arch my chest above the water to give him a better resting place. ▪
(From *Little Rascal* by Sterling North. Illustrated by Carl Burger.)

(From *Rascal: A Memoir of a Better Era* by Sterling North. Illustrated by John Schoenherr.)

Heyn, editors, *My Most Inspiring Moment*, Doubleday, 1965; *New York Times*, August 8, 1969; Martha E. Ward and Dorothy A. Marquardt, *Authors of Books for Young People*, 2nd edition, Scarecrow, 1971; Doris de Montreville and Donna Hill, editors, *Third Book of Junior Authors*, H. W. Wilson, 1972; D. L. Kirkpatrick, *Twentieth-Century Children's Writers*, St. Martin's, 1978.

Obituaries: *New York Times*, December 23, 1974; *AB Bookman's Weekly*, January 6, 1975; *Time*, January 6, 1975; *Publishers Weekly*, January 13, 1975; *Current Biography*, February, 1975.

OBLIGADO, Lilian (Isabel)   1931-

BRIEF ENTRY: Born April 12, 1931, in Buenos Aires, Argentina. Artist, author and illustrator of books for children. The granddaughter of poet Rafael Obligado, Lilian Obligado grew up in Argentina where she attended schools and later studied painting under artists like Vincent Puig. Part of her childhood was also spent in the United States, where she returned to make a living in 1958. Settling in New York City, Obligado worked as a free-lance illustrator for the Western Printing & Lithograph Co. until 1963 when she began executing book illustrations for a number of publishers, including Viking, Holiday House, Doubleday, and Dial. Through the years, Obligado has provided illustrations for over fifty children's books, among them three that she wrote herself: *Little Wolf and the Upstairs Bear* (Viking, 1979), *Faint Frogs Feeling Feverish: And Other Terrifically Tantalizing Tongue Twisters* (Viking, 1983), and *If I Had a Dog* (Golden Press, 1984). Her many illustrated works include Elspeth Bragdon's *One to Make*

Ready (Viking, 1959), Charlotte Zolotow's *The White Marble* (Abelard-Schuman, 1963), Albert G. Miller's *A Friend for Shadow* (L. W. Singer, 1969), Edna Barth's *The Day Luis Was Lost* (Little, Brown, 1971), Kathleen N. Daly's *A Child's Book of Animals* (Doubleday, 1975), and Marjorie Weinman Sharmat's *The Best Valentine in the World* (Holiday House, 1982).

PARTCH, Virgil Franklin II   1916-1984 (Vip)

PERSONAL: Born October 17, 1916, on St. Paul Island, Alaska; died in an automobile accident, August 10, 1984, near Valencia, Calif.; son of Paul C. (a U.S. Navy petty officer) and Anna (Pavaloff) Partch; married Helen Marie Aldridge, May, 1938; children: two sons, one daughter. *Education:* Attended University of Arizona and Chouinard Art Institute. *Residence:* Corona Del Mar, Calif.

CAREER: Walt Disney Studios, Hollywood, Calif., 1937-41, began as office boy, became assistant animator; free-lance cartoonist, 1942-84; creator of comic strips "Big George," 1960, and "The Captain's Gig," 1977; employed by Field Newspaper Syndicate to produce "Big George" comic strip. *Military service:* U.S. Army, 1944-46; staff artist, Ford Ord *Panorama. Awards, honors:* First prize, Brussels Cartoon Exhibit, 1964.

WRITINGS—Cartoon books with captions, unless otherwise indicated: *It's Hot in Here*, edited by Gurney Williams, R. M. McBride, 1944; *Water on the Brain*, R. M. McBride, 1945; *Bottle Fatigue*, Duell, Sloan & Pearce, 1950; *The Wild, Wild Women*, Duell, Sloan & Pearce, 1951; *Here We Go Again*, Duell, Sloan & Pearce, 1951; *Man the Beast*, Duell, Sloan & Pearce, 1953; *The Dead Game Sportsman*, Duell, Sloan & Pearce, 1954; *Hanging Way Over*, Duell, Sloan & Pearce, 1955; (under pseudonym Vip) *Crazy Cartoons*, Fawcett, 1956; (with William McIntyre) *Vip Tosses a Party*, Simon & Schuster, 1959.

(With John Armstrong) *Vip's All New Bar Guide*, Fawcett, 1960; *New Faces on the Barroom Floor*, Duell, Sloan & Pearce,

"*I took a thorn out of his paw a few years back.*"

One of Virgil Partch's many cartoons for *True* magazine.

(From *Joe, the Wounded Tennis Player* by Morton Thompson. Illustrated by Virgil Partch.)

1961; *Big George*, Duell, Sloan, & Pearce, 1962; (under pseudonym Vip; with Robert Kraus) *The Christmas Cookie Sprinkle Snitcher* (self-illustrated; juvenile story), Windmill Books, 1969.

(Under pseudonym Vip) *Vip's Mistake Book* (juvenile; puzzle book), Windmill Books, 1970; (contributor) *Dentists Are Funny People,* Gallery Books, 1972; (under pseudonym Vip) *Vip Quips* (juvenile), Windmill Books, 1975.

Other: *Gesellschaftsspiele mit Damen: Dreissig graphische Darstellungen mit einschlaegigen Randbemerkungen von Honore Balzác* (also see below; title means "Parlor Games with Women"), Diogenes Verlag (Zurich), 1956; *Gesellschaftsspiele mit Herren: Dreissig graphische Darstellungen mit einschlaegigen Randbemerkungen von Bettina von Arnim* (also see below; title means "Parlor Games with Men"), Diogenes Verlag, 1956; *Sport am Morgen: Ein Buch fuer Leute, die gesund bleiben wollen* (title means "Sport in the Morning: A Book for People Who Want to Remain Healthy"), Diogenes Verlag, 1960; *Wer will unter die Soldaten: Ein Buch fuer tapfere junge Menschen*, Diogenes Verlag, 1961; *Gesellschaftsspiele mit Damen und Herren* (title means "Parlor Games with Women and Men"; contains *Gesellschaftsspiele mit Damen* and *Gesellschaftsspiele mit Herren*), Diogenes Verlag, 1972.

Illustrator: Morton Thompson, *Joe, the Wounded Tennis Player*, introduction by Robert Benchley, Doubleday, Doran, 1945; Maurice Dolbier, *Nowhere Near Everest*, Knopf, 1955; Philip L. Gabriel, *The Executive*, Citadel, 1959; (under pseudonym Vip) Robert Kraus, *Shaggy Fur Face* (juvenile), Windmill Books, 1971; (under pseudonym Vip) R. Kraus, *Ludwig, the Dog Who Snored Symphonies* (juvenile), Windmill Books, 1971.

"Who can compose in the middle of all this snoring?" ■ (From *Ludwig, the Dog Who Snored Symphonies* by Robert Kraus. Illustrated by Vip.)

SIDELIGHTS: Partch first won recognition for his cartoons in the University of Arizona campus magazine. After one year of college, he enrolled at the Chouinard Art Institute for a term. He subsequently was hired as an office boy at the Walt Disney studios. After four years with Disney, Partch—by that time an assistant animator—participated in a strike at the Disney studios that led to his discharge.

For six weeks the young cartoonist supported his wife and infant son on $18 a week, while he continued to work on his cartoons, mailing some of them to *Collier's* magazine. Guerney Williams, *Collier's* cartoon edition, bought one of them. Beginning with that first sale in 1942 Partch's work was featured regularly in such magazines as *Saturday Evening Post, New Yorker,* and *Look.*

"Vip," as he signed his cartoons, was known as a black humorist with a sardonic touch. He was once described as "nuts ... but nuts in the nice American way." He had his first collection of cartoons published in 1944, and later wrote several books including self-illustrated books for children.

In 1960 "Big George," one of Partch's cartoon strips was syndicated. He also developed another syndicated cartoon strip, "The Captain's Gig," in 1977. His cartoons generally took a literal meaning to a colloquial phrase, thus creating sarcastic humor. "The actual process of achieving a funny drawing which will sell is a difficult thing to describe or explain. I spend little time at my desk during a week, perhaps 10 or 12 hours, and this is for the actual drawing of pictures. By the time I get to that they are pretty well set, either in my mind or in extremely rough pencil sketches on scraps of paper. They're so rough they would make no sense to anyone but me. The rest of the time I spend with people. I like people and from watching them I get my ideas. When I first started free-lancing I used to scribble small drawings and captions on scraps of paper which I stuffed in pockets as the ideas occurred to me. . . .

"Once in a while I write myself a memo, but habit is such that now I usually work on one of two plans. (1) I set myself a schedule for the week of two gags a day done quite roughly in pencil on typewriter paper. At the end of the week I have 10, working on a light-board (a habit formed at Disney's). Then I re-do them with a ball-point pen and get them into the mail on Saturday morning. (2) Or, I do absolutely nothing all week until Saturday, when I get up early, sit down at my desk and say, 'Okay, 10 gags before the noon mail leaves.' I haven't missed yet, although on some Saturdays I have to run all the way to the Post Office before it closes. In either case the batches often come bouncing back with a rejection slip.

"With Plan Two, I'll sometimes simply put the pen on a blank piece of paper and let the lines go where they may, so to speak. I'll draw a bathtub, perhaps, and spend five minutes staring at it. I'll put a man in the water—or maybe an octopus—or both. Then there will be a woman talking from the open door. What will he say? I stare at the sketch for another five minutes or so. What would be funny? Maybe I should have the man talking. I'll fill the woman's open mouth with teeth and open the man's mouth with a few heavy ink lines. Maybe he's fighting the octopus while talking. I put a few more arms on the man. By now the sketch is getting pretty incomprehensible. I might spend another long period of time studying the whole mess before coming up with something I think is pretty droll, or I might just decide the situation is completely idiotic without being in the least humorous. At that point I chuck it and start in on another blank piece of paper.

"When the Okayed sketch comes back, my usual procedure—unless the editor has indicated radical changes, and this seldom happens—is to place a piece of Strathmore paper over the rough, secure with paper clips and proceed with brush and ink. It's almost a tracing; I seldom make any drastic changes. This is where the light-board is essential. My light-board is simply a piece of frosted glass with two small fluorescent bulbs underneath and a switch for turning the lamps off and on. The glass is about 2 ½ by 3 feet and is slightly tilted.

"I say it is almost a tracing because in many cases, after not seeing a sketch for a week or so, I can view it with a fresh eye and make what changes I wish as I ink in the finish. Many times I'll change the actual placement of characters, closing them up or spreading them out, by moving the rough under the Strathmore after each character is finished. For example: if I have a drawing with three characters, with one fellow introducing the other two, and I decide that the drawing is too crowded, I will ink in the central man, then will take off the paper clips and slide the rough around under the Strathmore until I've found just the right position for the next character." [Virgil Partch, "Cartoonist at Work," *Design,* November, 1956.[1]]

Partch further elaborated on the materials he used for his cartoon work and described the "studio" in which he drew his cartoons. "The materials I use for finishes are simple. A couple of No. 4 Winsor Newton water color brushes, a bottle of India ink, two-ply kid Strathmore, a few paper clips or Scotch tape, a blue pencil for indicating Ben Day or areas to have color tint—and I'm off to the races.

"When the drawing is finished, I letter the caption in blue pencil at the bottom, put my name and address on the back, place it in an envelope with a couple pieces of cardboard and

"Something tells me he's going to try to steal home."

A *True* magazine cartoon by Partch.

air mail it. You can't beat free lancing for freedom. No matter where you are, a dime's worth of typewriter paper and a ball-point pen put you in business.

"My regular working set-up is at home. The loneliness of an office depresses me. Home gives me a feeling that human beings aren't too far away. I can hear the music of fighting kids, the wife's soap opera, neighbors visiting over back fences. My first 'studio' was in a closet in the main hall of a small house. Man, the traffic was terrific."[1]

Partch made his home in Corona Del Mar, California where he worked for many years as a free-lance cartoonist. He died at the age of sixty-seven in an automobile accident on August 10, 1984 near Valencia, California.

FOR MORE INFORMATION SEE: "Call Him Vip," *Newsweek,* June 14, 1943; *Collier's,* August 21, 1943, November 27, 1948; "Nuts but Nice," *Time,* July 3, 1944; *Look,* April 5, 1955, July 12, 1955; Virgil Partch, "Cartoonist at Work," *Design,* November, 1956; *The World Encyclopedia of Cartoons,* Gale, 1980. Obituaries: *Los Angeles Times,* August 12, 1984; *Chicago Tribune,* August 12, 1984; *New York Times,* August 12, 1984; *Washington Post,* August 12, 1984; *Newsweek,* August 27, 1984; *Current Biography,* October, 1984.

PENNINGTON, Lillian Boyer   1904-

PERSONAL: Born April 2, 1904, in Harrisburg, Pa.; daughter of Lynn Hutchinson (a railroad worker) and Eva Jane (Liggett) Boyer; married R. Corbin Pennington (a professor of speech), December 28, 1926; children: Corbin. *Education:* Graduated from Cumberland Valley State Normal School (now Shippensburg State College), teaching diploma, 1926; graduate study at Manhattan School of Music, 1937-39, and National Academy of Fine Arts, 1963-66. *Home and studio:* 777 Saturn Dr., Colorado Springs, Colo. 80906.

CAREER: Author of books for children, 1930—. Teacher at schools in Ickesburg, Pa., 1922, Windsor, Colo., 1926, Closter, N.J., 1927-33, 1935-37, and New York City, 1943; Riverdale Country School, New York City, teacher, 1947-58, 1960-63. Work has been exhibited in juried shows and one-artist shows. Paintings are included in private collections. *Member:* National League of American Pen Women, Society of Children's Book Writers, American Watercolor Society (associate), Photographic Society of America, Altrusa Club, Columbine Camera Club, Pikes Peak Camera Club, Colorado Artists Association, Pueblo Art Guild, Colorado Springs Art Guild, Daughters of the American Revolution, Palmer Lake Artists Association, Pikes Peak Artist Association, Miniature Art Society. *Awards, honors:* Maggie Award from Wonder Books, Inc., 1958, for *The Choo Choo Train;* recipient of photography awards, Photography Society of America, 1971; history award, National League of American Pen Women, 1974, for history of Pikes Peak Branch Map; award from National League of American Pen Women, 1974, for *Snafu, the Littlest Clown;* award from the National League of American Pen Women, 1977, for a play, "Shiprock"; Jessie S. Heiges Distinguished Alumnus Award, Shippensburg State College, 1978; music award from the National League of American Pen Women for original compositions, 1981.

WRITINGS: The Choo Choo Train (illustrated by Leonard Kessler), Wonder-Treasure Books, 1958; *Reading for Beginners,* Ottenheimer, 1963; *Treasure House of Bedtime Stories,* Ottenheimer, 1963; *Snafu, the Littlest Clown* (illustrated by

Earle Gardner; cassette also available), High Country Press, 1972. Also author of play, "Shiprock." Contributor of self-illustrated articles to *School Art Magazine, The Instructor, Grade Teacher, Primary Activities,* and *Audubon Jr. News.*

WORK IN PROGRESS: Blackfeet Indian legends as told by War Eagle; "Indian Why" stories.

SIDELIGHTS: "My very first accepted writing was by *Jack and Jill* magazine when I was teaching in New Jersey in the 1930s. It was about a miniature golf course made in our sand box by my first grade children. That was the time miniature golf was so popular. We received $4.00 and a one-year subscription to the *Jack and Jill* magazine. That $4.00 seemed very big then!

"While teaching at the Riverdale Country School in New York City I wrote many plays, poems, music arrangements and articles for *The Instructor, Grade Teacher* and *School Art* magazines as well as other educational magazines. I used my own photography or art work for these.

"One amusing incident was the time I wrote an article about a little squirrel Chippie—who started a newspaper in my second grade room. I sent this article 'Chippie Comes to Second Grade' to the *Grade Teacher,* but (quite by mistake) I used the address of *The Instructor* magazine. Soon afterward I received a special delivery letter from *The Instructor* saying that they received the manuscript, had read it and liked it very much . . . but it was addressed to the *Grade Teacher* . . . and did I want the *Grade Teacher* to have it? If not . . . they wanted it. Naturally, I gave it to *The Instructor* magazine.

"After a number of my articles were accepted by *The Instructor,* Ruth Birdsall of their staff often wrote to me asking for articles and plays.

LILLIAN BOYER PENNINGTON

(From *Snafu, the Littlest Clown* by Lillian Boyer Pennington. Illustrated by Earle Gardner.)

"I might mention that my plays were written in such a way that they served as a basis for a class activity and I think this was one reason that I was able to have so many of them accepted.

"This type of article required the classroom teacher and the children to develop and create the play. They were basic ideas and served to stimulate the imagination of the children so that when the play was given, the children felt it was theirs for they had a big part in the making of it.

"Scenery and costumes were planned and designed by the children and grade teacher. Suggestions were made in the article about the design, about the costumes and about the music. These suggestions helped the teacher and the children to create the completed play.

"Sometimes I would get an idea for a play by going to another classroom and by observing things they were doing there.

"A community project in the first grade gave me an idea for a play, 'Our Town.' This was definitely not the Thornton Wilder 'Our Town.' I drew up a skeleton for the play and the first grade teacher and I helped the children develop it. We gave the play at our school and I took photographs of it. Then I wrote it up and sent it with the photographs to Ruth Birdsall at *The Instructor* magazine. She accepted it. Whenever I used an idea from another classroom I always included that person as co-author and we divided whatever money we got for the article.

"I have always loved the various Indian legends and when I was teaching I enjoyed retelling these legends to my children who loved them as much as I did.

"One unit of work in my classroom was on the American Indian. Many of these legends were inspirations for plays.

"Truthfully, the children each day at 'Show and Tell' always gave me more ideas than I could follow through with.

"My very first book, *The Choo Choo Train* was published by Grosset and Dunlap in 1958. It was a small Wonder Book and won a Maggie award the year it was published. In 1967 it was made into a larger *Nursery Treasury Book*.

"*Reading for Beginners* and *Treasure House of Bedtime Stories* were published by Ottenheimer Publishers in Baltimore, Maryland in 1963 as 'Gold Star Books' and reissued some years later as 'Busy Bee' books.

"*Snafu, the Littlest Clown* book published by High Country Press in 1972, had a second printing that same year. It is now a third edition and Oddo Publishers in Fayetteville, Georgia have added this third printing, a library and school edition, to their 'Adventures in Reading' series with a cassette to go with the book. The cassette has circus sounds.

"I have been a volunteer with the Community Resource Center here in Colorado Springs since 1972 and I have gone to fifty or more schools, many of them four or five times, as I read my books, told stories, recited poems and did creative writing talks. I have also given creative writing talks to adult groups— Ft. Carson Officer's Wive's Club, Colorado College students, Air Force Academy High School students, etc.

"My love for children has made my retirement a very pleasant time."

Pennington's works are included in the children's literature program at Rutgers University.

PIERCE, Edith Gray   1893-1977
(Marian Gray)

PERSONAL: Born December 22, 1893, in Columbus Junction, Iowa; died October 11, 1977, in Columbus Junction, Iowa; daughter of James Edward (a farmer) and Margaret J. (Dawdy) Gray; married Chester Earl Pierce, May 31, 1912 (deceased); children: Alice Elizabeth (Mrs. Harold R. Pierce; deceased), James Gray, Robert Edward (deceased). *Education:* Attended University of Iowa. *Politics:* Republican. *Religion:* Methodist. *Home and office:* Evergreen Farm, Columbus Junction, Iowa 52738.

CAREER: County chairman of Louisa County Women's Farm Bureau, 1922-24, and Louisa County Girls 4-H Clubs, 1925-30. President of Iowa Council of Republican Women, 1951-52. *Member:* National League of American Pen Women (regional chairman, 1969-70), National Federation of Womens Clubs, National Federation of Music Clubs, Iowa Historical Society Etude Club, Shellbark Club. *Awards, honors:* Des Moines Register community service award, 1926.

WRITINGS: Horace Mann: Our Nation's First Educator (for young people) Lerner, 1972. Contributor, sometimes under pseudonym Marian Gray, to *Organic Gardening, Flower Grower, Flower and Garden, Popular Gardening, Capper's Farmer, Farmers Wife, Dog World, Lady's Circle, Farm Wife News,* and *Des Moines Register.* Author of pageant for Columbus Junction Centennial Celebration, 1974. Regional editor, *The Pen Woman* (of National League of American Pen Women), 1969-72.

SIDELIGHTS: Edith Pierce's ancestors came from England in 1840 to Iowa (then Wisconsin Territory), and settled on the farm where she lived.

EDITH GRAY PIERCE

PORTE, Barbara Ann

BRIEF ENTRY: An author of books for children, Porte also works as the Children's Services Specialist in New York's Nassau Library System. She has written three stories in Greenwillow's "Read-alone Books" series, aimed at early primary-grade readers. Beginning with *Harry's Visit* (1983), each book features the same small boy who *School Library Journal* described as "endearing and credible." *Horn Book* further observed that "Harry's dry, forthright narration is chock-full of humor, and the abundant, exuberant drawings washed with color perfectly match the feeling." *Harry's Visit* was followed by *Harry's Dog,* a 1984 ALA Notable Book, and *Harry's Mom* (1985).

For middle-grade readers, Porte provides an unsettling sense of mystery and the macabre in *Jesse's Ghost and Other Stories* (Greenwillow, 1983). The collection of eleven short stories is held together by a storyteller who, as the author states, "sits where three worlds meet, before and now and after." According to *Booklist,* the "sometimes elegant stories have a haunting quality to them. . . . A likely choice for perceptive readers." *Publishers Weekly* agreed, adding that this book should be read "in daylight, with people around; even the droll entries create an eerie aura." The same storytelling atmosphere is

present in *The Kidnapping of Aunt Elizabeth* (Greenwillow, 1985). As fifteen-year-old Ashley Baxter compiles her family history, a series of amusing anecdotes begins to emerge. "With this novel," noted *School Library Journal,* "Porte establishes herself as a masterful storyteller," capable of creating "memorable characters and a seemingly endless supply of engaging tales." Both *Jesse's Ghost and Other Stories* and *The Kidnapping of Aunt Elizabeth* contain a combination of the author's original stories and those based on folk and fairy tales. Porte has also written stories and poems for adults which have appeared in literary magazines nationwide. *Address:* P.O. Box 786, Mineola, N.Y. 11501.

RODDENBERRY, Eugene Wesley   1921- (Gene Roddenberry)

PERSONAL: Professional name, Gene Roddenberry; born August 19, 1921, in El Paso, Tex.; son of Eugene Edward (a master sergeant in U.S. Army) and Carolyn Glen (Golemon) Roddenberry; married Eileen Anita Rexroat, June 20, 1942 (divorced July, 1969); married Majel Barrett (an actress), August 6, 1969; children: (first marriage) Darleen R. Incopero, Dawn R. Compton; (second marriage) Eugene Wesley, Jr. *Education:* Received A.A. from Los Angeles City College; attended University of California, Los Angeles, University of Miami, and Columbia University. *Residence:* Beverly Hills, Calif. *Office:* c/o Paramount Pictures, 5555 Melrose Ave., Hollywood, Calif. 90038. *Agent:* Leonard Maizlish, 9255 Sunset Blvd., Los Angeles, Calif. 90069.

CAREER: Employed as a pilot for Pan American Airways, 1945-49; Los Angeles Police Department, Los Angeles, Calif., 1949-53, began as police officer, became sergeant; creator, producer, and writer of television programs and motion pictures, 1953—, including "The Lieutenant," National Broadcasting Co. (NBC), 1960-61, "Star Trek," NBC, 1966-69, "Pretty Maids All in a Row," Metro-Goldwyn-Mayer (MGM), 1970, "Genesis II" (made-for-television), 1973, "The Questor Tapes" (made-for-television), 1974, "Spectre" (made-for-television), 1977, "Star Trek: The Motion Picture," Paramount, 1979; executive consultant, "Star Trek II: The Wrath of Khan," Paramount, 1982; "Star Trek III: The Search for Spock," 1984. President of Norway Productions, Inc. *Military service:* U.S. Army Air Corps, 1941-45; became captain; received Distinguished Flying Cross and Air Medal.

MEMBER: Writers Guild of America, West (past member of executive council), Science Fiction Writers of America, Academy of Television Arts and Sciences (former member of board of governors), American Civil Liberties Union, Caucus for Producers, Writers, and Directors, Explorers Club (New York City), Bel Air Country Club, La Costa Country Club, Planetary Society, L-5 Society, Academy of Science Fiction, Fantasy and Horror Films, National Space Institute (member of board of directors), Los Angeles Police Band Association (member of board of directors).

AWARDS, HONORS: Commendation from Civil Aeronautics Board for rescue efforts; Writers Guild of America Award for best teleplay of the year, 1958, for "Helen of Abiginian," an episode of "Have Gun Will Travel"; Golden Reel awards from Film Council of America, 1962, and 1966; special award from Twenty-fourth World Science Fiction Convention, 1966; Hugo Award for best dramatic presentation from World Science Fiction Convention, 1967, for "The Menagerie," an episode of "Star Trek"; Brotherhood Award from National Association for the Advancement of Colored People (NAACP), 1967; Gold Medal from *Photoplay*, 1968, special plaque from Twenty-sixth World Science Fiction Convention, 1968, for "Star Trek"; D. H. L. from Emerson College, 1973; D.Litt., from Union College, 1977; Freedom Through Knowledge Award from National Space Club, 1979; American Freedom Award, 1980; D.Sc from Clarkson College, 1981.

WRITINGS: (With Stephen E. Whitfield) *The Making of "Star Trek,"* Ballantine, 1968; *The Questor Tapes,* adapted by D. C. Fontana, Ballantine, 1974, reprinted, Aeonian Press, 1975; *Star Trek—The Motion Picture,* Simon & Schuster, 1980; (with Susan Sackett) *The Making of "Star Trek; The Motion Picture,"* Simon & Schuster, 1980.

Author of over eighty scripts for television programs, including "Goodyear Theatre," "The Kaiser Aluminum Hour," "Chevron Theatre," "Four Star Theatre," "Dragnet," "The Jane Wyman Theatre," "Naked City," "Have Gun Will Travel," and "Star Trek."

Contributor of articles to aeronautical magazines. Contributor of poetry to *Embers* and *New York Times*. Poems included in anthologies.

ADAPTATIONS: "Star Trek," animated cartoon series, produced by Filmation Studios, NBC-TV, September 8, 1973-August 30, 1975.

SIDELIGHTS: Roddenberry held many jobs before becoming well known as the creator of "Star Trek." Among them were: commercial pilot for Pan Am; policeman; poet (his poems had been published in the *New York Times*); television writer; head writer for television program "Have Gun Will Travel"; and television producer.

After years of experience in the motion picture and television industry, he preferred to call himself a writer who produced. "I think that the purpose of all writing is to reach people and say something you believe in and think is important. You may do it as a scientific or philosophical tract, but with fiction and drama and a certain amount of adventure you reach them easier and you reach more of them and you can infiltrate your messages into them. I think people forget too often that literature—usually fiction—is responsible for more changes in public opinion than news articles or sermons. An excellent example of this is *Uncle Tom's Cabin*—actually it's not a very good book—which probably did more to propel us into the Civil War than any other writing of the time. So historically this has been true of literature and whether we like it or not, television is literature. It may not be very good literature usually, but of course not everything that is printed is very good, either.

"I'm a storyteller. And producing is merely an extension of the storytelling function. There's no difference between writing that 'he spoke slowly, uncertainly, unsure of himself' and being a director who makes sure the actor does it that way, or being

Gene Roddenberry (standing, second from left) on the set of "Star Trek: The Motion Picture."

the producer who hires an actor who is capable of doing it that way.

"When I first began writing, and I think many beginning writers go through this, I felt that the director and the producer and the actors were the enemy. They took, it seemed to me, these priceless visions I had in my head, these lovely, lovely sonnets that I had written and put them on the screen and destroyed them. Or warped them. As I became a more and more professional writer I began to realize that actors and directors indeed were taking some fairly average things that I had done and were making them very much better. So the longer you're in the business, the longer you're in television and film, the more you begin to respect all of the creative levels for what each of them brings to it. I had some strange ideas about Hollywood when I first came here. I had read these stories of the orgies and the pink Cadillacs and the flaming passions that erupt on set and all of that. But actually television and most independent motion picture production people are a group of very hardworking, dedicated, sensible people. This is not to say that we don't have our moods and arguments and disagreements, and often violent ones. But I think probably no more than take place at the top echelon of U.S. Steel or Prudential Life Insurance Company. Naturally people that care have strong feelings. But I've done a lot of odd jobs and I can say that the nicest group of people I have ever worked with in my life are the people in the creative levels of this industry. They're great fun to be with and great fun to work with." ["Star Trek's Gene Roddenberry," *Penthouse*, March, 1976.]

In the early 1960s Roddenberry created the science-fiction television program that was to propel him to celebrity status. The show debuted in 1966 to poor ratings, but the support of its audience and science fiction writers prevented studio executives from cancelling the series. In time, Roddenberry and "Star Trek" acquired a following of loyal fans—known as Trekkies—who started over 350 fan clubs and organized conventions, sometimes attended by as many as twenty thousand people. "I made 'Star Trek' for two reasons. One was that I thought science fiction hadn't been done well on television and it seemd to me, from a purely selfish, career point of view, that if I did it well I would be remembered. I suppose if a Western or a police story hadn't been done to my satisfaction I might have done that, too. The second reason is that I thought with science fiction I might do what Jonathan Swift did when he wrote *Gulliver's Travels*. He lived in a time when you could lose your head for making religious and political comments. I was working in a medium, television, which is heavily censored, and in contemporary shows I found I couldn't talk about sex, politics, religion, and all of the other things I wanted to talk about. It seemed to me that if I had things happen to little polka-dotted people on a far-off planet I might get past the network censors, as Swift did in his day. And indeed that's what we did.

"I get a huge charge out of doing a 'Star Trek' episode that demonstrates that petty nationalism must go if we're to survive and so on. Although there are certainly many network executives who are moral men, who give to charities and raise

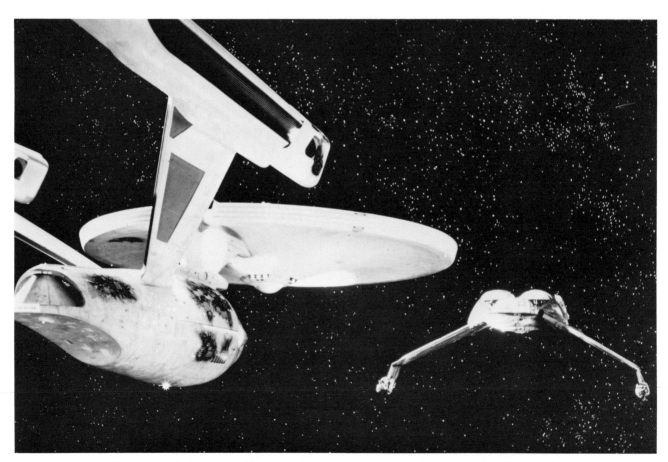

"**Space, the final frontier. These are the voyages of the Starship *Enterprise*. Her ongoing mission: to explore strange new worlds, to seek out new life and new civilizations, to boldly go where no man has gone before.**" ■ ("Star Trek" prologue.)

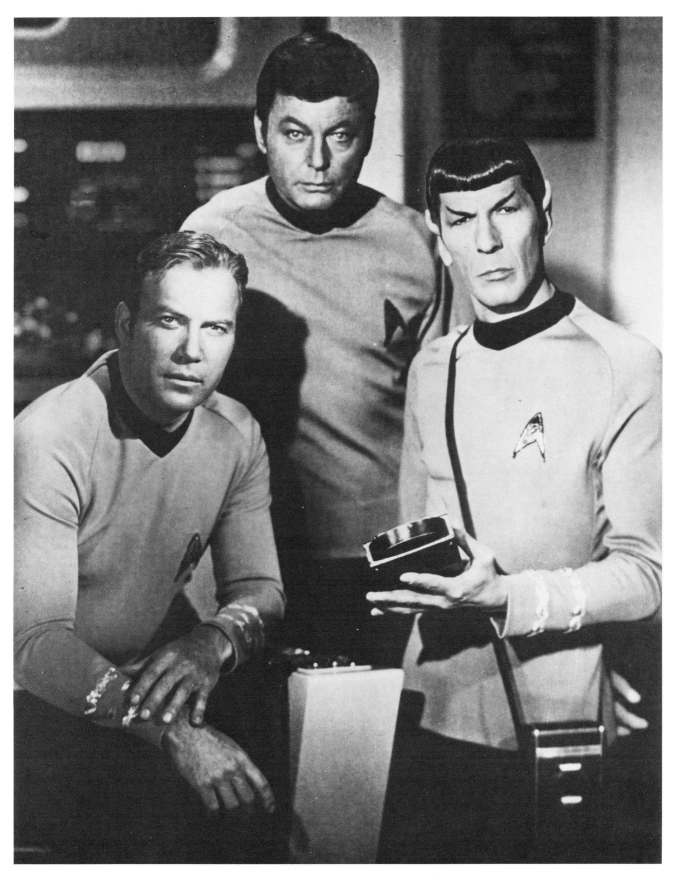

Cast of the television series "Star Trek."

Aboard the Klingon vessel, the warlord Kruge spoke to his officers. ■ (From the movie "Star Trek III: The Search for Spock," with Christopher Lloyd [left] as Kruge. Copyright © 1984 by Paramount Pictures Corp.)

their children decently, and who worry about these things too, this is not the main thrust of their jobs. Since they belong to a corporation, the main thrust of their jobs is to produce so many viewers for each sponsor and to turn a profit to the stockholders every year. So many of the arguments and fights that we have with them come out of just two different viewpoints, two different goals. I suppose that if writer/producers could have their way totally, I would try to do lovely things that would maybe attract an audience of two million people instead of the necessary eighteen million, and the network, of course, would go broke.''[1]

Television's filming techniques and technological advances in special effects made science fiction presentations increasingly realistic and appealing during the 1960s. Additionally, the U.S. space program stimulated interest in the sci-fi genre because people related more to space exploration. In Isaac Asimov's opinion, ''Star Trek'' signified television's effort to acquire a broad-based audience for science fiction series.

Roddenberry gave ''Star Trek'' a format similar to that of ''Wagon Train,'' a weekly television program about pioneers traveling westward armed with existing American myths. Although the western frontier was once regarded as the final frontier, the idea of people carrying American myths into the unknown persisted.

The program explored the issue of alienation from religion, morality, and government. In the process, some critics believe ''Star Trek'' appealed to the viewers' emotional needs and

revived their self-esteem as a nation. ''We live in a time in which everyone, and particularly young minds, are aware that we face huge troubles ahead. There are many people saying, 'I doubt if we'll make it through the next twenty or thirty years.' And indeed, if you read the newspapers it seems so. 'Star Trek' was a rare show that said, 'Hey, it's not all over. It hasn't all been invented. If we're wise, why the human adventure is just beginning.' And this is a powerful statement to young-minded people, to think that the explorations and discoveries and challenges ahead of us are greater than anything in the past. I think also 'Star Trek' was unusual in that it was about something. 'Star Trek' took points of view of tolerance, points of view against the petty meaningful things. And I think the audiences are a lot brighter than the networks believe. I think that the audience does like to have their minds challenged. I think that since 'Star Trek' came along there have been shows that have done that. . . .

''Thirdly, I think the reason for the popularity of 'Star Trek' is a really old-fashioned sort of reason. 'Star Trek' came along at a time in which most television leads were anti-heroes. On 'Star Trek' we decided to go for real heroes in an old-fashioned sense, people whose word was their bond, who believed that there were things more important in life than personal security or comfort. That, indeed, there are some things worth risking your life for, even dying for if necessary. As a result, our principal characters were ones about whom a person could say, 'Hey, I'd like to be like that.' Or, 'I'd like my children to be like that.' And it seems to me that possibly the greatest hunger there is in the world today is for heroes to admire and to emulate. When I grew up it was much simpler, it was the president of the United States. But we don't even have that left. One reason I don't object to the 'Star Trek' fan phenomenon is the fact that if there's got to be some show that people want to model their lives after, or point to for their children, I'd much rather they do it out of this show than some limited show that is saying that all doctors are Jesus Christ, or if we just let our police have more guns we could solve the crime problem."[1]

The "Star Trek" cast included three main characters, one of whom was an alien from the planet Vulcan, named Mr. Spock. "The reason for the creation of the three main characters—Captain Kirk, Dr. McCoy, and Mr. Spock—was that one thing you don't have in film literature that you do have in novels is stream of consciousness. In a novel you can get inside the character's mind and you can read, 'He thinks, ''Well should I do this or that, and there's this to say on this side and there's something else to say on the other side.''' So in 'Star Trek' the Captain would say, 'Which way shall we face up to this threat? And Spock would say, 'Well, from the logical point of view we'll do this.' The doctor would say, 'No, but that's not really humanitarian.' And the captain would say, 'As a man of action I'm bound by my orders.' They could have the whole discussion right there that in the novel would have been stream of consciousness.

"There are certain principles that I have and that other writers have that they will not violate even to get a show on the air. I don't like too much violence. I refuse to have the future run by the United States of America because I don't think that's the way it will be. I refuse to have an all lily-white, Anglo-Saxon crew. And I think if they had said, 'This ship really has to be an instrument of the CIA of the future, of keeping the galaxies safe for democracy,' I certainly would have said, 'You can shelve the whole project.'

"If there was one theme in all of 'Star Trek' it was that the glory of our universe is its infinite combinations of diversity. That all beauty comes out of its diversity. What a terrible, boring world it would be if everyone agreed with everyone else. And if there weren't different shapes and colors and ideas. When we are truly wise—and my test for a wise human is when they take a positive delight when someone says, 'I disagree with you because....' My God, what an opportunity this opens for dialogue, discussion, learning.'"[1]

Roddenberry left "Star Trek" during its third television season because of a disagreement with the network over scheduling. "The first year we were on at 8:30 P.M. on Thursdays. If we'd kept that time slot and evening I think our ratings would have slowly built because we built them all through that year. The second year, though, they put us on Friday, at 9 o'clock, which was a bad time. Our ratings dropped again. We slowly,

(From the movie "Star Trek: The Motion Picture," starring Leonard Nimoy. Copyright © 1979 by Paramount Pictures Corp.)

all year, fought to build them back up again. NBC was going to cancel us and then the fans protested, had marches all over the country, sent in over a million letters, and they put us on for a third year, but then they gave us Friday at ten o'clock, which is even worse. But it was the first time the fans had ever forced a network to keep a show on the air. But I went to the network and said, 'If you'll give us a decent time slot, I'll come back and personally produce the show.' I was at the time executive producer. 'And not only that, I will guarantee to work as I've never worked before to really make the show a hit.' And they said, 'Fine. We'd like you to come back and oversee it. Become the producer again and we'll give you Monday at seven,' I believe it was. A great time slot. And so I proceeded to prepare for the next season. But as they began

Isaac Asimov and Gene Roddenberry during their first meeting at the 1972 Star Trek convention.

Cartoon of a typical "Trek" convention opening. (Copyright © 1976 by Phil Foglio.)

(From the movie "Star Trek II: The Wrath of Khan," starring Ricardo Montalban. Copyright ©
1982 by Paramount Pictures Corp.)

to line up their schedules, a show came along called 'Laugh-In' that they felt they had a big bid on, and so they said, 'We're going to put "Laugh-In" there and we're going to give you Friday night at ten.'

"Well I knew this was death for the show. When you bargain with a network you have to use the only clout you have, the only single thing I had was agreeing to personally produce the show. And so, in an attempt to force them to give us some time period that would work, I said, 'I will not personally produce a show if you put it on Friday night at ten o'clock. There's just too much labor and effort and ultimate disappointment. If you do that I will stay executive producer. And, in fact, knowing that it's going to die, I'll be spending part of my time lining up what I'm going to do in the following year.' As it turned out, the network elected to keep us on at that time. And having made this threat, I felt that I had to stay true to my word, otherwise how could I, in the future, ever again make a bargain from any position of strength? It turned out it wasn't such a position of strength because they left it there.''[1]

"Star Trek" was cancelled in 1969, but returned in the 1970s in syndicated reruns, gaining increasing popularity and producing a "cult" following. "I think you probably can't go into ten- and twelve-hour days, six days a week, without at least the *hope* that someday, someone would tap your arm and say, 'I like what you did.' But of course, I never expected 'Star Trek' to become the cult that it became—the phenomenon!" [Michael Delon, "Star Trek," *Film* (London), number 128, September, 1984.[2]]

In 1973, Roddenberry wrote "Genesis II," a television movie, starring Alex Cord and Mariette Hartley. The "Genesis II" story concerned the adventures of a 20th-century NASA scientist who is resuscitated after being buried in a suspended animation chamber. He awakens to find himself in a future civilization. "Our civilization as we know it had been de-

stroyed. It had fallen apart. It had not been, however, due to nuclear warfare. Really, nuclear warfare is not necessary to cause a breakdown of society. You take large cities like Los Angeles, New York, Chicago—their water supply comes from hundreds of miles away and any interruption of that, or food, or power, for any period of time and you're going to have riots in the streets.

"Our society is so fragile, so dependent on the interworking of things to provide us with goods and services, that you don't need nuclear warfare to fragment us any more than the Romans needed it to cause their eventual downfall. It's important to know that I wasn't saying that 'Star Trek's' future, which would occur several hundred years after 'Genesis II,' never happened; I'm saying that humanity has always progressed by three steps forward and two steps back. The entire history of our civilization has been one society crumbling and a slightly better one, usually, being built on top of it. And on mankind's bumpy way to the 'Star Trek' era, we passed through this time, too." [Jess Szalay, "Gene Roddenberry: The Years Between, The Years Ahead," *Starlog,* October, 1981.[3]]

"Genesis II" was the first science-fiction story written and produced by Roddenberry since "Star Trek." It almost became a television series, but fell prey to another science-fiction movie turned television series, "Planet of the Apes." '''Genesis II' we almost sold. CBS had it penciled into their schedule. Fred Silverman had seen 'Planet of the Apes' and he thought the monkeys were so cute that he cancelled doing 'Genesis II' and decided to go for the monkeys. Several of us tried to warn him that it was a one-time joke. He didn't listen and it was a disaster and cost them many millions of dollars. It's a pity, too, because 'Genesis II' had the makings of a very exciting show. It had one thing in common with 'Star Trek' and that was that you could bring in a good writer and say to him, 'What bothers you about the world?' then go and invent a place in this new world and have it happening there. It's a

(From the weekly television series "Star Trek," starring William Shatner, shown above with guest star, Michael Dunn. The show, which ran three seasons, premiered on NBC-TV, September 8, 1966.)

tragedy that opportunities like this to do exciting things and to talk about exciting things are pulled out by the roots by business executives who have no desire at all to give writers, directors and actors a chance to explore and elevate the art of film and television. And it could have been more exciting than the monkeys which captured his attention, but he seemed to

be incapable of looking beyond and seeing the potential of something new and different.''[3]

Roddenberry made four television movies in the 1970s before creating ''Star Trek: The Motion Picture,'' which was released in 1979. The multimillion-dollar movie retained the same cast

(From the animated cartoon series "Star Trek," which featured the voices of the original cast. The show premiered on September 8, 1973, and won an Emmy Award for Children's Entertainment Series in 1975.)

that had made the television series so popular—Leonard Nimoy returned as Mr. Spock, William Shatner remained Captain Kirk and Leonard McCoy was played by DeForest Kelley. Besides retaining the same characters, the movie also tried to retain some of the original elements of "Star Trek." "I guess my biggest fear was that it would not be 'Star Trek.' I knew I couldn't go into a major picture with a fine director like Robert Wise and say to him, 'Don't change *anything*.' But at the same time, we had to ask ourselves, 'What are the things that made "Star Trek" what it was that we *don't* want to change?' That was a very tenuous and narrow path to walk, but I think we've done it successfully.

"Almost from the beginning we decided that we wanted to keep our characters intact; because we felt that in a time when the anti-hero seems most popular, we wanted to keep the old-fashioned type of heroes—people with great integrity. I personally feel that people tend to do what they see; and if you make integrity fashionable, I think maybe we could get rid of a lot of our problems.

"Bob Wise and I both believed that a story ought to be about people; and it doesn't matter whether it's set in the future, or in the past, or in the present. So we've put the same amount of effort into the movie as we did in the television show to make sure that the crew are alive. We didn't design this picture as a vehicle for spectacular opticals.... If you believe that there are real people there and can identify with them, then you can believe the rest." [Don Shay, "Star Trek: The Motion Picture," *Cinefantastique*, spring, 1979.[4]]

The success of the movie led to two sequels, "Star Trek II: The Wrath of Khan," in 1982 and "Star Trek III: The Search for Spock" in 1984. In 1985 Roddenberry was chosen as the first writer to be honored in the Hollywood Walk of Fame. "... I probably do tend to write for myself a little bit; and maybe sometimes I forget there's a mass audience out there. But I do think that that audience is a lot brighter than anyone gives them credit for being. All of us in science fiction, or those of us who have read it, know that science fiction also includes Huxley and Swift and so many others; but those who are not tend to think only of 'Buck Rogers' and 'Flash Gordon.' So you think you're talking about the same thing; but really, you're not."[2]

FOR MORE INFORMATION SEE—Books: David Gerrold, *The World of "Star Trek,"* Ballantine, 1972, reprinted by Bluejay Books, 1984; Jacqueline Lichtenberg, Sondra Marshak, and Joan Winston, *"Star Trek" Lives!*, Bantam, 1975; Karin Blair, *Meaning in "Star Trek,"* Anima Books, 1976; Betsy Caprio, *"Star Trek": Good News in Modern Images*, Sheed Andrews & McMeel, 1978; Susan Sackett, Fred and Stan Goldstein, *Star Trek Speaks!*, Pocket Books, 1979; S. Sackett and Gene Roddenberry, *The Making of "Star Trek— The Motion Picture,"* Pocket Books, 1980; *Contemporary Literary Criticism*, Volume 17, Gale, 1981.

Periodicals: *Saturday Review*, June 17, 1967, February 2, 1980; *Popular Science*, December, 1967; *New York Times*, October 15, 1967, August 25, 1968, February 18, 1969, June 4, 1969, January 21, 1979, November 23, 1979, December 8, 1979, January 14, 1980, October 9, 1980, December 23, 1981, May 23, 1982, June 8, 1982, June 27, 1982, July 4, 1982, September 8, 1982; *Newsweek*, January 29, 1968, December 19, 1979.

Show Business, May 9, 1970; *Daily News*, February 16, 1973, August 12, 1973, May 27, 1981; *New York Post*, March 15, 1973; *TV Guide*, April 27, 1974; Linda Merinoff, "Star Trek's Gene Roddenberry," *Penthouse*, March, 1976; *Variety*, Au-

(Jacket illustration from *Star Trek—The Motion Picture* by Gene Roddenberry.)

gust 25, 1976, June 12, 1985; *Journal of Popular Culture*, spring, 1977, fall, 1979; *Starlog*, March, 1978, November, 1980, October, 1981, January, 1983; *Time*, January 15, 1979, December 17, 1979, June 7, 1982; *Cinefantastique*, spring, 1979; Daniel L. Smith, "The Voyage of Starship Enterprise," *Saturday Evening Post*, May, 1979; *Science Fiction and Fantasy Book Review*, December 9, 1979; *Science Digest*, December, 1979; *Detroit News Magazine*, December 9, 1979; *Cincinnati Enquirer*, December 16, 1979; *New Yorker*, December 17, 1979, June 28, 1982; *New York*, December 24, 1979, June 21, 1982; *New Republic*, December 29, 1979.

Christian Century, January 16, 1980, August 18-25, 1982; *Washington Post Book World Progressive*, March, 1980; *Stereo Review*, March, 1980; *VOYA*, April, 1980, August, 1980; *School Library Journal*, May, 1980; *Best of Starlog*, Volume 2, 1981; *Maclean's Magazine*, June 14, 1982; *Rolling Stone*, July 22, 1982, September 2, 1982; *Nation*, August 21-28, 1982; *USA Today*, September, 1982; *Film* (London), September, 1984; *Futurist*, February, 1985.

Dreams, books, are each a world; and books,
    we know,
Are a substantial world, both pure and good:
Round these, with tendrils strong as flesh and blood,
Our pastime and our happiness will grow.
                —William Wordsworth

ROSENBLATT, Arthur S. 1938-

BRIEF ENTRY: Born April 21, 1938, in Boston, Mass. Advertising executive and author. Rosenblatt graduated from Princeton University in 1960 and, early in his career, worked as a copywriter and advertising manager. He later became an advertising executive for an international firm. Rosenblatt's first book was a young adult novel entitled *Smarty* (Little, Brown, 1981). Set in the fifties, the story concerns Marty, a seventh grader who longs to be popular with his classmates and lose the moniker of ''Smarty-Marty.'' *Smarty* was followed by several stories written for a younger reading audience and featuring characters popular with contemporary children, such as *Strawberry Shortcake and the Deep Dark Woods* (Parker Brothers, 1983) and *The Care Bears Battle the Freeze Machine* (Parker Brothers, 1984). Rosenblatt is also the author of two study guides published by Barron's Educational Series: *William Shakespeare's King Lear* and *William Shakespeare's Richard III. Residence:* Norfolk, Conn.

FOR MORE INFORMATION SEE: Who's Who in Advertising, 2nd edition, Redfield Publishing, 1972.

ROSS, John 1921-

PERSONAL: Born September 25, 1921, in New York, N.Y.; son of Ferdinand and Mary Agnes (Higgins) Ross; married Clare Romano (an artist and illustrator), November 23, 1943; children: Christopher, Timothy. *Education:* Attended Ecole des Beaux Arts (Fontainebleau, France), Instituto Statale d'Arte (Florence, Italy), and New School for Social Research; Cooper Union School of Art, B.F.A., 1948; attended Columbia University, 1953. *Home and office:* 110 Davison Pl., Englewood, N.J. 07631.

CAREER: Artist, printmaker, and educator. New School for Social Research, New York, N.Y., instructor in printmaking, 1957—; Pratt Institute Graphic Art Center, Brooklyn N.Y., instructor in printmaking, 1963—; U.S. Information Agency, Romania and Yugoslavia, artist-in-residence, demonstrator, and lecturer for exhibition ''Graphic Arts, U.S.A.,'' 1964-66; Manhattanville College, Purchase, N.Y., associate professor of art, 1964-70, professor of art, 1970—. Director of Art Center of Northern New Jersey, 1966-67; chairman of advisory panel of Cooper Union School of Art, 1967-69. Has executed commissions for Associated American Artists, 1964, 1966, and 1972, and New York State Council on the Arts, 1967, among others. Work has appeared in exhibitions, including Second International Color Print Exhibition, Grenchen, Switzerland, 1961, International Biennale Gravure, Cracow, Poland, 1968, ''Prize-Winning American Prints,'' Pratt Institute Graphic Art Center, Brooklyn, N.Y., 1968, and National Academy of Fine Arts, Amsterdam, Netherlands, 1968. Work represented in permanent collections, including National Collection of Fine Arts, Washington. D.C., Hirshhorn Collection, Metropolitan Museum of Art, New York City, Library of Congress, Washington, D.C., and Cincinnati Art Museum, Cincinnati, Ohio.

MEMBER: Society of American Graphic Artists (president, 1961-65; member of executive council, 1965—), National Academy of Design (associate), American Color Print Society, Boston Printmakers, Philadelphia Print Club. *Awards, honors:* Louis Comfort Tiffany Foundation grant, 1954, for printmaking; Second International Color Print Exhibit prize award, 1961, for ''Duomo,'' a collagraph; recipient of citation from Cooper Union School of Art, 1966, for professional achievement.

WRITINGS—All with wife, Clare Romano Ross; all nonfiction; all published by Free Press: *The Complete Printmaker,* 1972; *The Complete Intaglio Print,* 1974; *The Complete New Techniques in Printmaking,* 1974; *The Complete Relief Print,* 1974; *The Complete Screenprint and Lithograph,* 1974; *The Complete Collagraph: The Art and Technique of Printmaking from Collage Plates,* 1980.

Illustrator; all with Clare Romano Ross: May Garelick, *Manhattan Island,* Crowell, 1957; Gerald Doan McDonald, compiler, *A Way of Knowing: A Collection of Poems for Boys,* Crowell, 1959; Sophia Cedarbaum, *Chanukah, the Festival of Lights,* Union of American Hebrew Congregations, 1960; S. Cedarbaum, *Passover, the Festival of Freedom,* Union of American Hebrew Congregations, 1960; S. Cedarbaum, *Purim, a Joyous Holiday,* Union of American Hebrew Congregations, 1960; S. Cedarbaum, *Sabbath, a Day of Delight,* Union of American Hebrew Congregations, 1960; Clyde R. Bulla, *The Ring and the Fire: Stories From Wagner's Nibelung Operas,* Crowell, 1964; Walt Whitman, *Poems of Walt Whitman,* Crowell, 1964; W. Whitman, *Leaves of Grass* (poems), selected by Lawrence C. Powell, Crowell, 1964; Lillian Morrison, editor, *Sprints and Distances: Sports in Poetry and the Poetry in Sports,* Crowell, 1965; James Marnell, *Labor Day,* Crowell, 1966; Edmund Fuller, editor, *Poems of Henry Wadsworth Longfellow,* Crowell, 1967; Mira Brichto, *God Around Us,* Union of American Hebrew Congregations, 1969; Molly Cone, *About God,* edited by Jack D. Spiro, Union of American Hebrew Congregations, 1973; Charles W. Chesnutt, *Conjure Tales,* retold by Ray A. Shepard, Dutton, 1973; Helen Hill and Agnes Perkins, compilers, *New Coasts and Strange Harbors: Discovering Poems,* Crowell, 1974.

Contributor of articles to periodicals, including *American Artist, Artists Proof,* and *Art in America.*

SIDELIGHTS: Ross and his wife ''love to work in woodcuts, but have done many books making color separations on acetate, mainly, and also in line. *Leaves of Grass* was done with woodcuts, and *Labor Day* in collage.'' [Lee Kingman and others, compilers, *Illustrators of Children's Books: 1957-1966,* Horn Book, 1968.]

''The availability of everyday material makes the collagraph a simple and easy method of making prints. It can be used by beginners as well as accomplished artists.''

FOR MORE INFORMATION SEE: Art in America, fall, 1960, April, 1965; *Artist's Proof,* Volume 5, 1963; *At Cooper Union,* summer, 1964; Lee Kingman and others, compilers, *Illustrators of Children's Books: 1957-1966,* Horn Book, 1968; Martha E. Ward and Dorothy A. Marquardt, *Illustrators of Books for Young People,* 2nd edition, Scarecrow, 1975; L. Kingman and others, compilers, *Illustrators of Children's Books: 1967-76,* Horn Book, 1978; *American Artist,* August, 1981.

SADLER, Catherine Edwards

BRIEF ENTRY: Born in California. Sadler spent her childhood in England and Switzerland. Now an author of children's books, she has also worked as an editor. In 1979 Sadler and her husband, photographer Alan Sadler, spent a month in the Chinese city of Guilin where they lived with the Cheng and Heu families. The Sadlers recorded their observations in *Two Chinese Families* (Atheneum, 1981), an exploration of daily life in the structured, classless society of southern China. Sadler continued to reveal her interest in the Chinese culture with the publications of *Treasure Mountain: Folktales from Southern China* (Atheneum, 1982) and *Heaven's Reward; Fairy Tales from China* (Atheneum, 1985). Each contains six tales retold by Sadler and illustrated by Cheng Mung Yun. Aside from retellings of Chinese tales, Sadler produced Sir Arthur Conan Doyle's *The Adventures of Sherlock Holmes* (Avon/Camelot, 1981), four volumes of the renowned investigator's celebrated cases adapted for younger readers. She is also the author of *Sasha: The Life of Alexandra Tolstoy* (Putnam, 1982) in which she provides young adult readers with a look at the aristocratic yet unhappy childhood of the great Russian novelist's daughter. *Residence:* New York, N.Y.

ST. JOHN, Wylly Folk   1908-1985
(Eleanor Fox, Eve Larson, Katherine Pierce, Mary Keith Vincent, Michael Williams)

OBITUARY NOTICE—See sketch in *SATA* Volume 10: Born October 20, 1908, near Ehrhardt, S.C.; died of cancer, August 16, 1985, in High Shoals, Ga.; cremated. Journalist and author. A prolific author of articles, short stories, novels, and children's books, St. John wrote in genres ranging from murder mysteries and romances to science fiction. She was particularly well known as an author of mysteries for children and twice received a special award from the Mystery Writers of America, in 1973 for *Uncle Robert's Secret,* and in 1974 for *The Secret of the Seven Caves.* Another of her children's books, *Secrets of the Pirate Inn,* was adapted for television. St. John also published five novels in *Redbook* magazine and served as a staff writer for the *Atlantic Journal and Constitution Magazine* (now *Atlanta Weekly*) for more than twenty years.

FOR MORE INFORMATION SEE: Contemporary Authors, Volumes 21-24, revised, Gale, 1977; *Who's Who in the South and Southwest,* 18th edition, Marquis, 1982; *The Writers Directory: 1984-1986,* St. James Press, 1983. Obituaries: *Atlanta Journal,* August 22, 1985.

SAND, George X.

PERSONAL: Born in New Jersey; married Phyllis Philibert (deceased); married Lou Burke; children: (first marriage) Gail, Karen. *Home:* 1412 Winkler Ave., Ft. Myers, Fla. 33901.

CAREER: Free-lance writer and photojournalist for more than forty years, concentrating on fiction and articles for American and European magazine markets before turning to books. *Awards, honors:* First Florida recipient of Governor's Outstanding Conservationist award.

WRITINGS: Skin and Scuba Diving, Hawthorn, 1964; *Salt Water Fly Fishing,* Knopf, 1970; *The Everglades Today,* Four Winds Press, 1971; *Iron-Tail,* Scribner, 1971; *The Complete Beginner's Guide to Fishing,* Doubleday, 1974; (with Glenn Cunningham) *Never Quit,* Chosen Books, 1981.

SIDELIGHTS: "Looking back [on my writing career], it's been a wild, wonderful hodgepodge of victories and defeats, of shrieks and sighs. I've traveled over a million miles—by plane, bus, car, jeep, horse and dugout canoe. . . . I doubt that I'd do it over. And yet, there's nothing I'd rather do. I love adventure.

GEORGE X. SAND

"I'll always remember the grim early days when our noisy, growing youngsters forced me to flee the house, writing instead on a collapsible work table in the rear seat of the family jalopy parked behind big sand dunes. Some of my early sand-dune-fiction has been reprinted a dozen times, but I recall even more, the article that elevated a man from poverty to riches—and I received not even a handshake of thanks in return.

"Something about this life of utter freedom—even though it must be dulled with the discipline of typewriter and darkroom—mix-masters a man's blood intoxicatingly. You live by the day, by the hour, with the next phone call from New York deciding tomorrow." [George X. Sand, "Twenty Years of Wonderful Uncertainty," *Writer's Digest,* July 1961.[1]]

Both writer and photojournalist, Sand maintains that a photojournalist "*sees* a story before he tackles it. He works swiftly, smoothly, unobtrusively—so thoroughly acquainted with his equipment that during the decisive creative moments he's hardly aware of the cameras in his hands.

"Like the writer, in order to show life, the lensman must know life. Regardless of what the 'art' exponents may contend (and they can argue this point by the hour: "What is truth?', etc., etc.), I maintain that a good picture is simply something that serves its intended purpose, standing on its own merits—with or without a caption. *But first one must recognize it.*"[1]

"For the past thirty years I have donated my time (at least once each week) to young people whom I find in jail, halfway houses, on the streets, etc., showing them how the advice in the greatest of all guide books—the Bible—can help them find the right path. I've had some very rewarding experiences from this work and perhaps I'll write a book on that subject some day."

Many deer were drowned when members of the Flood Control District and the Army Engineers refused to lower the water level. ■ (From *The Everglades Today: Endangered Wilderness* by George X. Sand. Photograph by the author.)

WORK IN PROGRESS: An adventure book.

FOR MORE INFORMATION SEE: George Sand, "Twenty Years of Wonderful Uncertainty," *Writer's Digest,* July, 1961; Dick Powers, "George X. Sand: Conservationist," *Sun-Sentinel,* February 26, 1971; George X. Sand, "Return to Alaska, a Promise Fulfilled," *Sun-Sentinel,* February 26, 1971.

At Mr. Wackford Squeers' Academy, Dotheboys Hall . . . Youth are boarded, clothed, booked, furnished with pocket-money, provided with all necessaries, instructed in all languages living and dead . . . No extras, no vacations, and diet unparalleled.

—Charles Dickens
(From *Nicholas Nickleby*)

SCHOCK, Pauline 1928-
(Pauline Boyd)

PERSONAL: Born July 30, 1928, in Chicago, Ill.; daughter of Lucius Virgil (a carpenter) and Eloise (Stroupe) Boyd; married Richard John Schock, (a machinist) October 16, 1947; children: Rick, Susan, Carol, Debbie, Lisa. *Education:* Attended Western Carolina University, 1945-47, and University of Alabama. *Religion:* Lutheran. *Home:* 1401 Darnell St. SE, Huntsville, Ala. 35801.

CAREER: Langley Air Force Base, Hampton, Va., civilian computer operator, 1947-50; writer, 1979—. *Member:* Society of Children's Book Writers, Huntsville Literary Association.

WRITINGS: Under name Pauline Boyd; children's books; with sister, Selma Boyd: *The How: Making the Best of a Mistake* (illustrated by Peggy Luks), Human Sciences, 1981; *Footprints in the Refrigerator* (illustrated by Carol Nicklaus), F. Watts, 1982; *I Met a Polar Bear* (illustrated by Patience Brewster), Lothrop, 1983.

WORK IN PROGRESS: A children's novel, a picture book and an easy-to-read children's book, all with sister, Selma Boyd.

SIDELIGHTS: "My sister Selma and I were introduced very early to the world of books, and that world has always been the most fascinating part of our lives. Writing is the natural response. We believe that each book should be as different as possible, so that children can choose from a wide variety.

"After my children were born, I was a Sunday school teacher, home room mother, PTA officer, Cub Scout leader, Girl Scout leader, etc. We provided a home for a school year for a girl from Colombia so that she could graduate from an American school. I was the mother whose children always volunteered her services as, 'My mother doesn't work. She'll be glad to. . . .'

"I like to read and write. I enjoy art museums, the theatre, and I find children extremely interesting. I like to travel. I have visited England; it had always been a goal of mine. The museums, the theatres, the feeling of history as one stands in buildings dating back centuries, original manuscripts of admired writers all combined to fill me with a sense of wonder. Each time I visit, I encounter something new and magnificent.

"At the age of seven I started a diary. I thought everyone wrote and stashed their writing in drawers. In 1977 Selma and I took a creative writing class at the local university and were

The bus was crowded. ■ (From *I Met a Polar Bear* by Selma and Pauline Boyd. Illustrated by Patience Brewster.)

PAULINE SCHOCK

encouraged to submit our work to a publisher. We find it interesting that our lives, which have been so full of children and their activities, and our desire to write, should mesh together so beautifully.

"Ideas for books are always simmering. It's just a matter of the right one coming to a boil. The recurring thread in our books seems to be problem solving. If children are allowed to solve their early problems, they are more able to handle the larger ones they encounter later in life."

HOBBIES AND OTHER INTERESTS: Reading, traveling, and "grandmothering."

SCHWARTZ, Julius   1907-

PERSONAL: Born in 1907. *Residence:* New York, N.Y.

CAREER: Science teacher in New York City public schools; instructor in science education at Bank Street College of Education, New York City. Science consultant to Bureau of Curriculum Research for New York City schools and to Midwest Program on Airborn Television Instruction. *Awards, honors:* Honorable mention, New York Academy of Sciences Children's Book Award, 1974, for *It's Fun to Know Why: Experiments with Things around Us.*

WRITINGS—All for children, except as indicated: *It's Fun to Know Why: Experiments with Things around Us* (illustrated by Edwin Herron), Whittlesey House, 1952, 2nd edition (illustrated by E. Herron and Anne Marie Jauss), McGraw, 1973; *Through the Magnifying Glass: Little Things That Make a Big Difference* (illustrated by Jeanne Bendick), Whittlesey House,

1954; *Now I Know* (illustrated by Marc Simont), Whittlesey House, 1955; *I Know a Magic House* (illustrated by M. Simont), Whittlesey House, 1956; (with Glenn O. Blough) *Elementary School Science and How to Teach It* (adult), revised edition (Schwartz was not associated with original edition), Holt, 1958, 6th edition, 1979; (compiler with Herman Schneider) *Growing Up with Science Books,* [New York], 1959, 2nd edition compiled with Susan A. Kailin, Bowker, 1967; *The Earth Is Your Spaceship* (illustrated by M. Simont), Whittlesey House, 1963; *Uphill and Downhill* (illustrated by William McCaffery), Whittlesey House, 1965; *Go on Wheels* (illustrated by Arnold Roth), McGraw, 1966; *Magnify and Find Out Why* (illustrated by Richard Cuffari), McGraw, 1972; *Earthwatch: Space-Time Investigations with a Globe* (illustrated by Radu Vero), McGraw, 1977; (with Charles Tanzer) *Biology and Human Progress* (workbook and teacher's handbook), 5th edition, Prentice-Hall, 1977 (Schwartz was not involved in preparation of the text).

SIDELIGHTS: Schwartz writes to explain basic scientific concepts to children. His books have addressed a wide variety of topics, namely, the earth's orbit, wheels, inventions (including water faucets and phonographs), the sound of the wind, electric shocks, magnifying lenses, and time-space investigations. Critics, notably Alice Dalgliesh in the *Saturday Review,* have commented that Schwartz's works capture the imagination of a child. For example, the author explains the earth's orbit with references to birthdays instead of ordinary, calendar days. Most of Schwartz's books contain experiments for children to try at home or in the classroom.

FOR MORE INFORMATION SEE: Saturday Review, May 15, 1954, November 17, 1956, May 11, 1963; *New York Herald Tribune Books,* May 16, 1954, May 12, 1963; *New York Times,* June 6, 1954, November 11, 1956; Martha E. Ward and Dorothy A. Marquardt, *Authors of Books for Young People,* 2nd edition, Scarecrow, 1971; *Scientific American,* December, 1977.

SHELDON, Muriel   1926-
(Muriel Batherman)

PERSONAL: Born October 16, 1926, in New York, N.Y.; daughter of Samuel (an electrical contractor) and Shirley (Gold) Batherman; married Arthur Sheldon (a chemical engineer), January 4, 1953; children: Peter, Tina. *Education:* Attended Pratt Institute, 1944-47. *Home and office:* 20 East Main St., Brookside, N.J. 07926.

CAREER: Helena Rubinstein, New York City, promotional designer, 1947-48; *Charm,* New York City, assistant art editor, 1949-56; illustrator and writer. *Member:* Authors Guild, Authors League of America, Society of Children's Book Writers. *Awards, honors:* Certificates of excellence from American Institute of Graphic Arts, 1954, 1956-57; award of distinctive merit from Art Directors Club of New York, 1956; *New York Herald Tribune*'s Children's Spring Book Festival Award, 1964, for *Alphabet Tale,* which was also named among one hundred best children's books by American Institute of Graphic Arts, 1964; award from Printing Industries of America's graphic arts competition, 1972, for *Hey, Riddle Riddle; Some Things You Should Know About My Dog* was included in Children's Book Showcase of Children's Book Council, 1977; *Animals Live Here* was named one of the outstanding science trade books for children in 1979 by the National Science Teachers Association.

I explained to the chalk man that when you punch someone with your fist, it hurts the person you punch more than it hurts you. ■ (From *The Little Chalk Man* by Václav Čtvrtek. Illustrated by Muriel Batherman.)

WRITINGS—Self-illustrated children's books; all under name Muriel Batherman: *Big and Small, Short and Tall,* Scholastic Book Services, 1972; *Some Things You Should Know About My Dog,* Prentice-Hall, 1976; *Animals Live Here,* Greenwillow, 1979; *Before Columbus,* Houghton, 1981.

Illustrator; all under name, Muriel Batherman: Jan Garten, *The Alphabet Tale,* Random House, 1964; "Little Overcoat" (film), Silver Burdett Inc., 1969; "Sheep Shearing" (film), Silver Burdett, Inc., 1969; "One Little Blackbird" (film), Silver Burdett Inc., 1969; Bill Martin, Jr., *Sounds After Dark,* Holt, 1970; B. Martin, *Welcome Home Henry,* Holt, 1970; Vaclav Ctvrek, *The Little Chalk Man,* Knopf, 1970; Thomas Rockwell, *Humph!,* Pantheon, 1971; Ann Bishop, *Hey, Riddle Riddle,* Western Publishing, 1972; Elizabeth Levy, *Tips for Traveling in Space,* Holt, 1974; Blanche Dorsky, *Harry: A True Story,* Prentice-Hall, 1977; Deborah Hautzig, *The Handsomest Father,* Greenwillow, 1979; Mary Q. Steele, *Wish, Come True,* Greenwillow, 1979; Helen V. Griffith, *Mine Will, Said John,* Greenwillow, 1980.

SIDELIGHTS: "I came to publishing primarily as an illustrator though the total concept of a book was always uppermost in my mind. It wasn't till later that I published as an author. I do wish that my writing career had developed earlier in my life. I would have delighted in exploring and discovering the world of words with my children when they were younger. Now they are grown and I can only try to recall those impres-sionable years and in doing so think of the many questions they asked.

"I find being an author/illustrator wonderful. Not only do I have the pleasure of visualizing the complete book, I also have the job of sharing my interests with young people as well. I can think of nothing more rewarding."

SHENTON, Edward   1895-1977

PERSONAL: Born November 29, 1895, in Pottstown, Pa.; died June 17, 1977 in Augusta, Me.; married Barbara Webster (a writer and artist), March 29, 1930; children: Edward Heriot. *Education:* Attended Philadelphia Museum School of Industrial Art, 1916-17, Pennsylvania Academy of the Fine Arts, 1920-23; also studied in Paris with the Pennsylvania Academy of Fine Arts Cresson scholarship. *Home:* Sugarbridge Farm, West Chester, Pa.

CAREER: Illustrator, author, editor, and educator. Editor, Penn Publishing Co., Philadelphia, Penn., 1924; began as editor, became vice-president, Macrae Smith Co., Philadelphia, 1926-50; head of the illustration department, Moore College of Art; instructor in illustration, Pennsylvania Academy of the Fine Arts. Has exhibited at the Pennsylvania Academy of the Fine Arts, Philadelphia, 1956, and has executed murals for

Chester County Courthouse, West Chester, Pa., and Chapel of the War Memorial Cemetery at Saint James, Brittany, France. *Military service:* Corporal with the 103rd Engineers, 28th Division, A.E.F. *Awards, honors:* Cresson scholarships for study abroad, 1921 and 1922; Lee Prize, 1922.

WRITINGS: The Gray Beginning (adult novel), Penn, 1924; *Lean Twilight* (adult novel), Scribner, 1928; *Riders of the Wind* (juvenile nonfiction; self-illustrated), Macrae Smith, 1929; *Couriers of the Clouds: The Romance of Air Mail* (adult nonfiction), Macrae Smith, 1930, revised and enlarged edition, 1937; *The New Alphabet of Aviation* (juvenile nonfiction; self-illustrated), Macrae Smith, 1941; *On Wings for Freedom* (juvenile nonfiction; self-illustrated) Macrae Smith, 1942; *An Alphabet of the Army,* Macrae Smith, 1943; *The Rib and Adam* (adult nonfiction), Lippincott, 1959; *This Mortal Moment* (adult poetry), Dorrance, 1961; *150 Years of a Bank and People,* National Bank of Chester County and Trust Co., 1964.

Illustrator: Grace Humphrey, *The Story of the Marys,* Penn, 1923, reissued, 1928; Roy Addison Helton, *The Early Adventures of Peacham Grew,* Penn, 1925; Elizabeth Shackleton, *Touring through France,* Penn, 1925; Paul John Jones, *An Alphabet of Aviation,* Macrae Smith, 1928, reissued, 1934.

Rupert Sargent Holland, *Rescue,* Macrae Smith, 1932; F. Scott Fitzgerald, *Tender Is the Night: A Romance,* Scribner, 1934; R. S. Holland, *Big Bridge,* Macrae Smith, 1934, reissued, 1938; Ernest Hemingway, *Green Hills of Africa,* Scribner, 1935, reissued, 1953.

Desmond Holdridge, *Escape to the Tropics,* Harcourt, 1937; D. Holdridge, *The Witch in the Wilderness,* Harcourt, 1937; Stoyan Christowe, *This Is My Country: An Autobiography,* Carrick & Evans, 1938; Clyde Brion Davis, *Northend Wildcats,* Farrar & Rinehart, 1938; William Faulkner, *The Unvanquished,* Random House, 1938, Vintage, 1966; Stephen W. Meader, *T-Model Tommy,* Harcourt, 1938, reissued, 1966; Marjorie K. Rawlings, *The Yearling,* Scribner, 1938, large-type edition, complete and unabridged, F. Watts, 1966.

C. B. Davis, *Nebraska Coast,* Farrar & Rinehart, 1939; Clifford Dowdey, *Gamble's Hundred,* Little, Brown, 1939; D. Holdridge, *Northern Lights,* Viking, 1939; S. W. Meader, *Bat: The Story of a Bull Terrier,* Harcourt, 1939, Grosset, 1961; S. W. Meader, *Boy with a Pack,* Harcourt, 1939; Blair Niles, *The James,* Farrar & Rinehart, 1939, revised and enlarged edition published as *The James from Iron Gate to the Sea,* 1945; Donald Culross Peattie, *A Gathering of Birds: An*

Edward Shenton with student, Audrey Winston.

"Burning Ship." Pen-and-ink drawing by Edward Shenton.

Anthology of the Best Ornithological Prose, Dodd, 1939; Thomas Wolfe, *The Face of a Nation: Poetical Passages from the Writings of Thomas Wolfe*, Scribner, 1939.

Maristan Chapman, *Mill Creek Mystery*, Appleton-Century, 1940; Ernest Horn and others, *Following New Trails*, Ginn, 1940; Ruth Sawyer, *The Year of Jubilo*, Viking, 1940; M. Chapman, *Mountain Mystery*, Appleton-Century, 1941; S. W. Meader, *Blueberry Mountain*, Harcourt, 1941; Helen Griscom Hole, *Westtown through the Years, 1799-1942* (adult), Westtown Alumni Association (Penn.), 1942; S. W. Meader, *The Black Buccaneer*, Harcourt, 1942, reissued, 1948; S. W. Meader, *Shadow in the Pines*, Harcourt, 1942; Edd Winfield Parks, *Long Hunter*, Farrar & Rinehart, 1942; M. K. Rawlings, *Cross Creek* (adult), Scribner, 1942, Time, 1966; William E. Wilson, *Shooting Star: The Story of Tecumseh*, Farrar & Rinehart, 1942.

Thomas D. Clark, *Simon Kenton, Kentucky Scout*, Farrar & Rinehart, 1943; Meindert De Jong, *The Little Stray Dog*, Harper, 1943; S. W. Meader, *The Sea Snake*, Harcourt, 1943; Sam Mims, *Chennault of the Flying Tigers*, Macrae Smith, 1943; Margaret Isabel Ross, *A Farm in the Family*, Harper, 1943; Edwin Way Teale, *Dune Boy: The Early Years of a Naturalist*, Dodd, 1943, reissued, 1957; Judy van der Veer, *A Few Happy Ones*, Appleton-Century, 1943; Maribelle Cormack, *Road to Down Under*, Appleton-Century, 1944; Lavinia R. Davis, *Spinney and Spike and the B-29*, Scribner, 1944; Nicholas Kalashnikoff, *Jumper: The Life of a Siberian Horse*, Scribner, 1944; S. W. Meader, *The Long Trains Roll*, Harcourt, 1944; Stanley Young, *Mayflower Boy*, Farrar & Rinehart, 1944.

Barbara Webster, *Mrs. Heriot's House* (adult novel), Scribner, 1945; Martha Keller, *Brady's Bend, and Other Ballads* (adult), Rutgers University Press, 1946; S. W. Meader, *Jonathan Goes West*, Harcourt, 1946; Honoré Willsie Morrow, *On to Oregon!*, Morrow, 1946, published in England as *The Splendid Journey*, Heinemann, 1947; S. W. Meader, *Behind the Ranges*, Harcourt, 1947; B. Webster, *The Color of the Country* (adult), Scribner, 1947; John Bakeless, *Fighting Frontiersman: The Life of Daniel Boone*, Morrow, 1948; S. W. Meader, *River of the Wolves*, Harcourt, 1948; Gladys Taber, *The Book of Stillmeadow* (adult), Macrae Smith, 1948; Richard E. Banta, *The Ohio* (adult), Rinehart, 1949; Jeanette Eaton, *Buckey O'Neill of Arizona*, Morrow, 1949; Richard Johnson, *Saint George*

and the Dragon, retold by William H. G. Kingston, Limited Editions, 1949.

S. W. Meader, *Whaler 'Round the Horn*, Harcourt, 1950; Ralph Moody, *Little Britches: Father and I Were Ranchers*, Norton, 1950; G. Taber, *Stillmeadow Seasons* (adult), Macrae Smith, 1950; Jo Evalin Lundy, *Seek the Dark Gold: A Story of the Scots Fur Traders*, Winston, 1951; R. Moody, *Man of the Family*, Norton, 1951; Elisa Bialk, *Jill's Victory*, World, 1952; Elizabeth Jane Coatsworth, *The Last Fort: A Story of the French Voyageurs*, Winston, 1952; Almet Jenks, *The Huntsman at the Gate*, Lippincott, 1952; S. W. Meader, *The Fish Hawk's Nest*, Harcourt, 1952; E. Bialk, *The Colt of Cripple Creek*, World, 1953; Marjory Douglas, *Freedom River: Florida, 1845*, Scribner, 1953; Elizabeth Crosgrove Ladd, *Enchanted Island*, Morrow, 1953; R. Moody, *The Fields of Home*, Norton, 1953; R. Moody, *Little Britches: Man of the Family*, (contains selections from *Little Britches: Father and I Were Ranchers* and *Man of the Family*), edited and annotated by Egbert W. Nieman, Harcourt, 1953; G. Taber and B. Webster, *Stillmeadow and Sugarbridge* (adult), Lippincott, 1953; Page Cooper, *Thunder*, World, 1954.

W. Faulkner, *Big Woods* (adult), Random House, 1955; G. Taber, *Stillmeadow Daybook* (adult), Lippincott, 1955; R. Moody, *The Home Ranch*, Norton, 1956; B. Webster, *The Green Year* (adult), Norton, 1956; Samuel Hopkins Adams, *General Brock and Niagara Falls*, Random House, 1957; James A. Kjelgaard, *Swamp Cat*, Dodd, 1957; Jean Lee Latham, *On Stage, Mr. Jefferson!*, Harper, 1958; Henry Wadsworth Longfellow, *Hiawatha*, Nelson-Doubleday, 1958; J. Kjelgaard, *Rescue Dog of the High Pass*, Dodd, 1958; Elsa Pederson, *Victory at Bear Cove: A Story of Alaska*, Abingdon, 1959; G. Taber, *Stillmeadow Sampler* (adult), Lippincott, 1959; B. Webster, editor, *Country Matters: An Anthology* (adult), Lippincott, 1959.

Lillian J. Bragdon, *Abraham Lincoln: Courageous Leader*, Abingdon, 1960; Saxon R. Carver, *Ropes to Burma: The Story of Luther Rice*, Broadman, 1961; James Ralph Johnson, *Anyone Can Live Off the Land*, McKay, 1961, reissued, 1971; William M. Kendrick, *The Indian Fighters*, Follett, 1961; Ida R. Rifkin, *First Adventure at Sea*, Follett, 1961; Cottie Arthur Burland, *Finding Out about the Incas*, Lothrop, 1962; Robert H. Rankin, *Uniforms of the Sea Services: A Pictorial History*

Buck swung the ax into their huge, tough roots till his back ached. . . . ■ (From *Blueberry Mountain* by Stephen W. Meader. Illustrated by Edward Shenton.)

(adult), United States Naval Institute, 1962; G. Taber, *The Stillmeadow Road* (adult), Lippincott, 1962; Joseph E. Chipperfield, *The Gray Dog from Galtymore,* McKay, 1962; Jane S. McIlvaine, *Cammie's Cousin,* Bobbs-Merrill, 1963; Edwin Augustus Peeples, *Blue Boy,* Houghton, 1964.

Wyatt Blassingame, *Sacagawea, Indian Guide,* Garrard, 1965; Jane Levis Carter, *On a Theban Hill* (adult), [Penn.], 1965; B. Webster, *Creatures and Contentments: Ruminations on Living in the Country* (adult), Norton, 1965; Elizabeth R. Montgomery, *World Explorers: Lewis and Clark,* Garrard, 1966; Florence L. Sanville, *The Opening Door,* Franklin, 1967; J. L. Carter, *Edgmont: The Story of a Township* (adult), KNA Press, 1976; G. Taber, *The Best of Stillmeadow* (adult), Lippincott, 1976.

Author of text for cantata "Builders of America: Washington, Lincoln," 1953 and of song "O, Restless Race!," 1961. Contributor of articles, short stories, poems, and illustrations to periodicals, including *Scribner's, Colliers, Woman's Home Companion, Saturday Evening Post, American, New Yorker, Ladies' Home Journal, Reader's Digest,* and *Saturday Review.*

SIDELIGHTS: In *Illustrators of Children's Books: 1946-1956,* Shenton wrote: "At the age of fourteen or thereabouts, with

a great sheaf of drawings under my arm, I was taken to see Frederick Gruger. Nothing in my childish efforts could possibly have interested him but he took time from his work to talk to me about the knowledge, the curiosity for life and its wonders that an illustrator should have. Time has not dimmed or altered the truth of what he said, nor its value to me.

"From Henry McCarter I received the basic concepts of picture-making and, from the work of Vierge and Rockwell Kent, technical inspiration. But beyond such learning, nature is the perpetual source to which I return to refresh myself and my work. For this reason, living in the country as I do in West Chester, Pennsylvania, among the people who work with the earth, is a stimulating existence.

"Teaching is also an excellent means of keeping from falling into formulas and repetition. As instructor in illustration at the Pennsylvania Academy of Fine Arts, I am constantly jogged out of my habits by succeeding classes of eager young students."

FOR MORE INFORMATION SEE: Bertha E. Mahoney and others, compilers, *Illustrators of Children's Books: 1744-1945,* Horn Book, 1947; "The Undaunted Horseman," *Saturday Evening Post,* May 13, 1951; Robinson McIlvaine, "Edward Shenton," *Chester County Artist,* March, 1953; Bertha M.

Then he himself was running toward the group. He wouldn't object to getting in a few blows on his own account. ■ (From *Boy with a Pack* by Stephen W. Meader. Illustrated by Edward Shenton.)

The fog was gray with early daylight now, and beginning to lift in curling, wraith-like streamers. ■ (From *Shadow in the Pines* by Stephen W. Meader. Illustrated by Edward Shenton.)

Miller and others, compilers, *Illustrators of Children's Books: 1946-1956,* Horn Book, 1958; Henry C. Pitz, "The Book Illustration of Edward Shenton," *American Artist,* May, 1961; Walt Reed, editor, *The Illustrator in America: 1900-1960s,* Reinhold, 1966; Henry C. Pitz, *The Brandywine Tradition,* Houghton Mifflin, 1969.

SHIRER, William L(awrence) 1904-

PERSONAL: Surname is pronounced *Shy*-rer; born February 23, 1904, in Chicago, Ill.; son of Seward Smith (a lawyer) and Josephine (Tanner) Shirer; married Theresa Stiberitz, January 30, 1931 (divorced, 1970); children: Eileen Inga, Linda Elizabeth. *Education:* Coe College, B.A., 1925; College de France, Paris, courses in European history, 1925-27. *Politics:* Independent. *Religion:* Presbyterian. *Address:* Box 487, 34 Sunset Ave., Lenox, Mass. 01240. *Agent:* Don Congdon, Don Congdon Associates Inc., 177 E. 70th St., New York, N.Y. 10021.

CAREER: Chicago Tribune, Paris edition, reporter in Paris, France, 1925-27, foreign correspondent in Paris, London, England, Geneva, Switzerland, Rome, Italy, Dublin, Ireland, Vienna, Austria, and Prague, Czechoslovakia, 1927-29, chief of Central European bureau in Vienna, 1929-32; European correspondent for Paris edition of *New York Herald Tribune,* 1934; Universal News Service, foreign correspondent in Berlin, Germany, 1935-37; Columbia Broadcasting System (CBS), continental representative in Vienna, 1937-38, and in Prague and Berlin, 1938-40, war correspondent, 1939-45, radio commentator in the United States, 1941-47; radio commentator for Mutual Broadcasting System, 1947-49; full-time writer, 1950—. Columnist for *New York Herald Tribune* and its syndicate, 1942-48.

WILLIAM L. SHIRER

MEMBER: Authors Guild (president, 1953-57), P.E.N., Council on Foreign Relations, Foreign Policy Association, Phi Beta Kappa, Tau Kappa Epsilon, Century Club. *Awards, honors:* Headliners Club Award, 1938, for coverage of the Austrian Anschluss, and 1941, for general excellence in radio reporting; Litt. D., Coe College, 1941; Chevalier, Legion d'Honneur; George Foster Peabody Award, 1947; Wendell Willkie One World Award, 1948; National Book Award and Sidney Hillman Foundation Award, both 1961, both for *The Rise and Fall of the Third Reich;* Emmy Award for Outstanding Achievement in Cultural Documentaries, 1967-1968, for television series, "The Rise and Fall of the Third Reich."

WRITINGS: Berlin Diary: The Journal of a Foreign Correspondent, 1934-1941 (Book-of-the-Month Club selection), Knopf, 1941, reprinted, Penguin, 1979; *End of a Berlin Diary,* Knopf, 1947; *The Traitor* (novel), Farrar, Straus, 1950, reprinted, Pocket Books, 1971; *Midcentury Journey: The Western World through Its Years of Conflict* (Literary Guild selection), Farrar, Straus, 1952; *Stranger Come Home* (novel), Little, Brown, 1954; *The Challenge of Scandinavia: Norway, Sweden, Denmark, and Finland in Our Time,* Little, Brown, 1955, reprinted, Greenwood Press, 1977; *The Consul's Wife* (novel), Little, Brown, 1956.

The Rise and Fall of the Third Reich: A History of Nazi Germany (Book-of-the-Month Club selection), Simon & Schuster, 1960, reprinted, Fawcett, 1978; *The Rise and Fall of Adolf Hitler* (juvenile), Random House, 1961 (published in England as *All about the Rise and Fall of Adolf Hitler,* W. H. Allen, 1962); *The Sinking of the Bismarck* (juvenile), Random House, 1962 (published in England as *All about the Sinking of the Bismarck,* W. H. Allen, 1963); *The Collapse of the Third Republic: An Inquiry into the Fall of France in 1940* (Book-of-the-Month Club selection), Simon & Schuster, 1969; *Twentieth-Century Journey: A Memoir of a Life and the Times,* Volume I: *The Start, 1904-1930,* Simon & Schuster, 1976; *Gandhi: A Memoir,* Simon & Schuster, 1980; *Twentieth-Century Journey: A Memoir of a Life and the Times,* Volume II: *The Nightmare Years, 1930-1940,* Little, Brown, 1984.

Contributor to *Harper's, Atlantic, Reader's Digest, Look,* and other publications.

ADAPTATIONS: "The Rise and Fall of the Third Reich" (documentary; three-part television series), first broadcast on ABC-TV, March 6, 1968.

WORK IN PROGRESS: Volume III of *Twentieth-Century Journey.*

SIDELIGHTS: At the age of twenty-one, Shirer left his home in Cedar Rapids, Iowa to set out for Paris with two hundred dollars in his pocket and a dream of becoming a writer of fiction and poetry. He tried his luck at landing a newspaper job with major American newspapers with Paris editions, but was offered little encouragement. Dismayed and ready to return to the land of "Prohibition, fundamentalism, puritanism, coolidgeism, [and] Babbitry" when his money ran out, he woke the morning of his last day in the city to discover a note from the editor of the *Chicago Tribune* asking him to report to the newspaper office that evening for a possible job. Shirer spent the next seven years working for the *Tribune.*

"There was a great deal of talk of writing among the young writers at the newspaper offices of the Paris edition of the *Chicago Tribune* and the *New York Herald Tribune.* We talked about it all the time. There was a great ferment in those days about American writing.

(From the Emmy Award-winning documentary "The Rise and Fall of the Third Reich." First broadcast on ABC-TV, March 6, 1968.)

"I hadn't read much French literature. I learned French rather quickly—not because I have any great talent for languages, but I had to in order to hold my job. I think you lose about fifty percent when you read French (or any other foreign language) in translation. So I get very much interested in reading French literature in the original, starting with Voltaire, Balzac, and later Stendhal and Flaubert and some of the modern writers like Gide. I can't say I've kept up with anything as recent as the *noveau roman* writer, but I do a fair amount of reading in French. I have a library with the Pleiade editions of the French classics, and now quite a few of the contemporary writers like Camus and Sartre. At the moment I'm rereading Balzac and going over the Proust novels. There's always something new in them. You can reread Proust—I've read him half a dozen times—and it's amazing how many things may appear to you that you have forgotten.''

The very successful *The Rise and Fall of the Third Reich: A History of Nazi Germany* was published in 1960. The book went on to sell 1.5 million copies, becoming the Book of the Month Club's best seller ever. "Though I lived and worked in the Third Reich during the first half of its brief life, watching at first hand Adolf Hitler consolidate his power as dictator of this great but baffling nation and then lead it off to war and conquest, this personal experience would not have led me to

attempt to write this book had there not occurred at the end of World War II an event unique in history.

"This was the capture of most of the confidential archives of the German government and all its branches, including those of the Foreign Office, the Army and Navy, the National Socialist Party and Heinrich Himmler's secret police. Never before, I believe, has such a vast treasure fallen into the hands of contemporary historians. Hitherto the archives of a great state, even when it was defeated in war and its government overthrown by revolution, as happened to Germany and Russia in 1918, were preserved by it, and only those documents which served the interests of the subsequent ruling regime were ultimately published.

"I have not read, of course, all of this staggering amount of documentation—it would be far beyond the power of a single individual. But I have worked my way through a considerable part of it, slowed down, as all toilers in this rich vineyard must be, by the lack of any suitable indexes.

"In the case of the Third Reich, and it is a unique case, almost all of the documentary material became available at its fall, and it has been enriched by the testimony of all the surviving leaders, military and civilian, in some instances before their

SS troops proudly parade through Berlin, lifting their legs high in the familiar "goose step." ■
(From *The Rise and Fall of Adolf Hitler* by William L. Shirer. Photograph courtesy of United Press.)

death by execution. With such incomparable sources so soon available and with the memory of life in Nazi Germany and of the appearance and behavior and nature of the men who ruled it, Adolf Hitler above all, still fresh in my mind and bones, I decided, at any rate, to make an attempt to set down the history of the rise and fall of the Third Reich." [Foreword to *The Rise and Fall of the Third Reich: A History of Nazi Germany* by William L. Shirer, Simon & Schuster, 1960.[1]]

The Rise and Fall of Adolf Hitler and *The Sinking of the Bismarck* are Shirer's two books for children. "The problem was not to write down to them and yet to make your language and ideas simple enough to reach them. I sat before a blank piece of paper for a month without being able to write anything. I called people like Pearl Buck who had written a lot of children's books—I think she had written one on Luther—but I couldn't get the secret from her. I read a dozen books for children but I couldn't find the key. Finally I just sat down and wrote it as simply and as well as I could, but not condescendingly. I think that's the secret."

One of Shirer's concerns is "to see this country honor writers and artists and intellectuals—even philosophers!—as well as businessmen, bankers, and labor leaders."

FOR MORE INFORMATION SEE: William L. Shirer, *Berlin Diary: The Journal of a Foreign Correspondent, 1934-1941,* Knopf, 1941; *New Yorker,* June 21, 1941, October 29, 1960, September 27, 1976; *New York Times,* June 22, 1941, September 11, 1976, January 7, 1980; *Books,* June 22, 1941; *Saturday Review of Literature,* June 28, 1941; *Christian Science Monitor,* June 30, 1941, October 20, 1960; *New Republic,* June 30, 1941, November 14, 1960, February 12, 1977; *Nation,* July 19, 1941, October 29, 1960; *Living Age,* August, 1941; *Commonweal,* August 1, 1941; *Atlantic,* September, 1941, December, 1960, December, 1969; *Catholic World,* October, 1941; *Spectator,* October 3, 1941, November 18, 1960; *Time,* October 27, 1941, October 17, 1960, November 21, 1969.

Saturday Review, October 15, 1960, August 21, 1976, January 19, 1980; *Chicago Sunday Tribune,* October 16, 1960; *New York Herald Tribune Book Review,* October 16, 1960; *New York Times Book Review,* October 16, 1960, November 9, 1969, October 10, 1976, July 24, 1977, January 20, 1980; *New Statesman,* November 5, 1960; *Guardian,* November 11, 1960; *Times Literary Supplement,* December 2, 1960; *Washington Post Book World,* November 9, 1969; Shirer, *Twentieth-Century Journey: A Memoir of a Life and the Times,* Volume I: *The Start, 1904-1930,* Simon & Schuster, 1976;

National Review, November 26, 1976; *Best Sellers,* December, 1976; *Dictionary of Literary Biography: American Writers in Paris, 1920-1939,* Gale, 1980; *Newsweek,* January 28, 1980; *Washington Post,* January 29, 1980; *Los Angeles Times,* February 3, 1980.

SLEPIAN, Jan(ice B.)   1921-

BRIEF ENTRY: Born January 2, 1921, in New York, N.Y. Author of books for children and young adults. Unlike many authors, Slepian never planned to be a writer. A graduate of Brooklyn College, she holds two master's degrees—one in clinical psychology and the other in speech pathology. Slepian's vocational goal was to be a clinical psychologist, although she later entered the field of speech therapy. From 1947 to 1958 she worked as a speech therapist at hospitals in Massachusetts and New Jersey, as well as in her own private practice. Her career as a writer began with the publication of newspaper articles addressed to parents of speech inflicted children. When the series of articles proved to be a success, Slepian and her partner, Dr. Ann Seidler, went on to produce the "Listen-Hear" series of six picture books published by Follett in 1964. More picture books followed, including the "Junior Listen-Hear" series and *The Best Invention of All* (Crowell/Collier, 1967).

Slepian's young adult novel *The Alfred Summer* appeared in 1980. In this novel, Slepian created such memorable characters as Lester, a cerebral palsy victim; Alfred, lame and epileptic; and Myron and Claire, social misfits. As *New York Times Book Review* observed: "This is the story of a group of the walking wounded, and it is superb." Set in New York City during the late thirties, the novel evoked, according to *Booklist,* "powerful echoes." In 1981 *The Alfred Summer* was chosen a Boston Globe-Horn Book Award Honor Book and an American Book Award finalist. Slepian continued the story in her sequel, *Lester's Turn* (Macmillan, 1981), with a mixture of old and new characters. *Booklist* emphasized that the author "has achieved a major success in making the reader see Lester as a person first and a . . . victim second." Slepian's more recent works include *The Night of the Bozos* (Dutton, 1983) and *Getting On with It* (Four Winds, 1985).

FOR MORE INFORMATION SEE: Fifth Book of Junior Authors and Illustrators, H. W. Wilson, 1983.

SMITH, Samantha   1972-1985

OBITUARY NOTICE: Born in 1972; died in a plane crash, August 25, 1985, in Auburn, Me.; cremated. Student, actress, and author. Smith gained international attention in 1983 when the late Soviet leader Uri Andropov responded to a letter she wrote questioning him as to why he wanted to conquer the United States. In his reply, Andropov assured Smith that he only desired peace for both nations and invited the then eleven-year-old girl and her parents on a two week good-will tour of the Soviet Union. After her trip Smith became a celebrity, making numerous television appearances while traveling throughout the United States. She was a speaker at the Children's International Symposium for the Twenty-first Century in Japan, and she interviewed the 1984 Democratic candidates for president in association with the Disney cable channel. At the time of her death Smith was working as an actress on a new mystery-drama series, "Lime Street," for which she had

already completed four episodes. Smith wrote the book *Journey to the Soviet Union,* recounting her two-week visit with the Soviet people. Following her death, the Soviet Union issued a commemorative stamp in her honor.

FOR MORE INFORMATION SEE: Time, March 11, 1985; *People Weekly,* November 11, 1985. Obituaries: *Chicago Tribune,* August 27, August 28, August 30, 1985; *New York Times,* August 27, 1985; *Newsweek,* September 9, 1985; *Time,* September 9, 1985.

SMITH, Winsome   1935-

PERSONAL: Born April 7, 1935, in Sydney, Australia; daughter of Rupert Harold (a clergyman) and Willa (a bookkeeper; maiden name, Russell) Hayes; married Henry George Smith (an investor), June 26, 1954 (divorced); children: Lynette Smith Rennie, Joanne Smith Coromandel, Sharon Smith Manton. *Education:* Macquarie University, B.A., 1970; graduate study at University of New England, diploma in education, 1973. *Home:* 6 Warks Rd., Kurrajong Heights 2758, N.S.W., Australia. *Office:* Mount Druitt Technical College, Mount St. and North Parade, Mount Druitt 2770, N.S.W., Australia.

CAREER: Teacher of remedial reading in Sydney, N.S.W., Australia high schools, 1970-81. "Kindergarten of the Air" (radio program), ABC Radio, story writer, 1958-73; Moree Technical College, Moree, N.S.W., Australia, and Mount Druitt Technical College, Mount Druitt, N.S.W., Australia, adult literacy officer, 1981—. *Member:* Australian Society of Authors, Fellowship of Australian Writers. *Awards, honors:* PEN/

WINSOME SMITH

Cato broke off one of the leaves and tasted it. It had a crisp, cool, greenish taste. It was celery. ■ (From *Elephant in the Kitchen* by Winsome Smith. Illustrated by Carol Nicklaus.)

QANTAS short story competition runner-up for story entitled "There's a Good Girl," 1975.

WRITINGS—All for children: *Somewhere to Go, Something to Do*, McGraw, 1976; *Joy Ride*, McGraw, 1976; *Does Anyone Care?*, Macmillan, 1977; *Breakthrough*, Holt-Saunders, 1978; *Elephant in the Kitchen* (illustrated by Carol Nicklaus), Scholastic Book Services, 1980; *The Half-Dolls*, Ashton Scholastic, 1982.

Work represented in numerous anthologies, including *The Blindfolded Horse and Other Stories* (adult), The Australian Association for the Teaching of English, 1975, *The Kids' Own Book of Stories and Things to Do* (juvenile), T. Nelson, 1978, *More Stuff and Nonsense* (juvenile; poems), Collins, 1980, and *The True Life Story of . . .* (adult), University of Queensland Press, 1981.

WORK IN PROGRESS: "It is not really possible for me to describe work in progress because I am not an organised writer. I write all the time, mostly in the mornings. I keep diaries and I write down my dreams. I write down descriptions of things I see and my impressions. These are the things that I work into stories and sometimes into books. For me writing is a dynamic process, always changing and developing."

SIDELIGHTS: "I grew up in country parsonages as my father was a Methodist minister. Ours was a very strict and restricted home but we did have lots of books—and everyone did a lot of talking. My mother was an avid reader and, now in her seventies, still reads at least six books a week. My father was a great storyteller and raconteur. Every night he would tell us children a story, often one he had made up himself. He also told Bible stories, Aesop's fables, and Greek and Roman legends.

"I left school at fourteen and went to work at the local telephone exchange. My weekly wage was one pound sixteen shillings ($3.60). I loved my job so much that I often went to work on my day off.

"I got married at nineteen and subsequently had three daughters. When my youngest girl was five I went back to school. I eventually graduated from Macquarie University and became a teacher.

"My first jobs were teaching English and history in high schools. Then I became interested in remedial reading because I discovered that many high school students could not read. I am now an adult literacy officer with the Department of Technical and Further Education, teaching adults to read.

"My first writing was done for radio, writing stories for 'Kindergarten on the Air.' I think I began writing for children because my own children were young at the time.

"Although I write childrens books, I do not read childrens books, as I do not want to be influenced by them. I want all my ideas to be original. *Elephant in the Kitchen* was first told to my own children. During the long summer holidays we would sit around the breakfast table every morning and I would tell them a new episode every day. Sometimes we sat there till nearly lunchtime. My three favourite books are *Pride and Prejudice, The Great Gatsby*, and *The Catcher in the Rye*.

"I lived for many years in Sydney, the capital city of New South Wales, then lived for two and a half years in Moree, a town on the great north-west plains of that state. That is wheat- and cotton-growing country. It is also the home of large mobs of kangaroos and emus. It is the Australian outback. Life there was very interesting, but in 1973 I moved to Kurrajong Heights in the Blue Mountains. Here we have the beautiful Australian bush, with colourful birds such as rosellas and lorikeets. It is only an hour's drive from Sydney where there are theatres, the Opera House, a jazz club called Red Ned's, the beautiful harbour, and best of all, my family."

HOBBIES AND OTHER INTERESTS: "I am interested in many things. I love live theatre and going to the ballet and art exhibitions. I also love the movies, especially old movies. I enjoy photography, but I'm not very good at it, and I love music, mostly classical and jazz. I am addicted to cryptic crosswords."

I remember, I remember
The fir-trees dark and high;
I used to think their slender tops
Were close against the sky;
It was a childish ignorance,
But now 'tis little joy
To know I'm farther off from heav'n
Than when I was a boy.

—Thomas Hood
(From *I Remember, I Remember*)

SMITS, Theodore R(ichard) 1905-
(Teo Smits)

PERSONAL: Born April 24, 1905, in Jackson, Mich.; son of Bastian (a clergyman) and Helen (Hull) Smits; married Anna Mary Wells, September 5, 1931 (divorced June 13, 1952); married Pamela Ada Seward (an executive secretary), September 22, 1952; children: (first marriage) Jean Marie Smits Miles, Helen Lida, Gerrit (deceased); (second marriage) Richard Winston. *Education:* Attended Michigan State University, 1922-23. *Home:* 601 East 20th St., New York, N.Y. 10010.

CAREER: Lansing State Journal, Lansing, Mich., state and telegraph editor, 1924-29; International News Service, New York City, city editor, 1929-31, manager of Los Angeles bureau, 1931-34; Associated Press, New York City, city editor in Los Angeles, Calif., 1934-37, chief of bureaus in Salt Lake City, Utah, 1937-39, and Detroit, Mich., 1939-46, general sports editor in New York City, 1946-69; AMF, Inc., White Plains, N.Y., editorial adviser for Leisure Time Products, 1969-74; *Armchair Quarterback,* New York City, editor, 1976—.

WRITINGS—Under name Teo Smits: (Editor) *The Year in Sports,* Prentice-Hall, 1958; *The Game of Soccer,* Prentice-Hall, 1968; *Soccer for the American Boy* (illustrated by F. W. Turton), Prentice-Hall, 1970; *Soccer, American Style,* Doubleday, 1976.

SIDELIGHTS: While with Associated Press, Smits was in charge of world coverage for the Olympics from 1948 to 1968.

FOR MORE INFORMATION SEE: Choice, March, 1969; *Teacher,* May, 1978.

STEINBERG, Rafael (Mark) 1927-

PERSONAL: Born June 2, 1927, in Newark, N.J.; son of Isador N. (an artist) and Polly N. (Rifkind) Steinberg; married Tamiko Okamoto (a teacher of Japanese), November 21, 1953 (separated); children: Summer Eve, Joy Nathania. *Education:* Harvard University, A.B. (cum laude), 1950. *Home:* 1841 Broadway, New York, N.Y. 10023.

CAREER: Fire Island Reporter, Long Island, N.Y., editor and publisher, summers, 1949-50; International News Service, New York, N.Y., war correspondent from Korea, 1951-52; *Time* (magazine), New York, war correspondent from Korea and Japan, 1952, and New York, 1953-55, member of London Bureau, 1955-58; *Newsweek* (magazine), New York, Far Eastern correspondent and Tokyo bureau chief, 1959-63; free-lance journalist in Tokyo, Japan, serving as correspondent for *Washington Post* and *Saturday Evening Post,* 1963-67, and the United States, 1968-70; *Newsweek,* general editor, 1970-72, senior editor, 1972-73, managing editor of international edition, 1973; free-lance writer, 1973-75; *Cue* magazine, New York, editor, 1975-76. Executive director of Academic and Professional Alliance for a Responsible Congress, 1970. *Military service:* U.S. Naval Reserve, active duty, 1945-46. *Member:* Authors Guild of Authors League of America, Japan Society, Foreign Correspondents Club of Japan, Harvard Club (New York, N.Y.).

WRITINGS: Postscript from Hiroshima, Random House, 1966; *Japan,* Macmillan, 1969; (with Jacob Javits) *Javits: The Autobiography of a Public Man,* Houghton, 1981.

With the editors of Time-Life Books: *Cooking of Japan,* Time-Life, 1969; *Pacific and Southeast Asian Cooking,* Time-Life, 1970; *Man and the Organization,* Time-Life, 1975; *Island Fighting,* Time-Life, 1978; *Return to the Philippines,* Time-Life, 1979. Contributor of articles and stories to magazines, including *Playboy,* and newspapers.

STEINER, Charlotte 1900-1981

PERSONAL: Born in 1900 in Vienna, Austria; came to the United States in 1938, naturalized, 1944; died August 12, 1981; daughter of Bernard and Adele (Liechtenstein) Klein; married Frederick Steiner, June 17, 1922; *Education:* Attended schools in Austria, France, Czechoslovakia, and Germany. *Religion:* Roman Catholic.

CAREER: Author and illustrator of children's books.

WRITINGS—All for children; all self-illustrated: *Lulu,* Doubleday, Doran, 1939; *Pete and Peter,* Doubleday, Doran, 1941; *Lulu Meets Peter,* Doubleday, Doran, 1942; (with Mary Burlingham) *The Climbing Book,* Vanguard, 1943; *Kiki and Muffy,* Doubleday, Doran, 1943; *Daddy Comes Home,* Doubleday, Doran, 1944; (with M. Burlingham) *The Second Climbing Book,* Vanguard, 1944; *Find Us at the Children's Fair!,* Harper, 1945; *A Surprise for Mrs. Bunny,* Grosset, 1945; *The Sleepy Quilt,* Doubleday, Doran, 1945; *ABC,* F. Watts, 1946; *Wake Up! Wake Up!,* Grosset, 1946; *Where Are You Going?,* Doubleday, 1946; *The Little Train that Saved the Day,* Grosset, 1947; *Polka Dot,* Doubleday, 1947; *Lulu's Play School,* Doubleday, 1948; (with Margaret G. Otto) *The Big Laughing Book,* Grosset, 1949; *Kiki Dances,* Doubleday, 1949.

Kiki Skates, Doubleday, 1950; *Whose Baby? A Picture Book,* Crowell, 1950; *Giddy-Ap!, Giddy-Ap!,* Doubleday, 1951; *Little John Little,* Wonder Books, 1951; *Make-Believe Puppy* (illustrated with photographs by Helen Heller), Lothrop, 1952; *Pete's Puppets,* Doubleday, 1952; (compiler) *Happy Birthday Book: An Anthology of Verses and Stories,* Garden City Books, 1953; *Kiki Goes to Camp,* Doubleday, 1953; *Kiki Loves Music,* Doubleday, 1954; *Patsy's Pet,* Doubleday, 1955; *A Friend is "Amie",* Knopf, 1956; *Karoleena,* Doubleday, 1957; *My Slippers Are Red,* Knopf, 1957; *Kiki Is an Actress,* Doubleday, 1958; *My Bunny Feels Soft,* Knopf, 1958; *Terry Writes a Letter,* Macmillan, 1958; *Bobby Follows the Butterfly,* Macmillan, 1959; *Listen to My Seashell,* Knopf, 1959; *Lolly's Pony Ride,* Doubleday, 1959.

Good Day! Which Way?, Knopf, 1960; *Karoleena's Red Coat,* Doubleday, 1960; *Ten in a Family,* Knopf, 1960; *I Am Andy,* Knopf, 1961; *Tim and Tom Play Ball,* Macmillan, 1961; *Timmy Needs a Thinking Cap,* Macmillan, 1961; *Jack Is Glad, Jack Is Sad,* Knopf, 1962; *Kiki's Play House,* Doubleday, 1962; *Red Ridinghood Goes Sledding,* Macmillan, 1962; *The Fitfiddles Keep Fit,* Knopf, 1963; *Now That You Are Five,* Association Press, 1963; *Birthdays Are for Everyone,* Doubleday, 1964; *Red Ridinghood's Little Lamb,* Knopf, 1964; *Annie's ABC Kitten,* Knopf, 1965; *I'd Rather Stay with You,* Seabury, 1965; *The Hungry Book,* Knopf, 1967; *Square Bear and Cousin Bear,* Seabury, 1967; *What Do You Love: A Little Picture Book,* Knopf, 1968; *What's the Hurry, Harry?,* Lothrop, 1968; *Let Her Dance!,* Lothrop, 1969; *Tomboy's Doll,* Lothrop, 1969; *Look What Tracy Found,* Knopf, 1972.

Illustrator: Lena Barksdale, *Nilly and Her Dogs,* Doubleday, 1942; William Hall, *Watch the Pony Grow,* Crowell, 1942;

He saw the farmer's wife pour some warm, fresh milk into the cat's dish. ■ (From *The Hungry Book* by Charlotte Steiner. Illustrated by the author.)

Helen Sterling, *Choo Choo 'Round the World*, Pilot Press, 1946; Phyllis Britcher, *Five Little Finger Playmates*, Grosset, 1950; W. N. Hall and Robin Hall, *Telltime Goes A'Counting*, Crowell, 1956; W. N. Hall, *Telltime's Alphabet Book*, Crowell, 1958; *The Littlest Mother Goose*, Random House, 1964.

We are now at the point where we must educate people in what nobody knew yesterday, and prepare in our schools for what no one knows yet but what some people must know tomorrow.

—Margaret Mead

STRASSER, Todd 1950-
(Morton Rhue)

PERSONAL: Born May 5, 1950, in New York, N.Y.; son of Chester S. (a manufacturer of women's dresses) and Sheila (an artist; maiden name, Reisner) Strasser; married Pamela Older (a businesswoman), July 2, 1981; children: a daughter. *Education:* Beloit College, B.A., 1974. *Residence:* New York, N.Y. *Agent:* Ellen Levine, 432 Park Ave. S., New York, N.Y. 10016.

CAREER: Times Herald Record (newspaper), Middletown, N.Y., reporter, 1974-76; free-lance writer, 1975—; Compton

Advertising, New York, N.Y., copywriter, 1976-77; *Esquire,* New York, N.Y., researcher, 1977-78; owner of fortune cookie company, 1978—. Speaker at teachers' and librarians' conferences and at high schools. *Awards, honors: Friends Till the End* and *Rock 'n' Roll Nights* were both named best books for young adults by the American Library Association, 1981 and 1982; *Friends Till the End* was chosen as a notable children's trade book in Social Studies, 1982; *Rock 'n' Roll Nights* was chosen for the Acton Public Library Crabbery Award List, 1983.

WRITINGS—All young adult fiction; all published by Delacorte, except as indicated: *Angel Dust Blues* (teacher's guide available), Coward, 1979; *Friends Till the End,* 1981; (under pseudonym Morton Rhue) *The Wave* (novelization; based on the teleplay by Johnny Dawkins; teacher's guide available), 1981; *Rock 'n' Roll Nights,* 1982; *Workin' for Peanuts,* 1983; *The Complete Computer Popularity Program,* 1984; *Turn It Up!* (sequel to '*Rock 'n' Roll Nights*), 1984; *A Very Touchy Subject,* 1985.

Also contributor to various publications, including *New Yorker* and *Village Voice.*

WORK IN PROGRESS: A book about teenagers, drinking and driving; a third book in the 'Rock 'n' Roll' series; a book about malls from outer space.

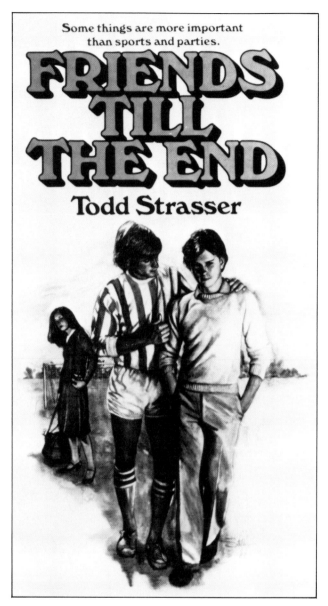

Some things are more important than sports and parties.

FRIENDS TILL THE END

Todd Strasser

(Jacket illustration from *Friends Till the End* by Todd Strasser.)

TODD STRASSER

SIDELIGHTS: "Since the birth of my daughter in 1984, I find myself working at a heightened pace, often all day and into the evening as well as parts of weekends. Since writing is not the most lucrative of employments, I am involved in other enterprises, including the fortune cookie business. Most of my time is spent writing, however, and I concentrate on books for teenagers.

"I write for teenagers for several reasons. First and foremost, I hope that they will find my books entertaining and perhaps even helpful as they go through the process of forming judgments and opinions on how they shall live. Secondly, I feel that books for teenagers have a longer shelf life than books for adults. One of the most depressing things in the world to me is the thought of a book going out of print."

"I am particularly interested in writing books for teenaged boys. By that I mean contemporary fiction and not sci fi or war stories. There are some very good writers writing for boys, but generally I'd say that most YA [young adult] literature for the teenaged male is still in the Dark Ages. Many writers seem to have ignored the idea that a teenaged boy can be just as sensitive, just as mixed-up, just as curious as a teenaged girl. Well, I think he can (at least I know I was).

''I also think that books for teenagers today have to be very entertaining. We are dealing with kids who have been fed entertainment by the shovel-full, whether it comes from television, video games, or whatever the next fad will be. Books for teenagers have to compete or they simply will not get read. So when I write about an important subject like drug abuse or disease, I try to write a compelling story with humor and romance as well as serious matters.'' [Alleen Pace Nilsen and Kenneth L. Donelson, *Literature for Today's Young Adults*, 2nd edition, Scott, Foresman, 1985.[1]]

The interests of teenagers today, Strasser feels, are basically the same as the interests of teenagers twenty years ago. ''I think the kind of music changes or what the wear may change, but dealing with being popular, friends or the opposite sex, or questions of morality and decency . . . [I don't think] those things really ever change. I hate to say this, but I think we tell the same stories—just in today's language and in today's settings.

''I've been writing almost exclusively for an age range that probably goes from about 11 to 15 or 16. I'd say it's for bright, sophisticated 11 year-olds and not as bright, nor as sophisticated 15 year-olds. There's a real difference in this country, depending on where you live.'' [Nina Piwoz, ''I Was a Teen-

age Boy: An Interview with Todd Strasser,'' *Media & Methods,* February, 1983.[2] Amended by Strasser.]

Strasser's aim is to write contemporary, realistic fiction for boys. ''My favorite example of this concerns that wonderful teenaged affliction called the 'crush.' There are millions of books about teenage girls with crushes. Teenage girls have crushes on everybody—the boy next door, the brother of the boy next door, the cousin of the boy next door. How many books are there about boys with crushes? There are so few. Does this mean that very few boys have teenaged crushes? *I* was a teenaged boy and I had lots of crushes—the girl next door, the cousin of the girl next door. . . .

''A teenage boy from the age of about 11 to 14 is discovering his masculinity and trying to understand the difference between himself as a male and others as females. In most families, the women are still *the readers*. The boy grows up saying to himself, 'Mom is reading and Dad is watching TV. I want to be like Dad.' A girl sees her mother reading and says, 'I can read just like Mom does.' Boys at that age aren't really *against* reading, but they want to do the things they envision as being masculine.

''What I try to do in my books is present *boyish* boys, but I try to make them *real* boys, with emotions and sensitivities. If a boy sees a book that says on the cover, 'Tommy is a sensitive, caring young boy in a tumultuous relationship with his best friend and his girlfriend,' he's not going to pick it up. But if Tommy is the star of the soccer team and is a tough,

(Jacket illustration by Judy Clifford from *Angel Dust Blues* by Todd Strasser.)

(From the movie "The Wave," starring Bruce Davison, on which Strasser based his novelization. Broadcast as an ABC Afterschool Special, March 30, 1983.)

good-looking guy, but is *still* in 'a tumultuous relationship with his best friend and his girlfriend,' *then* he's something kids will pick up on.

"[My] characters grow out of the story. Each story requires a certain group of characters to make it progress from beginning to end, and I supply them based on the story. I very rarely will pick a character and create a story around that character.

"I do not write books solely for teenage boys, but I write books that teenage boys will read. A greater percentage of my fan mail still comes from teenage girls, but at least I know that boys are reading my books, and that's important to me."[2]

Strasser's books are based on his own experiences as well as research. "My first book, *Angle Dust Blues,* is about a group of fairly well-to-do suburban teenagers who get into trouble with drugs. (I grew up in a fairly well-to-do, suburban community and a group of kids I knew got into trouble with drugs.) My first story was based on that experience . . . and watching it occur.

"My second book, *Friends Till the End,* is about a healthy teenager who has a friend who becomes extremely ill with leukemia. When I moved to New York, I got a roommate . . . an old friend of mine. Within a few weeks, he became very ill. I spent a year visiting him in the hospital, not knowing whether he was going to live or die. I thought it was an experience that teenagers could relate to and one they *should* relate to.

"My . . . book *Rock 'n' Roll Nights* [is] . . . about a teenage rock and roll band—something with which I have absolutely no *direct* experience. However, I grew up in the 1960s when rock and roll was really our 'national anthem.' I relate much better to rock stars than to movie stars. I always wanted to be in a rock band, as did just about everybody I knew."[2]

"I do a great deal of traveling and speaking both to students in high schools and to teachers and librarians at meetings and conferences. I find this an excellent way to keep in touch with teenagers and to do research. The opening scene of my book, *A Very Touchy Subject,* came from a story a librarian told me. I also find walking through schools and speaking with students gives me useful details for my work."

Strasser wrote *The Wave* under his pseudonym, Morton Rhue. "I didn't feel comfortable attaching my name to something that wasn't my original idea so I created 'Morton Rhue.' Anything on TV available in book form, kids will read. It has entertainment appeal, and for kids who are not natural readers, it gets them to enjoy reading as an entertainment."[2]

The message in Strasser's books is "honesty. Standing up for one's friends, self and beliefs. Even though I grew up in the 1960s with the 'new morality,' I'm old-fashioned in many ways. I want kids to have the same old-fashioned morals and values that I have. That doesn't mean I can't write about contemporary issues. If you have to deal with drugs or with teenage sexuality, you can have contemporary kids dealing with it, and those kids can still have what we call 'old-fashioned' values. The heroes in my books *A Very Touchy Subject* and *Workin' for Peanuts* are both modern boys with some old fashioned values.

"There are too many writers following trends. What we need is more contemporary, realistic, well-written fiction—expecially for boys and especially for minorities."[2]

"I work on a word processor, but still find the process of writing a book a long and arduous one. Generally I will rewrite all or parts of a manuscript five or six times before it is typeset and inevitably I will go on to make changes in the galleys.

"I like to fish, ski and play tennis, but don't have much time to do any of them. What free time I have I try to share with my wife and daugnter. I have enjoyed watching my daughter grow and develop into a little person. I guess when she's a teenager I'll use her for research."

FOR MORE INFORMATION SEE: Weekly Voice of Youth Advocates, June, 1981; Nina Powiz, "I Was a Teenage Boy: An Interview with Todd Strasser," *Media & Methods,* February, 1983; *New York Times,* October 2, 1983; Alleen Pace Nilsen and Kenneth L. Donelson, *Literature for Today's Young Adults,* 2nd edition, Scott, Foresman, 1985.

TELEKI, Geza   1943-

PERSONAL: Born December 7, 1943, in Kolozsvar, Hungary; came to the United States, 1949; naturalized U.S. citizen, 1956; son of Geza (a politician and scientist) and Hanna (Mikes) Teleki. *Education:* George Washington University, B.A., 1967; Pennsylvania State University, M.A., 1970, Ph.D., 1977. *Politics:* None. *Religion:* None. *Home Address:* 3819 48th St. N.W., Washington, D.C. 20016. *Office:* Department of Anthropology, George Washington University, Washington, D.C. 20052.

CAREER: University of New Mexico, Albuquerque, field assistant in archaeology at Sapawe (a Pueblo Indian site), 1966; Smithsonian Institution, Washington, D.C., laboratory assistant in physical anthropology, 1967; Gombe Stream Research Centre, Gombe National Park, Tanzania, field research assistant, 1968-69, senior field researcher in primatology, 1970-71; Hall's Island Gibbon Colony, Hall's Island, Bermuda, senior research assistant in primatology, 1971; George Washington University, Washington, D.C., assistant professional lecturer, 1978-79, associate professional lecturer, 1980—. Field assistant in ethology at Ngorogoro Crater, Tanzania, 1968, and Serengeti National Park, 1970; director, Wildlife Survey Project, Sierra Leone, 1979-80; director, Outamba-Kilimi National Park, Sierra Leone and project manager, World Wildlife Fund, 1981-84. Consultant for Survival Service Commission of the International Union for the Conservation of Nature, 1979—; research consultant on gibbon behavior.

MEMBER: International Primate Protection League, Audubon Society, American Society of Primatologists, American Anthropological Association, American Museum of Natural History. *Awards, honors: Goblin: A Wild Chimpanzee* was chosen as an Outstanding Science Book for Children from the National Science Teachers Association and the Children's Book Council, 1977, and *Leakey the Elder: A Chimpanzee and His Community,* was chosen in 1980.

WRITINGS: The Predatory Behavior of Wild Chimpanzees, Bucknell University Press, 1973; (contributor) D. M. Rum-

baugh, editor, *Gibbon and Siamang,* S. Karger, 1974; (with Karen Steffy) *Goblin: A Wild Chimpanzee,* Dutton, 1977; *Chimpanzee Behavior* (slide and study guide set), Educational Images, 1979; (with Lori Baldwin and Meredith Rucks) *Aerial Apes: Gibbons of Asia* (self-illustrated and illustrated with photographs by L. Baldwin), Coward, 1979; *Ecology of Gombe National Park* (slide and study guide set), Educational Images, 1979; (with K. Steffy and L. Baldwin) *Leakey the Elder: A Chimpanzee and His Community,* Dutton, 1980; (co-editor with R. S. O. Harding) *Omnivorous Primates: Gathering and Hunting in Human Evolution,* Columbia University Press, 1981.

Contributor of photographs: Pierre Rossion, *Science et vie* (title means "Science and Life"), Excelsior (Paris), 1973; R. S. Lazarus, *The Riddle of Man,* Prentice-Hall, 1974; *Animals in Action,* Reader's Digest Books, 1974; *East African Wildlife,* Time-Life, 1974; *Our Vanishing Wildlife,* Reader's Digest Books, 1974; John Alcock, *An Evolutionary Approach to Animal Behavior,* Sinauer, 1974; Helena Curtis, *Biology,* Worth Publishers, 1974; S. I. Rosen, *Introduction to Physical Anthropology,* McGraw, 1974. Has also made films of his field research on gibbons.

Author of research reports. Contributor of photographs to *Il Libro Del Anno* and *Encyclopaedia Britannica Yearbook.* Contributor of articles to journals, including *Scientific American, Primates, Journal of Human Evolution, Smithsonian, Zoonooz,* and *Folia Primatologica.* Editor of *Matrix* (interscience journal of George Washington University), 1965-67.

WORK IN PROGRESS: Accounts of "How to Set Up National Parks in West Africa," organizing an expedition to East Africa for *National Geographic* for the one hundred-year anniversary

Geza Teleki in 1984 at the national park in Sierra Leone with orphan chimpanzee, Rupert.

of great-uncle Count Samuel Teleki's discovery of Lakes Rudolf and Stefanie in 1887-1888.

SIDELIGHTS: ''In 1975, while still a graduate student in anthropology and after having already done several years of field work with Jane Goodall in Tanzania, I set out to write several books on wild chimpanzees. As a primatologist, I wanted to do more, however, than the usual professional series of papers and books for other specialized scientists, largely because my work with Goodall convinced me that preservation of African chimpanzees and their habitats was a vital necessity if my chosen career was to survive more than another decade or two. What was the point, in other words, of persuading college students to become primatologists if there remained nothing for them to study in the field by the time they became adults? It was a simple extension from that to asking myself how those wilderness areas can be protected in the long run if children are not encouraged to become aware of the dire need to preserve such fascinating animal species? So I decided that my professional responsibilities extended quite naturally into the field of writing for young readers, and all my works for that audience emphasize some aspect of nature conservation.

''The main task, so far as I was concerned, was to avoid lecturing readers on the subject. Too many authors are already preaching the necessities of conservation, and as a child I myself tended to reject most preachings of any kind. My intuition told me that chimpanzees can best tell their own story to readers, and that through telling that story in a narrative but completely factual way it would be possible to have readers voluntarily recognize the need for preserving species which share so many behavioral, social and mental features with humans. My approach, therefore, was to take authentic field observations and to do no more than arrange them into readable tales of ape life in the wild, using a liberal spread of photographs to show that everything described in these ''naturalist stories'' is absolutely real.

''I am pleased to say that the result was two volumes about chimpanzees and one volume about gibbons of which I am duly proud. *Goblin: A Wild Chimpanzee* and *Leakey the Elder: A Chimpanzee and His Community* won several awards, and were translated into French. Apparently there is a market for the type of naturalistic writing that I had in mind, and I intend to pursue the goal further with newer field work. Judging from the reactions of many young readers who wrote to me about *Goblin* and *Leakey,* I gather that my intuitions were quite correct in that children are quite capable of assimilating rather sophisticated ideas about wildlife. Sad to say, my view of the publishing world has deteriorated accordingly, as I feel that most publishers are committed to assuming that children are mentally inferior beings who must be fed standardized information in short bursts which conform to minimum attention spans. That is little more than a self-fulfilling prophesy, however, as our children are as we make them.''

HOBBIES AND OTHER INTERESTS: Nature photography, photovoltaic technology, philately.

Together, they lived in harmony with the land. . . . ■ (From *The Legend of Africania* by Dorothy W. Robinson. Illustrated by Herbert Temple.)

TEMPLE, Herbert   1919-

PERSONAL: Born July 6, 1919, in Gary, Ind.; married; children: Janel (daughter). *Education:* Attended Art Institute of Chicago, 1945-48. *Office:* 820 South Michigan Ave., Chicago, Ill. 60605.

CAREER: Graphic artist. Worked as an art director of *Ebony,* and *Ebony Jr.!* and *Black World* magazines, and as an advertising, promotional, and packaging designer for Supreme Beauty Products Co. Judge of art shows nationwide. *Awards, honors:* Coretta Scott King Award, 1975, for *The Legend of Africania.*

ILLUSTRATOR: Freda De Knight, *Ebony Cookbook: A Date with a Dish,* Johnson Publishing, 1962; A. S. "Doc" Young, *Negro Firsts in Sports,* Johnson Publishing, 1963; Dorothy W. Robinson, *The Legend of Africania* (juvenile), Johnson Publishing, 1974.

TERBAN, Marvin

BRIEF ENTRY: A teacher at the Columbia Grammar and Preparatory School in New York City, Terban is the author of four wordplay books designed to instruct children in the use of homonyms, idioms, verbs, and palindromes. Terban uses a light-hearted approach, making a game out of learning grammar. His first book, *Eight Ate: A Feast of Homonym Riddles* (Clarion Books, 1982), asks questions like "Who is married to Uncle Beetle? Aunt Ant." *Booklist* described it as "a well-executed concept," one that "teachers will welcome . . . especially those who work with primary graders." *In a Pickle and Other Funny Idioms* (Clarion Books, 1983) provides the meanings behind phrases such as "up a tree" and "to fly off the handle," while *I Think I Thought: And Other Tricky Verbs* (Clarion Books, 1984) humorously explores the present and past tenses of thirty irregular verbs. Terban's fourth book, *Too Hot to Hoot: Funny Palindrome Riddles* (Clarion Books, 1985) is a look at words, phrases, sentences, and numbers that read the same forward and backward. ("Madam, I'm Adam.") "While this has the look of a joke book," *Booklist* again noted, "it also challenges the reader to think about words creatively and analytically." During the summer, Terban directs children's plays at Cejwin Camps in Port Jervis, N.Y. He is married and the father of two children. *Residence:* New York, N.Y.

THIRY, Joan (Marie)   1926-

PERSONAL: Born October 27, 1926, in Chicago, Ill.; daughter of William Joseph and Mary Cecelia (Mertens) Thiry. *Education:* De Paul University, B.A., 1958, M.A. (with distinction), 1966; Mundelein College, M.A. in religious studies, 1974. *Politics:* Democrat. *Religion:* Roman Catholic. *Office:* Chateau Thierry Press, 1668 Olive Ave., Chicago, Ill. 60660, and Joan Thiry Enterprises Ltd., 2100 W. Estes, Chicago, Ill. 60645.

CAREER: Teacher in primary and secondary schools in Minneapolis, Minn., 1945-56, Piqua, Ohio, 1956-58, New Orleans, La., 1958-64, and Chicago, Ill., 1969; Archdiocese of New Orleans, New Orleans, diocesan director of religious education, 1964-68; St. Giles, Oak Park, Ill., parish coordinator or religious education, 1969-72; Urban Progress Center, Chicago, teacher of adult education, 1969-71; free-lance writer, 1971—; Roa Films, Inc., Milwaukee, Wis., program de-

JOAN THIRY

signer, 1971-78; Thiry Enterprises (communications company), Chicago, president, 1978—. *Member:* Women in Communications, Chicago Society of Creative Designers, Chicago Women in Publishing, The Executive Woman.

WRITINGS: All for children, except as noted: *Eucharist Is for Sharing,* Pflaum/Standard, 1977; (with mother, Mary Thiry) *You Must Tell Your Children: How To Capture Your Family Story with Help from Family and Friends* (adult), Chateau Thierry, 1978; *Creative Prayer,* Pflaum/Standard, 1981; *Sharing His Life,* Pflaum/Standard, 1981; *Sharing His Love,* Pflaum/ Standard, 1981.

"Manners for Living" series: *How to Cope with an Artichoke and Other Mannerly Mishaps* (illustrated by Karen J. Walsh), Chateau Thierry, 1982; *How to Entertain a Gnu and Not Disturb Your Family* (illustrated by K. J. Walsh), Chateau Thierry, 1982; *How to Make a Courtesy Butter Sandwich and Serve It Properly* (illustrated by K. J. Walsh), Chateau Thierry, 1982.

Also author of *Confirmation Is Saying Yes to God* (with Marilyn Burbach) for Pflaum/Standard and of many filmstrip and video series for children and families.

We can never know that a piece of writing is bad unless we have begun by trying to read it as if it was very good and ended by discovering that we were paying the author an undeserved compliment.

—C.S. Lewis

TRUESDELL, Susan G.
(Sue Truesdell)

BRIEF ENTRY: Illustrator. Truesdell spend her childhood in Glen Head, Long Island. She later graduated from Pratt Institute where she majored in communication design. Truesdell has produced pen-and-ink drawings in five books for children. *Horn Book* commented that her ''cartoonlike illustrations recall those of George Booth in *The New Yorker*—albeit without his frenzied zaniness.'' Her amusing sketches can be seen in Mitchell Sharmat's *The Seven Sloppy Days of Phineas Pig* (Harcourt, 1983), Alvin Schwartz's *Unriddling: All Sorts of Riddles to Puzzle Your Guessery* (Lippincott, 1983), and Anne Leo Ellis's *Dabble Duck* (Harper, 1984). In Dennis Haseley's *The Pirate Who Tried to Capture the Moon* (Harper, 1983), Truesdell used a two-color process that includes black-and-white drawings and a pale yellow moon which becomes more golden as the story progresses. *School Library Journal* observed: ''Truesdell's illustrations are marvelous. . . . It is rare that the mood and tone of the illustrations change so dramatically within a picture book.'' Her most recent work is Joan Robins's *Addie Meets Max* (Harper, 1985). *Residence:* Brooklyn, N.Y.

TUSIANI, Joseph   1924-

PERSONAL: Born January 14, 1924, in Foggia, Italy; came to United States in 1947, naturalized in 1956; son of Michael and Maria (Pisone) Tusiani. *Education:* University of Naples, Ph.D. (summa cum laude), 1947. *Religion:* Roman Catholic. *Home:* 2140 Tomlinson Ave., New York, N.Y. 10461.

CAREER: Liceo Classico, San Severo, Italy, teacher of Latin and Greek, 1944-47; College of Mount Saint Vincent, Riverdale, N.Y., chairman of Italian department, 1948-71; Hunter College (now Hunter College of the City University of New York), New York City, lecturer in Italian, 1950-63; New York University, New York City, lecturer in Italian literature, 1956-63; Herbert H. Lehman College of the City University of New York, Bronx, N.Y., professor of Italian literature, 1971-82. *Member:* Poetry Society of America (vice-president, 1958-68), Catholic Poetry Society of America (director, 1956-69), P.E.N., Dante Society of America, American Association of University Professors. *Awards, honors:* Greenwood Prize, Poetry Society of England, 1956; silver medal for Latin poetry (Rome), 1962; Alice Fay di Castagnola Award, Poetry Society of America, 1968; *Spirit* gold medal of Catholic Poetry Society of America, 1969; outstanding teacher award, College of Mount Saint Vincent, 1969; Litt.D., College of Mount Saint Vincent, 1971; Cavaliere Ufficiale in the Order of Merit of the Italian Republic, 1977; Leonard Covello Award, 1980; Leone di San Marco, 1982; Congressional Medal of Merit, 1984.

WRITINGS: (Translator and author of introduction and notes) *The Complete Poems of Michelangelo,* Noonday, 1960; *Rind and All: Fifty Poems,* Monastine Press, 1962; (translator and author of introduction and notes) *Lust and Liberty: The Poems of Machiavelli,* Obolensky, 1963; *The Fifth Season: Poems,* Obolensky, 1964; *Envoy from Heaven* (novel), Obolensky, 1965; *Dante's Inferno, as Told for Young People,* Obolensky, 1965; *Dante's Purgatorio, as Told for Young People,* Obolensky, 1966.

(Translator and author of introduction) Torquato Tasso, *Jerusalem Delivered,* Fairleigh Dickinson University Press, 1970;

(translator and author of introduction) Boccaccio, *Nymphs of Fiesole,* Fairleigh Dickinson University Press, 1971; *Italian Poets of the Renaissance,* Baroque Press, 1971; (editor and translator) *From Marino to Marinetti,* Baroque Press, 1972; (editor and translator) *The Age of Dante,* Baroque Press, 1972; (translator) *Alfieri's America the Free,* Italian-American Center, 1975; *Gente Mia and Other Poems,* Italian Cultural Center, 1978; T. Tasso, *Creation of the World,* State University of New York Press at Binghamton, 1982.

In Italian: *Flora* (poetry), Caputo, 1947; *Amore e morte* (poetry), Caputo, 1948; *Peccato e luce* (poetry), Venetian Press, 1949; *La Poesia amorosa di Emily Dickinson,* Venetian Press, 1950; *Dante in Licenza* (novel), Nigrizia, 1951; *Wordsworthiana,* Venetian Press, 1952; *Poesia missionaria in Inghilterra ed America: Storia critica ed antologica,* Nigrizia, 1952; *Sonettisti Americani,* introduction by Frances Winwar, Clemente Publishing Co., 1954; *Lacreme e Sciure,* Edizioni Cappetta, 1955; *L'Italia nell' opera di Frances Winwar,* [Chicago], 1956; *Lo Speco celeste* (poetry), Editrice Ciranna, 1956; *Odi Sacre* (poetry), Editrice Ciranna, 1959; *Influenza cristiana nella poesia Negro-Americana,* Nigrizia, 1971; *Tireca Tareca,* Quaderni del Sud, 1978.

In Latin: *Melos Cordis* (poems), Venetian Press, 1959; (editor) *Viva Camena* (verse anthology), Artemis (Stuttgart), 1961; *Rosa Rosarum* (poems), American Classical League, 1984; *In Exilio Rerum* (poems), Avignon (France), 1985.

Contributor of essays and reviews to *Modern Language Journal, Italica, Italian Quarterly, British Miscellany, La Fiera*

JOSEPH TUSIANI

Letteraria, Literary Review, Spirit, Catholic World, and *La Parola de Popolo,* and of poetry to *New Yorker, New York Times, Poetry* (London), *Voices, Yale Literary Magazine,* and other publications. Associate editor, *Spirit,* 1960-69; poetry editor, *Queen,* 1976—.

WORK IN PROGRESS: Dante's Minor Poems, for Baroque Press; the first English translation of Luigi Pulci's *Morgante.*

SIDELIGHTS: In his youth, Tusiani considered being a painter, then a composer; he passed, he says, "through all the forms of creative restlessness" before realizing that he sought to be a writer. As a child he remembers serving at Mass with Padre Pio, the Italian stigmatic. He arrived in America at the age of twenty-three, with the ability to read, but not speak, the English language. He had mastered the words, but found that was not adequate. "One must arrive at the point where mastery becomes creative atmosphere. I comforted myself with the thought that poetry had no linguistic barriers and that a poet . . . could write in any idiom he has mastered, for language is but a goblet bearing the wine, the ineffable essence which gives universality to his thought and feeling."

Tusiani's major area of interest is the Renaissance. "Perhaps [Italian poet Conte Giacomo] Leopardi has influenced me most. He was the literary god of my childhood. I am considering a verse translation of all his poetry.

"In the past four years I have published poetry in Latin. 'In Latin?' many people ask with less admiration than incredulity. 'Why Latin? And what's the use of it?' They believe, most wrongly of course, that Latin serves no purpose whatsoever in our modern, science-oriented civilization. And yet some of the greatest satisfaction I have had in my career as a writer has come—believe it or not—from my Latin verse through which I was able to reach more young people than I ever could through other publications. In my book, *Rosa Rosarum,* published in 1984 by the American Classical League, I deal with themes such as 'The Subway,' 'The Statue of Liberty,' 'Astronauts,' 'The Death of JFK,' and other contemporary issues, in the easiest Latin ever conceived—a Latin full of rhymes, alliterations and puns. Thus our high school students do not mind memorizing new rules and phrases and, while learning Latin, become more proficient in English. Some of their letters tell me so.

"But why do I really enjoy writing in Latin? Maybe because my very name is pure Latin. 'Tus Iani' means exactly 'Incense of Janus,' as a Latin freshman quickly learns after studying the third and second declension of nouns. Certainly, it is through Latin—the classical language I learned as a child—that I can now recapture the dreams and emotions of my childhood. Also, being a language we little use and never abuse, Latin enables me to give freshness to the expression of my thoughts and feelings."

HOBBIES AND OTHER INTERESTS: Music and painting.

VEVERS, (Henry) Gwynne 1916-

PERSONAL: Born November 13, 1916, in Girvan, Scotland; son of Geoffrey Marr (a surgeon and zoologist) and Catherine Rigby (Andrews) Vevers. *Education:* Magdalen College, Oxford, B.A., 1938, M.A., 1947, D.Phil., 1949. *Home:* Wood's House, Bampton, Oxfordshire, England.

CAREER: Marine Biologist Association, Plymouth, England, treasurer and zoologist, 1946-55; Zoological Society of Lon-

GWYNNE VEVERS

don, London, England, curator of aquarium, 1955-81, assistant director of science, 1966-81. Adviser for Bodley Head Natural Science Picture Books, 1962—. *Military service:* Royal Air Force, 1941-46; became squadron leader. *Member:* Institute of Biology, London (fellow), Linnean Society of London (fellow). *Awards, honors:* Member of the Order of the British Empire, 1942.

WRITINGS: The British Seashore, Routledge & Paul, 1954; (with H. Munro Fox) *The Nature of Animal Colours,* Macmillan, 1960; *Life in the Sea* (juvenile; illustrated by Barry Driscoll), Bodley Head, 1963, McGraw-Hill, 1965; *Animals of the Arctic* (juvenile; illustrated by Maurice Wilson), Bodley Head, 1964, McGraw-Hill, 1965; *Ants and Termites* (juvenile; illustrated by Colin Threadgall), McGraw-Hill, 1966 (published in England as *Ants and White Ants,* Bodley Head, 1966); *Elephants and Mammoths* (juvenile; illustrated by B. Driscoll), Bodley Head, 1968, McGraw-Hill, 1970; *Seashore Life in Colour,* Blandford, 1969; *The Underwater World* (illustrated by Lesley Marshall), Chatto & Windus, 1971, St. Martin's, 1972; *Birds and Their Nests* (juvenile; illustrated by C. Threadgall), Bodley Head, 1971, McGraw-Hill, 1973; *Fishes* (juvenile; illustrated by Alan Jessett), Bodley Head, 1974, McGraw-Hill, 1976; (compiler) *London's Zoo: An Anthology to Celebrate 150 Years of the Zoological Society of London, with Its Zoos at Regent's Park in London and Whipsnade in Bedfordshire,* Bodley Head, 1976; *Octopus, Cuttlefish, and Squid* (juvenile; illustrated by Joyce Bee), Bodley Head, 1977, McGraw-Hill, 1978; *Animals That Sleep in Winter* (juvenile; illustrated by C. Threadgall), Bodley Head, 1978, Merrimack, 1982; *Animals with Poison* (juvenile; illustrated by J. Bee), Bodley Head, 1978, Merrimack, 1982.

Aquarium Fishes: A Colour Guide to over 200 Fishes for the Freshwater Aquarium (illustrated by James Nicholls), Fontana, 1979; *Animal Parents* (juvenile; illustrated by C. Threadgall), Bodley Head, 1979; *Animal Weapons* (juvenile; illustrated by Wendy Bramall), Bodley Head, 1979, Merrimack, 1982; *Animal Disguises* (juvenile; illustrated by C. Threadgall), Bodley Head, 1980, Merrimack, 1982; *Animal Homes* (juvenile; illustrated by W. Bramall), Bodley Head, 1980; *An-*

imals of the Dark (juvenile; illustrated by W. Bramall), Bodley Head, 1980; *Animals That Store Food* (juvenile; illustrated by J. Bee), Bodley Head, 1980; *The Pocket Guide to Aquarium Fishes,* Simon & Schuster, 1980; *Animals That Live in Groups* (juvenile; illustrated by C. Threadgall), Bodley Head, 1981; *Animals That Travel* (juvenile; illustrated by Matthew Hillier), Bodley Head, 1981; *Animal Cleaners* (juvenile; illustrated by M. Hillier), Merrimack, 1982; *Animal Partners* (juvenile; illustrated by W. Bramall), Merrimack, 1982; *Animal Colors,* Edward Arnold, 1982 (published in England as *The Colours of Animals,* Edward Arnold, 1982); (editor with Dick Mills) *Practical Encyclopaedia of Freshwater Tropical Aquarium Fishes,* Salamander Books, 1982, published as *Tropical Aquarium Fishes* (juvenile), edited by Douglas G. Campbell, Golden Press, 1983; *Skin and Bone* (juvenile; illustrated by Sarah Pooley), Bodley Head, 1983, Lothrop, 1984; *Blood and Lungs* (juvenile; illustrated by S. Pooley), Bodley Head, 1983, Lothrop, 1984; *Feeding and Digestion* (juvenile; illustrated by S. Pooley), Lothrop, 1984; *Muscles and Movement* (juvenile; illustrated by S. Pooley), Lothrop, 1984.

Translator: (And adapter from the French) Jacques Forest, *The Animal World of the Sea,* Rathbone Books, 1957; (and adapter from the Danish) Georg Mandahl-Barth, *Tropical Aquarium Fishes in Colour,* Witherby, 1957; (from the Danish) Hans Hvass, *Mammals of the World* (illustrated by Wilhelm Eigener), Methuen, 1961; (from the French) Alwin J. H. Pedersen, *Polar Animals,* Harrap, 1962, Taplinger, 1966; (from the Danish) H. Hvass, *Birds of the World* (illustrated by W. Eigener), Methuen, 1963, new edition, 1978; (and adapter from the Danish) H. Hvass, *Fishes in Colour: Marine and Freshwater* (illustrated by Henning Anthon) Witherby, 1963, 2nd edition,

revised, 1978, State Mutual Bank, 1980; (and adapter from the Danish) H. Hvass, *Reptiles and Amphibians of the World* (illustrated by W. Eigener), Methuen, 1964; (from the German, and editor) Zdenek Vogel, *Reptiles and Amphibians, Their Care and Behaviour,* Viking, 1964; (from the Danish) Jorgen Bitsch, *Why Buddah Smiles,* Collins, 1964.

(From the Danish) H. Hvass, *Fishes of the World in Color* (illustrated by W. Eigener), Dutton, 1965; (from the German) Irenäus Eibl-Eibesfeldt, *Land of a Thousand Atolls: A Study of Marine Life in the Maldive and Nicobar Islands,* Mac-Gibbon & Kee, 1965; (with Winwood Reade, from the German) Gerhard Gronefeld, *Understanding Animals,* Heinemann, 1965; (from the German) Wilfried Weigel, *Planning and Decorating the Aquarium,* Studio Vista, 1966, published as *Aquarium Decorating and Planning,* T. F. H., 1973; (from the German) Gerhard Brünner, *Aquarium Plants,* Studio Vista, 1966, T. F. H., 1973; (from the German) Willy Jocher, *Food for the Aquarium and Vivarium,* Studio Vista, 1966, published as *Live Foods for Aquarium and Terrarium Animals,* T. F. H., 1973; (from the German) Horst Janus, *Pond Life in the Aquarium,* Studio Vista, 1966; (from the German) Hellmuth Wachtel, *Aquarium Hygiene,* Studio Vista, 1966, published as *Aquarium Ecology,* T. F. H., 1973; (from the German) Eigel Kiaer, *Methuen Handbook of Roses* (illustrated by Verner Hancke), Methuen, 1966; (from the German) Günther Sterba, *Aquarium Care,* Studio Vista, 1967; (from the German) Wolfgang Wickler, *The Marine Aquarium* (illustrated by Hermann Kacher), Studio Vista, 1967, T. F. H., 1973; (from the German) Gottfried Schubert, *Diseases of Fish,* Studio Vista, 1967; (from the German) *Hummingbirds: Flying Jewels* (illustrated with photographs by the author), Barker, 1967.

Monkeys

Every day monkeys spend some time grooming. One monkey, often a female or a young one, uses its fingers to rake through the fur of another monkey, to remove pieces of dirt, dry skin, thorns and, sometimes, also fleas.

The monkey that is being groomed evidently enjoys it. Grooming is very important as it helps to keep the members of the family group together.

(From *Animal Cleaners* by Gwynne Vevers. Illustrated by Matthew Hillier.)

(From the German) Heinrich Hediger, *Born in the Zoo* (illustrated with photographs by Jürg Klages), Collins, 1968; (with W. Reade, from the German) Eugen Schuhmacher, *The Last of the Wild: On the Track of Rare Animals*, Collins, 1968; (from the Swedish) Jan Lindblad, *Journey to Red Birds*, Collins, 1969; (from the German) Hermann Friedrich, *Marine Biology: An Introduction to Its Problems and Results*, Sidgwick & Jackson, 1969; (from the Danish, and editor) G. Mandahl-Barth, *Seashore Life in Colour* (illustrated by H. Anthon and Renate Klein-Rodder), Blandford, 1969; (and adapter with W. Reade, from the Danish) H. Clausen and E. J. Ipsen, *Farm Animals in Colour*, Blandford, 1970; (with W. Reade, from the German) H. Hediger, *Man and Animals in the Zoo: Zoo Biology*, Routledge & Kegan Paul, 1970; (from the German) Kurt Jacobs, *Livebearing Aquarium Fishes*, Studio Vista, 1971; (and adapter with W. Reade, from the Danish) Leif Lyneborg, *Mammals in Colour* (illustrated by H. Anthon), Blandford, 1971; (from the Danish) H. Hvass, *Reptiles and Amphibians in Colour* (illustrated by H. Anthon), Blanford Press, 1972; (and adapter from the Danish) Arne Schiotz, *Collins Guide to Aquarium Fishes and Plants* (illustrated by Preben Dahlstrom), Collins, 1972; (from the German, and editor) Günther Sterba, *Dr. Sterba's Aquarium Handbook*, Pet Library, 1973; (and adapter from the Danish) Preben Bang, *Collins Guide to Animal Tracks and Signs: The Tracks and Signs of British and European Mammals and Birds* (illustrated by Preben Dahlstrom), Collins, 1974; (from the Danish) Bent J. Muus, *Collins Guide to the Sea Fishes of Britain and North-Western Europe* (illustrated by P. Dahlstrom), Collins, 1974.

From the German, and editor) Klaus Paysan, *The Hamlyn Guide to Aquarium Fishes*, Hamlyn, 1975, published as *The Larousse Guide to Aquarium Fishes*, Larousse, 1981; (and adapter from the German) Hans J. Mayland, *The Complete Home Aquarium*, Grosset, 1976; (and adapter from the Danish) Leif Lyneborg, *Beetles in Colour* (illustrated by Niels Johnson), Blandford, 1977; (and adapter from the Danish) Henri Mourier and Ove Winding, *Collins Guide to Wild Life in House and Home* (illustrated by Ebbe Sunesen), Collins, 1977; (and adapter from the French) Henri Favre, *Dictionary of the Freshwater Aquarium*, Ward Lock, 1977, published as *Larousse Dictionary of the Freshwater Aquarium*, Barron's, 1978, (from the German, and editor) Gert Lindner, *Seashells of the World*, Blandford, 1977, published as *Field Guide to Seashells of the World*, Van Nostrand, 1978; (from the German, and editor) Siegfried Schmitz, *Aquarium Fishes* (illustrated with photographs by S. Schmitz), Chatto & Windus, 1978; (from the German, and editor) Wolfgang Dierl, *British and European Insects* (illustrated with photographs by W. Dierl), Chatto & Windus, 1978; (from the Danish, and adapter and editor with Philip Orkin) J. Moller Christensen, *Fishes of the British and Northern European Seas* (illustrated by Bente Nyström), Penguin, 1978; (and adapter from the German) H. J. Mayland, *Tropical Freshwater Aquarium Fishes*, Ward Lock, 1978; (and adapter from the Danish) Niels Jacobsen, *Aquarium Plants* (illustrated by Verner Hancke), Blandford, 1979; (from the German and editor) Fritz Terofal, *British and European Fishes: Freshwater and Marine Species* (illustrated with photographs by F. Terofal), Chatto & Windus, 1979; (from the German, and editor) Theodor Haltenorth, *British and European Mammals, Amphibians, and Reptiles* (illustrated with photographs by T. Haltenorth), Chatto & Windus, 1979.

(From the German, and editor) Horst Altmann, *Poisonous Plants and Animals*, Chatto & Windus, 1980; (from the German, and editor) Eckart Pott, *Rivers and Lakes: Plants and Animals* (illustrated with photographs by E. Pott), Chatto & Windus, 1980; (from the German, and editor) Kurt Harz, *Trees and Shrubs*, Chatto & Windus, 1980; (from the German, and ed-

itor) Walter Thiede, *Water and Shore Birds*, Chatto & Windus, 1980.

Contributor of articles to *Nature, New Science, Science America, Geographical Magazine*, British Broadcasting Corporation publications, and various biology journals; editor (with M. A. Edwards), *Zoological Record*, 1970-81.

WORK IN PROGRESS: Seeing, Hearing, Tasting and *Reproduction*, both juvenile, both illustrated by Sarah Pooley, for Bodley Head.

VOGT, Gregory

BRIEF ENTRY: An aerospace education specialist at the National Aeronautics and Space Administration (NASA), Vogt is the author of five young adult books published by F. Watts. Prior to his position at NASA, Vogt worked as a science teacher, curriculum writer, National Wildlife Federation educational consultant, and planetarium lecturer. The topics of his books quite naturally reflect his interest in the past, present, and future development of the space program. Among his titles are *Mars and the Inner Planets* (1982), *Model Rockets* (1982), *The Space Shuttle* (1983), and *A Twenty-Fifth Anniversary Album of NASA* (1983). Vogt's most recent work is *Electricity and Magnetism* (1985), a close look at electricity and its relationship to the force of magnetism. *Residence:* Annandale, Va.

VOGT, Marie Bollinger 1921-

PERSONAL: Born March 9, 1921, in Toledo, Ohio; daughter of Herman John (a physician) and Fannie (Millhaubt) Bollinger; married Theodore Vogt (an attorney), November 29, 1949. *Education:* University of Toledo, A.B., 1944. *Religion:* Protestant. *Home:* 5362 Main St., Sylvania, Ohio 43560.

CAREER: Toledo Ballet School, Toledo, Ohio, director, 1963—. Founder, director, and chief choreographer of Toledo Ballet; member of planning committee for Downtown Toledo Promenade Park, and Downtown Cultural Arts Center; president of Toledo Bar Association Auxiliary, 1974-75; University of Toledo Foundation (trustee, 1977-83, president, 1980-81). *Member:* National Association of Dance Companies, Northeast Regional Ballet Association, Ohioana Library Association. *Awards, honors:* Scripps-Howard Award for editorial in *Campus Collegian*, at University of Toledo, 1944.

WRITINGS—All self-illustrated: *The Ballet Book*, privately printed, 1963, 2nd edition, 1973; *The Businessman's Ballet Book*, privately printed, 1973; *Jill and the Nutcracker Ballet* (juvenile), Blair, 1974. Contributor to dance magazines and to *Toledo Blade*.

WORK IN PROGRESS: Choreography for Toledo Ballet; lecture demonstrations in public schools and before audiences of children and adults in theatre settings.

SIDELIGHTS: "My mother believed we should be exposed to the arts. She took us to concerts at the Toledo Museum of Art when I was five years old, and had to have a special permit because they couldn't believe that children would enjoy the Sunday afternoon concerts." [Marcia King, "Of Dance and Dreams," *Wayfarer*, Vol. 1, no. 8, December, 1985.¹]

Vogt also wrote songs and plays with the encouragement of her teachers at Whittier Elementary. "I was always the vil-

MARIE BOLLINGER VOGT

lain. . . . I had this marvelous cape which I made great use of—I was most often a slinking shadow."[1]

Ballet remains Vogt's first love. She is a dancer, teacher and choreographer. "I had these wonderful dancers, and it was exciting to present lovely, defined, disciplined performances."[1]

"*The Ballet Book* was written as an assist to ballet students in home practice. *The Businessman's Ballet Book* was written as a 'crash course' for the corporate male who suddenly finds his life style includes the art of ballet either as a pleasure pursuit or as a matter of corporate funding. It was meant for the man who knows much about a good many things but little about others.

"As director of the Toledo Ballet School, my focus is on preparing a vital community ballet company with a repertoire of standard and contemporary ballets. In addition, I see my role as an educator and as such focus our ballet company's lecture demonstrations on building audiences. We perform with the Toledo Symphony on subscription and family concerts and are preparing our Thirty-Fifth Annual Holiday Nutcracker Ballet.

"As advice for young persons engaged in the creative processes of Life, I suggest enlarging their scope through adventures in living by keeping eyes, ears, and mind open to new experiences; voracious reading in all fields; *experiencing* music, dance, arts, sports, politics, people; and siphoning all these experiences into written or other forms of communication, working at it, polishing and enjoying the process.

"Since Life offers no instant replays, young and old alike must be alert to life and opportunities around."

WALKER, (James) Braz(elton)   1934-1983

PERSONAL: Born May 29, 1934, in Waco, Tex.; died March 27, 1983; son of Virgil Harris and Marie (Brazelton) Walker. *Education:* University of Texas, student, 1952. *Religion:* Episcopalian. *Home:* 315 Crescent Rd., Waco, Tex. 76710.

CAREER: Writer and photographer, specializing in fish, 1955-83. *Member:* International Oceanographic Foundation, Cousteau Society, North American Native Fishes Association, Central Texas Professional Photographers Association (honorary life member). *Awards, honors:* Regional self-rehabilitation award from American Corrective Therapy Association, 1968, national achievement award, 1972; Anchor Award from San Francisco Aquarium Society, 1968; distinguished service award, 1968, from Waco Junior Chamber of Commerce; Outstanding Young Men of America award, 1969, from Outstanding Americans Foundation.

WRITINGS: Enjoy Native Fish, Pet Library, 1970; *Bouillabaisse: Aquatic Oddballs,* San Francisco Aquarium Society, 1971, revised edition published as *Oddball Fishes and Other Strange Creatures of the Deep* (illustrated by Shizu Matsuda and Gregory Thompson), Sterling, 1975; *Tropical Fish Identifier,* Sterling, 1973; *Angelfish,* T.F.H. Publications, 1974; *Sharks and Loaches,* T.F.H. Publications, 1974; (editor) *Marine Aquarium Fish Identifier,* Sterling, 1975; *Keeping and Breeding Cichlids,* T.F.H. Publications, 1977.

Author of columns "In the Fish Bowl" in *Waco Tribune-Herald,* "About Fish" in *Pets/Supplies/Marketing,* and "Aqua Life" in *Waco Tribune-Herald.* Contributor of articles and photographs to fish and wildlife magazines and to *Medical Research Engineering.* Former senior associate editor of *Aquarium Illustrated,* senior contributing editor of *Aquarium,* and associate editor of *Aquarist's Gazette.*

SIDELIGHTS: Paralyzed by polio in 1952, and dependent upon breathing equipment, Walker made himself a successful career with the aid of specially-designed photographic equipment, dictating machine, tape recorder, and typewriter. Once an avid sportsman—active in hunting, fishing, and athletics—he specialized in photographing and writing about these subjects, a successful and enthusiastic adaptation.

WALTER, Mildred Pitts

BRIEF ENTRY: An author of books for children and young adults, Walter graduated from Southern University in Louisiana and received her M.A. from Antioch College. For a number of years, she was employed as an elementary school teacher in Los Angeles, where she also served on the board of directors of the American Civil Liberties Union of Southern California. In 1977 Walter traveled to Lagos, Nigeria as a delegate to the Second World Black and African Festival of the Arts and Culture. She has also traveled extensively as an educational consultant. In her juvenile works, Walter addresses problems such as social integration between blacks and whites and also provides portrayals of blacks in simpler situations, such as the reaction of a child to a new baby in the family. Her young adult novels include *The Girl on the Outside* (Lothrop, 1982), a re-creation of the 1957 integration of Central High School in Little Rock, Arkansas, and *Because We Are* (Lothrop, 1983), which received honorable mention from the Coretta Scott King Award committee in 1984. For a younger reading audience, Walter has produced picture books like *Ty's One-Man Band* (Four Winds, 1980), an Irma Simonton Black Award runner up in 1981, *My Mama Needs Me* (Lothrop, 1983), and *Brother to the Wind* (Lothrop, 1985). *Residence:* Denver, Colo.

FOR MORE INFORMATION SEE: Authors of Books for Young People, supplement to the 2nd edition, Scarecrow, 1979.

WANGERIN, Walter, Jr. 1944-

PERSONAL: Born February 13, 1944, in Portland, Ore.; son of Walter M. (an educator) and Virginia (Stork) Wangerin; married Ruthanne Bohlmann, August 24, 1968; children: Joseph Andrew, Matthew Aaron, Mary Elisabeth, Talitha Michal. *Education:* Concordia Senior College (now Concordia Theological Seminary), Fort Wayne, Ind., B.A., 1966; Miami University, Oxford, Ohio. M.A., 1968; Christ Seminary, Seminex, M.Div., 1976. *Religion:* Lutheran. *Residence:* Evansville, Ind. *Office:* Grace Lutheran Church, 719 South Elliot, Evansville, Ind. 47713.

CAREER: Worked at a variety of jobs, including migrant pea-picker, lifeguard, and ghetto youth worker; KFUO-Radio, St. Louis, Mo., producer, announcer, 1969-70; University of Evansville, Evansville, Ind., instructor in English literature, 1970-74; ordained Lutheran minister, 1976; pastor of churches in Evansville, 1974—. *Awards, honors:* School Library Journal and *New York Times* chose *The Book of the Dun Cow* as a Best Children's Book of the Year, 1978; National Religious Book Award (children/youth category), 1980, and American Book Award for (paperback) science fiction, 1981, both for *The Book of the Dun Cow; Thistle* was chosen as a Best Book of 1983 by the *School Library Journal.*

WRITINGS: The Glory Story, Concordia, 1974; *God, I've Gotta Talk to You,* Concordia, 1974; (written with A. Jennings) *A Penny Is Everything,* Concordia, 1974; *The Baby God Promised,* Concordia, 1976; *The Book of the Dun Cow* (fantasy; ALA Notable Book), Harper, 1978; *The Bible: Its Story for Children,* Rand McNally, 1981; *Thistle* (illustrated by Marcia

WALTER WANGERIN, JR.

(Jacket illustration by Ronald Keller from *The Book of the Dun Cow* by Walter Wangerin, Jr.)

Sewall), Harper, 1983; *My First Bible Book about Jesus* (illustrated by Jim Cummins), Rand McNally, 1983; *Ragman and Other Cries of Faith,* Harper, 1984; *The Book of Sorrows* (sequel to *The Book of the Dun Cow*), Harper, 1985; *Potter, Come Fly to the First of the Earth,* Cook, 1985; *Elisabeth and the Water Troll,* Harper, 1986; *Faith: The Orphean Passages* (adult), Harper, 1986; *Once Upon a Time There Was No Sky,* T. Nelson, 1986; *A Miniature Cathedral, Poetical Exercises Presented in Three Cycles,* Harper, 1986.

SIDELIGHTS: Wangerin wrote his first novel when he was in the eighth grade and has since written poetry, short stories, science fiction, essays, and children's literature. During his twenties Wangerin worked at a variety of jobs, including stints as a migrant pea-picker, lifeguard, youth worker in a ghetto, and a radio announcer and producer. He also studied Medieval English literature, Greek, Latin, Anglo-Saxon, and German before he decided to pursue a religious vocation.

Although he has fulfilled several different career roles, throughout his life he wanted to be a writer. "In my case, which is probably not unusual, there are tendencies to do certain things, and either those tendencies wear themselves out, or they never have any approval or any success, so they naturally pass away. I always had a tendency to read, and it was very, very natural also to write. I always had the tendency to tell stories with the mouth, not just the pen. I can point to different times along the way where someone's encouragement shaped the tendency into a profession, a faithful act, something I could do with the hope that it would succeed. I remember a teacher in high school, in a creative writing course. We had written short stories and mine was one that he particularly

Six were four, then four were three. Now two alone were left, and one of these was crying. ∎
(From *Thistle* by Walter Wangerin, Jr. Illustrated by Marcia Sewall.)

singled out, and the phrase that he used was, 'Wangerin can write the eyes out of a turkey at fifty paces.' For him, that was just a tossed-off comment, but it was also a sensitive one that established in my mind that there was goodness in my work, I wasn't seeking praise, and I don't think I made a big thing out of it at the time. It was just one of those tiny little tacks that I think turned tendency into an art, an activity. That's how I would say it.

"It was many, many years that I thought that I would like to be an author, to support myself by it. That would be my life's work. I went to a college that was preparatory to the ministry, and instead of going with my class to seminary, I kicked out of that and went to graduate school in literature with the idea, not of commitment, but just that this was where I could learn writing better. So the thought was already there. There were times when I was teaching in college that I rather pined to be able to give full attention to writing.

"I think that probably at any one of those times, right up until the time when I became full-time pastor of the congregation where I am now, I might have seized the opportunity and quit whatever I was doing, and written only. But this place, when I came to it, was a very small parish, inner-city, and I knew even before I was given a call by this congregation that whoever should accept its call would not be right to leave it soon, that he needed to stay in this place. I knew that before I accepted it. I'm talking both in secular, and, I think, divine terms, that having accepted that call, I made a commitment both before these people and before my wife, and definitely before the Lord, that I would stay here for a good long time. And that has locked me. I'm not anguishing. It's no torment, it's just a very clear direction."

As pastor of a Lutheran church in Evansville, Indiana, Wangerin used his mornings to work on the manuscript for *The Book of the Dun Cow*. The book was published in 1978 by Harper, and became quite popular with children and adults. Joanne Ryder, an editor at Harper, said that the odds of the book's publication were more than a thousand to one because it arrived, unsolicited, in an envelope. "There's a lady here in Evansville, Marilyn Durham, who wrote *The Man Who Loved Cat Dancing*, and I talked with her a little bit to see how she sold her book. What she had done with her manuscript was to find an agent, which she did by going to a book in the library, and that worked for her. First I thought no, but when I failed with all the publishers, then I thought I would try it just like she did.

"So I got a book out of the library and I tried several agents, and I didn't have very good luck there either. First, agents told me that they had enough novels. I didn't know that agents rejected novels, but I think they did so without reading it— they didn't have time. Other agents took my novel and wrote me nice letters and told me that if I would send them sixty dollars, they would give me their editorial comments about the book, but they never promised to be an agent thereafter, and I pointed that out to them. I said, "I want an agent; I'll be glad to get your comments and give you sixty dollars if you'll assure me that you'll be my agent." They hesitated to give me that assurance, but they did want my money, so that wasn't a very good experience and it consumed a lot of time; I never thought on doing that again. I think these are people who make their money on their first comments on the manuscript."

In 1978 *The Book of the Dun Cow* was named a best children's book by the *New York Times*. The story was written as an animal fantasy that dealt with the ageless struggle between

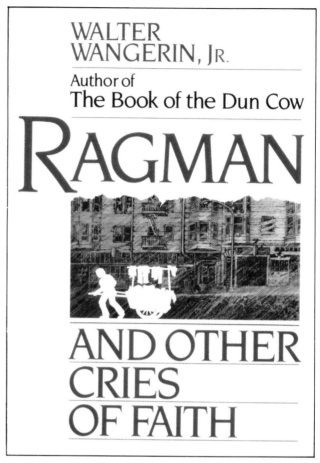

I noticed a young man, handsome and strong, walking the alleys of our City. He was pulling an old cart filled with clothes both bright and new.... ■ (Jacket illustration by Alan Mazzetti from *Ragman and Other Cries of Faith* by Walter Wangerin, Jr.)

good and evil. Wangerin did not intend the book as an allegory, however. "What I understand allegory to be is not what this book is. I'm not sure how clearly people use that term always, or how reviewers use that term. Maybe they're right in their definitions. But I understand an allegory to be a kind of code language, or even a codal use of character and event so that a character in a story equals some concept, some idea, or some character outside that story, and every quality neatly fits into the qualities of this thing outside. So you need an interpretive key to understand what's going on, and especially to understand it on a deeper level.

"I'm using that term, then, as one of the four interpretive patterns that have been handed down from St. Augustine to today. No, I did not write that way. I think sometimes people mean by allegory that meaning can be found in it. I'll accept that, although I would not accept an allegorical interpretation in the strictest sense. But even so, I would not say as an author that I first conceived meaning, then conceived a way to present it, then turned the meaning into a story and hoped that people would get the meaning. In fact, it's much simpler than that— I just wrote the story."

The popularity of *The Book of the Dun Cow* caused his Lutheran congregation and his family to relate to Wangerin a bit differently. "My wife liked it a lot. My kids are too young for it. They're aware of it and aware of some of the things that go on in it, but not because they've really read it. Here is the kind of response my kids have had to it. We were on a train . . . going out west, and one of the passengers sitting near us was reading it. My son Matthew about died to tell him that I was the one who wrote it, and I told him that he couldn't do that. I think they take a great pleasure in the fact that something that is familiar to them and something that comes out of our family is all over the country, and that they're able to see it in different places and point it out and say, 'I know that.'

"... I had been in another parish here in Evansville that was large, white, upper-middle-class. Because of the publication of the book, my relationship with those people had changed—in a good way, as long as they're my friends, but not if they were still my parishioners. It's good because there's a sense of adulation, a sense of possession, there; but all of that, as much as it might help friendship, hurts ministry. I don't think it's right—and it's certainly not easy—to minister to those who adore you. But here at Grace [Lutheran Church], very few people read the book. Some of them did, some tried, some were unable—and all of that is extraordinarily good. They take pleasure in the fact that I'm a writer, that they've received some notoriety. They've talked about it. We were given the occasion once in a council meeting to spend about an hour and a half on what this writing means to the parish as well as to me. I'm very, very pleased with their perspective."

Responses and criticism to his first popular book affected Wangerin's attitude toward his second book. "All responses, I find, have some kind of influence, both good and bad, more bad than good. Not that the people are doing something bad in responding, just that my freedom is reduced. When I suddenly see how other people have expectations and how they read this, unconsciously the freedom I have to move left or right is restricted. Some good things come from the response, and it always gives me pleasure when people are pleased, but I do have to be careful to keep the book on its own track and not be swayed by other people's expectations or even their own present interpretations, which may not have been what I had in mind. They have a right to those things, but I need to be careful that that right doesn't reduce my own right as author."

Since the success of *The Book of the Dun Cow*, Wangerin has written several more books, including a theological book for adults, several other children's books, and a sequel to *The Book of the Dun Cow* entitled *The Book of Sorrows*. He offered the following advice to would-be authors: "One thought I might share with those who (wisely) labor to possess writing skills: First the skill, then the significance. You can have dazzling skill without significance; but what a waste! Beauty that moves us without purpose is ultimately dangerous to us; we will give it our own purpose, and we will not be so careful as the artist might have been; we will allow evil designs to creep in, greed, racism, the division of the peoples (for example, Hitler's vile use of Wagner); we may go so far as to kill others in body and spirit by your beauty, dear artist. For God's sake, don't present us with works both sweet and hollow at the soul of them. On the other hand, significance presented without skill (the sweaty labor of a rich and proper craft!) will either expand into bombasts or diminish into petty squabble. Without skill, there will seem to be no significance at all; and, that, too, is a dreary waste."

FOR MORE INFORMATION SEE: Washington Post Book World, December 4, 1978; *New York Times Book Review*, December 10, 1978; *Detroit News*, January 20, 1980.

WELCH, Martha McKeen   1914-

BRIEF ENTRY: Born May 17, 1914, in Easton, Pa. Businesswoman, educator, photographer, and author. A free-lance photographer since 1947, Welch photographs children and animals for greeting cards, book jackets, and catalogs. She opened her shop, The Bookseller, in 1974. Welch's books for children include *Pudding and Pie* (Coward, 1968), *Nibbit* (Coward, 1969), *Just Like Puppies* (Coward, 1969), *Close Looks in a Spring Woods* (Dodd, 1982), and *Will That Wake Mother?* (Dodd, 1982). One of the author's books, *Sunflower!* (Dodd, 1980), was a New York Academy of Sciences Children's Science Award honor book in 1981. *Address:* Baldwin Rd., Route 2, Mount Kisco, N.Y. 10549; and The Bookseller, Arcade Building, Route 22, Bedford Village, N.Y. 10506.

WIBBERLEY, Leonard (Patrick O'Connor) 1915-1983 (Leonard Holton, Patrick O'Connor, Christopher Webb)

PERSONAL: Born April 9, 1915, in Dublin, Ireland; died of a heart attack, November 22, 1983, in Santa Monica, Calif.; came to the U.S. in 1943; son of Thomas (a professor of agriculture) and Sinaid (a teacher; maiden name; O'Connor) Wibberley; married Katherine Hazel Holton (a teacher), 1948; children: Kevin, Christopher, Rory, Cormac, Patricia Wibberley Sheehey, Arabella Wibberley Van Hoven. *Education:* Attended schools in Ireland and England. *Politics:* Liberal. *Religion:* Christian. *Residence:* Hermosa Beach, Calif.

CAREER: Author. William Collins (publishers), London, England, stock room apprentice, 1931; *Sunday Dispatch*, London, England, copy boy, 1931-32; *Sunday Express*, London, reporter, 1932-34; *Daily Mirror* and *Sunday Pictorial*, London, reporter, 1935-36; musician, 1936; *Malayan Straits Times*,

LEONARD WIBBERLEY

London, and *Singapore Free Press,* London, assistant editor, 1936; *Chronicle,* Trinidad, British West Indies, *Evening News,* Trinidad, and *Evening News,* Port of Spain, Trinidad, editor, 1936; worked for an oil company, Trinidad, 1939-41; Walsh Kaiser Shipyards, Providence, R.I., employee relations manager, 1943; Associated Press, New York, N.Y., cable editor, 1943-44; *Daily Mail,* London, U.S. correspondent, 1944; *Evening News,* London, New York correspondent and Bureau Chief, 1944-46; *Independent Journal,* San Rafael, Calif., editor, 1947-49; *Times,* Los Angeles, Calif., reporter and copy editor, 1950-54. *Military service:* Trinidad Artillery Volunteers, 1938-41, served as lance bombardier. *Member:* Authors Guild, Dramatists Guild.

AWARDS, HONORS: Commonwealth Club of California Silver Medal, 1954, for *The Epics of Everest;* Edison Mass Media Award for special excellence in portraying America's past, 1961, for *Peter Treegate's War;* Southern California Council on Literature for Children and Young People Notable Book Award, 1965, for *A Dawn in the Trees: Thomas Jefferson, the Years 1776 to 1789,* and Award for Excellence in a Series, 1977, for *The Last Battle* (''The Treegate Chronicles''); *Attar of the Ice Valley* was chosen as one of Child Study Association's Children's Books of the Year, 1968, *Leopard's Prey* was chosen, 1971, *Flint's Island,* 1972, *Guarneri: Story of a Genius,* 1974, and *The Last Battle,* 1976.

*WRITINGS—*Juvenile; all published by Farrar, Straus, except as indicated: *The King's Beard* (illustrated by Christine Price), 1952; *The Secret of the Hawk* (illustrated by C. Price), 1953;

Coco during the off season had picked up two bad faults. He was releasing the ball too early and he was trying to throw too hard. ■ (From *Little League Family* by Leonard Wibberley. Illustrated by Richard Cuffari.)

The Coronation Book: The Dramatic Story in History and Legend, 1953; *The Epics of Everest* (Junior Literary Guild selection; illustrated by Genevieve Vaughan-Jackson), 1954; *Deadmen's Cave* (illustrated by Tom Leamon), 1954; *The Wound of Peter Wayne,* 1955; *The Life of Winston Churchill,* 1956, revised edition, 1965; *John Barry: Father of the Navy,* 1957; *Kevin O'Connor and the Light Brigade,* 1957; *Wes Powell: Conqueror of the Grand Canyon,* 1958; *John Treegate's Musket,* 1959.

Peter Treegate's War, 1960; *Sea Captain from Salem* (ALA Notable Book), 1961; *The Time of the Lamb* (illustrated by Fritz Kredel), Ives Washburn, 1961; *The Ballad of the Pilgrim Cat* (verse; illustrated by Erik Blegvad), Ives Washburn, 1962; *Treegate's Raiders* (ALA Notable Book), 1962; *The Shepherd's Reward* (verse; illustrated by Thomas Fisher), Ives Washburn, 1963; ''Thomas Jefferson Biography'' series, Volume I: *Young Man from the Piedmont: The Youth of Thomas Jefferson,* 1963, Volume II: *A Dawn in the Trees: Thomas Jefferson, the Years 1776 to 1789* (Junior Literary Guild selection), 1964, Volume III: *The Gales of Spring: Thomas Jefferson, the Years 1789 to 1801,* 1965, Volume IV: *The Time of the Harvest: Thomas Jefferson, the Years 1801 to 1826,* 1966, series published in one volume as *Man of Liberty: A Life of Thomas Jefferson,* 1968; *Encounter near Venus* (Junior Literary Guild selection; illustrated by Alice Wadowski-Bak), 1967; *Attar of the Ice Valley,* 1968.

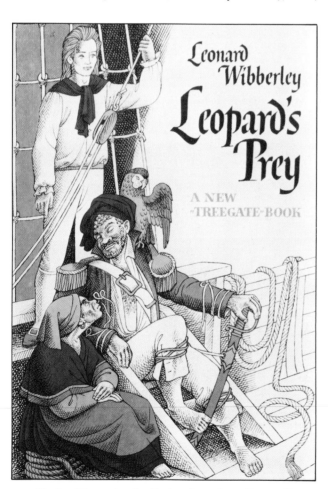

(Jacket illustration by Enrico Arno from *Leopard's Prey* by Leonard Wibberley.)

(Jacket illustration by Richard Cuffari from *Guarneri: Story of a Genius* by Leonard Wibberley.)

Journey to Untor, 1970; *Leopard's Prey* (Junior Literary Guild selection), 1971; *Flint's Island*, 1972; *The Red Pawns* (Junior Literary Guild selection), 1973; *Guarneri: Story of a Genius*, 1974, published in England as *Guarneri: Violin-Maker of Genius*, Macdonald & Jane's, 1976; *The Last Battle*, 1976; *Perilous Gold*, 1978; *Little League Family* (illustrated by Richard Cuffari), Doubleday, 1978; *The Crime of Martin Coverly*, 1980.

Juvenile; all under pseudonym Patrick O'Connor; all published by Ives Washburn: *The Flight of the Peacock* (illustrated by Rus Anderson), 1954; *The Society of Foxes* (illustrated by Rus Anderson), 1954; *The Watermelon Mystery*, 1955; *Gunpowder for Washington*, 1956; *The Black Tiger*, 1956; *Songs of Youth, and Later Poems*, Burns, Oates and Washbourne, 1957; *Mexican Road Race*, 1957; *The Lost Harpooner*, 1957; *The Black Tiger at LeMans*, 1958; *The Five-Dollar Watch Mystery*, 1959; *The Black Tiger at Bonneville*, 1960; *Treasure at Twenty Fathoms*, 1961; *The Black Tiger at Indianapolis*, 1962; *The Raising of the Dubhe*, 1964; *Seawind from Hawaii*, 1965; *South Swell*, 1967; *Beyond Hawaii*, 1969; *A Car Called Camellia*, 1970.

Juvenile; under pseudonym Christopher Webb; all published by Funk: *Matt Tyler's Chronicles*, 1958; *Mark Toyman's Inheritance*, 1960; *Zebulon Pike, Soldier and Explorer*, 1961; *The River of Pee Dee Jack*, 1962; *The Quest of the Otter*, 1963; *The "Ann and Hope" Mutiny*, 1966; *Eusebius, the Phoenician*, 1967.

Adult fiction: *Mrs. Searwood's Secret Weapon*, Little, Brown, 1954; *The Mouse That Roared*, Little, Brown, 1955 (published

in England as *The Wrath of Grapes*, Hale, 1955); *McGillicuddy McGotham*, Little, Brown, 1956; *Take Me to Your President*, Putnam, 1957; *Beware of the Mouse*, Putnam, 1957; *The Quest of Excalibur*, Putnam, 1959; *The Hands of Cormac Joyce*, Putnam, 1960; *Stranger at Killknock*, Putnam, 1961; *The Mouse on the Moon*, Morrow, 1962; *A Feast of Freedom*, Morrow, 1964; *The Island of the Angels* (illustrated by Leo Summers), Morrow, 1965; *The Centurion*, Morrow, 1966; *The Road from Toomi*, Morrow, 1967; *Adventures of an Elephant Boy*, Morrow, 1968; *The Mouse on Wall Street*, Morrow, 1969; *Meeting with a Great Beast*, Morrow, 1971; *The Testament of Theophilus: A Novel of Christ and Caesar*, Morrow, 1973 (published in England as *Merchant of Rome: A Novel of Christ and Caesar*, Cassell, 1974); *The Last Stand of Father Felix*, Morrow, 1974; *One in Four*, Morrow, 1976; *Homeward to Ithaka*, Morrow, 1978; *The Mouse That Poured*, Morrow, 1981; *The Mouse That Saved the West*, Morrow, 1981; *Shamrocks and Sea Silver and Other Illuminations*, Borgo Press, 1985.

Adult detective fiction; under pseudonym Leonard Holton; all published by Dodd, except as indicated: *The Saint Maker*, 1959; *A Pact with Satan*, 1960; *Secret of the Doubting Saint*, 1961; *Deliver Us from Wolves*, 1963; *Flowers by Request*, 1964; *Out of the Depths*, 1966; *A Touch of Jonah*, 1968; *A Problem in Angels*, 1970; *The Mirror of Hell*, 1972; *The Devil to Play*, 1974; *A Corner of Paradise*, St. Martin's, 1976.

Adult nonfiction; all published by Ives Washburn, except as indicated: *The Trouble with the Irish (or the English, De-*

(Jacket illustration by Enrico Arno from *The Gales of Spring: Thomas Jefferson, the Years 1789-1801* by Leonard Wibberley.)

He was halfway between a child and a boy.... ■ (From *The Hands of Cormac Joyce* by Leonard Wibberley. Illustrated by Lydia Rosier.)

pending on Your Point of View), Holt, 1956; *The Coming of the Green*, Holt, 1958; *No Garlic in the Soup!*, 1959; *The Land That Isn't There: An Irish Adventure*, 1959; *Yesterday's Land: A Baja California Adventure*, 1961; *Ventures into the Deep: The Thrill of Scuba Diving*, 1962; *Ah Julian! A Memoir of Julian Brodetsky*, 1963; *Fiji: Islands of the Dawn*, 1964; *Toward a Distant Island: A Sailor's Odyssey*, 1966; *Something to Read*, 1967; *Hound of the Sea*, 1969; *Voyage by Bus*, Morrow, 1971; *The Shannon Sailors: A Voyage to the Heart of Ireland*, Morrow, 1972; *The Good-Natured Man: A Portrait of Oliver Goldsmith*, Morrow, 1979.

Plays: *The Heavenly Quarterback,* Dramatic Publishing, 1968; *Gift of a Star* (one-act), Dramatic Publishing, 1969; *Black Jack Rides Again*, Dramatic Publishing, 1971; *1776—And All That*, Morrow, 1975; *Once, in a Garden*, Dramatic Publishing, 1975; *The Vicar of Wakefield* (based on novel by Oliver Goldsmith), Dramatic Publishing, 1976.

Contributor of short stories and articles to periodicals, including *Saturday Evening Post*, *Writer*, and *Horn Book*.

ADAPTATIONS: "The Mouse That Roared" (motion picture), starring Peter Sellers, copyright © 1959 by Open Road Films, Ltd. (England), released by Columbia, 1959; "The Mouse on the Moon" (motion picture), produced by Pinewood Studios (England), 1963, released by United Artists, 1963; "The Hands of Cormac Joyce" (television movie), starring Stephen Boyd, NBC-TV, November, 1972.

SIDELIGHTS: **April 9, 1915.** "I was born in Ireland and in Dublin, which is a city where beautiful white swans once glided on the river in the middle of the town and where you may leave a bicycle untended and unchained on the main street (a beautiful gold and red bicycle with the greatest appeal) and return to find it untouched five hours later.

"I don't remember much about Dublin in my childhood, except a glimpse of the sea, smooth and green as jade, at Blackrock or thereabouts. I remember Cork better, where we lived in a house opposite the Common, which seemed always to be flooded with rainwater and where I caught many leopard frogs

at great peril. They had lovely little golden tints in their eyes, and it was easy to see in the elegance of a frog that they were all of them princes bewitched. Bewitched or not, it was held a dangerous thing in my childhood to have your mouth open and a frog in your hands, for he would certainly pop down inside you and you would die in a moment. In Ireland, according to childhood lore, more children are destroyed by frogs jumping about in their vitals than are carried off by eagles in Switzerland or turned into stones in Norway by the horrid glance of a troll. Yet there is a great elegance to frogs and, if you were to take an impartial look at a frog and at a lemur, for example, you could not but decide that evolution had taken the wrong path." [Leonard Wibberley, *The Shannon Sailors: A Voyage to the Heart of Ireland,* Morrow, 1972.[1]]

Wibberley's father was a professor at the National University of Ireland and his mother was a schoolteacher. Thus, it was natural for the Wibberley home to be filled with books. "I had a very fortunate childhood, for I was one of six children, and being the youngest, I was quite properly thought not much worth bothering about. The happy result was that I was left splendidly alone to my fancies, and when I found myself interfered with, as sometimes happened with an older sister, I could secure my liberty by biting her. Like every child, I needed very much to be alone for a number of important rea-

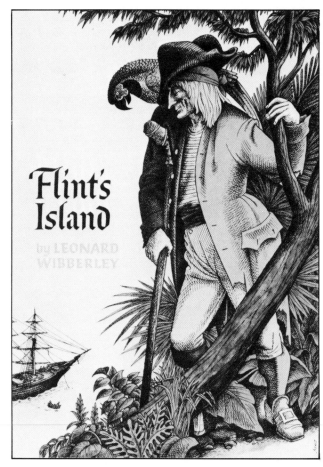

Some are brought up to fear Satan, and others to fear ghosts. But every child in New England, I think, feared Flint before any of them. . . . ■ (Jacket illustration by Enrico Arno from *Flint's Island* by Leonard Wibberley.)

(From the movie "The Mouse on the Moon," starring Ron Moody. Produced by Pinewood Studios, 1963. Released by United Artists, 1963.)

sons—mostly for exploration and observation. In the summer (we lived in the country and close to the sea) I delighted to lie in the long grass which rose about my head, watching tiny ants and beetles of different kinds climbing up a stalk. And when I did this, I was immediately an explorer in a tropical forest of giant bamboos, and the insects were unknown prehistoric creatures as big as elephants but capable of climbing trees.

"Sometimes lying in the grass, I could look up at the sky and the clouds slipping in graceful silence over my head until I got the feeling that the sky was actually down and I was up and, therefore, likely to fall into it. Then I would grasp the grass in my hands in delicious terror lest I fall out of the field to plunge forever into the blue heavens. This feeling at times became so acute that I had to turn on my face and press myself into the cool grass and the all-forgiving earth before I felt secure again. I have mentioned that we lived in those days by the sea. I remember it as being pale green, like glass bottles, and I looked for mother-of-pearl in the tidal pools and watched the seaweed swirling gracefully about the rocks, first this way and then that way, as if the sea were breathing; no movement in all the world has ever given me so much pleasure as this undulation of sea kelp.

"I was . . . of the last generation of children who were not the subjects of adult study. It was not thought vaguely evil of me that I liked to go alone through the woodlands listening to

the missel thrush and yellowhammer and high-piping blackbirds and was filled with sadness in the winter at the lonely cry of curlews mourning over a ploughed field. In those days the wizards had not yet got together to begin their assault on Tirna nOg, the Land of the Ever Young—the wizards who insist that all children must take part in group activities or be labeled antisocial and fiddled about with until, in desperation, they do take part in group activities. The wizards try to measure children according to intelligence and interests, as if the child were but a flask containing a measurable quantity of a liquid called intelligence. Nobody except one sister, whom I had to bite occasionally in self-protection—they did her quite a bit of good, those bites—nobody but that sister thought me antisocial, and even she would sit with me and read poetry on rainy days. Not what is called poetry these days but poems like 'The Highwayman' and 'Abou Ben Adhem' and 'The Traveller.'

"When I was young, children were reckoned to be pretty natural creatures. It was thought that children had been appearing in the world for thousands of generations and would continue to appear for thousands of generations more. They weren't problems; there was nothing the matter with them, and they didn't have to be measured like bottles of chemicals and their parts interfered with. . . .

"I do not know what were the psychological, social, ethical, moral, and economic aspects of my lying in the summer grass and marveling at the courage of a tiny ant climbing up one of the gigantic stalks. But it was by doing such things that I became a writer.'' [Leonard Wibberley, ''I Go There Quite Often,'' *Horn Book,* June, 1978.[2]]

1923. Family moved to England, where Wibberley finished school in London.

1931. Forced to drop out of school when his father died, Wibberley became a copy boy for a London newspaper.

During the depression, Wibberley worked as a street fiddler, ditch-digger, dishwasher, and cook. ''I was of an adventurous and romantic disposition, and reading one day that there was 8,000,000 unemployed in Great Britain, I began to be fearful of being fired. Nothing to do about fear but face it, so I quit and took to the road playing a violin in the streets. I did this for several weeks, sleeping in hedges, under haystacks, or in horrible lodging houses, returned to London, got clean somehow, and went to work in the London office of the *Straits Times of Malaya.*'' [Janet Podell, editor, *The Annual Obituary 1983,* St. Martin's, 1984.[3]]

1939-1941. Served as a lance bombardier in the Trinidad Artillery Volunteers.

1943. Came to the United States where he first worked for the Walsh Kaiser Shipyards, and then moved to New York to work as a cable editor for the Associated Press. Wibberley next became a U.S. correspondent for the London *Evening News.*

1948. Married Katherine Hazel Holton. The Wibberleys had four sons and two daughters. The family lived in California during the school year and often spent summers in Ireland.

1952. First book, *King's Beard* published by Farrar, Straus. It was followed by over fifty books in the next decade. ''Writing, it has been said, is the loneliest of professions, but the saying is spurious. No writer writes alone. However poor his work, he is in the presence of the characters about whom he is writing, who move freely before him, yawning, taking snuff, planning seduction or examining themselves in a mirror and wondering where their youth went. The deeper he is in the presence of these people, the better he will write, for the reality of their being will come out through him onto the paper in his typewriter.'' [Leonard Wibberley, ''The Writer as Conjurer,'' *The Writer,* February, 1962.[4]]

1955. *The Mouse That Roared* published. Wibberley was probably best known for his ''Mouse'' trilogy, which contained three satires: *The Mouse That Roared, The Mouse on the Moon,* and *The Mouse That Saved the West. The Mouse That Roared* and *The Mouse on the Moon* were both made into movies.

He considered writing, reading, and traveling his three major interests. ''Writing comes quite readily to me. I am never at

(From the movie ''The Mouse That Roared,'' starring Peter Sellers. Released by Columbia Pictures, 1959. Copyright © 1959 by Open Road Films, Ltd.)

a loss for an idea for a book and I write wherever I am. I like to travel about, and I find traveling stimulates my ideas and helps me to write.''

As Wibberley's fame as a writer of fiction, nonfiction, and children's books grew, the writer remained modest about his own style as a writer. He believed emphatically in the importance of reading fantasy. ''I feel that if you don't read works of pure imagination part of your mind goes dead. Such works are essential food for adults as well as children.

''Mediocre or poor children's books adults cannot abide nor children either. So what I am saying is that it takes just as much skill and talent to write a good book for children as it does to write a good novel for adults—and perhaps a little more . . . a child gets bored more quickly than an adult. You can't counteract the boredom by having something exciting happen on every page. That in itself gets boring. You must keep the characters real and interesting—even when the characters themselves are bored, their boredom has to be interesting. . . .

''Many people think of me as a writer of children's books, but I think of myself as a novelist who also likes to write children's books—that is books in which the plot is a bit more exciting, the colors a touch more vivid, the action faster and more direct, than in the adult novel. But I love most of all writing novels.[3]

1958. Travelled with his wife and growing family to Portugal. ''When a man decides to take his wife, his four children, his bulldog, his automobile, and about sixteen pieces of baggage to Portugal to live for an indefinite period, he certainly ought to have good reason for so doing.

''Perhaps the oddest part of my decision to go to Portugal is that I hadn't a good reason. I tried very hard to find one and did a great deal of utterly spurious rationalization in my search for a motive.

''But the candid fact is that I was simply obsessed with an overpowering desire to go to Portugal, as a man may be overtaken in the oddest moment by a strong urge to eat a banana split. In a sense a Portuguese ghost was haunting me and would not leave me be. I would set about writing a children's book, and into the pages would march some reference to Portugal or some character from Portugal demanding recognition.

''I would go down to San Pedro harbor to sail and would see the fleets of fishing boats manned by Portuguese and reflect that nobody really knows very much about the Portuguese. Between Vasco da Gama and Dr. António de Oliveira Salazar, Portugal is a big blank for most of us.

''Or I would go into the supermarket, and at the counter where all the odd varieties of canned fish are kept in their curiously shaped tins I would find a stack of canned sardines from Portugal.

''Having reached so drastic a decision, it was necessary to supply ourselves with sensible reasons for our actions—partly so that we could pretend we were acting in a sensible manner and partly to satisfy the curiosity of friends and business acquaintances who could hardly be expected to be satisfied with the explanation that I was haunted by a Portuguese ghost.

''An author, by the traditions of his profession, should be a cosmopolitan man. Southey visited Lisbon, Dickens went to Italy, Hemingway lives in Cuba and has spent many years in

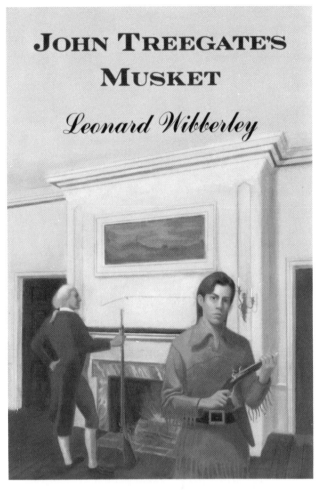

''I do not know how we are to get out of Boston armed,'' he said. ''But I will shoot my way out if need be.'' ■ (Jacket illustration by Eric Velasquez from *John Treegate's Musket* by Leonard Wibberley.)

France and Spain. Somerset Maugham moves as readily around the world as if each country were but a room in his house. What, then, was the matter with Wibberley plodding in his slippers to the supermarket for his pleasures? Had he not also an equal right as an author to view Capri and Madrid, and would not the very best place to start upon this more proper and fuller literary life be Portugal?

''I liked this argument best myself, for there is a touch of snobbery to my nature, and though timidly disposed, I like to fancy myself an international traveler, a cosmopolite, and perhaps something of an expert on Venetian glass or Dresden china—subjects of which I know nothing.

''The final reason we dredged up was that travel would be good for the children. There was some substance to this reason, for we are anxious that our children should not, because of a narrow nationalism, despise the people of other countries, or hold themselves superior to them because of the geographical accident of birth. It would do Kevin, for instance, good, to collect a black eye and a friend in some Portuguese village. . . . It would be helpful to Patricia and to Christopher and to Arabella to meet their counterparts in other lands.'' [Leonard Wibberley, *No Garlic in the Soup!*, Ives Washburn, 1959.[5]]

The Wibberley family found a house in Portugal, where a fifth child was born. Their adventures were recorded in *No Garlic in the Soup!*, which was published the following year.

1959. *Johnny Treegate's Musket,* the first of the "Treegate" books for children, was published. The Treegate family was chronicled in many historical novels for young people that depicted early events in the history of our country. Wibberley wrote four historical novels about the Treegate family and the Revolutionary War and three novels about the war of 1812 and the early 1800s. "I have always had a great interest in history—not the kind of litany of kings and presidents and knaves and heroes that is so frequently taught in schools—but the bright little incidents that gloriously illuminate landscape which is too often mouldy with the bone dusts of the dead. . . .

"In my youth I studied English history, and it was not until I came to the United States some eighteen years ago that I became first of all interested in and then captivated by American History.

"Of all the wars of which I have any knowledge from history, it gradually became evident to me that none was as important for the Western World as the War of the American Revolution. Indeed I regard it as the most important struggle in the history of what we can call Western Man.

"That is a big statement. But here are my reasons. There have been many wars fought to overthrow tyranny. Such wars are not exclusively a feature of American history. There was, for instance, the English Civil War which resulted in the beheading of Charles I (an appalling action—to try and to behead a king for crimes against his people), and earlier there was the Peasants' Revolt in what we call Germany now and Wat the Tyler's Rebellion in England. But the Revolutionary War not only sought to overthrow tyranny, it also established certain inalienable rights for people, rights which if preserved would protect mankind from tyranny in all the centuries ahead.

"What was fought on the North American continent then was a war for the rights of *all* men. The scope was wider than national. It embraced all mankind who loved freedom, and its effects are felt to this very day. Overshrill efforts have been made to deny that there was any connection between the French Revolution and the American Revolution. But the one stemmed from the other. Tom Paine was honored in Revolutionary France because he was part of Revolutionary America—because he adhered to principles of freedom enunciated clearly in America and passionately embraced by the French and later by the people of what were to become the Latin American Republics.

"The point I want to make here is that the American Revolution demonstrated that man needs constant protection from his own government—his house must be inviolate, his right to speak his mind at election unbreached, his right to bear arms unchallenged. He was not to be made to testify against himself nor be put in double jeopardy of his life by the courts. The more one examines the effect of the Revolutionary War not merely on Americans but on all peoples, the more one is amazed by the enormity of that effect. The shot was indeed heard around the world and is still heard today.

"The more I read about the Revolutionary War, the more these elements came clearly to me and the more I marveled at them and wanted to bring them to the attention of others. Out of this desire came the Treegate series of books in which I have attempted to trace the fortunes and feelings of a family of Americans of the Revolutionary War period.

"I asked for and was given large scope in writing these books. I didn't want to write books in which one hero got in and out of a series of scrapes. I wanted to paint a large mural which would embrace as many of the figures of the Revolution as could be usefully depicted. . . . Some of the figures are historic—some of them creatures of my imagination. These latter came to life as I wrote, standing as it were by my elbow and telling me of the weight of their muskets and how the birds sounded in the boding woods at Saratoga and how sharp was the January frost at Morristown.

"This of course is the work of the novelist in the field of history—not to instruct but to enrich that which is already known; not to distort but to listen to the insistent whisper of forgotten voices penetrating the centuries.

"There were, I am sure, people like Gabby and Master Gunner Simmons and Mr. Treaser in his Queen Anne coat, and Mr. Paddock—a self-appointed traveling university, and Peter Treegate and his stubborn, enduring father, John. History has no place for them. They belong in that other wing of history called the historical novel. They are the humble builders of the world, whose names are unknown, whose graves are lost, and whose lives made no stir beyond the circle of their friends.

"They are you and I and everyman, and I have tried to give them back their voices, so that they can speak across the centuries of their time on earth." [Leonard Wibberley, "The Treegate Series," *Horn Book Reflections on Children's Books and Reading,* edited by Elinor Whitney Field, Horn Book, 1969.°]

1963. Began the "Thomas Jefferson Biography" series with the publication of *Young Man from the Piedmont: The Youth of Thomas Jefferson,* which was followed by *A Dawn in the Trees,* a Junior Literary Guild selection. The Jefferson series grew to a four-volume biography of the famous statesman. "Jefferson is known as a man of the mind rather than of the heart. He early decided to be ruled by reason rather than by emotion and became, eminently, a man of the mind. But this, although it is the aspect of Jefferson most generally known, is not the whole man. He was very warmhearted and readily hurt. He loved his wife deeply, and when she died he had the problem of bringing up his daughters. They taught him a deeper understanding of women and without them he would have been, after his wife's death, the loneliest of men. He was not only a great statesman but a wonderful father.

"To my mind he was the most splendid of the founding giants of the nation. The America of today is the way it is largely because Jefferson made it so. When I think of him, however, it is in connection with Monticello. This was where his heart was—in his home. And I think it is this that makes Jefferson the greatest of Americans."

1972. *The Shannon Sailors: A Voyage to the Heart of Ireland* was published. The Book recorded Wibberley's return with his four sons to his homeland. '. . . My sons are all Americans, born and raised in western America, and there is then between us not only that generation gap which God in His wisdom put between Adam and his children, but also a cultural gap. We are come from differing though not inimical soil. I wanted them to know my roots as I know theirs.

"I have four sons. The year of my own venture, the eldest, Kevin . . . had already taken off for the Old World on his own to glory in the roses of Spain and marvel at the snake charmers of Algiers. He, then, was to meet me at Shannon Airport, and I sent a message to him to that effect at Biarritz, at Paris, and at Antwerp, for Americans do not realize, as do Europeans, that these places are very far apart, and scarcely to be visited in the same year. He visited them all in the same week, and my message finally reached him in London. Kevin was named both for St. Kevin of Glendalough and for Kevin Barry, who was hanged November 1, 1920, at the age of eighteen for taking part in the Irish Revolutionary War.

"My second son, Christopher . . . is named after that saint, beloved of all Christians, who carried Christ across a river. The Church has recently expressed some doubts as to whether St. Christopher ever existed, but the doubts refer to mortal existence. That he has existed for centuries in the minds and prayers of the faithful is beyond any question whatever, and the matter of his physical existence is purely academic. Reality is not bound up in flesh and blood and tangible matter. Much of it, like St. Christopher, exists beyond these confines. My son Christopher is big and dark-haired and would gladly, if called upon, take up the task of his namesake.

"My third son is Rory . . . who was named for Rory O'Connor, the last ard-ri or high king of Ireland. Rory O'Connor resigned his kingship and retired to a monastery, but the act was not as pious as it seems, for he was surrounded by enemies, most of them Normans, and the title of high king in such circumstances had little substance to it. Yet perhaps you will agree that it was a very Irish thing to go from King to monk, and I thought the act worthy of remembrance and so named my son for him. Kings do not do such things these days, nor Presidents either, and the conclusion to be reached is that in our times the material world is held more important than the world to come. Judge for yourself whether this is wisdom.

"My fourth son, Cormac . . . was also named for an Irish king—Cormac MacCarthy, who built a jewel of a chapel on the Rock of Cashel in Tipperary around 1134."[1]

1980. Fifty-eighth book for young people was published. During his long and prodigious career, Wibberley wrote various types of literature under several pseudonyms. He wrote mysteries, historical novels, satires, plays, nonfiction books, and stories for children. About his career, he once said that he spent the first thirty years getting his life together by reading and living, and the second thirty years by writing.

Wibberley believed that the desire to write "is born in childhood and has its birth in childhood reading." *Treasure Island* was read to him when he was a schoolboy, and it remained his favorite book.

November 22, 1983. Died of a heart attack in Santa Monica, California at the age of sixty-eight. "We are eternally children though strangely bearded, perhaps, and afflicted with bald heads. Whatever the exterior, we must nourish the innocent and hopeful child inside us."[6]

Wibberley's manuscript collection is at the University of Southern California in Los Angeles.

HOBBIES AND OTHER INTERESTS: Scuba diving, sailing, painting, music, and violin making.

FOR MORE INFORMATION SEE: Leonard Wibberley, *No Garlic in the Soup!*, Ives Washburn, 1959; *New York Times Book Review*, July 12, 1959, November 25, 1973; Huck and Young, *Children's Literature in the Elementary School*, Holt, 1961; *The Writer*, February, 1962, August, 1965, May, 1967; *Horn Book*, April, 1962, August, 1970, June, 1978; Muriel

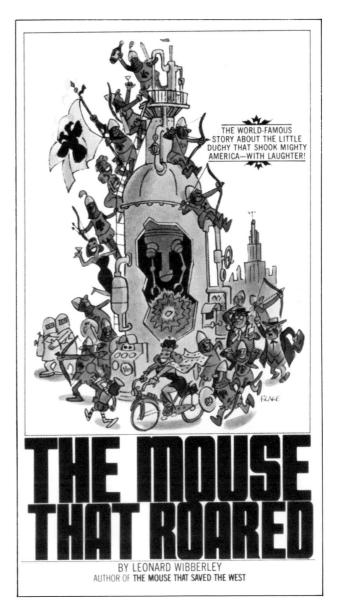

THE WORLD-FAMOUS STORY ABOUT THE LITTLE DUCHY THAT SHOOK MIGHTY AMERICA—WITH LAUGHTER!

THE MOUSE THAT ROARED

BY LEONARD WIBBERLEY
AUTHOR OF THE MOUSE THAT SAVED THE WEST

(Jacket illustration by Quentin Blake from *The Mouse That Roared* by Leonard Wibberley.)

Fuller, editor, *More Junior Authors*, H. W. Wilson, 1963; *Wilson Library Bulletin*, June, 1963; *Book Week*, November 1, 1964, July 2, 1967; *Travel*, April, 1965; G. Robert Carlson, *Books and the Teen-Age Reader*, Harper, 1967; *Best Sellers*, February 15, 1968, October 1976; *Books*, November, 1969; Leonard Wibberley, "The Treegate Series," *Horn Book Reflections on Children's Books and Reading*, edited by Elinor Whitney Field, Horn Book, 1969; *Christian Science Monitor*, November 6, 1974; John Wakeman, editor, *World Authors: 1950-1970*, H. W. Wilson, 1975; *Children's Book Review*, October, 1976; *Children's Literature Review*, Volume III, Gale, 1978; D. L. Kirkpatrick, *Twentieth-Century Children's Writers*, St. Martin's, 1978.

Obituaries: *Los Angeles Times*, November 24, 1983; *Washington Post*, November 24, 1983; *New York Times Biographical Service*, November, 1983; *Chicago Tribune*, November 25, 1983; *Variety*, November 30, 1983; *Time*, December 5, 1983; *School Library Journal*, February, 1984; Janet Podell, *The Annual Obituary 1983*, St. Martin's, 1984.

WINCHESTER, James H(ugh) 1917-1985

OBITUARY NOTICE—See sketch in *SATA* Volume 30: Born June 27, 1917, in Midlothian, Tex.; died November 20, 1985, in Waterbury, Conn.; buried in Pine Hill Cemetery. Journalist and author. Winchester worked as a reporter or writer for a variety of organizations, including the King Features Syndicate for fifteen years and, beginning in 1961, for the *Reader's Digest*. An extensive traveler and the contributor of more than one-thousand articles to major magazines, Winchester won the Trans-World Airlines aviation writing award eight times and the aviation safety writing award three times. He was also the author of radio and television scripts as well as juvenile books, including *Wonders of Water, Hit Parade of Flying Stories,* and *Hurricanes, Storms, Tornadoes.*

FOR MORE INFORMATION SEE: Contemporary Authors, Volumes 17-20, revised, Gale, 1976; *Who's Who in America,* 43rd edition, Marquis, 1984. Obituaries: *Waterbury Republican,* November 21, 1985.

WORK, Virginia 1946-

BRIEF ENTRY: Born September 26, 1946, in Moscow, Idaho. Since 1969 Work has been employed as a missionary at several locations, including Gresham, Oregon and Winnipeg, Manitoba. An author of books for young adults, she has written a series of mystery novels, among them *Jodi: The Mystery of the Missing Message* (Moody, 1980) and *Jodi: The Secret of the Alaskan Gift* (Moody, 1983), as well as *Apples of Gold: Proverbs for Today* and a historical novel entitled *Ruth: A Beautiful Friend.* As a writer, Work stated: 'I do not preach. I weave my message into the fabric of my story.'' She strives to provide ''real answers based on the biblical principles that have influenced my own life.'' Work is married and the mother of three children. *Home address:* P.O. Box 1145, Lillooet, British Columbia, Canada V0K 1V0.

FOR MORE INFORMATION SEE: Contemporary Authors, Volume 113, Gale, 1985.

CUMULATIVE INDEX TO ILLUSTRATIONS AND AUTHORS

Illustrations Index

(In the following index, the number of the volume in which an illustrator's work appears is given *before* the colon, and the page on which it appears is given *after* the colon. For example, a drawing by Adams, Adrienne appears in Volume 2 on page 6, another drawing by her appears in Volume 3 on page 80, another drawing in Volume 8 on page 1, and another drawing in Volume 15 on page 107.)

YABC

Index citations including this abbreviation refer to listings appearing in *Yesterday's Authors of Books for Children*, also published by the Gale Research Company, which covers authors who died prior to 1960.

Aas, Ulf, *5:* 174
Abbé, S. van. *See* van Abbé, S.
Abel, Raymond, *6:* 122; *7:* 195; *12:* 3; *21:* 86; *25:* 119
Abrahams, Hilary, *26:* 205; *29:* 24-25
Abrams, Kathie, *36:* 170
Accorsi, William, *11:* 198
Acs, Laszlo, *14:* 156; *42:* 22
Adams, Adrienne, *2:* 6; *3:* 80; *8:* 1; *15:* 107; *16:* 180; *20:* 65; *22:* 134-135; *33:* 75; *36:* 103, 112; *39:* 74
Adams, John Wolcott, *17:* 162
Adamson, George, *30:* 23, 24
Adkins, Alta, *22:* 250·
Adkins, Jan, *8:* 3
Adler, Peggy, *22:* 6; *29:* 31
Adler, Ruth, *29:* 29
Agard, Nadema, *18:* 1
Ahl, Anna Maria, *32:* 24
Aichinger, Helga, *4:* 5, 45
Aitken, Amy, *31:* 34
Akasaka, Miyoshi, *YABC 2:* 261
Akino, Fuku, *6:* 144
Alain, *40:* 41
Alajalov, *2:* 226
Albrecht, Jan, *37:* 176
Albright, Donn, *1:* 91
Alcorn, John, *3:* 159; *7:* 165; *31:* 22; *44:* 127
Alda, Arlene, *44:* 24
Alden, Albert, *11:* 103
Aldridge, Andy, *27:* 131
Alex, Ben, *45:* 25, 26
Alexander, Martha, *3:* 206; *11:* 103; *13:* 109; *25:* 100; *36:* 131
Alexeieff, Alexander, *14:* 6; *26:* 199
Aliki. *See* Brandenberg, Aliki
Allamand, Pascale, *12:* 9
Allan, Judith, *38:* 166
Alland, Alexander, *16:* 255
Alland, Alexandra, *16:* 255
Allen, Gertrude, *9:* 6
Allen, Graham, *31:* 145
Allison, Linda, *43:* 27
Almquist, Don, *11:* 8; *12:* 128; *17:* 46; *22:* 110

Aloise, Frank, *5:* 38; *10:* 133; *30:* 92
Althea. *See* Braithwaite, Althea
Altschuler, Franz, *11:* 185; *23:* 141; *40:* 48; *45:* 29
Ambrus, Victor G., *1:* 6-7, 194; *3:* 69; *5:* 15; *6:* 44; *7:* 36; *8:* 210; *12:* 227; *14:* 213; *15:* 213; *22:* 209; *24:* 36; *28:* 179; *30:* 178; *32:* 44, 46; *38:* 143; *41:* 25, 26, 27, 28, 29, 30, 31, 32; *42:* 87; *44:* 190
Ames, Lee J., *3:* 12; *9:* 130; *10:* 69; *17:* 214; *22:* 124
Amon, Aline, *9:* 9
Amoss, Berthe, *5:* 5
Amundsen, Dick, *7:* 77
Amundsen, Richard E., *5:* 10; *24:* 122
Ancona, George, *12:* 11
Anderson, Alasdair, *18:* 122
Anderson, Brad, *33:* 28
Anderson, C. W. , *11:* 10
Anderson, Carl, *7:* 4
Anderson, Doug, *40:* 111
Anderson, Erica, *23:* 65
Anderson, Laurie, *12:* 153, 155
Anderson, Wayne, *23:* 119; *41:* 239
Andrew, John, *22:* 4
Andrews, Benny, *14:* 251; *31:* 24
Angelo, Valenti, *14:* 8; *18:* 100; *20:* 232; *32:* 70
Anglund, Joan Walsh, *2:* 7, 250-251; *37:* 198, 199, 200
Anno, Mitsumasa, *5:* 7; *38:* 25, 26-27, 28, 29, 30, 31, 32
Antal, Andrew, *1:* 124; *30:* 145
Apple, Margot, *33:* 25; *35:* 206
Appleyard, Dev, *2:* 192
Araneus, *40:* 29
Archer, Janet, *16:* 69
Ardizzone, Edward, *1:* 11, 12; *2:* 105; *3:* 258; *4:* 78; *7:* 79; *10:* 100; *15:* 232; *20:* 69, 178; *23:* 223; *24:* 125; *28:* 25, 26, 27, 28, 29, 30, 31, 33, 34, 35, 36, 37; *31:* 192, 193; *34:* 215, 217; *YABC 2:* 25
Arenella, Roy, *14:* 9

Armer, Austin, *13:* 3
Armer, Laura Adams, *13:* 3
Armer, Sidney, *13:* 3
Armitage, Eileen, *4:* 16
Armstrong, George, *10:* 6; *21:* 72
Arno, Enrico, *1:* 217; *2:* 22, 210; *4:* 9; *5:* 43; *6:* 52; *29:* 217, 219; *33:* 152; *35:* 99; *43:* 31, 32, 33; *45:* 212, 213, 214
Arnosky, Jim, *22:* 20
Arrowood, Clinton, *12:* 193; *19:* 11
Arting, Fred J., *41:* 63
Artzybasheff, Boris, *13:* 143; *14:* 15; *40:* 152, 155
Aruego, Ariane, *6:* 4
    See also Dewey, Ariane
Aruego, Jose, *4:* 140; *6:* 4; *7:* 64; *33:* 195; *35:* 208
Asch, Frank, *5:* 9
Ashby, Gail, *11:* 135
Ashby, Gwynneth, *44:* 26
Ashley, C. W., *19:* 197
Ashmead, Hal, *8:* 70
Assel, Steven, *44:* 153
Astrop, John, *32:* 56
Atene, Ann, *12:* 18
Atherton, Lisa, *38:* 198
Atkinson, J. Priestman, *17:* 275
Atkinson, Wayne, *40:* 46
Attebery, Charles, *38:* 170
Atwood, Ann, *7:* 9
Augarde, Steve, *25:* 22
Austerman, Miriam, *23:* 107
Austin, Margot, *11:* 16
Austin, Robert, *3:* 44
Averill, Esther, *1:* 17; *28:* 39, 40, 41
Axeman, Lois, *2:* 32; *11:* 84; *13:* 165; *22:* 8; *23:* 49
Ayer, Jacqueline, *13:* 7
Ayer, Margaret, *15:* 12

B.T.B. *See* Blackwell, Basil T.
Babbitt, Bradford, *33:* 158
Babbitt, Natalie, *6:* 6; *8:* 220
Back, George, *31:* 161
Bacon, Bruce, *4:* 74

Bacon, Paul, *7:* 155; *8:* 121; *31:* 55
Bacon, Peggy, *2:* 11, 228
Baker, Alan, *22:* 22
Baker, Charlotte, *2:* 12
Baker, Jeannie, *23:* 4
Baker, Jim, *22:* 24
Baldridge, Cyrus LeRoy, *19:* 69;
    44: 50
Balet, Jan, *11:* 22
Balian, Lorna, *9:* 16
Ballantyne, R. M., *24:* 34
Ballis, George, *14:* 199
Baltzer, Hans, *40:* 30
Bang, Molly Garrett, *24:* 37, 38
Banik, Yvette Santiago, *21:* 136
Banner, Angela. *See* Maddison, Angela
    Mary
Bannerman, Helen, *19:* 13, 14
Bannon, Laura, *6:* 10; *23:* 8
Baptist, Michael, *37:* 208
Bare, Arnold Edwin, *16:* 31
Bare, Colleen Stanley, *32:* 33
Bargery, Geoffrey, *14:* 258
Barker, Carol, *31:* 27
Barkley, James, *4:* 13; *6:* 11; *13:* 112
Barks, Carl, *37:* 27, 28, 29, 30-31, 32,
    33, 34
Barling, Tom, *9:* 23
Barlow, Perry, *35:* 28
Barlowe, Dot, *30:* 223
Barlowe, Wayne, *37:* 72
Barner, Bob, *29:* 37
Barnes, Hiram P., *20:* 28
Barnett, Moneta, *16:* 89; *19:* 142;
    31: 102; *33:* 30, 31, 32; *41:* 153
Barney, Maginel Wright, *39:* 32, 33,
    34; *YABC 2:* 306
Barnum, Jay Hyde, *11:* 224; *20:* 5;
    37: 189, 190
Barrauds, *33:* 114
Barrer-Russell, Gertrude, *9:* 65; *27:* 31
Barrett, Angela, *40:* 136, 137
Barrett, John E., *43:* 119
Barrett, Ron, *14:* 24; *26:* 35
Barron, John N., *3:* 261; *5:* 101;
    14: 220
Barrows, Walter, *14:* 268
Barry, Ethelred B., *37:* 79;
    YABC 1: 229
Barry, James, *14:* 25
Barry, Katharina, *2:* 159; *4:* 22
Barry, Robert E., *6:* 12
Barry, Scott, *32:* 35
Bartenbach, Jean, *40:* 31
Barth, Ernest Kurt, *2:* 172; *3:* 160;
    8: 26; *10:* 31
Barton, Byron, *8:* 207; *9:* 18; *23:* 66
Barton, Harriett, *30:* 71
Bartram, Robert, *10:* 42
Bartsch, Jochen, *8:* 105; *39:* 38
Bascove, Barbara, *45:* 73
Baskin, Leonard, *30:* 42, 43, 46, 47
Bassett, Jeni, *40:* 99
Batchelor, Joy, *29:* 41, 47, 48
Bate, Norman, *5:* 16
Bates, Leo, *24:* 35
Batet, Carmen, *39:* 134
Batherman, Muriel, *31:* 79; *45:* 185
Batten, John D., *25:* 161, 162

Battles, Asa, *32:* 94, 95
Bauernschmidt, Marjorie, *15:* 15
Baum, Allyn, *20:* 10
Baum, Willi, *4:* 24-25; *7:* 173
Baumann, Jill, *34:* 170
Baumhauer, Hans, *11:* 218; *15:* 163,
    165, 167
Bayley, Dorothy, *37:* 195
Bayley, Nicola, *40:* 104; *41:* 34, 35
Baynes, Pauline, *2:* 244; *3:* 149;
    13: 133, 135, 137-141; *19:* 18,
    19, 20; *32:* 208, 213, 214;
    36: 105, 108
Beame, Rona, *12:* 40
Beard, Dan, *22:* 31, 32
Beard, J. H., *YABC 1:* 158
Bearden, Romare, *9:* 7; *22:* 35
Beardsley, Aubrey, *17:* 14; *23:* 181
Bearman, Jane, *29:* 38
Beaton, Cecil, *24:* 208
Beaucé, J. A., *18:* 103
Beck, Charles, *11:* 169
Beck, Ruth, *13:* 11
Becker, Harriet, *12:* 211
Beckett, Sheilah, *25:* 5; *33:* 37, 38
Beckhoff, Harry, *1:* 78; *5:* 163
Beckman, Kaj, *45:* 38, 39, 40, 41
Beckman, Per, *45:* 42, 43
Bedford, F. D., *20:* 118, 122; *33:* 170;
    41: 220, 221, 230, 233
Bee, Joyce, *19:* 62
Beeby, Betty, *25:* 36
Beech, Carol, *9:* 149
Beek, *25:* 51, 55, 59
Beerbohm, Max, *24:* 208
Behr, Joyce, *15:* 15; *21:* 132; *23:* 161
Behrens, Hans, *5:* 97
Belden, Charles J., *12:* 182
Belina, Renate, *39:* 132
Bell, Corydon, *3:* 20
Beltran, Alberto, *43:* 37
Bemelmans, Ludwig, *15:* 19, 21
Benda, Wladyslaw T., *15:* 256;
    30: 76, 77; *44:* 182
Bendick, Jeanne, *2:* 24
Bennett, F. I., *YABC 1:* 134
Bennett, Jill, *26:* 61; *41:* 38, 39;
    45: 54
Bennett, Rainey, *15:* 26; *23:* 53
Bennett, Richard, *15:* 45; *21:* 11, 12,
    13; *25:* 175
Bennett, Susan, *5:* 55
Bentley, Roy, *30:* 162
Benton, Thomas Hart, *2:* 99
Berelson, Howard, *5:* 20; *16:* 58;
    31: 50
Berenstain, Jan, *12:* 47
Berenstain, Stan, *12:* 47
Berg, Joan, *1:* 115; *3:* 156; *6:* 26, 58
Berg, Ron, *36:* 48, 49
Berger, William M., *14:* 143;
    YABC 1: 204
Bering, Claus, *13:* 14
Berkowitz, Jeanette, *3:* 249
Bernadette. *See* Watts, Bernadette
Bernath, Stefen, *32:* 76
Bernstein, Ted, *38:* 183
Bernstein, Zena, *23:* 46
Berrill, Jacquelyn, *12:* 50

Berry, Erick. *See* Best, Allena.
Berry, William A., *6:* 219
Berry, William D., *14:* 29; *19:* 48
Berson, Harold, *2:* 17-18; *4:* 28-29,
    220; *9:* 10; *12:* 19; *17:* 45;
    18: 193; *22:* 85; *34:* 172; *44:* 120
Bertschmann, Harry, *16:* 1
Beskow, Elsa, *20:* 13, 14, 15
Best, Allena, *2:* 26; *34:* 76
Bethers, Ray, *6:* 22
Bettina. *See* Ehrlich, Bettina
Betts, Ethel Franklin, *17:* 161,
    164-165; *YABC 2:* 47
Bewick, Thomas, *16:* 40-41, 43-45,
    47; *YABC 1:* 107
Biamonte, Daniel, *40:* 90
Bianco, Pamela, *15:* 31; *28:* 44, 45, 46
Bible, Charles, *13:* 15
Bice, Clare, *22:* 40
Biggers, John, *2:* 123
Bileck, Marvin, *3:* 102; *40:* 36-37
Bimen, Levent, *5:* 179
Binks, Robert, *25:* 150
Binzen, Bill, *24:* 47
Birch, Reginald, *15:* 150; *19:* 33, 34,
    35, 36; *37:* 196, 197; *44:* 182;
    YABC 1: 84; *YABC 2:* 34, 39
Bird, Esther Brock, *1:* 36; *25:* 66
Birmingham, Lloyd, *12:* 51
Biro, Val, *1:* 26; *41:* 42
Bischoff, Ilse, *44:* 51
Bjorklund, Lorence, *3:* 188, 252;
    7: 100; *9:* 113; *10:* 66; *19:* 178;
    33: 122, 123; *35:* 36, 37, 38, 39,
    41, 42, 43; *36:* 185; *38:* 93;
    YABC 1: 242
Blackwell, Basil T., *YABC 1:* 68, 69
Blades, Ann, *16:* 52; *37:* 213
Blair, Jay, *45:* 46
Blaisdell, Elinore, *1:* 121; *3:* 134;
    35: 63
Blake, Quentin, *3:* 170; *9:* 21; *10:* 48;
    13: 38; *21:* 180; *26:* 60; *28:* 228;
    30: 29, 31; *40:* 108; *45:* 219
Blake, Robert J., *37:* 90
Blake, William, *30:* 54, 56, 57, 58,
    59, 60
Blass, Jacqueline, *8:* 215
Blegvad, Erik, *2:* 59; *3:* 98; *5:* 117;
    7: 131; *11:* 149; *14:* 34, 35;
    18: 237; *32:* 219; *YABC 1:* 201
Bliss, Corinne Demas, *37:* 38
Bloch, Lucienne, *10:* 12
Bloom, Lloyd, *35:* 180; *36:* 149
Blossom, Dave, *34:* 29
Blumenschein, E. L., *YABC 1:* 113,
    115
Blumer, Patt, *29:* 214
Blundell, Kim, *29:* 36
Boardman, Gwenn, *12:* 60
Bobri, *30:* 138
Bock, Vera, *1:* 187; *21:* 41
Bock, William Sauts, *8:* 7; *14:* 37;
    16: 120; *21:* 141; *36:* 177
Bodecker, N. M., *8:* 13; *14:* 2;
    17: 55-57
Boehm, Linda, *40:* 31
Bohdal, Susi, *22:* 44

Bolian, Polly, *3:* 270; *4:* 30; *13:* 77; *29:* 197
Bolognese, Don, *2:* 147, 231; *4:* 176; *7:* 146; *17:* 43; *23:* 192; *24:* 50; *34:* 108; *36:* 133
Bond, Arnold, *18:* 116
Bond, Barbara Higgins, *21:* 102
Bond, Felicia, *38:* 197
Bonn, Pat, *43:* 40
Bonners, Susan, *41:* 40
Bonsall, Crosby, *23:* 6
Booth, Franklin, *YABC 2:* 76
Booth, Graham, *32:* 193; *37:* 41, 42
Bordier, Georgette, *16:* 54
Boren, Tinka, *27:* 128
Borja, Robert, *22:* 48
Bornstein, Ruth, *14:* 44
Borten, Helen, *3:* 54; *5:* 24
Bossom, Naomi, *35:* 48
Boston, Peter, *19:* 42
Bosustow, Stephen, *34:* 202
Bottner, Barbara, *14:* 46
Boucher, Joelle, *41:* 138
Boulat, Pierre, *44:* 40
Bourke-White, Margaret, *15:* 286-287
Boutet de Monvel, M., *30:* 61, 62, 63, 65
Bowen, Richard, *42:* 134
Bowen, Ruth, *31:* 188
Bower, Ron, *29:* 33
Bowser, Carolyn Ewing, *22:* 253
Boyd, Patti, *45:* 31
Boyle, Eleanor Vere, *28:* 50, 51
Bozzo, Frank, *4:* 154
Bradford, Ron, *7:* 157
Bradley, Richard D., *26:* 182
Bradley, William, *5:* 164
Brady, Irene, *4:* 31; *42:* 37
Bragg, Michael, *32:* 78
Braithwaite, Althea, *23:* 12-13
Bram, Elizabeth, *30:* 67
Bramley, Peter, *4:* 3
Brandenberg, Aliki, *2:* 36-37; *24:* 222; *35:* 49, 50, 51, 52, 53, 54, 56, 57
Brandi, Lillian, *31:* 158
Brandon, Brumsic, Jr., *9:* 25
Bransom, Paul, *17:* 121; *43:* 44
Brenner, Fred, *22:* 85; *36:* 34; *42:* 34
Brett, Bernard, *22:* 54
Brett, Harold M., *26:* 98, 99, 100
Brett, Jan, *30:* 135; *42:* 39
Brewer, Sally King, *33:* 44
Brewster, Patience, *40:* 68; *45:* 22, 183
Brick, John, *10:* 15
Bridge, David R., *45:* 28
Bridgman, L. J., *37:* 77
Bridwell, Norman, *4:* 37
Briggs, Raymond, *10:* 168; *23:* 20, 21
Brigham, Grace A., *37:* 148
Bright, Robert, *24:* 55
Brinckloe, Julie, *13:* 18; *24:* 79, 115; *29:* 35
Brisley, Joyce L., *22:* 57
Brock, Charles E., *15:* 97; *19:* 247, 249; *23:* 224, 225; *36:* 88; *42:* 41, 42, 43, 44, 45; *YABC 1:* 194, 196, 203
Brock, Emma, *7:* 21

Brock, Henry Matthew, *15:* 81; *16:* 141; *19:* 71; *34:* 115; *40:* 164; *42:* 47, 48, 49
Brodkin, Gwen, *34:* 135
Bromhall, Winifred, *5:* 11; *26:* 38
Brooke, L. Leslie, *16:* 181-183, 186; *17:* 15-17; *18:* 194
Brooker, Christopher, *15:* 251
Broomfield, Maurice, *40:* 141
Brotman, Adolph E., *5:* 21
Brown, Buck, *45:* 48
Brown, David, *7:* 47
Brown, Denise, *11:* 213
Brown, Judith Gwyn, *1:* 45; *7:* 5; *8:* 167; *9:* 182, 190; *20:* 16, 17, 18; *23:* 142; *29:* 117; *33:* 97; *36:* 23, 26; *43:* 184
Brown, Marc Tolon, *10:* 17, 197; *14:* 263
Brown, Marcia, *7:* 30; *25:* 203; *YABC 1:* 27
Brown, Margery W., *5:* 32-33; *10:* 3
Brown, Palmer, *36:* 40
Brown, Paul, *25:* 26; *26:* 107
Browne, Anthony, *45:* 50, 51, 52
Browne, Dik, *8:* 212
Browne, Gordon, *16:* 97
Browne, Hablot K., *15:* 65, 80; *21:* 14, 15, 16, 17, 18, 19, 20; *24:* 25
Browning, Coleen, *4:* 132
Browning, Mary Eleanor, *24:* 84
Bruce, Robert, *23:* 23
Brule, Al, *3:* 135
Bruna, Dick, *43:* 48, 49, 50
Brundage, Frances, *19:* 244
Brunhoff, Jean de, *24:* 57, 58
Brunhoff, Laurent de, *24:* 60
Brunson, Bob, *43:* 135
Bryan, Ashley, *31:* 44
Brychta, Alex, *21:* 21
Bryson, Bernarda, *3:* 88, 146; *39:* 26; *44:* 185
Buba, Joy, *12:* 83; *30:* 226; *44:* 56
Buchanan, Lilian, *13:* 16
Bucholtz-Ross, Linda, *44:* 137
Buchs, Thomas, *40:* 38
Buck, Margaret Waring, *3:* 30
Buehr, Walter, *3:* 31
Buff, Conrad, *19:* 52, 53, 54
Buff, Mary, *19:* 52, 53
Bull, Charles Livingston, *18:* 207
Bullen, Anne, *3:* 166, 167
Burbank, Addison, *37:* 43
Burchard, Peter, *3:* 197; *5:* 35; *6:* 158, 218
Burger, Carl, *3:* 33; *45:* 160, 162
Burgeson, Marjorie, *19:* 31
Burgess, Gelett, *32:* 39, 42
Burkert, Nancy Ekholm, *18:* 186; *22:* 140; *24:* 62, 63, 64, 65; *26:* 53; *29:* 60, 61; *YABC 1:* 46
Burn, Doris, *6:* 172
Burnett, Virgil, *44:* 42
Burningham, John, *9:* 68; *16:* 60-61
Burns, Howard M., *12:* 173
Burns, M. F., *26:* 69
Burns, Raymond, *9:* 29
Burns, Robert, *24:* 106

Burr, Dane, *12:* 2
Burra, Edward, *YABC 2:* 68
Burri, René, *41:* 143
Burridge, Marge Opitz, *14:* 42
Burris, Burmah, *4:* 81
Burroughs, John Coleman, *41:* 64
Burroughs, Studley O., *41:* 65
Burton, Virginia Lee, *2:* 43; *44:* 49, 51; *YABC 1:* 24
Busoni, Rafaello, *1:* 186; *3:* 224; *6:* 126; *14:* 5; *16:* 62-63
Butterfield, Ned, *1:* 153; *27:* 128
Buzonas, Gail, *29:* 88
Buzzell, Russ W., *12:* 177
Byard, Carole M., *39:* 44
Byfield, Barbara Ninde, *8:* 18
Byfield, Graham, *32:* 29
Byrd, Robert, *13:* 218; *33:* 46

Caddy, Alice, *6:* 41
Cady, Harrison, *17:* 21, 23; *19:* 57, 58
Caldecott, Randolph, *16:* 98, 103; *17:* 32-33, 36, 38-39; *26:* 90; *YABC 2:* 172
Calder, Alexander, *18:* 168
Calderon, W. Frank, *25:* 160
Caldwell, Doreen, *23:* 77
Callahan, Kevin, *22:* 42
Callahan, Philip S., *25:* 77
Cameron, Julia Margaret, *19:* 203
Campbell, Ann, *11:* 43
Campbell, Walter M., *YABC 2:* 158
Camps, Luis, *28:* 120-121
Canright, David, *36:* 162
Caras, Peter, *36:* 64
Caraway, James, *3:* 200-201
Carbe, Nino, *29:* 183
Carigiet, Alois, *24:* 67
Carle, Eric, *4:* 42; *11:* 121; *12:* 29
Carlson, Nancy L., *41:* 116
Carr, Archie, *37:* 225
Carrick, Donald, *5:* 194; *39:* 97
Carrick, Malcolm, *28:* 59, 60
Carrick, Valery, *21:* 47
Carroll, Lewis. *See* Dodgson, Charles L.
Carroll, Ruth, *7:* 41; *10:* 68
Carter, Harry, *22:* 179
Carter, Helene, *15:* 38; *22:* 202, 203; *YABC 2:* 220-221
Carty, Leo, *4:* 196; *7:* 163
Cary, *4:* 133; *9:* 32; *20:* 2; *21:* 143
Cary, Page, *12:* 41
Case, Sandra E., *16:* 2
Cassel, Lili. *See* Wronker, Lili Cassel
Cassel-Wronker, Lili. *See also* Wronker, Lili Cassel
Cassels, Jean, *8:* 50
Castle, Jane, *4:* 80
Cather, Carolyn, *3:* 83; *15:* 203; *34:* 216
Cauley, Lorinda Bryan, *44:* 135
Cayard, Bruce, *38:* 67
Cellini, Joseph, *2:* 73; *3:* 35; *16:* 116
Chabrian, Debbi, *45:* 55
Chagnon, Mary, *37:* 158
Chalmers, Mary, *3:* 145; *13:* 148; *33:* 125

Chamberlain, Christopher, 45: 57
Chambers, C. E., 17: 230
Chambers, Dave, 12: 151
Chambers, Mary, 4: 188
Chambliss, Maxie, 42: 186
Chandler, David P., 28: 62
Chapman, C. H., 13: 83, 85, 87
Chapman, Frederick T., 6: 27; 44: 28
Chapman, Gaynor, 32: 52, 53
Chappell, Warren, 3: 172; 21: 56;
    27: 125
Charles, Donald, 30: 154, 155
Charlip, Remy, 4: 48; 34: 138
Charlot, Jean, 1: 137, 138; 8: 23;
    14: 31
Charlton, Michael, 34: 50; 37: 39
Charmatz, Bill, 7: 45
Chartier, Normand, 9: 36
Chase, Lynwood M., 14: 4
Chastain, Madye Lee, 4: 50
Chauncy, Francis, 24: 158
Chen, Tony, 6: 45; 19: 131; 29: 126;
    34: 160
Cheney, T. A., 11: 47
Cheng, Judith, 36: 45
Cherry, Lynne, 34: 52
Chess, Victoria, 12: 6; 33: 42, 48, 49;
    40: 194; 41: 145
Chessare, Michele, 41: 50
Chesterton, G. K., 27: 43, 44, 45, 47
Chevalier, Christa, 35: 66
Chew, Ruth, 7: 46
Chin, Alex, 28: 54
Cho, Shinta, 8: 126
Chollick, Jay, 25: 175
Chorao, Kay, 7: 200-201; 8: 25;
    11: 234; 33: 187; 35: 239
Christelow, Eileen, 38: 44
Christensen, Gardell Dano, 1: 57
Christiansen, Per, 40: 24
Christy, Howard Chandler,
    17: 163-165, 168-169; 19: 186,
    187; 21: 22, 23, 24, 25
Chronister, Robert, 23: 138
Church, Frederick, YABC 1: 155
Chute, Marchette, 1: 59
Chwast, Jacqueline, 1: 63; 2: 275;
    6: 46-47; 11: 125; 12: 202;
    14: 235
Chwast, Seymour, 3: 128-129; 18: 43;
    27: 152
Cirlin, Edgard, 2: 168
Clark, Victoria, 35: 159
Clarke, Harry, 23: 172, 173
Claverie, Jean, 38: 46
Clayton, Robert, 9: 181
Cleaver, Elizabeth, 8: 204; 23: 36
Cleland, T. M., 26: 92
Clement, Charles, 20: 38
Clevin, Jörgen, 7: 50
Clifford, Judy, 34: 163; 45: 198
Coalson, Glo, 9: 72, 85; 25: 155;
    26: 42; 35: 212
Cober, Alan E., 17: 158; 32: 77
Cochran, Bobbye, 11: 52
CoConis, Ted, 4: 41
Coerr, Eleanor, 1: 64
Coes, Peter, 35: 172
Coggins, Jack, 2: 69

Cohen, Alix, 7: 53
Cohen, Vincent O., 19: 243
Cohen, Vivien, 11: 112
Colbert, Anthony, 15: 41; 20: 193
Colby, C. B., 3: 47
Cole, Herbert, 28: 104
Cole, Olivia H. H., 1: 134; 3: 223;
    9: 111; 38: 104
Collier, David, 13: 127
Collier, John, 27: 179
Colonna, Bernard, 21: 50; 28: 103;
    34: 140; 43: 180
Cone, Ferne Geller, 39: 49
Cone, J. Morton, 39: 49
Conklin, Paul, 43: 62
Connolly, Jerome P., 4: 128; 28: 52
Conover, Chris, 31: 52; 40: 184;
    41: 51; 44: 79
Converse, James, 38: 70
Cook, G. R., 29: 165
Cookburn, W. V., 29: 204
Cooke, Donald E., 2: 77
Coombs, Charles, 43: 65
Coombs, Patricia, 2: 82; 3: 52;
    22: 119
Cooney, Barbara, 6: 16-17, 50; 12: 42;
    13: 92; 15: 145; 16: 74, 111;
    18: 189; 23: 38, 89, 93; 32: 138;
    38: 105; YABC 2: 10
Cooper, Mario, 24: 107
Cooper, Marjorie, 7: 112
Copelman, Evelyn, 8: 61; 18: 25
Copley, Heather, 30: 86; 45: 57
Corbett, Grahame, 30: 114; 43: 67
Corbino, John, 19: 248
Corcos, Lucille, 2: 223; 10: 27; 34: 66
Corey, Robert, 9: 34
Corlass, Heather, 10: 7
Cornell, James, 27: 60
Cornell, Jeff, 11: 58
Corrigan, Barbara, 8: 37
Corwin, Judith Hoffman, 10: 28
Cory, Fanny Y., 20: 113
Cosgrove, Margaret, 3: 100
Costabel, Eva Deutsch, 45: 66, 67
Costello, David F., 23: 55
Courtney, R., 35: 110
Couture, Christin, 41: 209
Covarrubias, Miguel, 35: 118, 119,
    123, 124, 125
Coville, Katherine, 32: 57; 36: 167
Cox, 43: 93
Cox, Charles, 8: 20
Cox, Palmer, 24: 76, 77
Craft, Kinuko, 22: 182; 36: 220
Crane, Alan H., 1: 217
Crane, H. M., 13: 111
Crane, Jack, 43: 183
Crane, Walter, 18: 46-49, 53-54,
    56-57, 59-61; 22: 128; 24: 210,
    217
Crawford, Will, 43: 77
Credle, Ellis 1: 69
Crews, Donald, 32: 59, 60
Crofut, Susan, 23: 61
Crowell, Pers, 3: 125
Cruikshank, George, 15: 76, 83;
    22: 74, 75, 76, 77, 78, 79, 80,
    81, 82, 84, 137; 24: 22, 23

Crump, Fred H., 11: 62
Cruz, Ray, 6: 55
Cstari, Joe, 44: 82
Cuffari, Richard, 4: 75; 5: 98; 6: 56;
    7: 13, 84, 153; 8: 148, 155; 9: 89;
    11: 19; 12: 55, 96, 114; 15: 51,
    202; 18: 5; 20: 139; 21: 197;
    22: 14, 192; 23: 15, 106; 25: 97;
    27: 133; 28: 196; 29: 54; 30: 85;
    31: 35; 36: 101; 38: 171; 42: 97;
    44: 92, 192; 45: 212, 213
Cugat, Xavier, 19: 120
Cumings, Art, 35: 160
Cummings, Chris, 29: 167
Cummings, Pat, 42: 61
Cummings, Richard, 24: 119
Cunette, Lou, 20: 93; 22: 125
Cunningham, Aline, 25: 180
Cunningham, David, 11: 13
Cunningham, Imogene, 16: 122, 127
Curry, John Steuart, 2: 5; 19: 84;
    34: 36
Curtis, Bruce, 23: 96; 30: 88; 36: 22

Dabcovich, Lydia, 25: 105; 40: 114
Dain, Martin J., 35: 75
Dalton, Anne, 40: 62
Daly, Niki, 37: 53
Dalziel, Brothers, 33: 113
D'Amato, Alex, 9: 48; 20: 25
D'Amato, Janet, 9: 48; 20: 25; 26: 118
Daniel, Alan, 23: 59; 29: 110
Daniel, Lewis C., 20: 216
Daniels, Steve, 22: 16
Dann, Bonnie, 31: 83
Danska, Herbert, 24: 219
Danyell, Alice, 20: 27
Darley, F.O.C., 16: 145; 19: 79, 86,
    88, 185; 21: 28, 36; 35: 76, 77,
    78, 79, 80-81; YABC 2: 175
Darling, Lois, 3: 59; 23: 30, 31
Darling, Louis, 1: 40-41; 2: 63; 3: 59;
    23: 30, 31; 43: 54, 57, 59
Darrow, Whitney, Jr., 13: 25; 38: 220,
    221
Darwin, Beatrice, 43: 54
Darwin, Len, 24: 82
Dastolfo, Frank, 33: 179
Dauber, Liz, 1: 22; 3: 266; 30: 49
Daugherty, James, 3: 66; 8: 178;
    13: 27-28, 161; 18: 101; 19: 72;
    29: 108; 32: 156; 42: 84;
    YABC 1: 256; YABC 2: 174
d'Aulaire, Edgar, 5: 51
d'Aulaire, Ingri, 5: 51
David, Jonathan, 19: 37
Davidson, Kevin, 28: 154
Davidson, Raymond, 32: 61
Davis, Allen, 20: 11; 22: 45; 27: 222;
    29: 157; 41: 99
Davis, Bette J., 15: 53; 23: 95
Davis, Dimitris, 45: 95
Davis, Jim, 32: 63, 64
Davis, Marguerite, 31: 38; 34: 69, 70;
    YABC 1: 126, 230
Davisson, Virginia H., 44: 178
Dawson, Diane, 24: 127; 42: 126
Dean, Bob, 19: 211

de Angeli, Marguerite, *1:* 77; *27:* 62, 65, 66, 67, 69, 70, 72; *YABC 1:* 166
Deas, Michael, *27:* 219, 221; *30:* 156
de Bosschère, Jean, *19:* 252; *21:* 4
De Bruyn, M(onica) G., *13:* 30-31
De Cuir, John F., *1:* 28-29
Degen, Bruce, *40:* 227, 229
De Grazia, *14:* 59; *39:* 56, 57
de Groat, Diane, *9:* 39; *18:* 7; *23:* 123; *28:* 200-201; *31:* 58, 59; *34:* 151; *41:* 152; *43:* 88
de Groot, Lee, *6:* 21
Delacre, Lulu, *36:* 66
Delaney, A., *21:* 78
Delaney, Ned, *28:* 68
de Larrea, Victoria, *6:* 119, 204; *29:* 103
Delessert, Etienne, *7:* 140; *YABC 2:* 209
Delulio, John, *15:* 54
Demarest, Chris L., *45:* 68-69, 70
De Mejo, Oscar, *40:* 67
Denetsosie, Hoke, *13:* 126
Dennis, Morgan, *18:* 68-69
Dennis, Wesley, *2:* 87; *3:* 111; *11:* 132; *18:* 71-74; *22:* 9; *24:* 196, 200
Denslow, W. W., *16:* 84-87; *18:* 19-20, 24; *29:* 211
de Paola, Tomie, *8:* 95; *9:* 93; *11:* 69; *25:* 103; *28:* 157; *29:* 80; *39:* 52-53; *40:* 226
Detmold, Edward J., *22:* 104, 105, 106, 107; *35:* 120; *YABC 2:* 203
Detrich, Susan, *20:* 133
DeVelasco, Joseph E., *21:* 51
de Veyrac, Robert, *YABC 2:* 19
DeVille, Edward A., *4:* 235
Devito, Bert, *12:* 164
Devlin, Harry, *11:* 74
Dewey, Ariane, *7:* 64; *33:* 195; *35:* 208
See also Aruego, Ariane
Dewey, Kenneth, *39:* 62
de Zanger, Arie, *30:* 40
Diamond, Donna, *21:* 200; *23:* 63; *26:* 142; *35:* 83, 84, 85, 86-87, 88, 89; *38:* 78; *40:* 147; *44:* 152
Dick, John Henry, *8:* 181
Dickens, Frank, *34:* 131
Dickey, Robert L., *15:* 279
DiFate, Vincent, *37:* 70
DiFiori, Lawrence, *10:* 51; *12:* 190; *27:* 97; *40:* 219
Di Grazia, Thomas, *32:* 66; *35:* 241
Dillard, Annie, *10:* 32
Dillon, Corinne B., *1:* 139
Dillon, Diane, *4:* 104, 167; *6:* 23; *13:* 29; *15:* 99; *26:* 148; *27:* 136, 201
Dillon, Leo, *4:* 104, 167; *6:* 23; *13:* 29; *15:* 99; *26:* 148; *27:* 136, 201
DiMaggio, Joe, *36:* 22
Dinan, Carol, *25:* 169
Dines, Glen, *7:* 66-67
Dinesen, Thomas, *44:* 37

Dinnerstein, Harvey, *42:* 63, 64, 65, 66, 67, 68
Dinsdale, Mary, *10:* 65; *11:* 171
Disney, Walt, *28:* 71, 72, 73, 76, 77, 78, 79, 80, 81, 87, 88, 89, 90, 91, 94
Dixon, Maynard, *20:* 165
Doares, Robert G., *20:* 39
Dobias, Frank, *22:* 162
Dobrin, Arnold, *4:* 68
Docktor, Irv, *43:* 70
Dodd, Ed, *4:* 69
Dodd, Lynley, *35:* 92
Dodgson, Charles L., *20:* 148; *33:* 146; *YABC 2:* 98
Dodson, Bert, *9:* 138; *14:* 195; *42:* 55
Dohanos, Stevan, *16:* 10
Dolesch, Susanne, *34:* 49
Dolson, Hildegarde, *5:* 57
Domanska, Janina, *6:* 66-67; *YABC 1:* 166
Domjan, Joseph, *25:* 93
Donahue, Vic, *2:* 93; *3:* 190; *9:* 44
Donald, Elizabeth, *4:* 18
Donna, Natalie, *9:* 52
Doré, Gustave, *18:* 169, 172, 175; *19:* 93, 94, 95, 96, 97, 98, 99, 100, 101, 102, 103, 104, 105; *23:* 188; *25:* 197, 199
Doremus, Robert, *6:* 62; *13:* 90; *30:* 95, 96, 97; *38:* 97
Dorfman, Ronald, *11:* 128
Doty, Roy, *28:* 98; *31:* 32; *32:* 224
Dougherty, Charles, *16:* 204; *18:* 74
Douglas, Aaron, *31:* 103
Douglas, Goray, *13:* 151
Dowd, Vic, *3:* 244; *10:* 97
Dowden, Anne Ophelia, *7:* 70-71; *13:* 120
Dowdy, Mrs. Regera, *29:* 100. *See also* Gorey, Edward
Doyle, Richard, *21:* 31, 32, 33; *23:* 231; *24:* 177; *31:* 87
Draper, Angie, *43:* 84
Drath, Bill, *26:* 34
Drawson, Blair, *17:* 53
Drescher, Joan, *30:* 100, 101; *35:* 245
Drew, Patricia, *15:* 100
Drummond, V. H., *6:* 70
du Bois, William Pène, *4:* 70; *10:* 122; *26:* 61; *27:* 145, 211; *35:* 243; *41:* 216
Duchesne, Janet, *6:* 162
Dudash, Michael, *32:* 122
Duer, Douglas, *34:* 177
Duffy, Joseph, *38:* 203
Duffy, Pat, *28:* 153
Duke, Chris, *8:* 195
Dulac, Edmund, *19:* 108, 109, 110, 111, 112, 113, 114, 115, 117; *23:* 187; *25:* 152; *YABC 1:* 37; *YABC 2:* 147
Dulac, Jean, *13:* 64
Dunn, Harvey, *34:* 78, 79, 80, 81
Dunn, Phoebe, *5:* 175
Dunn, Iris, *5:* 175
Dunnington, Tom, *3:* 36; *18:* 281; *25:* 61; *31:* 159; *35:* 168
Dutz, *6:* 59

Duvoisin, Roger, *2:* 95; *6:* 76-77; *7:* 197; *28:* 125; *30:* 101, 102, 103, 104, 105, 107
Dypold, Pat, *15:* 37

E.V.B. *See* Boyle, Eleanor Vere (Gordon)
Eachus, Jennifer, *29:* 74
Eagle, Michael, *11:* 86; *20:* 9; *23:* 18; *27:* 122; *28:* 57; *34:* 201; *44:* 189
Earle, Olive L., *7:* 75
Earle, Vana, *27:* 99
Eastman, P. D., *33:* 57
Easton, Reginald, *29:* 181
Eaton, Tom, *4:* 62; *6:* 64; *22:* 99; *24:* 124
Ebel, Alex, *11:* 89
Ebert, Len, *9:* 191; *44:* 47
Echevarria, Abe, *37:* 69
Ede, Janina, *33:* 59
Edgar, Sarah E., *41:* 97
Edrien, *11:* 53
Edwards, Freya, *45:* 102
Edwards, George Wharton, *31:* 155
Edwards, Gunvor, *2:* 71; *25:* 47; *32:* 71
Edwards, Jeanne, *29:* 257
Edwards, Linda Strauss, *21:* 134; *39:* 123
Eggenhofer, Nicholas, *2:* 81
Egielski, Richard, *11:* 90; *16:* 208; *33:* 236; *38:* 35
Ehlert, Lois, *35:* 97
Ehrlich, Bettina, *1:* 83
Eichenberg, Fritz, *1:* 79; *9:* 54; *19:* 248; *23:* 170; *24:* 200; *26:* 208; *YABC 1:* 104-105; *YABC 2:* 213
Einsel, Naiad, *10:* 35; *29:* 136
Einsel, Walter, *10:* 37
Einzig, Susan, *3:* 77; *43:* 78
Eitzen, Allan, *9:* 56; *12:* 212; *14:* 226; *21:* 194; *38:* 162
Eldridge, Harold, *43:* 83
Elgaard, Greta, *19:* 241
Elgin, Kathleen, *9:* 188; *39:* 69
Ellacott, S. E., *19:* 118
Elliott, Sarah M., *14:* 58
Emberley, Ed, *8:* 53
Emberley, Michael, *34:* 83
Engle, Mort, *38:* 64
Englebert, Victor, *8:* 54
Enos, Randall, *20:* 183
Enright, Maginel Wright, *19:* 240, 243; *39:* 31, 35, 36
Enrique, Romeo, *34:* 135
Erhard, Walter, *1:* 152
Erickson, Phoebe, *11:* 83
Erikson, Mel, *31:* 69
Escourido, Joseph, *4:* 81
Esté, Kirk, *33:* 111
Estoril, Jean, *32:* 27
Estrada, Ric, *5:* 52, 146; *13:* 174
Etchemendy, Teje, *38:* 68
Ets, Marie Hall, *2:* 102
Eulalie, *YABC 2:* 315
Evans, Katherine, *5:* 64
Ewing, Juliana Horatia, *16:* 92

Falconer, Pearl, *34:* 23
Falls, C. B., *1:* 19; *38:* 71, 72, 73, 74
Falter, John, *40:* 169, 170
Farmer, Peter, *24:* 108; *38:* 75
Farrell, David, *40:* 135
Fatigati, Evelyn, *24:* 112
Faul-Jansen, Regina, *22:* 117
Faulkner, Jack, *6:* 169
Fava, Rita, *2:* 29
Fax, Elton C., *1:* 101; *4:* 2; *12:* 77; *25:* 107
Fay, *43:* 93
Federspiel, Marian, *33:* 51
Feelings, Tom, *5:* 22; *8:* 56; *12:* 153; *16:* 105; *30:* 196
Fehr, Terrence, *21:* 87
Feiffer, Jules, *3:* 91; *8:* 58
Feigeles, Neil, *41:* 242
Feller, Gene, *33:* 130
Fellows, Muriel H., *10:* 42
Felts, Shirley, *33:* 71
Fennelli, Maureen, *38:* 181
Fenton, Carroll Lane, *5:* 66; *21:* 39
Fenton, Mildred Adams, *5:* 66; *21:* 39
Ferguson, Walter W., *34:* 86
Fetz, Ingrid, *11:* 67; *12:* 52; *16:* 205; *17:* 59; *29:* 105; *30:* 108, 109; *32:* 149; *43:* 142
Fiammenghi, Gioia, *9:* 66; *11:* 44; *12:* 206; *13:* 57, 59
Field, Rachel, *15:* 113
Fine, Peter K., *43:* 210
Finger, Helen, *42:* 81
Fink, Sam, *18:* 119
Finlay, Winifred, *23:* 72
Fiorentino, Al, *3:* 240
Firmin, Charlotte, *29:* 75
Fischel, Lillian, *40:* 204
Fischer, Hans, *25:* 202
Fisher, Leonard Everett, *3:* 6; *4:* 72, 86; *6:* 197; *9:* 59; *16:* 151, 153; *23:* 44; *27:* 134; *29:* 26; *34:* 87, 89, 90, 91, 93, 94, 95, 96; *40:* 206; *YABC 2:* 169
Fisher, Lois, *20:* 62; *21:* 7
Fisk, Nicholas, *25:* 112
Fitschen, Marilyn, *2:* 20-21; *20:* 48
Fitzgerald, F. A., *15:* 116; *25:* 86-87
Fitzhugh, Louise, *1:* 94; *9:* 163; *45:* 75, 78
Fitzhugh, Susie, *11:* 117
Fitzsimmons, Arthur, *14:* 128
Fix, Philippe, *26:* 102
Flack, Marjorie, *21:* 67; *YABC 2:* 122
Flagg, James Montgomery, *17:* 227
Flax, Zeona, *2:* 245
Fleishman, Seymour, *14:* 232; *24:* 87
Fleming, Guy, *18:* 41
Floethe, Richard, *3:* 131; *4:* 90
Floherty, John J., Jr., *5:* 68
Flora, James, *1:* 96; *30:* 111, 112
Florian, Douglas, *19:* 122
Flory, Jane, *22:* 111
Floyd, Gareth, *1:* 74; *17:* 245
Fluchère, Henri A., *40:* 79
Flynn, Barbara, *7:* 31; *9:* 70
Fogarty, Thomas, *15:* 89
Folger, Joseph, *9:* 100

Folkard, Charles, *22:* 132; *29:* 128, 257-258
Foott, Jeff, *42:* 202
Forberg, Ati, *12:* 71, 205; *14:* 1; *22:* 113; *26:* 22
Ford, George, *24:* 120; *31:* 70, 177
Ford, H. J., *16:* 185-186
Ford, Pamela Baldwin, *27:* 104
Foreman, Michael, *2:* 110-111
Forrester, Victoria, *40:* 83
Fortnum, Peggy, *6:* 29; *20:* 179; *24:* 211; *26:* 76, 77, 78; *39:* 78; *YABC 1:* 148
Foster, Brad W., *34:* 99
Foster, Genevieve, *2:* 112
Foster, Gerald, *7:* 78
Foster, Laura Louise, *6:* 79
Foster, Marian Curtis, *23:* 74; *40:* 42
Fowler, Mel, *36:* 127
Fox, Charles Phillip, *12:* 84
Fox, Jim, *6:* 187
Fracé, Charles, *15:* 118
Frame, Paul, *2:* 45, 145; *9:* 153; *10:* 124; *21:* 71; *23:* 62; *24:* 123; *27:* 106; *31:* 48; *32:* 159; *34:* 195; *38:* 136; *42:* 55; *44:* 139
Francois, André, *25:* 117
Francoise. See Seignobosc, Francoise
Frank, Lola Edick, *2:* 199
Frank, Mary, *4:* 54; *34:* 100
Franke, Phil, *45:* 91
Frankel, Julie, *40:* 84, 85, 202
Frankenberg, Robert, *22:* 116; *30:* 50; *38:* 92, 94, 95
Franklin, John, *24:* 22
Frascino, Edward, *9:* 133; *29:* 229; *33:* 190
Frasconi, Antonio, *6:* 80; *27:* 208
Fraser, Betty, *2:* 212; *6:* 185; *8:* 103; *31:* 72, 73; *43:* 136
Fraser, Eric, *38:* 78; *41:* 149, 151
Fraser, F. A., *22:* 234
Frazetta, Frank, *41:* 72
Freas, John, *25:* 207
Freeman, Don, *2:* 15; *13:* 249; *17:* 62-63, 65, 67-68; *18:* 243; *20:* 195; *23:* 213, 217; *32:* 155
Fregosi, Claudia, *24:* 117
French, Fiona, *6:* 82-83
Friedman, Judith, *43:* 197
Friedman, Marvin, *19:* 59; *42:* 86
Frinta, Dagmar, *36:* 42
Frith, Michael K., *15:* 138; *18:* 120
Fromm, Lilo, *29:* 85; *40:* 197
Frost, A. B., *17:* 6-7; *19:* 123, 124, 125, 126, 127, 128, 129, 130; *YABC 1:* 156-157, 160; *YABC 2:* 107
Fry, Guy, *2:* 224
Fry, Rosalie, *3:* 72; *YABC 2:* 180-181
Fry, Rosalind, *21:* 153, 168
Fryer, Elmer, *34:* 115
Fuchs, Erich, *6:* 84
Fuchshuber, Annegert, *43:* 96
Fufuka, Mahiri, *32:* 146
Fujikawa, Gyo, *39:* 75, 76
Fulford, Deborah, *23:* 159
Fuller, Margaret, *25:* 189
Funai, Mamoru, *38:* 105

Funk, Tom, *7:* 17, 99
Furchgott, Terry, *29:* 86
Furukawa, Mel, *25:* 42

Gaberell, J., *19:* 236
Gackenbach, Dick, *19:* 168; *41:* 81
Gaetano, Nicholas, *23:* 209
Gag, Flavia, *17:* 49, 52
Gág, Wanda, *YABC 1:* 135, 137-138, 141, 143
Gagnon, Cécile, *11:* 77
Gal, Laszlo, *14:* 127
Galdone, Paul, *1:* 156, 181, 206; *2:* 40, 241; *3:* 42, 144; *4:* 141; *10:* 109, 158; *11:* 21; *12:* 118, 210; *14:* 12; *16:* 36-37; *17:* 70-74; *18:* 111, 230; *19:* 183; *21:* 154; *22:* 150, 245; *33:* 126; *39:* 136, 137; *42:* 57
Gallagher, Sears, *20:* 112
Galster, Robert, *1:* 66
Galsworthy, Gay John, *35:* 232
Gammell, Stephen, *7:* 48; *13:* 149; *29:* 82; *33:* 209; *41:* 88
Gannett, Ruth Chrisman, *3:* 74; *18:* 254; *33:* 77, 78
Gantschev, Ivan, *45:* 32
Garbutt, Bernard, *23:* 68
Garcia, *37:* 71
Gardner, Earle, *45:* 167
Gardner, Joan, *40:* 87
Gardner, Joel, *40:* 87, 92
Gardner, John, *40:* 87
Gardner, Lucy, *40:* 87
Gardner, Richard. See Cummings, Richard, *24:* 119
Garland, Michael, *36:* 29; *38:* 83; *44:* 168
Garnett, Eve, *3:* 75
Garnett, Gary, *39:* 184
Garraty, Gail, *4:* 142
Garrett, Edmund H., *20:* 29
Garrison, Barbara, *19:* 133
Gates, Frieda, *26:* 80
Gaughan, Jack, *26:* 79; *43:* 185
Gaver, Becky, *20:* 61
Gay, Zhenya, *19:* 135, 136
Geary, Clifford N., *1:* 122; *9:* 104
Gee, Frank, *33:* 26
Geer, Charles, *1:* 91; *3:* 179; *4:* 201; *6:* 168; *7:* 96; *9:* 58; *10:* 72; *12:* 127; *39:* 156, 157, 158, 159, 160; *42:* 88, 89, 90, 91
Gehm, Charlie, *36:* 65
Geisel, Theodor Seuss, *1:* 104-105, 106; *28:* 108, 109, 110, 111, 112, 113
Geldart, William, *15:* 121; *21:* 202
Genia, *4:* 84
Gentry, Cyrille R., *12:* 66
George, Jean, *2:* 113
Gérard, Jean Ignace, *45:* 80
Gérard, Rolf, *27:* 147, 150
Geritz, Franz, *17:* 135
Gerlach, Geff, *42:* 58
Gershinowitz, George, *36:* 27
Gerstein, Mordicai, *31:* 117
Gervase, *12:* 27

Getz, Arthur, *32:* 148

Gibbons, Gail, *23:* 78

Gibbs, Tony, *40:* 95

Gibran, Kahlil, *32:* 116

Giesen, Rosemary, *34:* 192-193

Giguère, George, *20:* 111

Gilbert, John, *19:* 184; *YABC 2:* 287

Gilbert, W. S., *36:* 83, 85, 96

Giles, Will, *41:* 218

Gill, Margery, *4:* 57; *7:* 7; *22:* 122; *25:* 166; *26:* 146, 147

Gillen, Denver, *28:* 216

Gillette, Henry J., *23:* 237

Gilliam, Stan, *39:* 64, 81

Gilman, Esther, *15:* 124

Giovanopoulos, Paul, *7:* 104

Githens, Elizabeth M., *5:* 47

Gladstone, Gary, *12:* 89; *13:* 190

Gladstone, Lise, *15:* 273

Glanzman, Louis S., *2:* 177; *3:* 182; *36:* 97, 98; *38:* 120, 122

Glaser, Milton, *3:* 5; *5:* 156; *11:* 107; *30:* 26; *36:* 112

Glass, Andrew, *36:* 38; *44:* 133

Glass, Marvin, *9:* 174

Glasser, Judy, *41:* 156

Glattauer, Ned, *5:* 84; *13:* 224; *14:* 26

Glauber, Uta, *17:* 76

Gleeson, J. M., *YABC 2:* 207

Glegg, Creina, *36:* 100

Gliewe, Unada, *3:* 78-79; *21:* 73; *30:* 220

Glovach, Linda, *7:* 105

Gobbato, Imero, *3:* 180-181; *6:* 213; *7:* 58; *9:* 150; *18:* 39; *21:* 167; *39:* 82, 83; *41:* 137, 251

Goble, Paul, *25:* 121; *26:* 86; *33:* 65

Godal, Eric, *36:* 93

Godfrey, Michael, *17:* 279

Goembel, Ponder, *42:* 124

Goffstein, M. B., *8:* 71

Golbin, Andrée, *15:* 125

Goldfeder, Cheryl, *11:* 191

Goldsborough, June, *5:* 154-155; *8:* 92, *14:* 226; *19:* 139

Goldstein, Leslie, *5:* 8; *6:* 60; *10:* 106

Goldstein, Nathan, *1:* 175; *2:* 79; *11:* 41, 232; *16:* 55

Goodall, John S., *4:* 92-93; *10:* 132; *YABC 1:* 198

Goode, Diane, *15:* 126

Goodelman, Aaron, *40:* 203

Goodenow, Earle, *40:* 97

Goodwin, Harold, *13:* 74

Goodwin, Philip R., *18:* 206

Goor, Nancy, *39:* 85, 86

Goor, Ron, *39:* 85, 86

Gordon, Gwen, *12:* 151

Gordon, Margaret, *4:* 147; *5:* 48-49; *9:* 79

Gorecka-Egan, Erica, *18:* 35

Gorey, Edward, *1:* 60-61; *13:* 169; *18:* 192; *20:* 201; *29:* 90, 91, 92-93, 94, 95, 96, 97, 98, 99, 100; *30:* 129; *32:* 90; *34:* 200. *See also* Dowdy, Mrs. Regera

Gorsline, Douglas, *1:* 98; *6:* 13; *11:* 113; *13:* 104; *15:* 14; *28:* 117, 118; *YABC 1:* 15

Gosner, Kenneth, *5:* 135

Gotlieb, Jules, *6:* 127

Gough, Philip, *23:* 47; *45:* 90

Govern, Elaine R., *26:* 94

Grabianski, *20:* 144

Grabiański, Janusz, *39:* 92, 93, 94, 95

Graboff, Abner, *35:* 103, 104

Graham, A. B., *11:* 61

Graham, L., *7:* 108

Graham, Margaret Bloy, *11:* 120; *18:* 305, 307

Grahame-Johnstone, Anne, *13:* 61

Grahame-Johnstone, Janet, *13:* 61

Grainger, Sam, *42:* 95

Gramatky, Hardie, *1:* 107; *30:* 116, 119, 120, 122, 123

Grandville, J. J., *45:* 81, 82, 83, 84, 85, 86, 87, 88

Granger, Paul, *39:* 153

Grant, Gordon, *17:* 230, 234; *25:* 123, 124, 125, 126; *YABC 1:* 164

Grant, (Alice) Leigh, *10:* 52; *15:* 131; *20:* 20; *26:* 119

Graves, Elizabeth, *45:* 101

Gray, Harold, *33:* 87, 88

Gray, Reginald, *6:* 69

Green, Eileen, *6:* 97

Green, Michael, *32:* 216

Greenaway, Kate, *17:* 275; *24:* 180; *26:* 107; *41:* 222, 232; *YABC 1:* 88-89; *YABC 2:* 131, 133, 136, 138-139, 141

Greenwald, Sheila, *1:* 34; *3:* 99; *8:* 72

Gregorian, Joyce Ballou, *30:* 125

Gregory, Frank M., *29:* 107

Greiffenhagen, Maurice, *16:* 137; *27:* 57; *YABC 2:* 288

Greiner, Robert, *6:* 86

Gretter, J. Clemens, *31:* 134

Gretz, Susanna, *7:* 114

Gretzer, John, *1:* 54; *3:* 26; *4:* 162; *7:* 125; *16:* 247; *18:* 117; *28:* 66; *30:* 85, 211; *33:* 235

Grey Owl, *24:* 41

Gri, *25:* 90

Grieder, Walter *9:* 84

Grifalconi, Ann, *2:* 126; *3:* 248; *11:* 18; *13:* 182

Griffin, Gillett Good, *26:* 96

Griffin, James, *30:* 166

Griffiths, Dave, *29:* 76

Gringhuis, Dirk, *6:* 98; *9:* 196

Gripe, Harald, *2:* 127

Grisha, *3:* 71

Gropper, William, *27:* 93; *37:* 193

Grose, Helen Mason, *YABC 1:* 260; *YABC 2:* 150

Grossman, Nancy, *24:* 130; *29:* 101

Grossman, Robert, *11:* 124

Groth, John, *15:* 79; *21:* 53, 54

Gruelle, Johnny, *35:* 107

Gschwind, William, *11:* 72

Guggenheim, Hans, *2:* 10; *3:* 37; *8:* 136

Guilbeau, Honoré, *22:* 69

Gundersheimer, Karen, *35:* 240

Gusman, Annie, *38:* 62

Gustafson, Scott, *34:* 111; *43:* 40

Guthrie, Robin, *20:* 122

Gwynne, Fred, *41:* 94, 95

Gyberg, Bo-Erik, *38:* 131

Haas, Irene, *17:* 77

Hader, Berta H., *16:* 126

Hader, Elmer S., *16:* 126

Hafner, Marylin, *22:* 196, 216; *24:* 44; *30:* 51; *35:* 95

Hague, Michael, *32:* 128

Halas, John, *29:* 41, 47, 48

Haldane, Roger, *13:* 76; *14:* 202

Hale, Irina, *26:* 97

Hale, Kathleen, *17:* 79

Haley, Gail E., *43:* 102, 103, 104, 105

Hall, Chuck, *30:* 189

Hall, Douglas, *15:* 184; *43:* 106, 107

Hall, H. Tom, *1:* 227; *30:* 210

Hall, Sydney P., *31:* 89

Hall, Vicki, *20:* 24

Hallinan, P. K., *39:* 98

Halpern, Joan, *10:* 25

Hamberger, John, *6:* 8; *8:* 32; *14:* 79; *34:* 136

Hamil, Tom, *14:* 80; *43:* 163

Hamilton, Bill and Associates, *26:* 215

Hamilton, Helen S., *2:* 238

Hamilton, J., *19:* 83, 85, 87

Hammond, Chris, *21:* 37

Hammond, Elizabeth, *5:* 36, 203

Hampshire, Michael, *5:* 187; *7:* 110-111

Hampson, Denman, *10:* 155; *15:* 130

Hampton, Blake, *41:* 244

Handforth, Thomas, *42:* 100, 101, 102, 103, 104, 105, 107

Handville, Robert, *1:* 89; *38:* 76; *45:* 108, 109

Hane, Roger, *17:* 239; *44:* 54

Haney, Elizabeth Mathieu, *34:* 84

Hanley, Catherine, *8:* 161

Hann, Jacquie, *19:* 144

Hannon, Mark, *38:* 37

Hanson, Joan, *8:* 76; *11:* 139

Hardy, David A., *9:* 96

Hardy, Paul, *YABC 2:* 245

Harlan, Jerry, *3:* 96

Harnischfeger, *18:* 121

Harper, Arthur, *YABC 2:* 121

Harrington, Richard, *5:* 81

Harris, Susan Yard, *42:* 121

Harrison, Florence, *20:* 150, 152

Harrison, Harry, *4:* 103

Harrison, Jack, *28:* 149

Hart, William, *13:* 72

Hartelius, Margaret, *10:* 24

Hartshorn, Ruth, *5:* 115; *11:* 129

Harvey, Gerry, *7:* 180

Hassall, Joan, *43:* 108, 109

Hassell, Hilton, *YABC 1:* 187

Hasselriis, Else, *18:* 87; *YABC 1:* 96

Hauman, Doris, *2:* 184; *29:* 58, 59; *32:* 85, 86, 87

Hauman, George, *2:* 184; *29:* 58, 59; *32:* 85, 86, 87

Hausherr, Rosmarie, *15:* 29

Hawkinson, John, *4:* 109; *7:* 83; *21:* 64

Hawkinson, Lucy, *21:* 64

Haxton, Elaine, 28: 131
Haydock, Robert, 4: 95
Hayes, Geoffrey, 26: 111; 44: 133
Haywood, Carolyn, 1: 112; 29: 104
Healy, Daty, 12: 143
Hearon, Dorothy, 34: 69
Hechtkopf, H., 11: 110
Hedderwick, Mairi, 30: 127; 32: 47;
    36: 104
Hefter, Richard, 28: 170; 31: 81, '82;
    33: 183
Heigh, James, 22: 98
Heighway, Richard, 25: 160
Heinly, John, 45: 113
Hellebrand, Nancy, 26: 57
Hellmuth, Jim, 38: 164
Helms, Georgeann, 33: 62
Helweg, Hans, 41: 118
Henderson, Keith, 35: 122
Henkes, Kevin, 43: 111
Henneberger, Robert, 1: 42; 2: 237;
    25: 83
Henriksen, Harold, 35: 26
Henry, Everett, 29: 191
Henry, Thomas, 5: 102
Hensel, 27: 119
Henstra, Friso, 8: 80; 36: 70; 40: 222;
    41: 250
Hepple, Norman, 28: 198
Herbert, Wally, 23: 101
Herbster, Mary Lee, 9: 33
Hergé. See Rémi, Georges
Hermanson, Dennis, 10: 55
Herrington, Roger, 3: 161
Heslop, Mike, 38: 60; 40: 130
Hess, Richard, 42: 31
Hester, Ronnie, 37: 85
Heustis, Louise L., 20: 28
Heyduck-Huth, Hilde, 8: 82
Heyer, Hermann, 20: 114, 115
Heyman, Ken, 8: 33; 34: 113
Hickling, P. B., 40: 165
Higginbottom, J. Winslow, 8: 170;
    29: 105, 106
Hildebrandt, Greg, 8: 191
Hildebrandt, Tim, 8: 191
Hilder, Rowland, 19: 207
Hill, Gregory, 35: 190
Hillier, Matthew, 45: 205
Himler, Ronald, 6: 114; 7: 162; 8: 17,
    84, 125; 14: 76; 19: 145; 26: 160;
    31: 43; 38: 116; 41: 44, 79;
    43: 52; 45: 120
Hinds, Bill, 37: 127, 130
Hiroshige, 25: 71
Hirsh, Marilyn, 7: 126
Hitz, Demi, 11: 135; 15: 245
Hnizdovsky, Jacques, 32: 96
Ho, Kwoncjan, 15: 132
Hoban, Lillian, 1: 114; 22: 157;
    26: 72; 29: 53; 40: 105, 107, 195;
    41: 80
Hoban, Tana, 22: 159
Hoberman, Norman, 5: 82
Hockerman, Dennis, 39: 22
Hodgell, P. C., 42: 114
Hodges, C. Walter, 2: 139; 11: 15;
    12: 25; 23: 34; 25: 96; 38: 165;
    44: 197; 45: 95; YABC 2: 62-63

Hodges, David, 9: 98
Hodgetts, Victoria, 43: 132
Hofbauer, Imre, 2: 162
Hoff, Syd, 9: 107; 10: 128; 33: 94
Hoffman, Rosekrans, 15: 133
Hoffman, Sanford, 38: 208
Hoffmann, Felix, 9: 109
Hofsinde, Robert, 21: 70
Hogan, Inez, 2: 141
Hogarth, Burne, 41: 58
Hogarth, Paul, 41: 102, 103, 104;
    YABC 1: 16
Hogarth, William, 42: 33
Hogenbyl, Jan, 1: 35
Hogner, Nils, 4: 122; 25: 144
Hogrogian, Nonny, 3: 221; 4: 106-107;
    5: 166; 7: 129; 15: 2; 16: 176;
    20: 154; 22: 146; 25: 217;
    27: 206; YABC 2: 84, 94
Hokusai, 25: 71
Holberg, Richard, 2: 51
Holdcroft, Tina, 38: 109
Holder, Heidi, 36: 99
Holiday, Henry, YABC 2: 107
Holl, F., 36: 91
Holland, Brad, 45: 59, 159
Holland, Janice, 18: 118
Holland, Marion, 6: 116
Holldobler, Turid, 26: 120
Holling, Holling C., 15: 136-137
Hollinger, Deanne, 12: 116
Holmes, B., 3: 82
Holmes, Bea, 7: 74; 24: 156; 31: 93
Holmgren, George Ellen, 45: 112
Holt, Norma, 44: 106
Holtan, Gene, 32: 192
Holz, Loretta, 17: 81
Homar, Lorenzo, 6: 2
Homer, Winslow, YABC 2: 87
Honigman, Marian, 3: 2
Honoré, Paul, 42: 77, 79, 81, 82
Hood, Susan, 12: 43
Hook, Frances, 26: 188; 27: 127
Hook, Jeff, 14: 137
Hook, Richard, 26: 188
Hoover, Carol A., 21: 77
Hoover, Russell, 12: 95; 17: 2;
    34: 156
Hoppin, Augustus, 34: 66
Horder, Margaret, 2: 108
Horen, Michael, 45: 121
Horvat, Laurel, 12: 201
Horvath, Ferdinand Kusati, 24: 176
Hotchkiss, De Wolfe, 20: 49
Hough, Charlotte, 9: 112; 13: 98;
    17: 83; 24: 195
Houlihan, Ray, 11: 214
Housman, Laurence, 25: 146, 147
Houston, James, 13: 107
How, W. E., 20: 47
Howard, Alan, 16: 80; 34: 58; 45: 114
Howard, J. N., 15: 234
Howard, John, 33: 179
Howard, Rob, 40: 161
Howe, Stephen, 1: 232
Howell, Pat, 15: 139
Howell, Troy, 23: 24; 31: 61; 36: 158;
    37: 184; 41: 76, 235
Howes, Charles, 22: 17

Hudnut, Robin, 14: 62
Huffaker, Sandy, 10: 56
Huffman, Joan, 13: 33
Huffman, Tom, 13: 180; 17: 212;
    21: 116; 24: 132; 33: 154; 38: 59;
    42: 147
Hughes, Arthur, 20: 148, 149, 150;
    33: 114, 148, 149
Hughes, David, 36: 197
Hughes, Shirley, 1: 20, 21; 7: 3;
    12: 217; 16: 163; 29: 154
Hülsmann, Eva, 16: 166
Hummel, Berta, 43: 137, 138, 139
Hummel, Lisl, 29: 109;
    YABC 2: 333-334
Humphrey, Henry, 16: 167
Humphreys, Graham, 25: 168
Hunt, James, 2: 143
Hurd, Clement, 2: 148, 149
Hurd, Peter; 24: 30, 31, YABC 2: 56
Hürlimann, Ruth, 32: 99
Hustler, Tom, 6: 105
Hutchins, Pat, 15: 142
Hutchinson, William M., 6: 3, 138
Hutchison, Paula, 23: 10
Hutton, Clarke, YABC 2: 335
Hutton, Kathryn, 35: 155
Hutton, Warwick, 20: 91
Huyette, Marcia, 29: 188
Hyman, Trina Schart, 1: 204; 2: 194;
    5: 153; 6: 106; 7: 138, 145; 8: 22;
    10: 196; 13: 96; 14: 114; 15: 204;
    16: 234; 20: 82; 22: 133; 24: 151;
    25: 79, 82; 26: 82; 29: 83; 31: 37,
    39; 34: 104; 38: 84, 100, 128;
    41: 49; 43: 146

Ichikawa, Satomi, 29: 152; 41: 52
Ide, Jacqueline, YABC 1: 39
Ilsley, Velma, 3: 1; 7: 55; 12: 109;
    37: 62; 38: 184
Inga, 1: 142
Ingraham, Erick, 21: 177
Innocenti, Roberto, 21: 123
Inoue, Yosuke, 24: 118
Ipcar, Dahlov, 1: 124-125
Irvin, Fred, 13: 166; 15: 143-144;
    27: 175
Irving, Jay, 45: 72
Irving, Laurence, 27: 50
Isaac, Joanne, 21: 76
Isadora, Rachel, 43: 159, 160
Ishmael, Woodi, 24: 111; 31: 99
Ives, Ruth, 15: 257

Jackson, Michael, 43: 42
Jacobs, Barbara, 9: 136
Jacobs, Lou, Jr., 9: 136; 15: 128
Jacques, Robin, 1: 70; 2: 1; 8: 46;
    9: 20; 15: 187; 19: 253; 32: 102,
    103, 104; 43: 184; YABC 1: 42
Jagr, Miloslav, 13: 197
Jakubowski, Charles, 14: 192
Jambor, Louis, YABC 1: 11
James, Derek, 35: 187; 44: 91

James, Gilbert, *YABC 1:* 43
James, Harold, *2:* 151; *3:* 62; *8:* 79; *29:* 113
James, Will, *19:* 150, 152, 153, 155, 163
Janosch. *See* Eckert, Horst
Jansson, Tove, *3:* 90; *41:* 106, 108, 109, 110, 111, 113, 114
Jaques, Faith, *7:* 11, 132-33; *21:* 83, 84
Jaques, Frances Lee, *29:* 224
Jauss, Anne Marie, *1:* 139; *3:* 34; *10:* 57, 119; *11:* 205; *23:* 194
Jeffers, Susan, *17:* 86-87; *25:* 164-165; *26:* 112
Jefferson, Louise E., *4:* 160
Jeruchim, Simon, *6:* 173; *15:* 250
Jeschke, Susan, *20:* 89; *39:* 161; *41:* 84; *42:* 120
Jessel, Camilla, *29:* 115
Joerns, Consuelo, *38:* 36; *44:* 94
John, Diana, *12:* 209
John, Helen, *1:* 215; *28:* 204
Johns, Jeanne, *24:* 114
Johnson, Bruce, *9:* 47
Johnson, Crockett. *See* Leisk, David
Johnson, D. William, *23:* 104
Johnson, Harper, *1:* 27; *2:* 33; *18:* 302; *19:* 61; *31:* 181; *44:* 46, 50, 95
Johnson, Ingrid, *37:* 118
Johnson, James David, *12:* 195
Johnson, James Ralph, *1:* 23, 127
Johnson, John E., *34:* 133
Johnson, Margaret S., *35:* 131
Johnson, Milton, *1:* 67; *2:* 71; *26:* 45; *31:* 107
Johnson, Pamela, *16:* 174
Johnson, William R., *38:* 91
Johnstone, Anne, *8:* 120; *36:* 89
Johnstone, Janet Grahame, *8:* 120; *36:* 89
Jones, Carol, *5:* 131
Jones, Elizabeth Orton, *18:* 124, 126, 128-129
Jones, Harold, *14:* 88
Jones, Jeff, *41:* 64
Jones, Laurian, *25:* 24, 27
Jones, Robert, *25:* 67
Jones, Wilfred, *35:* 115; *YABC 1:* 163
Joyner, Jerry, *34:* 138
Jucker, Sita, *5:* 93
Judkis, Jim, *37:* 38
Juhasz, Victor, *31:* 67
Jullian, Philippe, *24:* 206; *25:* 203
Jupo, Frank, *7:* 148-149
Justice, Martin, *34:* 72

Kahl, M. P., *37:* 83
Kakimoo, Kozo, *11:* 148
Kalin, Victor, *39:* 186
Kalmenoff, Matthew, *22:* 191
Kalow, Gisela, *32:* 105
Kamen, Gloria, *1:* 41; *9:* 119; *10:* 178; *35:* 157
Kandell, Alice, *35:* 133
Kane, Henry B., *14:* 90; *18:* 219-220
Kane, Robert, *18:* 131
Kappes, Alfred, *28:* 104

Karalus, Bob, *41:* 157
Karlin, Eugene, *10:* 63; *20:* 131
Kasuya, Masahiro, *41:* 206-207
Katona, Robert, *21:* 85; *24:* 126
Kauffer, E. McKnight, *33:* 103; *35:* 127
Kaufman, Angelika, *15:* 156
Kaufman, Joe, *33:* 119
Kaufman, John, *13:* 158
Kaufmann, John, *1:* 174; *4:* 159; *8:* 43, 1; *10:* 102; *18:* 133-134; *22:* 251
Kaye, Graham, *1:* 9
Kazalovski, Nata, *40:* 205
Keane, Bil, *4:* 135
Keats, Ezra Jack, *3:* 18, 105, 257; *14:* 101, 102; *33:* 129
Keegan, Marcia, *9:* 122; *32:* 93
Keely, John, *26:* 104
Keen, Eliot, *25:* 213
Keeping, Charles, *9:* 124, 185; *15:* 28, 134; *18:* 115; *44:* 194, 196
Keith, Eros, *4:* 98; *5:* 138; *31:* 29; *43:* 220
Kelen, Emery, *13:* 115
Keller, Arthur I., *26:* 106
Keller, Dick, *36:* 123, 125
Keller, Holly, *45:* 79
Keller, Ronald, *45:* 208
Kelley, True, *41:* 114, 115; *42:* 137
Kellogg, Steven, *8:* 96; *11:* 207; *14:* 130; *20:* 58; *29:* 140-141; *30:* 35; *41:* 141; *YABC 1:* 65, 73
Kelly, Walt, *18:* 136-141, 144-146, 148-149
Kemble, E. W., *34:* 75; *44:* 178; *YABC 2:* 54, 59
Kemp-Welsh, Lucy, *24:* 197
Kennedy, Paul Edward, *6:* 190; *8:* 132; *33:* 120
Kennedy, Richard, *3:* 93; *12:* 179; *44:* 193; *YABC 1:* 57
Kent, Jack, *24:* 136; *37:* 37; *40:* 81
Kent, Rockwell, *5:* 166; *6:* 129; *20:* 225, 226, 227, 229
Kepes, Juliet, *13:* 119
Kerr, Judity, *24:* 137
Kessler, Leonard, *1:* 108; *7:* 139; *14:* 107, 227; *22:* 101; *44:* 96
Kesteven, Peter, *35:* 189
Ketcham, Hank, *28:* 140, 141, 142
Kettelkamp, Larry, *2:* 164
Key, Alexander, *8:* 99
Kiakshuk, *8:* 59
Kiddell-Monroe, Joan, *19:* 201
Kidder, Harvey, *9:* 105
Kidwell, Carl, *43:* 145
Kieffer, Christa, *41:* 89
Kiff, Ken, *40:* 45
Kilbride, Robert, *37:* 100
Kimball, Yeffe, *23:* 116; *37:* 88
Kincade, Orin, *34:* 116
Kindred, Wendy, *7:* 151
King, Robin, *10:* 164-165
King, Tony, *39:* 121
Kingman, Dong, *16:* 287; *44:* 100, 102, 104
Kingsley, Charles, *YABC 2:* 182
Kipling, John Lockwood, *YABC 2:* 198

Kipling, Rudyard, *YABC 2:* 196
Kipniss, Robert, *29:* 59
Kirchhoff, Art, *28:* 136
Kirk, Ruth, *5:* 96
Kirk, Tim, *32:* 209, 211
Kirmse, Marguerite, *15:* 283; *18:* 153
Kirschner, Ruth, *22:* 154
Klapholz, Mel, *13:* 35
Kleinman, Zalman, *28:* 143
Kliban, B., *35:* 137, 138
Knight, Ann, *34:* 143
Knight, Christopher, *13:* 125
Knight, Hilary, *1:* 233; *3:* 21; *15:* 92, 158-159; *16:* 258-260; *18:* 235; *19:* 169; *35:* 242; *YABC 1:* 168-169, 172
Knotts, Howard, *20:* 4; *25:* 170; *36:* 163
Kobayashi, Ann, *39:* 58
Kocsis, J. C. *See* Paul, James
Koehn, Ilse, *34:* 198
Koering, Ursula, *3:* 28; *4:* 14; *44:* 53
Koerner, Henry. *See* Koerner, W.H.D.
Koerner, W.H.D., *14:* 216; *21:* 88, 89, 90, 91; *23:* 211
Koffler, Camilla, *36:* 113
Komoda, Kiyo, *9:* 128; *13:* 214
Konashevicha, V., *YABC 1:* 26
Konigsburg, E. L., *4:* 138
Korach, Mimi, *1:* 128-129; *2:* 52; *4:* 39; *5:* 159; *9:* 129; *10:* 21; *24:* 69
Koren, Edward, *5:* 100
Kossin, Sandy, *10:* 71; *23:* 105
Kostin, Andrej, *26:* 204
Kovacević, Zivojin, *13:* 247
Krahn, Fernando, *2:* 257; *34:* 206
Kramer, Anthony, *33:* 81
Kramer, Frank, *6:* 121
Krantz, Kathy, *35:* 83
Kraus, Robert, *13:* 217
Kredel, Fritz, *6:* 35; *17:* 93-96; *22:* 147; *24:* 175; *29:* 130; *35:* 77; *YABC 2:* 166, 300
Krementz, Jill, *17:* 98
Kresin, Robert, *23:* 19
Krush, Beth, *1:* 51, 85; *2:* 233; *4:* 115; *9:* 61; *10:* 191; *11:* 196; *18:* 164-165; *32:* 72; *37:* 203; *43:* 57
Krush, Joe, *2:* 233; *4:* 115; *9:* 61; *10:* 191; *11:* 196; *18:* 164-165; *32:* 72, 91; *37:* 203; *43:* 57
Kubinyi, Laszlo, *4:* 116; *6:* 113; *16:* 118; *17:* 100; *28:* 227; *30:* 172
Kuhn, Bob, *17:* 91; *35:* 235
Künstler, Mort, *10:* 73; *32:* 143
Kurchevsky, V., *34:* 61
Kurelek, William, *8:* 107
Kuriloff, Ron, *13:* 19
Kuskin, Karla, *2:* 170
Kutzer, Ernst, *19:* 249

LaBlanc, André, *24:* 146
Laboccetta, Mario, *27:* 120
Laceky, Adam, *32:* 121
La Croix, *YABC 2:* 4
Laimgruber, Monika, *11:* 153

Laite, Gordon, *1:* 130-131; *8:* 209; *31:* 113; *40:* 63
Lamb, Jim, *10:* 117
Lambert, J. K., *38:* 129; *39:* 24
Lambert, Saul, *23:* 112; *33:* 107
Lambo, Don, *6:* 156; *35:* 115; *36:* 146
Landa, Peter, *11:* 95; *13:* 177
Landau, Jacob, *38:* 111
Landshoff, Ursula, *13:* 124
Lane, John, *15:* 176-177; *30:* 146
Lane, John R., *8:* 145
Lang, Jerry, *18:* 295
Langner, Nola, *8:* 110; *42:* 36
Lantz, Paul, *1:* 82, 102; *27:* 88; *34:* 102; *45:* 123
Larrecq, John, *44:* 108
Larsen, Suzanne, *1:* 13
Larsson, Carl, *35:* 144, 145, 146, 147, 148-149, 150, 152, 153, 154
Larsson, Karl, *19:* 177
La Rue, Michael D., *13:* 215
Lasker, Joe, *7:* 186-187; *14:* 55; *38:* 115; *39:* 47
Latham, Barbara, *16:* 188-189; *43:* 71
Lathrop, Dorothy, *14:* 117, 118-119; *15:* 109; *16:* 78-79, 81; *32:* 201, 203; *33:* 112; *YABC 2:* 301
Lattimore, Eleanor Frances, *7:* 156
Lauden, Claire, *16:* 173
Lauden, George, Jr., *16:* 173
Laune, Paul, *2:* 235; *34:* 31
Lavis, Stephen, *43:* 143
Lawrence, John, *25:* 131; *30:* 141; *44:* 198, 200
Lawrence, Stephen, *20:* 195
Lawson, Carol, *6:* 38; *42:* 93, 131
Lawson, George, *17:* 280
Lawson, Robert, *5:* 26; *6:* 94; *13:* 39; *16:* 11; *20:* 100, 102, 103; *YABC 2:* 222, 224-225, 227-235, 237-241
Lazare, Jerry, *44:* 109
Lazarevich, Mila, *17:* 118
Lazarus, Keo Felker, *21:* 94
Lazzaro, Victor, *11:* 126
Lea, Tom, *43:* 72, 74
Leacroft, Richard, *6:* 140
Leaf, Munro, *20:* 99
Leander, Patricia, *23:* 27
Lear, Edward, *18:* 183-185
Lebenson, Richard, *6:* 209; *7:* 76; *23:* 145; *44:* 191
Le Cain, Errol, *6:* 141; *9:* 3; *22:* 142; *25:* 198; *28:* 173
Lee, Doris, *13:* 246; *32:* 183; *44:* 111
Lee, Manning de V., *2:* 200; *17:* 12; *27:* 87; *37:* 102, 103, 104; *YABC 2:* 304
Lee, Robert J., *3:* 97
Leech, John, *15:* 59
Leeman, Michael, *44:* 157
Lees, Harry, *6:* 112
Legrand, Edy, *18:* 89, 93
Lehrman, Rosalie, *2:* 180
Leichman, Seymour, *5:* 107
Leighton, Clare, *25:* 130; *33:* 168; *37:* 105, 106, 108, 109
Leisk, David, *1:* 140-141; *11:* 54; *30:* 137, 142, 143, 144

Leloir, Maurice, *18:* 77, 80, 83, 99
Lemke, Horst, *14:* 98; *38:* 117, 118, 119
Lemke, R. W., *42:* 162
Lemon, David Gwynne, *9:* 1
Lenski, Lois, *1:* 144; *26:* 135, 137, 139, 141
Lent, Blair, *1:* 116-117; *2:* 174; *3:* 206-207; *7:* 168-169; *34:* 62
Lerner, Sharon, *11:* 157; *22:* 56
Leslie, Cecil, *19:* 244
Levai, Blaise, *39:* 130
Levin, Ted, *12:* 148
Levine, David, *43:* 147, 149, 150, 151, 152
Levit, Herschel, *24:* 223
Levy, Jessica Ann, *19:* 225; *39:* 191
Lewin, Betsy, *32:* 114
Lewin, Ted, *4:* 77; *8:* 168; *20:* 110; *21:* 99, 100; *27:* 110; *28:* 96, 97; *31:* 49; *45:* 55
Lewis, Allen, *15:* 112
Leydon, Rita Flodén, *21:* 101
Lieblich, Irene, *22:* 173; *27:* 209, 214
Liese, Charles, *4:* 222
Lightfoot, Norman R., *45:* 47
Lignell, Lois, *37:* 114
Lilly, Charles, *8:* 73; *20:* 127
Lilly, Ken, *37:* 224
Lim, John, *43:* 153
Lincoln, Patricia Henderson, *27:* 27
Lindberg, Howard, *10:* 123; *16:* 190
Linden, Seymour, *18:* 200-201; *43:* 140
Linder, Richard, *27:* 119
Lindman, Maj, *43:* 154
Lindsay, Vachel, *40:* 118
Line, Les, *27:* 143
Linell. *See* Smith, Linell
Lionni, Leo, *8:* 115
Lipinsky, Lino, *2:* 156; *22:* 175
Lippman, Peter, *8:* 31; *31:* 119, 120, 160
Lisker, Sonia O., *16:* 274; *31:* 31; *44:* 113, 114
Lissim, Simon, *17:* 138
Little, Harold, *16:* 72
Little, Mary E., *28:* 146
Lively, Lorna, *19:* 216
Llerena, Carlos Antonio, *19:* 181
Lloyd, Errol, *11:* 39; *22:* 178
Lo, Koon-chiu, *7:* 134
Lobel, Anita, *6:* 87; *9:* 141; *18:* 248
Lobel, Arnold, *1:* 188-189; *5:* 12; *6:* 147; *7:* 167, 209; *18:* 190-191; *25:* 39, 43; *27:* 40; *29:* 174
Loefgren, Ulf, *3:* 108
Loescher, Ann, *20:* 108
Loescher, Gil, *20:* 108
Lofting, Hugh, *15:* 182-183
Loh, George, *38:* 88
Lonette, Reisie, *11:* 211; *12:* 168; *13:* 56; *36:* 122; *43:* 155
Long, Sally, *42:* 184
Longtemps, Ken, *17:* 123; *29:* 221
Looser, Heinz, *YABC 2:* 208
Lopshire, Robert, *6:* 149; *21:* 117; *34:* 166
Lord, John Vernon, *21:* 104; *23:* 25

Lorenz, Al, *40:* 146
Loretta, Sister Mary, *33:* 73
Lorraine, Walter H., *3:* 110; *4:* 123; *16:* 192
Loss, Joan, *11:* 163
Louderback, Walt, *YABC 1:* 164
Lousada, Sandra, *40:* 138
Low, Joseph, *14:* 124, 125; *18:* 68; *19:* 194; *31:* 166
Lowenheim, Alfred, *13:* 65-66
Lowitz, Anson, *17:* 124; *18:* 215
Lowrey, Jo, *8:* 133
Lubell, Winifred, *1:* 207; *3:* 15; *6:* 151
Lubin, Leonard B., *19:* 224; *36:* 79, 80; *45:* 128, 129, 131, 132, 133, 134, 135, 136, 137, 139, 140, 141; *YABC 2:* 96
Ludwig, Helen, *33:* 144, 145
Lufkin, Raymond, *38:* 138; *44:* 48
Luhrs, Henry, *7:* 123; *11:* 120
Lupo, Dom, *4:* 204
Lustig, Loretta, *30:* 186
Lydecker, Laura, *21:* 113; *42:* 53
Lynch, Charles, *16:* 33
Lynch, Marietta, *29:* 137; *30:* 171
Lyon, Elinor, *6:* 154
Lyon, Fred, *14:* 16
Lyons, Oren, *8:* 193
Lyster, Michael, *26:* 41

Maas, Dorothy, *6:* 175
Macdonald, Alister, *21:* 55
MacDonald, Norman, *13:* 99
MacDonald, Roberta, *19:* 237
Macguire, Robert Reid, *18:* 67
Machetanz, Fredrick, *34:* 147, 148
MacInnes, Ian, *35:* 59
MacIntyre, Elisabeth, *17:* 127-128
Mack, Stan, *17:* 129
Mackay, Donald, *17:* 60
MacKaye, Arvia, *32:* 119
MacKenzie, Garry, *33:* 159
Mackinlay, Miguel, *27:* 22
MacKinstry, Elizabeth, *15:* 110; *42:* 139, 140, 141, 142, 143, 144, 145
Maclise, Daniel, *YABC 2:* 257
Madden, Don, *3:* 112-113; *4:* 33, 108, 155; *7:* 193; *YABC 2:* 211
Maddison, Angela Mary, *10:* 83
Maestro, Giulio, *8:* 124; *12:* 17; *13:* 108; *25:* 182
Magnuson, Diana, *28:* 102; *34:* 190; *41:* 175
Maguire, Sheila, *41:* 100
Mahony, Will, *37:* 120
Mahood, Kenneth, *24:* 141
Maik, Henri, *9:* 102
Maisto, Carol, *29:* 87
Maitland, Antony, *1:* 100, 176; *8:* 41; *17:* 246; *24:* 46; *25:* 177, 178; *32:* 74
Makie, Pam, *37:* 117
Malvern, Corinne, *2:* 13; *34:* 148, 149
Mandelbaum, Ira, *31:* 115
Manet, Edouard, *23:* 170
Mangurian, David, *14:* 133
Manham, Allan, *42:* 109

Manniche, Lise, *31:* 121
Manning, Samuel F., *5:* 75
Maraja, *15:* 86; *YABC 1:* 28; *YABC 2:* 115
Marcellino, Fred, *20:* 125; *34:* 222
Marchesi, Stephen, *34:* 140
Marchiori, Carlos, *14:* 60
Margules, Gabriele, *21:* 120
Mariana. *See* Foster, Marian Curtis
Marino, Dorothy, *6:* 37; *14:* 135
Markham, R. L., *17:* 240
Marokvia, Artur, *31:* 122
Marriott, Pat, *30:* 30; *34:* 39; *35:* 164, 165, 166; *44:* 170
Mars, W. T., *1:* 161; *3:* 115; *4:* 208, 225; *5:* 92, 105, 186; *8:* 214; *9:* 12; *13:* 121; *27:* 151; *31:* 180; *38:* 102
Marsh, Christine, *3:* 164
Marsh, Reginald, *17:* 5; *19:* 89; *22:* 90, 96
Marshall, Anthony D., *18:* 216
Marshall, James, *6:* 160; *40:* 221; *42:* 24, 25, 29
Martin, David Stone, *23:* 232
Martin, Fletcher, *18:* 213; *23:* 151
Martin, René, *7:* 144; *42:* 148, 149, 150
Martin, Ron, *32:* 81
Martin, Stefan, *8:* 68; *32:* 124, 126
Martinez, John, *6:* 113
Marx, Robert F., *24:* 143
Masefield, Judith, *19:* 208, 209
Mason, George F., *14:* 139
Massie, Diane Redfield, *16:* 194
Massie, Kim, *31:* 43
Mathieu, Joseph, *14:* 33; *39:* 206; *43:* 167
Matsubara, Naoko, *12:* 121
Matsuda, Shizu, *13:* 167
Matte, L'Enc, *22:* 183
Mattelson, Marvin, *36:* 50, 51
Matthews, F. Leslie, *4:* 216
Matulay, Laszlo, *5:* 18; *43:* 168
Matus, Greta, *12:* 142
Mauldin, Bill, *27:* 23
Mawicke, Tran, *9:* 137; *15:* 191
Max, Peter, *45:* 146, 147, 148-149, 150
Maxie, Betty, *40:* 135
Maxwell, John Alan, *1:* 148
Mayan, Earl, *7:* 193
Mayer, Marianna, *32:* 132
Mayer, Mercer, *11:* 192; *16:* 195-196; *20:* 55, 57; *32:* 129, 130, 132, 133, 134; *41:* 144, 248, 252
Mayhew, Richard, *3:* 106
Mayo, Gretchen, *38:* 81
Mays, Victor, *5:* 127; *8:* 45, 153; *14:* 245; *23:* 50; *34:* 155; *40:* 79; *45:* 158
Mazza, Adriana Saviozzi, *19:* 215
Mazzetti, Alan, *45:* 210
McBride, Angus, *28:* 49
McBride, Will, *30:* 110
McCaffery, Janet, *38:* 145
McCann, Gerald, *3:* 50; *4:* 94; *7:* 54; *41:* 121

McCay, Winsor, *41:* 124, 126, 128-129, 130-131
McClary, Nelson, *1:* 111
McClintock, Theodore, *14:* 141
McCloskey, Robert, *1:* 184-185; *2:* 186-187; *17:* 209; *39:* 139, 140, 141, 142, 143, 146, 147, 148
McClung, Robert, *2:* 189
McClure, Gillian, *31:* 132
McConnel, Jerry, *31:* 75, 187
McCormick, A. D., *35:* 119
McCormick, Dell J., *19:* 216
McCrady, Lady, *16:* 198; *39:* 127
McCrea, James, *3:* 122; *33:* 216
McCrea, Ruth, *3:* 122; *27:* 102; *33:* 216
McCully, Emily, *2:* 89; *4:* 120-121, 146, 197; *5:* 2, 129; *7:* 191; *11:* 122; *15:* 210; *33:* 23; *35:* 244; *37:* 122; *39:* 88; *40:* 103
McCurdy, Michael, *13:* 153; *24:* 85
McDermott, Beverly Brodsky, *11:* 180
McDermott, Gerald, *16:* 201
McDonald, Jill, *13:* 155; *26:* 128
McDonald, Ralph J., *5:* 123, 195
McDonough, Don, *10:* 163
McEntee, Dorothy, *37:* 124
McFall, Christie, *12:* 144
McGee, Barbara, *6:* 165
McGregor, Malcolm, *23:* 27
McHugh, Tom, *23:* 64
McIntosh, Jon, *42:* 56
McKay, Donald, *2:* 118; *32:* 157; *45:* 151, 152
McKeating, Eileen, *44:* 58
McKee, David, *10:* 48; *21:* 9
McKie, Roy, *7:* 44
McKillip, Kathy, *30:* 153
McKinney, Ena, *26:* 39
McLachlan, Edward, *5:* 89
McLean, Sammis, *32:* 197
McMahon, Robert, *36:* 155
McMillan, Bruce, *22:* 184
McMullan, James, *40:* 33
McNaught, Harry, *12:* 80; *32:* 136
McNaughton, Colin, *39:* 149; *40:* 108
McNicholas, Maureen, *38:* 148
McPhail, David, *14:* 105; *23:* 135; *37:* 217, 218, 220, 221
McPhee, Richard B., *41:* 133
McQueen, Lucinda, *28:* 149; *41:* 249
McVay, Tracy, *11:* 68
McVicker, Charles, *39:* 150
Mead, Ben Carlton, *43:* 75
Mecray, John, *33:* 62
Meddaugh, Susan, *20:* 42; *29:* 143; *41:* 241
Melo, John, *16:* 285
Menasco, Milton, *43:* 85
Mendelssohn, Felix, *19:* 170
Meng, Heinz, *13:* 158
Mero, Lee, *34:* 68
Merrill, Frank T., *16:* 147; *19:* 71; *YABC 1:* 226, 229, 273
Meryman, Hope, *27:* 41
Meryweather, Jack, *10:* 179
Meth, Harold, *24:* 203
Meyer, Herbert, *19:* 189
Meyer, Renate, *6:* 170

Meyers, Bob, *11:* 136
Meynell, Louis, *37:* 76
Micale, Albert, *2:* 65; *22:* 185
Middleton-Sandford, Betty, *2:* 125
Mieke, Anne, *45:* 74
Mighell, Patricia, *43:* 134
Mikolaycak, Charles, *9:* 144; *12:* 101; *13:* 212; *21:* 121; *22:* 168; *30:* 187; *34:* 103, 150; *37:* 183; *43:* 179; *44:* 90
Miles, Jennifer, *17:* 278
Milhous, Katherine, *15:* 193; *17:* 51
Millais, John E., *22:* 230, 231
Millar, H. R., *YABC 1:* 194-195, 203
Millard, C. E., *28:* 186
Miller, Don, *15:* 195; *16:* 71; *20:* 106; *31:* 178
Miller, Edna, *29:* 148
Miller, Frank J., *25:* 94
Miller, Grambs, *18:* 38; *23:* 16
Miller, Jane, *15:* 196
Miller, Marcia, *13:* 233
Miller, Marilyn, *1:* 87; *31:* 69; *33:* 157
Miller, Mitchell, *28:* 183; *34:* 207
Miller, Shane, *5:* 140
Mills, Yaroslava Surmach, *35:* 169, 170
Minor, Wendell, *39:* 188
Mitsuhashi, Yoko, *45:* 153
Miyake, Yoshi, *38:* 141
Mizumura, Kazue, *10:* 143; *18:* 223; *36:* 159
Mochi, Ugo, *8:* 122; *38:* 150
Modell, Frank, *39:* 152
Mohr, Nicholasa, *8:* 139
Montresor, Beni, *2:* 91; *3:* 138; *38:* 152, 153, 154, 155, 156-157, 158, 159, 160
Moon, Carl, *25:* 183, 184, 185
Moon, Eliza, *14:* 40
Moon, Ivan, *22:* 39; *38:* 140
Moore, Agnes Kay Randall, *43:* 187
Moore, Mary, *29:* 160
Mora, Raul Mina, *20:* 41
Mordvinoff, Nicolas, *15:* 179
Morgan, Tom, *42:* 157
Morrill, Les, *42:* 127
Morrill, Leslie, *18:* 218; *29:* 177; *33:* 84; *38:* 147; *44:* 93
Morrison, Bill, *42:* 116
Morrow, Gray, *2:* 64; *5:* 200; *10:* 103, 114; *14:* 175
Morton, Lee Jack, *32:* 140
Morton, Marian, *3:* 185
Moses, Grandma, *18:* 228
Moskof, Martin Stephen, *27:* 152
Moss, Donald, *11:* 184
Moss, Geoffrey, *32:* 198
Moyers, William, *21:* 65
Moyler, Alan, *36:* 142
Mozley, Charles, *9:* 87; *20:* 176, 192, 193; *22:* 228; *25:* 205; *33:* 150; *43:* 170, 171, 172, 173, 174; *YABC 2:* 89
Mueller, Hans Alexander, *26:* 64; *27:* 52, 53
Mugnaini, Joseph, *11:* 35; *27:* 52, 53; *35:* 62
Müller, Jörg, *35:* 215

Muller, Steven, *32:* 167
Mullins, Edward S., *10:* 101
Munari, Bruno, *15:* 200
Munowitz, Ken, *14:* 148
Muñoz, William, *42:* 160
Munsinger, Lynn, *33:* 161
Munson, Russell, *13:* 9
Murphy, Bill, *5:* 138
Murphy, Jill, *37:* 142
Murr, Karl, *20:* 62
Murray, Ossie, *43:* 176
Mussino, Attilio, *29:* 131
Mutchler, Dwight, *1:* 25
Myers, Bernice, *9:* 147; *36:* 75
Myers, Lou, *11:* 2

Nachreiner, Tom, *29:* 182
Nakai, Michael, *30:* 217
Nakatani, Chiyoko, *12:* 124
Naso, John, *33:* 183
Nason, Thomas W., *14:* 68
Nast, Thomas, *21:* 29; *28:* 23
Natti, Susanna, *20:* 146; *32:* 141, 142;
    35: 178; *37:* 143
Navarra, Celeste Scala, *8:* 142
Naylor, Penelope, *10:* 104
Nebel, M., *45:* 154
Neebe, William, *7:* 93
Needler, Jerry, *12:* 93
Neel, Alice, *31:* 23
Negri, Rocco, *3:* 213; *5:* 67; *6:* 91,
    108; *12:* 159
Neill, John R., *18:* 8, 10-11, 21, 30
Ness, Evaline, *1:* 164-165; *2:* 39; *3:* 8;
    10: 147; *12:* 53; *26:* 150, 151,
    152, 153
Neville, Vera, *2:* 182
Newberry, Clare Turlay, *1.* 170
Newfeld, Frank, *14:* 121; *26:* 154
Newman, Ann, *43:* 90
Newsom, Carol, *40:* 159; *44:* 60
Ng, Michael, *29:* 171
Nicholson, William, *15:* 33-34; *16:* 48
Nicklaus, Carol, *45:* 194
Nickless, Will, *16:* 139
Nicolas, *17:* 130, 132-133;
    YABC 2: 215
Niebrugge, Jane, *6:* 118
Nielsen, Jon, *6:* 100; *24:* 202
Nielsen, Kay, *15:* 7; *16:* 211-213, 215,
    217; *22:* 143; *YABC 1:* 32-33
Niland, Deborah, *25:* 191; *27:* 156
Niland, Kilmeny, *25:* 191
Ninon, *1:* 5; *38:* 101, 103, 108
Nissen, Rie, *44:* 35
Nixon, K., *14:* 152
Noble, Trinka Hakes, *39:* 162
Noguchi, Yoshie, *30:* 99
Nolan, Dennis, *42:* 163
Noonan, Julia, *4:* 163; *7:* 207; *25:* 151
Nordenskjold, Birgitta, *2:* 208
Norman, Mary, *36:* 138, 147
Norman, Michael, *12:* 117; *27:* 168
Numeroff, Laura Joffe, *28:* 161;
    30: 177
Nussbaumer, Paul, *16:* 219; *39:* 117
Nyce, Helene, *19:* 219
Nygren, Tord, *30:* 148

Oakley, Graham, *8:* 112; *30:* 164, 165
Oakley, Thornton, *YABC 2:* 189
Obligado, Lilian, *2:* 28, 66-67; *6:* 30;
    14: 179; *15:* 103; *25:* 84
Obrant, Susan, *11:* 186
O'Brien, John, *41:* 253
Odell, Carole, *35:* 47
O'Donohue, Thomas, *40:* 89
Oechsli, Kelly, *5:* 144-145; *7:* 115;
    8: 83, 183; *13:* 117; *20:* 94
Offen, Hilda, *42:* 207
Ogden, Bill, *42:* 59
Ogg, Oscar, *33:* 34
Ohlsson, Ib, *4:* 152; *7:* 57; *10:* 20;
    11: 90; *19:* 217; *41:* 246
Ohtomo, Yasuo, *37:* 146; *39:* 212, 213
O'Kelley, Mattie Lou, *36:* 150
Oliver, Jenni, *23:* 121; *35:* 112
Olschewski, Alfred, *7:* 172
Olsen, Ib Spang, *6:* 178-179
Olugebefola, Ademola, *15:* 205
O'Neil, Dan IV, *7:* 176
O'Neill, Jean, *22:* 146
O'Neill, Steve, *21:* 118
Ono, Chiyo, *7:* 97
Orbaan, Albert, *2:* 31; *5:* 65, 171;
    9: 8; *14:* 241; *20:* 109
Orbach, Ruth, *21:* 112
Orfe, Joan, *20:* 81
Ormsby, Virginia H., *11:* 187
Orozco, José Clemente, *9:* 177
Orr, Forrest W., *23:* 9
Orr, N., *19:* 70
Osborne, Billie Jean, *35:* 209
Osmond, Edward, *10:* 111
O'Sullivan, Tom, *3:* 176; *4:* 55
Otto, Svend, *22:* 130, 141
Oudry, J. B., *18:* 167
Oughton, Taylor, *5:* 23
Övereng, Johannes, *44:* 36
Overlie, George, *11:* 156
Owens, Carl, *2:* 35; *23:* 521
Owens, Gail, *10:* 170; *12:* 157; *19:* 16;
    22: 70; *25:* 81; *28:* 203, 205;
    32: 221, 222; *36:* 132
Oxenbury, Helen, *3:* 150-151; *24:* 81

Padgett, Jim, *12:* 165
Page, Homer, *14:* 145
Paget, Sidney, *24:* 90, 91, 93, 95, 97
Pak, *12:* 76
Palazzo, Tony, *3:* 152-153
Palladini, David, *4:* 113; *40:* 176, 177,
    178-179, 181, 224-225
Pallarito, Don, *43:* 36
Palmer, Heidi, *15:* 207; *29:* 102
Palmer, Jan, *42:* 153
Palmer, Juliette, *6:* 89; *15:* 208
Palmer, Lemuel, *17:* 25, 29
Palmquist, Eric, *38:* 133
Panesis, Nicholas, *3:* 127
Papas, William, *11:* 223
Papin, Joseph, *26:* 113
Papish, Robin Lloyd, *10:* 80
Paradis, Susan, *40:* 216
Paraquin, Charles H., *18:* 166
Paris, Peter, *31:* 127
Park, Seho, *39:* 110

Park, W. B., *22:* 189
Parker, Lewis, *2:* 179
Parker, Nancy Winslow, *10:* 113;
    22: 164; *28:* 47, 144
Parker, Robert, *4:* 161; *5:* 74; *9:* 136;
    29: 39
Parker, Robert Andrew, *11:* 81;
    29: 186; *39:* 165; *40:* 25; *41:* 78;
    42: 123; *43:* 144
Parks, Gordon, Jr., *33:* 228
Parnall, Peter, *5:* 137; *16:* 221; *24:* 70;
    40: 78
Parnall, Virginia, *40:* 78
Parrish, Anne, *27:* 159, 160
Parrish, Dillwyn, *27:* 159
Parrish, Maxfield, *14:* 160, 161, 164,
    165; *16:* 109; *18:* 12-13;
    YABC 1: 149, 152, 267;
    YABC 2: 146, 149
Parry, David, *26:* 156
Parry, Marian, *13:* 176; *19:* 179
Partch, Virgil, *45:* 163, 165
Pascal, David, *14:* 174
Pasquier, J. A., *16:* 91
Paterson, Diane, *13:* 116; *39:* 163
Paterson, Helen, *16:* 93
Paton, Jane, *15:* 271; *35:* 176
Patterson, Robert, *25:* 118
Paul, James, *4:* 130; *23:* 161
Paull, Grace, *24:* 157
Payne, Joan Balfour, *1:* 118
Payson, Dale, *7:* 34; *9:* 151; *20:* 140;
    37: 22
Payzant, Charles, *21:* 147
Peake, Mervyn, *22:* 136, 149; *23:* 162,
    163, 164; *YABC 2:* 307
Pearson, Larry, *38:* 225
Peat, Fern B., *16:* 115
Peck, Anne Merriman, *18:* 241;
    24: 155
Pederson, Sharleen, *12:* 92
Pedersen, Vilhelm, *YABC 1:* 40
Peek, Merle, *39:* 168
Peet, Bill, *2:* 203; *41:* 159, 160, 161,
    162, 163
Peltier, Leslie C., *13:* 178
Pendle, Alexy, *7:* 159; *13:* 34;
    29: 161; *33:* 215
Pennington, Eunice, *27:* 162
Peppé, Mark, *28:* 142
Peppe, Rodney, *4:* 164-165
Perl, Susan, *2:* 98; *4:* 231; *5:* 44-45,
    118; *6:* 199; *8:* 137; *12:* 88;
    22: 193; *34:* 54-55; *YABC 1:* 176
Perry, Patricia, *29:* 137; *30:* 171
Perry, Roger, *27:* 163
Pesek, Ludek, *15:* 237
Petersham, Maud, *17:* 108, 147-153
Petersham, Miska, *17:* 108, 147-153
Peterson, R. F., *7:* 101
Peterson, Russell, *7:* 130
Petie, Haris, *2:* 3; *10:* 41, 118;
    11: 227; *12:* 70
Petrides, Heidrun, *19:* 223
Peyo, *40:* 56, 57
Peyton, K. M., *15:* 212
Pfeifer, Herman, *15:* 262
Phillips, Douglas, *1:* 19
Phillips, F. D., *6:* 202

Phillips, Thomas, *30:* 55
"Phiz." *See* Browne, Hablot K.
Piatti, Celestino, *16:* 223
Picarella, Joseph, *13:* 147
Pickard, Charles, *12:* 38; *18:* 203;
　36: 152
Picken, George A., *23:* 150
Pickens, David, *22:* 156
Pienkowski, Jan, *6:* 183; *30:* 32
Pimlott, John, *10:* 205
Pincus, Harriet, *4:* 186; *8:* 179;
　22: 148; *27:* 164, 165
Pinkney, Jerry, *8:* 218; *10:* 40;
　15: 276; *20:* 66; *24:* 121; *33:* 109;
　36: 222; *38:* 200; *41:* 165, 166,
　167, 168, 169, 170, 171, 173,
　174; *44:* 198
Pinkwater, Manus, *8:* 156
Pinto, Ralph, *10:* 131; *45:* 93
Pitz, Henry C., *4:* 168; *19:* 165;
　35: 128; *42:* 80; *YABC 2:* 95, 176
Pitzenberger, Lawrence J., *26:* 94
Plummer, William, *32:* 31
Pogány, Willy, *15:* 46, 49; *19:* 222,
　256; *25:* 214; *44:* 142, 143, 144,
　145, 146, 147, 148
Poirson, V. A., *26:* 89
Polgreen, John, *21:* 44
Politi, Leo, *1:* 178; *4:* 53; *21:* 48
Polonsky, Arthur, *34:* 168
Polseno, Jo, *1:* 53; *3:* 117; *5:* 114;
　17: 154; *20:* 87; *32:* 49; *41:* 245
Ponter, James, *5:* 204
Poortvliet, Rien, *6:* 212
Portal, Colette, *6:* 186; *11:* 203
Porter, George, *7:* 181
Potter, Beatrix, *YABC 1:* 208-210,
　212, 213
Potter, Miriam Clark, *3:* 162
Powers, Richard M., *1:* 230; *3:* 218;
　7: 194; *26:* 186
Powledge, Fred, *37:* 154
Pratt, Charles, *23:* 29
Price, Christine, *2:* 247; *3:* 163, 253;
　8: 166
Price, Edward, *33:* 34
Price, Garrett, *1:* 76; *2:* 42
Price, Hattie Longstreet, *17:* 13
Price, Norman, *YABC 1:* 129
Primavera, Elise, *26:* 95
Primrose, Jean, *36:* 109
Prince, Leonora E., *7:* 170
Prittie, Edwin J., *YABC 1:* 120
Provensen, Alice, *37:* 204, 215, 222
Provensen, Martin, *37:* 204, 215, 222
Pucci, Albert John, *44:* 154
Pudlo, *8:* 59
Purdy, Susan, *8:* 162
Puskas, James, *5:* 141
Pyk, Jan, *7:* 26; *38:* 123
Pyle, Howard, *16:* 225-228, 230-232,
　235; *24:* 27; *34:* 124, 125, 127,
　128

Quackenbush, Robert, *4:* 190; *6:* 166;
　7: 175, 178; *9:* 86; *11:* 65, 221;
　41: 154; *43:* 157

Quennell, Marjorie (Courtney),
　29: 163, 164
Quidor, John, *19:* 82
Quirk, Thomas, *12:* 81

Rackham, Arthur, *15:* 32, 78, 214-227;
　17: 105, 115; *18:* 233; *19:* 254;
　20: 151; *22:* 129, 131, 132, 133;
　23: 175; *24:* 161, 181; *26:* 91;
　32: 118; *YABC 1:* 25, 45, 55, 147;
　YABC 2: 103, 142, 173, 210
Rafilson, Sidney, *11:* 172
Raible, Alton, *1:* 202-203; *28:* 193;
　35: 181
Ramsey, James, *16:* 41
Rand, Paul, *6:* 188
Ransome, Arthur, *22:* 201
Rao, Anthony, *28:* 126
Raphael, Elaine, *23:* 192
Rappaport, Eva, *6:* 190
Raskin, Ellen, *2:* 208-209; *4:* 142;
　13: 183; *22:* 68; *29:* 139; *36:* 134;
　38: 173, 174, 175, 176, 177, 178,
　179, 180, 181
Ratzkin, Lawrence, *40:* 143
Rau, Margaret, *9:* 157
Raverat, Gwen, *YABC 1:* 152
Ravielli, Anthony, *1:* 198; *3:* 168;
　11: 143
Ray, Deborah, *8:* 164; *29:* 238
Ray, Ralph, *2:* 239; *5:* 73
Raymond, Larry, *31:* 108
Rayner, Mary, *22:* 207
Raynor, Dorka, *28:* 168
Raynor, Paul, *24:* 73
Razzi, James, *10:* 127
Read, Alexander D. "Sandy," *20:* 45
Reed, Tom, *34:* 171
Reid, Stephen, *19:* 213; *22:* 89
Reinertson, Barbara, *44:* 150
Reiniger, Lotte, *40:* 185
Reiss, John J., *23:* 193
Relf, Douglas, *3:* 63
Relyea, C. M., *16:* 29; *31:* 153
Rémi, Georges, *13:* 184
Remington, Frederic, *19:* 188; *41:* 178,
　179, 180, 181, 183, 184, 185,
　186, 187, 188
Renlie, Frank, *11:* 200
Reschofsky, Jean, *7:* 118
Réthi, Lili, *2:* 153; *36:* 156
Reusswig, William, *3:* 267
Rey, H. A., *1:* 182; *26:* 163, 164,
　166, 167, 169; *YABC 2:* 17
Reynolds, Doris, *5:* 71; *31:* 77
Rhead, Louis, *31:* 91
Rhodes, Andrew, *38:* 204
Ribbons, Ian, *3:* 10; *37:* 161; *40:* 76
Rice, Elizabeth, *2:* 53, 214
Rice, James, *22:* 210
Rice, Eve, *34:* 174, 175
Richards, George, *40:* 116, 119, 121;
　44: 179
Richards, Henry, *YABC 1:* 228, 231
Richardson, Ernest, *2:* 144
Richardson, Frederick, *18:* 27, 31
Richman, Hilda, *26:* 132
Richmond, George, *24:* 179

Rieniets, Judy King, *14:* 28
Riger, Bob, *2:* 166
Riley, Kenneth, *22:* 230
Ringi, Kjell, *12:* 171
Rios, Tere. *See* Versace, Marie
Ripper, Charles L., *3:* 175
Ritz, Karen, *41:* 117
Rivkin, Jay, *15:* 230
Rivoche, Paul, *45:* 125
Roach, Marilynne, *9:* 158
Robbin, Jodi, *44:* 156, 159
Robbins, Frank, *42:* 167
Roberts, Cliff, *4:* 126
Roberts, Doreen, *4:* 230; *28:* 105
Roberts, Jim, *22:* 166; *23:* 69; *31:* 110
Roberts, W., *22:* 2, 3
Robinson, Charles, *3:* 53; *5:* 14;
　6: 193; *7:* 150; *7:* 183; *8:* 38;
　9: 81; *13:* 188; *14:* 248-249;
　23: 149; *26:* 115; *27:* 48; *28:* 191;
　32: 28; *35:* 210; *36:* 37
Robinson, Charles [1870-1937],
　17: 157, 171-173, 175-176;
　24: 207; *25:* 204;
　YABC 2: 308-310, 331
Robinson, Jerry, *3:* 262
Robinson, Joan G., *7:* 184
Robinson, T. H., *17:* 179, 181-183;
　29: 254
Robinson, W. Heath, *17:* 185, 187,
　189, 191, 193, 195, 197, 199,
　202; *23:* 167; *25:* 194; *29:* 150;
　YABC 1: 44; *YABC 2:* 183
Roche, Christine, *41:* 98
Rocker, Fermin, *7:* 34; *13:* 21; *31:* 40;
　40: 190, 191
Rockwell, Anne, *5:* 147; *33:* 171, 173
Rockwell, Gail, *7:* 186
Rockwell, Harlow, *33:* 171, 173, 175
Rockwell, Norman, *23:* 39, 196, 197,
　199, 200, 203, 204, 207; *41:* 140,
　143; *YABC 2:* 60
Rodegast, Roland, *43:* 100
Rodriguez, Joel, *16:* 65
Roever, J. M., *4:* 119; *26:* 170
Roffey, Maureen, *33:* 142, 176, 177
Rogers, Carol, *2:* 262; *6:* 164; *26:* 129
Rogers, Frances, *10:* 130
Rogers, Walter S., *31:* 135, 138
Rogers, William A., *15:* 151, 153-154;
　33: 35
Rojankovsky, Feodor, *6:* 134, 136;
　10: 183; *21:* 128, 129, 130;
　25: 110; *28:* 42
Rorer, Abigail, *43:* 222
Rosamilia, Patricia, *36:* 120
Rose, Carl, *5:* 62
Rose, David S., *29:* 109
Rosenblum, Richard, *11:* 202; *18:* 18
Rosier, Lydia, *16:* 236; *20:* 104;
　21: 109; *22:* 125; *30:* 151, 158;
　42: 128; *45:* 214
Ross. *See* Thomson, Ross
Ross, Clare, *3:* 123; *21:* 45
Ross, Dave, *32:* 152
Ross, Herbert, *37:* 78
Ross, John, *3:* 123; *21:* 45
Ross, Johnny, *32:* 190
Ross, Tony, *17:* 204

Rossetti, Dante Gabriel, *20:* 151, 153
Roth, Arnold, *4:* 238; *21:* 133
Rotondo, Pat, *32:* 158
Roughsey, Dick, *35:* 186
Rouille, M., *11:* 96
Rounds, Glen, *8:* 173; *9:* 171; *12:* 56; *32:* 194; *40:* 230; *YABC 1:* 1-3
Rowe, Gavin, *27:* 144
Rowell, Kenneth, *40:* 72
Roy, Jeroo, *27:* 229; *36:* 110
Rubel, Nicole, *18:* 255; *20:* 59
Rubel, Reina, *33:* 217
Rud, Borghild, *6:* 15
Rudolph, Norman Guthrie, *17:* 13
Rue, Leonard Lee III, *37:* 164
Ruffins, Reynold, *10:* 134-135; *41:* 191, 192-193, 194-195, 196
Ruhlin, Roger, *34:* 44
Ruse, Margaret, *24:* 155
Rush, Peter, *42:* 75
Russell, E. B., *18:* 177, 182
Russo, Susan, *30:* 182; *36:* 144
Ruth, Rod, *9:* 161
Rutherford, Meg, *25:* 174; *34:* 178, 179
Rutland, Jonathan, *31:* 126
Ryden, Hope, *8:* 176
Rymer, Alta M., *34:* 181

Sabaka, Donna R., *21:* 172
Sabin, Robert, *45:* 35
Sacker, Amy, *16:* 100
Saffioti, Lino, *36:* 176
Sagsoorian, Paul, *12:* 183; *22:* 154; *33:* 106
Saint Exupéry, Antoine de, *20:* 157
St. John, J. Allen, *41:* 62
Saldutti, Denise, *39:* 186
Sale, Morton, *YABC 2:* 31
Sambourne, Linley, *YABC 2:* 181
Sampson, Katherine, *9:* 197
Samson, Anne S., *2:* 216
Sancha, Sheila, *38:* 185
Sand, George X., *45:* 182
Sandberg, Lasse, *15:* 239, 241
Sanders, Beryl, *39:* 173
Sanderson, Ruth, *21:* 126; *24:* 53; *28:* 63; *33:* 67; *41:* 48, 198, 199, 200, 201, 202, 203; *43:* 79
Sandin, Joan, *4:* 36; *6:* 194; *7:* 177; *12:* 145, 185; *20:* 43; *21:* 74; *26:* 144; *27:* 142; *28:* 224, 225; *38:* 86; *41:* 46; *42:* 35
Sandland, Reg, *39:* 215
Sandoz, Edouard, *26:* 45, 47
San Souci, Daniel, *40:* 200
Sapieha, Christine, *1:* 180
Sarg, Tony, *YABC 2:* 236
Sargent, Robert, *2:* 217
Saris, *1:* 33
Sarony, *YABC 2:* 170
Sasek, Miroslav, *16:* 239-242
Sassman, David, *9:* 79
Sätty, *29:* 203, 205
Sauber, Rob, *40:* 183
Savage, Steele, *10:* 203; *20:* 77; *35:* 28
Savitt, Sam, *8:* 66, 182; *15:* 278; *20:* 96; *24:* 192; *28:* 98

Say, Allen, *28:* 178
Scabrini, Janet, *13:* 191; *44:* 128
Scarry, Huck, *35:* 204-205
Scarry, Richard, *2:* 220-221; *18:* 20; *35:* 193, 194-195, 196, 197, 198, 199, 200-201, 202
Schaeffer, Mead, *18:* 81, 94; *21:* 137, 138, 139
Scharl, Josef, *20:* 132; *22:* 128
Scheel, Lita, *11:* 230
Scheib, Ida, *29:* 28
Schermer, Judith, *30:* 184
Schick, Joel, *16:* 160; *17:* 167; *22:* 12; *27:* 176; *31:* 147, 148; *36:* 23; *38:* 64; *45:* 116, 117
Schindelman, Joseph, *1:* 74; *4:* 101; *12:* 49; *26:* 51; *40:* 146
Schindler, Edith, *7:* 22
Schindler, S. D., *38:* 107
Schlesinger, Bret, *7:* 77
Schmid, Eleanore, *12:* 188
Schmiderer, Dorothy, *19:* 224
Schmidt, Elizabeth, *15:* 242
Schneider, Rex, *29:* 64; *44:* 171
Schoenherr, Ian, *32:* 83
Schoenherr, John, *1:* 146-147, 173; *3:* 39, 139; *17:* 75; *29:* 72; *32:* 83; *37:* 168, 169, 170; *43:* 164, 165; *45:* 160, 162
Schomburg, Alex, *13:* 23
Schongut, Emanuel, *4:* 102; *15:* 186
Schoonover, Frank, *17:* 107; *19:* 81, 190, 233; *22:* 88, 129; *24:* 189; *31:* 88; *41:* 69; *YABC 2:* 282, 316
Schottland, Miriam, *22:* 172
Schramm, Ulrik, *2:* 16; *14:* 112
Schreiber, Elizabeth Anne, *13:* 193
Schreiber, Ralph W., *13:* 193
Schreiter, Rick, *14:* 97; *23:* 171; *41:* 247
Schroeder, E. Peter, *12:* 112
Schroeder, Ted, *11:* 160; *15:* 189; *30:* 91; *34:* 43
Schrotter, Gustav, *22:* 212; *30:* 225
Schucker, James, *31:* 163
Schulz, Charles M., *10:* 137-142
Schwartz, Charles, *8:* 184
Schwartzberg, Joan, *3:* 208
Schweitzer, Iris, *2:* 137; *6:* 207
Schweninger, Ann, *29:* 172
Scott, Anita Walker, *7:* 38
Scott, Art, *39:* 41
Scott, Frances Gruse, *38:* 43
Scott, Julian, *34:* 126
Scott, Roszel, *33:* 238
Scott, Trudy, *27:* 172
Scribner, Joanne, *14:* 236; *29:* 78; *33:* 185; *34:* 208
Scrofani, Joseph, *31:* 65
Seaman, Mary Lott, *34:* 64
Searle, Ronald, *24:* 98; *42:* 172, 173, 174, 176, 177, 179
Searle, Townley, *36:* 85
Sebree, Charles, *18:* 65
Sedacca, Joseph M., *11:* 25; *22:* 36
Ségur, Adrienne, *27:* 121
Seignobosc, Francoise, *21:* 145, 146
Sejima, Yoshimasa, *8:* 187
Selig, Sylvie, *13:* 199

Seltzer, Isadore, *6:* 18
Seltzer, Meyer, *17:* 214
Sempé, *YABC 2:* 109
Sendak, Maurice, *1:* 135, 190; *3:* 204; *7:* 142; *15:* 199; *17:* 210; *27:* 181, 182, 183, 185, 186, 187, 189, 190-191, 192, 193, 194, 195, 197, 198, 199, 203; *28:* 181, 182; *32:* 108; *33:* 148, 149; *35:* 238; *44:* 180, 181; *45:* 97, 99; *YABC 1:* 167
Sengler, Johanna, *18:* 256
Seredy, Kate, *1:* 192; *14:* 20-21; *17:* 210
Sergeant, John, *6:* 74
Servello, Joe, *10:* 144; *24:* 139; *40:* 91
Seton, Ernest Thompson, *18:* 260-269, 271
Seuss, Dr. *See* Geisel, Theodor
Severin, John Powers, *7:* 62
Sewall, Marcia, *15:* 8; *22:* 170; *37:* 171, 172, 173; *39:* 73; *45:* 209
Seward, Prudence, *16:* 243
Sewell, Helen, *3:* 186; *15:* 308; *33:* 102; *38:* 189, 190, 191, 192
Shahn, Ben, *39:* 178
Shalansky, Len, *38:* 167
Shanks, Anne Zane, *10:* 149
Sharp, William, *6:* 131; *19:* 241; *20:* 112; *25:* 141
Shaw, Charles, *21:* 135; *38:* 187
Shaw, Charles G., *13:* 200
Shearer, Ted, *43:* 193, 194, 195, 196
Shecter, Ben, *16:* 244; *25:* 109; *33:* 188, 191; *41:* 77
Shekerjian, Haig, *16:* 245
Shekerjian, Regina, *16:* 245; *25:* 73
Shenton, Edward, *45:* 187, 188, 189; *YABC 1:* 218-219, 221
Shepard, Ernest H., *3:* 193; *4:* 74; *16:* 101; *17:* 109; *25:* 148; *33:* 152, 199, 200, 201, 202, 203, 204, 205, 206, 207; *YABC 1:* 148, 153, 174, 176, 180-181
Shepard, Mary, *4:* 210; *22:* 205; *30:* 132, 133
Sherman, Theresa, *27:* 167
Sherwan, Earl, *3:* 196
Shields, Charles, *10:* 150; *36:* 63
Shields, Leonard, *13:* 83, 85, 87
Shillabeer, Mary, *35:* 74
Shimin, Symeon, *1:* 93; *2:* 128-129; *3:* 202; *7:* 85; *11:* 177; *12:* 139; *13:* 202-203; *27:* 138; *28:* 65; *35:* 129; *36:* 130
Shinn, Everett, *16:* 148; *18:* 229; *21:* 149, 150, 151; *24:* 218
Shore, Robert, *27:* 54; *39:* 192, 193; *YABC 2:* 200
Shortall, Leonard, *4:* 144; *8:* 196; *10:* 166; *19:* 227, 228-229, 230; *25:* 78; *28:* 66, 167; *33:* 127
Shortt, T. M., *27:* 36
Shtainments, Leon, *32:* 161
Shulevitz, Uri, *3:* 198-199; *17:* 85; *22:* 204; *27:* 212; *28:* 184
Siberell, Anne, *29:* 193
Sibley, Don, *1:* 39; *12:* 196; *31:* 47

Sidjakov, Nicolas, *18:* 274
Siebel, Fritz, *3:* 120; *17:* 145
Siegl, Helen, *12:* 166; *23:* 216; *34:* 185, 186
Sills, Joyce, *5:* 199
Silverstein, Alvin, *8:* 189
Silverstein, Shel, *33:* 211
Silverstein, Virginia, *8:* 189
Simon, Eric M., *7:* 82
Simon, Hilda, *28:* 189
Simon, Howard, *2:* 175; *5:* 132; *19:* 199; *32:* 163, 164, 165
Simont, Marc, *2:* 119; *4:* 213; *9:* 168; *13:* 238, 240; *14:* 262; *16:* 179; *18:* 221; *26:* 210; *33:* 189, 194; *44:* 132
Sims, Blanche, *44:* 116
Singer, Edith G., *2:* 30
Singer, Gloria, *34:* 56; *36:* 43
Singer, Julia, *28:* 190
Sivard, Robert, *26:* 124
Skardinski, Stanley, *23:* 144; *32:* 84
Slackman, Charles B., *12:* 201
Slater, Rod, *25:* 167
Sloan, Joseph, *16:* 68
Sloane, Eric, *21:* 3
Slobodkin, Louis, *1:* 200; *3:* 232; *5:* 168; *13:* 251; *15:* 13, 88; *26:* 173, 174, 175, 176, 178, 179
Slobodkina, Esphyr, *1:* 201
Small, W., *33:* 113
Smalley, Janet, *1:* 154
Smedley, William T., *34:* 129
Smee, David, *14:* 78
Smith, A. G., Jr., *35:* 182
Smith, Alvin, *1:* 31, 229; *13:* 187; *27:* 216; *28:* 226
Smith, Anne Warren, *41:* 212
Smith, Carl, *36:* 41
Smith, Doris Susan, *41:* 139
Smith, E. Boyd, *19:* 70; *22:* 89; *26:* 63; *YABC 1:* 4-5, 240, 248-249
Smith, Edward J., *4:* 224
Smith, Eunice Young, *5:* 170
Smith, Howard, *19:* 196
Smith, Jacqueline Bardner, *27:* 108; *39:* 197
Smith, Jessie Willcox, *15:* 91; *16:* 95; *18:* 231; *19:* 57, 242; *21:* 29, 156, 157, 158, 159, 160, 161; *34:* 65; *YABC 1:* 6; *YABC 2:* 180, 185, 191, 311, 325
Smith, L. H., *35:* 174
Smith, Lee, *29:* 32
Smith, Linell Nash, *2:* 195
Smith, Maggie Kaufman, *13:* 205; *35:* 191
Smith, Moishe, *33:* 155
Smith, Philip, *44:* 134
Smith, Ralph Crosby, *2:* 267
Smith, Robert D., *5:* 63
Smith, Susan Carlton, *12:* 208
Smith, Terry, *12:* 106; *33:* 158
Smith, Virginia, *3:* 157; *33:* 72
Smith, William A., *1:* 36; *10:* 154; *25:* 65
Smollin, Mike, *39:* 203
Smyth, M. Jane, *12:* 15

Snyder, Andrew A., *30:* 212
Snyder, Jerome, *13:* 207; *30:* 173
Snyder, Joel, *28:* 163
Sofia, *1:* 62; *5:* 90; *32:* 166
Sokol, Bill, *37:* 178
Sokolov, Kirill, *34:* 188
Solbert, Ronni, *1:* 159; *2:* 232; *5:* 121; *6:* 34; *17:* 249
Solonevich, George, *15:* 246; *17:* 47
Sommer, Robert, *12:* 211
Sorel, Edward, *4:* 61; *36:* 82
Sotomayor, Antonio, *11:* 215
Soyer, Moses, *20:* 177
Spaenkuch, August, *16:* 28
Spanfeller, James, *1:* 72, 149; *2:* 183; *19:* 230, 231, 232; *22:* 66; *36:* 160, 161; *40:* 75
Sparks, Mary Walker, *15:* 247
Spence, Geraldine, *21:* 163
Spence, Jim, *38:* 89
Spiegel, Doris, *29:* 111
Spier, Jo, *10:* 30
Spier, Peter, *3:* 155; *4:* 200; *7:* 61; *11:* 78; *38:* 106
Spilka, Arnold, *5:* 120; *6:* 204; *8:* 131
Spivak, I. Howard, *8:* 10
Spollen, Christopher J., *12:* 214
Spooner, Malcolm, *40:* 142
Sprattler, Rob, *12:* 176
Spring, Bob, *5:* 60
Spring, Ira, *5:* 60
Springer, Harriet, *31:* 92
Spurrier, Steven, *28:* 198
Spy. *See* Ward, Leslie
Staffan, Alvin E., *11:* 56; *12:* 187
Stahl, Ben, *5:* 181; *12:* 91
Stair, Gobin, *35:* 214
Stamaty, Mark Alan, *12:* 215
Stanley, Diane, *3:* 45; *37:* 180
Steadman, Ralph, *32:* 180
Steichen, Edward, *30:* 79
Steig, William, *18:* 275-276
Stein, Harve, *1:* 109
Steinel, William, *23:* 146
Steiner, Charlotte, *45:* 196
Stephens, Charles H., *YABC 2:* 279
Stephens, William M., *21:* 165
Steptoe, John, *8:* 197
Stern, Simon, *15:* 249-250; *17:* 58; *34:* 192-193
Stevens, Janet, *40:* 126
Stevens, Mary, *11:* 193; *13:* 129; *43:* 95
Stevenson, James, *42:* 182, 183
Stewart, Arvis, *33:* 98; *36:* 69
Stewart, Charles, *2:* 205
Stiles, Fran, *26:* 85
Stillman, Susan, *44:* 130
Stinemetz, Morgan, *40:* 151
Stirnweis, Shannon, *10:* 164
Stobbs, William, *1:* 48-49; *3:* 68; *6:* 20; *17:* 117, 217; *24:* 150; *29:* 250
Stock, Catherine, *37:* 55
Stone, David, *9:* 173
Stone, David K., *4:* 38; *6:* 124; *9:* 180; *43:* 182
Stone, Helen, *44:* 121, 122, 126
Stone, Helen V., *6:* 209

Stratton, Helen, *33:* 151
Stratton-Porter, Gene, *15:* 254, 259, 263-264, 268-269
Streano, Vince, *20:* 173
Strong, Joseph D., Jr., *YABC 2:* 330
Ströyer, Poul, *13:* 221
Strugnell, Ann, *27:* 38
Stubis, Talivaldis, *5:* 182, 183; *10:* 45; *11:* 9; *18:* 304; *20:* 127
Stubley, Trevor, *14:* 43; *22:* 219; *23:* 37; *28:* 61
Stuecklen, Karl W., *8:* 34, 65; *23:* 103
Stull, Betty, *11:* 46
Suba, Susanne, *4:* 202-203; *14:* 261; *23:* 134; *29:* 222; *32:* 30
Sugarman, Tracy, *3:* 76; *8:* 199; *37:* 181, 182
Sugita, Yutaka, *36:* 180-181
Sullivan, Edmund J., *31:* 86
Sullivan, James F., *19:* 280; *20:* 192
Sumichrast, Jözef, *14:* 253; *29:* 168, 213
Summers, Leo, *1:* 177; *2:* 273; *13:* 22
Svolinsky, Karel, *17:* 104
Swain, Su Zan Noguchi, *21:* 170
Swan, Susan, *22:* 220-221; *37:* 66
Sweat, Lynn, *25:* 206
Sweet, Darryl, *1:* 163; *4:* 136
Sweet, Ozzie, *31:* 149, 151, 152
Sweetland, Robert, *12:* 194
Swope, Martha, *43:* 160
Sylvester, Natalie G., *22:* 222
Szafran, Gene, *24:* 144
Szasz, Susanne, *13:* 55, 226; *14:* 48
Szekeres, Cyndy, *2:* 218; *5:* 185; *8:* 85; *11:* 166; *14:* 19; *16:* 57, 159; *26:* 49, 214; *34:* 205

Taback, Simms, *40:* 207
Tafuri, Nancy, *39:* 210
Tait, Douglas, *12:* 220
Takakjian, Portia, *15:* 274
Takashima, Shizuye, *13:* 228
Talarczyk, June, *4:* 173
Tallon, Robert, *2:* 228; *43:* 200, 201, 202, 203, 204, 205, 206, 207, 209
Tamas, Szecskó, *29:* 135
Tamburine, Jean, *12:* 222
Tandy, H. R., *13:* 69
Tanobe, Miyuki, *23:* 221
Tarkington, Booth, *17:* 224-225
Taylor, Ann, *41:* 226
Taylor, Isaac, *41:* 228
Teale, Edwin Way, *7:* 196
Teason, James, *1:* 14
Teeple, Lyn, *33:* 147
Tee-Van, Helen Damrosch, *10:* 176; *11:* 182
Tempest, Margaret, *3:* 237, 238
Temple, Herbert, *45:* 201
Templeton, Owen, *11:* 77
Tenggren, Gustaf, *18:* 277-279; *19:* 15; *28:* 86; *YABC 2:* 145
Tenney, Gordon, *24:* 204
Tenniel, John, *YABC 2:* 99
Thacher, Mary M., *30:* 72
Thackeray, William Makepeace, *23:* 224, 228

Thamer, Katie, *42:* 187
Thelwell, Norman, *14:* 201
Theobalds, Prue, *40:* 23
Theurer, Marilyn Churchill, *39:* 195
Thistlethwaite, Miles, *12:* 224
Thollander, Earl, *11:* 47; *18:* 112; *22:* 224
Thomas, Allan, *22:* 13
Thomas, Eric, *28:* 49
Thomas, Harold, *20:* 98
Thomas, Mark, *42:* 136
Thomas, Martin, *14:* 255
Thompson, Arthur, *34:* 107
Thompson, George, *22:* 18; *28:* 150; *33:* 135
Thompson, George, W., *33:* 135
Thompson, Julie, *44:* 158
Thomson, Arline K., *3:* 264
Thomson, Hugh, *26:* 88
Thomson, Ross, *36:* 179
Thorne, Diana, *25:* 212
Thorvall, Kerstin, *13:* 235
Thurber, James, *13:* 239, 242-245, 248-249
Tibbles, Paul, *45:* 23
Tichenor, Tom, *14:* 207
Tiegreen, Alan, *36:* 143; *43:* 55, 56, 58
Tilney, F. C., *22:* 231
Timbs, Gloria, *36:* 90
Timmins, Harry, *2:* 171
Tinkelman, Murray, *12:* 225; *35:* 44
Titherington, Jeanne, *39:* 90
Tolford, Joshua, *1:* 221
Tolkien, J. R. R., *2:* 243; *32:* 215
Tolmie, Ken, *15:* 292
Tomes, Jacqueline, *2:* 117; *12:* 139
Tomes, Margot, *1:* 224; *2:* 120-121; *16:* 207; *18:* 250; *20:* 7; *25:* 62; *27:* 78, 79; *29:* 81, 199; *33:* 82; *36:* 186, 187, 188, 189, 190
Toner, Raymond John, *10:* 179
Toothill, Harry, *6:* 54; *7:* 49; *25:* 219; *42:* 192
Toothill, Ilse, *6:* 54
Topolski, Feliks, *44:* 48
Torbert, Floyd James, *22:* 226
Torrey, Marjorie, *34:* 105
Toschik, Larry, *6:* 102
Totten, Bob, *13:* 93
Tremain, Ruthven, *17:* 238
Tresilian, Stuart, *25:* 53; *40:* 212
Trez, Alain, *17:* 236
Trier, Walter, *14:* 96
Tripp, F. J., *24:* 167
Tripp, Wallace, *2:* 48; *7:* 28; *8:* 94; *10:* 54, 76; *11:* 92; *31:* 170, 171; *34:* 203; *42:* 57
Trnka, Jiri, *22:* 151; *43:* 212, 213, 214, 215; *YABC 1:* 30-31
Troughton, Joanna, *37:* 186
Troyer, Johannes, *3:* 16; *7:* 18
Trudeau, G. B., *35:* 220, 221, 222
Tsinajinie, Andy, *2:* 62
Tsugami, Kyuzo, *18:* 198-199
Tuckwell, Jennifer, *17:* 205
Tudor, Bethany, *7:* 103
Tudor, Tasha, *18:* 227; *20:* 185, 186, 187; *36:* 111; *YABC 2:* 46, 314

Tulloch, Maurice, *24:* 79
Tunis, Edwin, *1:* 218-219; *28:* 209, 210, 211, 212
Turkle, Brinton, *1:* 211, 213; *2:* 249; *3:* 226; *11:* 3; *16:* 209; *20:* 22; *YABC 1:* 79
Turska, Krystyna, *12:* 103; *31:* 173, 174-175
Tusan, Stan, *6:* 58; *22:* 236-237
Tzimoulis, Paul, *12:* 104

Uchida, Yoshiko, *1:* 220
Ulm, Robert, *17:* 238
Unada. *See* Gliewe, Unada
Underwood, Clarence, *40:* 166
Ungerer, Tomi, *5:* 188; *9:* 40; *18:* 188; *29:* 175; *33:* 221, 222-223, 225
Unwin, Nora S., *3:* 65, 234-235; *4:* 237; *44:* 173, 174; *YABC 1:* 59; *YABC 2:* 301
Utpatel, Frank, *18:* 114
Utz, Lois, *5:* 190

Van Abbé, S., *16:* 142; *18:* 282; *31:* 90; *YABC 2:* 157, 161
Van Allsburg, Chris, *37:* 205, 206
Vandivert, William, *21:* 175
Van Everen, Jay, *13:* 160; *YABC 1:* 121
Van Horn, William, *43:* 218
Van Loon, Hendrik Willem, *18:* 285, 289, 291
Van Sciver, Ruth, *37:* 162
Van Stockum, Hilda, *5:* 193
Van Wely, Babs, *16:* 50
Varga, Judy, *29:* 196
Vasiliu, Mircea, *2:* 166, 253; *9:* 166; *13:* 58
Vaughn, Frank, *34:* 157
Vavra, Robert, *8:* 206
Vawter, Will, *17:* 163
Veeder, Larry, *18:* 4
Velasquez, Eric, *45:* 217
Vendrell, Carme Solé, *42:* 205
Ver Beck, Frank, *18:* 16-17
Verney, John, *14:* 225
Verrier, Suzanne, *5:* 20; *23:* 212
Versace, Marie, *2:* 255
Vestal, H. B., *9:* 134; *11:* 101; *27:* 25; *34:* 158
Vickrey, Robert, *45:* 59, 64
Victor, Joan Berg, *30:* 193
Viereck, Ellen, *3:* 242; *14:* 229
Vigna, Judith, *15:* 293
Vilato, Gaspar E., *5:* 41
Vimnèra, A., *23:* 154
Vincent, Eric, *34:* 98
Vincent, Félix, *41:* 237
Vip, *45:* 164
Vo-Dinh, Mai, *16:* 272
Vogel, Ilse-Margret, *14:* 230
Voigt, Erna, *35:* 228
Vojtech, Anna, *42:* 190
von Schmidt, Eric, *8:* 62
von Schmidt, Harold, *30:* 80

Vosburgh, Leonard, *1:* 161; *7:* 32; *15:* 295-296; *23:* 110; *30:* 214; *43:* 181
Voter, Thomas W., *19:* 3, 9
Vroman, Tom, *10:* 29

Wagner, John, *8:* 200
Wagner, Ken, *2:* 59
Waide, Jan, *29:* 225; *36:* 139
Wainwright, Jerry, *14:* 85
Waldman, Bruce, *15:* 297; *43:* 178
Waldman, Neil, *35:* 141
Walker, Charles, *1:* 46; *4:* 59; *5:* 177; *11:* 115; *19:* 45; *34:* 74
Walker, Dugald Stewart, *15:* 47; *32:* 202; *33:* 112
Walker, Gil, *8:* 49; *23:* 132; *34:* 42
Walker, Jim, *10:* 94
Walker, Mort, *8:* 213
Walker, Norman, *41:* 37; *45:* 58
Walker, Stephen, *12:* 229; *21:* 174
Wallace, Beverly Dobrin, *19:* 259
Waller, S. E., *24:* 36
Wallner, Alexandra, *15:* 120
Wallner, John C., *9:* 77; *10:* 188; *11:* 28; *14:* 209; *31:* 56, 118; *37:* 64
Wallower, Lucille, *11:* 226
Walters, Audrey, *18:* 294
Walther, Tom, *31:* 179
Walton, Tony, *11:* 164; *24:* 209
Waltrip, Lela, *9:* 195
Waltrip, Mildred, *3:* 209; *37:* 211
Waltrip, Rufus, *9:* 195
Wan, *12:* 76
Ward, John, *42:* 191
Ward, Keith, *2:* 107
Ward, Leslie, *34:* 126; *36:* 87
Ward, Lynd, *1:* 99, 132, 133, 150; *2:* 108, 158, 196, 259; *18:* 86; *27:* 56; *29:* 79, 187, 253, 255; *36:* 199, 200, 201, 202, 203, 204, 205, 206, 207, 209; *43:* 34
Ward, Peter, *37:* 116
Warner, Peter, *14:* 87
Warren, Betsy, *2:* 101
Warren, Marion Cray, *14:* 215
Warshaw, Jerry, *30:* 197, 198; *42:* 165
Washington, Nevin, *20:* 123
Washington, Phyllis, *20:* 123
Waterman, Stan, *11:* 76
Watkins-Pitchford, D. J., *6:* 215, 217
Watson, Aldren A., *2:* 267; *5:* 94; *13:* 71; *19:* 253; *32:* 220; *42:* 193, 194, 195, 196, 197, 198, 199, 200, 201; *YABC 2:* 202
Watson, Gary, *19:* 147; *36:* 68; *41:* 122
Watson, J. D., *22:* 86
Watson, Karen, *11:* 26
Watson, Wendy, *5:* 197; *13:* 101; *33:* 116
Watts, Bernadette, *4:* 227
Watts, John, *37:* 149
Webber, Helen, *3:* 141
Webber, Irma E., *14:* 238
Weber, Florence, *40:* 153
Weber, William J., *14:* 239

Webster, Jean, *17:* 241
Wegner, Fritz, *14:* 250; *20:* 189; *44:* 165
Weidenear, Reynold H., *21:* 122
Weihs, Erika, *4:* 21; *15:* 299
Weil, Lisl, *7:* 203; *10:* 58; *21:* 95; *22:* 188, 217; *33:* 193
Weiner, Sandra, *14:* 240
Weisgard, Leonard, *1:* 65; *2:* 191, 197, 204, 264-265; *5:* 108; *21:* 42; *30:* 200, 201, 203, 204; *41:* 47; *44:* 125; *YABC 2:* 13
Weiss, Ellen, *44:* 202
Weiss, Emil, *1:* 168; *7:* 60
Weiss, Harvey, *1:* 145, 223; *27:* 224, 227
Weiss, Nicki, *33:* 229
Wells, Frances, *1:* 183
Wells, H. G., *20:* 194, 200
Wells, Rosemary, *6:* 49; *18:* 297
Wells, Susan, *22:* 43
Wendelin, Rudolph, *23:* 234
Wengenroth, Stow, *37:* 47
Werenskiold, Erik, *15:* 6
Werner, Honi, *24:* 110; *33:* 41
Werth, Kurt, *7:* 122; *14:* 157; *20:* 214; *39:* 128
Westerberg, Christine, *29:* 226
Weston, Martha, *29:* 116; *30:* 213; *33:* 85, 100
Wetherbee, Margaret, *5:* 3
Wheatley, Arabelle, *11:* 231; *16:* 276
Wheeler, Dora, *44:* 179
Wheelright, Rowland, *15:* 81; *YABC 2:* 286
Whistler, Rex, *16:* 75; *30:* 207, 208
White, David Omar, *5:* 56; *18:* 6
Whitear, *32:* 26
Whithorne, H. S., *7:* 49
Whitney, George Gillett, *3:* 24
Whittam, Geoffrey, *30:* 191
Wiberg, Harald, *38:* 127
Wiese, Kurt, *3:* 255; *4:* 206; *14:* 17; *17:* 18-19; *19:* 47; *24:* 152; *25:* 212; *32:* 184; *36:* 211, 213, 214, 215, 216, 217, 218; *45:* 161
Wiesner, David, *33:* 47
Wiesner, William, *4:* 100; *5:* 200, 201; *14:* 262
Wiggins, George, *6:* 133
Wikkelsoe, Otto, *45:* 25, 26
Wikland, Ilon, *5:* 113; *8:* 150; *38:* 124, 125, 130
Wilbur, C. Keith, M.D., *27:* 228
Wilcox, J.A.J., *34:* 122
Wilcox, R. Turner, *36:* 219
Wilde, George, *7:* 139
Wildsmith, Brian, *16:* 281-282; *18:* 170-171
Wilkin, Eloise, *36:* 173

Wilkinson, Gerald, *3:* 40
Wilkoń, Józef, *31:* 183, 184
Wilks, Mike, *34:* 24; *44:* 203
Williams, Ferelith Eccles, *22:* 238
Williams, Garth, *1:* 197; *2:* 49, 270; *4:* 205; *15:* 198, 302-304, 307; *16:* 34; *18:* 283, 298-301; *29:* 177, 178, 179, 232-233, 241-245, 248; *40:* 106; *YABC 2:* 15-16, 19
Williams, Kit, *44:* 206-207, 208, 209, 211, 212
Williams, Maureen, *12:* 238
Williams, Patrick, *14:* 218
Williams, Richard, *44:* 93
Wilson, Charles Banks, *17:* 92; *43:* 73
Wilson, Dagmar, *10:* 47
Wilson, Edward A., *6:* 24; *16:* 149; *20:* 220-221; *22:* 87; *26:* 67; *38:* 212, 214, 215, 216, 217
Wilson, Forrest, *27:* 231
Wilson, Gahan, *35:* 234; *41:* 136
Wilson, Jack, *17:* 139
Wilson, John, *22:* 240
Wilson, Patten, *35:* 61
Wilson, Peggy, *15:* 4
Wilson, Rowland B., *30:* 170
Wilson, Tom, *33:* 232
Wilson, W. N., *22:* 26
Wilwerding, Walter J., *9:* 202
Winchester, Linda, *13:* 231
Wind, Betty, *28:* 158
Windham, Kathryn Tucker, *14:* 260
Winslow, Will, *21:* 124
Winsten, Melanie Willa, *41:* 41
Winter, Milo, *15:* 97; *19:* 221; *21:* 181, 203, 204, 205; *YABC 2:* 144
Wise, Louis, *13:* 68
Wiseman, Ann, *31:* 187
Wiseman, B., *4:* 233
Wishnefsky, Phillip, *3:* 14
Wiskur, Darrell, *5:* 72; *10:* 50; *18:* 246
Wittman, Sally, *30:* 219
Woehr, Lois, *12:* 5
Wohlberg, Meg, *12:* 100; *14:* 197; *41:* 255
Woldin, Beth Weiner, *34:* 211
Wolf, J., *16:* 91
Wolf, Linda, *33:* 163
Wondriska, William, *6:* 220
Wonsetler, John C., *5:* 168
Wood, Grant, *19:* 198
Wood, Muriel, *36:* 119
Wood, Myron, *6:* 220
Wood, Owen, *18:* 187
Wood, Ruth, *8:* 11
Woodson, Jack, *10:* 201
Woodward, Alice, *26:* 89; *36:* 81
Wool, David, *26:* 27

Wooten, Vernon, *23:* 70
Worboys, Evelyn, *1:* 166-167
Worth, Jo, *34:* 143
Worth, Wendy, *4:* 133
Wosmek, Frances, *29:* 251
Wrenn, Charles L., *38:* 96; *YABC 1:* 20, 21
Wright, Dare, *21:* 206
Wright, George, *YABC 1:* 268
Wright, Joseph, *30:* 160
Wronker, Lili Cassel, *3:* 247; *10:* 204; *21:* 10
Wyeth, Andrew, *13:* 40; *YABC 1:* 133-134
Wyeth, Jamie, *41:* 257
Wyeth, N. C., *13:* 41; *17:* 252-259, 264-268; *18:* 181; *19:* 80, 191, 200; *21:* 57, 183; *22:* 91; *23:* 152; *24:* 28, 99; *35:* 61; *41:* 65; *YABC 1:* 133, 223; *YABC 2:* 53, 75, 171, 187, 317

Yang, Jay, *1:* 8; *12:* 239
Yap, Weda, *6:* 176
Yaroslava. See Mills, Yaroslava Surmach
Yashima, Taro, *14:* 84
Ylla. See Koffler, Camilla
Yohn, F. C., *23:* 128; *YABC 1:* 269
Young, Ed, *7:* 205; *10:* 206; *40:* 124; *YABC 2:* 242
Young, Noela, *8:* 221

Zacks, Lewis, *10:* 161
Zaffo, George, *42:* 208
Zaidenberg, Arthur, *34:* 218, 219, 220
Zalben, Jane Breskin, *7:* 211
Zallinger, Jean, *4:* 192; *8:* 8, 129; *14:* 273
Zallinger, Rudolph F., *3:* 245
Zeck, Gerry, *40:* 232
Zeiring, Bob, *42:* 130
Zelinsky, Paul O., *14:* 269; *43:* 56
Zemach, Margot, *3:* 270; *8:* 201; *21:* 210-211; *27:* 204, 205, 210; *28:* 185
Zemsky, Jessica, *10:* 62
Zepelinsky, Paul, *35:* 93
Zimmer, Dirk, *38:* 195
Zimnik, Reiner, *36:* 224
Zinkeisen, Anna, *13:* 106
Zoellick, Scott, *33:* 231
Zonia, Dhimitri, *20:* 234-235
Zweifel, Francis, *14:* 274; *28:* 187

Author Index

The following index gives the number of the volume in which an author's biographical sketch, Brief Entry, or Obituary appears.

This index includes references to all entries in the following series, which are also published by Gale Research Company.

YABC—*Yesterday's Authors of Books for Children: Facts and Pictures about Authors and Illustrators of Books for Young People from Early Times to 1960*, Volumes 1-2
CLR—*Children's Literature Review: Excerpts from Reviews, Criticism, and Commentary on Books for Children*, Volumes 1-10
SAAS—*Something about the Author Autobiography Series*, Volumes 1-2

A

Aardema, Verna 1911- *4*
Aaron, Chester 1923- *9*
Aaseng, Nate
  See Aaseng, Nathan
Aaseng, Nathan 1938-
  Brief Entry *38*
Abbott, Alice
  See Borland, Kathryn Kilby
Abbott, Alice
  See Speicher, Helen Ross (Smith)
Abbott, Jacob 1803-1879 .... *22*
Abbott, Manager Henry
  See Stratemeyer, Edward L.
Abbott, Sarah
  See Zolotow, Charlotte S.
Abdul, Raoul 1929- *12*
Abel, Raymond 1911- *12*
Abell, Kathleen 1938- *9*
Abercrombie, Barbara (Mattes)
  1939- *16*
Abernethy, Robert G. 1935- *5*
Abisch, Roslyn Kroop 1927- *9*
Abisch, Roz
  See Abisch, Roslyn Kroop
Abodaher, David J. (Naiph)
  1919- *17*
Abrahall, C. H.
  See Hoskyns-Abrahall, Clare
Abrahall, Clare Hoskyns
  See Hoskyns-Abrahall, Clare
Abrahams, Hilary (Ruth)
  1938- *29*
Abrahams, Robert D(avid)
  1905- *4*
Abrams, Joy 1941- *16*
Achebe, Chinua 1930- *40*
  Brief Entry *38*
Ackerman, Eugene 1888-1974 .... *10*
Acs, Laszlo (Bela) 1931- *42*
  Brief Entry *32*
Acuff, Selma Boyd 1924- *45*
Ada, Alma Flor 1938- *43*

Adair, Margaret Weeks
  (?)-1971 .... *10*
Adam, Cornel
  See Lengyel, Cornel Adam
Adams, Adrienne 1906- *8*
Adams, Andy
  1859-1935 ....*YABC 1*
Adams, Dale
  See Quinn, Elisabeth
Adams, Harriet S(tratemeyer)
  1893(?)-1982 .... *1*
  Obituary *29*
Adams, Harrison
  See Stratemeyer, Edward L.
Adams, Hazard 1926- *6*
Adams, Laurie 1941- *33*
Adams, Richard 1920- *7*
Adams, Ruth Joyce *14*
Adams, William Taylor
  1822-1897 .... *28*
Adamson, Gareth 1925-1982(?)
  Obituary *30*
Adamson, George Worsley
  1913- *30*
Adamson, Graham
  See Groom, Arthur William
Adamson, Joy 1910-1980 .... *11*
  Obituary *22*
Adamson, Wendy Wriston
  1942- *22*
Addona, Angelo F. 1925- *14*
Addy, Ted
  See Winterbotham, R(ussell) R(obert)
Adelberg, Doris
  See Orgel, Doris
Adelson, Leone 1908- *11*
Adkins, Jan 1944- *8*
  See also CLR 7
Adler, C(arole) S(chwerdtfeger)
  1932- *26*
Adler, David A. 1947- *14*
Adler, Irene
  See Penzler, Otto
  See Storr, Catherine (Cole)

Adler, Irving 1913- *29*
  Earlier sketch in SATA 1
Adler, Larry 1939- *36*
Adler, Peggy *22*
Adler, Ruth 1915-1968 .... *1*
Adoff, Arnold 1935- *5*
  See also CLR 7
Adorjan, Carol 1934- *10*
Adrian, Mary
  See Jorgensen, Mary Venn
Adshead, Gladys L. 1896- *3*
Aesop, Abraham
  See Newbery, John
Agapida, Fray Antonio
  See Irving, Washington
Agard, Nadema 1948- *18*
Agle, Nan Hayden 1905- *3*
Agnew, Edith J(osephine)
  1897- *11*
Ahern, Margaret McCrohan
  1921- *10*
Ahl, Anna Maria 1926- *32*
Ahlberg, Allan
  Brief Entry *35*
Ahlberg, Janet
  Brief Entry *32*
Aichinger, Helga 1937- *4*
Aiken, Clarissa (Lorenz)
  1899- *12*
Aiken, Conrad (Potter)
  1889-1973 .... *30*
  Earlier sketch in SATA 3
Aiken, Joan 1924- *30*
  Earlier sketch in SATA 2
  See also CLR 1
  See also SAAS 1
Ainsworth, Norma *9*
Ainsworth, Ruth 1908- *7*
Ainsworth, William Harrison
  1805-1882 .... *24*
Aistrop, Jack 1916- *14*
Aitken, Amy 1952-
  Brief Entry *40*
Aitken, Dorothy 1916- *10*

Akers, Floyd
  See Baum, L(yman) Frank
Alain
  See Brustlein, Daniel
Albert, Burton, Jr. 1936- 22
Alberts, Frances Jacobs 1907- 14
Albion, Lee Smith 29
Albrecht, Lillie (Vanderveer)
  1894- 12
Alcock, Gudrun
  Brief Entry 33
Alcock, Vivien 1924- 45
  Brief Entry 38
Alcorn, John 1935- 31
  Brief Entry 30
Alcott, Louisa May
  1832-1888 ....YABC 1
  See also CLR 1
Alda, Arlene 1933- 44
  Brief Entry 36
Alden, Isabella (Macdonald)
  1841-1930 ....YABC 2
Alderman, Clifford Lindsey
  1902- 3
Aldis, Dorothy (Keeley)
  1896-1966 2
Aldiss, Brian W(ilson) 1925- 34
Aldon, Adair
  See Meigs, Cornelia
Aldous, Allan (Charles) 1911- 27
Aldrich, Ann
  See Meaker, Marijane
Aldrich, Thomas Bailey
  1836-1907 17
Aldridge, Alan 1943(?)-
  Brief Entry 33
Aldridge, Josephine Haskell 14
Alegria, Ricardo E. 1921- 6
Aleksin, Anatolii (Georgievich)
  1924- 36
Alex, Ben [a pseudonym]
  1946- 45
Alex, Marlee [a pseudonym]
  1948- 45
Alexander, Anna Cooke 1913- 1
Alexander, Frances 1888- 4
Alexander, Jocelyn (Anne) Arundel
  1930- 22
Alexander, Linda 1935- 2
Alexander, Lloyd 1924- 3
  See also CLR 1, 5
Alexander, Martha 1920- 11
Alexander, Rae Pace
  See Alexander, Raymond Pace
Alexander, Raymond Pace
  1898-1974 22
Alexander, Sue 1933- 12
Alexander, Vincent Arthur 1925-1980
  Obituary 23
Alexeieff, Alexandre A.
  1901- 14
Alger, Horatio, Jr. 1832-1899 ...:. 16
Alger, Leclaire (Gowans)
  1898-1969 15
Aliki
  See Brandenberg, Aliki
  See also CLR 9
Alkema, Chester Jay 1932- 12
Allamand, Pascale 1942- 12

Allan, Mabel Esther 1915- 32
  Earlier sketch in SATA 5
Allard, Harry
  See Allard, Harry G(rover), Jr.
Allard, Harry G(rover), Jr.
  1928- 42
Allee, Marjorie Hill
  1890-1945 17
Allen, Adam [Joint pseudonym]
  See Epstein, Beryl and Epstein,
  Samuel
Allen, Alex B.
  See Heide, Florence Parry
Allen, Allyn
  See Eberle, Irmengarde
Allen, Betsy
  See Cavanna, Betty
Allen, Gertrude E(lizabeth)
  1888- 9
Allen, Jack 1899-
  Brief Entry 29
Allen, Jeffrey (Yale) 1948- 42
Allen, Leroy 1912- 11
Allen, Linda 1925- 33
Allen, Marjorie 1931- 22
Allen, Maury 1932- 26
Allen, Merritt Parmelee
  1892-1954 22
Allen, Nina (Strömgren)
  1935- 22
Allen, Rodney F. 1938- 27
Allen, Ruth
  See Peterson, Esther (Allen)
Allen, Samuel (Washington)
  1917- 9
Allen, T. D. [Joint pseudonym]
  See Allen, Terril Diener
Allen, Terril Diener 1908- 35
Allen, Terry D.
  See Allen, Terril Diener
Allen, Thomas B(enton)
  1929- 45
Allen, Tom
  See Allen, Thomas B(enton)
Allerton, Mary
  See Govan, Christine Noble
Alleyn, Ellen
  See Rossetti, Christina (Georgina)
Allington, Richard L(loyd)
  1947- 39
  Brief Entry 35
Allison, Bob 14
Allison, Linda 1948- 43
Allmendinger, David F(rederick), Jr.
  1938- 35
Allred, Gordon T. 1930- 10
Allsop, Kenneth 1920-1973 17
Almedingen, E. M.
  1898-1971 3
Almedingen, Martha Edith von
  See Almedingen, E. M.
Almquist, Don 1929- 11
Alsop, Mary O'Hara
  1885-1980 34
  Obituary 24
  Earlier sketch in SATA 5
Alter, Robert Edmond
  1925-1965 9

Althea
  See Braithwaite, Althea 23
Altschuler, Franz 1923- 45
Altsheler, Joseph A(lexander)
  1862-1919 ....YABC 1
Alvarez, Joseph A. 1930- 18
Ambler, C(hristopher) Gifford 1886-
  Brief Entry 29
Ambrose, Stephen E(dward)
  1936- 40
Ambrus, Gyozo (Laszlo)
  1935- 41
  Earlier sketch in SATA 1
Ambrus, Victor G.
  See Ambrus, Gyozo (Laszlo)
Amerman, Lockhart
  1911-1969 3
Ames, Evelyn 1908- 13
Ames, Gerald 1906- 11
Ames, Lee J. 1921- 3
Ames, Mildred 1919- 22
Amon, Aline 1928- 9
Amoss, Berthe 1925- 5
Anastasio, Dina 1941- 37
  Brief Entry 30
Anckarsvard, Karin
  1915-1969 6
Ancona, George 1929- 12
Andersdatter, Karla M(argaret)
  1938- 34
Andersen, Hans Christian
  1805-1875 ....YABC 1
  See also CLR 6
Andersen, Ted
  See Boyd, Waldo T.
Andersen, Yvonne 1932- 27
Anderson, Bernice G(oudy)
  1894- 33
Anderson, Brad(ley Jay)
  1924- 33
  Brief Entry 31
Anderson, C(larence) W(illiam)
  1891-1971 11
Anderson, Clifford [Joint pseudonym]
  See Gardner, Richard
Anderson, Ella
  See MacLeod, Ellen Jane (Anderson)
Anderson, Eloise Adell 1927- 9
Anderson, George
  See Groom, Arthur William
Anderson, Grace Fox 1932- 43
Anderson, J(ohn) R(ichard) L(ane)
  1911-1981 15
  Obituary 27
Anderson, Joy 1928- 1
Anderson, LaVere (Francis Shoenfelt)
  1907- 27
Anderson, (John) Lonzo
  1905- 2
Anderson, Lucia (Lewis)
  1922- 10
Anderson, Madelyn Klein 28
Anderson, Margaret J(ean)
  1931- 27
Anderson, Mary 1939- 7
Anderson, Mona 1910- 40
Anderson, Norman D(ean)
  1928- 22

Anderson, Poul (William) 1926-
  Brief Entry 39
Anderson, Rachel 1943- 34
Andre, Evelyn M(arie) 1924- 27
Andree, Louise
  See Coury, Louise Andree
Andrews, Benny 1930- 31
Andrews, F(rank) Emerson
  1902-1978 22
Andrews, J(ames) S(ydney)
  1934- 4
Andrews, Julie 1935- 7
Andrews, Laura
  See Coury, Louise Andree
Andrews, Roy Chapman
  1884-1960 19
Andrézel, Pierre
  See Blixen, Karen (Christentze
  Dinesen)
Andriola, Alfred J. 1912-1983
  Obituary 34
Andrist, Ralph K. 1914- 45
Angeles, Peter A. 1931- 40
Angell, Judie 1937- 22
Angell, Madeline 1919- 18
Angelo, Valenti 1897- 14
Angier, Bradford 12
Angle, Paul M(cClelland) 1900-1975
  Obituary 20
Anglund, Joan Walsh 1926- 2
  See also CLR 1
Angrist, Stanley W(olff)
  1933- 4
Anita
  See Daniel, Anita
Annett, Cora
  See Scott, Cora Annett
Annixter, Jane
  See Sturtzel, Jane Levington
Annixter, Paul
  See Sturtzel, Howard A.
Anno, Mitsumasa 1926- 38
  Earlier sketch in SATA 5
  See also CLR 2
Anrooy, Frans van
  See Van Anrooy, Francine
Antell, Will D. 1935- 31
Anthony, Barbara 1932- 29
Anthony, C. L.
  See Smith, Dodie
Anthony, Edward 1895-1971 21
Anticaglia, Elizabeth 1939- 12
Antolini, Margaret Fishback
  1904-1985
  Obituary 45
Anton, Michael (James) 1940- 12
Antonacci, Robert J(oseph)
  1916- 45
  Brief Entry 37
Aoki, Hisako 1942- 45
Apfel, Necia H(alpern) 1930-
  Brief Entry 41
Aphrodite, J.
  See Livingston, Carole
Appel, Benjamin 1907-1977 39
  Obituary 21
Appel, Martin E(liot) 1948- 45
Appel, Marty
  See Appel, Martin E(liot)

Appiah, Peggy 1921- 15
Apple, Margot
  Brief Entry 42
Applebaum, Stan 1929- 45
Appleton, Victor [Collective
  pseudonym] 1
Appleton, Victor II [Collective
  pseudonym] 1
  See also Adams, Harriet
  S(tratemeyer)
Apsler, Alfred 1907- 10
Aquillo, Don
  See Prince, J(ack) H(arvey)
Aragonés, Sergio 1937-
  Brief Entry 39
Arbuckle, Dorothy Fry 1910-1982
  Obituary 33
Arbuthnot, May Hill
  1884-1969 2
Archer, Frank
  See O'Connor, Richard
Archer, Jules 1915- 4
Archer, Marion Fuller 1917- 11
Archibald, Joseph S. 1898- 3
Arden, Barbie
  See Stoutenburg, Adrien
Arden, William
  See Lynds, Dennis
Ardizzone, Edward 1900-1979 ... 28
  Obituary 21
  Earlier sketch in SATA 1
  See also CLR 3
Ardley, Neil (Richard) 1937- 43
Arehart-Treichel, Joan 1942- 22
Arenella, Roy 1939- 14
Arkin, Alan (Wolf) 1934-
  Brief Entry 32
Armer, Alberta (Roller) 1904- 9
Armer, Laura Adams
  1874-1963 13
Armitage, David 1943-
  Brief Entry 38
Armitage, Ronda (Jacqueline) 1943-
  Brief Entry 38
Armour, Richard 1906- 14
Armstrong, George D. 1927- 10
Armstrong, Gerry (Breen)
  1929- 10
Armstrong, Louise 43
  Brief Entry 33
Armstrong, Richard 1903- 11
Armstrong, William H. 1914- 4
  See also CLR 1
Arndt, Ursula (Martha H.)
  Brief Entry 39
Arneson, D(on) J(on) 1935- 37
Arnett, Carolyn
  See Cole, Lois Dwight
Arno, Enrico 1913-1981 43
  Obituary 28
Arnold, Caroline 1944- 36
  Brief Entry 34
Arnold, Elliott 1912-1980 5
  Obituary 22
Arnold, Oren 1900- 4
Arnoldy, Julie
  See Bischoff, Julia Bristol
Arnosky, Jim 1946- 22
Arnott, Kathleen 1914- 20

Arnov, Boris, Jr. 1926- 12
Arnow, Harriette (Louisa Simpson)
  1908- 42
Arnstein, Helene S(olomon)
  1915- 12
Arntson, Herbert E(dward)
  1911- 12
Aronin, Ben 1904-1980
  Obituary 25
Arora, Shirley (Lease) 1930- 2
Arquette, Lois S(teinmetz)
  1934- 1
  See Duncan, Lois S(teinmetz)
Arrowood, (McKendrick Lee) Clinton
  1939- 19
Arthur, Robert
  See Feder, Robert Arthur
Arthur, Ruth M(abel)
  1905-1979 7
  Obituary 26
Artis, Vicki Kimmel 1945- 12
Artzybasheff, Boris (Miklailovich)
  1899-1965 14
Aruego, Ariane
  See Dewey, Ariane
Aruego, Jose 1932- 6
  See also CLR 5
Arundel, Honor (Morfydd)
  1919-1973 4
  Obituary 24
Arundel, Jocelyn
  See Alexander, Jocelyn (Anne)
  Arundel
Asbjörnsen, Peter Christen
  1812-1885 15
Asch, Frank 1946- 5
Ash, Jutta 1942- 38
Ashabranner, Brent (Kenneth)
  1921- 1
Ashby, Gwynneth 1922- 44
Ashe, Geoffrey (Thomas)
  1923- 17
Asher, Sandy (Fenichel)
  1942- 36
  Brief Entry 34
Ashey, Bella
  See Breinburg, Petronella
Ashford, Daisy
  See Ashford, Margaret Mary
Ashford, Margaret Mary
  1881-1972 10
Ashley, Bernard 1935-
  Brief Entry 39
  See also CLR 4
Ashley, Elizabeth
  See Salmon, Annie Elizabeth
Ashton, Warren T.
  See Adams, William Taylor
Asimov, Issac 1920- 26
  Earlier sketch in SATA 1
Asinof, Eliot 1919- 6
Astley, Juliet
  See Lofts, Nora (Robinson)
Aston, James
  See White, T(erence) H(anbury)
Atene, Ann
  See Atene, (Rita) Anna
Atene, (Rita) Anna 1922- 12

Atkinson, M. E.
 See Frankau, Mary Evelyn
Atkinson, Margaret Fleming *14*
Atticus
 See Davies, (Edward) Hunter
 See Fleming, Ian (Lancaster)
Atwater, Florence (Hasseltine
 Carroll) *16*
Atwater, Montgomery Meigs
 1904- *15*
Atwater, Richard Tupper 1892-1948
 Brief Entry *27*
Atwood, Ann 1913- *7*
Aubry, Claude B. 1914-1984 ..... *29*
 Obituary *40*
Augarde, Steve 1950- *25*
Ault, Phillip H. 1914- *23*
Ault, Rosalie Sain 1942- *38*
Ault, Roz
 See Ault, Rosalie Sain
Aung, (Maung) Htin 1910- *21*
Aung, U. Htin
 See Aung, (Maung) Htin
Auntie Deb
 See Coury, Louise Andree
Auntie Louise
 See Coury, Louise Andree
Austin, Elizabeth S. 1907- *5*
Austin, Margot *11*
Austin, Oliver L., Jr. 1903- *7*
Austin, Tom
 See Jacobs, Linda C.
Averill, Esther 1902- *28*
 Earlier sketch in SATA 1
Avery, Al
 See Montgomery, Rutherford
Avery, Gillian 1926- *7*
Avery, Kay 1908- *5*
Avery, Lynn
 See Cole, Lois Dwight
Avi
 See Wortis, Avi
Ayars, James S(terling) 1898- *4*
Ayer, Jacqueline 1930- *13*
Ayer, Margaret *15*
Aylesworth, Jim 1943- *38*
Aylesworth, Thomas G(ibbons)
 1927- *4*
 See also CLR 6
Aymar, Brandt 1911- *22*
Azaid
 See Zaidenberg, Arthur

B

B
 See Gilbert, W(illiam) S(chwenk)
B., Tania
 See Blixen, Karen (Christentze
 Dinesen)
BB
 See Watkins-Pitchford, D. J.
Baastad, Babbis Friis
 See Friis-Baastad, Babbis
Bab
 See Gilbert, W(illiam) S(chwenk)
Babbis, Eleanor
 See Friis-Baastad, Babbis

Babbitt, Natalie 1932- *6*
 See also CLR 2
Babcock, Dennis Arthur
 1948- *22*
Bach, Alice (Hendricks)
 1942- *30*
 Brief Entry *27*
Bach, Richard David 1936- *13*
Bachman, Fred 1949- *12*
Bacmeister, Rhoda W(arner)
 1893- *11*
Bacon, Elizabeth 1914- *3*
Bacon, Joan Chase
 See Bowden, Joan Chase
Bacon, Margaret Hope 1921- *6*
Bacon, Martha Sherman
 1917-1981 .... *18*
 Obituary *27*
 See also CLR 3
Bacon, Peggy 1895- *2*
Bacon, R(onald) L(eonard)
 1924- *26*
Baden-Powell, Robert (Stephenson
 Smyth) 1857-1941 .... *16*
Baerg, Harry J(ohn) 1909- *12*
Bagnold, Enid 1889-1981 .... *25*
 Earlier sketch in SATA 1
Bahr, Robert 1940- *38*
Bahti, Tom
 Brief Entry *31*
Bailey, Alice Cooper 1890- *12*
Bailey, Bernadine Freeman *14*
Bailey, Carolyn Sherwin
 1875-1961 .... *14*
Bailey, Jane H(orton) 1916- *12*
Bailey, Maralyn Collins (Harrison)
 1941- *12*
Bailey, Matilda
 See Radford, Ruby L.
Bailey, Maurice Charles
 1932- *12*
Bailey, Ralph Edgar 1893- *11*
Baird, Bil 1904- *30*
Baird, Thomas P. 1923- *45*
 Brief Entry *39*
Baity, Elizabeth Chesley
 1907- *1*
Bakeless, John (Edwin) 1894- *9*
Bakeless, Katherine Little
 1895- *9*
Baker, Alan 1951- *22*
Baker, Augusta 1911- *3*
Baker, Betty (Lou) 1928- *5*
Baker, Charlotte 1910- *2*
Baker, Elizabeth 1923- *7*
Baker, Gayle C(unningham)
 1950- *39*
Baker, James W. 1924- *22*
Baker, Janice E(dla) 1941- *22*
Baker, Jeannie 1950- *23*
Baker, Jeffrey J(ohn) W(heeler)
 1931- *5*
Baker, Jim
 See Baker, James W.
Baker, Laura Nelson 1911- *3*
Baker, Margaret 1890- *4*
Baker, Margaret J(oyce)
 1918- *12*

Baker, Mary Gladys Steel
 1892-1974 .... *12*
Baker, (Robert) Michael
 1938- *4*
Baker, Nina (Brown)
 1888-1957 .... *15*
Baker, Rachel 1904-1978 .... *2*
 Obituary *26*
Baker, Samm Sinclair 1909- *12*
Baker, Susan (Catherine)
 1942- *29*
Balaam
 See Lamb, G(eoffrey) F(rederick)
Balch, Glenn 1902- *3*
Baldridge, Cyrus LeRoy 1889-
 Brief Entry *29*
Balducci, Carolyn Feleppa
 1946- *5*
Baldwin, Anne Norris 1938- *5*
Baldwin, Clara *11*
Baldwin, Gordo
 See Baldwin, Gordon C.
Baldwin, Gordon C. 1908- *12*
Baldwin, James 1841-1925 .... *24*
Baldwin, James (Arthur)
 1924- *9*
Baldwin, Margaret
 See Weis, Margaret (Edith)
Baldwin, Stan(ley C.) 1929-
 Brief Entry *28*
Bales, Carol Ann 1940-
 Brief Entry *29*
Balet, Jan (Bernard) 1913- *11*
Balian, Lorna 1929- *9*
Ball, Zachary
 See Masters, Kelly R.
Ballantine, Lesley Frost
 See Frost, Lesley
Ballantyne, R(obert) M(ichael)
 1825-1894 .... *24*
Ballard, Lowell Clyne 1904- *12*
Ballard, (Charles) Martin
 1929- *1*
Balogh, Penelope 1916-1975 ...... *1*
 Obituary *34*
Balow, Tom 1931- *12*
Baltzer, Hans (Adolf) 1900- *40*
Bamfylde, Walter
 See Bevan, Tom
Bamman, Henry A. 1918- *12*
Bancroft, Griffing 1907- *6*
Bancroft, Laura
 See Baum, L(yman) Frank
Baner, Skulda V(anadis)
 1897-1964 .... *10*
Bang, Betsy (Garrett) 1912-
 Brief Entry *37*
Bang, Garrett
 See Bang, Molly Garrett
Bang, Molly Garrett 1943- *24*
 See also CLR 8
Banks, Laura Stockton Voorhees
 1908(?)-1980
 Obituary *23*
Banks, Sara (Jeanne Gordon Harrell)
 1937- *26*
Banner, Angela
 See Maddison, Angela Mary

Bannerman, Helen (Brodie Cowan
  Watson) 1863(?)-1946 19
Banning, Evelyn I. 1903- 36
Bannon, Laura (?)-1963 6
Barbary, James
  See Baumann, Amy (Brown)
Barbary, James
  See Beeching, Jack
Barbe, Walter Burke 1926- 45
Barber, Antonia
  See Anthony, Barbara
Barber, Linda
  See Graham-Barber, Lynda
Barber, Richard (William)
  1941- 35
Barbour, Ralph Henry
  1870-1944 16
Barclay, Isabel
  See Dobell, I.M.B.
Bare, Arnold Edwin 1920- 16
Bare, Colleen Stanley 32
Barish, Matthew 1907- 12
Barker, Albert W. 1900- 8
Barker, Carol (Minturn) 1938- 31
Barker, Cicely Mary 1895-1973
  Brief Entry 39
Barker, Melvern 1907- 11
Barker, S. Omar 1894- 10
Barker, Will 1908- 8
Barkin, Carol
  Brief Entry 42
Barkley, James Edward 1941- 6
Barks, Carl 1901- 37
Barnaby, Ralph S(tanton)
  1893- 9
Barner, Bob 1947- 29
Barnes, (Frank) Eric Wollencott
  1907-1962 22
Barnes, Malcolm 1909(?)-1984
  Obituary 41
Barnett, Lincoln (Kinnear)
  1909-1979 36
Barnett, Moneta 1922-1976 33
Barnett, Naomi 1927- 40
Barney, Maginel Wright
  1881-1966 39
  Brief Entry 32
Barnouw, Adriaan Jacob 1877-1968
  Obituary 27
Barnouw, Victor 1915- 43
  Brief Entry 28
Barnstone, Willis 1927- 20
Barnum, Jay Hyde
  1888(?)-1962 20
Barnum, Richard [Collective
  pseudonym] 1
Baron, Virginia Olsen 1931-
  Brief Entry 28
Barr, Donald 1921- 20
Barr, George 1907- 2
Barr, Jene 1900-1985 16
  Obituary 42
Barrer, Gertrude
  See Barrer-Russell, Gertrude
Barrer-Russell, Gertrude
  1921- 27
Barrett, Ethel
  Brief Entry 44
Barrett, Judith 1941- 26

Barrett, Ron 1937- 14
Barrie, J(ames) M(atthew)
  1860-1937 .... YABC 1
Barrol, Grady
  See Bograd, Larry
Barry, James P(otvin) 1918- 14
Barry, Katharina (Watjen)
  1936- 4
Barry, Robert 1931- 6
Barry, Scott 1952- 32
Bartenbach, Jean 1918- 40
Barth, Edna 1914-1980 7
  Obituary 24
Barthelme, Donald 1931- 7
Bartholomew, Barbara 1941-
  Brief Entry 42
Bartlett, Philip A. [Collective
  pseudonym] 1
Bartlett, Robert Merill 1899- 12
Barton, Byron 1930- 9
Barton, Harriett
  Brief Entry 43
Barton, May Hollis [Collective
  pseudonym] 1
  See also Adams, Harriet
  S(tratemeyer)
Bartos-Hoeppner, Barbara
  1923- 5
Bartsch, Jochen 1906- 39
Baruch, Dorothy W(alter)
  1899-1962 21
Bas, Rutger
  See Rutgers van der Loeff, An(na)
  Basenau
Bashevis, Isaac
  See Singer, Isaac Bashevis
Baskin, Leonard 1922- 30
  Brief Entry 27
Bason, Lillian 1913- 20
Bassett, Jeni 1960(?)-
  Brief Entry 43
Bassett, John Keith
  See Keating, Lawrence A.
Batchelor, Joy 1914-
  Brief Entry 29
Bate, Lucy 1939- 18
Bate, Norman 1916- 5
Bates, Barbara S(nedeker)
  1919- 12
Bates, Betty 1921- 19
Batey, Tom 1946-
  Brief Entry 41
Batherman, Muriel
  See Sheldon, Muriel
Batiuk, Thomas M(artin) 1947-
  Brief Entry 40
Batson, Larry 1930- 35
Battaglia, Aurelius
  Brief Entry 33
Batten, H(arry) Mortimer
  1888-1958 25
Batten, Mary 1937- 5
Batterberry, Ariane Ruskin
  1935- 13
Batterberry, Michael (Carver)
  1932- 32
Battles, Edith 1921- 7
Baudouy, Michel-Aime 1909- 7
Bauer, Fred 1934- 36

Bauer, Helen 1900- 2
Bauer, Marion Dane 1938- 20
Bauernschmidt, Marjorie
  1926- 15
Baum, Allyn Z(elton) 1924- 20
Baum, L(yman) Frank
  1856-1919 18
Baum, Willi 1931- 4
Baumann, Amy (Brown)
  1922- 10
Baumann, Elwood D.
  Brief Entry 33
Baumann, Hans 1914- 2
Baumann, Kurt 1935- 21
Bawden, Nina
  See Kark, Nina Mary
  See also CLR 2
Bayer, Jane E. (?)-1985
  Obituary 44
Bayley, Nicola 1949- 41
Baylor, Byrd 1924- 16
  See also CLR 3
Baynes, Pauline (Diana)
  1922- 19
Beach, Charles
  See Reid, (Thomas) Mayne
Beach, Charles Amory [Collective
  pseudonym] 1
Beach, Edward L(atimer)
  1918- 12
Beach, Stewart Taft 1899- 23
Beachcroft, Nina 1931- 18
Bealer, Alex W(inkler III)
  1921-1980 8
  Obituary 22
Beals, Carleton 1893- 12
Beals, Frank Lee 1881-1972
  Obituary 26
Beame, Rona 1934- 12
Beamer, (G.) Charles, (Jr.)
  1942- 43
Beaney, Jan
  See Udall, Jan Beaney
Beard, Charles Austin
  1874-1948 18
Beard, Dan(iel Carter)
  1850-1941 22
Bearden, Romare (Howard)
  1914- 22
Beardmore, Cedric
  See Beardmore, George
Beardmore, George
  1908-1979 20
Bearman, Jane (Ruth) 1917- 29
Beatty, Elizabeth
  See Holloway, Teresa (Bragunier)
Beatty, Hetty Burlingame
  1907-1971 5
Beatty, Jerome, Jr. 1918- 5
Beatty, John (Louis)
  1922-1975 6
  Obituary 25
Beatty, Patricia (Robbins) 30
  Earlier sketch in SATA 1
Bechtel, Louise Seaman
  1894-1985 4
  Obituary 43
Beck, Barbara L. 1927- 12
Becker, Beril 1901- 11

Becker, John (Leonard) 1901- *12*
Becker, Joyce 1936- *39*
Becker, May Lamberton
  1873-1958 .... *33*
Beckett, Sheilah 1913- *33*
Beckman, Gunnel 1910- *6*
Beckman, Kaj
  See Beckman, Karin
Beckman, Karin 1913- *45*
Beckman, Per (Frithiof) 1913- *45*
Bedford, A. N.
  See Watson, Jane Werner
Bedford, Annie North
  See Watson, Jane Werner
Beebe, B(urdetta) F(aye)
  1920- *1*
Beebe, (Charles) William
  1877-1962 .... *19*
Beeby, Betty 1923- *25*
Beech, Webb
  See Butterworth, W. E.
Beeching, Jack 1922- *14*
Beeler, Nelson F(rederick)
  1910- *13*
Beers, Dorothy Sands 1917- *9*
Beers, Lorna 1897- *14*
Beers, V(ictor) Gilbert 1928- *9*
Begley, Kathleen A(nne)
  1948- *21*
Behn, Harry 1898-1973 .... *2*
  Obituary *34*
Behnke, Frances L. *8*
Behr, Joyce 1929- *15*
Behrens, June York 1925- *19*
Behrman, Carol H(elen) 1925- *14*
Beiser, Arthur 1931- *22*
Beiser, Germaine 1931- *11*
Belair, Richard L. 1934- *45*
Belaney, Archibald Stansfeld
  1888-1938 .... *24*
Belknap, B. H.
  See Ellis, Edward S(ylvester)
Bell, Corydon 1894- *3*
Bell, Emily Mary
  See Cason, Mabel Earp
Bell, Gertrude (Wood) 1911- *12*
Bell, Gina
  See Iannone, Jeanne
Bell, Janet
  See Clymer, Eleanor
Bell, Margaret E(lizabeth)
  1898- *2*
Bell, Norman (Edward) 1899- *11*
Bell, Raymond Martin 1907- *13*
Bell, Robert S(tanley) W(arren)
  1871-1921
  Brief Entry *27*
Bell, Thelma Harrington
  1896- *3*
Bellairs, John 1938- *2*
Belloc, (Joseph) Hilaire (Pierre)
  1870-1953 ....*YABC 1*
Bell-Zano, Gina
  See Iannone, Jeanne
Belpré, Pura 1899-1982 .... *16*
  Obituary *30*
Belting, Natalie Maree 1915- *6*
Belton, John Raynor 1931- *22*
Beltran, Alberto 1923- *43*

Belvedere, Lee
  See Grayland, Valerie
Bemelmans, Ludwig
  1898-1962 .... *15*
  See also CLR 6
Benary, Margot
  See Benary-Isbert, Margot
Benary-Isbert, Margot
  1889-1979 .... *2*
  Obituary *21*
Benasutti, Marion 1908- *6*
Benchley, Nathaniel (Goddard)
  1915-1981 .... *25*
  Obituary *28*
  Earlier sketch in SATA 3
Benchley, Peter 1940- *3*
Bender, Lucy Ellen 1942- *22*
Bendick, Jeanne 1919- *2*
  See also CLR 5
Bendick, Robert L(ouis)
  1917- *11*
Benedict, Dorothy Potter
  1889-1979 .... *11*
  Obituary *23*
Benedict, Lois Trimble
  1902-1967 .... *12*
Benedict, Rex 1920- *8*
Benedict, Stewart H(urd)
  1924- *26*
Benét, Laura 1884-1979 .... *3*
  Obituary *23*
Benét, Stephen Vincent
  1898-1943 ....*YABC 1*
Benet, Sula 1903(?)-1982 .... *21*
  Obituary *33*
Benezra, Barbara 1921- *10*
Benjamin, Nora
  See Kubie, Nora (Gottheil) Benjamin
Bennett, Dorothea
  See Young, Dorothea Bennett
Bennett, Jay 1912- *41*
  Brief Entry *27*
Bennett, Jill (Crawford) 1934- *41*
Bennett, John 1865-1956 .....*YABC 1*
Bennett, Rachel
  See Hill, Margaret (Ohler)
Bennett, Rainey 1907- *15*
Bennett, Richard 1899- *21*
Bennett, Russell H(oradley)
  1896- *25*
Benson, Sally 1900-1972 .... *35*
  Obituary *27*
  Earlier sketch in SATA 1
Bentley, Judith (McBride)
  1945- *40*
Bentley, Nicolas Clerihew 1907-1978
  Obituary *24*
Bentley, Phyllis (Eleanor)
  1894-1977 .... *6*
  Obituary *25*
Berelson, Howard 1940- *5*
Berends, Polly Berrien 1939-
  Brief Entry *38*
Berenstain, Janice *12*
Berenstain, Michael 1951-
  Brief Entry *45*
Berenstain, Stan(ley) 1923- *12*
Beresford, Elisabeth *25*

Berg, Dave
  See Berg, David
Berg, David 1920- *27*
Berg, Jean Horton 1913- *6*
Berg, Joan
  See Victor, Joan Berg
Bergaust, Erik 1925-1978 .... *20*
Berger, Gilda
  Brief Entry *42*
Berger, Josef 1903-1971 .... *36*
Berger, Melvin H. 1927- *5*
  See also SAAS 2
Berger, Terry 1933- *8*
Bergey, Alyce (Mae) 1934- *45*
Berkebile, Fred D(onovan) 1900-1978
  Obituary *26*
Berkey, Barry Robert 1935- *24*
Berkowitz, Freda Pastor 1910- *12*
Berliner, Don 1930- *33*
Berliner, Franz 1930- *13*
Berlitz, Charles L. (Frambach)
  1913- *32*
Berman, Linda 1948- *38*
Berna, Paul 1910- *15*
Bernadette
  See Watts, Bernadette
Bernard, George I. 1949- *39*
Bernard, Jacqueline (de Sieyes)
  1921-1983 .... *8*
  Obituary *45*
Bernays, Anne
  See Kaplan, Anne Bernays
Bernstein, Joanne E(ckstein)
  1943- *15*
Bernstein, Theodore M(enline)
  1904-1979 .... *12*
  Obituary *27*
Berrien, Edith Heal
  See Heal, Edith
Berrill, Jacquelyn (Batsel)
  1905- *12*
Berrington, John
  See Brownjohn, Alan
Berry, B. J.
  See Berry, Barbara J.
Berry, Barbara J. 1937- *7*
Berry, Erick
  See Best, Allena Champlin
Berry, Jane Cobb 1915(?)-1979
  Obituary *22*
Berry, William D(avid) 1926- *14*
Berson, Harold 1926- *4*
Berwick, Jean
  See Meyer, Jean Shepherd
Beskow, Elsa (Maartman)
  1874-1953 .... *20*
Best, (Evangel) Allena Champlin
  1892-1974 .... *2*
  Obituary *25*
Best, (Oswald) Herbert 1894- *2*
Betancourt, Jeanne 1941-
  Brief Entry *43*
Beth, Mary
  See Miller, Mary Beth
Bethancourt, T. Ernesto 1932- *11*
  See also CLR 3
Bethell, Jean (Frankenberry)
  1922- *8*
Bethers, Ray 1902- *6*

Bethune, J. G.
   See Ellis, Edward S(ylvester)
Betteridge, Anne
   See Potter, Margaret (Newman)
Bettina
   See Ehrlich, Bettina
Betts, James [Joint pseudonym]
   See Haynes, Betsy
Betz, Eva Kelly 1897-1968 .... *10*
Bevan, Tom
   1868-1930(?) ....*YABC 2*
Bewick, Thomas 1753-1828 .... *16*
Beyer, Audrey White 1916- *9*
Bialk, Elisa *1*
Bianco, Margery (Williams)
   1881-1944 .... *15*
Bianco, Pamela 1906- *28*
Bibby, Violet 1908- *24*
Bible, Charles 1937- *13*
Bice, Clare 1909-1976 .... *22*
Bickerstaff, Isaac
   See Swift, Jonathan
Biegel, Paul 1925- *16*
Biemiller, Carl L(udwig)
   1912-1979 .... *40*
   Obituary *21*
Bienenfeld, Florence L(ucille)
   1929- *39*
Bierhorst, John 1936- *6*
Bileck, Marvin 1920- *40*
Bill, Alfred Hoyt 1879-1964 ...... *44*
Billings, Charlene W(interer)
   1941- *41*
Billington, Elizabeth T(hain)
   Brief Entry *43*
Billout, Guy René 1941- *10*
Binkley, Anne
   See Rand, Ann (Binkley)
Binzen, Bill *24*
Binzen, William
   See Binzen, Bill
Birch, Reginald B(athurst)
   1856-1943 .... *19*
Birmingham, Lloyd 1924- *12*
Biro, Val 1921- *1*
Bischoff, Julia Bristol
   1909-1970 .... *12*
Bishop, Bonnie 1943- *37*
Bishop, Claire (Huchet) *14*
Bishop, Curtis 1912-1967 .... *6*
Bishop, Elizabeth 1911-1979
   Obituary *24*
Bisset, Donald 1910- *7*
Bitter, Gary G(len) 1940- *22*
Bixby, William 1920- *6*
Bjerregaard-Jensen, Vilhelm Hans
   See Hillcourt, William
Bjorklund, Lorence F.
   1913-1978 .... *35*
   Brief Entry *32*
Black, Algernon David 1900- *12*
Black, Irma S(imonton)
   1906-1972 .... *2*
   Obituary *25*
Black, Mansell
   See Trevor, Elleston
Black, Susan Adams 1953- *40*
Blackburn, Claire
   See Jacobs, Linda C.

Blackburn, John(ny) Brewton
   1952- *15*
Blackburn, Joyce Knight
   1920- *29*
Blackett, Veronica Heath
   1927- *12*
Blackton, Peter
   See Wilson, Lionel
Blades, Ann 1947- *16*
Bladow, Suzanne Wilson
   1937- *14*
Blaine, John
   See Goodwin, Harold Leland
Blaine, John
   See Harkins, Philip
Blaine, Margery Kay 1937- *11*
Blair, Eric Arthur 1903-1950 ..... *29*
Blair, Helen 1910-
   Brief Entry *29*
Blair, Jay 1953- *45*
Blair, Ruth Van Ness 1912- *12*
Blair, Walter 1900- *12*
Blake, Olive
   See Supraner, Robyn
Blake, Quentin 1932- *9*
Blake, Robert 1949- *42*
Blake, Walker E.
   See Butterworth, W. E.
Blake, William 1757-1827 .... *30*
Bland, Edith Nesbit
   See Nesbit, E(dith)
Bland, Fabian [Joint pseudonym]
   See Nesbit, E(dith)
Blane, Gertrude
   See Blumenthal, Gertrude
Blassingame, Wyatt Rainey
   1909-1985 .... *34*
   Obituary *41*
   Earlier sketch in SATA 1
Bleeker, Sonia 1909-1971 .... *2*
   Obituary *26*
Blegvad, Erik 1923- *14*
Blegvad, Lenore 1926- *14*
Blishen, Edward 1920- *8*
Bliss, Corinne D(emas) 1947- *37*
Bliss, Reginald
   See Wells, H(erbert) G(eorge)
Bliss, Ronald G(ene) 1942- *12*
Bliven, Bruce, Jr. 1916- *2*
Blixen, Karen (Christentze Dinesen)
   1885-1962 .... *44*
Bloch, Lucienne 1909- *10*
Bloch, Marie Halun 1910- *6*
Bloch, Robert 1917- *12*
Blochman, Lawrence G(oldtree)
   1900-1975 .... *22*
Block, Irvin 1917- *12*
Blocksma, Mary
   Brief Entry *44*
Blood, Charles Lewis 1929- *28*
Bloom, Freddy 1914- *37*
Bloom, Lloyd
   Brief Entry *43*
Blos, Joan W(insor) 1928- *33*
   Brief Entry *27*
Blough, Glenn O(rlando)
   1907- *1*
Blue, Rose 1931- *5*
Blumberg, Rhoda 1917- *35*

Blume, Judy (Sussman) 1938- *31*
   Earlier sketch in SATA 2
   See also CLR 2
Blumenthal, Gertrude 1907-1971
   Obituary *27*
Blutig, Eduard
   See Gorey, Edward St. John
Bly, Janet Chester 1945- *43*
Bly, Stephen A(rthur) 1944- *43*
Blyton, Carey 1932- *9*
Blyton, Enid (Mary)
   1897-1968 .... *25*
Boardman, Fon Wyman, Jr.
   1911- *6*
Boardman, Gwenn R. 1924- *12*
Boase, Wendy 1944- *28*
Boatner, Mark Mayo III
   1921- *29*
Bobbe, Dorothie 1905-1975 .... *1*
   Obituary *25*
Bobri
   See Bobritsky, Vladimir
Bobri, Vladimir
   See Bobritsky, Vladimir
Bobritsky, Vladimir 1898-
   Brief Entry *32*
Bock, Hal
   See Bock, Harold I.
Bock, Harold I. 1939- *10*
Bock, William Sauts
   Netamux'we *14*
Bodecker, N. M. 1922- *8*
Boden, Hilda
   See Bodenham, Hilda Esther
Bodenham, Hilda Esther
   1901- *13*
Bodie, Idella F(allaw) 1925- *12*
Bodker, Cecil 1927- *14*
Bodsworth, (Charles) Fred(erick)
   1918- *27*
Boeckman, Charles 1920- *12*
Boegehold, Betty (Doyle) 1913-1985
   Obituary *42*
Boesch, Mark J(oseph) 1917- *12*
Boesen, Victor 1908- *16*
Boggs, Ralph Steele 1901- *7*
Bograd, Larry 1953- *33*
Bohdal, Susi 1951- *22*
Boles, Paul Darcy 1916-1984 ..... *9*
   Obituary *38*
Bolian, Polly 1925- *4*
Bollen, Roger 1941(?)-
   Brief Entry *29*
Bolliger, Max 1929- *7*
Bolognese, Don(ald Alan)
   1934- *24*
Bolton, Carole 1926- *6*
Bolton, Elizabeth
   See Johnston, Norma
Bolton, Evelyn
   See Bunting, Anne Evelyn
Bond, Gladys Baker 1912- *14*
Bond, J. Harvey
   See Winterbotham, R(ussell)
   R(obert)
Bond, Michael 1926- *6*
   See also CLR 1
Bond, Nancy (Barbara) 1945- *22*
Bond, Ruskin 1934- *14*

Bonehill, Captain Ralph
    See Stratemeyer, Edward L.
Bonham, Barbara 1926- 7
Bonham, Frank 1914- *1*
Bonn, Pat
    See Bonn, Patricia Carolyn
Bonn, Patricia Carolyn 1948- *43*
Bonner, Mary Graham
    1890-1974 .... *19*
Bonsall, Crosby (Barbara Newell)
    1921- *23*
Bontemps, Arna 1902-1973 .... *44*
    Obituary *24*
    Earlier sketch in SATA 2
    See also CLR 6
Bonzon, Paul-Jacques 1908- *22*
Booher, Dianna Daniels 1948- *33*
Bookman, Charlotte
    See Zolotow, Charlotte S.
Boone, Pat 1934- 7
Booth, Ernest Sheldon
    1915-1984 .... *43*
Booth, Graham (Charles)
    1935- *37*
Bordier, Georgette 1924- *16*
Boring, Mel 1939- *35*
Borja, Corinne 1929- *22*
Borja, Robert 1923- *22*
Borland, Hal 1900-1978 5
    Obituary *24*
Borland, Harold Glen
    See Borland, Hal
Borland, Kathryn Kilby 1916- *16*
Bornstein, Ruth 1927- *14*
Borski, Lucia Merecka *18*
Borten, Helen Jacobson 1930- 5
Borton, Elizabeth
    See Treviño, Elizabeth B. de
Bortstein, Larry 1942- *16*
Bosco, Jack
    See Holliday, Joseph
Boshell, Gordon 1908- *15*
Boshinski, Blanche 1922- *10*
Bosse, Malcolm J(oseph)
    1926- *35*
Bossom, Naomi 1933- *35*
Boston, Lucy Maria (Wood)
    1892- *19*
    See also CLR 3
Bosworth, J. Allan 1925- *19*
Bothwell, Jean *2*
Botkin, B(enjamin) A(lbert)
    1901-1975 .... *40*
Botting, Douglas (Scott)
    1934- *43*
Bottner, Barbara 1943- *14*
Boulle, Pierre (Francois Marie-Louis)
    1912- *22*
Bourne, Leslie
    See Marshall, Evelyn
Bourne, Miriam Anne 1931- *16*
Boutet De Monvel, (Louis) M(aurice)
    1850(?)-1913 .... *30*
Bova, Ben 1932- 6
    See also CLR 3
Bowden, Joan Chase 1925-
    Brief Entry *38*
Bowen, Betty Morgan
    See West, Betty

Bowen, Catherine Drinker
    1897-1973 7
Bowen, David
    See Bowen, Joshua David
Bowen, Joshua David 1930- *22*
Bowen, Robert Sidney 1900(?)-1977
    Obituary *21*
Bowie, Jim
    See Stratemeyer, Edward L.
Bowler, Jan Brett
    See Brett, Jan
Bowman, James Cloyd
    1880-1961 .... *23*
Bowman, John S(tewart)
    1931- *16*
Bowman, Kathleen (Gill) 1942-
    Brief Entry *40*
Boyce, George A(rthur) 1898- *19*
Boyd, Pauline
    See Schock, Pauline
Boyd, Selma
    See Acuff, Selma Boyd
Boyd, Waldo T. 1918- *18*
Boyer, Robert E(rnst) 1929- *22*
Boyle, Ann (Peters) 1916- *10*
Boyle, Eleanor Vere (Gordon)
    1825-1916 .... *28*
Boylston, Helen (Dore)
    1895-1984 .... *23*
    Obituary *39*
Boynton, Sandra 1953-
    Brief Entry *38*
Boz
    See Dickens, Charles
Bradbury, Bianca 1908- *3*
Bradbury, Ray (Douglas)
    1920- *11*
Bradford, Ann (Liddell) 1917-
    Brief Entry *38*
Bradford, Lois J(ean) 1936- *36*
Bradley, Duane
    See Sanborn, Duane
Bradley, Virginia 1912- *23*
Brady, Esther Wood 1905- *31*
Brady, Irene 1943- *4*
Brady, Lillian 1902- *28*
Bragdon, Elspeth 1897- *6*
Bragdon, Lillian (Jacot) *24*
Bragg, Mabel Caroline
    1870-1945 .... *24*
Braithwaite, Althea 1940- *23*
Bram, Elizabeth 1948- *30*
Brancato, Robin F(idler)
    1936- *23*
Brandenberg, Aliki (Liacouras)
    1929- *35*
    Earlier sketch in SATA 2
Brandenberg, Franz 1932- *35*
    Earlier sketch in SATA 8
Brandhorst, Carl T(heodore)
    1898- *23*
Brandon, Brumsic, Jr. 1927- 9
Brandon, Curt
    See Bishop, Curtis
Brandreth, Gyles 1948- *28*
Brandt, Catharine 1905- *40*
Brandt, Keith
    See Sabin, Louis

Branfield, John (Charles)
    1931- *11*
Branley, Franklyn M(ansfield)
    1915- *4*
Branscum, Robbie 1937- *23*
Bransom, (John) Paul
    1885-1979 .... *43*
Bratton, Helen 1899- *4*
Braude, Michael 1936- *23*
Braymer, Marjorie 1911- *6*
Brecht, Edith 1895-1975 .... *6*
    Obituary *25*
Breck, Vivian
    See Breckenfeld, Vivian Gurney
Breckenfeld, Vivian Gurney
    1895- *1*
Breda, Tjalmar
    See DeJong, David C(ornel)
Breinburg, Petronella 1927- *11*
Breisky, William J(ohn) 1928- *22*
Brennan, Joseph L. 1903- *6*
Brennan, Tim
    See Conroy, Jack (Wesley)
Brenner, Barbara (Johnes)
    1925- *42*
    Earlier sketch in SATA 4
Brenner, Fred 1920- *36*
    Brief Entry *34*
Brent, Hope 1935(?)-1984
    Obituary *39*
Brent, Stuart *14*
Brett, Bernard 1925- *22*
Brett, Grace N(eff) 1900-1975 .... *23*
Brett, Hawksley
    See Bell, Robert S(tanley) W(arren)
Brett, Jan 1949- *42*
Brewer, Sally King 1947- *33*
Brewster, Benjamin
    See Folsom, Franklin
Brewton, John E(dmund)
    1898- *5*
Brick, John 1922-1973 .... *10*
Bridgers, Sue Ellen 1942- *22*
    See also SAAS 1
Bridges, William (Andrew)
    1901- *5*
Bridwell, Norman 1928- *4*
Brier, Howard M(axwell)
    1903-1969 .... *8*
Briggs, Katharine Mary 1898-1980
    Obituary *25*
Briggs, Peter 1921-1975 .... *39*
    Obituary *31*
Briggs, Raymond (Redvers)
    1934- *23*
    See also CLR 10
Bright, Robert 1902- *24*
Brightwell, L(eonard) R(obert) 1889-
    Brief Entry *29*
Brimberg, Stanlee 1947- 9
Brin, Ruth F(irestone) 1921- *22*
Brinckloe, Julie (Lorraine)
    1950- *13*
Brindel, June (Rachuy) 1919- 7
Brindze, Ruth 1903- *23*
Brink, Carol Ryrie 1895-1981 ..... *31*
    Obituary *27*
    Earlier sketch in SATA 1

Brinsmead, H(esba) F(ay)
1922- *18*

Briquebec, John
See Rowland-Entwistle, (Arthur)
Theodore (Henry)

Brisco, Pat A.
See Matthews, Patricia

Brisco, Patty
See Matthews, Patricia

Brisley, Joyce Lankester
1896- *22*

Britt, Albert 1874-1969
Obituary *28*

Britt, Dell 1934- *1*

Brittain, William 1930- *36*

Britton, Louisa
See McGuire, Leslie (Sarah)

Bro, Margueritte (Harmon)
1894-1977 .... *19*
Obituary *27*

Broadhead, Helen Cross
1913- *25*

Brochmann, Elizabeth (Anne)
1938- *41*

Brock, Betty 1923- *7*

Brock, C(harles) E(dmund)
1870-1938 .... *42*
Brief Entry *32*

Brock, Emma L(illian)
1886-1974 .... *8*

Brock, H(enry) M(atthew)
1875-1960 .... *42*

Brockett, Eleanor Hall
1913-1967 .... *10*

Brockman, C(hristian) Frank
1902- *26*

Broderick, Dorothy M. 1929- *5*

Brodie, Sally
See Cavin, Ruth (Brodie)

Broekel, Rainer Lothar 1923- *38*

Broekel, Ray
See Broekel, Rainer Lothar

Bröger, Achim 1944- *31*

Brokamp, Marilyn 1920- *10*

Bromhall, Winifred *26*

Brommer, Gerald F(rederick)
1927- *28*

Brondfield, Jerome 1913- *22*

Brondfield, Jerry
See Brondfield, Jerome

Bronson, Lynn
See Lampman, Evelyn Sibley

Bronson, Wilfrid Swancourt
1894-1985
Obituary *43*

Brooke, L(eonard) Leslie
1862-1940 .... *17*

Brooke-Haven, P.
See Wodehouse, P(elham)
G(renville)

Brookins, Dana 1931- *28*

Brooks, Anita 1914- *5*

Brooks, Barbara
See Simons, Barbara B(rooks)

Brooks, Charlotte K. *24*

Brooks, Gwendolyn 1917- *6*

Brooks, Jerome 1931- *23*

Brooks, Lester 1924- *7*

Brooks, Maurice (Graham)
1900- *45*

Brooks, Polly Schoyer 1912- *12*

Brooks, Ron(ald George) 1948-
Brief Entry *33*

Brooks, Walter R(ollin)
1886-1958 .... *17*

Brosnan, James Patrick 1929- *14*

Brosnan, Jim
See Brosnan, James Patrick

Broun, Emily
See Sterne, Emma Gelders

Brower, Millicent *8*

Brower, Pauline (York) 1929- *22*

Browin, Frances Williams
1898- *5*

Brown, Alexis
See Baumann, Amy (Brown)

Brown, Bill
See Brown, William L.

Brown, Billye Walker
See Cutchen, Billye Walker

Brown, Bob
See Brown, Robert Joseph

Brown, Buck 1936- *45*

Brown, Conrad 1922- *31*

Brown, David
See Myller, Rolf

Brown, Dee (Alexander)
1908- *5*

Brown, Eleanor Frances 1908- *3*

Brown, Elizabeth M(yers)
1915- *43*

Brown, Fern G. 1918- *34*

Brown, (Robert) Fletch 1923- *42*

Brown, George Earl
1883-1964 .... *11*

Brown, George Mackay 1921- *35*

Brown, Irene Bennett 1932- *3*

Brown, Irving
See Adams, William Taylor

Brown, Ivor (John Carnegie)
1891-1974 .... *5*
Obituary *26*

Brown, Joe David 1915-1976 ..... *44*

Brown, Judith Gwyn 1933- *20*

Brown, Lloyd Arnold
1907-1966 .... *36*

Brown, Marc Tolon 1946- *10*

Brown, Marcia 1918- *7*

Brown, Margaret Wise
1910-1952 .... *YABC 2*
See also CLR 10

Brown, Margery *5*

Brown, Marion Marsh 1908- *6*

Brown, Myra Berry 1918- *6*

Brown, Palmer 1919- *36*

Brown, Pamela 1924- *5*

Brown, Robert Joseph 1907- *14*

Brown, Rosalie (Gertrude) Moore
1910- *9*

Brown, Roswell
See Webb, Jean Francis (III)

Brown, Roy (Frederick) 1921-1982
Obituary *39*

Brown, Vinson 1912- *19*

Brown, Walter R(eed) 1929- *19*

Brown, Will
See Ainsworth, William Harrison

Brown, William L(ouis)
1910-1964 .... *5*

Browne, Anthony (Edward Tudor)
1946- *45*
Brief Entry *44*

Browne, Dik
See Browne, Richard

Browne, Hablot Knight
1815-1882 .... *21*

Browne, Matthew
See Rands, William Brighty

Browne, Richard 1917-
Brief Entry *38*

Browning, Robert
1812-1889 .... *YABC 1*

Brownjohn, Alan 1931- *6*

Bruce, Dorita Fairlie 1885-1970
Obituary *27*

Bruce, Mary 1927- *1*

Bruchac, Joseph III 1942- *42*

Bruna, Dick 1927- *43*
Brief Entry *30*
See also CLR 7

Brunhoff, Jean de 1899-1937 ..... *24*
See also CLR 4

Brunhoff, Laurent de 1925- *24*
See also CLR 4

Brustlein, Daniel 1904- *40*

Brustlein, Janice Tworkov *40*

Bryan, Ashley F. 1923- *31*

Bryan, Dorothy (Marie) 1896(?)-1984
Obituary *39*

Bryant, Bernice (Morgan)
1908- *11*

Brychta, Alex 1956- *21*

Bryson, Bernarda 1905- *9*

Buba, Joy Flinsch 1904- *44*

Buchan, Bryan 1945- *36*

Buchan, John 1875-1940 ..... *YABC 2*

Buchheimer, Naomi Barnett
See Barnett, Naomi

Buchwald, Art(hur) 1925- *10*

Buchwald, Emilie 1935- *7*

Buck, Lewis 1925- *18*

Buck, Margaret Waring 1910- *3*

Buck, Pearl S(ydenstricker)
1892-1973 .... *25*
Earlier sketch in SATA 1

Buckeridge, Anthony 1912- *6*

Buckley, Helen E(lizabeth)
1918- *2*

Buckmaster, Henrietta *6*

Budd, Lillian 1897- *7*

Buehr, Walter 1897-1971 .... *3*

Buff, Conrad 1886-1975 .... *19*

Buff, Mary Marsh 1890-1970 ...... *19*

Bugbee, Emma 1888(?)-1981
Obituary *29*

Bulfinch, Thomas 1796-1867 ..... *35*

Bull, Angela (Mary) 1936- *45*

Bull, Norman John 1916- *41*

Bull, Peter (Cecil) 1912-1984
Obituary *39*

Bulla, Clyde Robert 1914- *41*
Earlier sketch in SATA 2

Bunin, Catherine 1967- *30*

Bunin, Sherry 1925- *30*

Bunting, A. E.
See Bunting, Anne Evelyn

Bunting, Anne Evelyn 1928- *18*
Bunting, Eve
  See Bunting, Anne Evelyn
Bunting, Glenn (Davison)
  1957- *22*
Burack, Sylvia K. 1916- *35*
Burbank, Addison (Buswell)
  1895-1961 .... *37*
Burch, Robert J(oseph) 1925- *1*
Burchard, Peter D(uncan) *5*
Burchard, Sue 1937- *22*
Burchardt, Nellie 1921- *7*
Burdick, Eugene (Leonard)
  1918-1965 .... *22*
Burford, Eleanor
  See Hibbert, Eleanor
Burger, Carl 1888-1967 .... *9*
Burgess, Anne Marie
  See Gerson, Noel B(ertram)
Burgess, Em
  See Burgess, Mary Wyche
Burgess, (Frank) Gelett
  1866-1951 .... *32*
  Brief Entry *30*
Burgess, Mary Wyche 1916- *18*
Burgess, Michael
  See Gerson, Noel B(ertram)
Burgess, Robert F(orrest)
  1927- *4*
Burgess, Thornton W(aldo)
  1874-1965 .... *17*
Burgess, Trevor
  See Trevor, Elleston
Burgwyn, Mebane H. 1914- *7*
Burke, John
  See O'Connor, Richard
Burkert, Nancy Ekholm 1933- *24*
Burland, Brian (Berkeley)
  1931- *34*
Burland, C. A.
  See Burland, Cottie A.
Burland, Cottie A. 1905- *5*
Burlingame, (William) Roger
  1889-1967 .... *2*
Burman, Alice Caddy 1896(?)-1977
  Obituary *24*
Burman, Ben Lucien
  1896-1984 .... *6*
  Obituary *40*
Burn, Doris 1923- *1*
Burnett, Constance Buel
  1893-1975 .... *36*
Burnett, Frances (Eliza) Hodgson
  1849-1924 ....*YABC 2*
Burnford, S. D.
  See Burnford, Sheila
Burnford, Sheila 1918-1984 .... *3*
  Obituary *38*
  See also CLR 2
Burningham, John (Mackintosh)
  1936- *16*
  See also CLR 9
Burns, Marilyn
  Brief Entry *33*
Burns, Paul C. *5*
Burns, Raymond (Howard)
  1924- *9*
Burns, William A. 1909- *5*

Burroughs, Edgar Rice
  1875-1950 .... *41*
Burroughs, Jean Mitchell
  1908- *28*
Burroughs, Polly 1925- *2*
Burroway, Janet (Gay) 1936- *23*
Burstein, John 1949-
  Brief Entry *40*
Burt, Jesse Clifton 1921-1976
  Obituary *20*
Burt, Olive Woolley 1894- *4*
Burton, Hester 1913- *7*
  See also CLR 1
Burton, Leslie
  See McGuire, Leslie (Sarah)
Burton, Maurice 1898- *23*
Burton, Robert (Wellesley)
  1941- *22*
Burton, Virginia Lee
  1909-1968 .... *2*
Burton, William H(enry)
  1890-1964 .... *11*
Busby, Edith (?)-1964
  Obituary *29*
Busch, Phyllis S. 1909- *30*
Bushmiller, Ernie 1905-1982
  Obituary *31*
Busoni, Rafaello 1900-1962 .... *16*
Butler, Beverly 1932- *7*
Butler, Suzanne
  See Perreard, Suzanne Louise Butler
Butters, Dorothy Gilman
  1923- *5*
Butterworth, Emma Macalik
  1928- *43*
Butterworth, Oliver 1915- *1*
Butterworth, W(illiam) E(dmund III)
  1929- *5*
Byars, Betsy 1928- *4*
  See also CLR 1
  See also SAAS 1
Byfield, Barbara Ninde 1930- *8*
Byrd, Elizabeth 1912- *34*
Byrd, Robert (John) 1942- *33*

C

C.3.3.
  See Wilde, Oscar (Fingal O'Flahertie Wills)
Cable, Mary 1920- *9*
Caddy, Alice
  See Burman, Alice Caddy
Cadwallader, Sharon 1936- *7*
Cady, (Walter) Harrison
  1877-1970 .... *19*
Cagle, Malcolm W(infield)
  1918- *32*
Cahn, Rhoda 1922- *37*
Cahn, William 1912-1976 .... *37*
Cain, Arthur H. 1913- *3*
Cain, Christopher
  See Fleming, Thomas J(ames)
Caines, Jeanette (Franklin)
  Brief Entry *43*
Cairns, Trevor 1922- *14*
Caldecott, Moyra 1927- *22*
Caldecott, Randolph (J.)
  1846-1886 .... *17*

Caldwell, John C(ope) 1913- *7*
Calhoun, Mary (Huiskamp)
  1926- *2*
Calkins, Franklin
  See Stratemeyer, Edward L.
Call, Hughie Florence
  1890-1969 .... *1*
Callahan, Dorothy M. 1934- *39*
  Brief Entry *35*
Callahan, Philip S(erna) 1923- *25*
Callaway, Kathy 1943- *36*
Callen, Larry
  See Callen, Lawrence Willard, Jr.
Callen, Lawrence Willard, Jr.
  1927- *19*
Calmenson, Stephanie 1952-
  Brief Entry *37*
Calvert, John
  See Leaf, (Wilbur) Munro
Calvert, Patricia 1931- *45*
Cameron, Ann 1943- *27*
Cameron, Edna M. 1905- *3*
Cameron, Eleanor (Butler)
  1912- *25*
  Earlier sketch in SATA 1
  See also CLR 1
Cameron, Elizabeth
  See Nowell, Elizabeth Cameron
Cameron, Elizabeth Jane
  1910-1976 .... *32*
  Obituary *30*
Cameron, Ian
  See Payne, Donald Gordon
Cameron, Polly 1928- *2*
Camp, Charles Lewis 1893-1975
  Obituary *31*
Camp, Walter (Chauncey)
  1859-1925 ....*YABC 1*
Campbell, Ann R. 1925- *11*
Campbell, Bruce
  See Epstein, Samuel
Campbell, Camilla 1905- *26*
Campbell, Hope *20*
Campbell, Jane
  See Edwards, Jane Campbell
Campbell, Patricia J(ean)
  1930- *45*
Campbell, Patty
  See Campbell, Patricia J(ean)
Campbell, R. W.
  See Campbell, Rosemae Wells
Campbell, Rod 1945-
  Brief Entry *44*
Campbell, Rosemae Wells
  1909- *1*
Campion, Nardi Reeder 1917- *22*
Candell, Victor 1903-1977
  Obituary *24*
Canfield, Dorothy
  See Fisher, Dorothy Canfield
Canfield, Jane White
  1897-1984 .... *32*
  Obituary *38*
Cannon, Cornelia (James) 1876-1969
  Brief Entry *28*
Cannon, Ravenna
  See Mayhar, Ardath
Canusi, Jose
  See Barker, S. Omar

Caplin, Alfred Gerald 1909-1979
  Obituary 21
Capp, Al
  See Caplin, Alfred Gerald
Cappel, Constance 1936- 22
Capps, Benjamin (Franklin)
  1922- 9
Captain Kangaroo
  See Keeshan, Robert J.
Carafoli, Marci
  See Ridlon, Marci
Caras, Roger A(ndrew) 1928- 12
Carbonnier, Jeanne 1894-1974 3
  Obituary 34
Care, Felicity
  See Coury, Louise Andree
Carew, Jan (Rynveld) 1925-
  Brief Entry 40
Carey, Bonnie 1941- 18
Carey, Ernestine Gilbreth
  1908- 2
Carey, M. V.
  See Carey, Mary (Virginia)
Carey, Mary (Virginia) 1925- 44
  Brief Entry 39
Carigiet, Alois 1902- 24
Carini, Edward 1923- 9
Carle, Eric 1929- 4
  See CLR 10
Carleton, Captain L. C.
  See Ellis, Edward S(ylvester)
Carley, V(an Ness) Royal 1906-1976
  Obituary 20
Carlisle, Clark, Jr.
  See Holding, James
Carlisle, Olga A(ndreyev)
  1930- 35
Carlsen, G(eorge) Robert
  1917- 30
Carlsen, Ruth C(hristoffer) 2
Carlson, Bernice Wells 1910- 8
Carlson, Dale Bick 1935- 1
Carlson, Daniel 1960- 27
Carlson, Nancy L(ee) 1953-
  Brief Entry 45
Carlson, Natalie Savage 2
Carlson, Vada F. 1897- 16
Carmer, Carl (Lamson)
  1893-1976 37
  Obituary 30
Carmer, Elizabeth Black
  1904- 24
Carmichael, Carrie 40
Carmichael, Harriet
  See Carmichael, Carrie
Carol, Bill J.
  See Knott, William Cecil, Jr.
Caroselli, Remus F(rancis)
  1916- 36
Carpelan, Bo (Gustaf Bertelsson)
  1926- 8
Carpenter, Allan 1917- 3
Carpenter, Frances 1890-1972 3
  Obituary 27
Carpenter, Patricia (Healy Evans)
  1920- 11
Carr, Glyn
  See Styles, Frank Showell
Carr, Harriett Helen 1899- 3

Carr, Mary Jane 2
Carrick, Carol 1935- 7
Carrick, Donald 1929- 7
Carrick, Malcolm 1945- 28
Carrighar, Sally 24
Carris, Joan Davenport 1938- 44
  Brief Entry 42
Carroll, Curt
  See Bishop, Curtis
Carroll, Elizabeth [Joint pseudonym]
  See James, Elizabeth
Carroll, Latrobe 7
Carroll, Laura
  See Parr, Lucy
Carroll, Lewis
  See Dodgson, Charles Lutwidge
  See also CLR 2
Carse, Robert 1902-1971 5
Carson, Captain James
  See Stratemeyer, Edward L.
Carson, John F. 1920- 1
Carson, Rachel (Louise)
  1907-1964 23
Carson, Rosalind
  See Chittenden, Margaret
Carson, S. M.
  See Gorsline, (Sally) Marie
Carter, Bruce
  See Hough, Richard (Alexander)
Carter, Dorothy Sharp 1921- 8
Carter, Forrest 1927(?)-1979 32
Carter, Helene 1887-1960 15
Carter, (William) Hodding
  1907-1972 2
  Obituary 27
Carter, Katharine J(ones)
  1905- 2
Carter, Nick
  See Lynds, Dennis
Carter, Phyllis Ann
  See Eberle, Irmengarde
Carter, Samuel III 1904- 37
Carter, William E. 1926-1983 1
  Obituary 35
Cartlidge, Michelle 1950-
  Brief Entry 37
Cartner, William Carruthers
  1910- 11
Cartwright, Sally 1923- 9
Carver, John
  See Gardner, Richard
Cary
  See Cary, Louis F(avreau)
Cary, Barbara Knapp 1912(?)-1975
  Obituary 31
Cary, Louis F(avreau) 1915- 9
Caryl, Jean
  See Kaplan, Jean Caryl Korn
Case, Marshal T(aylor) 1941- 9
Case, Michael
  See Howard, Robert West
Casewit, Curtis 1922- 4
Casey, Brigid 1950- 9
Casey, Winifred Rosen
  See Rosen, Winifred
Cason, Mabel Earp 1892-1965 10
Cass, Joan E(velyn) 1
Cassedy, Sylvia 1930- 27

Cassel, Lili
  See Wronker, Lili Cassell
Cassel-Wronker, Lili
  See Wronker, Lili Cassell
Castellanos, Jane Mollie (Robinson)
  1913- 9
Castillo, Edmund L. 1924- 1
Castle, Lee [Joint pseudonym]
  See Ogan, George F. and Ogan,
    Margaret E. (Nettles)
Castle, Paul
  See Howard, Vernon (Linwood)
Caswell, Helen (Rayburn)
  1923- 12
Cate, Dick
  See Cate, Richard (Edward Nelson)
Cate, Richard (Edward Nelson)
  1932- 28
Cather, Willa (Sibert)
  1873-1947 30
Catherall, Arthur 1906- 3
Cathon, Laura E(lizabeth)
  1908- 27
Catlin, Wynelle 1930- 13
Catton, (Charles) Bruce
  1899-1978 2
  Obituary 24
Catz, Max
  See Glaser, Milton
Caudill, Rebecca 1899-1985 1
  Obituary 44
Cauley, Lorinda Bryan 1951-
  Brief Entry 43
Causley, Charles 1917- 3
Cavallo, Diana 1931- 7
Cavanagh, Helen (Carol) 1939-
  Brief Entry 37
Cavanah, Frances 1899-1982 31
  Earlier sketch in SATA 1
Cavanna, Betty 1909- 30
  Earlier sketch in SATA 1
Cavin, Ruth (Brodie) 1918- 38
Cawley, Winifred 1915- 13
Caxton, Pisistratus
  See Lytton, Edward G(eorge) E(arle)
    L(ytton) Bulwer-Lytton, Baron
Cazet, Denys 1938-
  Brief Entry 41
Cebulash, Mel 1937- 10
Ceder, Georgiana Dorcas 10
Celestino, Martha Laing
  1951- 39
Cerf, Bennett 1898-1971 7
Cerf, Christopher (Bennett)
  1941- 2
Cervon, Jacqueline
  See Moussard, Jacqueline
Cetin, Frank (Stanley) 1921- 2
Chadwick, Lester [Collective
  pseudonym] 1
Chaffee, Allen 3
Chaffin, Lillie D(orton) 1925- .. 4
Chaikin, Miriam 1928- 24
Challans, Mary 1905-1983 23
  Obituary 36
Chalmers, Mary 1927- 6
Chambers, Aidan 1934- 1
Chambers, Bradford 1922-1984
  Obituary 39

Chambers, Catherine E.
  See Johnston, Norma
Chambers, Margaret Ada Eastwood
  1911- 2
Chambers, Peggy
  See Chambers, Margaret Ada
  Eastwood
Chandler, Caroline A(ugusta)
  1906-1979 22
  Obituary 24
Chandler, David Porter 1933- 28
Chandler, Edna Walker
  1908-1982 11
  Obituary 31
Chandler, Linda S(mith)
  1929- 39
Chandler, Robert 1953- 40
Chandler, Ruth Forbes
  1894-1978 2
  Obituary 26
Channel, A. R.
  See Catherall, Arthur
Chapian, Marie 1938- 29
Chapman, Allen [Collective
  pseudonym] 1
Chapman, (Constance) Elizabeth
  (Mann) 1919- 10
Chapman, Gaynor 1935- 32
Chapman, Jean 34
Chapman, John Stanton Higham
  1891-1972
  Obituary 27
Chapman, Maristan [Joint pseudonym]
  See Chapman, John Stanton Higham
Chapman, Vera 1898- 33
Chapman, Walker
  See Silverberg, Robert
Chappell, Warren 1904- 6
Chardiet, Bernice (Kroll) 27
Charles, Donald
  See Meighan, Donald Charles
Charles, Louis
  See Stratemeyer, Edward L.
Charlip, Remy 1929- 4
  See also CLR 8
Charlot, Jean 1898-1979 8
  Obituary 31
Charlton, Michael (Alan)
  1923- 34
Charmatz, Bill 1925- 7
Charosh, Mannis 1906- 5
Chase, Alice
  See McHargue, Georgess
Chase, Mary (Coyle)
  1907-1981 17
  Obituary 29
Chase, Mary Ellen 1887-1973 10
Chastain, Madye Lee 1908- 4
Chauncy, Nan 1900-1970 6
  See also CLR 6
Chaundler, Christine
  1887-1972 1
  Obituary 25
Chen, Tony 1929- 6
Chenault, Nell
  See Smith, Linell Nash
Chenery, Janet (Dai) 1923- 25
Cheney, Cora 1916- 3

Cheney, Ted
  See Cheney, Theodore Albert
Cheney, Theodore Albert
  1928- 11
Cheng, Judith 1955- 36
Chernoff, Dorothy A.
  See Ernst, (Lyman) John
Chernoff, Goldie Taub 1909- 10
Cherry, Lynne 1952- 34
Cherryholmes, Anne
  See Price, Olive
Chess, Victoria (Dickerson)
  1939- 33
Chessare, Michele
  Brief Entry 42
Chesterton, G(ilbert) K(eith)
  1874-1936 27
Chetin, Helen 1922- 6
Chevalier, Christa 1937- 35
Chew, Ruth 7
Chidsey, Donald Barr
  1902-1981 3
  Obituary 27
Childress, Alice 1920- 7
Childs, (Halla) Fay (Cochrane)
  1890-1971 1
  Obituary 25
Chimaera
  See Farjeon, Eleanor
Chinery, Michael 1938- 26
Chipperfield, Joseph E(ugene)
  1912- 2
Chittenden, Elizabeth F.
  1903- 9
Chittenden, Margaret 1933- 28
Chittum, Ida 1918- 7
Choate, Judith (Newkirk)
  1940- 30
Chorao, (Ann Mc)Kay (Sproat)
  1936- 8
Chorpenning, Charlotte (Lee Barrows)
  1872-1955
  Brief Entry 37
Chrisman, Arthur Bowie
  1889-1953 ....*YABC* 1
Christelow, Eileen 1943- 38
  Brief Entry 35
Christensen, Gardell Dano
  1907- 1
Christesen, Barbara 1940- 40
Christgau, Alice Erickson
  1902- 13
Christian, Mary Blount 1933- 9
Christie, Agatha (Mary Clarissa)
  1890-1976 36
Christopher, John
  See Youd, (Christopher) Samuel
  See also CLR 2
Christopher, Matt(hew F.)
  1917- 2
Christy, Howard Chandler
  1873-1952 21
Chu, Daniel 1933- 11
Chukovsky, Kornei (Ivanovich)
  1882-1969 34
  Earlier sketch in SATA 5
Church, Richard 1893-1972 3
Churchill, E. Richard 1937- 11
Chute, B(eatrice) J(oy) 1913- 2

Chute, Marchette (Gaylord)
  1909- 1
Chwast, Jacqueline 1932- 6
Chwast, Seymour 1931- 18
Ciardi, John (Anthony) 1916- 1
Clair, Andrée 19
Clampett, Bob
  Obituary 38
  See Clampett, Robert
Clampett, Robert
  1914(?)-1984 44
Clapp, Patricia 1912- 4
Clare, Helen
  See Hunter, Blair Pauline
Clark, Ann Nolan 1898- 4
Clark, David
  See Hardcastle, Michael
Clark, David Allen
  See Ernst, (Lyman) John
Clark, Frank J(ames) 1922- 18
Clark, Garel [Joint pseudonym]
  See Garelick, May
Clark, Leonard 1905-1981 30
  Obituary 29
Clark, Margaret Goff 1913- 8
Clark, Mavis Thorpe 8
Clark, Merle
  See Gessner, Lynne
Clark, Patricia (Finrow) 1929- 11
Clark, Ronald William 1916- 2
Clark, Van D(eusen) 1909- 2
Clark, Virginia
  See Gray, Patricia
Clark, Walter Van Tilburg
  1909-1971 8
Clarke, Arthur C(harles)
  1917- 13
Clarke, Clorinda 1917- 7
Clarke, Joan B. 1921- 42
  Brief Entry 27
Clarke, John
  See Laklan, Carli
Clarke, Mary Stetson 1911- 5
Clarke, Michael
  See Newlon, Clarke
Clarke, Pauline
  See Hunter Blair, Pauline
Clarkson, E(dith) Margaret
  1915- 37
Clarkson, Ewan 1929- 9
Claverie, Jean 1946- 38
Claypool, Jane
  See Miner, Jane Claypool
Cleary, Beverly (Bunn) 1916- 43
  Earlier sketch in SATA 2
  See also CLR 2, 8
Cleaver, Bill 1920-1981 22
  Obituary 27
  See also CLR 6
Cleaver, Carole 1934- 6
Cleaver, Elizabeth (Mrazik)
  1939-1985 23
  Obituary 43
Cleaver, Vera 22
  See also CLR 6
Cleishbotham, Jebediah
  See Scott, Sir Walter
Cleland, Mabel
  See Widdemer, Mabel Cleland

Clemens, Samuel Langhorne
1835-1910 ....*YABC* 2
Clemens, Virginia Phelps
1941- 35
Clements, Bruce 1931- 27
Clemons, Elizabeth
See Nowell, Elizabeth Cameron
Clerk, N. W.
See Lewis, C. S.
Cleveland, Bob
See Cleveland, George
Cleveland, George 1903(?)-1985
Obituary 43
Cleven, Cathrine
See Cleven, Kathryn Seward
Cleven, Kathryn Seward 2
Clevin, Jörgen 1920- 7
Clewes, Dorothy (Mary)
1907- 1
Clifford, Eth
See Rosenberg, Ethel
Clifford, Harold B. 1893- 10
Clifford, Margaret Cort 1929- 1
Clifford, Martin
See Hamilton, Charles H. St. John
Clifford, Mary Louise (Beneway)
1926- 23
Clifford, Peggy
See Clifford, Margaret Cort
Clifton, Harry
See Hamilton, Charles H. St. John
Clifton, Lucille 1936- 20
See also CLR 5
Clifton, Martin
See Hamilton, Charles H. St. John
Climo, Shirley 1928- 39
Brief Entry 35
Clinton, Jon
See Prince, J(ack) H(arvey)
Clish, (Lee) Marian 1946- 43
Clive, Clifford
See Hamilton, Charles H. St. John
Cloudsley-Thompson, J(ohn) L(eonard)
1921- 19
Clymer, Eleanor 1906- 9
Clyne, Patricia Edwards 31
Coalson, Glo 1946- 26
Coates, Belle 1896- 2
Coates, Ruth Allison 1915- 11
Coats, Alice M(argaret) 1905- 11
Coatsworth, Elizabeth 1893- 2
See also CLR 2
Cobb, Jane
See Berry, Jane Cobb
Cobb, Vicki 1938- 8
See also CLR 2
Cobbett, Richard
See Pluckrose, Henry (Arthur)
Cober, Alan E. 1935- 7
Cobham, Sir Alan
See Hamilton, Charles H. St. John
Cocagnac, A(ugustin) M(aurice-Jean)
1924- 7
Cochran, Bobbye A. 1949- 11
Cockett, Mary 3
Coe, Douglas [Joint pseudonym]
See Epstein, Beryl and Epstein,
Samuel

Coe, Lloyd 1899-1976
Obituary 30
Coen, Rena Neumann 1925- 20
Coerr, Eleanor 1922- 1
Coffin, Geoffrey
See Mason, F. van Wyck
Coffman, Ramon Peyton
1896- 4
Coggins, Jack (Banham)
1911- 2
Cohen, Barbara 1932- 10
Cohen, Daniel 1936- 8
See also CLR 3
Cohen, Jene Barr
See Barr, Jene
Cohen, Joan Lebold 1932- 4
Cohen, Miriam 1926- 29
Cohen, Peter Zachary 1931- 4
Cohen, Robert Carl 1930- 8
Cohn, Angelo 1914- 19
Coit, Margaret L(ouise) 2
Colbert, Anthony 1934- 15
Colby, C(arroll) B(urleigh)
1904-1977 35
Earlier sketch in SATA 3
Colby, Jean Poindexter 1909- 23
Cole, Annette
See Steiner, Barbara A(nnette)
Cole, Davis
See Elting, Mary
Cole, Jack
See Stewart, John (William)
Cole, Jackson
See Schisgall, Oscar
Cole, Joanna 1944-
Brief Entry 37
See also CLR 5
Cole, Lois Dwight
1903(?)-1979 10
Obituary 26
Cole, Sheila R(otenberg)
1939- 24
Cole, William (Rossa) 1919- 9
Coleman, William L(eRoy) 1938-
Brief Entry 34
Coles, Robert (Martin) 1929- 23
Collier, Christopher 1930- 16
Collier, Ethel 1903- 22
Collier, James Lincoln 1928- 8
See also CLR 3
Collier, Jane
See Collier, Zena
Collier, Zena 1926- 23
Collins, David 1940- 7
Collins, Hunt
See Hunter, Evan
Collins, Michael
See Lynds, Dennis
Collins, Pat Lowery 1932- 31
Collins, Ruth Philpott 1890-1975
Obituary 30
Collodi, Carlo
See Lorenzini, Carlo
See also CLR 5
Colloms, Brenda 1919- 40
Colman, Hila 1
Colman, Morris 1899(?)-1981
Obituary 25
Colonius, Lillian 1911- 3

Colorado (Capella), Antonio J(ulio)
1903- 23
Colt, Martin [Joint pseudonym]
See Epstein, Beryl and Epstein,
Samuel
Colum, Padraic 1881-1972 15
Columella
See Moore, Clement Clarke
Colver, Anne 1908- 7
Colwell, Eileen (Hilda) 1904- 2
Combs, Robert
See Murray, John
Comfort, Jane Levington
See Sturtzel, Jane Levington
Comfort, Mildred Houghton
1886- 3
Comins, Ethel M(ae) 11
Comins, Jeremy 1933- 28
Commager, Henry Steele
1902- 23
Comus
See Ballantyne, R(obert) M(ichael)
Conan Doyle, Arthur
See Doyle, Arthur Conan
Condit, Martha Olson 1913- 28
Cone, Ferne Geller 1921- 39
Cone, Molly (Lamken) 1918- 28
Earlier sketch in SATA 1
Conford, Ellen 1942- 6
See also CLR 10
Conger, Lesley
See Suttles, Shirley (Smith)
Conklin, Gladys (Plemon)
1903- 2
Conklin, Paul S. 43
Brief Entry 33
Conkling, Hilda 1910- 23
Conly, Robert Leslie
1918(?)-1973 23
Connell, Kirk [Joint pseudonym]
See Chapman, John Stanton Higham
Connelly, Marc(us Cook) 1890-1980
Obituary 25
Connolly, Jerome P(atrick)
1931- 8
Conover, Chris 1950- 31
Conquest, Owen
See Hamilton, Charles H. St. John
Conrad, Joseph 1857-1924 27
Conroy, Jack (Wesley) 1899- 19
Conroy, John
See Conroy, Jack (Wesley)
Constant, Alberta Wilson
1908-1981 22
Obituary 28
Conway, Gordon
See Hamilton, Charles H. St. John
Cook, Bernadine 1924- 11
Cook, Fred J(ames) 1911- 2
Cook, Joseph J(ay) 1924- 8
Cook, Lyn
See Waddell, Evelyn Margaret
Cooke, Ann
See Cole, Joanna
Cooke, David Coxe 1917- 2
Cooke, Donald Ewin
1916-1985 2
Obituary 45

Cookson, Catherine (McMullen)
   1906- 9
Coolidge, Olivia E(nsor)
   1908- 26
   Earlier sketch in SATA 1
Coombs, Charles I(ra) 1914- 43
   Earlier sketch in SATA 3
Coombs, Chick
   See Coombs, Charles I(ra)
Coombs, Patricia 1926- 3
Cooney, Barbara 1917- 6
Cooney, Caroline B. 1947-
   Brief Entry 41
Cooney, Nancy Evans 1932- 42
Coontz, Otto 1946- 33
Cooper, Gordon 1932- 23
Cooper, James Fenimore
   1789-1851 19
Cooper, James R.
   See Stratemeyer, Edward L.
Cooper, John R. [Collective
   pseudonym] 1
Cooper, Kay 1941- 11
Cooper, Lee (Pelham) 5
Cooper, Lester (Irving)
   1919-1985 32
   Obituary 43
Cooper, Lettice (Ulpha) 1897- 35
Cooper, Susan 1935- 4
   See also CLR 4
Copeland, Helen 1920- 4
Copeland, Paul W. 23
Copley, (Diana) Heather Pickering
   1918- 45
Coppard, A(lfred) E(dgar)
   1878-1957 ....YABC 1
Corbett, Grahame 43
   Brief Entry 36
Corbett, Scott 1913- 42
   Earlier sketch in SATA 2
   See also CLR 1
   See also SAAS 2
Corbett, W(illiam) J(esse) 1938-
   Brief Entry 44
Corbin, Sabra Lee
   See Malvern, Gladys
Corbin, William
   See McGraw, William Corbin
Corby, Dan
   See Catherall, Arthur
Corcoran, Barbara 1911- 3
Corcos, Lucille 1908-1973 10
Cordell, Alexander
   See Graber, Alexander
Coren, Alan 1938- 32
Corey, Dorothy 23
Corfe, Thomas Howell 1928- 27
Corfe, Tom
   See Corfe, Thomas Howell
Corlett, William 1938-
   Brief Entry 39
Cormack, M(argaret) Grant
   1913- 11
Cormack, Maribelle B.
   1902-1984 39
Cormier, Robert (Edmund)
   1925- 45
   Earlier sketch in SATA 10
Cornelius, Carol 1942- 40

Cornell, J.
   See Cornell, Jeffrey
Cornell, James (Clayton, Jr.)
   1938- 27
Cornell, Jean Gay 1920- 23
Cornell, Jeffrey 1945- 11
Cornish, Samuel James 1935- 23
Cornwall, Nellie
   See Sloggett, Nellie
Correy, Lee
   See Stine, G. Harry 10
Corrigan, (Helen) Adeline
   1909- 23
Corrigan, Barbara 1922- 8
Cort, M. C.
   See Clifford, Margaret Cort
Corwin, Judith Hoffman
   1946- 10
Cosgrave, John O'Hara II 1908-1968
   Obituary 21
Cosgrove, Stephen E(dward) 1945-
   Brief Entry 40
Coskey, Evelyn 1932- 7
Cosner, Shaaron 1940- 43
Costabel, Eva Deutsch 1924- 45
Costello, David F(rancis)
   1904- 23
Cott, Jonathan 1942- 23
Cottam, Clarence 1899-1974 25
Cottler, Joseph 1899- 22
Cottrell, Leonard 1913-1974 24
The Countryman
   See Whitlock, Ralph
Courlander, Harold 1908- 6
Courtis, Stuart Appleton 1874-1969
   Obituary 29
Coury, Louise Andree 1895(?)-1983
   Obituary 34
Cousins, Margaret 1905- 2
Cousteau, Jacques-Yves 1910- 38
Coville, Bruce 1950- 32
Cowen, Eve
   See Werner, Herma
Cowie, Leonard W(allace)
   1919- 4
Cowles, Kathleen
   See Krull, Kathleen
Cowley, Joy 1936- 4
Cox, Donald William 1921- 23
Cox, Jack
   See Cox, John Roberts
Cox, John Roberts 1915- 9
Cox, Palmer 1840-1924 24
Cox, Victoria
   See Garretson, Victoria Diane
Cox, Wally 1924-1973 25
Cox, William R(obert) 1901-
   Brief Entry 31
Coy, Harold 1902- 3
Craft, Ruth
   Brief Entry 31
Craig, A. A.
   See Anderson, Poul (William)
Craig, Alisa
   See MacLeod, Charlotte (Matilda
   Hughes)
Craig, John Eland
   See Chipperfield, Joseph
Craig, John Ernest 1921- 23

Craig, M. Jean 17
Craig, Margaret Maze
   1911-1964 9
Craig, Mary Francis 1923- 6
Craik, Dinah Maria (Mulock)
   1826-1887 34
Crane, Barbara J. 1934- 31
Crane, Caroline 1930- 11
Crane, M. A.
   See Wartski, Maureen (Ann Crane)
Crane, Roy
   See Crane, Royston Campbell
Crane, Royston Campbell 1901-1977
   Obituary 22
Crane, Stephen (Townley)
   1871-1900 ....YABC 2
Crane, Walter 1845-1915 18
Crane, William D(wight)
   1892- 1
Crary, Elizabeth (Ann) 1942-
   Brief Entry 43
Crary, Margaret (Coleman)
   1906- 9
Craven, Thomas 1889-1969 22
Crawford, Charles P. 1945- 28
Crawford, Deborah 1922- 6
Crawford, John E. 1904-1971 3
Crawford, Mel 1925- 44
   Brief Entry 33
Crawford, Phyllis 1899- 3
Craz, Albert G. 1926- 24
Crayder, Dorothy 1906- 7
Crayder, Teresa
   See Colman, Hila
Crayon, Geoffrey
   See Irving, Washington
Crecy, Jeanne
   See Williams, Jeanne
Credle, Ellis 1902- 1
Cresswell, Helen 1934- 1
Cretan, Gladys (Yessayan)
   1921- 2
Crew, Helen (Cecilia) Coale
   1866-1941 ....YABC 2
Crews, Donald 1938- 32
   Brief Entry 30
   See also CLR 7
Crichton, (J.) Michael 1942- 9
Crofut, Bill
   See Crofut, William E. III
Crofut, William E. III 1934- 23
Croman, Dorothy Young
   See Rosenberg, Dorothy
Cromie, Alice Hamilton 1914- 24
Cromie, William J(oseph)
   1930- 4
Crompton, Anne Eliot 1930- 23
Crompton, Richmal
   See Lamburn, Richmal Crompton
Cronbach, Abraham
   1882-1965 11
Crone, Ruth 1919- 4
Cronin, A(rchibald) J(oseph)
   1896-1981
   Obituary 25
Crook, Beverly Courtney 38
   Brief Entry 35
Cros, Earl
   See Rose, Carl

Crosby, Alexander L.
1906-1980 2
Obituary 23
Crosher, G(eoffry) R(obins)
1911- 14
Cross, Gillian (Clare) 1945- 38
Cross, Helen Reeder
See Broadhead, Helen Cross
Cross, Wilbur Lucius III
1918- 2
Crossley-Holland, Kevin 5
Crouch, Marcus 1913- 4
Crout, George C(lement)
1917- 11
Crow, Donna Fletcher 1941- 40
Crowe, Bettina Lum 1911- 6
Crowe, John
See Lynds, Dennis
Crowell, Grace Noll
1877-1969 34
Crowell, Pers 1910- 2
Crowfield, Christopher
See Stowe, Harriet (Elizabeth)
Beecher
Crowley, Arthur M(cBlair)
1945- 38
Crownfield, Gertrude
1867-1945 .... YABC 1
Crowther, James Gerald 1899- 14
Cruikshank, George
1792-1878 22
Crump, Fred H., Jr. 1931- 11
Crump, J(ames) Irving 1887-1979
Obituary 21
Cruz, Ray 1933- 6
Ctvrtek, Vaclav 1911-1976
Obituary 27
Cuffari, Richard 1925-1978 6
Obituary 25
Cullen, Countee 1903-1946 18
Culliford, Pierre 1928- 40
Culp, Louanna McNary
1901-1965 2
Cumming, Primrose (Amy)
1915- 24
Cummings, Betty Sue 1918- 15
Cummings, Parke 1902- 2
Cummings, Pat 1950- 42
Cummings, Richard
See Gardner, Richard
Cummins, Maria Susanna
1827-1866 .... YABC 1
Cunliffe, John Arthur 1933- 11
Cunliffe, Marcus (Falkner)
1922- 37
Cunningham, Captain Frank
See Glick, Carl (Cannon)
Cunningham, Cathy
See Cunningham, Chet
Cunningham, Chet 1928- 23
Cunningham, Dale S(peers)
1932- 11
Cunningham, E.V.
See Fast, Howard
Cunningham, Julia W(oolfolk)
1916- 26
Earlier sketch in SATA 1
See also SAAS 2

Cunningham, Virginia
See Holmgren, Virginia
C(unningham)
Curiae, Amicus
See Fuller, Edmund (Maybank)
Curie, Eve 1904- 1
Curley, Daniel 1918- 23
Curry, Jane L(ouise) 1932- 1
Curry, Peggy Simson 1911- 8
Curtis, Bruce (Richard) 1944- 30
Curtis, Patricia 1921- 23
Curtis, Peter
See Lofts, Norah (Robinson)
Curtis, Richard (Alan) 1937- 29
Curtis, Wade
See Pournelle, Jerry (Eugene)
Cushman, Jerome 2
Cutchen, Billye Walker 1930- 15
Cutler, (May) Ebbitt 1923- 9
Cutler, Ivor 1923- 24
Cutler, Samuel
See Folsom, Franklin
Cutt, W(illiam) Towrie 1898- 16
Cuyler, Margery Stuyvesant
1948- 39
Cuyler, Stephen
See Bates, Barbara S(nedeker)

D

Dahl, Borghild 1890-1984 7
Obituary 37
Dahl, Roald 1916- 26
Earlier sketch in SATA 1
See also CLR 1; 7
Dahlstedt, Marden 1921- 8
Dain, Martin J. 1924- 35
Dale, Jack
See Holliday, Joseph
Dale, Margaret J(essy) Miller
1911- 39
Dale, Norman
See Denny, Norman (George)
Dalgliesh, Alice 1893-1979 17
Obituary 21
Dalton, Anne 1948- 40
Daly, Jim
See Stratemeyer, Edward L.
Daly, Kathleen N(orah)
Brief Entry 37
Daly, Maureen 2
See also SAAS 1
Daly, Nicholas 1946- 37
Daly, Niki
See Daly, Nicholas
D'Amato, Alex 1919- 20
D'Amato, Janet 1925- 9
Damrosch, Helen Therese
See Tee-Van, Helen Damrosch
Dana, Barbara 1940- 22
Dana, Richard Henry, Jr.
1815-1882 26
Danachair, Caoimhin O.
See Danaher, Kevin
Danaher, Kevin 1913- 22
D'Andrea, Kate
See Steiner, Barbara A(nnette)
Dangerfield, Balfour
See McCloskey, Robert

Daniel, Anita 1893(?)-1978 23
Obituary 24
Daniel, Anne
See Steiner, Barbara A(nnette)
Daniel, Hawthorne 1890- 8
Daniels, Guy 1919- 11
Dank, Leonard D(ewey)
1929- 44
Dank, Milton 1920- 31
Danziger, Paula 1944- 36
Brief Entry 30
Darby, J. N.
See Govan, Christine Noble
Darby, Patricia (Paulsen) 14
Darby, Ray K. 1912- 7
Daringer, Helen Fern 1892- 1
Darke, Marjorie 1929- 16
Darley, F(elix) O(ctavius) C(arr)
1822-1888 35
Darling, David J.
Brief Entry 44
Darling, Kathy
See Darling, Mary Kathleen
Darling, Lois M. 1917- 3
Darling, Louis, Jr. 1916-1970 3
Obituary 23
Darling, Mary Kathleen 1943- 9
Darrow, Whitney, Jr. 1909- 13
Darwin, Len
See Darwin, Leonard
Darwin, Leonard 1916- 24
Dasent, Sir George Webbe 1817-1896
Brief Entry 29
Dauer, Rosamond 1934- 23
Daugherty, Charles Michael
1914- 16
Daugherty, James (Henry)
1889-1974 13
Daugherty, Richard D(eo)
1922- 35
Daugherty, Sonia Medwedeff (?)-1971
Obituary 27
d'Aulaire, Edgar Parin 1898- 5
d'Aulaire, Ingri (Maartenson Parin)
1904-1980 5
Obituary 24
Daveluy, Paule Cloutier 1919- 11
Davenport, Spencer
See Stratemeyer, Edward L.
Daves, Michael 1938- 40
David, Jonathan
See Ames, Lee J.
Davidson, Alice Joyce 1932-
Brief Entry 45
Davidson, Basil 1914- 13
Davidson, Jessica 1915- 5
Davidson, Judith 1953- 40
Davidson, Margaret 1936- 5
Davidson, Marion
See Garis, Howard R(oger)
Davidson, Mary R.
1885-1973 9
Davidson, R.
See Davidson, Raymond
Davidson, Raymond 1926- 32
Davidson, Rosalie 1921- 23
Davies, Andrew (Wynford)
1936- 27
Davies, Bettilu D(onna) 1942- 33

Davies, (Edward) Hunter 1936-
  Brief Entry *45*
Davis, Bette J. 1923- *15*
Davis, Burke 1913- *4*
Davis, Christopher 1928- *6*
Davis, D(elbert) Dwight
  1908-1965 .... *33*
Davis, Daniel S(heldon) 1936- *12*
Davis, Gibbs 1953-
  Brief Entry *41*
Davis, Hubert J(ackson) 1904- *31*
Davis, James Robert 1945- *32*
Davis, Jim
  See Davis, James Robert
Davis, Julia 1904- *6*
Davis, Louise Littleton 1921- *25*
Davis, Marguerite 1889- *34*
Davis, Mary L(ee) 1935- *9*
Davis, Mary Octavia 1901- *6*
Davis, Paxton 1925- *16*
Davis, Robert
  1881-1949 .... *YABC 1*
Davis, Russell G. 1922- *3*
Davis, Verne T. 1889-1973 .... *6*
Dawson, Elmer A. [Collective
  pseudonym] *1*
Dawson, Mary 1919- *11*
Day, Beth (Feagles) 1924- *33*
Day, Maurice 1892-
  Brief Entry *30*
Day, Thomas 1748-1789 ..... *YABC 1*
Dazey, Agnes J(ohnston) *2*
Dazey, Frank M. *2*
Deacon, Eileen
  See Geipel, Eileen
Deacon, Richard
  See McCormick, (George) Donald
  (King)
Dean, Anabel 1915- *12*
de Angeli, Marguerite 1889- *27*
  Earlier sketch in SATA 1
  See also CLR 1
DeArmand, Frances Ullmann
  1904(?)-1984 .... *10*
  Obituary *38*
Deary, Terry 1946-
  Brief Entry *41*
deBanke, Cecile 1889-1965 .... *11*
De Bruyn, Monica 1952- *13*
de Camp, Catherine C(rook)
  1907- *12*
DeCamp, L(yon) Sprague
  1907- *9*
Decker, Duane 1910-1964 .... *5*
DeClements, Barthe 1920- *35*
Deedy, John 1923- *24*
Deegan, Paul Joseph 1937-
  Brief Entry *38*
Defoe, Daniel 1660(?)-1731 .... *22*
deFrance, Anthony
  See Di Franco, Anthony (Mario)
DeGering, Etta 1898- *7*
De Grazia
  See De Grazia, Ted
De Grazia, Ted 1909-1982 .... *39*
De Grazia, Ettore
  See De Grazia, Ted
De Groat, Diane 1947- *31*
de Grummond, Lena Young *6*

Deiss, Joseph J. 1915- *12*
DeJong, David C(ornel)
  1905-1967 .... *10*
de Jong, Dola *7*
De Jong, Meindert 1906- *2*
  See also CLR 1
de Kay, Ormonde, Jr. 1923- *7*
de Kiriline, Louise
  See Lawrence, Louise de Kiriline
Dekker, Carl
  See Laffin, John (Alfred Charles)
Dekker, Carl
  See Lynds, Dennis
deKruif, Paul (Henry)
  1890-1971 .... *5*
Delacre, Lulu 1957- *36*
De Lage, Ida 1918- *11*
de la Mare, Walter 1873-1956 .... *16*
Delaney, Harry 1932- *3*
Delaney, Ned 1951- *28*
Delano, Hugh 1933- *20*
De La Ramée, (Marie) Louise
  1839-1908 .... *20*
Delaune, Lynne *7*
DeLaurentis, Louise Budde
  1920- *12*
Delderfield, Eric R(aymond)
  1909- *14*
Delderfield, R(onald) F(rederick)
  1912-1972 .... *20*
De Leeuw, Adele Louise
  1899- *30*
  Earlier sketch in SATA 1
Delessert, Etienne 1941-
  Brief Entry *27*
Delmar, Roy
  See Wexler, Jerome (LeRoy)
Deloria, Vine (Victor), Jr.
  1933- *21*
Del Rey, Lester 1915- *22*
Delton, Judy 1931- *14*
Delulio, John 1938- *15*
Delving, Michael
  See Williams, Jay
Demarest, Chris(topher) L(ynn)
  1951- *45*
  Brief Entry *44*
Demarest, Doug
  See Barker, Will
Demas, Vida 1927- *9*
De Mejo, Oscar 1911- *40*
de Messières, Nicole 1930- *39*
Deming, Richard 1915- *24*
Dengler, Sandy 1939-
  Brief Entry *40*
Denmark, Harrison
  See Zelazny, Roger (Joseph
  Christopher)
Denney, Diana 1910- *25*
Dennis, Morgan 1891(?)-1960 .... *18*
Dennis, Wesley 1903-1966 .... *18*
Denniston, Elinore 1900-1978
  Obituary *24*
Denny, Norman (George)
  1901-1982 .... *43*
Denslow, W(illiam) W(allace)
  1856-1915 .... *16*
Denzel, Justin F(rancis) 1917-
  Brief Entry *38*

Denzer, Ann Wiseman
  See Wiseman, Ann (Sayre)
de Paola, Thomas Anthony
  1934- *11*
de Paola, Tomie
  See de Paola, Thomas Anthony
  See also CLR 4
DePauw, Linda Grant 1940- *24*
deRegniers, Beatrice Schenk
  (Freedman) 1914- *2*
Derleth, August (William)
  1909-1971 .... *5*
Derman, Sarah Audrey 1915- *11*
de Roo, Anne Louise 1931- *25*
De Roussan, Jacques 1929-
  Brief Entry *31*
Derry Down Derry
  See Lear, Edward
Derwent, Lavinia *14*
Desbarats, Peter 1933- *39*
De Selincourt, Aubrey
  1894-1962 .... *14*
Desmond, Alice Curtis 1897- *8*
Detine, Padre
  See Olsen, Ib Spang
Deutsch, Babette 1895-1982 ...... *1*
  Obituary *33*
De Valera, Sinead 1870(?)-1975
  Obituary *30*
Devaney, John 1926- *12*
Devereux, Frederick L(eonard), Jr.
  1914- *9*
Devlin, Harry 1918- *11*
Devlin, (Dorothy) Wende
  1918- *11*
DeWaard, E. John 1935- *7*
DeWeese, Gene
  See DeWeese, Thomas Eugene
DeWeese, Jean
  See DeWeese, Thomas Eugene
DeWeese, Thomas Eugene 1934-
  Brief Entry *45*
Dewey, Ariane 1937- *7*
Dewey, Ken(neth Francis)
  1940- *39*
DeWit, Dorothy (May Knowles)
  1916-1980 .... *39*
  Obituary *28*
Deyneka, Anita 1943- *24*
Deyrup, Astrith Johnson
  1923- *24*
Diamond, Donna 1950- *35*
  Brief Entry *30*
Dias, Earl Joseph 1916- *41*
Dick, Cappy
  See Cleveland, George
Dick, Trella Lamson
  1889-1974 .... *9*
Dickens, Charles 1812-1870 ...... *15*
Dickens, Frank
  See Huline-Dickens, Frank William
Dickens, Monica 1915- *4*
Dickerson, Roy Ernest 1886-1965
  Obituary *26*
Dickinson, Emily (Elizabeth)
  1830-1886 .... *29*
Dickinson, Mary 1949-
  Brief Entry *41*
Dickinson, Peter 1927- *5*

Dickinson, Susan 1931- 8
Dickinson, William Croft
  1897-1973 13
Dickson, Helen
  See Reynolds, Helen Mary
  Greenwood Campbell
Dickson, Naida 1916- 8
Dietz, David H(enry)
  1897-1984 10
  Obituary 41
Dietz, Lew 1907- 11
Di Franco, Anthony (Mario)
  1945- 42
Digges, Jeremiah
  See Berger, Josef
D'Ignazio, Fred 1949- 39
  Brief Entry 35
Di Grazia, Thomas (?)-1983 32
Dillard, Annie 1945- 10
Dillard, Polly (Hargis) 1916- 24
Dillon, Barbara 1927- 44
  Brief Entry 39
Dillon, Diane 1933- 15
Dillon, Eilis 1920- 2
Dillon, Leo 1933- 15
Dilson, Jesse 1914- 24
Dines, Glen 1925- 7
Dinesen, Isak
  See Blixen, Karen (Christentze
  Dinesen)
Dinnerstein, Harvey 1928- 42
Dinsdale, Tim 1924- 11
Dirks, Rudolph 1877-1968
  Brief Entry 31
Disney, Walt(er Elias)
  1901-1966 28
  Brief Entry 27
DiValentin, Maria 1911- 7
Dixon, Dougal 1947- 45
Dixon, Franklin W. [Collective
  pseudonym] 1
  See also Adams, Harriet
  S(tratemeyer); McFarlane, Leslie;
  Stratemeyer, Edward L.; Svenson,
  Andrew E.
Dixon, Jeanne 1936- 31
Dixon, Peter L. 1931- 6
Doane, Pelagie 1906-1966 7
Dobell, I(sabel) M(arian) B(arclay)
  1909- 11
Dobie, J(ames) Frank
  1888-1964 43
Dobkin, Alexander 1908-1975
  Obituary 30
Dobler, Lavinia G. 1910- 6
Dobrin, Arnold 1928- 4
Dockery, Wallene T. 1941- 27
"Dr. A"
  See Silverstein, Alvin
Dodd, Ed(ward) Benton 1902- 4
Dodd, Lynley (Stuart) 1941- 35
Dodge, Bertha S(anford)
  1902- 8
Dodge, Mary (Elizabeth) Mapes
  1831-1905 21
Dodgson, Charles Lutwidge
  1832-1898 .... *YABC* 2
Dodson, Kenneth M(acKenzie)
  1907- 11

Dodson, Susan 1941-
  Brief Entry 40
Doherty, C. H. 1913- 6
Dolan, Edward F(rancis), Jr.
  1924- 45
  Brief Entry 31
Dolson, Hildegarde 1908- 5
Domanska, Janina 6
Domino, John
  See Averill, Esther
Domjan, Joseph 1907- 25
Donalds, Gordon
  See Shirreffs, Gordon D.
Donna, Natalie 1934- 9
Donovan, Frank (Robert) 1906-1975
  Obituary 30
Donovan, John 1928-
  Brief Entry 29
  See also CLR 3
Donovan, William
  See Berkebile, Fred D(onovan)
Doob, Leonard W(illiam)
  1909- 8
Dor, Ana
  See Ceder, Georgiana Dorcas
Doré, (Louis Christophe Paul) Gustave
  1832-1883 19
Doremus, Robert 1913- 30
Dorian, Edith M(cEwen)
  1900- 5
Dorian, Harry
  See Hamilton, Charles H. St. John
Dorian, Marguerite 7
Dorman, Michael 1932- 7
Dorman, N. B. 1927- 39
Dorson, Richard M(ercer)
  1916-1981 30
Doss, Helen (Grigsby) 1918- 20
Doss, Margot Patterson 6
dos Santos, Joyce Audy
  Brief Entry 42
Dottig
  See Grider, Dorothy
Dotts, Maryann J. 1933- 35
Doty, Jean Slaughter 1929- 28
Doty, Roy 1922- 28
Doubtfire, Dianne (Abrams)
  1918- 29
Dougherty, Charles 1922- 18
Douglas, James McM.
  See Butterworth, W. E.
Douglas, Kathryn
  See Ewing, Kathryn
Douglas, Marjory Stoneman
  1890- 10
Douglass, Barbara 1930- 40
Douglass, Frederick
  1817(?)-1895 29
Douty, Esther M(orris)
  1911-1978 8
  Obituary 23
Dow, Emily R. 1904- 10
Dowdell, Dorothy (Florence) Karns
  1910- 12
Dowden, Anne Ophelia 1907- 7
Dowdey, Landon Gerald
  1923- 11
Dowdy, Mrs. Regera
  See Gorey, Edward St. John

Downer, Marion 1892(?)-1971 25
Downey, Fairfax 1893- 3
Downie, Mary Alice 1934- 13
Doyle, Arthur Conan
  1859-1930 24
Doyle, Donovan
  See Boegehold, Betty (Doyle)
Doyle, Richard 1824-1883 21
Draco, F.
  See Davis, Julia
Dragonwagon, Crescent 1952- 41
  Earlier sketch in SATA 11
Drake, Frank
  See Hamilton, Charles H. St. John
Drapier, M. B.
  See Swift, Jonathan
Drawson, Blair 1943- 17
Dresang, Eliza (Carolyn Timberlake)
  1941- 19
Drescher, Joan E(lizabeth)
  1939- 30
Drew, Patricia (Mary) 1938- 15
Drewery, Mary 1918- 6
Drial, J. E.
  See Laird, Jean E(louise)
Drucker, Malka 1945- 39
  Brief Entry 29
Drummond, V(iolet) H. 1911- 6
Drummond, Walter
  See Silverberg, Robert
Drury, Roger W(olcott) 1914- 15
Dryden, Pamela
  See Johnston, Norma
du Blanc, Daphne
  See Groom, Arthur William
DuBois, Rochelle Holt
  See Holt, Rochelle Lynn
Du Bois, Shirley Graham
  1907-1977 24
Du Bois, W(illiam) E(dward)
  B(urghardt) 1868-1963 42
du Bois, William Pène 1916- 4
  See also CLR 1
DuBose, LaRocque (Russ)
  1926- 2
Du Chaillu, Paul (Belloni)
  1831(?)-1903 26
Duchesne, Janet 1930-
  Brief Entry 32
Ducornet, Erica 1943- 7
Dudley, Martha Ward 1909(?)-1985
  Obituary 45
Dudley, Nancy
  See Cole, Lois Dwight
Dudley, Robert
  See Baldwin, James
Dudley, Ruth H(ubbell) 1905- 11
Dueland, Joy V(ivian) 27
Duff, Maggie
  See Duff, Margaret K.
Duff, Margaret K. 37
Dugan, Michael (Gray) 1947- 15
Duggan, Alfred Leo
  1903-1964 25
Duggan, Maurice (Noel)
  1922-1974 40
  Obituary 30
du Jardin, Rosamond (Neal)
  1902-1963 2

Dulac, Edmund 1882-1953 .... *19*
Dumas, Alexandre (the elder)
   1802-1870 .... *18*
du Maurier, Daphne 1907- *27*
Dunbar, Paul Laurence
   1872-1906 .... *34*
Dunbar, Robert E(verett)
   1926- *32*
Duncan, Gregory
   See McClintock, Marshall
Duncan, Jane
   See Cameron, Elizabeth Jane
Duncan, Julia K. [Collective
   pseudonym] *1*
Duncan, Lois S(teinmetz)
   1934- *36*
   Earlier sketch in SATA 1
   See also SAAS 2
Duncan, Norman
   1871-1916 ....*YABC 1*
Duncombe, Frances (Riker)
   1900- *25*
Dunlop, Agnes M.R. *3*
Dunlop, Eileen (Rhona) 1938- *24*
Dunn, Harvey T(homas)
   1884-1952 .... *34*
Dunn, Judy
   See Spangenberg, Judith Dunn
Dunn, Mary Lois 1930- *6*
Dunnahoo, Terry 1927- *7*
Dunne, Mary Collins 1914- *11*
Dunnett, Margaret (Rosalind)
   1909-1977 .... *42*
Dupuy, T(revor) N(evitt)
   1916- *4*
Durant, John 1902- *27*
Durrell, Gerald (Malcolm)
   1925- *8*
Du Soe, Robert C.
   1892-1958 ....*YABC 2*
Dutz
   See Davis, Mary Octavia
Duval, Katherine
   See James, Elizabeth
Duvall, Evelyn Millis 1906- *9*
Duvoisin, Roger (Antoine)
   1904-1980 .... *30*
   Obituary *23*
   Earlier sketch in SATA 2
Dwiggins, Don 1913- *4*
Dwight, Allan
   See Cole, Lois Dwight
Dyer, James (Frederick) 1934- *37*
Dygard, Thomas J. 1931- *24*
Dyke, John 1935- *35*

E

E.V.B.
   See Boyle, Eleanor Vere (Gordon)
Eagar, Frances 1940- *11*
Eager, Edward (McMaken)
   1911-1964 .... *17*
Eagle, Mike 1942- *11*
Earle, Olive L. *7*
Earnshaw, Brian 1929- *17*
Eastman, Charles A(lexander)
   1858-1939 ....*YABC 1*
Eastman, P(hilip) D(ey) 1909- *33*

Eastwick, Ivy O. *3*
Eaton, Anne T(haxter)
   1881-1971 .... *32*
Eaton, George L.
   See Verral, Charles Spain
Eaton, Jeanette 1886-1968 .... *24*
Eaton, Tom 1940- *22*
Ebel, Alex 1927- *11*
Eber, Dorothy (Margaret) Harley
   1930- *27*
Eberle, Irmengarde 1898-1979 .... *2*
   Obituary *23*
Eccles
   See Williams, Ferelith Eccles
Eckblad, Edith Berven 1923- *23*
Ecke, Wolfgang 1927-1983
   Obituary *37*
Eckert, Allan W. 1931- *29*
   Brief Entry *27*
Eckert, Horst 1931- *8*
Ede, Janina 1937- *33*
Edell, Celeste *12*
Edelman, Lily (Judith) 1915- *22*
Edens, (Bishop) David 1926- *39*
Edey, Maitland A(rmstrong)
   1910- *25*
Edgeworth, Maria 1767-1849 ..... *21*
Edmonds, I(vy) G(ordon)
   1917- *8*
Edmonds, Walter D(umaux)
   1903- *27*
   Earlier sketch in SATA 1
Edmund, Sean
   See Pringle, Laurence
Edsall, Marian S(tickney)
   1920- *8*
Edwards, Anne 1927- *35*
Edwards, Audrey 1947-
   Brief Entry *31*
Edwards, Bertram
   See Edwards, Herbert Charles
Edwards, Bronwen Elizabeth
   See Rose, Wendy
Edwards, Cecile (Pepin)
   1916- *25*
Edwards, Dorothy 1914-1982 ..... *4*
   Obituary *31*
Edwards, Gunvor *32*
Edwards, Harvey 1929- *5*
Edwards, Herbert Charles
   1912- *12*
Edwards, Jane Campbell
   1932- *10*
Edwards, Julie
   See Andrews, Julie
Edwards, Julie
   See Stratemeyer, Edward L.
Edwards, Linda Strauss
   Brief Entry *42*
Edwards, Monica le Doux Newton
   1912- *12*
Edwards, Olwen
   See Gater, Dilys
Edwards, Sally 1929- *7*
Edwards, Samuel
   See Gerson, Noel B(ertram)
Egan, E(dward) W(elstead)
   1922- *35*
Eggenberger, David 1918- *6*

Eggleston, Edward 1837-1902 ..... *27*
Egielski, Richard 1952- *11*
Egypt, Ophelia Settle
   1903-1984 .... *16*
   Obituary *38*
Ehlert, Lois (Jane) 1934- *35*
Ehrlich, Amy 1942- *25*
Ehrlich, Bettina (Bauer) 1903- *1*
Eichberg, James Bandman
   See Garfield, James B.
Eichenberg, Fritz 1901- *9*
Eichler, Margrit 1942- *35*
Eichner, James A. 1927- *4*
Eifert, Virginia S(nider)
   1911-1966 .... *2*
Einsel, Naiad *10*
Einsel, Walter 1926- *10*
Einzig, Susan 1922- *43*
Eiseman, Alberta 1925- *15*
Eisenberg, Azriel 1903- *12*
Eisenberg, Phyllis Rose 1924- *41*
Eisner, Will(iam Erwin) 1917- *31*
Eitzen, Allan 1928- *9*
Eitzen, Ruth (Carper) 1924- *9*
Elam, Richard M(ace, Jr.)
   1920- *9*
Elfman, Blossom 1925- *8*
Elgin, Kathleen 1923- *39*
Elia
   See Lamb, Charles
Eliot, Anne
   See Cole, Lois Dwight
Elisofon, Eliot 1911-1973
   Obituary *21*
Elkin, Benjamin 1911- *3*
Elkins, Dov Peretz 1937- *5*
Ellacott, S(amuel) E(rnest)
   1911- *19*
Elliott, Sarah M(cCarn) 1930- *14*
Ellis, Anyon
   See Rowland-Entwistle, (Arthur)
   Theodore (Henry)
Ellis, Edward S(ylvester)
   1840-1916 ....*YABC 1*
Ellis, Ella Thorp 1928- *7*
Ellis, Harry Bearse 1921- *9*
Ellis, Herbert
   See Wilson, Lionel
Ellis, Mel 1912-1984 .... *7*
   Obituary *39*
Ellison, Lucile Watkins 1907(?)-1979
   Obituary *22*
Ellison, Virginia Howell
   1910- *4*
Ellsberg, Edward 1891- *7*
Elmore, (Carolyn) Patricia
   1933- *38*
   Brief Entry *35*
Elspeth
   See Bragdon, Elspeth
Elting, Mary 1906- *2*
Elwart, Joan Potter 1927- *2*
Emberley, Barbara A(nne) *8*
   See also CLR 5
Emberley, Ed(ward Randolph)
   1931- *8*
   See also CLR 5
Emberley, Michael 1960- *34*

Embry, Margaret (Jacob) 1919- 5
Emerson, Alice B. [Collective pseudonym] 1
Emerson, William K(eith) 1925- 25
Emery, Anne (McGuigan) 1907- 33
   Earlier sketch in SATA 1
Emmens, Carol Ann 1944- 39
Emmons, Della (Florence) Gould 1890-1983
   Obituary 39
Emrich, Duncan (Black Macdonald) 1908- 11
Emslie, M. L.
   See Simpson, Myrtle L(illias)
Ende, Michael 1930(?)-
   Brief Entry 42
Enderle, Judith (Ann) 1941- 38
Engdahl, Sylvia Louise 1933- 4
   See also CLR 2
Engle, Eloise Katherine 1923- 9
Englebert, Victor 1933- 8
English, James W(ilson) 1915- 37
Enright, D(ennis) J(oseph) 1920- 25
Enright, Elizabeth 1909-1968 9
   See also CLR 4
Enright, Maginel Wright
   See Barney, Maginel Wright
Enys, Sarah L.
   See Sloggett, Nellie
Epp, Margaret A(gnes) 20
Epple, Anne Orth 1927- 20
Epstein, Anne Merrick 1931- 20
Epstein, Beryl (Williams) 1910- 31
   Earlier sketch in SATA 1
Epstein, Perle S(herry) 1938- 27
Epstein, Samuel 1909- 31
   Earlier sketch in SATA 1
Erdman, Loula Grace 1
Erdoes, Richard 1912- 33
   Brief Entry 28
Erhard, Walter 1920-
   Brief Entry 30
Erickson, Russell E(verett) 1932- 27
Erickson, Sabra R(ollins) 1912- 35
Ericson, Walter
   See Fast, Howard
Erikson, Mel 1937- 31
Erlanger, Baba
   See Trahey, Jane
Erlich, Lillian (Feldman) 1910- 10
Ernest, William
   See Berkebile, Fred D(onovan)
Ernst, (Lyman) John 1940- 39
Ernst, Kathryn (Fitzgerald) 1942- 25
Ernst, Lisa Campbell 1957-
   Brief Entry 44
Ervin, Janet Halliday 1923- 4
Erwin, Will
   See Eisner, Will(iam Erwin)

Eshmeyer, R(einhart) E(rnst) 1898- 29
Espeland, Pamela (Lee) 1951-
   Brief Entry 38
Espy, Willard R(ichardson) 1910- 38
Estep, Irene (Compton) 5
Estes, Eleanor 1906- 7
   See also CLR 2
Estoril, Jean
   See Allan, Mabel Esther
Etchemendy, Nancy 1952- 38
Etchison, Birdie L(ee) 1937- 38
Ets, Marie Hall 2
Eunson, Dale 1904- 5
Evans, Eva Knox 1905- 27
Evans, Katherine (Floyd) 1901-1964 5
Evans, Mari 10
Evans, Mark 19
Evans, Patricia Healy
   See Carpenter, Patricia
Evarts, Esther
   See Benson, Sally
Evarts, Hal G. (Jr.) 1915- 6
Evernden, Margery 1916- 5
Evslin, Bernard 1922- 45
   Brief Entry 28
Ewen, David 1907- 4
Ewing, Juliana (Horatia Gatty) 1841-1885 16
Ewing, Kathryn 1921- 20
Eyerly, Jeannette Hyde 1908- 4
Eyre, Dorothy
   See McGuire, Leslie (Sarah)
Eyre, Katherine Wigmore 1901-1970 26
Ezzell, Marilyn 1937- 42
   Brief Entry 38

F

Fabe, Maxene 1943- 15
Faber, Doris 1924- 3
Faber, Harold 1919- 5
Fabre, Jean Henri (Casimir) 1823-1915 22
Facklam, Margery Metz 1927- 20
Fadiman, Clifton (Paul) 1904- 11
Fair, Sylvia 1933- 13
Fairfax-Lucy, Brian (Fulke Cameron-Ramsay) 1898-1974 6
   Obituary 26
Fairlie, Gerard 1899-1983
   Obituary 34
Fairman, Joan A(lexandra) 1935- 10
Faithfull, Gail 1936- 8
Falconer, James
   See Kirkup, James
Falkner, Leonard 1900- 12
Fall, Thomas
   See Snow, Donald Clifford
Falls, C(harles) B(uckles) 1874-1960 38
   Brief Entry 27
Falstein, Louis 1909- 37
Fanning, Leonard M(ulliken) 1888-1967 5

Faralla, Dana 1909- 9
Faralla, Dorothy W.
   See Faralla, Dana
Farb, Peter 1929-1980 12
   Obituary 22
Farber, Norma 1909-1984 25
   Obituary 38
Farge, Monique
   See Grée, Alain
Farjeon, (Eve) Annabel 1919- 11
Farjeon, Eleanor 1881-1965 2
Farley, Carol 1936- 4
Farley, Walter 1920- 43
   Earlier sketch in SATA 2
Farmer, Penelope (Jane) 1939- 40
   Brief Entry 39
   See also CLR 8
Farmer, Peter 1950- 38
Farnham, Burt
   See Clifford, Harold B.
Farquhar, Margaret C(utting) 1905- 13
Farquharson, Martha
   See Finley, Martha
Farr, Finis (King) 1904- 10
Farrar, Susan Clement 1917- 33
Farrell, Ben
   See Cebulash, Mel
Farrington, Benjamin 1891-1974
   Obituary 20
Farrington, Selwyn Kip, Jr. 1904- 20
Farthing, Alison 1936- 45
   Brief Entry 36
Fassler, Joan (Grace) 1931- 11
Fast, Howard 1914- 7
Fatchen, Max 1920- 20
Father Xavier
   See Hurwood, Bernhardt J.
Fatigati, (Frances) Evelyn de Buhr 1948- 24
Fatio, Louise 6
Faulhaber, Martha 1926- 7
Faulkner, Anne Irvin 1906- 23
Faulkner, Nancy
   See Faulkner, Anne Irvin
Fax, Elton Clay 1909- 25
Feagles, Anita MacRae 9
Feagles, Elizabeth
   See Day, Beth (Feagles)
Feague, Mildred H. 1915- 14
Fecher, Constance 1911- 7
Feder, Paula (Kurzband) 1935- 26
Feder, Robert Arthur 1909-1969
   Brief Entry 35
Feelings, Muriel (Grey) 1938- 16
   See also CLR 5
Feelings, Thomas 1933- 8
Feelings, Tom
   See Feelings, Thomas
   See also CLR 5
Fehrenbach, T(heodore) R(eed, Jr.) 1925- 33
Feiffer, Jules 1929- 8
Feig, Barbara Krane 1937- 34
Feikema, Feike
   See Manfred, Frederick F(eikema)

Feil, Hila 1942- *12*
Feilen, John
  See May, Julian
Feldman, Anne (Rodgers)
  1939- *19*
Félix
  See Vincent, Félix
Fellows, Muriel H. *10*
Felsen, Henry Gregor 1916- *1*
  See also SAAS 2
Felton, Harold William 1902- *1*
Felton, Ronald Oliver 1909- *3*
Felts, Shirley 1934- *33*
Fenderson, Lewis H. 1907-1983
  Obituary *37*
Fenner, Carol 1929- *7*
Fenner, Phyllis R(eid)
  1899-1982 .... *1*
  Obituary *29*
Fenten, Barbara D(oris) 1935- *26*
Fenten, D. X. 1932- *4*
Fenton, Carroll Lane
  1900-1969 .... *5*
Fenton, Edward 1917- *7*
Fenton, Mildred Adams 1899- *21*
Fenwick, Patti
  See Grider, Dorothy
Feravolo, Rocco Vincent
  1922- *10*
Ferber, Edna 1887-1968 .... *7*
Ferguson, Bob
  See Ferguson, Robert Bruce
Ferguson, Cecil 1931- *45*
Ferguson, Robert Bruce 1927- *13*
Ferguson, Walter (W.) 1930- *34*
Fergusson, Erna 1888-1964 .... *5*
Fermi, Laura (Capon)
  1907-1977 .... *6*
  Obituary *28*
Fern, Eugene A. 1919- *10*
Ferrier, Lucy
  See Penzler, Otto
Ferris, Helen Josephine
  1890-1969 .... *21*
Ferris, James Cody [Collective
  pseudonym] *1*
  See also McFarlane, Leslie;
  Stratemeyer, Edward L.
Ferry, Charles 1927- *43*
Fetz, Ingrid 1915- *30*
Feydy, Anne Lindbergh
  Brief Entry *32*
  See Sapieyevski, Anne Lindbergh
Fiammenghi, Gioia 1929- *9*
Fiarotta, Noel 1944- *15*
Fiarotta, Phyllis 1942- *15*
Fichter, George S. 1922- *7*
Fidler, Kathleen (Annie)
  1899-1980 .... *3*
  Obituary *45*
Fiedler, Jean *4*
Field, Edward 1924- *8*
Field, Elinor Whitney 1889-1980
  Obituary *28*
Field, Eugene 1850-1895 .... *16*
Field, Rachel (Lyman)
  1894-1942 .... *15*
Fife, Dale (Odile) 1910- *18*

Fighter Pilot, A
  See Johnston, H(ugh) A(nthony)
  S(tephen)
Figueroa, Pablo 1938- *9*
Fijan, Carol 1918- *12*
Fillmore, Parker H(oysted)
  1878-1944 .... *YABC 1*
Filstrup, Chris
  See Filstrup, E(dward) Christian
Filstrup, E(dward) Christian
  1942- *43*
Filstrup, Jane Merrill
  See Merrill, Jane
Filstrup, Janie
  See Merrill, Jane
Finder, Martin
  See Salzmann, Siegmund
Fine, Anne 1947- *29*
Finger, Charles J(oseph)
  1869(?)-1941 .... *42*
Fink, William B(ertrand)
  1916- *22*
Finke, Blythe F(oote) 1922- *26*
Finkel, George (Irvine)
  1909-1975 .... *8*
Finlay, Winifred 1910- *23*
Finlayson, Ann 1925- *8*
Finley, Martha 1828-1909 .... *43*
Firmin, Charlotte 1954- *29*
Firmin, Peter 1928- *15*
Fischbach, Julius 1894- *10*
Fischler, Stan(ley I.)
  Brief Entry *36*
Fishback, Margaret
  See Antolini, Margaret Fishback
Fisher, Aileen (Lucia) 1906- *25*
  Earlier sketch in SATA 1
Fisher, Barbara 1940- *44*
  Brief Entry *34*
Fisher, Clavin C(argill) 1912- *24*
Fisher, Dorothy Canfield
  1879-1958 .... *YABC 1*
Fisher, John (Oswald Hamilton)
  1909- *15*
Fisher, Laura Harrison 1934- *5*
Fisher, Leonard Everett 1924- *34*
  Earlier sketch in SATA 4
  See also SAAS 1
Fisher, Lois I. 1948- *38*
  Brief Entry *35*
Fisher, Margery (Turner)
  1913- *20*
Fisk, Nicholas 1923- *25*
Fitch, Clarke
  See Sinclair, Upton (Beall)
Fitch, John IV
  See Cormier, Robert (Edmund)
Fitschen, Dale 1937- *20*
Fitzalan, Roger
  See Trevor, Elleston
Fitzgerald, Captain Hugh
  See Baum, L(yman) Frank
Fitzgerald, Edward Earl 1919- *20*
Fitzgerald, F(rancis) A(nthony)
  1940- *15*
Fitzgerald, John D(ennis)
  1907- *20*
  See also CLR 1

Fitzhardinge, Joan Margaret
  1912- *2*
Fitzhugh, Louise (Perkins)
  1928-1974 .... *45*
  Obituary *24*
  Earlier sketch in SATA 1
  See also CLR 1
Flack, Marjorie
  1899-1958 .... *YABC 2*
Flack, Naomi John (White) *40*
  Brief Entry *35*
Flash Flood
  See Robinson, Jan M.
Fleischer, Max 1889-1972
  Brief Entry *30*
Fleischhauer-Hardt, Helga
  1936- *30*
Fleischman, Paul 1952- *39*
  Brief Entry *32*
Fleischman, (Albert) Sid(ney)
  1920- *8*
  See also CLR 1
Fleishman, Seymour 1918-
  Brief Entry *32*
Fleming, Alice Mulcahey
  1928- *9*
Fleming, Ian (Lancaster)
  1908-1964 .... *9*
Fleming, Susan 1932- *32*
Fleming, Thomas J(ames)
  1927- *8*
Fletcher, Charlie May 1897- *3*
Fletcher, Colin 1922- *28*
Fletcher, Helen Jill 1911- *13*
Fletcher, Richard E. 1917(?)-1983
  Obituary *34*
Fletcher, Rick
  See Fletcher, Richard E.
Fleur, Anne 1901-
  Brief Entry *31*
Flexner, James Thomas 1908- *9*
Flitner, David P. 1949- *7*
Floethe, Louise Lee 1913- *4*
Floethe, Richard 1901- *4*
Floherty, John Joseph
  1882-1964 .... *25*
Flood, Flash
  See Robinson, Jan M.
Flora, James (Royer) 1914- *30*
  Earlier sketch in SATA 1
Florian, Douglas 1950- *19*
Flory, Jane Trescott 1917- *22*
Flowerdew, Phyllis *33*
Floyd, Gareth 1940-
  Brief Entry *31*
Fluchère, Henri A(ndré) 1914- *40*
Flynn, Barbara 1928- *9*
Flynn, Jackson
  See Shirreffs, Gordon D.
Flynn, Mary
  See Welsh, Mary Flynn
Fodor, Ronald V(ictor) 1944- *25*
Foley, (Anna) Bernice Williams
  1902- *28*
Foley, June 1944- *44*
Foley, (Mary) Louise Munro 1933-
  Brief Entry *40*
Foley, Rae
  See Denniston, Elinore

Folkard, Charles James 1878-1963
  Brief Entry 28
Follett, Helen (Thomas) 1884(?)-1970
  Obituary 27
Folsom, Franklin (Brewster)
  1907- 5
Folsom, Michael (Brewster)
  1938- 40
Fontenot, Mary Alice 1910- 34
Fooner, Michael 22
Forberg, Ati 1925- 22
Forbes, Bryan 1926- 37
Forbes, Cabot L.
  See Hoyt, Edwin P(almer), Jr.
Forbes, Esther 1891-1967 2
Forbes, Graham B. [Collective
  pseudonym] 1
Forbes, Kathryn
  See McLean, Kathryn (Anderson)
Ford, Albert Lee
  See Stratemeyer, Edward L.
Ford, Barbara
  Brief Entry 34
Ford, Elbur
  See Hibbert, Eleanor
Ford, George (Jr.) 31
Ford, Hilary
  See Youd, (Christopher) Samuel
Ford, Hildegarde
  See Morrison, Velma Ford
Ford, Marcia
  See Radford, Ruby L.
Ford, Nancy K(effer) 1906-1961
  Obituary 29
Foreman, Michael 1938- 2
Forest, Antonia 29
Forester, C(ecil) S(cott)
  1899-1966 13
Forman, Brenda 1936- 4
Forman, James Douglas 1932- 8
Forrest, Sybil
  See Markun, Patricia M(aloney)
Forrester, Marian
  See Schachtel, Roger
Forrester, Victoria 1940- 40
  Brief Entry 35
Forsee, (Frances) Aylesa 1
Fort, Paul
  See Stockton, Francis Richard
Fortnum, Peggy 1919- 26
Foster, Brad W. 1955- 34
Foster, Doris Van Liew 1899- 10
Foster, E(lizabeth) C(onnell)
  1902- 9
Foster, Elizabeth 1905-1963 10
Foster, Elizabeth Vincent
  1902- 12
Foster, F. Blanche 1919- 11
Foster, G(eorge) Allen
  1907-1969 26
Foster, Genevieve (Stump)
  1893-1979 2
  Obituary 23
  See also CLR 7
Foster, Hal
  See Foster, Harold Rudolf
Foster, Harold Rudolf 1892-1982
  Obituary 31
Foster, John T(homas) 1925- 8

Foster, Laura Louise 1918- 6
Foster, Margaret Lesser 1899-1979
  Obituary 21
Foster, Marian Curtis
  1909-1978 23
Fourth Brother, The
  See Aung, (Maung) Htin
Fowke, Edith (Margaret)
  1913- 14
Fowles, John 1926- 22
Fox, Charles Philip 1913- 12
Fox, Eleanor
  See St. John, Wylly Folk
Fox, Fontaine Talbot, Jr. 1884-1964
  Obituary 23
Fox, Fred 1903(?)-1981
  Obituary 27
Fox, Freeman
  See Hamilton, Charles H. St. John
Fox, Grace
  See Anderson, Grace Fox
Fox, Larry 30
Fox, Lorraine 1922-1975 11
  Obituary 27
Fox, Mary Virginia 1919- 44
  Brief Entry 39
Fox, Michael Wilson 1937- 15
Fox, Paula 1923- 17
  See also CLR 1
Fox, Petronella
  See Balogh, Penelope
Fox, Robert J. 1927- 33
Fradin, Dennis Brindel 1945- 29
Frame, Paul 1913-
  Brief Entry 33
Frances, Miss
  See Horwich, Frances R.
Franchere, Ruth 18
Francis, Charles
  See Holme, Bryan
Francis, Dee
  See Haas, Dorothy F.
Francis, Dorothy Brenner
  1926- 10
Francis, Pamela (Mary) 1926- 11
Franco, Marjorie 38
Francois, André 1915- 25
Francoise
  See Seignobosc, Francoise
Frank, Anne 1929-1945(?)
  Brief Entry 42
Frank, Josette 1893- 10
Frank, Mary 1933- 34
Frank, R., Jr.
  See Ross, Frank (Xavier), Jr.
Frankau, Mary Evelyn 1899- 4
Frankel, Bernice 9
Frankel, Edward 1910- 44
Frankel, Julie 1947- 40
  Brief Entry 34
Frankenberg, Robert 1911- 22
Franklin, Harold 1920- 13
Franklin, Max
  See Deming, Richard
Franklin, Steve
  See Stevens, Franklin
Franzén, Nils-Olof 1916- 10
Frascino, Edward 193(?)-
  Brief Entry 33

Frasconi, Antonio 1919- 6
Fraser, Antonia (Pakenham) 1932-
  Brief Entry 32
Fraser, Betty
  See Fraser, Elizabeth Marr
Fraser, Elizabeth Marr 1928- 31
Fraser, Eric (George)
  1902-1983 38
Frazier, Neta Lohnes 7
Freed, Alvyn M. 1913- 22
Freedman, Benedict 1919- 27
Freedman, Nancy 1920- 27
Freedman, Russell (Bruce)
  1929- 16
Freeman, Barbara C(onstance)
  1906- 28
Freeman, Don 1908-1978 17
Freeman, Ira M(aximilian)
  1905- 21
Freeman, Lucy (Greenbaum)
  1916- 24
Freeman, Mae (Blacker)
  1907- 25
Freeman, Peter J.
  See Calvert, Patricia
Freeman, Tony
  Brief Entry 44
Fregosi, Claudia (Anne Marie)
  1946- 24
French, Allen 1870-1946 ..... YABC 1
French, Dorothy Kayser 1926- 5
French, Fiona 1944- 6
French, Kathryn
  See Mosesson, Gloria R(ubin)
French, Michael 1944-
  Brief Entry 38
French, Paul
  See Asimov, Isaac
Freund, Rudolf 1915-1969
  Brief Entry 28
Frewer, Glyn 1931- 11
Frick, C. H.
  See Irwin, Constance Frick
Frick, Constance
  See Irwin, Constance Frick
Friedlander, Joanne K(ohn)
  1930- 9
Friedman, Estelle 1920- 7
Friedman, Frieda 1905- 43
Friedman, Ina R(osen) 1926-
  Brief Entry 41
Friedman, Marvin 1930- 42
  Brief Entry 33
Friedrich, Otto (Alva) 1929- 33
Friedrich, Priscilla 1927- 39
Friendlich, Dick
  See Friendlich, Richard J.
Friendlich, Richard J. 1909- 11
Friermood, Elisabeth Hamilton
  1903- 5
Friis, Babbis
  See Friis-Baastad, Babbis
Friis-Baastad, Babbis
  1921-1970 7
Frimmer, Steven 1928- 31
Friskey, Margaret Richards
  1901- 5

Fritz, Jean (Guttery) 1915- *29*
  Earlier sketch in SATA 1
  See also CLR 2
  See also SAAS 2
Froissart, Jean
  1338(?)-1410(?) *28*
Froman, Elizabeth Hull
  1920-1975 .... *10*
Froman, Robert (Winslow)
  1917- *8*
Fromm, Lilo 1928- *29*
Frommer, Harvey 1937- *41*
Frost, A(rthur) B(urdett)
  1851-1928 .... *19*
Frost, Erica
  See Supraner, Robyn
Frost, Lesley 1899(?)-1983 .... *14*
  Obituary *34*
Frost, Robert (Lee) 1874-1963 .... *14*
Fry, Edward Bernard 1925- *35*
Fry, Rosalie 1911- *3*
Fuchs, Erich 1916- *6*
Fuchshuber, Annegert 1940- *43*
Fujikawa, Gyo 1908- *39*
  Brief Entry *30*
Fujita, Tamao 1905- *7*
Fujiwara, Michiko 1946- *15*
Fuka, Vladimir 1926-1977
  Obituary *27*
Fuller, Catherine L(euthold)
  1916- *9*
Fuller, Edmund (Maybank)
  1914- *21*
Fuller, Iola
  See McCoy, Iola Fuller
Fuller, Lois Hamilton 1915- *11*
Fuller, Margaret
  See Ossoli, Sarah Margaret (Fuller)
  marchesa d'
Fults, John Lee 1932- *33*
Funk, Thompson
  See Funk, Tom
Funk, Tom 1911- *7*
Funke, Lewis 1912- *11*
Furchgott, Terry 1948- *29*
Furukawa, Toshi 1924- *24*
Fyleman, Rose 1877-1957 .... *21*
Fyson, J(enny) G(race) 1904- *42*

G

Gackenbach, Dick
  Brief Entry *30*
Gaddis, Vincent H. 1913- *35*
Gadler, Steve J. 1905- *36*
Gaeddert, Lou Ann (Bigge)
  1931- *20*
Gàg, Flavia 1907-1979
  Obituary *24*
Gàg, Wanda (Hazel)
  1893-1946 .... *YABC 1*
  See also CLR 4
Gage, Wilson
  See Steele, Mary Q.
Gagliardo, Ruth Garver 1895(?)-1980
  Obituary *22*
Gal, Laszlo 1933-
  Brief Entry *32*
Galdone, Paul 1914- *17*

Galinsky, Ellen 1942- *23*
Gallant, Roy (Arthur) 1924- *4*
Gallico, Paul 1897-1976 .... *13*
Galt, Thomas Franklin, Jr.
  1908- *5*
Galt, Tom
  See Galt, Thomas Franklin, Jr.
Gamerman, Martha 1941- *15*
Gannett, Ruth Chrisman (Arens)
  1896-1979 .... *33*
Gannett, Ruth Stiles 1923- *3*
Gannon, Robert (Haines)
  1931- *8*
Gans, Roma 1894- *45*
Gantos, Jack
  See Gantos, John (Bryan), Jr.
Gantos, John (Bryan), Jr.
  1951- *20*
Garbutt, Bernard 1900-
  Brief Entry *31*
Gard, Joyce
  See Reeves, Joyce
Gard, Robert Edward 1910- *18*
Gardam, Jane 1928- *39*
  Brief Entry *28*
Garden, Nancy 1938- *12*
Gardner, Dic
  See Gardner, Richard
Gardner, Jeanne LeMonnier *5*
Gardner, John (Champlin, Jr.)
  1933-1982 .... *40*
  Obituary *31*
Gardner, Martin 1914- *16*
Gardner, Richard 1931- *24*
Gardner, Richard A. 1931- *13*
Gardner, Robert 1929-
  Brief Entry *43*
Gardner, Sheldon 1934- *33*
Garelick, May *19*
Garfield, James B. 1881-1984 ..... *6*
  Obituary *38*
Garfield, Leon 1921- *32*
  Earlier sketch in SATA 1
Garis, Howard R(oger)
  1873-1962 .... *13*
Garner, Alan 1934- *18*
Garnett, Eve C. R. *3*
Garraty, John A. 1920- *23*
Garret, Maxwell R. 1917- *39*
Garretson, Victoria Diane
  1945- *44*
Garrett, Helen 1895- *21*
Garrigue, Sheila 1931- *21*
Garrison, Barbara 1931- *19*
Garrison, Frederick
  See Sinclair, Upton (Beall)
Garrison, Webb B(lack) 1919- *25*
Garst, Doris Shannon 1894- *1*
Garst, Shannon
  See Garst, Doris Shannon
Garthwaite, Marion H. 1893- *7*
Garton, Malinda D(ean) (?)-1976
  Obituary *26*
Gater, Dilys 1944- *41*
Gates, Doris 1901- *34*
  Earlier sketch in SATA 1
  See also SAAS 1
Gates, Frieda 1933- *26*

Gathorne-Hardy, Jonathan G.
  1933- *26*
Gatty, Juliana Horatia
  See Ewing, Juliana (Horatia Gatty)
Gatty, Margaret Scott 1809-1873
  Brief Entry *27*
Gauch, Patricia Lee 1934- *26*
Gault, Clare S. 1925- *36*
Gault, Frank 1926-1982 .... *36*
  Brief Entry *30*
Gault, William Campbell
  1910- *8*
Gaver, Becky
  See Gaver, Rebecca
Gaver, Rebecca 1952- *20*
Gay, Francis
  See Gee, H(erbert) L(eslie)
Gay, Kathlyn 1930- *9*
Gay, Zhenya 1906-1978 .... *19*
Gee, H(erbert) L(eslie) 1901-1977
  Obituary *26*
Geer, Charles 1922- *42*
  Brief Entry *32*
Gehr, Mary *32*
Geipel, Eileen 1932- *30*
Geis, Darlene *7*
Geisel, Helen 1898-1967 .... *26*
Geisel, Theodor Seuss 1904- *28*
  Earlier sketch in SATA 1
  See also CLR 1
Geldart, William 1936- *15*
Gelinas, Paul J. 1911- *10*
Gelman, Steve 1934- *3*
Gemming, Elizabeth 1932- *11*
Gendel, Evelyn W. 1916(?)-1977
  Obituary *27*
Gentleman, David 1930- *7*
George, Jean Craighead 1919- *2*
  See also CLR 1
George, John L(othar) 1916- *2*
George, S(idney) C(harles)
  1898- *11*
George, W(illiam) Lloyd 1900(?)-1975
  Obituary *30*
Georgiou, Constantine 1927- *7*
Gérard, Jean Ignace Isidore
  1803-1847 .... *45*
Geras, Adele (Daphne) 1944- *23*
Gergely, Tibor 1900-1978
  Obituary *20*
Geringer, Laura 1948- *29*
Gernstein, Mordicai
  Brief Entry *36*
Gerrard, Roy 1935-
  Brief Entry *45*
Gerson, Corinne *37*
Gerson, Noel B(ertram) 1914- *22*
Gesner, Clark 1938- *40*
Gessner, Lynne 1919- *16*
Gewe, Raddory
  See Gorey, Edward St. John
Gibbons, Gail 1944- *23*
  See also CLR 8
Gibbs, Alonzo (Lawrence)
  1915- *5*
Gibbs, (Cecilia) May 1877-1969
  Obituary *27*
Gibbs, Tony
  See Gibbs, Wolcott, Jr.

Gibbs, Wolcott, Jr. 1935- 40
Giblin, James Cross 1933- 33
Gibson, Josephine
  See Joslin, Sesyle
Gidal, Sonia 1922- 2
Gidal, Tim N(ahum) 1909- 2
Giegling, John A(llan) 1935- 17
Giff, Patricia Reilly 1935- 33
Gifford, Griselda 1931- 42
Gilbert, Ann
  See Taylor, Ann
Gilbert, Harriett 1948- 30
Gilbert, (Agnes) Joan (Sewell)
  1931- 10
Gilbert, John (Raphael) 1926- 36
Gilbert, Miriam
  See Presberg, Miriam Goldstein
Gilbert, Nan
  See Gilbertson, Mildred
Gilbert, Sara (Dulaney) 1943- 11
Gilbert, W(illiam) S(chwenk)
  1836-1911 36
Gilbertson, Mildred Geiger
  1908- 2
Gilbreath, Alice (Thompson)
  1921- 12
Gilbreth, Frank B., Jr. 1911- 2
Gilfond, Henry 2
Gilge, Jeanette 1924- 22
Gill, Derek L(ewis) T(heodore)
  1919- 9
Gill, Margery Jean 1925- 22
Gillett, Mary 7
Gillette, Henry Sampson
  1915- 14
Gillham, Bill
  See Gillham, William Edwin Charles
Gillham, William Edwin Charles
  1936- 42
Gilliam, Stan 1946- 39
  Brief Entry 35
Gilman, Dorothy
  See Butters, Dorothy Gilman
Gilman, Esther 1925- 15
Gilmore, Iris 1900- 22
Gilson, Barbara
  See Gilson, Charles James Louis
Gilson, Charles James Louis
  1878-1943 ....YABC 2
Gilson, Jamie 1933- 37
  Brief Entry 34
Ginsburg, Mirra 6
Giovanni, Nikki 1943- 24
  See also CLR 6
Giovanopoulos, Paul 1939- 7
Gipson, Frederick B.
  1908-1973 2
  Obituary 24
Girard, Linda Walvoord 1942- 41
Girion, Barbara 1937- 26
Gittings, Jo Manton 1919- 3
Gittings, Robert 1911- 6
Gladstone, Gary 1935- 12
Gladstone, M(yron) J. 1923- 37
Gladwin, William Zachary
  See Zollinger, Gulielma
Glanville, Brian (Lester)
  1931- 42
Glanzman, Louis S. 1922- 36

Glaser, Dianne E(lizabeth) 1937-
  Brief Entry 31
Glaser, Milton 1929- 11
Glaspell, Susan
  1882-1948 ....YABC 2
Glauber, Uta (Heil) 1936- 17
Glazer, Tom 1914- 9
Gleasner, Diana (Cottle)
  1936- 29
Gleason, Judith 1929- 24
Glendinning, Richard 1917- 24
Glendinning, Sally
  See Glendinning, Sara W(ilson)
Glendinning, Sara W(ilson)
  1913- 24
Glenn, Mel 1943-
  Brief Entry 45
Gles, Margaret Breitmaier
  1940- 22
Glick, Carl (Cannon)
  1890-1971 14
Glick, Virginia Kirkus 1893-1980
  Obituary 23
Gliewe, Unada 1927- 3
Glines, Carroll V(ane), Jr.
  1920- 19
Globe, Leah Ain 1900- 41
Glovach, Linda 1947- 7
Glubok, Shirley 6
  See also CLR 1
Gluck, Felix 1924(?)-1981
  Obituary 25
Glynne-Jones, William 1907- 11
Gobbato, Imero 1923- 39
Goble, Dorothy 26
Goble, Paul 1933- 25
Godden, Rumer 1907- 36
  Earlier sketch in SATA 3
Gode, Alexander
  See Gode von Aesch, Alexander
  (Gottfried Friedrich)
Gode von Aesch, Alexander (Gottfried
  Friedrich) 1906-1970 14
Godfrey, Jane
  See Bowden, Joan Chase
Godfrey, William
  See Youd, (Christopher) Samuel
Goettel, Elinor 1930- 12
Goetz, Delia 1898- 22
Goffstein, M(arilyn) B(rooke)
  1940- 8
  See also CLR 3
Golann, Cecil Paige 1921- 11
Golbin, Andrée 1923- 15
Gold, Phyllis 1941- 21
Gold, Sharlya 9
Goldberg, Herbert S. 1926- 25
Goldberg, Stan J. 1939- 26
Goldfeder, Cheryl
  See Pahz, Cheryl Suzanne
Goldfeder, Jim
  See Pahz, James Alon
Goldfrank, Helen Colodny
  1912- 6
Goldin, Augusta 1906- 13
Goldsborough, June 1923- 19
Goldsmith, Howard 1943- 24
Goldsmith, Oliver 1728-1774 26
Goldstein, Philip 1910- 23

Goldston, Robert (Conroy)
  1927- 6
Goll, Reinhold W(eimar)
  1897- 26
Gonzalez, Gloria 1940- 23
Goodall, John S(trickland)
  1908- 4
Goodbody, Slim
  See Burstein, John
Goode, Diane 1949- 15
Goode, Stephen 1943-
  Brief Entry 40
Goodenow, Earle 1913- 40
Goodman, Elaine 1930- 9
Goodman, Walter 1927- 9
Goodrich, Samuel Griswold
  1793-1860 23
Goodwin, Hal
  See Goodwin, Harold Leland
Goodwin, Harold Leland
  1914- 13
Goor, Nancy (Ruth Miller)
  1944- 39
  Brief Entry 34
Goor, Ron(ald Stephen) 1940- 39
  Brief Entry 34
Goossen, Agnes
  See Epp, Margaret A(gnes)
Gordon, Bernard Ludwig
  1931- 27
Gordon, Colonel H. R.
  See Ellis, Edward S(ylvester)
Gordon, Donald
  See Payne, Donald Gordon
Gordon, Dorothy 1893-1970 20
Gordon, Esther S(aranga)
  1935- 10
Gordon, Frederick [Collective
  pseudonym] 1
Gordon, Hal
  See Goodwin, Harold Leland
Gordon, John 1925- 6
Gordon, John
  See Gesner, Clark
Gordon, Lew
  See Baldwin, Gordon C.
Gordon, Margaret (Anna)
  1939- 9
Gordon, Mildred 1912-1979
  Obituary 24
Gordon, Selma
  See Lanes, Selma G.
Gordon, Shirley 1921-
  Brief Entry 41
Gordon, Sol 1923- 11
Gordon, Stewart
  See Shirreffs, Gordon D.
Gordons, The [Joint pseudonym]
  See Gordon, Mildred
Gorelick, Molly C. 1920- 9
Gorey, Edward St. John
  1925- 29
  Brief Entry 27
Gorham, Charles Orson
  1911-1975 36
Gorham, Michael
  See Folsom, Franklin
Gormley, Beatrice 1942- 39
  Brief Entry 35

Gorog, Judith (Allen) 1938- *39*
Gorsline, Douglas (Warner)
  1913-1985 .... *11*
  Obituary *43*
Gorsline, (Sally) Marie 1928- *28*
Gorsline, S. M.
  See Gorsline, (Sally) Marie
Goryan, Sirak
  See Saroyan, William
Goscinny, René 1926-1977
  Brief Entry *39*
Gottlieb, Bill
  See Gottlieb, William P(aul)
Gottlieb, Gerald 1923- *7*
Gottlieb, William P(aul) *24*
Goudey, Alice E. 1898- *20*
Goudge, Elizabeth 1900-1984 ..... *2*
  Obituary *38*
Gough, Catherine 1931- *24*
Gough, Philip 1908- *45*
Goulart, Ron 1933- *6*
Gould, Chester 1900-1985
  Obituary *43*
Gould, Jean R(osalind) 1919- *11*
Gould, Lilian 1920- *6*
Gould, Marilyn 1923- *15*
Govan, Christine Noble 1898- *9*
Govern, Elaine 1939- *26*
Graber, Alexander *7*
Graber, Richard (Fredrick)
  1927- *26*
Grabiański, Janusz 1929-1976 ..... *39*
  Obituary *30*
Graboff, Abner 1919- *35*
Grace, F(rances Jane) *45*
Graeber, Charlotte Towner
  Brief Entry *44*
Graff, Polly Anne
  See Colver, Anne
Graff, (S.) Stewart 1908- *9*
Graham, Ada 1931- *11*
Graham, Brenda Knight 1942- *32*
Graham, Charlotte
  See Bowden, Joan Chase
Graham, Eleanor 1896-1984 ...... *18*
  Obituary *38*
Graham, Frank, Jr. 1925- *11*
Graham, John 1926- *11*
Graham, Kennon
  See Harrison, David Lee
Graham, Lorenz B(ell) 1902- *2*
  See also CLR 10
Graham, Margaret Bloy 1920- *11*
Graham, Robin Lee 1949- *7*
Graham, Shirley
  See Du Bois, Shirley Graham
Graham-Barber, Lynda 1944- *42*
Graham-Cameron, M(alcolm) G(ordon)
  1931-
  Brief Entry *45*
Graham-Cameron, Mike
  See Graham-Cameron, M(alcolm)
  G(ordon)
Grahame, Kenneth
  1859-1932 ....*YABC 1*
  See also CLR 5
Gramatky, Hardie 1907-1979 ..... *30*
  Obituary *23*
  Earlier sketch in SATA 1

Grand, Samuel 1912- *42*
Grandville, J. J.
  See Gérard, Jean Ignace Isidore
Grandville, Jean Ignace Isidore Gérard
  See Gérard, Jean Ignace Isidore
Grange, Peter
  See Nicole, Christopher Robin
Granger, Margaret Jane 1925(?)-1977
  Obituary *27*
Granger, Peggy
  See Granger, Margaret Jane
Granstaff, Bill 1925- *10*
Grant, Bruce 1893-1977 .... *5*
  Obituary *25*
Grant, Cynthia D. 1950- *33*
Grant, Eva 1907- *7*
Grant, Evva H. 1913-1977
  Obituary *27*
Grant, Gordon 1875-1962 .... *25*
Grant, (Alice) Leigh 1947- *10*
Grant, Matthew C.
  See May, Julian
Grant, Maxwell
  See Lynds, Dennis
Grant, Myrna (Lois) 1934- *21*
Grant, Neil 1938- *14*
Gravel, Fern
  See Hall, James Norman
Graves, Charles Parlin
  1911-1972 .... *4*
Graves, Robert (von Ranke)
  1895-1985 .... *45*
Gray, Elizabeth Janet 1902- *6*
Gray, Genevieve S. 1920- *4*
Gray, Harold (Lincoln)
  1894-1968 .... *33*
  Brief Entry *32*
Gray, Jenny
  See Gray, Genevieve S.
Gray, Marian
  See Pierce, Edith Gray
Gray, Nicholas Stuart
  1922-1981 .... *4*
  Obituary *27*
Gray, Nigel 1941- *33*
Gray, Patricia *7*
Gray, Patsey
  See Gray, Patricia
Grayland, V. Merle
  See Grayland, Valerie
Grayland, Valerie *7*
Great Comte, The
  See Hawkesworth, Eric
Greaves, Margaret 1914- *7*
Grée, Alain 1936- *28*
Green, Adam
  See Weisgard, Leonard
Green, D.
  See Casewit, Curtis
Green, Hannah
  See Greenberg, Joanne (Goldenberg)
Green, Jane 1937- *9*
Green, Mary Moore 1906- *11*
Green, Morton 1937- *8*
Green, Norma B(erger) 1925- *11*
Green, Phyllis 1932- *20*
Green, Roger (Gilbert) Lancelyn
  1918- *2*
Green, Sheila Ellen 1934- *8*

Greenaway, Kate
  1846-1901 ....*YABC 2*
  See also CLR 6
Greenbank, Anthony Hunt
  1933- *39*
Greenberg, Harvey R. 1935- *5*
Greenberg, Joanne (Goldenberg)
  1932- *25*
Greenberg, Polly 1932-
  Brief Entry *43*
Greene, Bette 1934- *8*
  See also CLR 2
Greene, Carla 1916- *1*
Greene, Carol
  Brief Entry *44*
Greene, Constance C(larke)
  1924- *11*
Greene, Ellin 1927- *23*
Greene, Graham 1904- *20*
Greene, Laura 1935- *38*
Greene, Wade 1933- *11*
Greenfeld, Howard *19*
Greenfield, Eloise 1929- *19*
  See also CLR 4
Greenhaus, Thelma Nurenberg
  1903-1984 .... *45*
Greening, Hamilton
  See Hamilton, Charles H. St. John
Greenleaf, Barbara Kaye
  1942- *6*
Greenleaf, Peter 1910- *33*
Greenwald, Sheila
  See Green, Sheila Ellen
Gregg, Walter H(arold) 1919- *20*
Gregor, Arthur 1923- *36*
Gregori, Leon 1919- *15*
Gregorian, Joyce Ballou
  1946- *30*
Gregorowski, Christopher
  1940- *30*
Gregory, Diana (Jean) 1933-
  Brief Entry *42*
Gregory, Stephen
  See Penzler, Otto
Greisman, Joan Ruth 1937- *31*
Grendon, Stephen
  See Derleth, August (William)
Grenville, Pelham
  See Wodehouse, P(elham)
  G(renville)
Gretz, Susanna 1937- *7*
Gretzer, John *18*
Grey, Jerry 1926- *11*
Grey Owl
  See Belaney, Archibald Stansfeld
Gri
  See Denney, Diana
Grice, Frederick 1910- *6*
Grider, Dorothy 1915- *31*
Gridley, Marion E(leanor)
  1906-1974 .... *35*
  Obituary *26*
Grieder, Walter 1924- *9*
Griese, Arnold A(lfred) 1921- *9*
Grifalconi, Ann 1929- *2*
Griffin, Gillett Good 1928- *26*
Griffin, Judith Berry *34*
Griffith, Helen V(irginia)
  1934- *39*

Griffith, Jeannette
  See Eyerly, Jeanette
Griffiths, G(ordon) D(ouglas)
  1910-1973
  Obituary 20
Griffiths, Helen 1939- 5
Grimm, Cherry Barbara Lockett 1930-
  Brief Entry 43
Grimm, Jacob Ludwig Karl
  1785-1863 22
Grimm, Wilhelm Karl
  1786-1859 22
Grimm, William C(arey)
  1907- 14
Grimshaw, Nigel (Gilroy)
  1925- 23
Grimsley, Gordon
  See Groom, Arthur William
Gringhuis, Dirk
  See Gringhuis, Richard H.
Gringhuis, Richard H.
  1918-1974 6
  Obituary 25
Grinnell, George Bird
  1849-1938 16
Gripe, Maria (Kristina) 1923- 2
  See also CLR 5
Groch, Judith (Goldstein)
  1929- 25
Grode, Redway
  See Gorey, Edward St. John
Grohskopf, Bernice 7
Grol, Lini Richards 1913- 9
Grollman, Earl A. 1925- 22
Groom, Arthur William
  1898-1964 10
Gross, Alan 1947-
  Brief Entry 43
Gross, Ruth Belov 1929- 33
Gross, Sarah Chokla
  1906-1976 9
  Obituary 26
Grossman, Nancy 1940- 29
Grossman, Robert 1940- 11
Groth, John 1908- 21
Groves, Georgina
  See Symons, (Dorothy) Geraldine
Gruelle, John (Barton)
  1880-1938 35
  Brief Entry 32
Gruelle, Johnny
  See Gruelle, John
Gruenberg, Sidonie M(atsner)
  1881-1974 2
  Obituary 27
Guck, Dorothy 1913- 27
Gugliotta, Bobette 1918- 7
Guillaume, Jeanette G. (Flierl)
  1899- 8
Guillot, Rene 1900-1969 7
Gundersheimer, Karen
  Brief Entry 44
Gundrey, Elizabeth 1924- 23
Gunn, James E(dwin) 1923- 35
Gunston, Bill
  See Gunston, William Tudor
Gunston, William Tudor
  1927- 9

Gunterman, Bertha Lisette
  1886(?)-1975
  Obituary 27
Gunther, John 1901-1970 2
Gurko, Leo 1914- 9
Gurko, Miriam 9
Gustafson, Anita 1942-
  Brief Entry 45
Gustafson, Sarah R.
  See Riedman, Sarah R.
Gustafson, Scott 1956- 34
Guthrie, Anne 1890-1979 28
Gutman, Bill
  Brief Entry 43
Gutman, Naham 1899(?)-1981
  Obituary 25
Guy, Rosa (Cuthbert) 1928- 14
Gwynne, Fred(erick Hubbard)
  1926- 41
  Brief Entry 27

H

Haas, Carolyn Buhai 1926- 43
Haas, Dorothy F.
  Brief Entry 43
Haas, Irene 1929- 17
Haas, James E(dward) 1943- 40
Haas, Merle S. 1896(?)-1985
  Obituary 41
Habenstreit, Barbara 1937- 5
Haber, Louis 1910- 12
Hader, Berta (Hoerner)
  1891(?)-1976 16
Hader, Elmer (Stanley)
  1889-1973 16
Hadley, Franklin
  See Winterbotham, R(ussell)
  R(obert)
Hadley, Lee 1934-
  Brief Entry 38
Hafner, Marylin 1925- 7
Hager, Alice Rogers 1894-1969
  Obituary 26
Haggard, H(enry) Rider
  1856-1925 16
Haggerty, James J(oseph)
  1920- 5
Hagon, Priscilla
  See Allan, Mabel Esther
Hague, Kathleen
  Brief Entry 45
Hague, Michael (R.)
  Brief Entry 32
Hahn, Emily 1905- 3
Hahn, Hannelore 1926- 8
Hahn, James (Sage) 1947- 9
Hahn, (Mona) Lynn 1949- 9
Hahn, Mary Downing 1937-
  Brief Entry 44
Haig-Brown, Roderick (Langmere)
  1909-1976 12
Haight, Anne Lyon 1895-1977
  Obituary 30
Haines, Gail Kay 1943- 11
Haining, Peter 1940- 14
Halacy, D(aniel) S(tephen), Jr.
  1919- 36
Haldane, Roger John 1945- 13

Hale, Edward Everett
  1822-1909 16
Hale, Helen
  See Mulcahy, Lucille Burnett
Hale, Irina 1932- 26
Hale, Kathleen 1898- 17
Hale, Linda 1929- 6
Hale, Lucretia Peabody
  1820-1900 26
Hale, Nancy 1908- 31
Haley, Gail E(inhart) 1939- 43
  Brief Entry 28
Hall, Adam
  See Trevor, Elleston
Hall, Adele 1910- 7
Hall, Anna Gertrude
  1882-1967 8
Hall, Borden
  See Yates, Raymond F(rancis)
Hall, Brian P(atrick) 1935- 31
Hall, Caryl
  See Hansen, Caryl (Hall)
Hall, Donald (Andrew, Jr.)
  1928- 23
Hall, Douglas 1931- 43
Hall, Elvajean 6
Hall, James Norman
  1887-1951 21
Hall, Jesse
  See Boesen, Victor
Hall, Lynn 1937- 2
Hall, Malcolm 1945- 7
Hall, Marjory
  See Yeakley, Marjory Hall
Hall, Rosalys Haskell 1914- 7
Hallard, Peter
  See Catherall, Arthur
Hallas, Richard
  See Knight, Eric (Mowbray)
Hall-Clarke, James
  See Rowland-Entwistle, (Arthur)
  Theodore (Henry)
Halliburton, Warren J. 1924- 19
Hallin, Emily Watson 1919- 6
Hallinan, P(atrick) K(enneth)
  1944- 39
  Brief Entry 37
Hallman, Ruth 1929- 43
  Brief Entry 28
Hall-Quest, Olga W(ilbourne)
  1899- 11
Hallstead, William F(inn) III
  1924- 11
Hallward, Michael 1889- 12
Halsell, Grace 1923- 13
Halsted, Anna Roosevelt 1906-1975
  Obituary 30
Halter, Jon C(harles) 1941- 22
Hamalian, Leo 1920- 41
Hamberger, John 1934- 14
Hamblin, Dora Jane 1920- 36
Hamerstrom, Frances 1907- 24
Hamil, Thomas Arthur 1928- 14
Hamil, Tom
  See Hamil, Thomas Arthur
Hamill, Ethel
  See Webb, Jean Francis (III)
Hamilton, Alice
  See Cromie, Alice Hamilton

Hamilton, Charles Harold St. John
  1875-1961 .... *13*
Hamilton, Clive
  See Lewis, C. S.
Hamilton, Dorothy 1906-1983 ..... *12*
  Obituary *35*
Hamilton, Edith 1867-1963 .... *20*
Hamilton, Elizabeth 1906- *23*
Hamilton, Morse 1943- *35*
Hamilton, Robert W.
  See Stratemeyer, Edward L.
Hamilton, Virginia 1936- *4*
  See also CLR 1
Hamley, Dennis 1935- *39*
Hammer, Richard 1928- *6*
Hammerman, Gay M(orenus)
  1926- *9*
Hammond, Winifred G(raham)
  1899- *29*
Hammontree, Marie (Gertrude)
  1913- *13*
Hampson, (Richard) Denman
  1929- *15*
Hamre, Leif 1914- *5*
Hamsa, Bobbie 1944-
  Brief Entry *38*
Hancock, Mary A. 1923- *31*
Hancock, Sibyl 1940- *9*
Handforth, Thomas (Schofield)
  1897-1948 .... *42*
Handville, Robert (Tompkins)
  1924- *45*
Hane, Roger 1940-1974
  Obituary *20*
Haney, Lynn 1941- *23*
Hanff, Helene *11*
Hanlon, Emily 1945- *15*
Hann, Jacquie 1951- *19*
Hanna, Paul R(obert) 1902- *9*
Hano, Arnold 1922- *12*
Hansen, Caryl (Hall) 1929- *39*
Hansen, Joyce 1942-
  Brief Entry *39*
Hanser, Richard (Frederick)
  1909- *13*
Hanson, Joan 1938- *8*
Hanson, Joseph E. 1894(?)-1971
  Obituary *27*
Harald, Eric
  See Boesen, Victor
Harcourt, Ellen Knowles 1890(?)-1984
  Obituary *36*
Hardcastle, Michael 1933-
  Brief Entry *38*
Harding, Lee 1937- *32*
  Brief Entry *31*
Hardwick, Richard Holmes, Jr.
  1923- *12*
Hardy, Alice Dale [Collective
  pseudonym] *1*
Hardy, David A(ndrews)
  1936- *9*
Hardy, Stuart
  See Schisgall, Oscar
Hardy, Thomas 1840-1928 .... *25*
Hare, Norma Q(uarles) 1924-
  Brief Entry *41*
Harford, Henry
  See Hudson, W(illiam) H(enry)

Hark, Mildred
  See McQueen, Mildred Hark
Harkaway, Hal
  See Stratemeyer, Edward L.
Harkins, Philip 1912- *6*
Harlan, Elizabeth 1945- *41*
  Brief Entry *35*
Harlan, Glen
  See Cebulash, Mel
Harman, Fred 1902(?)-1982
  Obituary *30*
Harman, Hugh 1903-1982
  Obituary *33*
Harmelink, Barbara (Mary) *9*
Harmer, Mabel 1894- *45*
Harmon, Margaret 1906- *20*
Harnan, Terry 1920- *12*
Harnett, Cynthia (Mary)
  1893-1981 .... *5*
  Obituary *32*
Harper, Anita 1943- *41*
Harper, Mary Wood
  See Dixon, Jeanne
Harper, Wilhelmina
  1884-1973 .... *4*
  Obituary *26*
Harrah, Michael 1940- *41*
Harrell, Sara Gordon
  See Banks, Sara (Jeanne Gordon
  Harrell)
Harries, Joan 1922- *39*
Harrington, Lyn 1911- *5*
Harris, Aurand 1915- *37*
Harris, Christie 1907- *6*
Harris, Colver
  See Colver, Anne
Harris, Dorothy Joan 1931- *13*
Harris, Janet 1932-1979 .... *4*
  Obituary *23*
Harris, Joel Chandler
  1848-1908 .... *YABC 1*
Harris, Lavinia
  See Johnston, Norma
Harris, Leon A., Jr. 1926- *4*
Harris, Lorle K(empe) 1912- *22*
Harris, Mark Jonathan 1941- *32*
Harris, Rosemary (Jeanne) *4*
Harris, Sherwood 1932- *25*
Harrison, C. William 1913- *35*
Harrison, David Lee 1937- *26*
Harrison, Deloris 1938- *9*
Harrison, Harry 1925- *4*
Harrison, Molly 1909- *41*
Harshaw, Ruth H(etzel)
  1890-1968 .... *27*
Hart, Bruce 1938-
  Brief Entry *39*
Hart, Carole 1943-
  Brief Entry *39*
Harte, (Francis) Bret(t)
  1836-1902 .... *26*
Hartley, Ellen (Raphael)
  1915- *23*
Hartley, Fred Allan III 1953- ... *41*
Hartley, William B(rown)
  1913- *23*
Hartman, Evert 1937- *38*
  Brief Entry *35*

Hartman, Louis F(rancis)
  1901-1970 .... *22*
Hartshorn, Ruth M. 1928- *11*
Harvey, Edith 1908(?)-1972
  Obituary *27*
Harwin, Brian
  See Henderson, LeGrand
Harwood, Pearl Augusta (Bragdon)
  1903- *9*
Haseley, Dennis
  Brief Entry *44*
Haskell, Arnold 1903- *6*
Haskins, James 1941- *9*
  See also CLR 3
Haskins, Jim
  See Haskins, James
Hasler, Joan 1931- *28*
Hassall, Joan 1906- *43*
Hassler, Jon (Francis) 1933- *19*
Hastings, Beverly [Joint pseudonym]
  See Barkin, Carol
  See James, Elizabeth
Hatch, Mary Cottam 1912-1970
  Brief Entry *28*
Hatlo, Jimmy 1898-1963
  Obituary *23*
Haugaard, Erik Christian
  1923- *4*
Hauman, Doris 1898- *32*
Hauman, George 1890-1961 .... *32*
Hauser, Margaret L(ouise)
  1909- *10*
Hausman, Gerald 1945- *13*
Hausman, Gerry
  See Hausman, Gerald
Hautzig, Deborah 1956- *31*
Hautzig, Esther 1930- *4*
Havenhand, John
  See Cox, John Roberts
Havighurst, Walter (Edwin)
  1901- *1*
Haviland, Virginia 1911- *6*
Hawes, Judy 1913- *4*
Hawk, Virginia Driving
  See Sneve, Virginia Driving Hawk
Hawkesworth, Eric 1921- *13*
Hawkins, Arthur 1903- *19*
Hawkins, Quail 1905- *6*
Hawkinson, John 1912- *4*
Hawkinson, Lucy (Ozone)
  1924-1971 .... *21*
Hawley, Mable C. [Collective
  pseudonym] *1*
Hawthorne, Captain R. M.
  See Ellis, Edward S(ylvester)
Hawthorne, Nathaniel
  1804-1864 .... *YABC 2*
Hay, John 1915- *13*
Hay, Timothy
  See Brown, Margaret Wise
Haycraft, Howard 1905- *6*
Haycraft, Molly Costain
  1911- *6*
Hayden, Gwendolen Lampshire
  1904- *35*
Hayden, Robert C(arter), Jr. 1937-
  Brief Entry *28*

Hayden, Robert E(arl)
1913-1980 .... *19*
Obituary *26*
Hayes, Carlton J. H.
1882-1964 .... *11*
Hayes, Geoffrey 1947- *26*
Hayes, John F. 1904- *11*
Hayes, Will *7*
Hayes, William D(imitt)
1913- *8*
Haynes, Betsy 1937-
Brief Entry *37*
Hays, H(offman) R(eynolds)
1904-1980 .... *26*
Hays, Wilma Pitchford 1909- *28*
Hayward, Linda 1943-
Brief Entry *39*
Haywood, Carolyn 1898- *29*
Earlier sketch in SATA 1
Hazen, Barbara Shook 1930- *27*
Head, Gay
See Hauser, Margaret L(ouise)
Headley, Elizabeth
See Cavanna, Betty
Headstrom, Richard 1902- *8*
Heady, Eleanor B(utler) 1917- *8*
Heal, Edith 1903- *7*
Healey, Brooks
See Albert, Burton, Jr.
Healey, Larry 1927- *44*
Brief Entry *42*
Heaps, Willard (Allison)
1909- *26*
Hearne, Betsy Gould 1942- *38*
Heath, Veronica
See Blackett, Veronica Heath
Heaven, Constance
See Fecher, Constance
Hecht, George J(oseph) 1895-1980
Obituary *22*
Hecht, Henri Joseph 1922- *9*
Hechtkopf, Henryk 1910- *17*
Heck, Bessie Holland 1911- *26*
Hedderwick, Mairi 1939- *30*
Hedges, Sid(ney) G(eorge)
1897-1974 .... *28*
Hefter, Richard 1942- *31*
Hegarty, Reginald Beaton
1906-1973 .... *10*
Heide, Florence Parry 1919- *32*
Heiderstadt, Dorothy 1907- *6*
Hein, Lucille Eleanor 1915- *20*
Heinemann, George Alfred 1918-
Brief Entry *31*
Heinlein, Robert A(nson)
1907- *9*
Heins, Paul 1909- *13*
Heintze, Carl 1922- *26*
Heinz, W(ilfred) C(harles)
1915- *26*
Heinzen, Mildred
See Masters, Mildred
Helfman, Elizabeth S(eaver)
1911- *3*
Helfman, Harry 1910- *3*
Hellberg, Hans-Eric 1927- *38*
Heller, Linda 1944-
Brief Entry *40*

Hellman, Hal
See Hellman, Harold
Hellman, Harold 1927- *4*
Helps, Racey 1913-1971 .... *2*
Obituary *25*
Helweg, Hans H. 1917-
Brief Entry *33*
Hemming, Roy 1928- *11*
Hemphill, Martha Locke
1904-1973 .... *37*
Henderley, Brooks [Collective
pseudonym] *1*
Henderson, LeGrand
1901-1965 .... *9*
Henderson, Nancy Wallace
1916- *22*
Henderson, Zenna (Chlarson)
1917- *5*
Hendrickson, Walter Brookfield, Jr.
1936- *9*
Henkes, Kevin 1960- *43*
Henriod, Lorraine 1925- *26*
Henry, Joanne Landers 1927- *6*
Henry, Marguerite *11*
See also CLR 4
Henry, O.
See Porter, William Sydney
Henry, Oliver
See Porter, William Sydney
Henry, T. E.
See Rowland-Entwistle, (Arthur)
Theodore (Henry)
Henson, James Maury 1936- *43*
Henson, Jim
See Henson, James Maury
Henstra, Friso 1928- *8*
Hentoff, Nat(han Irving)
1925- *42*
Brief Entry *27*
See also CLR 1
Herald, Kathleen
See Peyton, Kathleen (Wendy)
Herbert, Cecil
See Hamilton, Charles H. St. John
Herbert, Don 1917- *2*
Herbert, Frank (Patrick) 1920- *37*
Earlier sketch in SATA 9
Herbert, Wally
See Herbert, Walter William
Herbert, Walter William
1934- *23*
Hergé
See Rémi, Georges
See also CLR 6
Herkimer, L(awrence) R(ussell)
1925- *42*
Herman, Charlotte 1937- *20*
Hermanson, Dennis (Everett)
1947- *10*
Hermes, Patricia 1936- *31*
Herriot, James
See Wight, James Alfred
Herrmanns, Ralph 1933- *11*
Herron, Edward A(lbert)
1912- *4*
Hersey, John (Richard) 1914- *25*
Hertz, Grete Janus 1915- *23*
Hess, Lilo 1916- *4*
Heuer, Kenneth John 1927- *44*

Heuman, William 1912-1971 ...... *21*
Hewes, Agnes Danforth
1874-1963 .... *35*
Hewett, Anita 1918- *13*
Hext, Harrington
See Phillpotts, Eden
Hey, Nigel S(tewart) 1936- *20*
Heyduck-Huth, Hilde 1929- *8*
Heyerdahl, Thor 1914- *2*
Heyliger, William
1884-1955 .... *YABC 1*
Heyman, Ken(neth Louis)
1930- *34*
Heyward, Du Bose 1885-1940 .... *21*
Hibbert, Christopher 1924- *4*
Hibbert, Eleanor Burford
1906- *2*
Hickman, Janet 1940- *12*
Hickman, Martha Whitmore
1925- *26*
Hickok, Lorena A.
1892(?)-1968 .... *20*
Hickok, Will
See Harrison, C. William
Hicks, Eleanor B.
See Coerr, Eleanor
Hicks, Harvey
See Stratemeyer, Edward L.
Hieatt, Constance B(artlett)
1928- *4*
Hiebert, Ray Eldon 1932- *13*
Higdon, Hal 1931- *4*
Higginbottom, J(effrey) Winslow
1945- *29*
Highet, Helen
See MacInnes, Helen
Hightower, Florence Cole
1916-1981 .... *4*
Obituary *27*
Highwater, Jamake 1942- *32*
Brief Entry *30*
Hildebrandt, Greg 1939-
Brief Entry *33*
Hildebrandt, Tim 1939-
Brief Entry *33*
Hilder, Rowland 1905- *36*
Hildick, E. W.
See Hildick, Wallace
Hildick, (Edmund) Wallace
1925- *2*
Hill, Donna (Marie) *24*
Hill, Douglas (Arthur) 1935- *39*
Hill, Elizabeth Starr 1925- *24*
Hill, Grace Brooks [Collective
pseudonym] *1*
Hill, Grace Livingston
1865-1947 .... *YABC 2*
Hill, Helen M(orey) 1915- *27*
Hill, Kathleen Louise 1917- *4*
Hill, Kay
See Hill, Kathleen Louise
Hill, Lorna 1902- *12*
Hill, Margaret (Ohler) 1915- *36*
Hill, Meg
See Hill, Margaret (Ohler)
Hill, Monica
See Watson, Jane Werner

Hill, Robert W(hite)
  1919-1982 .... *12*
  Obituary *31*
Hill, Ruth A.
  See Viguers, Ruth Hill
Hill, Ruth Livingston
  See Munce, Ruth Hill
Hillcourt, William 1900- *27*
Hillerman, Tony 1925- *6*
Hillert, Margaret 1920- *8*
Hillman, Martin
  See Hill, Douglas (Arthur)
Hillman, Priscilla 1940-
  Brief Entry *39*
Hills, C(harles) A(lbert) R(eis)
  1955- *39*
Hilton, Irene (P.) 1912- *7*
Hilton, James 1900-1954 .... *34*
Hilton, Ralph 1907- *8*
Hilton, Suzanne 1922- *4*
Him, George 1900-1982
  Obituary *30*
Himler, Ann 1946- *8*
Himler, Ronald 1937- *6*
Hinckley, Helen
  See Jones, Helen Hinckley
Hines, Anna G(rossnickle) 1946-
  Brief Entry *45*
Hinton, S(usan) E(loise)
  1950- *19*
  See also CLR 3
Hinton, Sam 1917- *43*
Hintz, (Loren) Martin 1945-
  Brief Entry *39*
Hirsch, Phil 1926- *35*
Hirsch, S. Carl 1913- *2*
Hirschmann, Linda (Ann)
  1941- *40*
Hirsh, Marilyn 1944- *7*
Hirshberg, Al(bert Simon)
  1909-1973 .... *38*
Hiser, Iona Seibert 1901- *4*
Hitchcock, Alfred (Joseph)
  1899-1980 .... *27*
  Obituary *24*
Hitte, Kathryn 1919- *16*
Hitz, Demi 1942- *11*
Hnizdovsky, Jacques 1915- *32*
Ho, Minfong 1951- *15*
Hoare, Robert J(ohn)
  1921-1975 .... *38*
Hoban, Lillian 1925- *22*
Hoban, Russell C(onwell)
  1925- *40*
  Earlier sketch in SATA 1
  See also CLR 3
Hoban, Tana *22*
Hobart, Lois *7*
Hoberman, Mary Ann 1930- *5*
Hobson, Burton (Harold)
  1933- *28*
Hochschild, Arlie Russell
  1940- *11*
Hockaby, Stephen
  See Mitchell, Gladys (Maude
  Winifred)
Hockenberry, Hope
  See Newell, Hope (Hockenberry)

Hodge, P(aul) W(illiam)
  1934- *12*
Hodgell, P(atricia) C(hristine)
  1951- *42*
Hodges, C(yril) Walter 1909- *2*
Hodges, Carl G. 1902-1964 .... *10*
Hodges, Elizabeth Jamison *1*
Hodges, Margaret Moore
  1911- *33*
  Earlier sketch in SATA 1
Hodgetts, Blake Christopher
  1967- *43*
Hoexter, Corinne K. 1927- *6*
Hoff, Carol 1900- *11*
Hoff, Syd(ney) 1912- *9*
Hoffman, Phyllis M. 1944- *4*
Hoffman, Rosekrans 1926- *15*
Hoffmann, E(rnst) T(heodor)
  A(madeus) 1776-1822 .... *27*
Hoffmann, Felix 1911-1975 .... *9*
Hofsinde, Robert 1902-1973 .... *21*
Hogan, Bernice Harris 1929- *12*
Hogan, Inez 1895- *2*
Hogarth, Jr.
  See Kent, Rockwell
Hogarth, Paul 1917- *41*
Hogg, Garry 1902- *2*
Hogner, Dorothy Childs *4*
Hogner, Nils 1893-1970 .... *25*
Hogrogian, Nonny 1932- *7*
  See also CLR 2
  See also SAAS 1
Hoke, Helen (L.) 1903- *15*
Hoke, John 1925- *7*
Holbeach, Henry
  See Rands, William Brighty
Holberg, Ruth Langland
  1889- *1*
Holbrook, Peter
  See Glick, Carl (Cannon)
Holbrook, Sabra
  See Erickson, Sabra R(ollins)
Holbrook, Stewart Hall
  1893-1964 .... *2*
Holden, Elizabeth Rhoda
  See Lawrence, Louise
Holding, James 1907- *3*
Holisher, Desider 1901-1972 ...... *6*
Holl, Adelaide (Hinkle) *8*
Holland, Isabelle 1920- *8*
Holland, Janice 1913-1962 .... *18*
Holland, John L(ewis) 1919- *20*
Holland, Lys
  See Gater, Dilys
Holland, Marion 1908- *6*
Hollander, John 1929- *13*
Hollander, Phyllis 1928- *39*
Holldobler, Turid 1939- *26*
Holliday, Joe
  See Holliday, Joseph
Holliday, Joseph 1910- *11*
Holling, Holling C(lancy)
  1900-1973 .... *15*
  Obituary *26*
Hollingsworth, Alvin C(arl)
  1930- *39*
Holloway, Teresa (Bragunier)
  1906- *26*

Holm, (Else) Anne (Lise)
  1922- *1*
Holman, Felice 1919- *7*
Holme, Bryan 1913- *26*
Holmes, Marjorie 1910- *43*
Holmes, Oliver Wendell
  1809-1894 .... *34*
Holmes, Rick
  See Hardwick, Richard Holmes, Jr.
Holmgren, George Ellen
  See Holmgren, Helen Jean
Holmgren, Helen Jean 1930- *45*
Holmgren, Virginia C(unningham)
  1909- *26*
Holmquist, Eve 1921- *11*
Holt, Margaret 1937- *4*
Holt, Margaret Van Vechten
  (Saunders) 1899-1963 .... *32*
Holt, Michael (Paul) 1929- *13*
Holt, Rackham
  See Holt, Margaret Van Vechten
  (Saunders)
Holt, Rochelle Lynn 1946- *41*
Holt, Stephen
  See Thompson, Harlan H.
Holt, Victoria
  See Hibbert, Eleanor
Holton, Leonard
  See Wibberley, Leonard (Patrick
  O'Connor)
Holyer, Erna Maria 1925- *22*
Holyer, Ernie
  See Holyer, Erna Maria
Holz, Loretta (Marie) 1943- *17*
Homze, Alma C. 1932- *17*
Honig, Donald 1931- *18*
Honness, Elizabeth H. 1904- *2*
Hoobler, Dorothy *28*
Hoobler, Thomas *28*
Hood, Joseph F. 1925- *4*
Hood, Robert E. 1926- *21*
Hook, Frances 1912- *27*
Hook, Martha 1936- *27*
Hooker, Ruth 1920- *21*
Hooks, William H(arris)
  1921- *16*
Hooper, Byrd
  See St. Clair, Byrd Hooper
Hooper, Meredith (Jean)
  1939- *28*
Hoopes, Lyn Littlefield 1953-
  Brief Entry *44*
Hoopes, Ned E(dward) 1932- *21*
Hoopes, Roy 1922- *11*
Hoople, Cheryl G.
  Brief Entry *32*
Hoover, H(elen) M(ary) 1935- *44*
  Brief Entry *33*
Hoover, Helen (Drusilla Blackburn)
  1910-1984 .... *12*
  Obituary *39*
Hope, Laura Lee [Collective
  pseudonym] *1*
  See also Adams, Harriet
  S(tratemeyer)
Hope Simpson, Jacynth 1930- *12*
Hopf, Alice L(ightner) 1904- *5*
Hopkins, A. T.
  See Turngren, Annette

Hopkins, Clark 1895-1976
  Obituary 34
Hopkins, Joseph G(erard) E(dward)
  1909- 11
Hopkins, Lee Bennett 1938- 3
Hopkins, Lyman
  See Folsom, Franklin
Hopkins, Marjorie 1911- 9
Hoppe, Joanne 1932- 42
Hopper, Nancy J. 1937- 38
  Brief Entry 35
Horgan, Paul 1903- 13
Hornblow, Arthur (Jr.)
  1893-1976 15
Hornblow, Leonora (Schinasi)
  1920- 18
Horne, Richard Henry
  1803-1884 29
Horner, Althea (Jane) 1926- 36
Horner, Dave 1934- 12
Hornos, Axel 1907- 20
Horvath, Betty 1927- 4
Horwich, Frances R(appaport)
  1908- 11
Horwitz, Elinor Lander 45
  Brief Entry 33
Hosford, Dorothy (Grant)
  1900-1952 22
Hosford, Jessie 1892- 5
Hoskyns-Abrahall, Clare 13
Houck, Carter 1924- 22
Hough, (Helen) Charlotte
  1924- 9
Hough, Richard (Alexander)
  1922- 17
Houghton, Eric 1930- 7
Houlehen, Robert J. 1918- 18
Household, Geoffrey (Edward West)
  1900- 14
Houselander, (Frances) Caryll
  1900-1954
  Brief Entry 31
Housman, Laurence
  1865-1959 25
Houston, James A(rchibald)
  1921- 13
  See also CLR 3
Houton, Kathleen
  See Kilgore, Kathleen
Howard, Alan 1922- 45
Howard, Elizabeth
  See Mizner, Elizabeth Howard
Howard, Prosper
  See Hamilton, Charles H. St. John
Howard, Robert West 1908- 5
Howard, Vernon (Linwood)
  1918- 40
Howarth, David 1912- 6
Howe, Deborah 1946-1978 29
Howe, James 1946- 29
  See also CLR 9
Howell, Pat 1947- 15
Howell, S.
  See Styles, Frank Showell
Howell, Virginia Tier
  See Ellison, Virginia Howell
Howes, Barbara 1914- 5
Hoy, Nina
  See Roth, Arthur J(oseph)

Hoyle, Geoffrey 1942- 18
Hoyt, Edwin P(almer), Jr.
  1923- 28
Hoyt, Olga (Gruhzit) 1922- 16
Hubbell, Patricia 1928- 8
Hubley, John 1914-1977
  Obituary 24
Hudson, Jeffrey
  See Crichton, (J.) Michael
Hudson, (Margaret) Kirsty
  1947- 32
Hudson, W(illiam) H(enry)
  1841-1922 35
Huffaker, Sandy 1943- 10
Huffman, Tom 24
Hughes, Dean 1943- 33
Hughes, (James) Langston
  1902-1967 33
  Earlier sketch in SATA 4
Hughes, Matilda
  See MacLeod, Charlotte (Matilda
  Hughes)
Hughes, Monica 1925- 15
  See also CLR 9
Hughes, Richard (Arthur Warren)
  1900-1976 8
  Obituary 25
Hughes, Shirley 1929- 16
Hughes, Ted 1930-
  Brief Entry 27
  See also CLR 3
Hughes, Thomas 1822-1896 31
Hughes, Walter (Llewellyn)
  1910- 26
Huline-Dickens, Frank William
  1931- 34
Hull, Eleanor (Means) 1913- 21
Hull, Eric Traviss
  See Harnan, Terry
Hull, H. Braxton
  See Jacobs, Helen Hull
Hull, Katharine 1921-1977 23
Hülsmann, Eva 1928- 16
Hults, Dorothy Niebrugge
  1898- 6
Hume, Lotta Carswell 7
Hume, Ruth (Fox) 1922-1980 26
  Obituary 22
Hummel, Berta 1909-1946 43
Hummel, Sister Maria Innocentia
  See Hummel, Berta
Humphrey, Henry (III) 1930- 16
Humphreys, Graham 1945-
  Brief Entry 32
Hungerford, Pixie
  See Brinsmead, H(esba) F(ay)
Hunt, Francis
  See Stratemeyer, Edward L.
Hunt, Irene 1907- 2
  See also CLR 1
Hunt, Joyce 1927- 31
Hunt, Linda Lawrence 1940- 39
Hunt, Mabel Leigh 1892-1971 1
  Obituary 26
Hunt, Morton 1920- 22
Hunt, Nigel
  See Greenbank, Anthony Hunt
Hunter, Bernice Thurman 1922-
  Brief Entry 45

Hunter, Clingham, M.D.
  See Adams, William Taylor
Hunter, Dawe
  See Downie, Mary Alice
Hunter, Edith Fisher 1919- 31
Hunter, Evan 1926- 25
Hunter, Hilda 1921- 7
Hunter, Kristin (Eggleston)
  1931- 12
  See also CLR 3
Hunter, Leigh
  See Etchison, Birdie L(ee)
Hunter, Mel 1927- 39
Hunter, Mollie
  See McIllwraith, Maureen
Hunter, Norman (George Lorimer)
  1899- 26
Hunter Blair, Pauline 1921- 3
Huntington, Harriet E(lizabeth)
  1909- 1
Huntsberry, William E(mery)
  1916- 5
Hurd, Clement 1908- 2
Hurd, Edith Thacher 1910- 2
Hurd, Thacher 1949-
  Brief Entry 45
Hürlimann, Bettina 1909-1983 39
  Obituary 34
Hürlimann, Ruth 1939- 32
  Brief Entry 31
Hurwitz, Johanna 1937- 20
Hurwood, Bernhardt J. 1926- 12
Hutchens, Paul 1902-1977 31
Hutchins, Carleen Maley
  1911- 9
Hutchins, Pat 1942- 15
Hutchins, Ross E(lliott) 1906- 4
Hutchmacher, J. Joseph 1929- 5
Hutto, Nelson (Allen) 1904- 20
Hutton, Warwick 1939- 20
Hyde, Dayton O(gden) 9
Hyde, Hawk
  See Hyde, Dayton O(gden)
Hyde, Margaret Oldroyd
  1917- 42
  Earlier sketch in SATA 1
Hyde, Shelley
  See Reed, Kit
Hyde, Wayne F. 1922- 7
Hylander, Clarence J.
  1897-1964 7
Hyman, Robin P(hilip) 1931- 12
Hyman, Trina Schart 1939- 7
Hymes, Lucia M. 1907- 7
Hyndman, Jane Andrews
  1912-1978 1
  Obituary 23
Hyndman, Robert Utley
  1906(?)-1973 18

I

Iannone, Jeanne 7
Ibbotson, Eva 1925- 13
Ibbotson, M. C(hristine)
  1930- 5
Ichikawa, Satomi
  Brief Entry 36
Ilowite, Sheldon A. 1931- 27

Ilsley, Dent [Joint pseudonym]
  See Chapman, John Stanton Higham
Ilsley, Velma (Elizabeth)
  1918- *12*
Immel, Mary Blair 1930- *28*
Ingelow, Jean 1820-1897 .... *33*
Ingham, Colonel Frederic
  See Hale, Edward Everett
Ingraham, Leonard W(illiam)
  1913- *4*
Ingrams, Doreen 1906- *20*
Inyart, Gene 1927- *6*
Ionesco, Eugene 1912- *7*
Ipcar, Dahlov (Zorach) 1917- *1*
Irvin, Fred 1914- *15*
Irving, Alexander
  See Hume, Ruth (Fox)
Irving, Robert
  See Adler, Irving
Irving, Washington
  1783-1859 .... *YABC 2*
Irwin, Ann(abelle Bowen)
  1915- *44*
  Brief Entry *38*
Irwin, Constance Frick 1913- *6*
Irwin, Hadley [Joint pseudonym]
  See Hadley, Lee and Irwin, Ann
Irwin, Keith Gordon
  1885-1964 .... *11*
Isaac, Joanne 1934- *21*
Isaacs, Jacob
  See Kranzler, George G(ershon)
Isadora, Rachel 1953(?)-
  Brief Entry *32*
  See also CLR 7
Isham, Charlotte H(ickox)
  1912- *21*
Ish-Kishor, Judith 1892-1972 ..... *11*
Ish-Kishor, Sulamith
  1896-1977 .... *17*
Ishmael, Woodi 1914- *31*
Israel, Elaine 1945- *12*
Israel, Marion Louise 1882-1973
  Obituary *26*
Iwamatsu, Jun Atsushi 1908- *14*

J

Jac, Lee
  See Morton, Lee Jack, Jr.
Jackson, Anne 1896(?)-1984
  Obituary *37*
Jackson, C. Paul 1902- *6*
Jackson, Caary
  See Jackson, C. Paul
Jackson, Jesse 1908- *29*
  Earlier sketch in SATA 2
Jackson, O. B.
  See Jackson, C. Paul
Jackson, Robert B(lake) 1926- *8*
Jackson, Sally
  See Kellogg, Jean
Jackson, Shirley 1919-1965 .... *2*
Jacob, Helen Pierce 1927- *21*
Jacobi, Kathy
  Brief Entry *42*
Jacobs, Flora Gill 1918- *5*
Jacobs, Francine 1935- *43*
  Brief Entry *42*

Jacobs, Frank 1929- *30*
Jacobs, Helen Hull 1908- *12*
Jacobs, Joseph 1854-1916 .... *25*
Jacobs, Leland Blair 1907- *20*
Jacobs, Linda C. 1943- *21*
Jacobs, Lou(is), Jr. 1921- *2*
Jacobs, Susan 1940- *30*
Jacobs, William Jay 1933- *28*
Jacobson, Daniel 1923- *12*
Jacobson, Morris K(arl) 1906- *21*
Jacopetti, Alexandra 1939- *14*
Jacques, Robin 1920- *32*
  Brief Entry *30*
Jaffee, Al(lan) 1921-
  Brief Entry *37*
Jagendorf, Moritz (Adolf)
  1888-1981 .... *2*
  Obituary *24*
Jahn, (Joseph) Michael 1943- *28*
Jahn, Mike
  See Jahn, (Joseph) Michael
Jahsmann, Allan Hart 1916- *28*
James, Andrew
  See Kirkup, James
James, Dynely
  See Mayne, William
James, Edwin
  See Gunn, James E(dwin)
James, Elizabeth 1942- *45*
  Brief Entry *39*
James, Harry Clebourne 1896- *11*
James, Josephine
  See Sterne, Emma Gelders
James, T. F.
  See Fleming, Thomas J(ames)
James, Will(iam Roderick)
  1892-1942 .... *19*
Jane, Mary Childs 1909- *6*
Janes, Edward C. 1908- *25*
Janeway, Elizabeth (Hall)
  1913- *19*
Janice
  See Brustlein, Janice Tworkov
Janosch
  See Eckert, Horst
Jansen, Jared
  See Cebulash, Mel
Janson, Dora Jane 1916- *31*
Janson, H(orst) W(oldemar)
  1913- *9*
Jansson, Tove (Marika) 1914- *41*
  Earlier sketch in SATA 3
  See also CLR 2
Janus, Grete
  See Hertz, Grete Janus
Jaques, Faith 1923- *21*
Jaques, Francis Lee 1887-1969
  Brief Entry *28*
Jarman, Rosemary Hawley
  1935- *7*
Jarrell, Mary von Schrader
  1914- *35*
Jarrell, Randall 1914-1965 .... *7*
  See also CLR 6
Jauss, Anne Marie 1907- *10*
Jayne, Lieutenant R. H.
  See Ellis, Edward S(ylvester)
Jaynes, Clare [Joint pseudonym]
  See Mayer, Jane Rothschild

Jeake, Samuel, Jr.
  See Aiken, Conrad
Jefferies, (John) Richard
  1848-1887 .... *16*
Jeffers, Susan *17*
Jefferson, Sarah
  See Farjeon, Annabel
Jeffries, Roderic 1926- *4*
Jenkins, Marie M. 1909- *7*
Jenkins, William A(twell)
  1922- *9*
Jennings, Gary (Gayne) 1928- *9*
Jennings, Robert
  See Hamilton, Charles H. St. John
Jennings, S. M.
  See Meyer, Jerome Sydney
Jennison, C. S.
  See Starbird, Kaye
Jennison, Keith Warren 1911- *14*
Jensen, Niels 1927- *25*
Jensen, Virginia Allen 1927- *8*
Jeschke, Susan *42*
  Brief Entry *27*
Jessel, Camilla (Ruth) 1937- *29*
Jewell, Nancy 1940-
  Brief Entry *41*
Jewett, Eleanore Myers
  1890-1967 .... *5*
Jewett, Sarah Orne 1849-1909 .... *15*
Jezard, Alison 1919-
  Brief Entry *34*
Jiler, John 1946- *42*
  Brief Entry *35*
Jobb, Jamie 1945- *29*
Joerns, Consuelo *44*
  Brief Entry *33*
John, Naomi
  See Flack, Naomi John (White)
Johns, Avery
  See Cousins, Margaret
Johnson, A. E. [Joint pseudonym]
  See Johnson, Annabell and Johnson,
  Edgar
Johnson, Annabell Jones
  1921- *2*
Johnson, Benj. F., of Boone
  See Riley, James Whitcomb
Johnson, Charles R. 1925- *11*
Johnson, Chuck
  See Johnson, Charles R.
Johnson, Crockett
  See Leisk, David (Johnson)
Johnson, D(ana) William
  1945- *23*
Johnson, Dorothy M(arie)
  1905-1984 .... *6*
  Obituary *40*
Johnson, E(ugene) Harper *44*
Johnson, Edgar Raymond
  1912- *2*
Johnson, Elizabeth 1911-1984 ..... *7*
  Obituary *39*
Johnson, Eric W(arner) 1918- *8*
Johnson, Evelyne 1932- *20*
Johnson, Gaylord 1884- *7*
Johnson, Gerald White
  1890-1980 .... *19*
  Obituary *28*

Johnson, Harper
　See Johnson, E(ugene) Harper
Johnson, James Ralph 1922- *1*
Johnson, James Weldon
　See Johnson, James William
Johnson, James William
　1871-1938 .... *31*
Johnson, John E(mil) 1929- *34*
Johnson, LaVerne B(ravo)
　1925- *13*
Johnson, Lois S(mith) *6*
Johnson, Lois W(alfrid) 1936- *22*
Johnson, Margaret S(weet)
　1893-1964 .... *35*
Johnson, Mary Frances K.
　1929(?)-1979
　Obituary *27*
Johnson, Milton 1932- *31*
Johnson, Natalie
　See Robison, Nancy L(ouise)
Johnson, (Walter) Ryerson
　1901- *10*
Johnson, Shirley K(ing) 1927- *10*
Johnson, Siddie Joe 1905-1977
　Obituary *20*
Johnson, Spencer 1938-
　Brief Entry *38*
Johnson, William R. *38*
Johnson, William Weber
　1909- *7*
Johnston, Agnes Christine
　See Dazey, Agnes J.
Johnston, Annie Fellows
　1863-1931 .... *37*
Johnston, H(ugh) A(nthony) S(tephen)
　1913-1967 .... *14*
Johnston, Johanna
　1914(?)-1982 .... *12*
　Obituary *33*
Johnston, Norma *29*
Johnston, Portia
　See Takakjian, Portia
Johnston, Tony 1942- *8*
Jonas, Ann
　Brief Entry *42*
Jones, Adrienne 1915- *7*
Jones, Diana Wynne 1934- *9*
Jones, Elizabeth Orton 1910- *18*
Jones, Evan 1915- *3*
Jones, Geraldine 1951- *43*
Jones, Gillingham
　See Hamilton, Charles H. St. John
Jones, Harold 1904- *14*
Jones, Helen Hinckley 1903- *26*
Jones, Helen L. 1904(?)-1973
　Obituary *22*
Jones, Hettie 1934- *42*
　Brief Entry *27*
Jones, Hortense P. 1918- *9*
Jones, Jessie Mae Orton 1887(?)-1983
　Obituary *37*
Jones, Margaret Boone
　See Zarif, Margaret Min'imah
Jones, Mary Alice *6*
Jones, McClure *34*
Jones, Penelope 1938- *31*
Jones, Rebecca C(astaldi)
　1947- *33*
Jones, Weyman 1928- *4*

Jonk, Clarence 1906- *10*
Jordan, Don
　See Howard, Vernon (Linwood)
Jordan, E(mil) L(eopold) 1900-
　Brief Entry *31*
Jordan, Hope (Dahle) 1905- *15*
Jordan, Jael (Michal) 1949- *30*
Jordan, June 1936- *4*
　See also CLR 10
Jordan, Mildred 1901- *5*
Jorgensen, Mary Venn *36*
Jorgenson, Ivar
　See Silverberg, Robert
Joseph, Joan 1939- *34*
Joseph, Joseph M(aron)
　1903-1979 .... *22*
Joslin, Sesyle 1929- *2*
Joyce, J(ames) Avery *11*
Joyner, Jerry 1938- *34*
Jucker, Sita 1921- *5*
Judd, Denis (O'Nan) 1938- *33*
Judd, Frances K. [Collective
　pseudonym] *1*
Judson, Clara Ingram
　1879-1960 .... *38*
　Brief Entry *27*
Jukes, Mavis
　Brief Entry *43*
Jumpp, Hugo
　See MacPeek, Walter G.
Jupo, Frank J. 1904- *7*
Juster, Norton 1929- *3*
Justus, May 1898- *1*
Juvenilia
　See Taylor, Ann

K

Kabdebo, Tamas
　See Kabdebo, Thomas
Kabdebo, Thomas 1934- *10*
Kabibble, Osh
　See Jobb, Jamie
Kadesch, Robert R(udstone)
　1922- *31*
Kahl, M(arvin) P(hilip) 1934- *37*
Kahl, Virginia (Caroline) 1919-
　Brief Entry *38*
Kahn, Roger 1927- *37*
Kakimoto, Kozo 1915- *11*
Kalashnikoff, Nicholas
　1888-1961 .... *16*
Kalb, Jonah 1926- *23*
Kaler, James Otis 1848-1912 ...... *15*
Kalnay, Francis 1899- *7*
Kalow, Gisela 1946- *32*
Kamen, Gloria 1923- *9*
Kamerman, Sylvia E.
　See Burack, Sylvia K.
Kamm, Josephine (Hart)
　1905- *24*
Kandell, Alice S. 1938- *35*
Kane, Henry Bugbee
　1902-1971 .... *14*
Kane, Robert W. 1910- *18*
Kanetzke, Howard W(illiam)
　1932- *38*
Kanzawa, Toshiko
　See Furukawa, Toshi

Kaplan, Anne Bernays 1930- *32*
Kaplan, Bess 1927- *22*
Kaplan, Boche 1926- *24*
Kaplan, Irma 1900- *10*
Kaplan, Jean Caryl Korn
　1926- *10*
Karageorge, Michael
　See Anderson, Poul (William)
Karasz, Ilonka 1896-1981
　Obituary *29*
Karen, Ruth 1922- *9*
Kark, Nina Mary 1925- *4*
Karl, Jean E(dna) 1927- *34*
Karlin, Eugene 1918- *10*
Karp, Naomi J. 1926- *16*
Kashiwagi, Isami 1925- *10*
Kästner, Erich 1899-1974 .... *14*
　See also CLR 4
Katchen, Carole 1944- *9*
Kathryn
　See Searle, Kathryn Adrienne
Katona, Robert 1949- *21*
Katsarakis, Joan Harries
　See Harries, Joan
Katz, Bobbi 1933- *12*
Katz, Fred 1938- *6*
Katz, Jane 1934- *33*
Katz, Marjorie P.
　See Weiser, Marjorie P(hillis) K(atz)
Katz, William Loren 1927- *13*
Kaufman, Joe 1911- *33*
Kaufman, Mervyn D. 1932- *4*
Kaufmann, Angelika 1935- *15*
Kaufmann, John 1931- *18*
Kaula, Edna Mason 1906- *13*
Kavaler, Lucy 1930- *23*
Kay, Helen
　See Goldfrank, Helen Colodny
Kay, Mara *13*
Kaye, Geraldine 1925- *10*
Keane, Bil 1922- *4*
Keating, Bern
　See Keating, Leo Bernard
Keating, Lawrence A.
　1903-1966 .... *23*
Keating, Leo Bernard 1915- *10*
Keats, Ezra Jack 1916-1983 ...... *14*
　Obituary *34*
　See also CLR 1
Keegan, Marcia 1943- *9*
Keen, Martin L. 1913- *4*
Keene, Carolyn [Collective
　pseudonym]
　See Adams, Harriet S.
Keeping, Charles (William James)
　1924- *9*
Keeshan, Robert J. 1927- *32*
Keir, Christine
　See Pullein-Thompson, Christine
Keith, Carlton
　See Robertson, Keith
Keith, Hal 1934- *36*
Keith, Harold (Verne) 1903- *2*
Keith, Robert
　See Applebaum, Stan
Kelen, Emery 1896-1978 .... *13*
　Obituary *26*
Kelleam, Joseph E(veridge)
　1913-1975 .... *31*

Keller, B(everly) L(ou) *13*
Keller, Charles 1942- *8*
Keller, Dick 1923- *36*
Keller, Gail Faithfull
  See Faithfull, Gail
Keller, Holly
  Brief Entry *42*
Keller, Irene (Barron) 1927- *36*
Kelley, Leo P(atrick) 1928- *32*
  Brief Entry *31*
Kelley, True Adelaide 1946- *41*
  Brief Entry *39*
Kellin, Sally Moffet 1932- *9*
Kelling, Furn L. 1914- *37*
Kellogg, Gene
  See Kellogg, Jean
Kellogg, Jean 1916- *10*
Kellogg, Steven 1941- *8*
  See also CLR 6
Kellow, Kathleen
  See Hibbert, Eleanor
Kelly, Eric P(hilbrook)
  1884-1960 .... *YABC 1*
Kelly, Martha Rose
  1914-1983 .... *37*
Kelly, Marty
  See Kelly, Martha Rose
Kelly, Ralph
  See Geis, Darlene
Kelly, Regina Z. *5*
Kelly, Rosalie (Ruth) *43*
Kelly, Walt(er Crawford)
  1913-1973 .... *18*
Kelsey, Alice Geer 1896- *1*
Kemp, Gene 1926- *25*
Kempner, Mary Jean
  1913-1969 .... *10*
Kempton, Jean Welch 1914- *10*
Kendall, Carol (Seeger) 1917- *11*
Kendall, Lace
  See Stoutenburg, Adrien
Kenealy, James P. 1927-
  Brief Entry *29*
Kenealy, Jim
  See Kenealy, James P.
Kennedy, John Fitzgerald
  1917-1963 .... *11*
Kennedy, Joseph 1929- *14*
Kennedy, Paul E(dward)
  1929- *33*
Kennedy, (Jerome) Richard
  1932- *22*
Kennedy, T(eresa) A. 1953- *42*
  Brief Entry *35*
Kennedy, X. J.
  See Kennedy, Joseph
Kennell, Ruth E(pperson)
  1893-1977 .... *6*
  Obituary *25*
Kenny, Ellsworth Newcomb
  1909-1971
  Obituary *26*
Kenny, Herbert A(ndrew)
  1912- *13*
Kenny, Kathryn
  See Bowden, Joan Chase
  See Krull, Kathleen
Kenny, Kevin
  See Krull, Kathleen

Kent, Alexander
  See Reeman, Douglas Edward
Kent, Deborah Ann 1948-
  Brief Entry *41*
Kent, Jack
  See Kent, John Wellington
Kent, John Wellington
  1920-1985 .... *24*
  Obituary *45*
Kent, Margaret 1894- *2*
Kent, Rockwell 1882-1971 .... *6*
Kent, Sherman 1903- *20*
Kenward, Jean 1920- *42*
Kenworthy, Leonard S. 1912- *6*
Kenyon, Ley 1913- *6*
Kepes, Juliet A(ppleby) 1919- *13*
Kerigan, Florence 1896- *12*
Kerman, Gertrude Lerner
  1909- *21*
Kerr, Jessica 1901- *13*
Kerr, (Anne) Judith 1923- *24*
Kerr, M. E.
  See Meaker, Marijane
  See also SAAS 1
Kerry, Frances
  See Kerigan, Florence
Kerry, Lois
  See Duncan, Lois S(teinmetz)
Ker Wilson, Barbara 1929- *20*
Kessel, Joyce Karen 1937- *41*
Kessler, Ethel 1922- *44*
  Brief Entry *37*
Kessler, Leonard P. 1921- *14*
Kesteven, G. R.
  See Crosher, G(eoffry) R(obins)
Ketcham, Hank
  See Ketcham, Henry King
Ketcham, Henry King 1920- *28*
  Brief Entry *27*
Kettelkamp, Larry 1933- *2*
Kevles, Bettyann 1938- *23*
Key, Alexander (Hill)
  1904-1979 .... *8*
  Obituary *23*
Keyes, Daniel 1927- *37*
Keyes, Fenton 1915- *34*
Keyser, Marcia 1933- *42*
Keyser, Sarah
  See McGuire, Leslie (Sarah)
Khanshendel, Chiron
  See Rose, Wendy
Kherdian, David 1931- *16*
Kidd, Ronald 1948- *42*
Kiddell, John 1922- *3*
Kidwell, Carl 1910- *43*
Kiefer, Irene 1926- *21*
Kiesel, Stanley 1925- *35*
Kikukawa, Cecily H. 1919- *44*
  Brief Entry *35*
Kilgore, Kathleen 1946- *42*
Kilian, Crawford 1941- *35*
Killilea, Marie (Lyons) 1913- *2*
Kilreon, Beth
  See Walker, Barbara K.
Kimball, Yeffe 1914-1978 .... *37*
Kimbrough, Emily 1899- *2*
Kimmel, Eric A. 1946- *13*

Kimmel, Margaret Mary
  1938- *43*
  Brief Entry *33*
Kindred, Wendy 1937- *7*
Kines, Pat Decker 1937- *12*
King, Adam
  See Hoare, Robert J(ohn)
King, Arthur
  See Cain, Arthur H.
King, Billie Jean 1943- *12*
King, (David) Clive 1924- *28*
King, Cynthia 1925- *7*
King, Frank O. 1883-1969
  Obituary *22*
King, Marian *23*
King, Martin
  See Marks, Stan(ley)
King, Martin Luther, Jr.
  1929-1968 .... *14*
King, Reefe
  See Barker, Albert W.
King, Stephen 1947- *9*
King, Tony 1947- *39*
Kingman, Dong (Moy Shu)
  1911- *44*
Kingman, (Mary) Lee 1919- *1*
Kingsland, Leslie William
  1912- *13*
Kingsley, Charles
  1819-1875 .... *YABC 2*
Kingsley, Emily Perl 1940- *33*
King-Smith, Dick 1922-
  Brief Entry *38*
Kinney, C. Cle 1915- *6*
Kinney, Harrison 1921- *13*
Kinney, Jean Stout 1912- *12*
Kinsey, Elizabeth
  See Clymer, Eleanor
Kipling, (Joseph) Rudyard
  1865-1936 .... *YABC 2*
Kirk, Ruth (Kratz) 1925- *5*
Kirkup, James 1927- *12*
Kirkus, Virginia
  See Glick, Virginia Kirkus
Kirtland, G. B.
  See Joslin, Sesyle
Kishida, Eriko 1929- *12*
Kisinger, Grace Gelvin
  1913-1965 .... *10*
Kissin, Eva H. 1923- *10*
Kjelgaard, James Arthur
  1910-1959 .... *17*
Kjelgaard, Jim
  See Kjelgaard, James Arthur
Klagsbrun, Francine (Lifton) *36*
Klaperman, Gilbert 1921- *33*
Klaperman, Libby Mindlin
  1921-1982 .... *33*
  Obituary *31*
Klass, Morton 1927- *11*
Klass, Sheila Solomon 1927- *45*
Kleberger, Ilse 1921- *5*
Klein, Aaron E. 1930- *45*
  Brief Entry *28*
Klein, Gerda Weissmann
  1924- *44*
Klein, H. Arthur *8*
Klein, Leonore 1916- *6*
Klein, Mina C(ooper) *8*

Klein, Norma 1938- 7
  See also CLR 2
  See also SAAS 1
Klein, Robin 1936-
  Brief Entry 45
Klemm, Edward G., Jr. 1910- 30
Klemm, Roberta K(ohnhorst)
  1884- 30
Klevin, Jill Ross 1935- 39
  Brief Entry 38
Kliban, B. 1935- 35
Klimowicz, Barbara 1927- 10
Klug, Ron(ald) 1939- 31
Knapp, Ron 1952- 34
Knebel, Fletcher 1911- 36
Knickerbocker, Diedrich
  See Irving, Washington
Knifesmith
  See Cutler, Ivor
Knight, Anne (Katherine)
  1946- 34
Knight, Damon 1922- 9
Knight, David C(arpenter) 14
Knight, Eric (Mowbray)
  1897-1943 18
Knight, Francis Edgar 14
Knight, Frank
  See Knight, Francis Edgar
Knight, Hilary 1926- 15
Knight, Mallory T.
  See Hurwood, Bernhardt J.
Knight, Ruth Adams 1898-1974
  Obituary 20
Knott, Bill
  See Knott, William Cecil, Jr.
Knott, William Cecil, Jr.
  1927- 3
Knotts, Howard (Clayton, Jr.)
  1922- 25
Knowles, Anne 1933- 37
Knowles, John 1926- 8
Knox, Calvin
  See Silverberg, Robert
Knox, (Mary) Eleanor Jessie
  1909- 30
Knox, James
  See Brittain, William
Knudsen, James 1950- 42
Knudson, Richard L(ewis)
  1930- 34
Knudson, R. R.
  See Knudson, Rozanne
Knudson, Rozanne 1932- 7
Koch, Dorothy Clarke 1924- 6
Kocsis, J. C.
  See Paul, James
Koehn, Ilse
  See Van Zwienen, Ilse (Charlotte
  Koehn)
Koerner, W(illiam) H(enry) D(avid)
  1878-1938 21
Kohler, Julilly H(ouse) 1908-1976
  Obituary 20
Kohn, Bernice (Herstein)
  1920- 4
Kohner, Frederick 1905- 10
Kolba, Tamara 22
Komisar, Lucy 1942- 9
Komoda, Beverly 1939- 25

Komoda, Kiyo 1937- 9
Komroff, Manuel 1890-1974 2
  Obituary 20
Konigsburg, E(laine) L(obl)
  1930- 4
  See also CLR 1
Koning, Hans
  See Koningsberger, Hans
Koningsberger, Hans 1921- 5
Konkle, Janet Everest 1917- 12
Koob, Theodora (Johanna Foth)
  1918- 23
Korach, Mimi 1922- 9
Koren, Edward 1935- 5
Korinetz, Yuri (Iosifovich)
  1923- 9
  See also CLR 4
Korman, Gordon 1963-
  Brief Entry 41
Korty, Carol 1937- 15
Kossin, Sandy (Sanford)
  1926- 10
Kotzwinkle, William 1938- 24
  See also CLR 6
Koutoukas, H. M.
  See Rivoli, Mario
Kouts, Anne 1945- 8
Krahn, Fernando 1935-
  Brief Entry 31
  See also CLR 3
Kramer, Anthony
  Brief Entry 42
Kramer, George
  See Heuman, William
Kramer, Nora 1896(?)-1984 26
  Obituary 39
Krantz, Hazel (Newman)
  1920- 12
Kranzler, George G(ershon)
  1916- 28
Kranzler, Gershon
  See Kranzler, George G(ershon)
Krasilovsky, Phyllis 1926- 38
  Earlier sketch in SATA 1
Kraske, Robert
  Brief Entry 36
Kraus, Robert 1925- 4
Krauss, Ruth (Ida) 1911- 30
  Earlier sketch in SATA 1
Krautter, Elisa
  See Bialk, Elisa
Kredel, Fritz 1900-1973 17
Krementz, Jill 1940- 17
  See also CLR 5
Krensky, Stephen (Alan) 1953-
  Brief Entry 41
Kripke, Dorothy Karp 30
Kristof, Jane 1932- 8
Kroeber, Theodora (Kracaw)
  1897- 1
Kroll, Francis Lynde
  1904-1973 10
Kroll, Steven 1941- 19
Kropp, Paul (Stephen) 1948- 38
  Brief Entry 34
Krull, Kathleen 1952-
  Brief Entry 39
Krumgold, Joseph 1908-1980 1
  Obituary 23

Krush, Beth 1918- 18
Krush, Joe 1918- 18
Krüss, James 1926- 8
  See also CLR 9
Kubie, Nora (Gottheil) Benjamin
  1899- 39
Kubinyi, Laszlo 1937- 17
Kuh, Charlotte 1892(?)-1985
  Obituary 43
Kujoth, Jean Spealman 1935-1975
  Obituary 30
Kullman, Harry 1919-1982 35
Kumin, Maxine (Winokur)
  1925- 12
Kunhardt, Dorothy Meserve
  1901(?)-1979
  Obituary 22
Künstler, Morton 1927- 10
Kupferberg, Herbert 1918- 19
Kuratomi, Chizuko 1939- 12
Kurelek, William 1927-1977 8
  Obituary 27
  See also CLR 2
Kurland, Gerald 1942- 13
Kuskin, Karla (Seidman)
  1932- 2
  See also CLR 4
Kuttner, Paul 1931- 18
Kuzma, Kay 1941- 39
Kvale, Velma R(uth) 1898- 8
Kyle, Elisabeth
  See Dunlop, Agnes M. R.
Kyte, Kathy S. 1946-
  Brief Entry 44

L

Lacy, Leslie Alexander 1937- 6
Ladd, Veronica
  See Miner, Jane Claypool
Lader, Lawrence 1919- 6
Lady, A
  See Taylor, Ann
Lady Mears
  See Tempest, Margaret Mary
Lady of Quality, A
  See Bagnold, Enid
La Farge, Oliver (Hazard Perry)
  1901-1963 19
La Farge, Phyllis 14
Laffin, John (Alfred Charles)
  1922- 31
La Fontaine, Jean de
  1621-1695 18
Lagercrantz, Rose (Elsa)
  1947- 39
Lagerlöf, Selma (Ottiliana Lovisa)
  1858-1940 15
  See also CLR 7
Laiken, Deirdre S(usan) 1948-
  Brief Entry 40
Laimgruber, Monika 1946- 11
Laing, Martha
  See Celestino, Martha Laing
Laird, Jean E(louise) 1930- 38
Laite, Gordon 1925- 31
Laklan, Carli 1907- 5
la Mare, Walter de
  See de la Mare, Walter

Lamb, Beatrice Pitney 1904- 21
Lamb, Charles 1775-1834 17
Lamb, Elizabeth Searle 1917- 31
Lamb, G(eoffrey) F(rederick) 10
Lamb, Lynton 1907- 10
Lamb, Mary Ann 1764-1847 17
Lamb, Robert (Boyden) 1941- 13
Lambert, Janet (Snyder)
    1894-1973 25
Lambert, Saul 1928- 23
Lamburn, Richmal Crompton
    1890-1969 5
Lamorisse, Albert (Emmanuel)
    1922-1970 23
Lamplugh, Lois 1921- 17
Lampman, Evelyn Sibley
    1907-1980 4
    Obituary 23
Lamprey, Louise
    1869-1951 ....YABC 2
Lancaster, Bruce 1896-1963 9
Lancaster, Matthew 1973(?)-1983
    Obituary 45
Land, Barbara (Neblett) 1923- 16
Land, Jane [Joint pseudonym]
    See Borland, Kathryn Kilby and
    Speicher, Helen Ross (Smith)
Land, Myrick (Ebben) 1922- 15
Land, Ross [Joint pseudonym]
    See Borland, Kathryn Kilby and
    Speicher, Helen Ross (Smith)
Landau, Elaine 1948- 10
Landau, Jacob 1917- 38
Landeck, Beatrice 1904- 15
Landin, Les(lie) 1923- 2
Landshoff, Ursula 1908- 13
Lane, Carolyn 1926- 10
Lane, Jerry
    See Martin, Patricia Miles
Lane, John 1932- 15
Lane, Margaret 1907-
    Brief Entry 38
Lane, Rose Wilder 1886-1968 29
    Brief Entry 28
Lanes, Selma G. 1929- 3
Lang, Andrew 1844-1912 16
Lange, John
    See Crichton, (J.) Michael
Lange, Suzanne 1945- 5
Langley, Noel 1911-1980
    Obituary 25
Langner, Nola 1930- 8
Langone, John (Michael) 1929-
    Brief Entry 38
Langstaff, John 1920- 6
    See also CLR 3
Langstaff, Launcelot
    See Irving, Washington
Langton, Jane 1922- 3
Lanier, Sidney 1842-1881 18
Lansing, Alfred 1921-1975 35
Lantz, Paul 1908- 45
Lantz, Walter 1900- 37
Lappin, Peter 1911- 32
Larom, Henry V. 1903(?)-1975
    Obituary 30
Larrecq, John M(aurice)
    1926-1980 44
    Obituary 25

Larrick, Nancy G. 1910- 4
Larsen, Egon 1904- 14
Larson, Eve
    See St. John, Wylly Folk
Larson, Norita D. 1944- 29
Larson, William H. 1938- 10
Larsson, Carl (Olof)
    1853-1919 35
Lasell, Elinor H. 1929- 19
Lasell, Fen H.
    See Lasell, Elinor H.
Lash, Joseph P. 1909- 43
Lasher, Faith B. 1921- 12
Lasker, David 1950- 38
Lasker, Joe 1919- 9
Lasky, Kathryn 1944- 13
Lassalle, C. E.
    See Ellis, Edward S(ylvester)
Latham, Barbara 1896- 16
Latham, Frank B. 1910- 6
Latham, Jean Lee 1902- 2
Latham, Mavis
    See Clark, Mavis Thorpe
Latham, Philip
    See Richardson, Robert S(hirley)
Lathrop, Dorothy P(ulis)
    1891-1980 14
    Obituary 24
Lathrop, Francis
    See Leiber, Fritz
Lattimore, Eleanor Frances
    1904- 7
Lauber, Patricia (Grace) 1924- ... 33
    Earlier sketch in SATA 1
Laugesen, Mary E(akin)
    1906- 5
Laughbaum, Steve 1945- 12
Laughlin, Florence 1910- 3
Lauré, Jason 1940-
    Brief Entry 44
Laurence, Ester Hauser 1935- 7
Laurin, Anne
    See McLaurin, Anne
Lauritzen, Jonreed 1902- 13
Lavine, David 1928- 31
Lavine, Sigmund A. 1908- 3
Lawrence, Ann (Margaret)
    1942- 41
Lawrence, Isabelle (Wentworth)
    Brief Entry 29
Lawrence, J. T.
    See Rowland-Entwistle, (Arthur)
    Theodore (Henry)
Lawrence, John 1933- 30
Lawrence, Josephine 1890(?)-1978
    Obituary 24
Lawrence, Linda
    See Hunt, Linda Lawrence
Lawrence, Louise 1943- 38
Lawrence, Louise de Kiriline
    1894- 13
Lawrence, Mildred 1907- 3
Lawson, Carol (Antell) 1946- 42
Lawson, Don(ald Elmer)
    1917- 9
Lawson, Marion Tubbs 1896- 22
Lawson, Robert
    1892-1957 ....YABC 2
    See also CLR 2

Laycock, George (Edwin)
    1921- 5
Lazare, Gerald John 1927- 44
Lazare, Jerry
    See Lazare, Gerald John
Lazarevich, Mila 1942- 17
Lazarus, Keo Felker 1913- 21
Lea, Alec 1907- 19
Lea, Richard
    See Lea, Alec
Leach, Maria 1892-1977 39
    Brief Entry 28
Leacroft, Helen 1919- 6
Leacroft, Richard 1914- 6
Leaf, (Wilbur) Munro
    1905-1976 20
Leaf, VaDonna Jean 1929- 26
Leakey, Richard E(rskine Frere)
    1944- 42
Leander, Ed
    See Richelson, Geraldine
Lear, Edward 1812-1888 18
    See also CLR 1
Leavitt, Jerome E(dward)
    1916- 23
LeBar, Mary E(velyn)
    1910-1982 35
LeCain, Errol 1941- 6
Lee, Benjamin 1921- 27
Lee, Betsy 1949- 37
Lee, Carol
    See Fletcher, Helen Jill
Lee, Dennis (Beynon) 1939- 14
    See also CLR 3
Lee, Doris (Emrick)
    1905-1983 44
    Obituary 35
Lee, (Nelle) Harper 1926- 11
Lee, John R(obert) 1923-1976 27
Lee, Manning de V(illeneuve)
    1894-1980 37
    Obituary 22
Lee, Marian
    See Clish, (Lee) Marian
Lee, Mary Price 1934- 8
Lee, Mildred 1908- 6
Lee, Robert C. 1931- 20
Lee, Robert J. 1921- 10
Lee, Roy
    See Hopkins, Clark
Lee, Tanith 1947- 8
Leekley, Thomas B(riggs)
    1910- 23
Leeming, Jo Ann
    See Leeming, Joseph
Leeming, Joseph 1897-1968 26
Leeson, R. A.
    See Leeson, Robert (Arthur)
Leeson, Robert (Arthur) 1928- 42
Lefler, Irene (Whitney) 1917- 12
Le Gallienne, Eva 1899- 9
Legg, Sarah Martha Ross Bruggeman
    (?)-1982
    Obituary 40
LeGrand
    See Henderson, LeGrand
Le Guin, Ursula K(roeber)
    1929- 4
    See also CLR 3

Legum, Colin 1919- *10*
Lehr, Delores 1920- *10*
Leiber, Fritz 1910- *45*
Leichman, Seymour 1933- *5*
Leigh-Pemberton, John 1911- *35*
Leighton, Clare (Veronica Hope)
   1900(?)- *37*
Leighton, Margaret 1896- *1*
Leipold, L. Edmond 1902- *16*
Leisk, David (Johnson)
   1906-1975 .... *30*
   Obituary *26*
   Earlier sketch in SATA 1
Leister, Mary 1917- *29*
Leitch, Patricia 1933- *11*
LeMair, H(enriette) Willebeek
   1889-1966
   Brief Entry *29*
Lemke, Horst 1922- *38*
Lenanton, C.
   See Oman, Carola (Mary Anima)
Lenard, Alexander 1910-1972
   Obituary *21*
L'Engle, Madeleine 1918- *27*
   Earlier sketch in SATA 1
   See also CLR 1
Lengyel, Cornel Adam 1915- *27*
Lengyel, Emil 1895-1985 .... *3*
   Obituary *42*
Lens, Sidney 1912- *13*
Lenski, Lois 1893-1974 .... *26*
   Earlier sketch in SATA 1
Lent, Blair 1930- *2*
Lent, Henry Bolles 1901-1973 .... *17*
Leodhas, Sorche Nic
   See Alger, Leclaire (Gowans)
Leokum, Arkady 1916(?)- *45*
Leonard, Constance (Brink)
   1923- *42*
   Brief Entry *40*
Leonard, Jonathan N(orton)
   1903-1975 .... *36*
Leong Gor Yun
   See Ellison, Virginia Howell
Lerner, Aaron B(unsen) 1920- *35*
Lerner, Carol 1927- *33*
Lerner, Marguerite Rush
   1924- *11*
Lerner, Sharon (Ruth)
   1938-1982 .... *11*
   Obituary *29*
LeRoy, Gen
   Brief Entry *36*
Lerrigo, Marion Olive 1898-1968
   Obituary *29*
LeShan, Eda J(oan) 1922- *21*
   See also CLR 6
LeSieg, Theo
   See Geisel, Theodor Seuss
Leslie, Robert Franklin 1911- *7*
Leslie, Sarah
   See McGuire, Leslie (Sarah)
Lesser, Margaret 1899(?)-1979
   Obituary *22*
Lester, Julius B. 1939- *12*
   See also CLR 2
Le Sueur, Meridel 1900- *6*
Leutscher, Alfred (George)
   1913- *23*

Levai, Blaise 1919- *39*
Levin, Betty 1927- *19*
Levin, Marcia Obrasky 1918- *13*
Levin, Meyer 1905-1981 .... *21*
   Obituary *27*
Levine, David 1926- *43*
   Brief Entry *35*
Levine, Edna S(imon) *35*
Levine, I(srael) E. 1923- *12*
Levine, Joan Goldman *11*
Levine, Joseph 1910- *33*
Levine, Rhoda *14*
Levinson, Nancy Smiler
   1938- *33*
Levitin, Sonia 1934- *4*
   See also SAAS 2
Levoy, Myron
   Brief Entry *37*
Levy, Elizabeth 1942- *31*
Lewees, John
   See Stockton, Francis Richard
Lewin, Betsy 1937- *32*
Lewin, Hugh (Francis) 1939-
   Brief Entry *40*
   See also CLR 9
Lewin, Ted 1935- *21*
Lewis, Alfred E. 1912-1968
   Brief Entry *32*
Lewis, Alice Hudson 1895(?)-1971
   Obituary *29*
Lewis, (Joseph) Anthony
   1927- *27*
Lewis, C(live) S(taples)
   1898-1963 .... *13*
   See also CLR 3
Lewis, Claudia (Louise) 1907- *5*
Lewis, E. M. *20*
Lewis, Elizabeth Foreman
   1892-1958 ....*YABC 2*
Lewis, Francine
   See Wells, Helen
Lewis, Hilda (Winifred) 1896-1974
   Obituary *20*
Lewis, Lucia Z.
   See Anderson, Lucia (Lewis)
Lewis, Marjorie 1929- *40*
   Brief Entry *35*
Lewis, Paul
   See Gerson, Noel B(ertram)
Lewis, Richard 1935- *3*
Lewis, Roger
   See Zarchy, Harry
Lewis, Shari 1934- *35*
   Brief Entry *30*
Lewis, Thomas P(arker) 1936- ... *27*
Lewiton, Mina 1904-1970 .... *2*
Lexau, Joan M. *36*
   Earlier sketch in SATA 1
Ley, Willy 1906-1969 .... *2*
Leydon, Rita (Flodén) 1949- *21*
Leyland, Eric (Arthur) 1911- *37*
L'Hommedieu, Dorothy K(easley)
   1885-1961
   Obituary *29*
Libby, Bill
   See Libby, William M.
Libby, William M. 1927-1984 .... *5*
   Obituary *39*
Liberty, Gene 1924- *3*

Liebers, Arthur 1913- *12*
Lieblich, Irene 1923- *22*
Liers, Emil E(rnest)
   1890-1975 .... *37*
Lietz, Gerald S. 1918- *11*
Lifton, Betty Jean *6*
Lightner, A. M.
   See Hopf, Alice L.
Lignell, Lois 1911- *37*
Lillington, Kenneth (James)
   1916- *39*
Lilly, Charles
   Brief Entry *33*
Lilly, Ray
   See Curtis, Richard (Alan)
Lim, John 1932- *43*
Liman, Ellen (Fogelson)
   1936- *22*
Limburg, Peter R(ichard)
   1929- *13*
Lincoln, C(harles) Eric 1924- *5*
Lindbergh, Anne
   See Sapieyevski, Anne Lindbergh
Lindbergh, Anne Morrow (Spencer)
   1906- *33*
Lindbergh, Charles A(ugustus, Jr.)
   1902-1974 .... *33*
Lindblom, Steven (Winther)
   1946- *42*
   Brief Entry *39*
Linde, Gunnel 1924- *5*
Lindgren, Astrid 1907- *38*
   Earlier sketch in SATA 2
   See also CLR 1
Lindman, Maj (Jan)
   1886-1972 .... *43*
Lindop, Edmund 1925- *5*
Lindquist, Jennie Dorothea
   1899-1977 .... *13*
Lindquist, Willis 1908- *20*
Lindsay, Norman (Alfred William)
   1879-1969
   See CLR 8
Lindsay, (Nicholas) Vachel
   1879-1931 .... *40*
Line, Les 1935- *27*
Linfield, Esther *40*
Lingard, Joan *8*
Link, Martin 1934- *28*
Lionni, Leo 1910- *8*
   See also CLR 7
Lipinsky de Orlov, Lino S.
   1908- *22*
Lipkind, William 1904-1974 ...... *15*
Lipman, David 1931- *21*
Lipman, Matthew 1923- *14*
Lippincott, Bertram 1898(?)-1985
   Obituary *42*
Lippincott, Joseph Wharton
   1887-1976 .... *17*
Lippincott, Sarah Lee 1920- *22*
Lippman, Peter J. 1936- *31*
Lipsyte, Robert 1938- *5*
Lisker, Sonia O. 1933- *44*
Lisle, Seward D.
   See Ellis, Edward S(ylvester)
Lisowski, Gabriel 1946-
   Brief Entry *31*
Liss, Howard 1922- *4*

Lissim, Simon 1900-1981
  Brief Entry 28
List, Ilka Katherine 1935- 6
Liston, Robert A. 1927- 5
Litchfield, Ada B(assett)
  1916- 5
Litowinsky, Olga (Jean) 1936- 26
Little, A. Edward
  See Klein, Aaron E.
Little, (Flora) Jean 1932- 2
  See also CLR 4
Little, Mary E. 1912- 28
Littledale, Freya (Lota) 2
Lively, Penelope 1933- 7
  See also CLR 7
Liversidge, (Henry) Douglas
  1913- 8
Livingston, Carole 1941- 42
Livingston, Myra Cohn 1926- 5
  See also CLR 7
  See also SAAS 1
Livingston, Richard R(oland)
  1922- 8
Llerena-Aguirre, Carlos Antonio
  1952- 19
Llewellyn, Richard
  See Llewellyn Lloyd, Richard
  Dafydd Vyvyan
Llewellyn, T. Harcourt
  See Hamilton, Charles H. St. John
Llewellyn Lloyd, Richard Dafydd
  Vyvyan 1906-1983 11
  Obituary 37
Lloyd, E. James
  See James, Elizabeth
Lloyd, James
  See James, Elizabeth
Lloyd, Errol 1943- 22
Lloyd, Norman 1909-1980
  Obituary 23
Lloyd, (Mary) Norris 1908- 10
Lobel, Anita 1934- 6
Lobel, Arnold 1933- 6
  See also CLR 5
Lobsenz, Amelia 12
Lobsenz, Norman M. 1919- 6
Lochak, Michèle 1936- 39
Lochlons, Colin
  See Jackson, C. Paul
Locke, Clinton W. [Collective
  pseudonym] 1
Locke, Lucie 1904- 10
Lockwood, Mary
  See Spelman, Mary
Lodge, Bernard 1933- 33
Lodge, Maureen Roffey
  See Roffey, Maureen
Loeb, Robert H., Jr. 1917- 21
Loeper, John J(oseph) 1929- 10
Loescher, Ann Dull 1942- 20
Loescher, Gil(burt Damian)
  1945- 20
Loewenstein, Bernice
  Brief Entry 40
Löfgren, Ulf 1931- 3
Lofting, Hugh 1886-1947 15
Lofts, Norah (Robinson)
  1904-1983 8
  Obituary 36

Logue, Christopher 1926- 23
Loken, Newton (Clayton)
  1919- 26
Lomas, Steve
  See Brennan, Joseph L.
Lomask, Milton 1909- 20
London, Jack 1876-1916 18
London, Jane
  See Geis, Darlene
London, John Griffith
  See London, Jack
Lonergan, (Pauline) Joy (Maclean)
  1909- 10
Lonette, Reisie (Dominee)
  1924- 43
Long, Helen Beecher [Collective
  pseudonym] 1
Long, Judith Elaine 1953- 20
Long, Judy
  See Long, Judith Elaine
Long, Laura Mooney 1892-1967
  Obituary 29
Longfellow, Henry Wadsworth
  1807-1882 19
Longman, Harold S. 1919- 5
Longsworth, Polly 1933- 28
Longtemps, Kenneth 1933- 17
Longway, A. Hugh
  See Lang, Andrew
Loomis, Robert D. 5
Lopshire, Robert 1927- 6
Lord, Athena V. 1932- 39
Lord, Beman 1924- 5
Lord, (Doreen Mildred) Douglas
  1904- 12
Lord, John Vernon 1939- 21
Lord, Nancy
  See Titus, Eve
Lord, Walter 1917- 3
Lorenz, Lee (Sharp) 1932(?)-
  Brief Entry 39
Lorenzini, Carlo 1826-1890 29
Lorraine, Walter (Henry)
  1929- 16
Loss, Joan 1933- 11
Lot, Parson
  See Kingsley, Charles
Lothrop, Harriet Mulford Stone
  1844-1924 20
Louie, Ai-Ling 1949- 40
  Brief Entry 34
Louisburgh, Sheila Burnford
  See Burnford, Sheila
Lourie, Helen
  See Storr, Catherine (Cole)
Love, Katherine 1907- 3
Love, Sandra (Weller) 1940- 26
Lovelace, Delos Wheeler
  1894-1967 7
Lovelace, Maud Hart
  1892-1980 2
  Obituary 23
Lovett, Margaret (Rose) 1915- 22
Low, Alice 1926- 11
Low, Elizabeth Hammond
  1898- 5
Low, Joseph 1911- 14
Lowe, Jay, Jr.
  See Loper, John J(oseph)

Lowenstein, Dyno 1914- 6
Lowitz, Anson C.
  1901(?)-1978 18
Lowitz, Sadyebeth (Heath)
  1901-1969 17
Lowrey, Janette Sebring
  1892- 43
Lowry, Lois 1937- 23
  See also CLR 6
Lowry, Peter 1953- 7
Lowther, George F. 1913-1975
  Obituary 30
Lozier, Herbert 1915- 26
Lubell, Cecil 1912- 6
Lubell, Winifred 1914- 6
Lubin, Leonard B. 1943- 45
  Brief Entry 37
Lucas, E(dward) V(errall)
  1868-1938 20
Lucas, Jerry 1940- 33
Luce, Celia (Geneva Larsen)
  1914- 38
Luce, Willard (Ray) 1914- 38
Luckhardt, Mildred Corell
  1898- 5
Ludden, Allen (Ellsworth)
  1918(?)-1981
  Obituary 27
Ludlam, Mabel Cleland
  See Widdemer, Mabel Cleland
Ludwig, Helen 33
Lueders, Edward (George)
  1923- 14
Lufkin, Raymond H. 1897- 38
Lugard, Flora Louisa Shaw
  1852-1929 21
Luger, Harriett M(andelay)
  1914- 23
Luhrmann, Winifred B(ruce)
  1934- 11
Luis, Earlene W. 1929- 11
Lum, Peter
  See Crowe, Bettina Lum
Lund, Doris (Herold) 1919- 12
Lunn, Janet 1928- 4
Luther, Frank 1905-1980
  Obituary 25
Luttrell, Guy L. 1938- 22
Luttrell, Ida (Alleene) 1934- 40
  Brief Entry 35
Lutzker, Edythe 1904- 5
Luzzati, Emanuele 1912- 7
Luzzatto, Paola (Caboara)
  1938- 38
Lydon, Michael 1942- 11
Lyfick, Warren
  See Reeves, Lawrence F.
Lyle, Katie Letcher 1938- 8
Lynch, Lorenzo 1932- 7
Lynch, Marietta 1947- 29
Lynch, Patricia (Nora)
  1898-1972 9
Lynds, Dennis 1924-
  Brief Entry 37
Lynn, Mary
  See Brokamp, Marilyn
Lynn, Patricia
  See Watts, Mabel Pizzey
Lyon, Elinor 1921- 6

Lyon, Lyman R.
  See De Camp, L(yon) Sprague
Lyons, Dorothy 1907- *3*
Lyons, Grant 1941- *30*
Lystad, Mary (Hanemann)
  1928- *11*
Lyttle, Richard B(ard) 1927- *23*
Lytton, Edward G(eorge) E(arle)
  L(ytton) Bulwer-Lytton, Baron
  1803-1873 .... *23*

M

Maar, Leonard (F., Jr.) 1927- *30*
Maas, Selve *14*
Mac
  See MacManus, Seumas
Mac Aodhagáin, Eamon
  See Egan, E(dward) W(elstead)
MacArthur-Onslow, Annette
  (Rosemary) 1933- *26*
Macaulay, David Alexander 1946-
  Brief Entry *27*
  See also CLR 3
MacBeth, George 1932- *4*
MacClintock, Dorcas 1932- *8*
MacDonald, Anson
  See Heinlein, Robert A(nson)
MacDonald, Betty (Campbell Bard)
  1908-1958 ....*YABC 1*
Macdonald, Blackie
  See Emrich, Duncan
Macdonald, Dwight
  1906-1982 .... *29*
  Obituary *33*
MacDonald, George
  1824-1905 .... *33*
Mac Donald, Golden
  See Brown, Margaret Wise
Macdonald, Marcia
  See Hill, Grace Livingston
Macdonald, Mary
  See Gifford, Griselda
Macdonald, Shelagh 1937- *25*
Macdonald, Zillah K(atherine)
  1885- *11*
Mace, Elisabeth 1933- *27*
MacFarlan, Allan A.
  1892-1982 .... *35*
MacFarlane, Iris 1922- *11*
MacGregor, Ellen 1906-1954 ..... *39*
  Brief Entry *27*
MacGregor-Hastie, Roy 1929- *3*
Machetanz, Frederick 1908- *34*
Machin Goodall, Daphne
  (Edith) *37*
MacInnes, Helen 1907-1985 ..... *22*
  Obituary *44*
MacIntyre, Elisabeth 1916- *17*
Mack, Stan(ley) *17*
Mackay, Claire 1930- *40*
MacKaye, Percy (Wallace)
  1875-1956 .... *32*
MacKellar, William 1914- *4*
Macken, Walter 1915-1967 .... *36*
Mackenzie, Dr. Willard
  See Stratemeyer, Edward L.
MacKenzie, Garry 1921-
  Brief Entry *31*

MacKinstry, Elizabeth
  1879-1956 .... *42*
MacLachlan, Patricia
  Brief Entry *42*
MacLean, Alistair (Stuart)
  1923- *23*
MacLeod, Beatrice (Beach)
  1910- *10*
MacLeod, Charlotte (Matilda Hughes)
  1922- *28*
MacLeod, Ellen Jane (Anderson)
  1916- *14*
MacManus, James
  See MacManus, Seumas
MacManus, Seumas
  1869-1960 .... *25*
MacMillan, Annabelle
  See Quick, Annabelle
MacPeek, Walter G.
  1902-1973 .... *4*
  Obituary *25*
MacPherson, Margaret 1908- *9*
MacPherson, Thomas George
  1915-1976
  Obituary *30*
Macrae, Hawk
  See Barker, Albert W.
MacRae, Travi
  See Feagles, Anita (MacRae)
Macumber, Mari
  See Sandoz, Mari
Madden, Don 1927- *3*
Maddison, Angela Mary
  1923- *10*
Maddock, Reginald 1912- *15*
Madian, Jon 1941- *9*
Madison, Arnold 1937- *6*
Madison, Winifred *5*
Maestro, Betsy 1944-
  Brief Entry *30*
Maestro, Giulio 1942- *8*
Magorian, James 1942- *32*
Maguire, Anne
  See Nearing, Penny
Maguire, Gregory 1954- *28*
Maher, Ramona 1934- *13*
Mählqvist, (Karl) Stefan
  1943- *30*
Mahon, Julia C(unha) 1916- *11*
Mahony, Elizabeth Winthrop
  1948- *8*
Mahood, Kenneth 1930- *24*
Mahy, Margaret 1936- *14*
  See also CLR 7
Maidoff, Ilka List
  See List, Ilka Katherine
Maik, Henri
  See Hecht, Henri Joseph
Maiorano, Robert 1946- *43*
Maitland, Antony (Jasper)
  1935- *25*
Major, Kevin 1949- *32*
Makie, Pam 1943- *37*
Malcolmson, Anne
  See Storch, Anne B. von
Malcolmson, David 1899- *6*
Mali, Jane Lawrence 1937-
  Brief Entry *44*

Mallowan, Agatha Christie
  See Christie, Agatha (Mary Clarissa)
Malmberg, Carl 1904- *9*
Malo, John 1911- *4*
Malory, (Sir) Thomas 1410(?)-1471(?)
  Brief Entry *33*
Maltese, Michael 1908(?)-1981
  Obituary *24*
Malvern, Corinne 1905-1956 ...... *34*
Malvern, Gladys (?)-1962 .... *23*
Manchel, Frank 1935- *10*
Manes, Stephen 1949- *42*
  Brief Entry *40*
Manfred, Frederick F(eikema)
  1912- *30*
Mangione, Jerre 1909- *6*
Mangurian, David 1938- *14*
Maniscalco, Joseph 1926- *10*
Manley, Deborah 1932- *28*
Manley, Seon *15*
  See also CLR 3
  See also SAAS 2
Mann, Peggy *6*
Mannheim, Grete (Salomon)
  1909- *10*
Manniche, Lise 1943- *31*
Manning, Rosemary 1911- *10*
Manning-Sanders, Ruth 1895- *15*
Manson, Beverlie 1945-
  Brief Entry *44*
Manton, Jo
  See Gittings, Jo Manton
Manushkin, Fran 1942- *7*
Mapes, Mary A.
  See Ellison, Virginia Howell
Mara, Barney
  See Roth, Arthur J(oseph)
Mara, Jeanette
  See Cebulash, Mel
Marais, Josef 1905-1978
  Obituary *24*
Marasmus, Seymour
  See Rivoli, Mario
Marcellino
  See Agnew, Edith J.
Marchant, Bessie
  1862-1941 ....*YABC 2*
Marchant, Catherine
  See Cookson, Catherine (McMulen)
Marcher, Marion Walden
  1890- *10*
Marcus, Rebecca B(rian)
  1907- *9*
Margaret, Karla
  See Andersdatter, Karla M(argaret)
Margolis, Richard J(ules)
  1929- *4*
Mariana
  See Foster, Marian Curtis
Marino, Dorothy Bronson
  1912- *14*
Maris, Ron
  Brief Entry *45*
Mark, Jan 1943- *22*
Mark, Pauline (Dahlin) 1913- *14*
Mark, Polly
  See Mark, Pauline (Dahlin)
Markins, W. S.
  See Jenkins, Marie M.

Markle, Sandra L(ee) 1946-
  Brief Entry 41
Marko, Katherine D(olores) 28
Marks, Burton 1930-
  Brief Entry 43
Marks, J
  See Highwater, Jamake
Marks, J(ames) M(acdonald)
  1921- 13
Marks, Margaret L. 1911(?)-1980
  Obituary 23
Marks, Mickey Klar 12
Marks, Peter
  See Smith, Robert Kimmel
Marks, Stan(ley) 1929- 14
Marks-Highwater, J
  See Highwater, Jamake
Markun, Patricia M(aloney)
  1924- 15
Marlowe, Amy Bell [Collective
  pseudonym] 1
Marokvia, Artur 1909- 31
Marokvia, Mireille (Journet)
  1918- 5
Marrin, Albert 1936-
  Brief Entry 43
Marriott, Alice Lee 1910- 31
Marriott, Pat(ricia) 1920- 35
Mars, W. T.
  See Mars, Witold Tadeusz J.
Mars, Witold Tadeusz J.
  1912- 3
Marsh, J. E.
  See Marshall, Evelyn
Marsh, Jean
  See Marshall, Evelyn
Marshall, Anthony D(ryden)
  1924- 18
Marshall, (Sarah) Catherine
  1914-1983 2
  Obituary 34
Marshall, Douglas
  See McClintock, Marshall
Marshall, Evelyn 1897- 11
Marshall, James 1942- 6
Marshall, James Vance
  See Payne, Donald Gordon
Marshall, Kim
  See Marshall, Michael (Kimbrough)
Marshall, Michael (Kimbrough)
  1948- 37
Marshall, Percy
  See Young, Percy M(arshall)
Marshall, S(amuel) L(yman) A(twood)
  1900-1977 21
Marsten, Richard
  See Hunter, Evan
Marston, Hope Irvin 1935- 31
Martignoni, Margaret E. 1908(?)-1974
  Obituary 27
Martin, Ann M(atthews)
  1955- 44
  Brief Entry 41
Martin, Bill, Jr.
  See Martin, William Ivan
Martin, David Stone 1913- 39
Martin, Eugene [Collective
  pseudonym] 1

Martin, Frances M(cEntee)
  1906- 36
Martin, Fredric
  See Christopher, Matt
Martin, J(ohn) P(ercival)
  1880(?)-1966 15
Martin, Jeremy
  See Levin, Marcia Obransky
Martin, Lynne 1923- 21
Martin, Marcia
  See Levin, Marcia Obransky
Martin, Nancy
  See Salmon, Annie Elizabeth
Martin, Patricia Miles 1899- 43
  Earlier sketch in SATA 1
Martin, Peter
  See Chaundler, Christine
Martin, René 1891-1977 42
  Obituary 20
Martin, Rupert (Claude) 1905- 31
Martin, Stefan 1936- 32
Martin, Vicky
  See Storey, Victoria Carolyn
Martin, William Ivan 1916-
  Brief Entry 40
Martineau, Harriet
  1802-1876 ....YABC 2
Martini, Teri 1930- 3
Marx, Robert F(rank) 1936- 24
Marzani, Carl (Aldo) 1912- 12
Marzollo, Jean 1942- 29
Masefield, John 1878-1967 19
Mason, Edwin A. 1905-1979
  Obituary 32
Mason, F. van Wyck
  1901-1978 3
  Obituary 26
Mason, Frank W.
  See Mason, F. van Wyck
Mason, George Frederick
  1904- 14
Mason, Miriam (Evangeline)
  1900-1973 2
  Obituary 26
Mason, Tally
  See Derleth, August (William)
Mason, Van Wyck
  See Mason, F. van Wyck
Masselman, George
  1897-1971 19
Massie, Diane Redfield 16
Masters, Kelly R. 1897- 3
Masters, Mildred 1932- 42
Masters, William
  See Cousins, Margaret
Matchette, Katharine E. 1941- 38
Math, Irwin 1940- 42
Mathews, Janet 1914- 41
Mathews, Louise
  See Tooke, Louise Mathews
Mathiesen, Egon 1907-1976
  Obituary 28
Mathieu, Joe
  See Mathieu, Joseph P.
Mathieu, Joseph P. 1949- 43
  Brief Entry 36
Mathis, Sharon Bell 1937- 7
  See also CLR 3

Matson, Emerson N(els)
  1926- 12
Matsui, Tadashi 1926- 8
Matsuno, Masako 1935- 6
Matte, (Encarnacion) L'Enc
  1936- 22
Matthews, Ann
  See Martin, Ann M(atthews)
Matthews, Ellen 1950- 28
Matthews, Jacklyn Meek
  See Meek, Jacklyn O'Hanlon
Matthews, Patricia 1927- 28
Matthews, William Henry III
  1919- 45
  Brief Entry 28
Matthias, Catherine 1945-
  Brief Entry 41
Matthiessen, Peter 1927- 27
Mattingley, Christobel (Rosemary)
  1931- 37
Matulay, Laszlo 1912- 43
Matulka, Jan 1890-1972
  Brief Entry 28
Matus, Greta 1938- 12
Mauser, Patricia Rhoads
  1943- 37
Maves, Mary Carolyn 1916- 10
Maves, Paul B(enjamin)
  1913- 10
Mawicke, Tran 1911- 15
Max, Peter 1939- 45
Maxon, Anne
  See Best, Allena Champlin
Maxwell, Arthur S.
  1896-1970 11
Maxwell, Edith 1923- 7
May, Charles Paul 1920- 4
May, Julian 1931- 11
May, Robert Lewis 1905-1976
  Obituary 27
Mayberry, Florence V(irginia
  Wilson) 10
Mayer, Albert Ignatius, Jr. 1906-1960
  Obituary 29
Mayer, Ann M(argaret) 1938- 14
Mayer, Jane Rothschild 1903- 38
Mayer, Marianna 1945- 32
Mayer, Mercer 1943- 32
  Earlier sketch in SATA 16
Mayerson, Charlotte Leon 36
Mayhar, Ardath 1930- 38
Maynard, Chris
  See Maynard, Christopher
Maynard, Christopher 1949-
  Brief Entry 43
Maynard, Olga 1920- 40
Mayne, William 1928- 6
Maynes, Dr. J. O. Rocky
  See Maynes, J. Oscar, Jr.
Maynes, J. O. Rocky, Jr.
  See Maynes, J. Oscar, Jr.
Maynes, J. Oscar, Jr. 1929- 38
Mayo, Margaret (Mary) 1935- 38
Mays, (Lewis) Victor, (Jr.)
  1927- 5
Mazer, Harry 1925- 31
Mazer, Norma Fox 1931- 24
  See also SAAS 1
Mazza, Adriana 1928- 19

McBain, Ed
  See Hunter, Evan
McCaffery, Janet 1936- *38*
McCaffrey, Anne 1926- *8*
McCain, Murray (David, Jr.)
  1926-1981 .... *7*
  Obituary *29*
McCall, Edith S. 1911- *6*
McCall, Virginia Nielsen
  1909- *13*
McCallum, Phyllis 1911- *10*
McCann, Gerald 1916- *41*
McCannon, Dindga Fatima
  1947- *41*
McCarthy, Agnes 1933- *4*
McCarty, Rega Kramer 1904- *10*
McCaslin, Nellie 1914- *12*
McCaughrean, Geraldine
  See Jones, Geraldine
McCay, Winsor 1869-1934 .... *41*
McClintock, Marshall
  1906-1967 .... *3*
McClintock, Mike
  See McClintock, Marshall
McClintock, Theodore
  1902-1971 .... *14*
McClinton, Leon 1933- *11*
McCloskey, (John) Robert
  1914- *39*
  Earlier sketch in SATA 2
  See also CLR 7
McClung, Robert M. 1916- *2*
McClure, Gillian Mary 1948- *31*
McConnell, James Douglas
  (Rutherford) 1915- *40*
McCord, Anne 1942- *41*
McCord, David (Thompson Watson)
  1897- *18*
  See also CLR 9
McCord, Jean 1924- *34*
McCormick, Brooks
  See Adams, William Taylor
McCormick, Dell J.
  1892-1949 .... *19*
McCormick, (George) Donald (King)
  1911- *14*
McCormick, Edith (Joan)
  1934- *30*
McCourt, Edward (Alexander)
  1907-1972
  Obituary *28*
McCoy, Iola Fuller *3*
McCoy, J(oseph) J(erome)
  1917- *8*
McCoy, Lois (Rich) 1941- *38*
McCrady, Lady 1951- *16*
McCrea, James 1920- *3*
McCrea, Ruth 1921- *3*
McCullers, (Lula) Carson
  1917-1967 .... *27*
McCulloch, Derek (Ivor Breashur)
  1897-1967
  Obituary *29*
McCullough, Frances Monson
  1938- *8*
McCully, Emily Arnold 1939- *5*
McCurdy, Michael 1942- *13*
McDearmon, Kay *20*

McDermott, Beverly Brodsky
  1941- *11*
McDermott, Gerald 1941- *16*
  See also CLR 9
McDole, Carol
  See Farley, Carol
McDonald, Gerald D.
  1905-1970 .... *3*
McDonald, Jamie
  See Heide, Florence Parry
McDonald, Jill (Masefield)
  1927-1982 .... *13*
  Obituary *29*
McDonald, Lucile Saunders
  1898- *10*
McDonnell, Christine 1949- *34*
McDonnell, Lois Eddy 1914- *10*
McEntee, Dorothy (Layng)
  1902- *37*
McEwen, Robert (Lindley) 1926-1980
  Obituary *23*
McFall, Christie 1918- *12*
McFarland, Kenton D(ean)
  1920- *11*
McFarlane, Leslie 1902-1977 ..... *31*
McGaw, Jessie Brewer 1913- *10*
McGee, Barbara 1943- *6*
McGiffin, (Lewis) Lee (Shaffer)
  1908- *1*
McGill, Marci
  See Ridlon, Marci
McGinley, Phyllis 1905-1978 ..... *44*
  Obituary *24*
  Earlier sketch in SATA 2
McGinnis, Lila S(prague)
  1924- *44*
McGough, Elizabeth (Hemmes)
  1934- *33*
McGovern, Ann *8*
McGowen, Thomas E. 1927- *2*
McGowen, Tom
  See McGowen, Thomas
McGrady, Mike 1933- *6*
McGrath, Thomas 1916- *41*
McGraw, Eloise Jarvis 1915- *1*
McGraw, William Corbin
  1916- *3*
McGregor, Craig 1933- *8*
McGregor, Iona 1929- *25*
McGuire, Edna 1899- *13*
McGuire, Leslie (Sarah) 1945-
  Brief Entry *45*
McGurk, Slater
  See Roth, Arthur J(oseph)
McHargue, Georgess *4*
  See also CLR 2
McHugh, (Berit) Elisabet 1941-
  Brief Entry *44*
McIlwraith, Maureen 1922- *2*
McKay, Donald 1895- *45*
McKay, Robert W. 1921- *15*
McKeever, Marcia
  See Laird, Jean E(louise)
McKenzie, Dorothy Clayton
  1910-1981
  Obituary *28*
McKillip, Patricia A(nne)
  1948- *30*

McKinley, (Jennifer Carolyn) Robin
  Brief Entry *32*
  See also CLR 10
McKown, Robin *6*
McLaurin, Anne 1953- *27*
McLean, Kathryn (Anderson)
  1909-1966 .... *9*
McLeish, Kenneth 1940- *35*
McLenighan, Valjean 1947-
  Brief Entry *40*
McLeod, Emilie Warren
  1926-1982 .... *23*
  Obituary *31*
McLeod, Kirsty
  See Hudson, (Margaret) Kirsty
McLeod, Margaret Vail
  See Holloway, Teresa (Bragunier)
McMahan, Ian
  Brief Entry *45*
McMeekin, Clark
  See McMeekin, Isabel McLennan
McMeekin, Isabel McLennan
  1895- *3*
McMillan, Bruce 1947- *22*
McMullen, Catherine
  See Cookson, Catherine (McMullen)
McMurtrey, Martin A(loysius)
  1921- *21*
McNair, Kate *3*
McNamara, Margaret C(raig)
  1915-1981
  Obituary *24*
McNaught, Harry *32*
McNaughton, Colin 1951- *39*
McNeely, Jeannette 1918- *25*
McNeer, May *1*
McNeill, Janet 1907- *1*
McNickle, (William) D'Arcy
  1904-1977
  Obituary *22*
McNulty, Faith 1918- *12*
McPhail, David M(ichael) 1940-
  Brief Entry *32*
McPharlin, Paul 1903-1948
  Brief Entry *31*
McPhee, Richard B(yron)
  1934- *41*
McPherson, James M. 1936- *16*
McQueen, Mildred Hark
  1908- *12*
McShean, Gordon 1936- *41*
McSwigan, Marie 1907-1962 ..... *24*
McVicker, Charles (Taggart)
  1930- *39*
McVicker, Chuck
  See McVicker, Charles (Taggart)
McWhirter, Norris (Dewar)
  1925- *37*
McWhirter, (Alan) Ross
  1925-1975 .... *37*
  Obituary *31*
Mead, Margaret 1901-1978
  Obituary *20*
Mead, Russell (M., Jr.) 1935- *10*
Mead, Stella (?)-1981
  Obituary *27*
Meade, Ellen (Roddick) 1936- *5*
Meade, Marion 1934- *23*

Meader, Stephen W(arren)
1892- *1*

Meadow, Charles T(roub)
1929- *23*

Meadowcroft, Enid LaMonte
See Wright, Enid Meadowcroft

Meaker, M. J.
See Meaker, Marijane

Meaker, Marijane 1927- *20*

Means, Florence Crannell
1891-1980 .... *1*
Obituary *25*

Medary, Marjorie 1890- *14*

Meddaugh, Susan 1944- *29*

Medearis, Mary 1915- *5*

Mee, Charles L., Jr. 1938- *8*

Meek, Jacklyn O'Hanlon 1933-
Brief Entry *34*

Meek, S(terner St.) P(aul) 1894-1972
Obituary *28*

Meeker, Oden 1918(?)-1976 ...... *14*

Meeks, Esther MacBain *1*

Meggendorfer, Lothar 1847-1925
Brief Entry *36*

Mehdevi, Alexander 1947- *7*

Mehdevi, Anne (Marie)
Sinclair *8*

Meighan, Donald Charles
1929- *30*

Meigs, Cornelia Lynde
1884-1973 .... *6*

Meilach, Dona Z(weigoron)
1926- *34*

Melcher, Daniel 1912-1985
Obituary *43*

Melcher, Frederic Gershom 1879-1963
Obituary *22*

Melcher, Marguerite Fellows
1879-1969 .... *10*

Melin, Grace Hathaway
1892-1973 .... *10*

Mellersh, H(arold) E(dward) L(eslie)
1897- *10*

Meltzer, Milton 1915- *1*
See also SAAS 1

Melville, Anne
See Potter, Margaret (Newman)

Melwood, Mary
See Lewis, E. M.

Melzack, Ronald 1929- *5*

Memling, Carl 1918-1969 .... *6*

Mendel, Jo [House pseudonym]
See Bond, Gladys Baker

Mendonca, Susan 1950-
Brief Entry *45*

Mendoza, George 1934- *41*
Brief Entry *39*

Meng, Heinz (Karl) 1924- *13*

Menotti, Gian Carlo 1911- *29*

Menuhin, Yehudi 1916- *40*

Mercer, Charles (Edward)
1917- *16*

Meredith, David William
See Miers, Earl Schenck

Meriwether, Louise 1923-
Brief Entry *31*

Merriam, Eve 1916- *40*
Earlier sketch in SATA 3

Merrill, Jane 1946- *42*

Merrill, Jean (Fairbanks)
1923- *1*

Merrill, Phil
See Merrill, Jane

Merwin, Decie 1894-1961
Brief Entry *32*

Messmer, Otto 1892(?)-1983 ..... *37*

Metcalf, Suzanne
See Baum, L(yman) Frank

Metos, Thomas H(arry) 1932- *37*

Meyer, Carolyn 1935- *9*

Meyer, Edith Patterson 1895- *5*

Meyer, F(ranklyn) E(dward)
1932- *9*

Meyer, Jean Shepherd 1929- *11*

Meyer, Jerome Sydney
1895-1975 .... *3*
Obituary *25*

Meyer, June
See Jordan, June

Meyer, Louis A(lbert) 1942- *12*

Meyer, Renate 1930- *6*

Meyers, Susan 1942- *19*

Meynier, Yvonne (Pollet)
1908- *14*

Mezey, Robert 1935- *33*

Micale, Albert 1913- *22*

Michel, Anna 1943-
Brief Entry *40*

Micklish, Rita 1931- *12*

Miers, Earl Schenck
1910-1972 .... *1*
Obituary *26*

Miklowitz, Gloria D. 1927- *4*

Mikolaycak, Charles 1937- *9*

Mild, Warren (Paul) 1922- *41*

Miles, Betty 1928- *8*

Miles, Miska
See Martin, Patricia Miles

Miles, (Mary) Patricia 1930- *29*

Miles, Patricia A.
See Martin, Patricia Miles

Milgrom, Harry 1912- *25*

Milhous, Katherine 1894-1977 .... *15*

Militant
See Sandburg, Carl (August)

Millar, Barbara F. 1924- *12*

Miller, Albert G(riffith)
1905-1982 .... *12*
Obituary *31*

Miller, Alice P(atricia
McCarthy) *22*

Miller, Don 1923- *15*

Miller, Doris R.
See Mosesson, Gloria R(ubin)

Miller, Eddie
See Miller, Edward

Miller, Edna (Anita) 1920- *29*

Miller, Edward 1905-1974 .... *8*

Miller, Elizabeth 1933- *41*

Miller, Eugene 1925- *33*

Miller, Helen M(arkley) *5*

Miller, Helen Topping 1884-1960
Obituary *29*

Miller, Jane (Judith) 1925- *15*

Miller, John
See Samachson, Joseph

Miller, Margaret J.
See Dale, Margaret J(essy) Miller

Miller, Marilyn (Jean) 1925- *33*

Miller, Mary Beth 1942- *9*

Miller, Natalie 1917-1976 .... *35*

Miller, Ruth White
See White, Ruth C.

Miller, Sandy (Peden) 1948- *41*
Brief Entry *35*

Milligan, Spike
See Milligan, Terence Alan

Milligan, Terence Alan 1918- *29*

Mills, Claudia 1954- *44*
Brief Entry *41*

Mills, Yaroslava Surmach
1925- *35*

Millstead, Thomas Edward *30*

Milne, A(lan) A(lexander)
1882-1956 .... *YABC 1*
See also CLR 1

Milne, Lorus J. *5*

Milne, Margery *5*

Milonas, Rolf
See Myller, Rolf

Milotte, Alfred G(eorge)
1904- *11*

Milton, Hilary (Herbert)
1920- *23*

Milton, John R(onald) 1924- *24*

Milton, Joyce 1946-
Brief Entry *41*

Milverton, Charles A.
See Penzler, Otto

Minarik, Else Holmelund
1920- *15*

Miner, Jane Claypool 1933- *38*
Brief Entry *37*

Miner, Lewis S. 1909- *11*

Minier, Nelson
See Stoutenburg, Adrien

Mintonye, Grace *4*

Mirsky, Jeannette 1903- *8*

Mirsky, Reba Paeff
1902-1966 .... *1*

Miskovits, Christine 1939- *10*

Miss Francis
See Horwich, Francis R.

Miss Read
See Saint, Dora Jessie

Mister Rogers
See Rogers, Fred (McFeely)

Mitchell, Cynthia 1922- *29*

Mitchell, (Sibyl) Elyne (Keith)
1913- *10*

Mitchell, Gladys (Maude Winifred)
1901-1983
Obituary *35*

Mitchell, Joyce Slayton 1933-
Brief Entry *43*

Mitchell, Yvonne 1925-1979
Obituary *24*

Mitchison, Naomi Margaret (Haldane)
1897- *24*

Mitchnik, Helen 1901- *41*
Brief Entry *35*

Mitsuhashi, Yoko *45*
Brief Entry *33*

Mizner, Elizabeth Howard
1907- *27*

Mizumura, Kazue *18*

Moché, Dinah (Rachel) L(evine)
    1936- 44
    Brief Entry 40
Mochi, Ugo (A.) 1889-1977 38
Modell, Frank B. 1917- 39
    Brief Entry 36
Moe, Barbara 1937- 20
Moeri, Louise 1924- 24
Moffett, Martha (Leatherwood)
    1934- 8
Mofsie, Louis B. 1936-
    Brief Entry 33
Mohn, Peter B(urnet) 1934- 28
Mohn, Viola Kohl 1914- 8
Mohr, Nicholasa 1935- 8
Molarsky, Osmond 1909- 16
Mole, John 1941- 36
Molloy, Anne Baker 1907- 32
Molloy, Paul 1920- 5
Momaday, N(avarre) Scott 1934-
    Brief Entry 30
Moncure, Jane Belk 23
Monjo, F(erdinand) N.
    1924-1978 16
    See also CLR 2
Monroe, Lyle
    See Heinlein, Robert A(nson)
Monroe, Marion 1898-1983
    Obituary 34
Monsell, Helen (Albee)
    1895-1971 24
Montana, Bob 1920-1975
    Obituary 21
Montgomerie, Norah Mary
    1913- 26
Montgomery, Constance
    See Cappell, Constance
Montgomery, Elizabeth Rider
    1902-1985 34
    Obituary 41
    Earlier sketch in SATA 3
Montgomery, L(ucy) M(aud)
    1874-1942 .... YABC 1
    See also CLR 8
Montgomery, R(aymond) A., (Jr.)
    1936- 39
Montgomery, Rutherford George
    1894- 3
Montgomery, Vivian 36
Montresor, Beni 1926- 38
    Earlier sketch in SATA 3
Moody, Ralph Owen 1898- 1
Moon, Carl 1879-1948 25
Moon, Grace 1877(?)-1947 25
Moon, Sheila (Elizabeth)
    1910- 5
Moor, Emily
    See Deming, Richard
Moore, Anne Carroll
    1871-1961 13
Moore, Clement Clarke
    1779-1863 18
Moore, Eva 1942- 20
Moore, Fenworth
    See Stratemeyer, Edward L.
Moore, Jack (William) 1941-
    Brief Entry 32
Moore, Janet Gaylord 1905- 18
Moore, Jim 1946- 42

Moore, John Travers 1908- 12
Moore, Lamont 1909-
    Brief Entry 29
Moore, Margaret Rumberger
    1903- 12
Moore, Marianne (Craig)
    1887-1972 20
Moore, Patrick (Alfred) 1923-
    Brief Entry 39
Moore, Ray (S.) 1905(?)-1984
    Obituary 37
Moore, Regina
    See Dunne, Mary Collins
Moore, Rosalie
    See Brown, Rosalie (Gertrude)
    Moore
Moore, Ruth 23
Moore, Ruth Nulton 1923- 38
Moore, S. E. 23
Mooser, Stephen 1941- 28
Mordvinoff, Nicolas
    1911-1973 17
More, Caroline [Joint pseudonym]
    See Cone, Molly Lamken and
    Strachan, Margaret Pitcairn
Morey, Charles
    See Fletcher, Helen Jill
Morey, Walt 1907- 3
Morgan, Alfred P(owell)
    1889-1972 33
Morgan, Alison Mary 1930- 30
Morgan, Helen (Gertrude Louise)
    1921- 29
Morgan, Helen Tudor
    See Morgan, Helen (Gertrude
    Louise)
Morgan, Jane
    See Cooper, James Fenimore
Morgan, Lenore 1908- 8
Morgan, Louise
    See Morgan, Helen (Gertrude
    Louise)
Morgan, Shirley 1933- 10
Morgan, Tom 1942- 42
Morgenroth, Barbara
    Brief Entry 36
Morrah, Dave
    See Morrah, David Wardlaw, Jr.
Morrah, David Wardlaw, Jr.
    1914- 10
Morressy, John 1930- 23
Morrill, Leslie H.
    Brief Entry 33
Morris, Desmond (John)
    1928- 14
Morris, Robert A. 1933- 7
Morris, William 1913- 29
Morrison, Bill 1935-
    Brief Entry 37
Morrison, Dorothy Nafus 29
Morrison, Gert W.
    See Stratemeyer, Edward L.
Morrison, Lillian 1917- 3
Morrison, Lucile Phillips
    1896- 17
Morrison, Roberta
    See Webb, Jean Francis (III)
Morrison, Velma Ford 1909- 21

Morrison, William
    See Samachson, Joseph
Morriss, James E(dward)
    1932- 8
Morrow, Betty
    See Bacon, Elizabeth
Morse, Carol
    See Yeakley, Marjory Hall
Morse, Dorothy B(ayley) 1906-1979
    Obituary 24
Morse, Flo 1921- 30
Mort, Vivian
    See Cromie, Alice Hamilton
Mortimer, Mary H.
    See Coury, Louise Andree
Morton, Lee Jack, Jr. 1928- 32
Morton, Miriam 1918- 9
Moscow, Alvin 1925- 3
Mosel, Arlene 1921- 7
Moser, Don
    See Moser, Donald Bruce
Moser, Donald Bruce 1932- 31
Mosesson, Gloria R(ubin) 24
Moskin, Marietta D(unston)
    1928- 23
Moskof, Martin Stephen
    1930- 27
Moss, Don(ald) 1920- 11
Moss, Elaine Dora 1924-
    Brief Entry 31
Most, Bernard 1937-
    Brief Entry 40
Motz, Lloyd 20
Mountain, Robert
    See Montgomery, R(aymond) A.,
    (Jr.)
Mountfield, David
    See Grant, Neil
Moussard, Jacqueline 1924- 24
Mowat, Farley 1921- 3
Moyler, Alan (Frank Powell)
    1926- 36
Mozley, Charles 1915- 43
    Brief Entry 32
Mrs. Fairstar
    See Horne, Richard Henry
Mueller, Virginia 1924- 28
Muir, Frank 1920- 30
Mukerji, Dhan Gopal
    1890-1936 40
    See also CLR 10
Mulcahy, Lucille Burnett 12
Mulford, Philippa Greene
    1948- 43
Mulgan, Catherine
    See Gough, Catherine
Muller, Billex
    See Ellis, Edward S(ylvester)
Mullins, Edward S(wift)
    1922- 10
Mulock, Dinah Maria
    See Craik, Dinah Maria (Mulock)
Mulvihill, William Patrick
    1923- 8
Mun
    See Leaf, (Wilbur) Munro
Munari, Bruno 1907- 15
    See also CLR 9
Munce, Ruth Hill 1898- 12

Munowitz, Ken 1935-1977 .... *14*
Muñoz, William 1949- *42*
Munro, Alice 1931- *29*
Munro, Eleanor 1928- *37*
Munsinger, Lynn 1951- *33*
Munson(-Benson), Tunie
  1946- *15*
Munves, James (Albert) 1922- *30*
Munzer, Martha E. 1899- *4*
Murch, Mel and Starr, Ward [Joint
  double pseudonym]
  See Manes, Stephen
Murphy, Barbara Beasley
  1933- *5*
Murphy, E(mmett) Jefferson
  1926- *4*
Murphy, Jill 1949- *37*
Murphy, Jim 1947- *37*
  Brief Entry *32*
Murphy, Pat
  See Murphy, E(mmett) Jefferson
Murphy, Robert (William)
  1902-1971 .... *10*
Murphy, Shirley Rousseau
  1928- *36*
Murray, John 1923- *39*
Murray, Marian *5*
Murray, Michele 1933-1974 ...... *7*
Murray, Ossie 1938- *43*
Musgrave, Florence 1902- *3*
Musgrove, Margaret W(ynkoop)
  1943- *26*
Mussey, Virginia T. H.
  See Ellison, Virginia Howell
Mutz
  See Kunstler, Morton
Myers, Arthur 1917- *35*
Myers, Bernice *9*
Myers, Caroline Elizabeth (Clark)
  1887-1980 .... *28*
Myers, Elisabeth P(erkins)
  1918- *36*
Myers, Hortense (Powner)
  1913- *10*
Myers, Walter Dean 1937- *41*
  Brief Entry *27*
  See also CLR 4
  See also SAAS 2
Myller, Rolf 1926- *27*
Myra, Harold L(awrence) 1939-
  Brief Entry *42*
Myrus, Donald (Richard)
  1927- *23*

N

Nakatani, Chiyoko 1930-
  Brief Entry *40*
Namioka, Lensey 1929- *27*
Napier, Mark
  See Laffin, John (Alfred Charles)
Nash, Bruce M(itchell) 1947- *34*
Nash, Linell
  See Smith, Linell Nash
Nash, Mary (Hughes) 1925- *41*
Nash, (Frediric) Ogden
  1902-1971 .... *2*
Nast, Elsa Ruth
  See Watson, Jane Werner

Nast, Thomas 1840-1902
  Brief Entry *33*
Nastick, Sharon 1954- *41*
Nathan, Dorothy (Goldeen)
  (?)-1966 .... *15*
Nathan, Robert (Gruntal)
  1894-1985 .... *6*
  Obituary *43*
Natti, Susanna 1948- *32*
Navarra, John Gabriel 1927- *8*
Naylor, Penelope 1941- *10*
Naylor, Phyllis Reynolds
  1933- *12*
Nazaroff, Alexander I. 1898- *4*
Neal, Harry Edward 1906- *5*
Nearing, Penny 1916-
  Brief Entry *42*
Nebel, Gustave E. *45*
  Brief Entry *33*
Nebel, Mimouca
  See Nebel, Gustave E.
Nee, Kay Bonner *10*
Needle, Jan 1943- *30*
Needleman, Jacob 1934- *6*
Negri, Rocco 1932- *12*
Neigoff, Anne *13*
Neigoff, Mike 1920- *13*
Neilson, Frances Fullerton (Jones)
  1910- *14*
Neimark, Anne E. 1935- *4*
Neimark, Paul G. 1934-
  Brief Entry *37*
Nelson, Cordner (Bruce) 1918-
  Brief Entry *29*
Nelson, Esther L. 1928- *13*
Nelson, Lawrence E(rnest) 1928-1977
  Obituary *28*
Nelson, Mary Carroll 1929- *23*
Nesbit, E(dith)
  1858-1924 .... *YABC 1*
  See also CLR 3
Nesbit, Troy
  See Folsom, Franklin
Nespojohn, Katherine V.
  1912- *7*
Ness, Evaline (Michelow)
  1911- *26*
  Earlier sketch in SATA 1
  See also CLR 6
  See also SAAS 1
Neufeld, John 1938- *6*
Neumeyer, Peter F(lorian)
  1929- *13*
Neurath, Marie (Reidemeister)
  1898- *1*
Neusner, Jacob 1932- *38*
Neville, Emily Cheney 1919- *1*
  See also SAAS 2
Neville, Mary
  See Woodrich, Mary Neville
Nevins, Albert J. 1915- *20*
Newberry, Clare Turlay
  1903-1970 .... *1*
  Obituary *26*
Newbery, John 1713-1767 .... *20*
Newcomb, Ellsworth
  See Kenny, Ellsworth Newcomb
Newcombe, Jack *45*
  Brief Entry *33*

Newell, Crosby
  See Bonsall, Crosby (Barbara
  Newell)
Newell, Edythe W. 1910- *11*
Newell, Hope (Hockenberry)
  1896-1965 .... *24*
Newfeld, Frank 1928- *26*
Newlon, (Frank) Clarke
  1905(?)-1982 .... *6*
  Obituary *33*
Newman, Daisy 1904- *27*
Newman, Gerald 1939-
  Brief Entry *42*
Newman, Robert (Howard)
  1909- *4*
Newman, Shirlee Petkin
  1924- *10*
Newsom, Carol 1948- *40*
Newton, James R(obert)
  1935- *23*
Newton, Suzanne 1936- *5*
Ney, John 1923- *43*
  Brief Entry *33*
Nic Leodhas, Sorche
  See Alger, Leclaire (Gowans)
Nichols, Cecilia Fawn 1906- *12*
Nichols, Peter
  See Youd, (Christopher) Samuel
Nichols, (Joanna) Ruth 1948- *15*
Nicholson, Joyce Thorpe
  1919- *35*
Nickelsburg, Janet 1893- *11*
Nickerson, Betty
  See Nickerson, Elizabeth
Nickerson, Elizabeth 1922- *14*
Nicklaus, Carol
  Brief Entry *33*
Nicol, Ann
  See Turnbull, Ann (Christine)
Nicolas
  See Mordvinoff, Nicolas
Nicolay, Helen
  1866-1954 .... *YABC 1*
Nicole, Christopher Robin
  1930- *5*
Nielsen, Kay (Rasmus)
  1886-1957 .... *16*
Nielsen, Virginia
  See McCall, Virginia Nielsen
Niland, Deborah 1951- *27*
Nixon, Hershell Howard
  1923- *42*
Nixon, Joan Lowery 1927- *44*
  Earlier sketch in SATA 8
Nixon, K.
  See Nixon, Kathleen Irene (Blundell)
Nixon, Kathleen Irene
  (Blundell) *14*
Noble, Iris 1922- *5*
Noble, Trinka Hakes
  Brief Entry *37*
Nodset, Joan L.
  See Lexau, Joan M.
Noguere, Suzanne 1947- *34*
Nolan, Dennis 1945- *42*
  Brief Entry *34*
Nolan, Jeannette Covert
  1897-1974 .... *2*
  Obituary *27*

Nolan, William F(rancis) 1928-
    Brief Entry 28
Noonan, Julia 1946- 4
Norcross, John
    See Conroy, Jack (Wesley)
Nordhoff, Charles (Bernard)
    1887-1947 23
Nordlicht, Lillian 29
Nordstrom, Ursula 3
Norman, Charles 1904- 38
Norman, James
    See Schmidt, James Norman
Norman, Mary 1931- 36
Norman, Steve
    See Pashko, Stanley
Norris, Gunilla B(rodde)
    1939- 20
North, Andrew
    See Norton, Alice Mary
North, Captain George
    See Stevenson, Robert Louis
North, Joan 1920- 16
North, Robert
    See Withers, Carl A.
North, Sterling 1906-1974 45
    Obituary 26
    Earlier sketch in SATA 1
Norton, Alice Mary 1912- 43
    Earlier sketch in SATA 1
Norton, André
    See Norton, Alice Mary
Norton, Browning
    See Norton, Frank R(owland)
    B(rowning)
Norton, Frank R(owland) B(rowning)
    1909- 10
Norton, Mary 1903- 18
    See also CLR 6
Nöstlinger, Christine 1936-
    Brief Entry 37
Nowell, Elizabeth Cameron 12
Numeroff, Laura Joffe 1953- 28
Nurenberg, Thelma
    See Greenhaus, Thelma Nurenberg
Nurnberg, Maxwell
    1897-1984 27
    Obituary 41
Nussbaumer, Paul (Edmond)
    1934- 16
Nyce, (Nellie) Helene von Strecker
    1885-1969 19
Nyce, Vera 1862-1925 19
Nye, Harold G.
    See Harding, Lee
Nye, Robert 1939- 6

O

Oakes, Vanya 1909-1983 6
    Obituary 37
Oakley, Don(ald G.) 1927- 8
Oakley, Graham 1929- 30
    See also CLR 7
Oakley, Helen 1906- 10
Oana, Katherine D. 1929-
    Brief Entry 37
Oana, Kay D.
    See Oana, Katherine D.

Obligado, Lilian (Isabel) 1931-
    Brief Entry 45
Obrant, Susan 1946- 11
O'Brien, Esse Forrester 1895(?)-1975
    Obituary 30
O'Brien, Robert C.
    See Conly, Robert Leslie
    See also CLR 2
O'Brien, Thomas C(lement)
    1938- 29
O'Carroll, Ryan
    See Markun, Patricia M(aloney)
O'Connell, Margaret F(orster)
    1935-1977
    Obituary 30
O'Connell, Peg
    See Ahern, Margaret McCrohan
O'Connor, Karen 1938- 34
O'Connor, Patrick
    See Wibberley, Leonard (Patrick
    O'Connor)
O'Connor, Richard 1915-1975
    Obituary 21
O'Daniel, Janet 1921- 24
O'Dell, Scott 1903- 12
    See also CLR 1
Odenwald, Robert P(aul)
    1899-1965 11
Odor, Ruth Shannon 1926-
    Brief Entry 44
Oechsli, Kelly 1918- 5
Ofek, Uriel 1926- 36
Offit, Sidney 1928- 10
Ofosu-Appiah, L(awrence) H(enry)
    1920- 13
Ogan, George F. 1912- 13
Ogan, M. G. [Joint pseudonym]
    See Ogan, George F. and Ogan,
    Margaret E. (Nettles)
Ogan, Margaret E. (Nettles)
    1923- 13
Ogburn, Charlton, Jr. 1911- 3
Ogilvie, Elisabeth May 1917- 40
    Brief Entry 29
O'Hagan, Caroline 1946- 38
O'Hanlon, Jacklyn
    See Meek, Jacklyn O'Hanlon
O'Hara, Mary
    See Alsop, Mary O'Hara
Ohlsson, Ib 1935- 7
Ohtomo, Yasuo 1946- 37
O'Kelley, Mattie Lou 1908- 36
Okimoto, Jean Davies 1942- 34
Olcott, Frances Jenkins
    1872(?)-1963 19
Old Boy
    See Hughes, Thomas
Old Fag
    See Bell, Robert S(tanley) W(arren)
Oldenburg, E(gbert) William
    1936-1974 35
Olds, Elizabeth 1896- 3
Olds, Helen Diehl 1895-1981 9
    Obituary 25
Oldstyle, Jonathan
    See Irving, Washington
O'Leary, Brian 1940- 6
Oleksy, Walter 1930- 33

Olesky, Walter
    See Oleksy, Walter
Oliver, John Edward 1933- 21
Olmstead, Lorena Ann 1890- 13
Olney, Ross R. 1929- 13
Olschewski, Alfred 1920- 7
Olsen, Ib Spang 1921- 6
Olson, Gene 1922- 32
Olugebefola, Ademole 1941- 15
Oman, Carola (Mary Anima)
    1897-1978 35
Ommanney, F(rancis) D(ownes)
    1903-1980 23
O Mude
    See Gorey, Edward St. John
Oneal, Elizabeth 1934- 30
Oneal, Zibby
    See Oneal, Elizabeth
O'Neill, Judith (Beatrice)
    1930- 34
O'Neill, Mary L(e Duc) 1908- 2
Opie, Iona 1923- 3
Opie, Peter (Mason)
    1918-1982 3
    Obituary 28
Oppenheim, Joanne 1934- 5
Oppenheimer, Joan L(etson)
    1925- 28
Optic, Oliver
    See Adams, William Taylor
Orbach, Ruth Gary 1941- 21
Orczy, Emmuska, Baroness
    1865-1947 40
Orgel, Doris 1929- 7
Orleans, Ilo 1897-1962 10
Ormerod, Jan(ette Louise) 1946-
    Brief Entry 44
Ormondroyd, Edward 1925- 14
Ormsby, Virginia H(aire) 11
Orris
    See Ingelow, Jean
Orth, Richard
    See Gardner, Richard
Orwell, George
    See Blair, Eric Arthur
Osborne, Chester G. 1915- 11
Osborne, David
    See Silverberg, Robert
Osborne, Leone Neal 1914- 2
Osborne, Mary Pope 1949-
    Brief Entry 41
Osceola
    See Blixen, Karen (Christentze
    Dinesen)
Osgood, William E(dward)
    1926- 37
Osmond, Edward 1900- 10
Ossoli, Sarah Margaret (Fuller)
    marchesa d' 1810-1850 25
Otis, James
    See Kaler, James Otis
O'Trigger, Sir Lucius
    See Horne, Richard Henry
Ottley, Reginald (Leslie) 26
Otto, Margaret Glover 1909-1976
    Obituary 30
Ouida
    See De La Ramée, (Marie) Louise
Ousley, Odille 1896- 10

Overton, Jenny (Margaret Mary) 1942-
Brief Entry 36
Owen, Caroline Dale
See Snedecker, Caroline Dale
(Parke)
Owen, Clifford
See Hamilton, Charles H. St. John
Owen, Dilys
See Gater, Dilys
Owen, (Benjamin) Evan
1918-1984 38
Oxenbury, Helen 1938- 3

P

Pace, Mildred Mastin 1907-
Brief Entry 29
Packer, Vin
See Meaker, Marijane
Page, Eileen
See Heal, Edith
Page, Eleanor
See Coerr, Eleanor
Page, Lou Williams 1912- 38
Paget-Fredericks, Joseph E. P. Rous-
Marten 1903-1963
Brief Entry 30
Pahz, (Anne) Cheryl Suzanne
1949- 11
Pahz, James Alon 1943- 11
Paice, Margaret 1920- 10
Paige, Harry W. 1922- 41
Brief Entry 35
Paine, Roberta M. 1925- 13
Paisley, Tom
See Bethancourt, T. Ernesto
Palazzo, Anthony D.
1905-1970 3
Palazzo, Tony
See Palazzo, Anthony D.
Palder, Edward L. 1922- 5
Palladini, David (Mario)
1946- 40
Brief Entry 32
Pallas, Norvin 1918- 23
Pallister, John C(lare) 1891-1980
Obituary 26
Palmer, Bernard 1914- 26
Palmer, C(yril) Everard 1930- 14
Palmer, (Ruth) Candida 1926- 11
Palmer, Heidi 1948- 15
Palmer, Helen Marion
See Geisel, Helen
Palmer, Juliette 1930- 15
Palmer, Robin 1911- 43
Panetta, George 1915-1969 15
Pansy
See Alden, Isabella (Macdonald)
Pantell, Dora (Fuchs) 1915- 39
Panter, Carol 1936- 9
Papashvily, George
1898-1978 17
Papashvily, Helen (Waite)
1906- 17
Pape, D(onna) L(ugg) 1930- 2
Paperny, Myra (Green) 1932-
Brief Entry 33
Paradis, Adrian A(lexis)
1912- 1

Paradis, Marjorie (Bartholomew)
1886(?)-1970 17
Parenteau, Shirley (Laurolyn) 1935-
Brief Entry 40
Parish, Peggy 1927- 17
Park, Barbara 1947- 40
Brief Entry 35
Park, Bill
See Park, W(illiam) B(ryan)
Park, Ruth 25
Park, W(illiam) B(ryan) 1936- ... 22
Parker, Elinor 1906- 3
Parker, Lois M(ay) 1912- 30
Parker, Nancy Winslow 1930- 10
Parker, Richard 1915- 14
Parker, Robert
See Boyd, Waldo T.
Parkinson, Ethelyn M(inerva)
1906- 11
Parks, Edd Winfield
1906-1968 10
Parks, Gordon (Alexander Buchanan)
1912- 8
Parley, Peter
See Goodrich, Samuel Griswold
Parlin, John
See Graves, Charles Parlin
Parnall, Peter 1936- 16
Parr, Letitia (Evelyn) 1906- 37
Parr, Lucy 1924- 10
Parrish, Anne 1888-1957 27
Parrish, Mary
See Cousins, Margaret
Parrish, (Frederick) Maxfield
1870-1966 14
Parry, Marian 1924- 13
Parsons, Tom
See MacPherson, Thomas George
Partch, Virgil Franklin II
1916-1984 45
Obituary 39
Partridge, Benjamin W(aring), Jr.
1915- 28
Partridge, Jenny (Lilian) 1947-
Brief Entry 37
Pascal, David 1918- 14
Pascal, Francine 1938-
Brief Entry 37
Paschal, Nancy
See Trotter, Grace V(iolet)
Pashko, Stanley 1913- 29
Patent, Dorothy Hinshaw
1940- 22
Paterson, Diane (R. Cole) 1946-
Brief Entry 33
Paterson, Katherine (Womeldorf)
1932- 13
See also CLR 7
Paton, Alan (Stewart) 1903- 11
Paton, Jane (Elizabeth) 1934- ... 35
Paton Walsh, Gillian 1939- 4
Patten, Brian 1946- 29
Patterson, Geoffrey 1943-
Brief Entry 44
Patterson, Lillie G. 14
Paul, Aileen 1917- 12
Paul, Elizabeth
See Crow, Donna Fletcher
Paul, James 1936- 23

Paul, Robert
See Roberts, John G(aither)
Pauli, Hertha (Ernestine)
1909-1973 3
Obituary 26
Paull, Grace A. 1898- 24
Paulsen, Gary 1939- 22
Paulson, Jack
See Jackson, C. Paul
Pavel, Frances 1907- 10
Payne, Donald Gordon 1924- 37
Payne, Emmy
See West, Emily G(ovan)
Payson, Dale 1943- 9
Payzant, Charles 18
Payzant, Jessie Mercer Knechtel
See Shannon, Terry
Paz, A.
See Pahz, James Alon
Paz, Zan
See Pahz, Cheryl Suzanne
Peake, Mervyn 1911-1968 23
Peale, Norman Vincent 1898- 20
Pearce, (Ann) Philippa 1920- 1
See also CLR 9
Peare, Catherine Owens 1911- 9
Pears, Charles 1873-1958
Brief Entry 30
Pearson, Susan 1946- 39
Brief Entry 27
Pease, Howard 1894-1974 2
Obituary 25
Peck, Anne Merriman 1884- 18
Peck, Richard 1934- 18
See also SAAS 2
Peck, Robert Newton III
1928- 21
See also SAAS 1
Peek, Merle 1938- 39
Peel, Norman Lemon
See Hirsch, Phil
Peeples, Edwin A. 1915- 6
Peet, Bill
See Peet, William Bartlett
Peet, Creighton B. 1899-1977 30
Peet, William Bartlett 1915- 41
Earlier sketch in SATA 2
Peirce, Waldo 1884-1970
Brief Entry 28
Pelaez, Jill 1924- 12
Pellowski, Anne 1933- 20
Pelta, Kathy 1928- 18
Peltier, Leslie C(opus) 1900- ... 13
Pembury, Bill
See Gronon, Arthur William
Pemsteen, Hans
See Manes, Stephen
Pendennis, Arthur, Esquire
See Thackeray, William Makepeace
Pender, Lydia 1907- 3
Pendery, Rosemary 7
Pendle, Alexy 1943- 29
Pendle, George 1906-1977
Obituary 28
Penn, Ruth Bonn
See Rosenberg, Ethel
Pennage, E. M.
See Finkel, George (Irvine)
Penney, Grace Jackson 1904- 35

Pennington, Eunice 1923- 27
Pennington, Lillian Boyer
  1904- 45
Penrose, Margaret
  See Stratemeyer, Edward L.
Penzler, Otto 1942- 38
Pepe, Phil(ip) 1935- 20
Peppe, Rodney 1934- 4
Percy, Charles Henry
  See Smith, Dodie
Perera, Thomas Biddle 1938- 13
Perkins, Al(bert Rogers)
  1904-1975 30
Perkins, Marlin 1905- 21
Perl, Lila 6
Perl, Susan 1922-1983 22
  Obituary 34
Perlmutter, O(scar) William
  1920-1975 8
Perrault, Charles 1628-1703 25
Perreard, Suzanne Louise Butler 1919-
  Brief Entry 29
Perrine, Mary 1913- 2
Perry, Barbara Fisher
  See Fisher, Barbara
Perry, Patricia 1949- 30
Perry, Roger 1933- 27
Pershing, Marie
  See Schultz, Pearle Henriksen
Peters, Caroline
  See Betz, Eva Kelly
Peters, S. H.
  See Porter, William Sydney
Petersen, P(eter) J(ames) 1941-
  Brief Entry 43
Petersham, Maud (Fuller)
  1890-1971 17
Petersham, Miska 1888-1960 17
Peterson, Esther (Allen) 1934- ... 35
Peterson, Hans 1922- 8
Peterson, Harold L(eslie)
  1922- 8
Peterson, Helen Stone 1910- 8
Peterson, Jeanne Whitehouse
  See Whitehouse, Jeanne
Peterson, Lorraine 1940-
  Brief Entry 44
Petie, Haris 1915- 10
Petrides, Heidrun 1944- 19
Petrie, Catherine 1947-
  Brief Entry 41
Petrovich, Michael B(oro)
  1922- 40
Petrovskaya, Kyra
  See Wayne, Kyra Petrovskaya
Petry, Ann (Lane) 5
Pevsner, Stella 8
Peyo
  See Culliford, Pierre
Peyton, K. M.
  See Peyton, Kathleen (Wendy)
  See also CLR 3
Peyton, Kathleen (Wendy)
  1929- 15
Pfeffer, Susan Beth 1948- 4
Phelan, Josephine 1905-
  Brief Entry 30
Phelan, Mary Kay 1914- 3
Phelps, Ethel Johnston 1914- 35

Philbrook, Clem(ent E.) 1917- 24
Phillips, Irv
  See Phillips, Irving W.
Phillips, Irving W. 1908- 11
Phillips, Jack
  See Sandburg, Carl (August)
Phillips, Leon
  See Gerson, Noel B(ertram)
Phillips, Loretta (Hosey)
  1893- 10
Phillips, Louis 1942- 8
Phillips, Mary Geisler
  1881-1964 10
Phillips, Prentice 1894- 10
Phillpotts, Eden 1862-1960 24
Phipson, Joan
  See Fitzhardinge, Joan M.
  See also CLR 5
Phiz
  See Browne, Hablot Knight
Phleger, Fred B. 1909- 34
Phleger, Marjorie Temple 1
Phypps, Hyacinthe
  See Gorey, Edward St. John
Piaget, Jean 1896-1980
  Obituary 23
Piatti, Celestino 1922- 16
Picard, Barbara Leonie 1917- 2
Pickard, Charles 1932- 36
Pickering, James Sayre
  1897-1969 36
  Obituary 28
Pienkowski, Jan 1936- 6
  See also CLR 6
Pierce, Edith Gray 1893-1977 45
Pierce, Katherine
  See St. John, Wylly Folk
Pierce, Ruth (Ireland) 1936- 5
Pierik, Robert 1921- 13
Pig, Edward
  See Gorey, Edward St. John
Pike, E(dgar) Royston 1896- 22
Pilarski, Laura 1926- 13
Pilgrim, Anne
  See Allan, Mabel Esther
Pilkington, Francis Meredyth
  1907- 4
Pilkington, Roger (Windle)
  1915- 10
Pinchot, David 1914(?)-1983
  Obituary 34
Pincus, Harriet 1938- 27
Pine, Tillie S(chloss) 1897- 13
Pinkerton, Kathrene Sutherland
  (Gedney) 1887-1967
  Obituary 26
Pinkney, Jerry 1939- 41
  Brief Entry 32
Pinkwater, Manus 1941- 8
  See also CLR 4
Pinner, Joma
  See Werner, Herma
Pioneer
  See Yates, Raymond F(rancis)
Piper, Roger
  See Fisher, John (Oswald Hamilton)
Piper, Watty
  See Bragg, Mabel Caroline
Piro, Richard 1934- 7

Pirsig, Robert M(aynard)
  1928- 39
Pitrone, Jean Maddern 1920- 4
Pitz, Henry C(larence)
  1895-1976 4
  Obituary 24
Pizer, Vernon 1918- 21
Place, Marian T. 1910- 3
Plaidy, Jean
  See Hibbert, Eleanor
Plaine, Alfred R. 1898(?)-1981
  Obituary 29
Platt, Kin 1911- 21
Plimpton, George (Ames)
  1927- 10
Plomer, William (Charles Franklin)
  1903-1973 24
Plotz, Helen (Ratnoff) 1913- 38
Plowhead, Ruth Gipson
  1877-1967 43
Plowman, Stephanie 1922- 6
Pluckrose, Henry (Arthur)
  1931- 13
Plum, J.
  See Wodehouse, P(elham)
  G(renville)
Plumb, Charles P. 1900(?)-1982
  Obituary 29
Plume, Ilse
  Brief Entry 43
Plummer, Margaret 1911- 2
Podendorf, Illa E.
  1903(?)-1983 18
  Obituary 35
Poe, Edgar Allan 1809-1849 23
Pogány, William Andrew
  1882-1955 44
Pogány, Willy
  Brief Entry 30
  See Pogány, William Andrew
Pohl, Frederik 1919- 24
Pohlmann, Lillian (Grenfell)
  1902- 11
Pointon, Robert
  See Rooke, Daphne (Marie)
Pola
  See Watson, Pauline
Polatnick, Florence T. 1923- 5
Polder, Markus
  See Krüss, James
Polette, Nancy (Jane) 1930- 42
Polhamus, Jean Burt 1928- 21
Politi, Leo 1908- 1
Polking, Kirk 1925- 5
Polland, Barbara K(ay) 1939- 44
Polland, Madeleine A. 1918- 6
Pollock, Mary
  See Blyton, Enid (Mary)
Pollock, Penny 1935- 44
  Brief Entry 42
Pollowitz, Melinda (Kilborn)
  1944- 26
Polonsky, Arthur 1925- 34
Polseno, Jo 17
Pomerantz, Charlotte 20
Pomeroy, Pete
  See Roth, Arthur J(oseph)
Pond, Alonzo W(illiam) 1894- 5
Pontiflet, Ted 1932- 32

Poole, Gray Johnson 1906- *1*
Poole, Josephine 1933- *5*
   See also SAAS 2
Poole, Lynn 1910-1969 .... *1*
Poole, Peggy 1925- *39*
Poortvliet, Marien
   See Poortvliet, Rien
Poortvliet, Rien 1933(?)-
   Brief Entry *37*
Pope, Elizabeth Marie 1917- *38*
   Brief Entry *36*
Portal, Colette 1936- *6*
Porte, Barbara Ann
   Brief Entry *45*
Porter, Katherine Anne
   1890-1980 .... *39*
   Obituary *23*
Porter, Sheena 1935- *24*
Porter, William Sydney
   1862-1910 .... YABC *2*
Portteus, Eleanora Marie Manthei
   (?)-1983
   Obituary *36*
Posell, Elsa Z. *3*
Posten, Margaret L(ois) 1915- *10*
Potok, Chaim 1929- *33*
Potter, (Helen) Beatrix
   1866-1943 .... YABC *1*
   See also CLR 1
Potter, Margaret (Newman)
   1926- *21*
Potter, Marian 1915- *9*
Potter, Miriam Clark
   1886-1965 .... *3*
Pournelle, Jerry (Eugene)
   1933- *26*
Powell, A. M.
   See Morgan, Alfred P(owell)
Powell, Richard Stillman
   See Barbour, Ralph Henry
Powers, Anne
   See Schwartz, Anne Powers
Powers, Bill 1931-
   Brief Entry *31*
Powers, Margaret
   See Heal, Edith
Powledge, Fred 1935- *37*
Poynter, Margaret 1927- *27*
Prager, Arthur *44*
Preiss, Byron (Cary)
   Brief Entry *42*
Prelutsky, Jack *22*
Presberg, Miriam Goldstein 1919-1978
   Brief Entry *38*
Preston, Edna Mitchell *40*
Preussler, Otfried 1923- *24*
Prevert, Jacques (Henri Marie)
   1900-1977
   Obituary *30*
Price, Christine 1928-1980 .... *3*
   Obituary *23*
Price, Garrett 1896-1979
   Obituary *22*
Price, Jennifer
   See Hoover, Helen (Drusilla
   Blackburn)
Price, Lucie Locke
   See Locke, Lucie

Price, Margaret (Evans) 1888-1973
   Brief Entry *28*
Price, Olive 1903- *8*
Price, Susan 1955- *25*
Price, Willard 1887-
   Brief Entry *38*
Prideaux, Tom 1908- *37*
Priestley, Lee (Shore) 1904- *27*
Prieto, Mariana B(eeching)
   1912- *8*
Prime, Derek (James) 1931- *34*
Prince, Alison 1931- *28*
Prince, J(ack) H(arvey) 1908- *17*
Pringle, Laurence 1935- *4*
   See also CLR 4
Pritchett, Elaine H(illyer)
   1920- *36*
Proctor, Everitt
   See Montgomery, Rutherford
Professor Zingara
   See Leeming, Joseph
Provensen, Alice 1918- *9*
Provensen, Martin 1916- *9*
Pryor, Helen Brenton
   1897-1972 .... *4*
Pucci, Albert John 1920- *44*
Pudney, John (Sleigh)
   1909-1977 .... *24*
Pugh, Ellen T. 1920- *7*
Pullein-Thompson, Christine
   1930- *3*
Pullein-Thompson, Diana *3*
Pullein-Thompson, Josephine *3*
Puner, Helen W(alker) 1915- *37*
Purdy, Susan Gold 1939- *8*
Purscell, Phyllis 1934- *7*
Putnam, Arthur Lee
   See Alger, Horatio, Jr.
Putnam, Peter B(rock) 1920- *30*
Pyle, Howard 1853-1911 .... *16*
Pyne, Mable Mandeville
   1903-1969 .... *9*

Q

Quackenbush, Robert M.
   1929- *7*
Quammen, David 1948- *7*
Quarles, Benjamin 1904- *12*
Queen, Ellery, Jr.
   See Holding, James
Quennell, Marjorie (Courtney)
   1884-1972 .... *29*
Quick, Annabelle 1922- *2*
Quin-Harkin, Janet 1941- *18*
Quinn, Elisabeth 1881-1962 .... *22*
Quinn, Susan
   See Jacobs, Susan
Quinn, Vernon
   See Quinn, Elisabeth

R

Rabe, Berniece 1928- *7*
Rabe, Olive H(anson)
   1887-1968 .... *13*
Rabinowich, Ellen 1946- *29*

Rabinowitz, Sandy 1954-
   Brief Entry *39*
Raboff, Ernest Lloyd
   Brief Entry *37*
Rackham, Arthur 1867-1939 ...... *15*
Radford, Ruby L(orraine)
   1891-1971 .... *6*
Radlauer, David 1952- *28*
Radlauer, Edward 1921- *15*
Radlauer, Ruth (Shaw) 1926- *15*
Radley, Gail 1951- *25*
Rae, Gwynedd 1892-1977 .... *37*
Raebeck, Lois 1921- *5*
Raftery, Gerald (Bransfield)
   1905- *11*
Rahn, Joan Elma 1929- *27*
Raible, Alton (Robert) 1918- *35*
Raiff, Stan 1930- *11*
Rainey, W. B.
   See Blassingame, Wyatt Rainey
Ralston, Jan
   See Dunlop, Agnes M. R.
Ramal, Walter
   See de la Mare, Walter
Ranadive, Gail 1944- *10*
Rand, Ann (Binkley) *30*
Rand, Paul 1914- *6*
Randall, Florence Engel 1917- *5*
Randall, Janet [Joint pseudonym]
   See Young, Janet Randall and
   Young, Robert W.
Randall, Robert
   See Silverberg, Robert
Randall, Ruth Painter
   1892-1971 .... *3*
Randolph, Lieutenant J. H.
   See Ellis, Edward S(ylvester)
Rands, William Brighty
   1823-1882 .... *17*
Ranney, Agnes V. 1916- *6*
Ransome, Arthur (Michell)
   1884-1967 .... *22*
   See also CLR 8
Rapaport, Stella F(read) *10*
Raphael, Elaine (Chionchio)
   1933- *23*
Rappaport, Eva 1924- *6*
Rarick, Carrie 1911- *41*
Raskin, Edith (Lefkowitz)
   1908- *9*
Raskin, Ellen 1928-1984 .... *38*
   Earlier sketch in SATA 2
   See also CLR 1
Raskin, Joseph 1897-1982 .... *12*
   Obituary *29*
Rasmussen, Knud Johan Victor
   1879-1933
   Brief Entry *34*
Rathjen, Carl H(enry) 1909- *11*
Rattray, Simon
   See Trevor, Elleston
Rau, Margaret 1913- *9*
   See also CLR 8
Rauch, Mabel Thompson 1888-1972
   Obituary *26*
Raucher, Herman 1928- *8*
Ravielli, Anthony 1916- *3*
Rawlings, Marjorie Kinnan
   1896-1953 .... YABC *1*

Rawls, (Woodrow) Wilson
  1913- 22
Ray, Deborah 1940- 8
Ray, Irene
  See Sutton, Margaret Beebe
Ray, JoAnne 1935- 9
Ray, Mary (Eva Pedder)
  1932- 2
Raymond, James Crossley 1917-1981
  Obituary 29
Raymond, Robert
  See Alter, Robert Edmond
Rayner, Mary 1933- 22
Rayner, William 1929-
  Brief Entry 36
Raynor, Dorka 28
Rayson, Steven 1932- 30
Razzell, Arthur (George)
  1925- 11
Razzi, James 1931- 10
Read, Elfreida 1920- 2
Read, Piers Paul 1941- 21
Ready, Kirk L. 1943- 39
Reaney, James 1926- 43
Reck, Franklin Mering 1896-1965
  Brief Entry 30
Redding, Robert Hull 1919- 2
Redway, Ralph
  See Hamilton, Charles H. St. John
Redway, Ridley
  See Hamilton, Charles H. St. John
Reed, Betty Jane 1921- 4
Reed, Gwendolyn E(lizabeth)
  1932- 21
Reed, Kit 1932- 34
Reed, Philip G. 1908-
  Brief Entry 29
Reed, Thomas (James) 1947- 34
Reed, William Maxwell
  1871-1962 15
Reeder, Colonel Red
  See Reeder, Russell P., Jr.
Reeder, Russell P., Jr. 1902- 4
Reeman, Douglas Edward 1924-
  Brief Entry 28
Rees, David Bartlett 1936- 36
Rees, Ennis 1925- 3
Reeve, Joel
  See Cox, William R(obert)
Reeves, James 1909- 15
Reeves, Joyce 1911- 17
Reeves, Lawrence F. 1926- 29
Reeves, Ruth Ellen
  See Ranney, Agnes V.
Regehr, Lydia 1903- 37
Reggiani, Renée 18
Reid, Barbara 1922- 21
Reid, Dorothy M(arion) (?)-1974
  Brief Entry 29
Reid, Eugenie Chazal 1924- 12
Reid, John Calvin 21
Reid, (Thomas) Mayne
  1818-1883 24
Reid, Meta Mayne 1905-
  Brief Entry 36
Reid Banks, Lynne 1929- 22
Reiff, Stephanie Ann 1948-
  Brief Entry 28
Reig, June 1933- 30

Reigot, Betty Polisar 1924-
  Brief Entry 41
Reinach, Jacquelyn (Krasne)
  1930- 28
Reiner, William B(uck) 1910-1976
  Obituary 30
Reinfeld, Fred 1910-1964 3
Reiniger, Lotte 1899-1981 40
  Obituary 33
Reiss, Johanna de Leeuw
  1932- 18
Reiss, John J. 23
Reit, Seymour 21
Reit, Sy
  See Reit, Seymour
Rémi, Georges 1907-1983 13
  Obituary 32
Remington, Frederic (Sackrider)
  1861-1909 41
Renault, Mary
  See Challans, Mary
Rendell, Joan 28
Rendina, Laura Cooper 1902- 10
Renick, Marion (Lewis) 1905- 1
Renken, Aleda 1907- 27
Renlie, Frank H. 1936- 11
Rensie, Willis
  See Eisner, Will(iam Erwin)
Renvoize, Jean 1930- 5
Resnick, Michael D(iamond)
  1942- 38
Resnick, Mike
  See Resnick, Michael D(iamond)
Resnick, Seymour 1920- 23
Retla, Robert
  See Alter, Robert Edmond
Reuter, Carol (Joan) 1931- 2
Rey, H(ans) A(ugusto)
  1898-1977 26
  Earlier sketch in SATA 1
  See also CLR 5
Rey, Margret (Elizabeth)
  1906- 26
  See also CLR 5
Reyher, Becky
  See Reyher, Rebecca Hourwich
Reyher, Rebecca Hourwich
  1897- 18
Reynolds, Dickson
  See Reynolds, Helen Mary
  Greenwood Campbell
Reynolds, Helen Mary Greenwood
  Campbell 1884-1969
  Obituary 26
Reynolds, John
  See Whitlock, Ralph
Reynolds, Madge
  See Whitlock, Ralph
Reynolds, Malvina 1900-1978 44
  Obituary 24
Reynolds, Pamela 1923- 34
Rhodes, Bennie (Loran) 1927- 35
Rhodes, Frank H(arold Trevor)
  1926- 37
Rhue, Morton
  See Strasser, Todd
Rhys, Megan
  See Williams, Jeanne

Ribbons, Ian 1924- 37
  Brief Entry 30
Ricciuti, Edward R(aphael)
  1938- 10
Rice, Charles D(uane) 1910-1971
  Obituary 27
Rice, Dale R(ichard) 1948- 42
Rice, Edward E. 1918-
  Brief Entry 42
Rice, Elizabeth 1913- 2
Rice, Eve (Hart) 1951- 34
Rice, Inez 1907- 13
Rice, James 1934- 22
Rich, Elaine Sommers 1926- 6
Rich, Josephine 1912- 10
Richard, Adrienne 1921- 5
Richards, Curtis
  See Curtis, Richard (Alan)
Richards, Frank
  See Hamilton, Charles H. St. John
Richards, Hilda
  See Hamilton, Charles H. St. John
Richards, Kay
  See Baker, Susan (Catherine)
Richards, Laura E(lizabeth Howe)
  1850-1943 ....*YABC 1*
Richards, R(onald) C(harles) W(illiam)
  1923-
  Brief Entry 43
Richardson, Frank Howard 1882-1970
  Obituary 27
Richardson, Grace Lee
  See Dickson, Naida
Richardson, Robert S(hirley)
  1902- 8
Richelson, Geraldine 1922- 29
Richler, Mordecai 1931- 44
  Brief Entry 27
Richoux, Pat 1927- 7
Richter, Alice 1941- 30
Richter, Conrad 1890-1968 3
Richter, Hans Peter 1925- 6
Rico, Don(ato) 1917-1985
  Obituary 43
Ridge, Antonia (Florence)
  (?)-1981 7
  Obituary 27
Ridge, Martin 1923- 43
Ridley, Nat, Jr.
  See Stratemeyer, Edward L.
Ridlon, Marci 1942- 22
Riedman, Sarah R(egal) 1902- 1
Riesenberg, Felix, Jr.
  1913-1962 23
Rieu, E(mile) V(ictor) 1887-1972
  Obituary 26
Riggs, Sidney Noyes 1892-1975
  Obituary 28
Rikhoff, Jean 1928- 9
Riley, James Whitcomb
  1849-1916 17
Rinard, Judith E(llen) 1947- 44
Ringi, Kjell Arne Sörensen
  1939- 12
Rinkoff, Barbara (Jean)
  1923-1975 4
  Obituary 27
Riordan, James 1936- 28

Rios, Tere
  See Versace, Marie Teresa
Ripley, Elizabeth Blake
  1906-1969 5
Ripper, Charles L. 1929- 3
Ritchie, Barbara (Gibbons) 14
Ritts, Paul 1920(?)-1980
  Obituary 25
Rivera, Geraldo 1943-
  Brief Entry 28
Riverside, John
  See Heinlein, Robert A(nson)
Rivkin, Ann 1920- 41
Rivoli, Mario 1943- 10
Roach, Marilynne K(athleen)
  1946- 9
Roach, Portia
  See Takakjian, Portia
Robbins, Frank 1917- 42
  Brief Entry 32
Robbins, Raleigh
  See Hamilton, Charles H. St. John
Robbins, Ruth 1917(?)- 14
Robbins, Tony
  See Pashko, Stanley
Roberts, Bruce (Stuart) 1930-
  Brief Entry 39
Roberts, Charles G(eorge) D(ouglas)
  1860-1943
  Brief Entry 29
Roberts, David
  See Cox, John Roberts
Roberts, Elizabeth Madox
  1886-1941 33
  Brief Entry 27
Roberts, Jim
  See Bates, Barbara S(nedeker)
Roberts, John G(aither) 1913- 27
Roberts, Nancy Correll 1924-
  Brief Entry 28
Roberts, Terence
  See Sanderson, Ivan T.
Roberts, Willo Davis 1928- 21
Robertson, Barbara (Anne)
  1931- 12
Robertson, Don 1929- 8
Robertson, Dorothy Lewis
  1912- 12
Robertson, Jennifer (Sinclair)
  1942- 12
Robertson, Keith 1914- 1
Robinet, Harriette Gillem
  1931- 27
Robins, Seelin
  See Ellis, Edward S(ylvester)
Robinson, Adjai 1932- 8
Robinson, Barbara (Webb)
  1927- 8
Robinson, C(harles) A(lexander), Jr.
  1900-1965 36
Robinson, Charles 1870-1937 17
Robinson, Charles 1931- 6
Robinson, Jan M. 1933- 6
Robinson, Jean O. 1934- 7
Robinson, Jerry 1922-
  Brief Entry 34
Robinson, Joan (Mary) G(ale Thomas)
  1910- 7
Robinson, Marileta 1942- 32

Robinson, Maudie (Millian Oller)
  1914- 11
Robinson, Maurice R. 1895-1982
  Obituary 29
Robinson, Nancy K(onheim)
  1942- 32
  Brief Entry 31
Robinson, Ray(mond Kenneth)
  1920- 23
Robinson, Shari
  See McGuire, Leslie (Sarah)
Robinson, T(homas) H(eath)
  1869-1950 17
Robinson, (Wanda) Veronica
  1926- 30
Robinson, W(illiam) Heath
  1872-1944 17
Robison, Bonnie 1924- 12
Robison, Nancy L(ouise)
  1934- 32
Robottom, John 1934- 7
Roche, A. K. [Joint pseudonym]
  See Abisch, Roslyn Kroop and
  Kaplan, Boche
Roche, P(atricia) K.
  Brief Entry 34
Roche, Terry
  See Poole, Peggy
Rock, Gail
  Brief Entry 32
Rocker, Fermin 1907- 40
Rockwell, Anne F. 1934- 33
Rockwell, Gail
  Brief Entry 36
Rockwell, Harlow 33
Rockwell, Norman (Percevel)
  1894-1978 23
Rockwell, Thomas 1933- 7
  See also CLR 6
Rockwood, Joyce 1947- 39
Rockwood, Roy [Collective
  pseudonym] 1
  See also McFarlane, Leslie;
  Stratemeyer, Edward L.
Roddenberry, Eugene Wesley
  1921- 45
Roddenberry, Gene
  See Roddenberry, Eugene Wesley
Rodgers, Mary 1931- 8
Rodman, Emerson
  See Ellis, Edward S(ylvester)
Rodman, Maia
  See Wojciechowska, Maia
Rodman, Selden 1909- 9
Rodowsky, Colby 1932- 21
Roe, Harry Mason
  See Stratemeyer, Edward L.
Roever, J(oan) M(arilyn)
  1935- 26
Roffey, Maureen 1936- 33
Rogers, (Thomas) Alan (Stinchcombe)
  1937- 2
Rogers, Frances 1888-1974 10
Rogers, Fred (McFeely) 1928- ... 33
Rogers, Matilda 1894-1976 5
  Obituary 34
Rogers, Pamela 1927- 9
Rogers, Robert
  See Hamilton, Charles H. St. John

Rogers, W(illiam) G(arland)
  1896-1978 23
Rojan
  See Rojankovsky, Feodor
  (Stepanovich)
Rojankovsky, Feodor (Stepanovich)
  1891-1970 21
Rokeby-Thomas, Anna E(lma)
  1911- 15
Roland, Albert 1925- 11
Rolerson, Darrell A(llen)
  1946- 8
Roll, Winifred 1909- 6
Rollins, Charlemae Hill
  1897-1979 3
  Obituary 26
Romano, Louis 1921- 35
Rongen, Björn 1906- 10
Rood, Ronald (N.) 1920- 12
Rooke, Daphne (Marie) 1914- ... 12
Roos, Stephen (Kelley) 1945-
  Brief Entry 41
Roper, Laura Wood 1911- 34
Roscoe, D(onald) T(homas)
  1934- 42
Rose, Anna Perrot
  See Wright, Anna (Maria Louisa
  Perrot) Rose
Rose, Anne 8
Rose, Carl 1903-1971
  Brief Entry 31
Rose, Elizabeth Jane (Pretty) 1933-
  Brief Entry 28
Rose, Florella
  See Carlson, Vada F.
Rose, Gerald (Hembdon Seymour)
  1935-
  Brief Entry 30
Rose, Wendy 1948- 12
Rosen, Michael (Wayne) 1946-
  Brief Entry 40
Rosen, Sidney 1916- 1
Rosen, Winifred 1943- 8
Rosenbaum, Maurice 1907- 6
Rosenberg, Dorothy 1906- 40
Rosenberg, Ethel 3
Rosenberg, Nancy Sherman
  1931- 4
Rosenberg, Sharon 1942- 8
Rosenblatt, Arthur S. 1938-
  Brief Entry 45
Rosenbloom, Joseph 1928- 21
Rosenblum, Richard 1928- 11
Rosenburg, John M. 1918- 6
Rosenthal, Harold 1914- 35
Ross, Alan
  See Warwick, Alan R(oss)
Ross, Alex(ander) 1909-
  Brief Entry 29
Ross, Dave 1949- 32
Ross, David 1896-1975
  Obituary 20
Ross, Diana
  See Denney, Diana
Ross, Frank (Xavier), Jr.
  1914- 28
Ross, John 1921- 45
Ross, Tony 1938- 17

Ross, Wilda (S.) 1915-
  Brief Entry *39*
Rossel, Seymour 1945- *28*
Rössel-Waugh, C. C. [Joint
  pseudonym]
  See Waugh, Carol-Lynn Rössel
Rossetti, Christiana (Georgina)
  1830-1894 .... *20*
Roth, Arnold 1929- *21*
Roth, Arthur J(oseph) 1925- *43*
  Brief Entry *28*
Roth, David 1940- *36*
Rothkopf, Carol Z. 1929- *4*
Rothman, Joel 1938- *7*
Roueché, Berton 1911- *28*
Roughsey, Dick 1921(?)- *35*
Rounds, Glen (Harold) 1906- *8*
Rourke, Constance (Mayfield)
  1885-1941 .... *YABC 1*
Rowe, Viola Carson 1903-1969
  Obituary *26*
Rowland, Florence Wightman
  1900- *8*
Rowland-Entwistle, (Arthur) Theodore
  (Henry) 1925- *31*
Rowsome, Frank (Howard), Jr.
  1914-1983 .... *36*
Roy, Liam
  See Scarry, Patricia
Roy, Ron(ald) 1940- *40*
  Brief Entry *35*
Rubel, Nicole 1953- *18*
Rubin, Eva Johanna 1925- *38*
Ruby, Lois 1942- *35*
  Brief Entry *34*
Ruchlis, Hy 1913- *3*
Ruckman, Ivy 1931- *37*
Ruck-Pauquèt, Gina 1931- *40*
  Brief Entry *37*
Rudeen, Kenneth
  Brief Entry *36*
Rudley, Stephen 1946- *30*
Rudolph, Marguerita 1908- *21*
Rudomin, Esther
  See Hautzig, Esther
Rue, Leonard Lee III 1926- *37*
Ruedi, Norma Paul
  See Ainsworth, Norma
Ruffell, Ann 1941- *30*
Ruffins, Reynold 1930- *41*
Rugoff, Milton 1913- *30*
Ruhen, Olaf 1911- *17*
Rukeyser, Muriel 1913-1980
  Obituary *22*
Rumsey, Marian (Barritt)
  1928- *16*
Runyan, John
  See Palmer, Bernard
Rush, Alison 1951- *41*
Rush, Peter 1937- *32*
Rushmore, Helen 1898- *3*
Rushmore, Robert (William)
  1926- *8*
Ruskin, Ariane
  See Batterberry, Ariane Ruskin
Ruskin, John 1819-1900 .... *24*
Russell, Charlotte
  See Rathjen, Carl H(enry)
Russell, Franklin 1926- *11*

Russell, Helen Ross 1915- *8*
Russell, Patrick
  See Sammis, John
Russell, Solveig Paulson
  1904- *3*
Russo, Susan 1947- *30*
Ruth, Rod 1912- *9*
Rutherford, Douglas
  See McConnell, James Douglas
  (Rutherford)
Rutherford, Meg 1932- *34*
Ruthin, Margaret *4*
Rutgers van der Loeff, An(na) Basenau
  1910- *22*
Rutz, Viola Larkin 1932- *12*
Ruzicka, Rudolph 1883-1978
  Obituary *24*
Ryan, Betsy
  See Ryan, Elizabeth (Anne)
Ryan, Cheli Durán *20*
Ryan, Elizabeth (Anne) 1943- *30*
Ryan, John (Gerald Christopher)
  1921- *22*
Ryan, Peter (Charles) 1939- *15*
Rydberg, Ernest E(mil) 1901- *21*
Rydberg, Lou(isa Hampton)
  1908- *27*
Rydell, Wendell
  See Rydell, Wendy
Rydell, Wendy *4*
Ryden, Hope *8*
Ryder, Joanne
  Brief Entry *34*
Rye, Anthony
  See Youd, (Christopher) Samuel
Rylant, Cynthia 1954-
  Brief Entry *44*
Rymer, Alta May 1925- *34*

S

Saberhagen, Fred (Thomas)
  1930- *37*
Sabin, Edwin Legrand
  1870-1952 .... *YABC 2*
Sabin, Francene *27*
Sabin, Louis 1930- *27*
Sabre, Dirk
  See Laffin, John (Alfred Charles)
Sabuso
  See Phillips, Irving W.
Sachs, Marilyn 1927- *3*
  See also CLR 2
  See also SAAS 2
Sackett, S(amuel) J(ohn)
  1928- *12*
Sackson, Sid 1920- *16*
Saddler, Allen
  See Richards, R(onald) C(harles)
  W(illiam)
Saddler, K. Allen
  See Richards, R(onald) C(harles)
  W(illiam)
Sadie, Stanley (John) 1930- *14*
Sadler, Catherine Edwards
  Brief Entry *45*
Sadler, Mark
  See Lynds, Dennis

Sage, Juniper [Joint pseudonym]
  See Brown, Margaret Wise and
  Hurd, Edith
Sagsoorian, Paul 1923- *12*
Saida
  See LeMair, H(enriette) Willebeek
Saint, Dora Jessie 1913- *10*
St. Briavels, James
  See Wood, James Playsted
St. Clair, Byrd Hooper 1905-1976
  Obituary *28*
Saint Exupéry, Antoine de
  1900-1944 .... *20*
  See also CLR 10
St. George, Judith 1931- *13*
St. John, Nicole
  See Johnston, Norma
St. John, Philip
  See Del Rey, Lester
St. John, Wylly Folk
  1908-1985 .... *10*
  Obituary *45*
St. Meyer, Ned
  See Stratemeyer, Edward L.
St. Tamara
  See Kolba, Tamara
Saito, Michiko
  See Fujiwara, Michiko
Salassi, Otto R(ussell) 1939- *38*
Saldutti, Denise 1953- *39*
Salkey, (Felix) Andrew (Alexander)
  1928- *35*
Salmon, Annie Elizabeth
  1899- *13*
Salten, Felix
  See Salzmann, Siegmund
Salter, Cedric
  See Knight, Francis Edgar
Salvadori, Mario (George)
  1907- *40*
Salzer, L. E.
  See Wilson, Lionel
Salzman, Yuri
  Brief Entry *42*
Salzmann, Siegmund
  1869-1945 .... *25*
Samachson, Dorothy 1914- *3*
Samachson, Joseph 1906- *3*
Sammis, John 1942- *4*
Sampson, Fay (Elizabeth)
  1935- *42*
  Brief Entry *40*
Samson, Anne S(tringer)
  1933- *2*
Samson, Joan 1937-1976 .... *13*
Samuels, Charles 1902- *12*
Samuels, Gertrude *17*
Sanborn, Duane 1914- *38*
Sancha, Sheila 1924- *38*
Sanchez, Sonia 1934- *22*
Sanchez-Silva, Jose Maria
  1911- *16*
Sand, George X. *45*
Sandak, Cass R(obert) 1950-
  Brief Entry *37*
Sandberg, (Karin) Inger 1930- ... *15*
Sandberg, Karl C. 1931- *35*
Sandberg, Lasse (E. M.)
  1924- *15*

Sandburg, Carl (August)
   1878-1967 8
Sandburg, Charles A.
   See Sandburg, Carl (August)
Sandburg, Helga 1918- 3
Sanderlin, George 1915- 4
Sanderlin, Owenita (Harrah)
   1916- 11
Sanders, Winston P.
   See Anderson, Poul (William)
Sanderson, Ivan T. 1911-1973 6
Sanderson, Ruth (L.) 1951- 41
Sandin, Joan 1942- 12
Sandison, Janet
   See Cameron, Elizabeth Jane
Sandoz, Mari (Susette)
   1901-1966 5
Sanger, Marjory Bartlett
   1920- 8
Sankey, Alice (Ann-Susan)
   1910- 27
San Souci, Robert D. 1946- 40
Santesson, Hans Stefan 1914(?)-1975
   Obituary 30
Sapieyevski, Anne Lindbergh
   1940- 35
Sarac, Roger
   See Caras, Roger A(ndrew)
Sarg, Anthony Fredrick
   See Sarg, Tony
Sarg, Tony 1880-1942 ....*YABC 1*
Sargent, Pamela 29
Sargent, Robert 1933- 2
Sargent, Sarah 1937- 44
   Brief Entry 41
Sargent, Shirley 1927- 11
Sari
   See Fleur, Anne
Sarnoff, Jane 1937- 10
Saroyan, William 1908-1981 23
   Obituary 24
Sarton, Eleanore Marie
   See Sarton, (Eleanor) May
Sarton, (Eleanor) May 1912- 36
Sasek, Miroslav 1916-1980 16
   Obituary 23
   See also CLR 4
Sattler, Helen Roney 1921- 4
Sauer, Julia (Lina) 1891-1983 ... 32
   Obituary 36
Saul, (E.) Wendy 1946- 42
Saunders, Caleb
   See Heinlein, Robert A(nson)
Saunders, Keith 1910- 12
Saunders, Rubie (Agnes)
   1929- 21
Saunders, Susan 1945-
   Brief Entry 41
Savage, Blake
   See Goodwin, Harold Leland
Savery, Constance (Winifred)
   1897- 1
Saville, (Leonard) Malcolm
   1901-1982 23
   Obituary 31
Saviozzi, Adriana
   See Mazza, Adriana
Savitt, Sam 8
Savitz, Harriet May 1933- 5

Sawyer, Ruth 1880-1970 17
Say, Allen 1937- 28
Sayers, Frances Clarke 1897- 3
Sazer, Nina 1949- 13
Scabrini, Janet 1953- 13
Scagnetti, Jack 1924- 7
Scanlon, Marion Stephany 11
Scarf, Maggi
   See Scarf, Maggie
Scarf, Maggie 1932- 5
Scarry, Huck
   See Scarry, Richard, Jr.
Scarry, Patricia (Murphy)
   1924- 2
Scarry, Patsy
   See Scarry, Patricia
Scarry, Richard (McClure)
   1919- 35
   Earlier sketch in SATA 2
   See also CLR 3
Scarry, Richard, Jr. 1953- 35
Schachtel, Roger (Bernard)
   1949- 38
Schaefer, Jack 1907- 3
Schaeffer, Mead 1898- 21
Schaller, George B(eals)
   1933- 30
Schatzki, Walter 1899-
   Brief Entry 31
Schechter, Betty (Goodstein)
   1921- 5
Scheer, Julian (Weisel) 1926- ... 8
Scheffer, Victor B. 1906- 6
Scheier, Michael 1943- 40
   Brief Entry 36
Schell, Mildred 1922- 41
Schell, Orville H. 1940- 10
Schellie, Don 1932- 29
Schemm, Mildred Walker
   1905- 21
Scherf, Margaret 1908- 10
Schermer, Judith (Denise)
   1941- 30
Schertle, Alice 1941- 36
Schick, Alice 1946- 27
Schick, Eleanor 1942- 9
Schick, Joel 1945- 31
   Brief Entry 30
Schiff, Ken 1942- 7
Schiller, Andrew 1919- 21
Schiller, Barbara (Heyman)
   1928- 21
Schiller, Justin G. 1943-
   Brief Entry 31
Schindelman, Joseph 1923-
   Brief Entry 32
Schisgall, Oscar 1901-1984 12
   Obituary 38
Schlee, Ann 1934- 44
   Brief Entry 36
Schlein, Miriam 1926- 2
Schloat, G. Warren, Jr. 1914- ... 4
Schmid, Eleonore 1939- 12
Schmiderer, Dorothy 1940- 19
Schmidt, Elizabeth 1915- 15
Schmidt, James Norman
   1912- 21
Schneider, Herman 1905- 7

Schneider, Laurie
   See Adams, Laurie
Schneider, Nina 1913- 2
Schneider, Rex 1937- 44
Schnirel, James R(einhold)
   1931- 14
Schock, Pauline 1928- 45
Schoen, Barbara 1924- 13
Schoenherr, John (Carl) 1935- ... 37
Scholastica, Sister Mary
   See Jenkins, Marie M.
Scholefield, Edmund O.
   See Butterworth, W. E.
Scholey, Arthur 1932- 28
Schone, Virginia 22
Schongut, Emanuel
   Brief Entry 36
Schoonover, Frank (Earle)
   1877-1972 24
Schoor, Gene 1921- 3
Schraff, Anne E(laine) 1939- 27
Schrank, Joseph 1900-1984
   Obituary 38
Schreiber, Elizabeth Anne (Ferguson)
   1947- 13
Schreiber, Georges 1904-1977
   Brief Entry 29
Schreiber, Ralph W(alter)
   1942- 13
Schroeder, Ted 1931(?)-1973
   Obituary 20
Schulman, Janet 1933- 22
Schulman, L(ester) M(artin)
   1934- 13
Schulte, Elaine L(ouise) 1934- .. 36
Schultz, Gwendolyn 21
Schultz, James Willard
   1859-1947 ....*YABC 1*
Schultz, Pearle Henriksen
   1918- 21
Schulz, Charles M(onroe)
   1922- 10
Schurfranz, Vivian 1925- 13
Schutzer, A. I. 1922- 13
Schuyler, Pamela R(icka)
   1948- 30
Schwartz, Alvin 1927- 4
   See also CLR 3
Schwartz, Amy 1954-
   Brief Entry 41
Schwartz, Ann Powers 1913- 10
Schwartz, Charles W(alsh)
   1914- 8
Schwartz, Daniel (Bennet) 1929-
   Brief Entry 29
Schwartz, Elizabeth Reeder
   1912- 8
Schwartz, Julius 1907- 45
Schwartz, Sheila (Ruth) 1929- ... 27
Schwartz, Stephen (Lawrence)
   1948- 19
Schweitzer, Iris
   Brief Entry 36
Schweninger, Ann 1951- 29
Scoggin, Margaret C. 1905-1968
   Brief Entry 28
Scoppettone, Sandra 1936- 9
Scott, Ann Herbert 1926-
   Brief Entry 29

Scott, Cora Annett (Pipitone)
1931- *11*
Scott, Dan [House pseudonym]
See Barker, S. Omar; Stratemeyer,
Edward L.
Scott, Elaine 1940- *36*
Scott, Jack Denton 1915- *31*
Scott, John 1912-1976 .... *14*
Scott, John Anthony 1916- *23*
Scott, John M(artin) 1913- *12*
Scott, Sally (Elisabeth) 1948- *44*
Scott, Sally Fisher 1909-1978 ..... *43*
Scott, Tony
See Scott, John Anthony
Scott, Sir Walter
1771-1832 ....*YABC 2*
Scott, Warwick
See Trevor, Elleston
Scribner, Charles, Jr. 1921- *13*
Scribner, Joanne L. 1949- *33*
Scrimsher, Lila Gravatt 1897-1974
Obituary *28*
Scuro, Vincent 1951- *21*
Seabrooke, Brenda 1941- *30*
Seaman, Augusta Huiell
1879-1950 .... *31*
Seamands, Ruth (Childers)
1916- *9*
Searcy, Margaret Zehmer 1926-
Brief Entry *39*
Searight, Mary W(illiams)
1918- *17*
Searle, Kathryn Adrienne
1942- *10*
Searle, Ronald (William Fordham)
1920- *42*
Sears, Stephen W. 1932- *4*
Sebastian, Lee
See Silverberg, Robert
Sebestyen, Igen
See Sebestyen, Ouida
Sebestyen, Ouida 1924- *39*
Sechrist, Elizabeth Hough
1903- *2*
Sedges, John
See Buck, Pearl S.
Seed, Jenny 1930- *8*
Seed, Sheila Turner 1937(?)-1979
Obituary *23*
Seeger, Elizabeth 1889-1973
Obituary *20*
Seeger, Pete(r) 1919- *13*
Seever, R.
See Reeves, Lawrence F.
Sefton, Catherine
See Waddell, Martin
Segal, Joyce 1940- *35*
Segal, Lore 1928- *4*
Seidelman, James Edward
1926- *6*
Seiden, Art(hur)
Brief Entry *42*
Seidman, Laurence (Ivan)
1925- *15*
Seigel, Kalman 1917- *12*
Seignobosc, Francoise
1897-1961 .... *21*
Seixas, Judith S. 1922- *17*
Sejima, Yoshimasa 1913- *8*

Selden, George
See Thompson, George Selden
See also CLR 8
Self, Margaret Cabell 1902- *24*
Selig, Sylvie 1942- *13*
Selkirk, Jane [Joint pseudonym]
See Chapman, John Stanton
Higham
Sellers, Naomi John
See Flack, Naomi John (White)
Selsam, Millicent E(llis)
1912- *29*
Earlier sketch in SATA 1
See also CLR 1
Seltzer, Meyer 1932- *17*
Seltzer, Richard (Warren, Jr.)
1946- *41*
Sendak, Jack *28*
Sendak, Maurice (Bernard)
1928- *27*
Earlier sketch in SATA 1
See also CLR 1
Sengler, Johanna 1924- *18*
Serage, Nancy 1924- *10*
Seredy, Kate 1899-1975 .... *1*
Obituary *24*
See also CLR 10
Seroff, Victor I(lyitch)
1902-1979 .... *12*
Obituary *26*
Serraillier, Ian (Lucien) 1912- *1*
See also CLR 2
Servello, Joe 1932- *10*
Service, Robert W(illiam)
1874(?)-1958 .... *20*
Serwadda, William Moses
1931- *27*
Serwer, Blanche L. 1910- *10*
Seth, Marie
See Lexau, Joan M.
Seton, Anya *3*
Seton, Ernest Thompson
1860-1946 .... *18*
Seuling, Barbara 1937- *10*
Seuss, Dr.
See Geisel, Theodor Seuss
See also CLR 9
Severn, Bill
See Severn, William Irving
Severn, David
See Unwin, David S(torr)
Severn, William Irving 1914- *1*
Sewall, Marcia 1935- *37*
Seward, Prudence 1926- *16*
Sewell, Anna 1820-1878 .... *24*
Sewell, Helen (Moore)
1896-1957 .... *38*
Sexton, Anne (Harvey)
1928-1974 .... *10*
Seymour, Alta Halverson *10*
Shackleton, C. C.
See Aldiss, Brian W(ilson)
Shafer, Robert E(ugene)
1925- *9*
Shahn, Ben(jamin) 1898-1969
Obituary *21*
Shahn, Bernarda Bryson
See Bryson, Bernarda
Shane, Harold Gray 1914- *36*

Shanks, Ann Zane (Kushner) *10*
Shannon, George (William Bones)
1952- *35*
Shannon, Monica (?)-1965 .... *28*
Shannon, Terry *21*
Shapiro, Irwin 1911-1981 .... *32*
Shapiro, Milton J. 1926- *32*
Shapp, Martha 1910- *3*
Sharfman, Amalie *14*
Sharma, Partap 1939- *15*
Sharmat, Marjorie Weinman
1928- *33*
Earlier sketch in SATA 4
Sharmat, Mitchell 1927- *33*
Sharp, Margery 1905- *29*
Earlier sketch in SATA 1
Sharp, Zerna A. 1889-1981
Obituary *27*
Sharpe, Mitchell R(aymond)
1924- *12*
Shaw, Arnold 1909- *4*
Shaw, Charles (Green)
1892-1974 .... *13*
Shaw, Evelyn 1927- *28*
Shaw, Flora Louisa
See Lugard, Flora Louisa Shaw
Shaw, Ray *7*
Shaw, Richard 1923- *12*
Shay, Arthur 1922- *4*
Shay, Lacey
See Shebar, Sharon Sigmond
Shea, George 1940-
Brief Entry *42*
Shearer, John 1947- *43*
Brief Entry *27*
Shearer, Ted 1919- *43*
Shebar, Sharon Sigmond
1945- *36*
Shecter, Ben 1935- *16*
Sheedy, Alexandra (Elizabeth)
1962- *39*
Earlier sketch in SATA 19
Sheedy, Ally
See Sheedy, Alexandra (Elizabeth)
Sheehan, Ethna 1908- *9*
Sheffield, Janet N. 1926- *26*
Shekerjian, Regina Tor *16*
Sheldon, Ann [Collective
pseudonym] *1*
Sheldon, Aure 1917-1976 .... *12*
Sheldon, Muriel 1926- *45*
Brief Entry *39*
Shelley, Mary Wollstonecraft
(Godwin) 1797-1851 .... *29*
Shelton, William Roy 1919- *5*
Shemin, Margaretha 1928- *4*
Shenton, Edward 1895-1977 ...... *45*
Shepard, Ernest Howard
1879-1976 .... *33*
Obituary *24*
Earlier sketch in SATA 3
Shepard, Mary
See Knox, (Mary) Eleanor Jessie
Shephard, Esther 1891-1975 ...... *5*
Obituary *26*
Shepherd, Elizabeth *4*
Sherburne, Zoa 1912- *3*
Sherman, D(enis) R(onald) 1934-
Brief Entry *29*

Sherman, Diane (Finn) 1928- *12*
Sherman, Elizabeth
  See Friskey, Margaret Richards
Sherman, Harold (Morrow)
  1898- *37*
Sherman, Nancy
  See Rosenberg, Nancy Sherman
Sherrod, Jane
  See Singer, Jane Sherrod
Sherry, (Dulcie) Sylvia 1932- *8*
Sherwan, Earl 1917- *3*
Shiefman, Vicky *22*
Shields, Brenda Desmond (Armstrong)
  1914- *37*
Shields, Charles 1944- *10*
Shimin, Symeon 1902- *13*
Shinn, Everett 1876-1953 ..... *21*
Shippen, Katherine B(inney)
  1892-1980 ..... *1*
  Obituary *23*
Shipton, Eric 1907- *10*
Shirer, William L(awrence)
  1904- *45*
Shirreffs, Gordon D(onald)
  1914- *11*
Sholokhov, Mikhail A. 1905-1984
  Obituary *36*
Shore, June Lewis *30*
Shore, Robert 1924- *39*
Shortall, Leonard W. *19*
Shotwell, Louisa R. 1902- *3*
Showalter, Jean B(reckinridge) *12*
Showell, Ellen Harvey 1934- *33*
Showers, Paul C. 1910- *21*
  See also CLR 6
Shreve, Susan Richards 1939-
  Brief Entry *41*
Shtainmets, Leon *32*
Shub, Elizabeth *5*
Shulevitz, Uri 1935- *3*
  See also CLR 5
Shulman, Alix Kates 1932- *7*
Shulman, Irving 1913- *13*
Shumsky, Zena
  See Collier, Zena
Shura, Mary Francis
  See Craig, Mary Francis
Shuttlesworth, Dorothy *3*
Shyer, Marlene Fanta *13*
Siberell, Anne *29*
Sibley, Don 1922- *12*
Siculan, Daniel 1922- *12*
Sidjakov, Nicolas 1924- *18*
Sidney, Frank [Joint pseudonym]
  See Warwick, Alan R(oss)
Sidney, Margaret
  See Lothrop, Harriet Mulford Stone
Siebel, Fritz (Frederick) 1913-
  Brief Entry *44*
Siegal, Aranka 1930-
  Brief Entry *37*
Siegel, Beatrice *36*
Siegel, Helen
  See Siegl, Helen
Siegel, Robert (Harold) 1939- *39*
Siegl, Helen 1924- *34*
Silas
  See McCay, Winsor
Silcock, Sara Lesley 1947- *12*

Silver, Ruth
  See Chew, Ruth
Silverberg, Robert *13*
Silverman, Mel(vin Frank)
  1931-1966 ..... *9*
Silverstein, Alvin 1933- *8*
Silverstein, Shel(by) 1932- *33*
  Brief Entry *27*
  See also CLR 5
Silverstein, Virginia B(arbara
  Opshelor) 1937- *8*
Silverthorne, Elizabeth 1930- *35*
Simon, Charlie May
  See Fletcher, Charlie May
Simon, Hilda (Rita) 1921- *28*
Simon, Howard 1903-1979 ..... *32*
  Obituary *21*
Simon, Joe
  See Simon, Joseph H.
Simon, Joseph H. 1913- *7*
Simon, Martin P(aul William)
  1903-1969 ..... *12*
Simon, Mina Lewiton
  See Lewiton, Mina
Simon, Norma 1927- *3*
Simon, Seymour 1931- *4*
  See also CLR 9
Simon, Shirley (Schwartz)
  1921- *11*
Simon, Solomon 1895-1970 ..... *40*
Simonetta, Linda 1948- *14*
Simonetta, Sam 1936- *14*
Simons, Barbara B(rooks)
  1934- *41*
Simont, Marc 1915- *9*
Simpson, Colin 1908- *14*
Simpson, Myrtle L(illias)
  1931- *14*
Sinclair, Clover
  See Gater, Dilys
Sinclair, Upton (Beall)
  1878-1968 ..... *9*
Singer, Isaac Bashevis 1904- *27*
  Earlier sketch in SATA 3
  See also CLR 1
Singer, Jane Sherrod
  1917-1985 ..... *4*
  Obituary *42*
Singer, Julia 1917- *28*
Singer, Kurt D(eutsch) 1911- *38*
Singer, Marilyn 1948-
  Brief Entry *38*
Singer, Susan (Mahler) 1941- *9*
Sirof, Harriet 1930- *37*
Sisson, Rosemary Anne 1923- *11*
Sitomer, Harry 1903- *31*
Sitomer, Mindel 1903- *31*
Sive, Helen R. 1951- *30*
Sivulich, Sandra (Jeanne) Stoner
  1941- *9*
Skelly, James R(ichard) 1927- *17*
Skinner, Constance Lindsay
  1882-1939 ..... *YABC 1*
Skinner, Cornelia Otis 1901- *2*
Skipper, G. C. 1939-
  Brief Entry *38*
Skofield, James
  Brief Entry *44*
Skold, Betty Westrom 1923- *41*

Skorpen, Liesel Moak 1935- *3*
Skurzynski, Gloria (Joan)
  1930- *8*
Slackman, Charles B. 1934- *12*
Slade, Richard 1910-1971 ..... *9*
Slate, Joseph (Frank) 1928- *38*
Slater, Jim 1929-
  Brief Entry *34*
Slaughter, Jean
  See Doty, Jean Slaughter
Sleator, William 1945- *3*
Sleigh, Barbara 1906-1982 ..... *3*
  Obituary *30*
Slepian, Jan(ice B.) 1921-
  Brief Entry *45*
Slicer, Margaret O. 1920- *4*
Sloane, Eric 1910(?)-1985
  Obituary *42*
Slobodkin, Florence (Gersh)
  1905- *5*
Slobodkin, Louis 1903-1975 ..... *26*
  Earlier sketch in SATA 1
Slobodkina, Esphyr 1909- *1*
Sloggett, Nellie 1851-1923 ..... *44*
Slote, Alfred 1926- *8*
  See also CLR 4
Small, Ernest
  See Lent, Blair
Smallwood, Norah (Evelyn)
  1910(?)-1984
  Obituary *41*
Smaridge, Norah 1903- *6*
Smiley, Virginia Kester 1923- *2*
Smith, Anne Warren 1938- *41*
  Brief Entry *34*
Smith, Beatrice S(chillinger) *12*
Smith, Betsy Covington 1937-
  Brief Entry *43*
Smith, Betty 1896-1972 ..... *6*
Smith, Bradford 1909-1964 ..... *5*
Smith, Caesar
  See Trevor, Elleston
Smith, Datus C(lifford), Jr.
  1907- *13*
Smith, Dodie *4*
Smith, Doris Buchanan 1934- *28*
Smith, Dorothy Stafford
  1905- *6*
Smith, E(lmer) Boyd
  1860-1943 ..... *YABC 1*
Smith, E(dric) Brooks 1917- *40*
Smith, Elva S(ophronia) 1871-1965
  Brief Entry *31*
Smith, Emma 1923-
  Brief Entry *36*
Smith, Eunice Young 1902- *5*
Smith, Frances C. 1904- *3*
Smith, Fredrika Shumway 1877-1968
  Brief Entry *30*
Smith, Gary R(ichard) 1932- *14*
Smith, George Harmon 1920- *5*
Smith, H(arry) Allen 1907-1976
  Obituary *20*
Smith, Howard Everett, Jr.
  1927- *12*
Smith, Hugh L(etcher)
  1921-1968 ..... *5*
Smith, Imogene Henderson
  1922- *12*

Smith, Jacqueline B. 1937- *39*
Smith, Jean
  See Smith, Frances C.
Smith, Jean Pajot 1945- *10*
Smith, Jessie Willcox
  1863-1935 .... *21*
Smith, Jim 1920-
  Brief Entry *36*
Smith, Johnston
  See Crane, Stephen (Townley)
Smith, Lafayette
  See Higdon, Hal
Smith, Lee
  See Albion, Lee Smith
Smith, Lillian H(elena) 1887-1983
  Obituary *32*
Smith, Linell Nash 1932- *2*
Smith, Lucia B. 1943- *30*
Smith, Marion Hagens 1913- *12*
Smith, Marion Jaques 1899- *13*
Smith, Mary Ellen *10*
Smith, Mike
  See Smith, Mary Ellen
Smith, Nancy Covert 1935- *12*
Smith, Norman F. 1920- *5*
Smith, Pauline C(oggeshall)
  1908- *27*
Smith, Robert Kimmel 1930- *12*
Smith, Robert Paul 1915-1977
  Obituary *30*
Smith, Ruth Leslie 1902- *2*
Smith, Samantha 1972-1985
  Obituary *45*
Smith, Sarah Stafford
  See Smith, Dorothy Stafford
Smith, Susan Carlton 1923- *12*
Smith, Susan Mathias 1950- *43*
  Brief Entry *35*
Smith, Vian (Crocker)
  1919-1969 .... *11*
Smith, Ward
  See Goldsmith, Howard
Smith, William A. *10*
Smith, William Jay 1918- *2*
Smith, Winsome 1935- *45*
Smith, Z. Z.
  See Westheimer, David
Smits, Teo
  See Smits, Theodore R(ichard)
Smits, Theodore R(ichard)
  1905- *45*
  Brief Entry *28*
Smucker, Barbara (Claassen)
  1915- *29*
  See also CLR 10
Snedeker, Caroline Dale (Parke)
  1871-1956 ....*YABC 2*
Snell, Nigel (Edward Creagh) 1936-
  Brief Entry *40*
Sneve, Virginia Driving Hawk
  1933- *8*
  See also CLR 2
Sniff, Mr.
  See Abisch, Roslyn Kroop
Snodgrass, Thomas Jefferson
  See Clemens, Samuel Langhorne
Snook, Barbara (Lillian)
  1913-1976 .... *34*
Snow, Donald Clifford 1917- *16*

Snow, Dorothea J(ohnston)
  1909- *9*
Snow, Richard F(olger) 1947-
  Brief Entry *37*
Snyder, Anne 1922- *4*
Snyder, Carol 1941- *35*
Snyder, Gerald S(eymour) 1933-
  Brief Entry *34*
Snyder, Jerome 1916-1976
  Obituary *20*
Snyder, Zilpha Keatley 1927- *28*
  Earlier sketch in SATA 1
  See also SAAS 2
Snyderman, Reuven K. 1922- *5*
Soble, Jennie
  See Cavin, Ruth (Brodie)
Sobol, Donald J. 1924- *31*
  Earlier sketch in SATA 1
  See also CLR 4
Sobol, Harriet Langsam 1936-
  Brief Entry *34*
Soderlind, Arthur E(dwin)
  1920- *14*
Softly, Barbara (Frewin)
  1924- *12*
Soglow, Otto 1900-1975
  Obituary *30*
Sohl, Frederic J(ohn) 1916- *10*
Sokol, Bill
  See Sokol, William
Sokol, William 1923- *37*
Sokolov, Kirill 1930- *34*
Solbert, Romaine G. 1925- *2*
Solbert, Ronni
  See Solbert, Romaine G.
Solomon, Joan 1930(?)-
  Brief Entry *40*
Solomons, Ikey, Esquire, Jr.
  See Thackeray, William Makepeace
Solonevich, George 1915- *15*
Solot, Mary Lynn 1939- *12*
Sommer, Elyse 1929- *7*
Sommer, Robert 1929- *12*
Sommerfelt, Aimee 1892- *5*
Sonneborn, Ruth (Cantor) A.
  1899-1974 .... *4*
  Obituary *27*
Sorche, Nic Leodhas
  See Alger, Leclaire (Gowans)
Sorel, Edward 1929-
  Brief Entry *37*
Sorensen, Virginia 1912- *2*
Sorley Walker, Kathrine *41*
Sorrentino, Joseph N. *6*
Sortor, June Elizabeth 1939- *12*
Sortor, Toni
  See Sortor, June Elizabeth
Soskin, V. H.
  See Ellison, Virginia Howell
Sotomayor, Antonio 1902- *11*
Soudley, Henry
  See Wood, James Playsted
Soule, Gardner (Bosworth)
  1913- *14*
Soule, Jean Conder 1919- *10*
Southall, Ivan 1921- *3*
  See also CLR 2
Spanfeller, James J(ohn)
  1930- *19*

Spangenberg, Judith Dunn
  1942- *5*
Spar, Jerome 1918- *10*
Sparks, Beatrice Mathews
  1918- *44*
  Brief Entry *28*
Sparks, Mary W. 1920- *15*
Spaulding, Leonard
  See Bradbury, Ray
Speare, Elizabeth George
  1908- *5*
  See also CLR 8
Spearing, Judith (Mary Harlow)
  1922- *9*
Specking, Inez 1890-196(?) *11*
Speicher, Helen Ross (Smith)
  1915- *8*
Spellman, John W(illard)
  1934- *14*
Spelman, Mary 1934- *28*
Spence, Eleanor (Rachel)
  1927- *21*
Spencer, Ann 1918- *10*
Spencer, Cornelia
  See Yaukey, Grace S.
Spencer, Donald D(ean) 1931- *41*
Spencer, Elizabeth 1921- *14*
Spencer, William 1922- *9*
Spencer, Zane A(nn) 1935- *35*
Sperry, Armstrong W.
  1897-1976 .... *1*
  Obituary *27*
Sperry, Raymond, Jr. [Collective
  pseudonym] *1*
Spicer, Dorothy (Gladys)
  (?)-1975 .... *32*
Spiegelman, Judith M. *5*
Spielberg, Steven 1947- *32*
Spier, Peter (Edward) 1927- *4*
  See also CLR 5
Spilhaus, Athelstan 1911- *13*
Spilka, Arnold 1917- *6*
Spinelli, Eileen 1942- *38*
Spinelli, Jerry 1941- *39*
Spink, Reginald (William)
  1905- *11*
Spinner, Stephanie 1943- *38*
Spinossimus
  See White, William
Splaver, Sarah 1921-
  Brief Entry *28*
Spollen, Christopher 1952- *12*
Sprague, Gretchen (Burnham)
  1926- *27*
Sprigge, Elizabeth 1900-1974 ..... *10*
Spring, (Robert) Howard
  1889-1965 .... *28*
Springstubb, Tricia 1950-
  Brief Entry *40*
Spykman, E(lizabeth) C.
  19(?)-1965 .... *10*
Spyri, Johanna (Heusser)
  1827-1901 .... *19*
Squire, Miriam
  See Sprigge, Elizabeth
Squires, Phil
  See Barker, S. Omar
S-Ringi, Kjell
  See Ringi, Kjell

Srivastava, Jane Jonas
   Brief Entry 37
Stadtler, Bea 1921- 17
Stafford, Jean 1915-1979
   Obituary 22
Stahl, Ben(jamin) 1910- 5
Stair, Gobin (John) 1912- 35
Stalder, Valerie 27
Stamaty, Mark Alan 1947- 12
Stambler, Irwin 1924- 5
Stanek, Muriel (Novella) 1915-
   Brief Entry 34
Stang, Judit 1921-1977 29
Stang, Judy
   See Stang, Judit
Stanhope, Eric
   See Hamilton, Charles H. St. John
Stankevich, Boris 1928- 2
Stanley, Diana 1909-
   Brief Entry 30
Stanley, Diane 1943- 37
   Brief Entry 32
Stanley, Robert
   See Hamilton, Charles H. St. John
Stanli, Sue
   See Meilach, Dona Z(weigoron)
Stanstead, John
   See Groom, Arthur William
Stapleton, Marjorie (Winifred)
   1932- 28
Stapp, Arthur D(onald)
   1906-1972 4
Starbird, Kaye 1916- 6
Stark, James
   See Goldston, Robert
Starkey, Marion L. 1901- 13
Starr, Ward and Murch, Mel [Joint
   double pseudonym]
   See Manes, Stephen
Starret, William
   See McClintock, Marshall
Stauffer, Don
   See Berkebile, Fred D(onovan)
Staunton, Schuyler
   See Baum, L(yman) Frank
Steadman, Ralph (Idris) 1936- 32
Stearns, Monroe (Mather)
   1913- 5
Steele, Chester K.
   See Stratemeyer, Edward L.
Steele, Mary Q. 3
Steele, (Henry) Max(well)
   1922- 10
Steele, William O(wen)
   1917-1979 1
   Obituary 27
Steig, William 1907- 18
   See also CLR 2
Stein, Harvé 1904-
   Brief Entry 30
Stein, M(eyer) L(ewis) 6
Stein, Mini 2
Stein, R(ichard) Conrad 1937- 31
Stein, Sara Bonnett
   Brief Entry 34
Steinbeck, John (Ernst)
   1902-1968 9
Steinberg, Alfred 1917- 9
Steinberg, Fannie 1899- 43

Steinberg, Fred J. 1933- 4
Steinberg, Phillip Orso 1921- 34
Steinberg, Rafael (Mark)
   1927- 45
Steiner, Barbara A(nnette)
   1934- 13
Steiner, Charlotte 1900-1981 45
Steiner, Jörg 1930- 35
Steiner, Stan(ley) 1925- 14
Steiner-Prag, Hugo 1880-1945
   Brief Entry 32
Stephens, Mary Jo 1935- 8
Stephens, William M(cLain)
   1925- 21
Stephensen, A. M.
   See Manes, Stephen
Stepp, Ann 1935- 29
Steptoe, John (Lewis) 1950- 8
   See also CLR 2
Sterling, Dorothy 1913- 1
   See also CLR 1
   See also SAAS 2
Sterling, Helen
   See Hoke, Helen (L.)
Sterling, Philip 1907- 8
Stern, Ellen N(orman) 1927- 26
Stern, Madeleine B(ettina)
   1912- 14
Stern, Philip Van Doren
   1900-1984 13
   Obituary 39
Stern, Simon 1943- 15
Sterne, Emma Gelders
   1894-1971 6
Steurt, Marjorie Rankin 1888- 10
Stevens, Carla M(cBride)
   1928- 13
Stevens, Franklin 1933- 6
Stevens, Gwendolyn 1944- 33
Stevens, Patricia Bunning
   1931- 27
Stevens, Peter
   See Geis, Darlene
Stevenson, Anna (M.) 1905- 12
Stevenson, Augusta
   1869(?)-1976 2
   Obituary 26
Stevenson, Burton E(gbert)
   1872-1962 25
Stevenson, James 1929- 42
   Brief Entry 34
Stevenson, Janet 1913- 8
Stevenson, Robert Louis
   1850-1894 .... YABC 2
   See also CLR 10
Stewart, A(gnes) C(harlotte) 15
Stewart, Charles
   See Zurhorst, Charles (Stewart, Jr.)
Stewart, Elizabeth Laing
   1907- 6
Stewart, George Rippey
   1895-1980 3
   Obituary 23
Stewart, John (William) 1920- 14
Stewart, Mary (Florence Elinor)
   1916- 12
Stewart, Robert Neil
   1891-1972 7

Stewart, Scott
   See Zaffo, George J.
Stewig, John Warren 1937- 26
Stiles, Martha Bennett 6
Stiles, Norman B. 1942-
   Brief Entry 36
Still, James 1906- 29
Stillerman, Robbie 1947- 12
Stilley, Frank 1918- 29
Stine, G(eorge) Harry 1928- 10
Stine, Jovial Bob
   See Stine, Robert Lawrence
Stine, Robert Lawrence 1943- 31
Stinetorf, Louise 1900- 10
Stirling, Arthur
   See Sinclair, Upton (Beall)
Stirling, Nora B. 3
Stirnweis, Shannon 1931- 10
Stobbs, William 1914- 17
Stockton, Francis Richard
   1834-1902 44
Stockton, Frank R(ichard)
   Brief Entry 32
   See Stockton, Francis Richard
Stoddard, Edward G. 1923- 10
Stoddard, Hope 1900- 6
Stoddard, Sandol
   See Warburg, Sandol Stoddard
Stoiko, Michael 1919- 14
Stoker, Abraham 1847-1912 29
Stoker, Bram
   See Stoker, Abraham
Stokes, Cedric
   See Beardmore, George
Stokes, Jack (Tilden) 1923- 13
Stokes, Olivia Pearl 1916- 32
Stolz, Mary (Slattery) 1920- 10
Stone, Alan [Collective
   pseudonym] 1
   See also Svenson, Andrew E.
Stone, D(avid) K(arl) 1922- 9
Stone, Eugenia 1879-1971 7
Stone, Gene
   See Stone, Eugenia
Stone, Helen V. 6
Stone, Irving 1903- 3
Stone, Jon 1931- 39
Stone, Josephine Rector
   See Dixon, Jeanne
Stone, Raymond [Collective
   pseudonym] 1
Stone, Richard A.
   See Stratemeyer, Edward L.
Stonehouse, Bernard 1926- 13
Stong, Phil(ip Duffield)
   1899-1957 32
Storch, Anne B. von
   See von Storch, Anne B.
Storey, (Elizabeth) Margaret (Carlton)
   1926- 9
Storey, Victoria Carolyn
   1945- 16
Storme, Peter
   See Stern, Philip Van Doren
Storr, Catherine (Cole) 1913- 9
Stoutenburg, Adrien 1916- 3
Stover, Allan C(arl) 1938- 14
Stover, Marjorie Filley 1914- 9

Stowe, Harriet (Elizabeth) Beecher
  1811-1896 ....*YABC 1*
Strachan, Margaret Pitcairn
  1908- *14*
Strait, Treva Adams 1909- *35*
Strand, Mark 1934- *41*
Strange, Philippa
  See Coury, Louise Andree
Stranger, Joyce
  See Wilson, Joyce M(uriel Judson)
Strasser, Todd 1950- *45*
  Brief Entry *41*
Stratemeyer, Edward L.
  1862-1930 .... *1*
Stratton, Thomas [Joint pseudonym]
  See DeWeese, Thomas Eugene
Stratton-Porter, Gene
  1863-1924 .... *15*
Strayer, E. Ward
  See Stratemeyer, Edward L.
Streano, Vince(nt Catello)
  1945- *20*
Streatfeild, Noel 1897- *20*
Street, Julia Montgomery
  1898- *11*
Stren, Patti 1949-
  Brief Entry *41*
  See also CLR 5
Strete, Craig Kee 1950- *44*
Stretton, Barbara (Humphrey)
  1936- *43*
  Brief Entry *35*
Strong, Charles [Joint pseudonym]
  See Epstein, Beryl and Epstein,
  Samuel
Strong, David
  See McGuire, Leslie (Sarah)
Strong, J. J.
  See Strong, Jeremy
Strong, Jeremy 1949- *36*
Ströyer, Poul 1923- *13*
Stuart, David
  See Hoyt, Edwin P(almer), Jr.
Stuart, Forbes 1924- *13*
Stuart, Ian
  See MacLean, Alistair (Stuart)
Stuart, (Hilton) Jesse
  1907-1984 .... *2*
  Obituary *36*
Stuart, Sheila
  See Baker, Mary Gladys Steel
Stuart-Clark, Christopher
  1940- *32*
Stubis, Talivaldis 1926- *5*
Stubley, Trevor (Hugh) 1932- *22*
Stultifer, Morton
  See Curtis, Richard (Alan)
Sture-Vasa, Mary
  See Alsop, Mary O'Hara
Sturton, Hugh
  See Johnston, H(ugh) A(nthony)
  S(tephen)
Sturtzel, Howard A(llison)
  1894- *1*
Sturtzel, Jane Levington
  1903- *1*
Styles, Frank Showell 1908- *10*
Suba, Susanne *4*

Subond, Valerie
  See Grayland, Valerie
Sudbery, Rodie 1943- *42*
Sugarman, Tracy 1921- *37*
Sugita, Yutaka 1930- *36*
Suhl, Yuri 1908- *8*
  See also CLR 2
  See also SAAS 1
Suid, Murray 1942- *27*
Sullivan, George E(dward)
  1927- *4*
Sullivan, Mary W(ilson)
  1907- *13*
Sullivan, Thomas Joseph, Jr.
  1947- *16*
Sullivan, Tom
  See Sullivan, Thomas Joseph, Jr.
Sumichrast, Józef 1948- *29*
Summers, James L(evingston) 1910-
  Brief Entry *28*
Sunderlin, Sylvia 1911- *28*
Sung, Betty Lee *26*
Supraner, Robyn 1930- *20*
Surge, Frank 1931- *13*
Susac, Andrew 1929- *5*
Sutcliff, Rosemary 1920- *44*
  Earlier sketch in SATA 6
  See also CLR 1
Sutherland, Efua (Theodora Morgue)
  1924- *25*
Sutherland, Margaret 1941- *15*
Sutherland, Zena B(ailey)
  1915- *37*
Suttles, Shirley (Smith) 1922- *21*
Sutton, Ann (Livesay) 1923- *31*
Sutton, Eve(lyn Mary) 1906- *26*
Sutton, Felix 1910(?)- *31*
Sutton, Jane 1950-
  Brief Entry *43*
Sutton, Larry M(atthew)
  1931- *29*
Sutton, Margaret (Beebe)
  1903- *1*
Sutton, Myron Daniel 1925- *31*
Svenson, Andrew E.
  1910-1975 .... *2*
  Obituary *26*
Swain, Su Zan (Noguchi)
  1916- *21*
Swan, Susan 1944- *22*
Swarthout, Glendon (Fred)
  1918- *26*
Swarthout, Kathryn 1919- *7*
Sweeney, James B(artholomew)
  1910- *21*
Sweeney, Karen O'Connor
  See O'Connor, Karen
Swenson, Allan A(rmstrong)
  1933- *21*
Swenson, May 1919- *15*
Swift, David
  See Kaufmann, John
Swift, Hildegarde Hoyt 1890(?)-1977
  Obituary *20*
Swift, Jonathan 1667-1745 .... *19*
Swift, Merlin
  See Leeming, Joseph
Swiger, Elinor Porter 1927- *8*
Swinburne, Laurence 1924- *9*

Swindells, Robert E(dward) 1939-
  Brief Entry *34*
Sydney, Frank [Joint pseudonym]
  See Warwick, Alan R(oss)
Sylvester, Natalie G(abry)
  1922- *22*
Syme, (Neville) Ronald 1913- *2*
Symons, (Dorothy) Geraldine
  1909- *33*
Synge, (Phyllis) Ursula 1930- *9*
Sypher, Lucy Johnston 1907- *7*
Szasz, Suzanne Shorr 1919- *13*
Szekeres, Cyndy 1933- *5*
Szulc, Tad 1926- *26*

T

Taback, Simms 1932- *40*
  Brief Entry *36*
Taber, Gladys (Bagg) 1899-1980
  Obituary *22*
Tabrah, Ruth Milander 1921- *14*
Tafuri, Nancy 1946- *39*
Tait, Douglas 1944- *12*
Takakjian, Portia 1930- *15*
Takashima, Shizuye 1928- *13*
Talbot, Charlene Joy 1928- *10*
Talbot, Toby 1928- *14*
Talker, T.
  See Rands, William Brighty
Tallcott, Emogene *10*
Tallon, Robert 1939- *43*
  Brief Entry *28*
Talmadge, Marian *14*
Tamarin, Alfred *13*
Tamburine, Jean 1930- *12*
Tannen, Mary 1943- *37*
Tannenbaum, Beulah 1916- *3*
Tannenbaum, D(onald) Leb
  1948- *42*
Tanner, Louise S(tickney)
  1922- *9*
Tanobe, Miyuki 1937- *23*
Tapio, Pat Decker
  See Kines, Pat Decker
Tarkington, (Newton) Booth
  1869-1946 .... *17*
Tarry, Ellen 1906- *16*
Tarshis, Jerome 1936- *9*
Tarsky, Sue 1946- *41*
Tashjian, Virginia A. 1921- *3*
Tasker, James *9*
Tate, Eleanora E(laine) 1948- *38*
Tate, Ellalice
  See Hibbert, Eleanor
Tate, Joan 1922- *9*
Tatham, Campbell
  See Elting, Mary
Taves, Isabella 1915- *27*
Taylor, Ann 1782-1866 .... *41*
  Brief Entry *35*
Taylor, Barbara J. 1927- *10*
Taylor, Carl 1937- *14*
Taylor, David 1900-1965 .... *10*
Taylor, Elizabeth 1912-1975 ...... *13*
Taylor, Florence Walton *9*
Taylor, Florence M(arion Tompkins)
  1892- *9*

Author Index

Taylor, Herb(ert Norman, Jr.)
  1942- 22
Taylor, Jane 1783-1824 .... *41*
  Brief Entry 35
Taylor, Kenneth N(athaniel)
  1917- 26
Taylor, L(ester) B(arbour), Jr.
  1932- 27
Taylor, Mark 1927- *32*
  Brief Entry 28
Taylor, Mildred D. 15
  See also CLR 9
Taylor, Paula (Wright) 1942-
  Brief Entry 33
Taylor, Robert Lewis 1912- 10
Taylor, Sydney (Brenner)
  1904(?)-1978 28
  Obituary 26
  Earlier sketch in SATA 1
Taylor, Theodore 1924- 5
Teague, Bob
  See Teague, Robert
Teague, Robert 1929- *32*
  Brief Entry 31
Teal, Val 1903- 10
Teale, Edwin Way 1899-1980 7
  Obituary 25
Teasdale, Sara 1884-1933 .... *32*
Tebbel, John (William) 1912- 26
Tee-Van, Helen Damrosch
  1893-1976 10
  Obituary 27
Teleki, Geza 1943- 45
Telemaque, Eleanor Wong
  1934- 43
Telescope, Tom
  See Newbery, John
Temkin, Sara Anne (Schlossberg)
  1913- 26
Temko, Florence *13*
Tempest, Margaret Mary 1892-1982
  Obituary 33
Templar, Maurice
  See Groom, Arthur William
Temple, Herbert 1919- 45
Temple, Paul [Joint pseudonym]
  See McConnell, James Douglas
    (Rutherford)
Tenggren, Gustaf 1896-1970 ...... *18*
  Obituary 26
Tennant, Kylie 1912- 6
Tennant, Veronica 1946- 36
Tenniel, Sir John 1820-1914
  Brief Entry 27
Terban, Marvin
  Brief Entry 45
ter Haar, Jaap 1922- 6
Terhune, Albert Payson
  1872-1942 15
Terlouw, Jan (Cornelis) 1931- 30
Terris, Susan 1937- 3
Terry, Luther L(eonidas)
  1911-1985 11
  Obituary 42
Terry, Walter 1913- 14
Terzian, James P. 1915- 14
Tester, Sylvia Root 1939-
  Brief Entry 37

Tether, (Cynthia) Graham 1950-
  Brief Entry 36
Thacher, Mary McGrath
  1933- 9
Thackeray, William Makepeace
  1811-1863 23
Thamer, Katie 1955- 42
Thane, Elswyth 1900- 32
Tharp, Louise Hall 1898- 3
Thayer, Jane
  See Woolley, Catherine
Thayer, Marjorie
  Brief Entry 37
Thayer, Peter
  See Wyler, Rose
Thelwell, Norman 1923- *14*
Theroux, Paul 1941- 44
Thieda, Shirley Ann 1943- *13*
Thiele, Colin (Milton) 1920- *14*
  See also SAAS 2
Thiry, Joan (Marie) 1926- 45
Thistlethwaite, Miles 1945- *12*
Thollander, Earl 1922- 22
Thomas, Andrea
  See Hill, Margaret (Ohler)
Thomas, Art(hur Lawrence) 1952-
  Brief Entry 38
Thomas, Estelle Webb 1899- 26
Thomas, H. C.
  See Keating, Lawrence A.
Thomas, Ianthe 1951-
  Brief Entry 42
  See also CLR 8
Thomas, J. F.
  See Fleming, Thomas J(ames)
Thomas, Jane Resh 1936- 38
Thomas, Joan Gale
  See Robinson, Joan G.
Thomas, Joyce Carol 1938- 40
Thomas, Lowell (Jackson), Jr.
  1923- 15
Thomas, Victoria [Joint pseudonym]
  See DeWeese, Thomas Eugene
Thompson, Brenda 1935- 34
Thompson, Christine Pullein
  See Pullein-Thompson, Christine
Thompson, David H(ugh)
  1941- 17
Thompson, Diana Pullein
  See Pullein-Thompson, Diana
Thompson, George Selden
  1929- 4
Thompson, Harlan H. 1894- 10
Thompson, Josephine
  See Pullein-Thompson, Josephine
Thompson, Julian F(rancis) 1927-
  Brief Entry 40
Thompson, Kay 1912- *16*
Thompson, Stith 1885-1976
  Obituary 20
Thompson, Vivian L. 1911- 3
Thomson, David (Robert Alexander)
  1914- 40
Thomson, Peggy 1922- *31*
Thorndyke, Helen Louise
  [Collective pseudonym] 1
Thorne, Ian
  See May, Julian

Thornton, W. B.
  See Burgess, Thornton Waldo
Thorpe, E(ustace) G(eorge)
  1916- *21*
Thorvall, Kerstin 1925- *13*
Thrasher, Crystal (Faye)
  1921- 27
Thum, Gladys 1920- 26
Thum, Marcella 28
  Earlier sketch in SATA 3
Thundercloud, Katherine
  See Witt, Shirley Hill
Thurber, James (Grover)
  1894-1961 .... *13*
Thurman, Judith 1946- 33
Thwaite, Ann (Barbara Harrop)
  1932- *14*
Ticheburn, Cheviot
  See Ainsworth, William Harrison
Tichenor, Tom 1923- *14*
Tichy, William 1924- *31*
Tiegreen, Alan F. 1935-
  Brief Entry 36
Tilton, Madonna Elaine 1929- 41
Tilton, Rafael
  See Tilton, Madonna Elaine
Timmins, William F. 10
Tiner, John Hudson 1944- *32*
Tinkelman, Murray 1933- *12*
Tinkle, (Julien) Lon
  1906-1980 36
Titler, Dale M(ilton) 1926- 35
  Brief Entry 28
Titmarsh, Michael Angelo
  See Thackeray, William Makepeace
Titus, Eve 1922- 2
Tobias, Tobi 1938- 5
  See also CLR 4
Todd, Anne Ophelia
  See Dowden, Anne Ophelia
Todd, Barbara K. 1917- 10
Todd, H(erbert) E(atton)
  1908- *11*
Todd, Loreto 1942- 30
Tolan, Stephanie S. 1942- 38
Toland, John (Willard) 1912- 38
Tolkien, J(ohn) R(onald) R(euel)
  1892-1973 .... *32*
  Obituary 24
  Earlier sketch in SATA 2
Tolles, Martha 1921- 8
Tolliver, Ruby C(hangos) 1922-
  Brief Entry 41
Tolmie, Ken(neth Donald)
  1941- 15
Tolstoi, Leo (Nikolaevich)
  1828-1910 26
Tomalin, Ruth 29
Tomes, Margot (Ladd) 1917- *36*
  Brief Entry 27
Tomfool
  See Farjeon, Eleanor
Tomkins, Jasper
  See Batey, Tom
Tomline, F. Latour
  See Gilbert, W(illiam) S(chwenk)
Tomlinson, Jill 1931-1976 3
  Obituary 24

Tomlinson, Reginald R(obert)
   1885-1979(?)
   Obituary 27
Tompert, Ann 1918- 14
Toner, Raymond John 1908- 10
Took, Belladonna
   See Chapman, Vera
Tooke, Louise Mathews 1950- 38
Toonder, Martin
   See Groom, Arthur William
Toothaker, Roy Eugene 1928- 18
Tooze, Ruth 1892-1972 4
Topping, Audrey R(onning)
   1928- 14
Tor, Regina
   See Shekerjian, Regina Tor
Torbert, Floyd James 1922- 22
Torgersen, Don Arthur 1934-
   Brief Entry 41
Torrie, Malcolm
   See Mitchell, Gladys (Maude
   Winifred)
Totham, Mary
   See Breinburg, Petronella
Tournier, Michel 1924- 23
Towne, Mary
   See Spelman, Mary
Townsend, John Rowe 1922- 4
   See also CLR 2
   See also SAAS 2
Toye, Clive 1933(?)-
   Brief Entry 30
Toye, William E(ldred) 1926- 8
Traherne, Michael
   See Watkins-Pitchford, D. J.
Trahey, Jane 1923- 36
Trapp, Maria (Augusta) von
   1905- 16
Travers, P(amela) L(yndon)
   1906- 4
   See also CLR 2
   See also SAAS 2
Trease, (Robert) Geoffrey
   1909- 2
Tredez, Alain 1926- 17
Treece, Henry 1911-1966 2
   See also CLR 2
Tregarthen, Enys
   See Sloggett, Nellie
Tregaskis, Richard 1916-1973 3
   Obituary 26
Trell, Max 1900- 14
Tremain, Ruthven 1922- 17
Trent, Robbie 1894- 26
Trent, Timothy
   See Malmberg, Carl
Tresilian, (Cecil) Stuart
   1891-19(?) 40
Tresselt, Alvin 1916- 7
Treviño, Elizabeth B(orton) de
   1904- 29
   Earlier sketch in SATA 1
Trevor, Elleston 1920- 28
Trevor, Glen
   See Hilton, James
Trevor, (Lucy) Meriol 1919- 10
Trez, Alain
   See Tredez, Alain

Trimby, Elisa 1948-
   Brief Entry 40
Tripp, Eleanor B. 1936- 4
Tripp, Paul 8
Tripp, Wallace (Whitney)
   1940- 31
Trivett, Daphne (Harwood)
   1940- 22
Trnka, Jiri 1912-1969 43
   Brief Entry 32
Trollope, Anthony 1815-1882 22
Trost, Lucille Wood 1938- 12
Trotter, Grace V(iolet) 1900- 10
Troughton, Joanna (Margaret)
   1947- 37
Troyer, Johannes 1902-1969
   Brief Entry 40
Trudeau, G(arretson) B(eekman)
   1948- 35
Trudeau, Garry B.
   See Trudeau, G(arretson) B(eekman)
Truesdell, Sue
   See Truesdell, Susan G.
Truesdell, Susan G.
   Brief Entry 45
Truss, Jan 1925- 35
Tucker, Caroline
   See Nolan, Jeannette
Tudor, Tasha 20
Tully, John (Kimberley)
   1923- 14
Tunis, Edwin (Burdett)
   1897-1973 28
   Obituary 24
   Earlier sketch in SATA 1
   See also CLR 2
Tunis, John R(oberts)
   1889-1975 37
   Brief Entry 30
Turkle, Brinton 1915- 2
Turlington, Bayly 1919- 5
Turnbull, Agnes Sligh 14
Turnbull, Ann (Christine)
   1943- 18
Turner, Alice K. 1940- 10
Turner, Ann W(arren) 1945- 14
Turner, Elizabeth
   1774-1846 ....YABC 2
Turner, Josie
   See Crawford, Phyllis
Turner, Philip 1925- 11
Turner, Sheila R.
   See Seed, Sheila Turner
Turngren, Annette 1902(?)-1980
   Obituary 23
Turngren, Ellen (?)-1964 3
Turska, Krystyna Zofia 1933- 31
   Brief Entry 27
Tusan, Stan 1936- 22
Tusiani, Joseph 1924- 45
Twain, Mark
   See Clemens, Samuel Langhorne
Tweedsmuir, Baron
   See Buchan, John
Tworkov, Jack 1900-1982
   Obituary 31
Tyler, Anne 1941- 7

U

Ubell, Earl 1926- 4
Uchida, Yoshiko 1921- 1
   See also CLR 6
   See also SAAS 1
Udall, Jan Beaney 1938- 10
Uden, (Bernard Gilbert) Grant
   1910- 26
Udry, Janice May 1928- 4
Ullman, James Ramsey
   1907-1971 7
Ulm, Robert 1934-1977 17
Ulyatt, Kenneth 1920- 14
Unada
   See Gliewe, Unada
Uncle Gus
   See Rey, H. A.
Uncle Mac
   See McCulloch, Derek (Ivor
   Breashur)
Uncle Ray
   See Coffman, Ramon Peyton
Uncle Shelby
   See Silverstein, Shel(by)
Underhill, Alice Mertie 1900-1971
Ungerer, (Jean) Thomas 1931- 33
   Earlier sketch in SATA 5
Ungerer, Tomi
   See Ungerer, (Jean) Thomas
   See also CLR 3
Unkelbach, Kurt 1913- 4
Unnerstad, Edith 1900- 3
Unrau, Ruth 1922- 9
Unstead, R(obert) J(ohn)
   1915- 12
Unsworth, Walt 1928- 4
Untermeyer, Louis 1885-1977 37
   Obituary 26
   Earlier sketch in SATA 2
Unwin, David S(torr) 1918- 14
Unwin, Nora S. 1907- 3
Usher, Margo Scegge
   See McHargue, Georgess
Uttley, Alice Jane (Taylor) 1884-1976
   Obituary 26
Uttley, Alison
   See Uttley, Alice Jane (Taylor)
Utz, Lois 1932- 5
Uzair, Salem ben
   See Horne, Richard Henry

V

Vaeth, J(oseph) Gordon 1921- 17
Valen, Nanine 1950- 21
Valencak, Hannelore 1929- 42
Valens, Evans G., Jr. 1920- 1
Van Abbé, Salaman
   1883-1955 18
Van Allsburg, Chris 1949- 37
   See also CLR 5
Van Anrooy, Francine 1924- 2
Van Anrooy, Frans
   See Van Anrooy, Francine
Vance, Eleanor Graham 1908- 11
Vance, Marguerite 1889-1965 29
Vandenburg, Mary Lou 1943- 17

Vander Boom, Mae M. *14*
Van der Veer, Judy
  1912-1982 .... *4*
  Obituary *33*
Vandivert, Rita (Andre) 1905- *21*
Van Duyn, Janet 1910- *18*
Van Dyne, Edith
  See Baum, L(yman) Frank
Van Horn, William 1939- *43*
Van Iterson, S(iny) R(ose) *26*
Van Leeuwen, Jean 1937- *6*
Van Lhin, Erik
  See Del Rey, Lester
Van Loon, Hendrik Willem
  1882-1944 .... *18*
Van Orden, M(erton) D(ick)
  1921- *4*
Van Rensselaer, Alexander (Taylor
  Mason) 1892-1962 .... *14*
Van Riper, Guernsey, Jr.
  1909- *3*
Van Steenwyk, Elizabeth Ann
  1928- *34*
Van Stockum, Hilda 1908- *5*
Van Tuyl, Barbara 1940- *11*
Van Vogt, A(lfred) E(lton)
  1912- *14*
Van Woerkom, Dorothy (O'Brien)
  1924- *21*
Van Wormer, Joe
  See Van Wormer, Joseph Edward
Van Wormer, Joseph Edward
  1913- *35*
Van-Wyck Mason, F.
  See Mason, F. van Wyck
Van Zwienen, Ilse (Charlotte Koehn)
  1929- *34*
  Brief Entry *28*
Varga, Judy
  See Stang, Judit
Varley, Dimitry V. 1906- *10*
Vasiliu, Mircea 1920- *2*
Vass, George 1927-
  Brief Entry *31*
Vaughan, Carter A.
  See Gerson, Noel B(ertram)
Vaughan, Harold Cecil 1923- *14*
Vaughan, Sam(uel) S. 1928- *14*
Vaughn, Ruth 1935- *14*
Vavra, Robert James 1944- *8*
Vecsey, George 1939- *9*
Veglahn, Nancy (Crary) 1937- *5*
Venable, Alan (Hudson)
  1944- *8*
Venn, Mary Eleanor
  See Jorgensen, Mary Venn
Ventura, Piero (Luigi) 1937-
  Brief Entry *43*
Vequin, Capini
  See Quinn, Elisabeth
Verne, Jules 1828-1905 .... *21*
Verner, Gerald 1897(?)-1980
  Obituary *25*
Verney, John 1913- *14*
Vernon, (Elda) Louise A(nderson)
  1914- *14*
Vernor, D.
  See Casewit, Curtis
Verral, Charles Spain 1904- *11*

Verrone, Robert J. 1935(?)-1984
  Obituary *39*
Versace, Marie Teresa Rios
  1917- *2*
Vesey, Paul
  See Allen, Samuel (Washington)
Vestly, Anne-Cath(arina)
  1920- *14*
Vevers, (Henry) Gwynne
  1916- *45*
Viator, Vacuus
  See Hughes, Thomas
Vicarion, Count Palmiro
  See Logue, Christopher
Vicker, Angus
  See Felsen, Henry Gregor
Vickery, Kate
  See Kennedy, T(eresa) A.
Victor, Edward 1914- *3*
Victor, Joan Berg 1937- *30*
Viereck, Ellen K. 1928- *14*
Viereck, Phillip 1925- *3*
Viertel, Janet 1915- *10*
Vigna, Judith 1936- *15*
Viguers, Ruth Hill 1903-1971 ..... *6*
Villiard, Paul 1910-1974
  Obituary *20*
Villiers, Alan (John) 1903- *10*
Vincent, Eric Douglas 1953- *40*
Vincent, Félix 1946- *41*
Vincent, Mary Keith
  See St. John, Wylly Folk
Vinge, Joan D(ennison) 1948- *36*
Vining, Elizabeth Gray
  See Gray, Elizabeth Janet
Vinson, Kathryn 1911- *21*
Vinton, Iris *24*
Viorst, Judith *7*
  See also CLR 3
Vip
  See Partch, Virgil Franklin II
Visser, W(illiam) F(rederick)
  H(endrik) 1900-1968 .... *10*
Vlahos, Olivia 1924- *31*
Vlasic, Bob
  See Hirsch, Phil
Vo-Dinh, Mai 1933- *16*
Vogel, Ilse-Margret 1914- *14*
Vogel, John H(ollister), Jr.
  1950- *18*
Vogt, Esther Loewen 1915- *14*
Vogt, Gregory
  Brief Entry *45*
Vogt, Marie Bollinger 1921- *45*
Voight, Virginia Frances
  1909- *8*
Voigt, Cynthia 1942-
  Brief Entry *33*
Voigt, Erna 1925- *35*
Voigt-Rother, Erna
  See Voigt, Erna
Vojtech, Anna 1946- *42*
von Almedingen, Martha Edith
  See Almedingen, E. M.
Von Hagen, Victor Wolfgang
  1908- *29*
von Klopp, Vahrah
  See Malvern, Gladys

Von Schmidt, Eric 1931-
  Brief Entry *36*
von Storch, Anne B. 1910- *1*
Vosburgh, Leonard (W.)
  1912- *15*
Voyle, Mary
  See Manning, Rosemary

W

Waber, Bernard 1924-
  Brief Entry *40*
Waddell, Evelyn Margaret
  1918- *10*
Waddell, Martin 1941- *43*
Wade, Theodore E., Jr. 1936- *37*
Wagenheim, Kal 1935- *21*
Wagner, Jane *33*
Wagner, Sharon B. 1936- *4*
Wagoner, David (Russell)
  1926- *14*
Wahl, Jan 1933- *34*
  Earlier sketch in SATA 2
Waide, Jan 1952- *29*
Waitley, Douglas 1927- *30*
Wakefield, Jean L.
  See Laird, Jean E(louise)
Wakin, Edward 1927- *37*
Walck, Henry Z(eigler) 1908-1984
  Obituary *40*
Walden, Amelia Elizabeth *3*
Waldman, Bruce 1949- *15*
Waldron, Ann Wood 1924- *16*
Walker, Alice 1944- *31*
Walker, Barbara K. 1921- *4*
Walker, (James) Braz(elton)
  1934-1983 .... *45*
Walker, David Harry 1911- *8*
Walker, Diana 1925- *9*
Walker, Frank 1930- *36*
Walker, Holly Beth
  See Bond, Gladys Baker
Walker, Louise Jean 1891-1976
  Obituary *35*
Walker, Mildred
  See Schemm, Mildred Walker
Walker, (Addison) Mort
  1923- *8*
Walker, Pamela 1948- *24*
Walker, Stephen J. 1951- *12*
Wallace, Barbara Brooks *4*
Wallace, Beverly Dobrin
  1921- *19*
Wallace, Daisy
  See Cuyler, Margery Stuyvesant
Wallace, John A. 1915- *3*
Wallace, Nigel
  See Hamilton, Charles H. St. John
Wallace, Robert A. 1932-
  Brief Entry *37*
Wallace-Brodeur, Ruth 1941-
  Brief Entry *41*
Waller, Leslie 1923- *20*
Wallis, G. McDonald
  See Campbell, Hope
Wallner, Alexandra 1946-
  Brief Entry *41*
Wallner, John C. 1945- *10*
Wallower, Lucille *11*

Walsh, Jill Paton
See Paton Walsh, Gillian
See also CLR 2
Walter, Mildred Pitts
Brief Entry 45
Walter, Villiam Christian
See Andersen, Hans Christian
Walters, Audrey 1929- 18
Walters, Hugh
See Hughes, Walter (Llewellyn)
Walther, Thomas A. 1950- 31
Walther, Tom
See Walther, Thomas A.
Waltner, Elma 1912- 40
Waltner, Willard H. 1909- 40
Walton, Richard J. 1928- 4
Waltrip, Lela (Kingston)
1904- 9
Waltrip, Mildred 1911- 37
Waltrip, Rufus (Charles)
1898- 9
Walworth, Nancy Zinsser
1917- 14
Wangerin, Walter, Jr. 1944- 45
Brief Entry 37
Wannamaker, Bruce
See Moncure, Jane Belk
Warbler, J. M.
See Cocagnac, A. M.
Warburg, Sandol Stoddard
1927- 14
Ward, John (Stanton) 1917- 42
Ward, Lynd (Kendall)
1905-1985 36
Obituary 42
Earlier sketch in SATA 2
Ward, Martha (Eads) 1921- 5
Ward, Melanie
See Curtis, Richard (Alan)
Wardell, Dean
See Prince, J(ack) H(arvey)
Ware, Leon (Vernon) 1909- 4
Warner, Frank A. [Collective
pseudonym] 1
Warner, Gertrude Chandler
1890- 9
Warner, Lucille Schulberg 30
Warner, Oliver 1903-1976 29
Warren, Betsy
See Warren, Elizabeth Avery
Warren, Billy
See Warren, William Stephen
Warren, Elizabeth
See Supraner, Robyn
Warren, Elizabeth Avery 1916-
Brief Entry 38
Warren, Joyce W(illiams)
1935- 18
Warren, Mary Phraner 1929- 10
Warren, William Stephen
1882-1968 9
Warrick, Patricia Scott 1925- 35
Warsh
See Warshaw, Jerry
Warshaw, Jerry 1929- 30
Warshofsky, Fred 1931- 24
Warshofsky, Isaac
See Singer, Isaac Bashevis

Wartski, Maureen (Ann Crane) 1940-
Brief Entry 37
Warwick, Alan R(oss)
1900-1973 42
Wa-sha-quon-asin
See Belaney, Archibald Stansfeld
Washburn, (Henry) Bradford (Jr.)
1910- 38
Washburne, Heluiz Chandler
1892-1970 10
Obituary 26
Washington, Booker T(aliaferro)
1858(?)-1915 28
Watanabe, Shigeo 1928- 39
Brief Entry 32
See also CLR 8
Waters, John F(rederick)
1930- 4
Waterton, Betty (Marie) 1923- 37
Brief Entry 34
Watkins-Pitchford, D. J.
1905- 6
Watson, Aldren A(uld) 1917- 42
Brief Entry 36
Watson, Clyde 1947- 5
See also CLR 3
Watson, Helen Orr 1892-1978
Obituary 24
Watson, James 1936- 10
Watson, Jane Werner 1915- 3
Watson, Nancy Dingman 32
Watson, Pauline 1925- 14
Watson, Sally 1924- 3
Watson, Wendy (McLeod)
1942- 5
Watson Taylor, Elizabeth
1915- 41
Watt, Thomas 1935- 4
Watts, Bernadette 1942- 4
Watts, Ephraim
See Horne, Richard Henry
Watts, Franklin (Mowry) 1904-1978
Obituary 21
Watts, Mabel Pizzey 1906- 11
Waugh, Carol-Lynn Rössel
1947- 41
Waugh, Dorothy 11
Wayland, Patrick
See O'Connor, Richard
Wayne, (Anne) Jenifer
1917-1982 32
Wayne, Kyra Petrovskaya
1918- 8
Wayne, Richard
See Decker, Duane
Waystaff, Simon
See Swift, Jonathan
Weales, Gerald (Clifford)
1925- 11
Weary, Ogdred
See Gorey, Edward St. John
Weaver, John L. 1949- 42
Weaver, Ward
See Mason, F. van Wyck
Webb, Christopher
See Wibberley, Leonard (Patrick
O'Connor)
Webb, Jean Francis (III)
1910- 35

Webb, Sharon 1936- 41
Webber, Irma E(leanor Schmidt)
1904- 14
Weber, Alfons 1921- 8
Weber, Lenora Mattingly
1895-1971 2
Obituary 26
Weber, William John 1927- 14
Webster, Alice (Jane Chandler)
1876-1916 17
Webster, David 1930- 11
Webster, Frank V. [Collective
pseudonym] 1
Webster, Gary
See Garrison, Webb B(lack)
Webster, James 1925-1981 17
Obituary 27
Webster, Jean
See Webster, Alice (Jane Chandler)
Wechsler, Herman 1904-1976
Obituary 20
Weddle, Ethel H(arshbarger)
1897- 11
Wegen, Ron(ald)
Brief Entry 44
Wegner, Fritz 1924- 20
Weihs, Erika 1917- 15
Weik, Mary Hays
1898(?)-1979 3
Obituary 23
Weil, Ann Yezner 1908-1969 9
Weil, Lisl 7
Weilerstein, Sadie Rose 1894- 3
Weiner, Sandra 1922- 14
Weingarten, Violet (Brown)
1915-1976 3
Obituary 27
Weingartner, Charles 1922- 5
Weir, LaVada 2
Weir, Rosemary (Green)
1905- 21
Weis, Margaret (Edith) 1948- 38
Weisberger, Bernard A(llen)
1922- 21
Weiser, Marjorie P(hillis) K(atz)
1934- 33
Weisgard, Leonard (Joseph)
1916- 30
Earlier sketch in SATA 2
Weiss, Adelle 1920- 18
Weiss, Ann E(dwards) 1943- 30
Weiss, Ellen 1953- 44
Weiss, Harvey 1922- 27
Earlier sketch in SATA 1
See also CLR 4
Weiss, Malcolm E. 1928- 3
Weiss, Miriam
See Schlein, Miriam
Weiss, Nicki 1954- 33
Weiss, Renee Karol 1923- 5
Weissenborn, Hellmuth 1898-1982
Obituary 31
Welber, Robert 26
Welch, D'Alte Aldridge 1907-1970
Obituary 27
Welch, Jean-Louise
See Kempton, Jean Welch
Welch, Martha McKeen 1914-
Brief Entry 45

Welch, Pauline
See Bodenham, Hilda Esther
Welch, Ronald
See Felton, Ronald Oliver
Weller, George (Anthony)
1907- 31
Welles, Winifred 1893-1939
Brief Entry 27
Wellman, Alice 1900-
Brief Entry 36
Wellman, Manly Wade 1903- 6
Wellman, Paul I. 1898-1966 3
Wells, H(erbert) G(eorge)
1866-1946 20
Wells, Helen 1910- 2
Wells, J. Wellington
See DeCamp, L(yon) Sprague
Wells, Rosemary 18
See also SAAS 1
Wels, Byron G(erald) 1924- 9
Welsh, Mary Flynn 1910(?)-1984
Obituary 38
Weltner, Linda R(iverly)
1938- 38
Welty, S. F.
See Welty, Susan F.
Welty, Susan F. 1905- 9
Wendelin, Rudolph 1910- 23
Werner, Herma 1926-
Brief Entry 41
Werner, Jane
See Watson, Jane Werner
Werner, K.
See Casewit, Curtis
Wersba, Barbara 1932- 1
See also CLR 3
See also SAAS 2
Werstein, Irving 1914-1971 14
Werth, Kurt 1896- 20
West, Anna 1938- 40
West, Barbara
See Price, Olive
West, Betty 1921- 11
West, C. P.
See Wodehouse, P(elham)
G(renville)
West, Emily G(ovan) 1919- 38
West, Emmy
See West, Emily G(ovan)
West, James
See Withers, Carl A.
West, Jerry
See Stratemeyer, Edward L.
West, Jerry
See Svenson, Andrew E.
West, (Mary) Jessamyn 1902(?)-1984
Obituary 37
West, Ward
See Borland, Hal
Westall, Robert (Atkinson)
1929- 23
See also SAAS 2
Westerberg, Christine 1950- 29
Westervelt, Virginia (Veeder)
1914- 10
Westheimer, David 1917- 14
Westmacott, Mary
See Christie, Agatha (Mary Clarissa)

Westman, Paul (Wendell)
1956- 39
Weston, Allen [Joint pseudonym]
See Norton, Alice Mary
Weston, John (Harrison)
1932- 21
Westwood, Jennifer 1940- 10
Wexler, Jerome (LeRoy)
1923- 14
Wharf, Michael
See Weller, George (Anthony)
Wheatley, Arabelle 1921- 16
Wheeler, Captain
See Ellis, Edward S(ylvester)
Wheeler, Cindy 1955-
Brief Entry 40
Wheeler, Janet D. [Collective
pseudonym] 1
Wheeler, Opal 1898- 23
Whelan, Elizabeth M(urphy)
1943- 14
Whistler, Reginald John
1905-1944 30
Whistler, Rex
See Whistler, Reginald John
Whitcomb, Jon 1906- 10
White, Anne Hitchcock 1902-1970
Brief Entry 33
White, Anne Terry 1896- 2
White, Dale
See Place, Marian T.
White, Dori 1919- 10
White, E(lwyn) B(rooks)
1899-1985 29
Obituary 44
Earlier sketch in SATA 2
See also CLR 1
White, Eliza Orne
1856-1947 ....YABC 2
White, Florence M(eiman)
1910- 14
White, Laurence B., Jr. 1935- 10
White, Ramy Allison [Collective
pseudonym] 1
White, Robb 1909- 1
See also CLR 3
See also SAAS 1
White, Ruth C. 1942- 39
White, T(erence) H(anbury)
1906-1964 12
White, William, Jr. 1934- 16
Whitehead, Don(ald) F. 1908- 4
Whitehouse, Arch
See Whitehouse, Arthur George
Whitehouse, Arthur George
1895-1979 14
Obituary 23
Whitehouse, Elizabeth S(cott)
1893-1968 35
Whitehouse, Jeanne 1939- 29
Whitinger, R. D.
See Place, Marian T.
Whitlock, Pamela 1921(?)-1982
Obituary 31
Whitlock, Ralph 1914- 35
Whitman, Walt(er) 1819-1892 20
Whitney, Alex(andra) 1922- 14
Whitney, David C(harles) 1921-
Brief Entry 29

Whitney, Phyllis A(yame)
1903- 30
Earlier sketch in SATA 1
Whitney, Thomas P(orter)
1917- 25
Wibberley, Leonard (Patrick
O'Connor) 1915-1983 45
Obituary 36
Earlier sketch in SATA 2
See also CLR 3
Wiberg, Harald (Albin) 1908-
Brief Entry 40
Widdemer, Mabel Cleland
1902-1964 5
Widenberg, Siv 1931- 10
Wier, Ester 1910- 3
Wiese, Kurt 1887-1974 36
Obituary 24
Earlier sketch in SATA 3
Wiesner, Portia
See Takakjian, Portia
Wiesner, William 1899- 5
Wiggin, Kate Douglas (Smith)
1856-1923 ....YABC 1
Wight, James Alfred 1916-
Brief Entry 44
Wikland, Ilon 1930-
Brief Entry 32
Wilber, Donald N(ewton)
1907- 35
Wilbur, C. Keith 1923- 27
Wilbur, Richard (Purdy)
1921- 9
Wilcox, R(uth) Turner
1888-1970 36
Wilde, Gunther
See Hurwood, Bernhardt J.
Wilde, Oscar (Fingal O'Flahertie
Wills) 1854-1900 24
Wilder, Cherry
See Grimm, Cherry Barbara Lockett
Wilder, Laura Ingalls
1867-1957 29
See also CLR 2
Wildsmith, Brian 1930- 16
See also CLR 2
Wilkie, Katharine E(lliott)
1904-1980 31
Wilkins, Frances 1923- 14
Wilkins, Marilyn (Ruth)
1926- 30
Wilkins, Marne
See Wilkins, Marilyn (Ruth)
Wilkinson, (Thomas) Barry 1923-
Brief Entry 32
Wilkinson, Brenda 1946- 14
Wilkinson, Burke 1913- 4
Wilkinson, Sylvia (J.) 1940-
Brief Entry 39
Wilkoń, Józef 1930- 31
Wilks, Michael Thomas 1947- 44
Wilks, Mike
See Wilks, Michael Thomas
Will
See Lipkind, William
Willard, Barbara (Mary)
1909- 17
See also CLR 2
Willard, Mildred Wilds 1911- 14

Willard, Nancy 1936- *37*
　Brief Entry *30*
　See also CLR 5
Willcox, Isobel 1907- *42*
Willey, Robert
　See Ley, Willy
Williams, Barbara 1925- *11*
Williams, Beryl
　See Epstein, Beryl
Williams, Charles
　See Collier, James Lincoln
Williams, Clyde C.
　1881-1974 .... *8*
　Obituary *27*
Williams, Coe
　See Harrison, C. William
Williams, Eric (Ernest)
　1911-1983 .... *14*
　Obituary *38*
Williams, Ferelith Eccles
　1920- *22*
Williams, Frances B.
　See Browin, Frances Williams
Williams, Garth (Montgomery)
　1912- *18*
Williams, Guy R. 1920- *11*
Williams, Hawley
　See Heyliger, William
Williams, J. R.
　See Williams, Jeanne
Williams, J. Walker
　See Wodehouse, P(elham)
　G(renville)
Williams, Jay 1914-1978 .... *41*
　Obituary *24*
　Earlier sketch in SATA 3
　See also CLR 8
Williams, Jeanne 1930- *5*
Williams, Kit 1946(?)- *44*
　See also CLR 4
Williams, Leslie 1941- *42*
Williams, Louise Bonino 1904(?)-1984
　Obituary *39*
Williams, Maureen 1951- *12*
Williams, Michael
　See St. John, Wylly Folk
Williams, Patrick J.
　See Butterworth, W. E.
Williams, Selma R(uth) 1925- *14*
Williams, Slim
　See Williams, Clyde C.
Williams, Ursula Moray
　1911- *3*
Williams, Vera B. 1927-
　Brief Entry *33*
　See also CLR 9
Williams-Ellis, (Mary) Amabel
　(Nassau) 1894-1984 .... *29*
　Obituary *41*
Williamson, Henry 1895-1977 .... *37*
　Obituary *30*
Williamson, Joanne Small
　1926- *3*
Willson, Robina Beckles (Ballard)
　1930- *27*
Wilma, Dana
　See Faralla, Dana
Wilson, Beth P(ierre) *8*
Wilson, Carter 1941- *6*

Wilson, Charles Morrow
　1905-1977 .... *30*
Wilson, Dagmar 1916-
　Brief Entry *31*
Wilson, Dorothy Clarke 1904- *16*
Wilson, Edward A(rthur)
　1886-1970 .... *38*
Wilson, Ellen (Janet Cameron)
　(?)-1976 .... *9*
　Obituary *26*
Wilson, Eric H. 1940- *34*
　Brief Entry *32*
Wilson, Forrest 1918- *27*
Wilson, Gahan 1930- *35*
　Brief Entry *27*
Wilson, Gina 1943- *36*
　Brief Entry *34*
Wilson, (Leslie) Granville
　1912- *14*
Wilson, Hazel 1898- *3*
Wilson, John 1922- *22*
Wilson, Joyce M(uriel Judson) *21*
Wilson, Lionel 1924- *33*
　Brief Entry *31*
Wilson, Ron(ald William) *38*
Wilson, Tom 1931- *33*
　Brief Entry *30*
Wilson, Walt(er N.) 1939- *14*
Wilton, Elizabeth 1937- *14*
Wilwerding, Walter Joseph
　1891-1966 .... *9*
Winchester, James H(ugh)
　1917-1985 .... *30*
　Obituary *45*
Winders, Gertrude Hecker *3*
Windham, Basil
　See Wodehouse, P(elham)
　G(renville)
Windham, Kathryn T(ucker)
　1918- *14*
Windsor, Claire
　See Hamerstrom, Frances
Windsor, Patricia 1938- *30*
Winfield, Arthur M.
　See Stratemeyer, Edward L.
Winfield, Edna
　See Stratemeyer, Edward L.
Winn, Chris 1952- *42*
Winn, Janet Bruce 1928- *43*
Winn, Marie 1936- *38*
Winston, Clara 1921-1983
　Obituary *39*
Winter, Milo (Kendall)
　1888-1956 .... *21*
Winter, R. R.
　See Winterbotham, R(ussell)
　R(obert)
Winterbotham, R(ussell) R(obert)
　1904-1971 .... *10*
Winterton, Gayle
　See Adams, William Taylor
Winthrop, Elizabeth
　See Mahony, Elizabeth Winthrop
Wirtenberg, Patricia Z. 1932- *10*
Wise, William 1923- *4*
Wise, Winifred E. *2*
Wiseman, Ann (Sayre) 1926- *31*
Wiseman, B(ernard) 1922- *4*

Wiseman, David 1916- *43*
　Brief Entry *40*
Wisner, Bill
　See Wisner, William L.
Wisner, William L.
　1914(?)-1983 .... *42*
Witham, (Phillip) Ross 1917- *37*
Withers, Carl A. 1900-1970 .... *14*
Witt, Shirley Hill 1934- *17*
Wittels, Harriet Joan 1938- *31*
Wittman, Sally (Anne Christensen)
　1941- *30*
Witty, Paul A(ndrew) 1898-1976
　Obituary *30*
Wizard, Mr.
　See Herbert, Don
Wodehouse, P(elham) G(renville)
　1881-1975 .... *22*
Wodge, Dreary
　See Gorey, Edward St. John
Wohlberg, Meg 1905- *41*
Wohlrabe, Raymond A. 1900- *4*
Wojciechowska, Maia 1927- *28*
　Earlier sketch in SATA 1
　See also CLR 1
　See also SAAS 1
Wolcott, Patty 1929- *14*
Wold, Jo Anne 1938- *30*
Woldin, Beth Weiner 1955- *34*
Wolf, Bernard 1930-
　Brief Entry *37*
Wolfe, Burton H. 1932- *5*
Wolfe, Louis 1905- *8*
Wolfe, Rinna (Evelyn) 1925- *38*
Wolfenden, George
　See Beardmore, George
Wolff, Diane 1945- *27*
Wolff, Robert Jay 1905- *10*
Wolitzer, Hilma 1930- *31*
Wolkoff, Judie (Edwards)
　Brief Entry *37*
Wolkstein, Diane 1942- *7*
Wolters, Richard A. 1920- *35*
Wondriska, William 1931- *6*
Wood, Audrey
　Brief Entry *44*
Wood, Catherine
　See Etchison, Birdie L(ee)
Wood, Don 1945-
　Brief Entry *44*
Wood, Edgar A(llardyce)
　1907- *14*
Wood, Esther
　See Brady, Esther Wood
Wood, Frances Elizabeth *34*
Wood, James Playsted 1905- *1*
Wood, Kerry
　See Wood, Edgar A(llardyce)
Wood, Laura N.
　See Roper, Laura Wood
Wood, Nancy 1936- *6*
Wood, Phyllis Anderson
　1923- *33*
　Brief Entry *30*
Wood, Wallace 1927-1981
　Obituary *33*
Woodard, Carol 1929- *14*
Woodburn, John Henry 1914- *11*
Woodford, Peggy 1937- *25*

Woodrich, Mary Neville
1915- *2*
Woods, George A(llan) 1926- *30*
Woods, Geraldine 1948-
Brief Entry *42*
Woods, Harold 1945-
Brief Entry *42*
Woods, Margaret 1921- *2*
Woods, Nat
See Stratemeyer, Edward L.
Woodson, Jack
See Woodson, John Waddie, Jr.
Woodson, John Waddie, Jr. *10*
Woodward, Cleveland 1900- *10*
Woody, Regina Jones 1894- *3*
Wooldridge, Rhoda 1906- *22*
Woolley, Catherine 1904- *3*
Woolsey, Janette 1904- *3*
Worcester, Donald Emmet
1915- *18*
Work, Virginia 1946-
Brief Entry *45*
Worline, Bonnie Bess 1914- *14*
Wormser, Sophie 1896- *22*
Worth, Valerie 1933- *8*
Wortis, Avi 1937- *14*
Wosmek, Frances 1917- *29*
Wriggins, Sally Hovey 1922 ...... *17*
Wright, Anna (Maria Louisa Perrot)
Rose 1890-1968
Brief Entry *35*
Wright, Dare 1926(?)- *21*
Wright, Enid Meadowcroft
1898-1966 .... *3*
Wright, Esmond 1915- *10*
Wright, Frances Fitzpatrick
1897- *10*
Wright, Judith 1915- *14*
Wright, Katrina
See Gater, Dilys
Wright, Kenneth
See Del Rey, Lester
Wright, Nancy Means *38*
Wright, R(obert) H. 1906- *6*
Wrightson, Patricia 1921- *8*
See also CLR 4
Wronker, Lili Cassel 1924- *10*
Wulffson, Don L. 1943- *32*
Wuorio, Eva-Lis 1918- *34*
Brief Entry *28*
Wyeth, Betsy James 1921- *41*
Wyeth, N(ewell) C(onvers)
1882-1945 .... *17*
Wyler, Rose 1909- *18*
Wylie, Laura
See Matthews, Patricia
Wymer, Norman George
1911- *25*
Wynants, Miche 1934-
Brief Entry *31*
Wyndham, Lee
See Hyndman, Jane Andrews
Wyndham, Robert
See Hyndman, Robert Utley
Wynter, Edward (John) 1914- *14*
Wynyard, Talbot
See Hamilton, Charles H. St. John
Wyss, Johann David Von
1743-1818 .... *29*
Brief Entry *27*

Wyss, Thelma Hatch 1934- *10*

Y

Yaffe, Alan
See Yorinks, Arthur
Yamaguchi, Marianne 1936- *7*
Yang, Jay 1941- *12*
Yarbrough, Ira 1910(?)-1983
Obituary *35*
Yaroslava
See Mills, Yaroslava Surmach
Yashima, Taro
See Iwamatsu, Jun Atsushi
See also CLR 4
Yates, Elizabeth 1905- *4*
Yates, Raymond F(rancis)
1895-1966 .... *31*
Yaukey, Grace S(ydenstricker)
1899- *5*
Yeakley, Marjory Hall 1908- *21*
Yeatman, Linda 1938- *42*
Yensid, Retlaw
See Disney, Walt(er Elias)
Yeo, Wilma (Lethem) 1918- *24*
Yeoman, John (Brian) 1934- *28*
Yep, Laurence M. 1948- *7*
See also CLR 3
Yerian, Cameron John *21*
Yerian, Margaret A. *21*
Yolen, Jane H. 1939- *40*
Earlier sketch in SATA 4
See also CLR 4
See also SAAS 1
Yonge, Charlotte Mary
1823-1901 .... *17*
Yorinks, Arthur 1953- *33*
York, Andrew
See Nicole, Christopher Robin
York, Carol Beach 1928- *6*
Yost, Edna 1889-1971
Obituary *26*
Youd, (Christopher) Samuel 1922-
Brief Entry *30*
Young, Bob
See Young, Robert W.
Young, Clarence [Collective
pseudonym] *1*
Young, Dorothea Bennett
1924- *31*
Young, Ed 1931- *10*
Young, Edward
See Reinfeld, Fred
Young, Elaine L.
See Schulte, Elaine L(ouise)
Young, Jan
See Young, Janet Randall
Young, Janet Randall 1919- *3*
Young, Lois Horton
1911-1981 .... *26*
Young, Margaret B(uckner)
1922- *2*
Young, Miriam 1913-1934 .... *7*
Young, (Rodney Lee) Patrick (Jr.)
1937- *22*
Young, Percy M(arshall)
1912- *31*
Young, Robert W. 1916-1969 ..... *3*

Young, Scott A(lexander)
1918- *5*
Young, Vivien
See Gater, Dilys
Youngs, Betty 1934-1985
Obituary *42*

Z

Zaffo, George J. (?)-1984 .... *42*
Zaidenberg, Arthur 1908(?)- *34*
Zalben, Jane Breskin 1950- *7*
Zallinger, Jean (Day) 1918- *14*
Zappler, Lisbeth 1930- *10*
Zarchy, Harry 1912- *34*
Zarif, Margaret Min'imah
(?)-1983 .... *33*
Zaring, Jane (Thomas) 1936-
Brief Entry *40*
Zaslavsky, Claudia 1917- *36*
Zeck, Gerald Anthony 1939- *40*
Zeck, Gerry
See Zeck, Gerald Anthony
Zei, Alki *24*
See also CLR 6
Zelazny, Roger (Joseph Christopher)
1937-
Brief Entry *39*
Zelinsky, Paul O.
Brief Entry *33*
Zellan, Audrey Penn 1950- *22*
Zemach, Harve 1933- *3*
Zemach, Kaethe 1958-
Brief Entry *39*
Zemach, Margot 1931- *21*
Ziemienski, Dennis 1947- *10*
Zillah
See Macdonald, Zillah K.
Zim, Herbert S(pencer) 1909- *30*
Earlier sketch in SATA 1
See also CLR 2
See also SAAS 2
Zim, Sonia Bleeker
See Bleeker, Sonia
Zimelman, Nathan
Brief Entry *37*
Zimmerman, Naoma 1914- *10*
Zimnik, Reiner 1930- *36*
See also CLR 3
Zindel, Bonnie 1943- *34*
Zindel, Paul 1936- *16*
See also CLR 3
Ziner, (Florence) Feenie
1921- *5*
Zion, (Eu)Gene 1913-1975 .... *18*
Zollinger, Gulielma 1856-1917
Brief Entry *27*
Zolotow, Charlotte S. 1915- *35*
Earlier sketch in SATA 1
See also CLR 2
Zonia, Dhimitri 1921- *20*
Zubrowski, Bernard 1939- *35*
Zupa, G. Anthony
See Zeck, Gerald Anthony
Zurhorst, Charles (Stewart, Jr.)
1913- *12*
Zuromskis, Diane
See Stanley, Diane
Zweifel, Frances 1931- *14*